W9-AVK-529

Tsung-mi and the
Sinification of Buddhism

Tsung-mi and the
Sinification of Buddhism

Peter N. Gregory

PRINCETON UNIVERSITY PRESS

PRINCETON, NEW JERSEY

Library of Congress Cataloging-in-Publication Data

Gregory, Peter N., 1945–
Tsung-mi and the sinification of Buddhism /
Peter N. Gregory.
p. cm.
Includes bibliographical references and index.
1. Tsung-mi, 780–841. I. Title.
BQ8249.T787G74 1991 294.3′92—dc20 90-27299

ISBN 0-691-07373-2

This book is dedicated to my father

John Roy Gregory, M.D.
1 April 1919–19 February 1986

यदन पुण्यं तद् भवतु पितृश्चसवसत्नानाम्

CONTENTS

ACKNOWLEDGMENTS

THIS BOOK has evolved in fits and starts over the last decade. I began work on Tsung-mi as part of my 1981 Harvard University dissertation, which centered on a study and translation of his *Inquiry into the Origin of Man*. A 1983–84 grant from the Joint Committee for Chinese Studies of the American Council of Learned Societies and the Social Science Research Council, with funds provided by the Andrew M. Mellon Foundation, enabled me to conduct significant subsequent research and to extend my knowledge of Tsung-mi beyond the limited range of sources used in my dissertation. In 1986, with a National Endowment for the Humanities Summer Stipend and Hewlitt Summer International Research Grant, I began to write the manuscript that inadvertently developed into this book. Although these two summer grants were awarded to prepare my annotated translation of the *Inquiry into the Origin of Man* for publication, the introduction soon began to expand far beyond the scope of the original project and turned into drafts for what became chapters 3 and 4 of the present book. I thank these granting agencies for their support, without which this volume could never have been completed.

Over the 1980s my thinking on Tsung-mi evolved through a series of papers, and some of the material that appears in this book has been published in different form in various journal articles or book chapters. I accordingly thank *Philosophy East and West*, *Journal of the International Association of Buddhist Studies*, *Journal of the American Academy of Religion*, and the Kuroda Institute and the University of Hawaii Press for permission to use sections of previously published work.

At various points in the course of my slow and unsteady progress I have received valuable feedback from many colleagues and friends. Unfortunately, the intellectual and other debts that I have accumulated in a decade of work are too numerous to acknowledge individually. Still, I would like to single out a few of these *kalyāṇamitra* for special thanks: Masatoshi Nagatomi, who guided my doctoral research at Harvard and pushed me in ways that I only later came to appreciate; Maezumi Rōshi, who opened up a dimension of Buddhism as a living practice that I never could have gotten from books alone; and Rob Gimello, who extended his friendship to me at a particularly vulnerable point in my career and whose own work provided a standard of excellence toward which to aspire. I also thank John

McRae for his detailed comments on an early draft; Pat Ebrey and Kai-wing Chow for their patient reading and constructive criticisms of my penultimate draft; and Robert Buswell and Buzzy Teiser for their careful reviews for the press, which offered many valuable suggestions that I have incorporated into my final draft.

ABBREVIATIONS

B   Broughton, Jeffrey, "Kuei-feng Tsung-mi: The Convergence of Ch'an and the Teachings"

CTL   *Ching-te ch'uan-teng lu*, by Tao-yüan, T no. 2076

K   Kamata, Shigeo, *Zengen shosenshū tojo*, Zen no goroku, vol. 9

HKSC   *Hsü kao-seng chuan*, by Tao-hsüan, T no. 2060

HTC   *Hsü tsang ching*, reprint of *Dainippon zokuzōkyō*

KSC   *Kao-seng chuan*, by Hui-chiao, T no. 2059

LS   *Yüan-chüeh ching lüeh-shu*, by Tsung-mi, T no. 1759

LSC   *Yüan-chüeh ching lüeh-shu ch'ao*, by Tsung-mi, HTC, vol. 15

LTFPC   *Li-tai fa-pao chi*, T no. 2075

SKSC   *Sung kao-seng chuan*, by Tsan-ning, T no. 2061

SPPY   *Ssu-pu pei-yao*, revised edition

SPTK   *Ssu-pu ts'ung-k'an*

T   *Taishō shinshū daizōkyō*, edited by Takakusu Junjirō and Watanabe Kaigyoku

TS   *Yüan-chüeh ching ta-shu*, by Tsung-mi, HTC, vol. 14

TSC   *Yüan-chüeh ching ta-shu ch'ao*, by Tsung-mi, HTC, vols. 14–15

Tsung-mi and the
Sinification of Buddhism

Chapter One

INTRODUCTION

WITHIN Chinese Buddhism, Kuei-feng Tsung-mi (780–841) has been traditionally honored as the fifth "patriarch" in both the Hua-yen scholastic tradition and the Ho-tse line of Southern Ch'an. Hua-yen and Ch'an, the Buddhist traditions with which Tsung-mi was affiliated, represent two of the major forms of Chinese Buddhism that took shape during the Sui (581–617) and T'ang (618–907) dynasties. It was during this time that Chinese Buddhist thought reached its apogee and that the main modes of Chinese Buddhist practice developed into some of their most characteristic forms. Together with T'ien-t'ai and Pure Land, Hua-yen and Ch'an exemplify what Yūki Reimon has characterized as the "new Buddhism of the Sui and T'ang."[1] Indeed, the Sui–T'ang period marks an important shift in the history of Buddhism in China. For it was then that the fully acculturated forms of Chinese Buddhism assumed their mature state, one that was at once authentically Buddhist and uniquely Chinese.

These Sui–T'ang traditions represent a significant departure from the Buddhism of the preceding Six Dynasties period (222–589), and to appreciate what was "new" about them, and to understand Tsung-mi's role in forging that tradition, one must briefly take stock of what had come before. By the founding of the Sui dynasty at the end of the sixth century, Chinese Buddhism had already undergone several centuries of development and assimilation. Toward the end of the fourth century it had begun to become apparent to some of the more perspicacious among the clerical elite how earlier attempts to understand Buddhism through the lens of their indigenous traditions, particularly arcane learning or so-called Neo-Taoism (*hsüan-hsüeh*), had

---

[1] Yūki has developed his theory in a number of articles. The two most pertinent in the present context are his "Shotō bukkyō no shisōshi-teki mujun to kokka kenryoku to no kōsaku" and "Chūgoku bukkyō no keisei." The basic outline of Yūki's theory is well summarized in Stanley Weinstein's classic article, "Imperial Patronage in the Formation of T'ang Buddhism." Robert M. Gimello has done a brilliant job of drawing out the implications of Yūki's theory as it applies to the Hua-yen tradition in his "Chih-yen (602–668) and the Foundations of Hua-yen Buddhism." Gimello's work is without qualification the best study of Chinese Buddhism during the sixth and seventh centuries in any language, and the following discussion of early Hua-yen is much indebted to it.

only yielded a distorted perception of their religion. Chinese Buddhists of the fifth and sixth centuries accordingly laid aside their *Lao-
tzu* and *Chuang-tzu* and looked instead to the western regions whence
Buddhism had come. They immersed themselves in the learned treatises and scholastic compendia of the great Indian doctors of the
church. Much of their effort was directed toward the study of the
imposing Yogācāra treatises with their intricate epistemological analy-
ses of the mind. Although what medieval Chinese Buddhists made
of these texts was often quite novel, the important point is that their
efforts were directed toward mastering Buddhism on its own terms.
In its attempt to be faithful to the received tradition, the Buddhism
of this period is characterized by its encyclopedic concern with the
detail and technical arcana of Buddhist learning.

The new traditions that emerged during the Sui and T'ang can be
seen in part as a reaction against the mounting weight of Chinese
Buddhist scholasticism. The sheer bulk and daunting complexity of
the scholastic enterprise contributed to a sense of crisis among some
of the learned Buddhists during the Sui and early T'ang. The texts
that they strove to comprehend were by no means univocal. Nor did
they address what many felt to be the more urgent religious issues of
the day. In times when the very existence of the religion was threatened, as many felt it had been by the Northern Chou persecution
(574–577), Chinese Buddhists' anxiety was not assuaged by the dis-
maying prospect of the bodhisattva career that the Indian treatises
portrayed as requiring three incalculable eons. In an evil and corrupt
age of the decline of the dharma (*mo-fa*), new practices and a new
theology to justify them were called for.

In an effort to make Buddhism speak to more immediate spiritual
needs, the Sui–T'ang innovators discarded foreign models of the
path, rejecting the authority of the Indian scholastic tradition in favor
of a return to those texts believed to contain the word of the Buddha,
the sūtras. In this move one can see a nascent sense of assurance beginning to assert itself. The prior centuries of scholastic appropriation had gradually earned Chinese Buddhists a hard-won confidence
in their own authority to interpret the tradition in accord with their
own experience. This reorientation also opened up a new dimension
of interpretive possibilities. Not only was much of the discourse
found within the Indian scholastic tradition foreign to Chinese religious concerns, but its method—which was concerned to provide definitive interpretations and rule out ambiguity—also did not always
leave room to discover a meaning that was relevant to the religious
needs of Chinese Buddhists of the sixth and seventh centuries. By
contrast, the sūtras, which more often resorted to parable and meta-

phor than to argument and syllogism, offered a range of interpretive possibilities that could be made to speak more directly to Chinese experience. Accordingly, the new traditions of Chinese Buddhism preferred to designate themselves in terms of the scripture on which they based their authority rather than on a body of scholastic literature, as was more typically the case with the exegetical traditions of the fifth and sixth centuries.[2] This rejection of Indian authority can also be seen in their gradual construction of a Chinese patriarchate. The "patriarchs" were no longer hallowed Indian exegetes or foreign translators but the charismatic Chinese masters who were retrospectively judged as "founders" of the new traditions.

Many of the features of the new Buddhism are represented by Tu-shun (557–640), the shadowy figure in whom the later Hua-yen tradition was to discover its first patriarch. He is now perhaps best known as the putative author of the *Fa-chieh kuan-men* (Discernments of the dharmadhātu).[3] Yet, despite the enormous contribution that this text made to the subsequent development of Hua-yen thought, it

[2] Five of what are traditionally reckoned as the six exegetical traditions of the fifth and six centuries were based on Indian scholastic treatises. Only the so-called Nirvāṇa (Nieh-p'an) tradition was based on a scripture. The other five exegetical traditions are the Ti-lun, based on Bodhiruci's translation of Vasubandhu's *Daśabhūmikabhāṣya* (*Shih-ti ching lun*); the She-lun, based on Paramārtha's translation of the *Mahāyānasaṃgraha* (*Ta-sheng she lun*); the San-lun, based on three treatises of Nāgārjuna; the Abhidharma, based on the Sarvāstivādin Abhidharma; and the Ch'eng-shih, based on a translation (*Ch'eng-shih lun*) of an otherwise unknown Indian Buddhist treatise, whose Sanskrit title may have been either *Tattvasiddhi* or *Satyasiddhi*. By contrast, T'ien-t'ai, Hua-yen, and Pure Land all legitimate their teachings by appealing to a single scripture or scriptural corpus. Although the Ch'an claim to be based on extra-canonical authority appears to be an exception, one should note that it, too, rejects the scholastic tradition and looks back to the authority of the Buddha. Its major difference from traditions like T'ien-t'ai and Hua-yen is that, whereas they look back to the words of the Buddha, Ch'an claims special access to the Buddha's enlightenment.

[3] This text occurs in two slightly different versions in Ch'eng-kuan's and Tsung-mi's commentary, *Hua-yen fa-chieh hsüan-ching* (no. 1883) and *Chu hua-yen fa-chieh kuan-men* (no. 1884), in T 45. It is available in several translations, the most recent of which is that of Thomas Cleary, who includes it along with Ch'eng-kuan's commentary in his *Entry into the Inconceivable*, pp. 69–124. The best translation, which is also thoroughly annotated, is that of Gimello, included as an appendix to his "Chih-yen," pp. 454–510. Tu-shun's authorship of this text has been much controverted. For a good summary of the various arguments, and a strong argument in favor of Tu-shun's authorship, see Gimello, "Chih-yen," pp. 80–93. Kimura Kiyotaka has reopened the issue in his *Shoki chūgoku kegon shisō no kenkyū*, pp. 328–370. Despite the strong case Gimello makes for Tu-shun's authorship, I agree with Kimura that the evidence is ultimately inconclusive, and that we must suspend final judgment on the matter. Nevertheless, for simplicity's sake, in what follows I will talk as if Tu-shun were the author of the *Fa-chieh kuan-men*, while noting here for the record that the controversy has yet to be definitively settled.

was primarily as a charismatic miracle-working monk, and not as a scholar or philosophical innovator, that Tu-shun was remembered in the T'ang. Tao-hsüan (596–667), for instance, places his biography in the section dealing with thaumaturges (*kan-t'ung*), and not that dealing with exegetes (*i-chieh*), in his *Hsü kao-seng chuan* (Continued biographies of eminent monks).[4] In contrast to the learned monks of the large metropolitan temples who devoted their energies to the scholastic exegesis of the *Hua-yen* (*Avataṃsaka*) *Sūtra*, Tu-shun lived among the people in the countryside, where he gained a reputation as a monk skilled in exorcizing demons and curing the sick. His thaumaturgical feats, of course, were palpable proof of his meditative prowess. His religious practice presumably involved the recitation of the *Hua-yen Sūtra*, as he urges this practice on one of his disciples.[5] Indeed, many of the figures associated with the early Hua-yen cult at the end of the sixth century were known for the extraordinary powers they developed as a result of reciting the sūtra.[6]

The text that is associated with Tu-shun, the *Fa-chieh kuan-men*, contained in seminal form many of the ideas and themes that were developed within the subsequent Hua-yen tradition, and its style and content exhibit features typical of the new Buddhism. The work is divided into three main sections: the discernment of true emptiness (*chen-k'ung kuan-fa*), the discernment of the mutual nonobstruction of principle and phenomena (*li-shih wu-ai kuan*), and the discernment of total pervasion and inclusion (*chou-pien han-jung kuan*).[7]

The progression of Tu-shun's three discernments reflects typically Chinese reservations about the negative conative implications of the teaching of emptiness. But unlike the misguided attempts to understand emptiness in "Neo-Taoist" ontological terms characteristic of the foregoing centuries, Tu-shun demonstrates an accurate and authoritative comprehension of this cardinal Mahāyāna notion. Indeed, the first discernment represents a concise distillation of standard Madhyamaka understanding of the relationship of emptiness (*k'ung*; *śūnyatā*) and form (*se*; *rūpa*). However, whereas the first discernment demonstrates the true emptiness of reality, it does not yet reveal its marvelous actuality (*miao-yu*). This is only accomplished in the next two discernments, which introduce the terms principle (*li*)[8] and phe-

---

[4] See T 50.653b15–654a13.

[5] See *Hua-yen ching chuan-chi*, T 51.166c10.

[6] See my "The Teaching of Men and Gods," pp. 278–296. See also Kamata Shigeo's *Chūgoku kegon shisōshi no kenkyū*, pp. 42–47 and 235–248, to which my study is indebted.

[7] My comments on this text are based on Gimello, "Chih-yen," chap. 1, a portion of which was published in Gimello, "Apopathic and Kataphatic Discourse in Mahāyāna."

[8] The meaning that *li* has for the Hua-yen tradition changes in the course of the

nomena (*shih*). These terms, which became defining features of the Hua-yen lexicon, are drawn from the Chinese philosophical tradition and, as they appear in the second discernment, represent a significant development in the appropriation of emptiness. The replacement of "emptiness" by "principle" signals an important step in the direction of evolving a more affirmative discourse—a theme that will recur as a major leit motif in the chapters to come.

Tu-shun's replacement of "form" by "phenomenon" marks a comparably important shift toward an affirmation of the phenomenal world.[9] The second discernment elucidates various ways in which phenomena and principle interrelate. Because they instantiate principle, all phenomena are thereby validated. This positive valuation of the phenomenal world culminates in the third discernment, that of total pervasion and inclusion. With this final discernment principle itself is ultimately transcended, and one enters the world of total interpenetration for which the Hua-yen tradition is justly famous. Each and every phenomenon is not only seen to contain each and every other phenomenon, but all phenomena are also seen to contain the totality of the unobstructed interpenetration of all phenomena. It is this vision that the Hua-yen tradition avers as uniquely its own. The ten "gates" in terms of which Tu-shun elucidates this discernment were adapted by his disciple Chih-yen (602–668) as the ten profundities (*shih-hsüan*), which were taken by Fa-tsang (643–712) to represent content of the Buddha's enlightenment. Ch'eng-kuan (738–839) later claimed the ten profundities exemplify the distinctively Hua-yen teaching of the unobstructed interpenetration of phenomena (*shih-shih wu-ai*), the rubric by which this vision is subsequently most commonly known.

Such are some of the main ideas that assured the *Fa-chieh kuan-men* a central place in the Hua-yen tradition. The tradition prizes Tu-shun's text as a concise exposition of the essential purport of the *Hua-yen Sūtra,* and here it is worth noting how dissimilar it is in style from

---

T'ang. In the *Fa-chieh kuan-men* it is the principle that all forms are empty. As Gimello explains: "The term *li* reveals the true modal status of the concept of emptiness or indeterminability more clearly than did the word *śūnyatā* and without its negative conative impact" ("Apophatic and Kataphatic Discourse," p. 128). With Fa-tsang, however, *li* becomes associated with the one mind of the *Awakening of Faith*, an association that becomes even stronger with Ch'eng-kuan and Tsung-mi, in which case it is more appropriately translated as "absolute."

[9] Gimello notes that "discourse in terms of emptiness and forms seems still to dissolve the world of common experience and derogate its variety" ("Apophatic and Kataphatic Discourse," p. 123). In contrast to a more typically Indian term such as dharma (*fa*), *shih* refers to the world of phenomenal experience, not to its subpersonal constituents (ibid., pp. 124–125).

more traditional commentaries. As Robert Gimello observes, it "contains little of what we would normally associate with Buddhist exegetics. There are no labored 'chapter and verse' explanations, no paraphrases of obscure pasages, no definitions of technical vocabulary."[10] Rather, as Tsung-mi claims in his commentary, the text represents Tu-shun's distillation of the essential meaning of the *Hua-yen Sūtra* within the light of his own meditative experience.[11] Indeed, the text presents the truths of the sūtra from the standpoint of religious practice: its insights are put forth not as speculative propositions to be weighed in the balance of reason but as meditative discernments (*kuan*) whose meaning can only be realized in practice. Tu-shun's bold hermeneutical approach, so different from scholastic exegesis, as well as his emphasis on the "practical" content of the discernments, are characteristic of the innovations of the new Buddhism of the Sui and T'ang.

The dharmadhātu (*fa-chieh*) that Tu-shun takes as the central focus of his discernment is a concept that plays an important role in the *Hua-yen Sūtra* itself. The term, of course, has a long history in Buddhism, and its multiple connotations cannot adequately be conveyed by any single English translation.[12] "Dhātu" has a range of meaning almost as broad as "dharma."[13] Among other things, it can mean "el-

---

[10] Gimello, "Chih-yen," p. 125.

[11] T 45.684c14–18; for a translation see Gimello, "Chih-yen," p. 127.

[12] A good survey of the wide range of meanings that "dharmadhātu" has throughout Buddhist thought can be found in Kang Nam Oh's dissertation, "A Study of Chinese Hua-yen Buddhism with Special Reference to the *Dharmadhātu* (*fa-chieh*) Doctrine," pp. 11–35; Oh summarizes the main points of his dissertation in his article "*Dharmadhātu*: An Introduction to Hua-yen Buddhism."

[13] Fa-tsang indicates some of the ways in which dharmadhātu could be interpreted in his discussion at the beginning of his commentary on the "Ju fa-chieh p'in" (Entering the Dharmadhātu chapter) of the *Hua-yen Sūtra* in his *T'an-hsüan chi* (T 35.440b11ff.—cf. T 44.63b18–21). He points out that in the compound "dharmadhātu" (*fa-chieh*), "dharma" (*fa*) can have three meanings: that which upholds (*ch'ih*), that which serves as a norm (*kuei-tse*), and mental object (*tui-i*). "Dhātu" (*chieh*) likewise has three meanings: the cause (*yin*) (upon which noble path is realized), the nature (*hsing*) (upon which all dharmas are based), and the differentiated (*fen-ch'i*) (since all conditionally originated phenomena are distinct from one another). According to the first and second senses of dhātu, "dharmadhātu" refers to either the cause for the realization of the noble path or the underlying nature of phenomenal reality. In either case, its meaning is closely related to the tathāgatagarbha, and, indeed, in tathāgatagarbha texts such as the *Ratnagotravibhāga* the two terms are used synonymously. In the third sense of dhātu, however, Fa-tsang points out that dharma is equivalent to dhātu; "dharmadhātu" can thus also be understood to refer to differentiated phenomena. It is in this last sense that Fa-tsang uses the term in his *Treatise on the Five Teachings* (*Wu-chiao chang*); see Liu Ming-Wood, "The Teaching of Fa-tsang," pp. 391–396. Tsung-mi, as will be seen, understands the dharmadhātu in terms of the tathāgatagarbha.

ement," "cause," "essence," and "realm"; hence the compound "dharmadhātu" can refer to the "dharma-element" that inheres in all beings as the "cause" of their enlightenment as well as the "essence of all dharmas" or the "realm of dharma" that is realized in enlightenment. "Dharmadhātu" is particularly associated with the last chapter of the *Hua-yen Sūtra*, the "Ju fa-chieh p'in" (Chapter on entering the dharmadhātu). This chapter, which originated as an independent scripture (the *Gaṇḍavyūha*), was regarded by Chinese Buddhists as the culmination of the sūtra, wherein the philosophical content elaborated in the preceding chapters was reenacted in an allegory of the Buddhist path. It describes the visits of a young pilgrim, Sudhana, to fifty-three "good friends" (*kalyāṇamitra*) in his quest for enlightenment. Sudhana's pilgrimage reaches its dramatic climax with his meeting of Maitreya, the future Buddha, who snaps his fingers, thereby opening the door to his marvelous tower. When Sudhana enters, he experiences the totality of the dharmadhātu, which contains all world systems, in a mind-boggling succession of increasingly fantastic visions of interpenetration.[14]

The *Hua-yen Sūtra* that inspired Tu-shun's vision of interpenetration is a prodigious work, being the longest of all Mahāyāna scriptures. It is actually a compendium of a number of texts, many of which originally circulated as sūtras in their own right, that were combined sometime around or before the beginning of the fifth century when it was first brought to China from Khotan (408) and subsequently translated by Buddhabhadra (418–422).[15] A more developed version of the text was later translated by the Khotanese master Śikṣānanda at the very end of the seventh century (695–699). It would be futile, and not particularly useful, to try to summarize the contents of the sūtra here, for the Hua-yen tradition that took its name and spiritual warrant from this text was not primarily concerned with a careful exegesis of the original meaning of the scripture. Rather, what it discovered in the text was the justification for a number of ideas and metaphors in terms of which it elaborated its

[14] This episode represents the conclusion of Sudhana's pilgrimage in Buddhabhadra's translation of the text. Even though Śikṣānanda's translation adds a second and final visit to Mañjuśrī, Sudhana's entrance into Maitreya's tower remains the dramatic climax of his pilgrimage. For an English translation of the Śikṣānanda version (T 10.434c–437c), see Thomas Cleary, trans., *The Flower Ornament Scripture*, 3: 365–374. For a summary of Sudhana's pilgrimage, see Jan Fontein, *The Pilgrimage of Sudhana*, pp. 5–14. For an interesting discussion of Maitreya's tower as the possible inspiration for Barabuḍur, see Luis O. Gomez, "Observations of the Role of the *Gaṇḍavyūha* in the Design of Barabuḍur." See also Gomez, "Selected Verses from the *Gaṇḍavyūha*."

[15] A good summary of the research on the origins of this text can be found in Liu's "The Teaching of Fa-tsang," pp. 34–59.

own body of doctrine. Many of the key Hua-yen doctrines that were inspired by the scripture (such as nature origination, the conditioned origination of the dharmadhātu, the samādhi of oceanic reflection, or the six aspects of all dharmas) played only a peripheral role in or had a tenuous connection with the actual *Hua-yen Sūtra* itself. The great commentaries written on the text by Fa-tsang and Ch'eng-kuan were not so much concerned with tendering a faithful and judicious interpretation of the words of the text as they were with using the text as a basis from which to advance a doctrinal agenda that was determined by the context of Sui–T'ang Buddhism.

The career of the second Hua-yen "patriarch," Chih-yen, illustrates other aspects of the new Buddhism. His biography, as recorded in Fa-tsang's *Hua-yen ching chuan-chi* (Record of the transmission of the *Hua-yen Sūtra*), presents a dramatic account of his spiritual development.[16] It informs us that Chih-yen was inducted into the sangha in his twelfth year by Tu-shun. Tu-shun apparently laid his hand on the boy's head and told his parents that he belonged to him. He accordingly took Chih-yen back with him to the Chih-hsiang temple on Mount Chung-nan, where he entrusted his education to one of his senior disciples. Chih-yen subsequently moved on to study under some of the leading scholars in the capital. His early curriculum consisted in a comprehensive study of almost all of the major currents of the scholastic thought that had evolved during the fifth and sixth centuries.[17] Chih-yen proved himself a deft student, quickly mastering the complexities of this abstruse fare. However, far from endowing him with self-confidence, his command of these teachings only awakened a profound sense of despair. Perplexed over their lack of unanimity, Chih-yen then decided, in a gesture emblematic of the spirit of the new Buddhism, to reject the scholastic tradition and turn to the scriptures for the resolution of his doubts. Entrusting his fate to the "hand of faith," he selected the *Hua-yen Sūtra* from the collection of scriptures and embarked on a thorough study of the text and its commentaries. Yet even this did not fully settle his mind. Then, according to Fa-tsang, a strange monk, who mysteriously vanished as soon as he had spoken, directed him to meditate for two months on the meaning of the six aspects (*liu-hsiang*) of all dharmas expounded in the chapter on the ten bodhisattva stages. In less than a month of strenuous meditation, Chih-yen attained a profound understanding and accordingly, at the age of twenty-six, wrote a five-fascicle com-

[16] See T 51.163b18–164b13. For a translation see Gimello, "Chih-yen," pp. 59–60, 148–153, and 343–345.

[17] Of the six exegetical traditions, Chih-yen's biography mentions all but the San-lun, which, significantly, represents the Chinese appropriation of Madhyamaka.

mentary on the sūtra known as the *Sou-hsüan chi* (Record inquiring into the profundities [of the *Hua-yen Sūtra*]).[18] After any lingering uncertainty over the correctness of his interpretation was dispelled by a dream, he abandoned the life of the cloister to "wander in the hinterlands," in an apparent decision to follow in the footsteps of his original master, Tu-shun.[19]

The following three decades of Chih-yen's life are lost in obscurity, and he does not reemerge into public view until the end of his life. Some of the features of Chih-yen's early years can be noted here, however. His rejection of the scholastic tradition that had been a major component of his youthful training, his turning to the authority of the Buddha's word for the resolution of his doubts, and his reliance on his own meditational experience as the final basis for penetrating the meaning of the sūtra are all characteristic of the spirit of the new Buddhism. The "six aspects," which formed the content of the meditation that led to his hermeneutical breakthrough, appear only incidently in the *Hua-yen Sūtra* as part of an enumeration of the virtues of the novice bodhisattva and in no way constitute a discernible theme within the original text.[20] Such a creative appropriation of scripture is another distinguishing feature of the new Buddhism.

After leaving Chih-yen in 628, Fa-tsang's biography resumes in 661, when Chih-yen was awarded an imperial appointment as a chief lecturer. Chih-yen's final years brought recognition and acclaim. It was also during the last decade of his life that he completed two of his major works, the *Wu-shih yao wen-ta* (Fifty essential questions and answers)[21] and *K'ung-mu chang* (Hua-yen miscellany).[22] As the content of these works suggests, the event that seems to have precipitated Chih-yen's active reinvolvement in the world of Buddhist scholarship was Hsüan-tsang's return to China in 645 with a new version of Yogā-cāra teachings.[23] Indeed, the doctrinal efforts of the last decade of

---

[18] T 35.13b-106b, the full title of which is *Ta-fang-kuang fo hua-yen ching sou-hsüan fen-ch'i t'ung-chih fang-kuei* (The *Mahāvaipulyabuddhāvataṃsaka-sūtra*, a categorization of doctrine for the inquiry into its mysteries and a broad avenue for the access of penetrating insight into its meanings); for a synopsis, see Gimello, "Chih-yen," pp. 532–534.

[19] For an insightful discussion of Chih-yen's early career, see Gimello, "Chih-yen," pp. 154–170.

[20] Ibid., pp. 166–168.

[21] T 45.519a–536b; for a synopsis, see Gimello, "Chih-yen," pp. 536–537.

[22] T 45.536c–589b, the full title of which is *Hua-yen ching-nei chang-men teng-tsa k'ung-mu chang* (Essays on sundry topics in the *Hua-yen Sūtra*); for a synopsis see Gimello, "Chih-yen," pp. 539–542.

[23] For an authoritative summary of Hsüan-tsang's new version of Yogācāra, see Weinstein, "Imperial Patronage," pp. 291–297.

Chih-yen's career can be best understood as directed toward upholding the new Buddhism against the influence of Hsüan-tsang's views.[24]

Hsüan-tsang (596–664) was one of the most celebrated monks of the entire T'ang period, and the story of his pilgrimage to the western regions has been elaborated in over a thousand years of popular literature of all genres. After his return, Hsüan-tsang was enthusiastically patronized by the emperor T'ai-tsung, who helped him establish a translation bureau that in the next two decades rendered a large body of texts into Chinese, many of which belonged to the Yogācāra tradition of Indian Mahāyāna. Hsüan-tsang used these texts to introduce a new version of Yogācāra that was in many ways at odds with what previously had become accepted as the established Yogācāra tradition in China. The most flagrant point of controversy had to do with the claim that there was a special class of beings who were irrevocably banned from the prospect of attaining enlightenment. This doctrine in particular struck at the heart of what had become a cardinal tenet of all the Chinese Buddhist traditions (namely, that all beings have the capacity to achieve Buddhahood), and it was largely on this score that Chih-yen and the subsequent Hua-yen tradition classified Hsüan-tsang's brand of Buddhism as only a quasi-Mahāyāna teaching.

Thus, even though Hsüan-tsang's teaching chronologically falls within the T'ang period, its overall approach to Buddhism, especially its reliance on Indian sources of authority,[25] is more characteristic of the exegetical traditions of the fifth and sixth centuries. Moreover, in doctrinal terms, Chinese Buddhists saw it as harking back to a more primitive understanding of Mahāyāna. Chih-yen's reaction to Hsüan-tsang's new teachings, which the Hua-yen tradition referred to as Fa-hsiang, underscores the importance of a doctrine that had become a central article of faith among all the traditions of the new Buddhism.

This doctrine was the Buddha-nature or, as it is known in more technical nomenclature, the tathāgatagarbha (ju-lai-tsang). Meaning both the "embryo" or "womb of the Tathāgata," this doctrine referred to the potentiality for Buddhahood that existed embryonically

[24] For a thorough discussion of this point, see Gimello, "Chih-yen," pp. 338–414.

[25] This is well illustrated by an episode Gimello notes in Hsüan-tsang's biography. Hsüan-tsang seems to have experienced a crisis not unlike Chih-yen's, but his response was completely different. Instead of turning to the scriptures for a resolution of the doubts brought about by his awareness of the conflicting interpretations of Buddhist doctrine found in the scholastic tradition, he left for India to find the definitive version of Yogācārabhūmi (see ibid., pp. 348–350). Indeed, their different responses can be taken as emblematic of the difference between the earlier exegetical Buddhism and the new Buddhism represented by Tu-shun and Chih-yen.

within all sentient beings as well as the pure principle of Buddhahood that appeared enwombed within defiled sentient existence. Even though this doctrine seems to have been of relatively minor importance in Indian Buddhism, it assumed a significance in Chinese Buddhism that enabled it to stand on its own as a distinct tradition of Mahāyāna alongside of the two great Indian traditions of Madhyamaka and Yogācāra. This doctrine resonated with some of the perennial preoccupations of indigenous Chinese thought, such as its attempt to define human nature, clarify the sources of ethical action, and uncover the underlying ontological matrix from which the phenomenal world evolves. Chinese Buddhists not only valued the tathāgatagarbha doctrine for providing a basis for faith in the universal accessibility of enlightenment but also found within it a rationale for qualifying the radical apophasis of the Madhyamaka teaching of emptiness and thus developing a vision of Buddhism that affirmed life in this world. The Chinese appropriation of this doctrine was elaborated in a number of apocryphal texts, most notably the *Awakening of Faith in Mahāyāna* (*Ta-sheng ch'i-hsin lun*), a treatise that will figure heavily in the chapters to come.

The tathāgatagarbha doctrine was central to the earlier Chinese Yogācāra tradition to which Chih-yen appealed in his refutation of Hsüan-tsang's new Yogācāra teaching. In his *Wu-shih yao wen-ta* and *K'ung-mu chang*, Chih-yen drew from the doctrinal arsenal that had previously been developed within the Ti-lun and She-lun traditions and reformulated them so as to defend Tu-shun's new vision. The tathāgatagarbha, especially as it was developed in the *Awakening of Faith*, was also important in Fa-tsang's systematization of Hua-yen. Fa-tsang studied under Chih-yen in the imperial capital of Ch'ang-an from 662 until 668. In 670, only two years after Chih-yen's death, Fa-tsang was installed as abbot of the T'ai-yüan temple, which the future empress Wu dedicated to the memory of her deceased mother, thus beginning the imperial patronage that was to continue throughout the rest of his life.[26]

Fa-tsang is usually credited with bringing Hua-yen thought to its final culmination, and the subsequent history of the tradition is often treated as a footnote to his grand achievement. The contributions of later T'ang figures such as Ch'eng-kuan and Tsung-mi (not to mention the layman Li T'ung-hsüan) thus frequently tend to be overlooked or minimalized. But such a picture of the tradition ignores the dynamic and many-faceted character of Hua-yen thought by slight-

[26] For a study of Fa-tsang's life, see Yoshizu Yoshihide, "Hōzō-den no kenkyū"; see also Liu, "The Teaching of Fa-tsang," pp. 2–18.

ing the importance of the changing historical context in which Hua-yen ideas evolved and changed throughout the course of the T'ang dynasty. It also presupposes a standard of orthodoxy that is based on a static and one-dimensional understanding of the nature of a religious tradition (*tsung*). Such an approach is wont to presume that because the thought of a later figure like Tsung-mi deviates from the classical norm defined by Fa-tsang, it can be of only marginal importance. Although the notion of a religious tradition (*tsung*) implies a shared sense of historical continuity, it does not thereby also imply that its concerns and goals are not subject to change. To gain a more rounded understanding of Hua-yen as a living historical tradition, one must set aside the value judgments implicit in such an ideological approach to Chinese Buddhism.

A study of Tsung-mi's thought is thus valuable for clarifying the extent to which Hua-yen changed during the eighth and early ninth centuries. By expanding our understanding of the diversity encompassed within the tradition, it thereby also provides a corrective to the tendency to define the essence of a tradition such as Hua-yen in terms of a normative doctrine wholly detached from any historical context. Later chapters will take Fa-tsang's formulation of Hua-yen as a base from which to gauge the scope of such change by comparing his hierarchical classification of Buddhist teachings with that of Tsung-mi. Such a comparison shows that Tsung-mi's revalorization of Hua-yen thought extended to some of the most fundamental orientations of the tradition. Most notably, Tsung-mi deleted from his system of classification the very teaching that Fa-tsang had ranked highest—that is, the vision of the unobstructed interpenetration of phenomena that the earlier tradition had deemed to be the defining characteristic of Hua-yen thought. And it was precisely this vision that set Hua-yen apart from all other traditions of Buddhism and justified its claim to be the most profound teaching of the Buddha. Tsung-mi thereby displaced the *Hua-yen Sūtra*, the scripture from which the tradition took its name, and ceded pride of place to the teaching exemplified by the *Awakening of Faith*.

The differences between Tsung-mi's and Fa-tsang's formulation of Hua-yen not only bring into focus the unique character of Tsung-mi's contribution, they also point to some of the larger forces to which the tradition had to adapt, the most important of which was the rise of Ch'an, the other major Chinese Buddhist tradition with which Tsung-mi was affiliated. Just as a study of Tsung-mi's writings yields a more balanced understanding of the Hua-yen tradition, it also helps to form a clearer picture of Ch'an during the late T'ang. Tsung-mi wrote two major works on Ch'an that survive: the *Preface to the Collected Writings on the Source of Ch'an (Ch'an-yüan chu-ch'üan-chi tu-hsü*, referred to hereafter as *Ch'an Preface)*[27] and the *Chart of the Master-Disciple Succession of the Ch'an Gate that Transmits the Mind Ground in China (Chung-hua ch'uan-hsin-ti ch'an-men shih-tzu ch'eng-hsi t'u*, referred to hereafter as *Ch'an Chart).*[28] These works are especially valuable because they offer a contemporary account of Ch'an during the late T'ang and so provide a corrective to the traditional picture of Ch'an that only assumed its definitive form during the Sung (960–1279). Tsung-mi describes several traditions that, because they did not survive into the Sung, were not recorded in the standard Sung histories of the transmission of the lamp. Modern historians have thus been able to use Tsung-mi's writings along with the Tun-huang manuscripts to reconstruct the history of T'ang-dynasty Ch'an.

The traditional picture of Ch'an history is encapsulated in the well-known formula retrospectively attributed to Bodhidharma, the legendary figure believed to have brought Ch'an to China—namely, that Ch'an is "a special transmission independent of the doctrinal teachings (*chiao-wai pieh-ch'uan*) that does not rely on the written word (*pu-li wen-tzu*) but, by directly pointing to the human mind (*chih-chih jen-hsin*), enables humans to see their nature and realize their Buddhahood (*chien-hsing ch'eng-fo*)." These four phrases express the tradition's claim to represent "mind-to-mind transmission" (*i-hsin-*

---

[27] T 48, no. 2015. For a critically edited, annotated version of the text with Japanese translation, see Kamata Shigeo, trans., *Zengen shosenshū tojo*, which will be cited as "K" hereafter. Jeffrey Broughton has translated this text as part of his 1975 Columbia University Ph.D. dissertation, "Kuei-feng Tsung-mi: The Convergence of Ch'an and the Teachings," which will be cited as "B" hereafter. For a discussion of the Tun-huang version of this text, see Tanaka Ryōshō, "Tonkōbon *Zengen shosenshū tojo* zankan kō" (the original version of which has been reprinted in his *Tonkō zenshū bunken no kenkyū*).

[28] HTC 110.433c–438b. A critically edited, annotated version of the text with Japanese translation is also contained in Kamata's *Zengen shosenshū tojo*. Based on a comparison with the quotations from this text that appear in Chinul's *Pŏpchip pyŏrhaeng nok chŏryo pyŏngip sagi* (hereafter referred to as *Chŏryo*), Ui Hakuju has pointed out that the HTC edition is missing some 288 characters; see *Zenshūshi kenkyū*, 3:477–510. Kamata has accordingly incorporated the missing section into his edition. The text seems to have originally borne the title of *P'ei Hsiu shih-i wen*, as a version with that title was recently discovered in Shinpuku-ji in Japan and has been published by Ishii Shūdō in *Zengaku kenkyū*. The Shinpuku-ji text contains the missing section quoted by Chinul as well as three other short essays by Tsung-mi. These were all originally published together as part of a collection of essays Tsung-mi had written in response to questions from his lay and clerical followers that his disciples compiled shortly after his death under the title of *Tao-su ch'ou-ta wen-chi*. At some point the *Ch'an Chart* came to circulate in a separate edition (*pieh-hsing*; K. *pyŏrhaeng*) under the title of *Fa-chi* (K. *Pŏpchip*), and, as Jan Yün-hua has argued persuasively in his "*Fa-chi* and Chinul's Understanding of Tsung-mi," it was that edition that formed the basis of Chinul's *Pŏpchip pyŏrhaeng nok chŏryo pyŏngip sagi*.

ch'uan-hsin) that links Chinese Ch'an masters through an unbroken patriarchal succession all the way back to the historical Buddha. The "mind" that is passed on is, of course, the Buddha's enlightened understanding, and it is for that reason that the tradition does not need to base its authority on written texts, which, after all, are merely a reflection of the Buddha's experience. The ideas on which this theory are based can be traced back to the late seventh or early eighth century, but the theory itself did not assume final form as a set formula until the Sung.[29] The Sung Ch'an historians looked back to the T'ang period as a golden age and celebrated the sayings and doings of the great masters of the late eighth and ninth centuries as embodying its spirit. This picture also assumes that Ch'an had somehow fallen from its once pristine state when the exemplars of the late T'ang lived and taught.

Such a vision, of course, is a myth that tells us more about the ideals and self-conception of Ch'an in the Sung than it does about its actual history in the T'ang, and modern scholars, utilizing the window on early Ch'an history opened up by the Tun-huang documents, have directed their efforts toward deconstructing it. Yet, despite the enormous amount of work and the high quality of critical scholarship that has gone into rewriting the early history of Ch'an, Griffith Foulk has shown that much of that scholarship is still framed by preconceptions implicit in Sung Ch'an historiography.[30] As such it assumes a notion of "Ch'an" for which there is little evidence in the T'ang sources; nor has it yet succeeded in freeing itself from value judgments based on Ch'an theology of a mind-to-mind transmission and mythical notions of a "pure" Ch'an from which the later tradition fell.

It is in this context that Tsung-mi's Ch'an writings are particularly valuable. One could even argue that they yield a better picture of the Ch'an landscape in the T'ang than does any other single source. Tun-huang "Ch'an histories" like the *Ch'uan fa-pao chi* (Annals of the transmission of the dharma-treasure),[31] *Leng-ch'ieh shih-tzu chi* (Records of the masters and disciples of the Laṅka[avatāra]),[32] and *Li-tai*

[29] These four phrases first appear as a set formula in the *Tsu-t'ing shih-yüan* compiled by Shan-ch'ing in 1108; see HTC 113.66c10–13; see also Isshū Miura and Ruth Fuller Sasaki, *Zen Dust*, pp. 229–230.

[30] See his 1987 University of Michigan Ph.D. dissertation, "The 'Ch'an School' and Its Place in the Buddhist Monastic Tradition."

[31] T 85, no. 2838, compiled by Tu Fei sometime during the first decade of the eighth century. For a critically edited, annotated version of the text with a Japanese translation, see Yanagida Seizan, *Shoki no zenshi I*. John McRae has translated this text in his *The Northern School and the Formation of Early Ch'an Buddhism*, pp. 255–269.

[32] T 85, no. 2837, written by Ching-chüeh between 713 and 716. For a critically edited, annotated version of the text with a Japanese translation, see Yanagida, *Shoki no*

fa-pao chi (Records of the dharma-treasure down through the generations)[33] chronicle the teachings and dharma succession within a particular tradition. Such works are blatantly partisan, their main goal
being to legitimate a particular tradition of Ch'an and either directly
or indirectly impugn the claims of their rivals. Tsung-mi's work is
unique in that it attempts a synthetic overview of the various Ch'an
traditions of his day. Although the framework within which Tsung-
mi discusses these traditions reflects his own sectarian standpoint, it
is nevertheless creditable in its overall picture of the rich diversity
that characterized the Ch'an of the late T'ang. His account indicates
that there was no particular teaching or approach to meditation that
all the competing Ch'an traditions had in common. Tsung-mi, in fact,
takes pains to show how various traditions were based on different
Buddhist teachings and how they accordingly drew different conclusions about the implications of those teachings for Buddhist practice.
His writings demonstrate that "Ch'an" in the late T'ang was still a
relatively amorphous phenomenon. While the different traditions all
shared a common claim of lineal connection with Bodhidharma,
there was as yet no clear idea of a "Ch'an" school. Nor is there any
evidence of a distinctively "Ch'an" institution. What seems to emerge
as unique is a new rhetoric expressing a heightened sensitivity to the
danger of dualistic formulations that was occasioned by Shen-hui's
attack on the Northern tradition associated with Shen-hsiu and his
followers.[34]

With Shen-hsiu's (606?–706) grand welcome to the court at the beginning of the eighth century, Ch'an[35] began to emerge from an isolated and self-contained phenomenon into a national movement.
Shen-hsiu's East Mountain tradition was lavishly patronized by empress Wu (r. 690–705), and his cohorts and disciples were honored
by subsequent monarchs. Although Shen-hsiu's tradition continued
to thrive throughout the eighth century,[36] the particular form of
Ch'an that is most important for understanding Tsung-mi's background grew out of a rival movement begun by Ho-tse Shen-hui
(684–758), the master from whom Tsung-mi claimed descent. In a
series of public lectures beginning in 730, Shen-hui denounced the

---

zenshi I. J. C. Cleary has translated this text in his *Zen Dawn*; see review by John McRae
in *The Eastern Buddhist.*

[33] T 51, no. 2075, compiled around 780. For a critically edited, annotated version of
the text with a Japanese translation, see Yanagida Seizan, *Shoki no zenshi II.*

[34] See John McRae, "Shen-hui and the Teaching of Sudden Enlightenment in Early
Ch'an Buddhism."

[35] Or, more accurately, what retrospectively came to be seen as Ch'an.

[36] The best account of this line of Ch'an can be found in McRae's *The Northern School.*

tradition represented by Shen-hsiu's successors on two main counts. The first called into question the credentials of Shen-hsiu's lineage. Shen-hui charged that the fifth patriarch Hung-jen (601–674) had not transmitted the dharma to Shen-hsiu, as his followers claimed, but had secretly transmitted it to an obscure disciple named Hui-neng (638–713), who was therefore the sole legitimate sixth patriarch of Ch'an. As proof of the transmission, Shen-hui alleged that the fifth patriarch had given Hui-neng the robe that had been passed down from Bodhidharma.

Shen-hui went on to claim that Shen-hsiu had not received the transmission from the fifth patriarch because his understanding of Ch'an was defective. Whereas Shen-hsiu taught a "gradualistic" approach to meditation practice that was fundamentally dualistic, Hui-neng advocated the true "sudden" teaching of no-thought (wu-nien). Shen-hui's criticisms were later developed in the Platform Sūtra, where the famous story over the exchange of verses between Shen-hsiu and Hui-neng became the accepted explanation for the split between the Northern and Southern lines of Ch'an. Shen-hui's attack initiated a period of sectarian rivalry that characterizes much of the history of Ch'an in the eighth century. In addition to the Northern and Southern rift, the Ox-head (Niu-t'ou) tradition arose as an alternative untainted by the invective associated with Northern and Southern controversy.[37]

With the An Lu-shan rebellion in the middle of the eighth century, the Chinese political order became fragmented, patterns of patronage changed, and Ch'an began to develop in a number of regional forms. Among these, the Szechwan traditions documented by Tsung-mi were particularly important, for it was out of that milieu that the style of Ch'an that was later to emerge as orthodox in the Sung developed. Shen-hui's influence was particularly strong in Szechwan. His teaching of no-thought was a central element in the teachings of both Wu-hsiang (694–762) and Wu-chu (714–774), two of the major figures in this region, and his story of the transmission of the patriarchal robe was further elaborated in the Li-tai fa-pao chi, where it was used to legitimate the claims of the Pao-t'ang tradition of Wu-chu.

Tsung-mi was sharply critical of the Pao-t'ang tradition, and it is in light of his qualms about its radical extension of the meaning of nondualism that his criticism of the Hung-chou tradition is best understood. The Hung-chou tradition derived from Ma-tsu Tao-i (709–788), who, like Tsung-mi, hailed from Szechwan. It boasted a succession of great teachers—such as Pai-chang, Huang-po, and Lin-chi—and

---

[37] See John McRae, "The Ox-head School of Chinese Ch'an Buddhism."

was the tradition from which four out of the five main lineages of Sung Ch'an claimed descent. The essential criticism that Tsung-mi leveled against the Hung-chou tradition was that its attitude that Ch'an practice consisted in "entrusting oneself to act freely according to the nature of one's feelings" had dangerous antinomian implications. Tsung-mi's sensitivity to such ethical concerns gains importance when seen in the context of his reaction to the Pao-t'ang tradition, which had, according to his account, interpreted Shen-hui's teaching of "no-thought" to entail the rejection of all forms of traditional Buddhist ethical practice and ritual observance. In exploring this theme in later chapters I shall argue that Tsung-mi saw a similarity in the ethical import of the Hung-chou line of Ch'an and the religious paradigm associated with the *Hua-yen Sūtra*, which helps explain why he displaced that text in favor of the *Awakening of Faith* in his systematic evaluation of Buddhist teachings.

Tsung-mi's response to the Ch'an movements of his day—especially his critique of the Hung-chou tradition—thus provides the context for understanding his reformulation of Hua-yen theory. The various revisions that he made in Hua-yen thought can all be seen in terms of his attempt to provide an ontological basis and philosophical rationale for Ch'an practice. For this purpose the *Awakening of Faith* provided a more appropriate model than the *Hua-yen Sūtra*. It at once offered an ontology that locates enlightenment within the original nature of man and at the same time furnished an explanation of how the process of delusion arises and perpetuates itself. As chapter 7 will detail, Tsung-mi took this text to provide a "cosmogony" that he made serve as a "map" for Buddhist practice.

Tsung-mi's adaptation of the cosmogony he derived from the *Awakening of Faith* thus served to establish a clear linkage between the ontological basis of reality and ethical behavior and thereby to check the antinomian dangers that he perceived in the Pao-t'ang and Hung-chou teachings. The ethical tenor of Tsung-mi's critique also points to the lasting influence of the Confucian moral vision that he had absorbed in his early studies before his Ch'an conversion at the age of twenty-four. Moreover, his attempt to articulate the ultimate ground for religious practice, and his related criticism of the more radical interpretations of Ch'an, foreshadow both the general concerns and specific moves seen in Chu Hsi's (1130–1200) Neo-Confucian criticism of Buddhism in the Sung. Indeed, the kind of theory articulated in Tsung-mi's interpretation of the *Awakening of Faith* refined the set of issues in terms of which Neo-Confucian thinkers formulated their response to Buddhism. Not only does the specifically ethical thrust of Tsung-mi's critique of Hung-chou Ch'an parallel

Chu Hsi's subsequent critique of Buddhism, but the very form that Tsung-mi's defense takes anticipates in fascinating ways Chu Hsi's theory of human nature. The last chapter of this study will accordingly show how Chu Hsi's critique of the Buddhist understanding of human nature paralleled Tsung-mi's critique of the Hung-chou tradition.

A study of Tsung-mi's thought is thus not only important for understanding some of the major developments within the Chinese Buddhist world of the late T'ang but also for bringing into focus some of the recurring themes in Chinese intellectual history that are important for understanding the complex process by which Buddhism accommodated itself to Chinese cultural values at the same time that it thereby also transformed those values. An examination of the life and thought of Tsung-mi therefore offers a pivotal vantage point for understanding how the Chinese adapted Buddhism to their own religious and philosophical concerns as well as clarifying the ways in which Buddhism expanded the realm of discourse in which those concerns were conceived.

. . .

Tsung-mi's interests were not confined to Hua-yen and Ch'an. His scholarship was broad ranging, and he wrote commentaries to a variety of Buddhist texts. The ones for which he is best known deal with the *Scripture of Perfect Enlightenment* (*Yüan-chüeh ching*). But he also wrote commentaries on an array of texts as diverse as the *Diamond Sūtra*, the *Nirvāṇa Sūtra*, the *Ch'eng wei-shih lun*, the *Yü-lan-p'en ching*, and the *Pien-tsung lun*—a sample covering a spectrum of interests from the paradoxes of the Perfection of Wisdom, the universality of Buddha-nature within all beings, a technical exposition of the meaning of the Yogācāra doctrine of representation-only, the story of Maudgalyāyana's rescue of his mother from hell as an expression of Buddhist filiality enacted in the popular ghost festival, to Hsieh Ling-yün's famous early fifth-century defense of Tao-sheng's theory of sudden enlightenment.[38]

[38] Of these five last mentioned works, only Tsung-mi's commentary to the *Yü-lan-p'en ching* survives (T no. 1792). For a discussion of this text, see Stephen Teiser, *The Ghost Festival in Medieval China*. Tsung-mi mentions his commentaries to the *Diamond Sūtra* and the *Ch'eng wei-shih lun* in his own autobiographical comments (see chapter 2). The other commentaries are listed in an appendix to the Tun-huang version of the *Ch'an Preface*; see Tanaka, "Tonkōbon *Zengen shosenshū tojo* zankan kō." See appendix II for a discussion of Tsung-mi's oeuvre.

In addition to such predominantly doctrinal interests, Tsung-mi was also deeply concerned with Buddhist practice. He not only took pains to articulate the theoretical basis of Buddhist practice but also wrote extensively on its details as well. Most noteworthy in this regard is his massive eighteen-fascicle ritual manual, the *Yüan-chüeh ching tao-t'ang hsiu-cheng i*, which drew extensively from Chih-i's (538–597) various ritual and meditation manuals in order to elaborate a complex program of ritual and meditation practice in terms of the *Scripture of Perfect Enlightenment*.[39] Tsung-mi also wrote a four-fascicle commentary on the *Ssu-fen lü*, based on the Dharmagupta vinaya adapted by Tao-hsüan, and composed hymns to be used in Buddhist liturgy.

While his commentaries and ritual manuals were aimed at a largely monastic audience, he also composed works with a broader appeal, including a number of essays written in response to queries posed by prominent literati of his day. The most famous of these was undoubtedly his *Inquiry into the Origin of Man* (*Yüan jen lun*), with which later chapters will be much concerned.

Such a diversity of interest drew fire from more sectarian quarters, and Tsung-mi was criticized for it by both contemporaries and later generations. On the question of whether Tsung-mi was rightly to be regarded as a Ch'an practitioner, vinaya specialist, or textual exegete, Tsan-ning (919–100l') commented: "Tsung-mi is a country fought over on all sides. Yet none has succeeded in laying claim to him."[40] He then quoted from Tsung-mi's epitaph, written by his lay disciple P'ei Hsiu (787?–860):

> Critics claim that the great master did not observe *ch'an* practice but lectured widely on [Buddhist] scriptures and treatises, traveled about to famous cities and the great capitals, and took his task to be the promotion [of Buddhism]. Does this not show that he was a slave to his erudition? Is it not that he had not yet forgotten fame and profit?

[39] HTC 128.361a–498c. In his *Tendai shō shikan no kenkyū*, Sekiguchi Shindai has shown that the discussions of meditation found in the first and last two fascicles of this text consist almost entirely of excerpts from Chih-i's *Hsiao chih-kuan* reassembled in a different order; see also Kamata Shigeo, *Shūmitsu kyōgaku no shisōshi-teki kenkyū*, pp. 499–608. The first two fascicles of the text draw on Chih-i's *Fa-hua san-mei ch'an-i*, as Ikeda Rosan has pointed out in his "*Engakukyō dōjō shūshōgi* no reizanhō." For a discussion of the influence of this text on Tsung-tse's twelfth-century manual of seated meditation, see Carl Bielefeldt's "Ch'ang-lu Tsung-tse's *Tso-ch'an i* and the 'Secret' of Zen Meditation."

[40] SKSC 742b5–7.

P'ei Hsiu faithfully went on to rebut such criticism:

> Alas! How could such critics understand the purpose of the great Way?
> Now, the one mind is that which encompasses the myriad dharmas.
> When separated, it becomes discipline (śīla), concentration (samādhi),
> and wisdom (prajñā); when opened, it becomes the six perfections; and
> when divided, it becomes the myriad practices. The myriad practices
> never go against the one mind, and the one mind never opposes the
> myriad practices. Since *ch'an* [i.e., dhyāna] is but one of the six perfec-
> tions, how could it encompass all dharmas?[41]

The impressive scope of Tsung-mi's scholarship stands in apparent
contradiction to Ch'an's professed rejection of scriptural authority
based on its claim to have privileged access to the Buddha's enlightenment. Such a conceit not only played an important role in the process by which Ch'an legitimated itself as an authentic form of Buddhism but also expressed some of its most central religious values. Yet
one must not be so naive as to take it at face value. Protestations to
the contrary, Ch'an was based on the kinds of doctrinal innovations
effected by the new Buddhists of the Sui and T'ang,[42] and a study of
Tsung-mi's thought helps to clarify the doctrinal foundation on
which Ch'an was predicated. When one lays aside the historiograph-
ical presumptions of Sung Ch'an, the evidence suggests that scriptural study, repentance ritual, and seated meditation all formed an
important part of "Ch'an" practice during T'ang. While Tsung-mi
may have been exceptional in the degree to which he was versed in
them all, these interests were all integral aspects of "Ch'an" practice,
which in the T'ang cannot be dissociated from Chinese monastic
practice as a whole. Although Ch'an rhetoric, seen in Shen-hui's subitist criticism of Shen-hsiu's dualistic approach to meditation, may
have served to undercut *ch'an* (i.e., meditation) practice on a theoretical level, there is little indication that it had much effect on a practical level. The Pao-t'ang tradition's attempt to apply its implications
literally seems to have been an exception, and even here there is good
reason to suppose that Tsung-mi's portrayal of its radical character
may have been overdrawn.

---

[41] P'ei Hsiu's epitaph can be found in *Chin-shih ts'ui-pien* 114.6b-7c and CTW
743.12b-17b. Kamata has conveniently listed the variations in his reproduction of the
CTW text in his *Shūmitsu kyōgaku no shisōshi-teki kenkyū*, pp. 49–52. All references to P'ei
Hsiu's epitaph will be cited from Kamata's *Shūmitsu* by page and line number. The
present passage comes from p. 50.9–12. Cf. Jan Yün-hua, "Tsung-mi: His Analysis of
Ch'an Buddhism," p. 25, and B 63.

[42] This is also a major theme in Robert Buswell's excellent new book, *The Formation
of Ch'an Ideology in China and Korea.*

The issue of Tsung-mi's diverse interests also raises once again the question of sectarian affiliation. Even though he identified with Shen-hui's Ho-tse tradition and equated it with the highest teaching of Buddhism, he did not view himself as a specifically "Ch'an" or "Hua-yen" figure. Indeed, much of his work can only be understood as a reaction against the sectarian divisions that rent the Buddhist world of the eighth and early ninth centuries. One of the avowed aims of his *Ch'an Preface*, after all, was to articulate an all-encompassing intellectual framework in which such apparent differences could all be shown to be but different perspectives within a broader, unified vision. Thus, as will be shown in chapter 9, Tsung-mi contended that the teachings passed down by the Ch'an patriarchs did not conflict with the doctrinal teachings preserved in the Buddhist canon, because both derived from Śākyamuni Buddha. Tsung-mi was therefore able to equate the principles espoused by the various Ch'an traditions with different doctrinal teachings, thereby allowing him to classify them in a hierarchical order just as the Buddhist teachings were classified. While such a method enabled him to justify the superiority of his own tradition, it also created a framework in which all of the other traditions could be incorporated and thereby validated. Their error lay in the fact that they did not recognize their own partiality. Their truth was validated, however, once they were seen as integral parts of the larger whole to which they belonged. The logic by which such a synthetic approach worked was dialectical. Each teaching overcame the particular shortcoming of the one that preceded it, and the highest teaching was accorded that vaunted position precisely because it succeeded in sublating all of the other teachings within itself.

Tsung-mi is also important for extending his synthetic reach to Confucianism and Taoism, as will be discussed in chapter 10. His thought thus represents a significant milestone in the development of the theory of the essential unity of the three traditions (of Buddhism, Confucianism, and Taoism), which was an important feature of Sung discourse before achieving its full development in the Ming (1368–1644).[43]

The later Ch'an tradition regarded Tsung-mi with ambivalence. For one thing, the Ho-tse tradition with which he identified did not survive into the Sung. Since it was centered around the capital of

[43] The classical discussions of the "three religions" remain Tokiwa Daijō, *Shina ni okeru bukkyō to jukyō dōkyō*; Kubota Ryōon, *Shina ju dō butsu sankyō shiron*; and Kubota, *Shina ju dō butsu kōshō-shi*. For more recent summaries, see Miriam Levering, "Ch'an Enlightenment for Laymen," pp. 103–170, and Judith Berling, *The Syncretic Religion of Lin Chao-en*, pp. 14–61.

Ch'ang-an, it was particularly vulnerable to the depredations of the great persecution carried out by Wu-tsung shortly after Tsung-mi's death. Other traditions, such as the Hung-chou, which were located in areas in which the central government had little direct control, were more fortunate. Moreover, Tsung-mi's critique of the Hung-chou tradition, from which the dominant lineages of Sung Ch'an claimed descent, made his assessment of Ch'an awkward in the eyes of Sung Buddhists. Nevertheless, his texts continued to be studied and commented upon, and, as Foulk has argued, it was Tsung-mi's ecumenical vision of Ch'an as a many-branched family tree that was taken over in the Sung lamp histories.

The place where Tsung-mi's thought had the greatest long term influence was Korea, where it became a cornerstone in Chinul's (1158–1210) systematic formulation of Sŏn practice, as has been documented in Robert Buswell's authoritative study.[44] Chinul's thought still continues to provide a major template for Korean Buddhist practice today. The applicability of models of Ch'an/Sŏn practice Chinul appropriated from Tsung-mi is a central focus of debate within the modern sangha and, as I was surprised to discover in a visit in 1988, can even be the topic of feature newspaper articles and television comment.

[44] See his *The Korean Approach to Zen*.

PART ONE

Tsung-mi's Life

Chapter Two

A BIOGRAPHY OF TSUNG-MI

Tsung-mi's life (780–841) falls between the An Lu-shan rebellion (755–763) and the Hui-ch'ang persecution of Buddhism (841–845). This was a period of momentous political, economic, social, and intellectual change. The fragmentation and centrifugal shift of power that occurred in the wake of the rebellion necessitated major readjustments in political and economic organization that altered the structure of Chinese society and called forth a profound response among the intelligentsia.

Such changes also affected patterns of patronage. Although different T'ang emperors continued to support Buddhism to varying degrees, regional political and military magnates came to play an increasingly important role in the direction in which Buddhism evolved during the second part of the T'ang. Kamata Shigeo has suggested that these figures were less likely to support the more "philosophical" type of Buddhism that had been patronized by the court before the rebellion than they were the more "practice-oriented" varieties of Ch'an that proliferated during the second half of the eighth and first half of the ninth centuries and hence were a major factor in the shift in Hua-yen thought that will be described in subsequent chapters.[1] Whatever the validity of Kamata's hypothesis, such figures, as the present chapter will show, were instrumental in shaping Szechwanese Buddhism during the late T'ang.

The first forty years of Tsung-mi's life coincided with the attempts of two powerful emperors to restore T'ang power, although their struggle to bring recalcitrant provinces back within imperial control met with only limited success. Their efforts to reassert T'ang authority led to their increasing reliance on institutions outside of the regular bureaucracy, especially the eunuchs, who, at the height of Tsung-mi's career in the late 820s and early 830s, had come to dominate court politics. From the beginning of the ninth century, eunuchs had also extended their control over the supervision of the Buddhist church, and mounting anti-eunuch sentiment among the literati, who filled the important ranks within the regular bureau-

[1] See, for example, his "Chūtō no bukkyō no hendō to kokka kenryoku." He makes the same point in his *Chūgoku kegon shisōshi no kenkyū*.

cracy, consequently was often directed against the privileges of the church. Buddhism was criticized on other fronts as well, as given voice in Han Yü's (768–824) strident brand of Confucianism. These factors contributed to the massive persecution of the religion, whose beginnings began to gather momentum in the last year of Tsung-mi's life, carried out by Wu-tsung (r. 840–846).

Classical Background (780–804)

Tsung-mi was born in 780 in Hsi-ch'ung County in Kuo-chou in what was then known as the province of Chien-nan East (corresponding to the western part of present-day Nan-ch'ung County in central Szechwan) between the Fu and Chia-ling rivers some fifteen to twenty miles northwest of the prefectural capital (see fig. 2.1). His family, the Ho, evidently belonged to the local elite. Yet other than P'ei Hsiu's laconic remark, repeated in subsequent biographies, that he came from a powerful family (*hao chia*),[2] little else is known about his social background. Although P'ei Hsiu's choice of terms suggests that his family were not traditional members of the literati, they nevertheless had the means, and saw fit, to provide their son with a proper Confucian education. Such an education was necessary in order to succeed in the civil service examinations that were one of the main channels through which members of the provincial elite could enter into the national elite. Even though it would have been difficult for someone of Tsung-mi's social background to succeed in the national examinations without substantial literati connections,[3] such an education would surely have opened the doors to a career in the provincial government, which in Szechwan in the late eighth and early ninth centuries operated with a large degree of independence. The powerful regional commanders who controlled the area recruited their own staffs outside of the imperial bureaucracy. Although such an alternative may have been less attractive than gaining a post in the national government, it was one to which a number of promising young scholars in the post–An Lu-shan era were forced to turn—the most notable example being Han Yü. Alluding to Tsung-mi's youthful ambition to enter public service, P'ei Hsiu's epitaph notes that he studied

[2] Kamata, *Shūmitsu*, p. 50.3. SKSC (741c23) and CTL (205c12) add "prosperous" (*sheng*).

[3] See Arthur Waley, *The Life and Times of Po Chü-i*, pp. 18–19, for a description of the importance of candidates winning patronage of prominent literati to success in the examinations. For an account of Han Yü's difficulties with the examination system, see Charles Hartman's *Han Yü and the T'ang Search for Unity*, pp. 24–34.

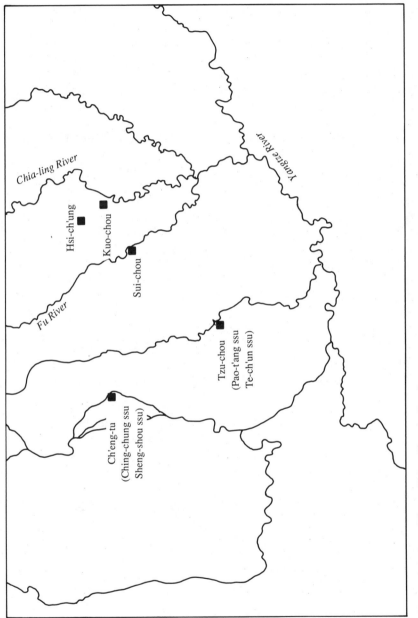

Figure 2.1. Late T'ang Ch'an Sites in Szechwan

Confucian texts when young, "desiring to take part in the world in order to benefit living beings."[4]

Besides these sparse facts, Tsung-mi's official biographies yield scant independent information on his early life. Where they do contain details that help to flesh out a picture of his development, they draw from his own autobiographical comments, which remain the most important source for his life up until the age of forty-three, when he completed his *Commentary to the Scripture of Perfect Enlightenment*. Tsung-mi summarizes his early years in his preface to that work: "When young, I concentrated on the announcements of Lu [i.e., Confucian studies]. At the age of capping [around twenty], I inquired into Indian tomes [i.e., Buddhism]. In both cases I was sunk in traps and snares and only tasted chaff and dregs."[5]

Tsung-mi's subcommentary fortunately unpacks the allusions in this highly compacted passage.[6] There he notes that from the age of six to fifteen or sixteen he devoted himself to Confucian studies (*ju-hsüeh*). For the next three years, from seventeen or eighteen to twenty or twenty-one, while wearing plain (mourning?) garments (*su-fu*) and living on his family's estate (*chuang chu*), he studied Buddhist scriptures and treatises. From twenty-two to twenty-four he once again concentrated his efforts on Confucian texts, studying at the I-hsüeh yüan, a Confucian academy in Sui-chou.[7] Tsung-mi's initial letter to Ch'eng-kuan, written in October 811, adds that during his three years of retirement he "gave up eating meat, examined [Buddhist] scriptures and treatises, became familiar with the virtues of meditation, and sought out the acquaintance of noted monks. Living on our estate, I frequently took part in dharma gatherings and, wearing plain garments, I gave myself over to discussing their meaning."[8]

Jan Yün-hua has speculated that this time coincided with the traditional three-year period of ritual mourning,[9] in which case Tsung-mi would have lost his father when he was seventeen or eighteen. This supposition seems highly probable. The plain garments that

---

[4] Kamata, *Shūmitsu*, p. 50.3–4; repeated in SKSC 741c24.

[5] TS 109c12–13; LS 524b20–21.

[6] Tsung-mi traces his allusion to "traps and snares" from Wang Pi's commentary to the *I ching* to the following well-known passage from the *Chuang-tzu*: "The fish trap exists because of the fish; once you've gotten the fish, you can forget the trap. The rabbit snare exists because of the rabbit; once you've gotten the rabbit, you can forget the snare. Words exist because of meaning; once you've gotten the meaning, you can forget the words" (75/26/48–49; Watson, trans., *The Complete Works of Chuang Tzu*, p. 302).

[7] TSC 222a1–d8; LSC 105d8–106d1.

[8] T 39.576c12–14.

[9] "Tsung-mi," p. 6.

Tsung-mi described himself as wearing can refer to the clothes worn during mourning; hence *su-fu* was an expression often used as an euphemism for being in mourning.[10] That Tsung-mi intended such an implication is further suggested by a statement in his introduction to his commentary to the *Yü-lan-p'en ching*: "I, Tsung-mi, must have committed a sin, as I lost my parents in my early age. Whenever I suffered from hard experience, I had eternal remorse for being unable to recall my parents to life and to look after them."[11]

The plaint of grief sounded in this passage, and the timing of Tsung-mi's interest in Buddhism, suggests that the sorrow he suffered at the loss of his father provided a strong impetus for his interest in Buddhism. The passage from Tsung-mi's commentary to the *Yü-lan-p'en ching* is also noteworthy in other respects. Its deft use of classical allusions suggests the thoroughness and quality of his early Confucian education.[12] More important, its content reveals his preoccupation with Confucian values. As the canonical basis for the festival for feeding hungry ghosts celebrated on the fifteenth day of the seventh lunar month, the *Yü-lan-p'en ching* provided a means by which Buddhist ritual practice could be fused with the expression of filial devotion to one's deceased parents and ancestors. Tsung-mi's commentary focuses on the centrality of filial piety, arguing that Buddhist practice of "leaving home"—often cited by Confucian critics as epitomizing Buddhist rejection of filial duty—represents an even higher level of filiality than the traditional expressions of filial devo-

---

[10] Morohashi Tetsuji, *Daikanwa jiten*, 8:9121d. Broughton interprets the passage in which this expression occurs to mean he "wore white garments [i.e., the apparel of a Buddhist layman]" (B 41). Had Tsung-mi intended this meaning he would surely have used the expression *po-i* instead of *su-fu*. Po Chü-i, for instance, refers to himself as a layman in white robes (*chü-shih po-i*) (*Po-shih Ch'ang-ch'ing-chi* 18.2a). The paradigmatic layman, Vimalakīrti, is described as wearing white robes (*po-i*) (T 14.539a19). See also *Li-tai fa-pao chi*, where Ch'en Ch'u-chang (called Vimalakīrti Ch'en) is described as the "white-robed layman" (*po-i chü-shih*) (T 51.186a21; *Shoki II*, p. 168).

[11] T 39.505a8–10, as translated by Jan, "Tsung-mi," p. 6.

[12] In his footnote to this passage, Jan shows how Tsung-mi's use of *feng-shu* (wind-tree) skillfully draws on a passage from the *Han-shih wai-chuan*, which James R. Hightower renders as follows: "The tree would be still, but the wind would not stop, the son wishes to look after them, but his parents will not tarry" (p. 292). Yüan-chao, Tsung-mi's Sung-dynasty subcommentator, traces *feng-shu* back to the *Tso-chuan* (*Yü-lan-p'en ching shu hsin-chi*, HTC 35.101c). The passage Jan translates as "whenever I suffered from hard experience" (*mei lu hsüeh-shuang chih pei*) literally means "whenever I experienced the sorrow of treading on hoar-frost" and alludes to a passage in the chapter of the *Li chi* on the meaning of ancestral sacrifices. Explaining why the sacrifices are to be performed during the autumn and spring, the text says: "When he treads on the dew that has descended as hoar-frost he cannot help a feeling of sadness, which arises in his mind, and cannot be ascribed to the cold" (James Legge, trans., *Li Chi: The Book of Rites*, 2:210).

tion.[13] The prominence of Confucian values throughout Tsung-mi's Buddhist writings is lasting testament to the influence that his early studies played in shaping his character.

From the impressive array of classical allusions Tsung-mi employs throughout his oeuvre, as well as from what we know about the content of the imperial examinations in the late T'ang, it is not difficult to surmise the general content of his early education. At that time there were two major national examinations held annually: the *ming-ching* (understanding the classics) and *chin-shih* (advanced scholar).[14] The former tested the candidates' knowledge of the classics. Although it had the largest number of both candidates and graduates, its emphasis on rote knowledge made it the less prestigious of the two. The *chin-shih* examination, in addition to demanding familiarity with the classics, also tested the candidates' literary talent and ability to discuss policy issues.[15] Although recruitment through the examination system accounted for only a small portion of the civil servants within the T'ang bureaucracy (estimates range from 6 to 16 percent),[16] the career prospects of those who succeeded were high, especially for those earning the *chin-shih* degree. Success in the *chin-shih* examination opened up an elite stream within the bureaucracy, and *chin-shih* graduates tended to dominate the highest echelons of the government in the later T'ang.

Whichever examination Tsung-mi had prepared for would have entailed a detailed familiarity with the classics. In his letter to Ch'eng-kuan, he mentions that his youthful curriculum included the classics of *Poetry* and *History*. Although he singles out these two works for mention, they are probably merely a locution for the classics in general. Tsung-mi was thoroughly acquainted with the other classics as well and quotes freely from the *Confucian Analects*, the *Classic of Filial Piety*, the *Book of Rites*, the *Classic of History*, and the *Classic of Change*.

---

[13] See Teiser's *The Ghost Festival*. For a discussion of the significance of filial piety in Tsung-mi's commentary, see Okabe Kazuo, "Shūmitsu ni okeru kōron no tenkai to sono hōhō"; Michihata Ryōshū, *Tōdai bukkyō-shi no kenkyū*, pp. 320–324; and Kenneth Ch'en, *The Chinese Transformation of Buddhism*, pp. 29–31.

[14] For a general account of the examination system during the T'ang, see Robert des Retours, *Le Traité des examens*.

[15] See Waley, *Po Chü-i*, pp. 20–23, for an interesting discussion of the content of the *chin-shih* examination that Po Chü-i passed in 800.

[16] See John Chaffee, *The Thorny Gates of Learning in Sung China*, p. 15, which cites studies by Twitchett and Sun Kuo-tung, the former estimating that the exams accounted for approximately 15–16 percent of the bureaucracy in the ninth century while the latter gives an estimate of 6 percent (p. 214, n. 66). Richard Guisso says that the examinations provided for only about 10 percent of the bureaucracy ("The Reigns of Empress Wu, Chung-tsung and Jui-tsung," p. 329).

His writings also abound with allusions to the two great Taoist classics, the *Lao-tzu* and *Chuang-tzu*. In addition to such standard works, he was conversant with various historical records, such as the *Tso chuan*, *Han shu*, *Shih chi*, and *Chin shu*, as well as a variety of lesser Confucian and Taoist writings.

Both Tsung-mi's social background and his classical education were crucial factors in the connections he was to form later on in his life with a number of the most prominent literary and political figures of his generation. Tsung-mi came from the provincial elite, which in the later T'ang had begun to temper the dominant role that the great aristocratic clans had exercised over national politics in the early part of the dynasty. Such a change in the composition of the elite was, of course, a result of many factors. Although its role has often been exaggerated, the examination system clearly contributed to this process by providing a major channel by which access to the ruling class was expanded. The curriculum of study dictated by the examinations also did much to instill a sense of shared values among the educated elite. Many of the literati with whom Tsung-mi was associated were degree-holders who belonged to this group.

CH'AN TRAINING AND THE
SCRIPTURE OF PERFECT ENLIGHTENMENT (804–810)

Tsung-mi's autobiographical summary continues: "Fortunately, I was attracted to Fu-shang [i.e., Tao-yüan] as a needle [to a magnet] or a tiny particle [to amber]. In meditation (*ch'an*) I encountered the Southern tradition, and in doctrine (*chiao*) I met this text [i.e., the *Scripture of Perfect Enlightenment*]. At one word [from Tao-yüan] my mind-ground opened thoroughly, and with one scroll [of the *Scripture of Perfect Enlightenment*] its meaning was as clear and bright as the heavens."[17] In his subcommentary, Tsung-mi reports that after having studied at the I-hsüeh yüan for two years, he met the Ch'an priest Tao-yüan, who was returning to Sui-chou from the west.[18] This event was one of the major turning points in Tsung-mi's life. It occurred in 804 when he was twenty-four, as is made clear by his earlier statement: "At twenty-two I once again resumed my earlier efforts, concentrating on Confucian studies until the age of twenty-four, whereupon I encountered propitious conditions and left the household."[19] This passage is important because it definitively establishes the date of Tsung-mi's conversion as having taken place in 804. Most bio-

[17] TS 109a13–15; LS 524b21–23.
[18] TSC 222b12–14; LSC 106d5–7.
[19] LSC 106a3–4; cf. TSC 222b7–8.

graphical sources (both ancient and modern) follow the *Sung kao-seng chuan*,[20] which gives the date as 807—an error most likely deriving from P'ei Hsiu's comment that "in the second year of the Yüan-ho period [i.e., 807] his mind was sealed [*yin-hsin*; i.e., his understanding was sanctioned] by the priest [Tao]-yüan."[21]

Tsung-mi was immediately drawn to Tao-yüan as if by magnetic attraction, to borrow his simile, and the two men had a natural rapport. "When I questioned him about the dharma, our minds meshed."[22] Tsung-mi later told Ch'eng-kuan that after this meeting he realized that his worldly pursuits were no longer relevant. He thereupon decided to become Tao-yüan's disciple, taking the tonsure and donning Buddhist robes.[23]

Aside from Tsung-mi's testimony, nothing is known about the monk who so impressed him. Tsung-mi claims that Tao-yüan had inherited the essential teaching (*tsung-chi*) transmitted by the sixth patriarch Hui-neng.[24] According to Tsung-mi, Tao-yüan stood in the fourth generation of the Ho-tse line of Ch'an, which took its name from the temple in Lo-yang with which Shen-hui[25] was closely associated. Shen-hui was, of course, the figure famous for championing the cause of the Hui-neng as the true sixth patriarch against what he denounced as the false claims of the disciples of Shen-hsiu that their master had inherited the mantle of the patriarchate. His criticism of Shen-hsiu and his disciples for teaching an inferior "gradual" approach to enlightenment against the authentic "sudden" teaching upheld by Hui-neng resulted in the split between what came to be known as the Northern and Southern lines of Ch'an. Elsewhere Tsung-mi records the determination of an imperial commission in

[20] 741c25. See also CTL 205c13 and *Fa-chieh tsung wu-tsu lüeh-chi*, HTC 134.277a14.

[21] Kamata, *Shūmitsu*, p. 51.8.

[22] TSC 222d14; LSC 106d7.

[23] T 39.576c17–18.

[24] TSC 222d17–18; LSC 106d11–12.

[25] The recent discovery of Shen-hui's epitaph has established his dates as 684–758. The discovery was first announced by Wen Yü-ch'eng in his "Chi hsin ch'u-t'u-te Ho-tse ta-shih Shen-hui t'a-ming." Takeuchi Kōdō has summarized Wen's article and included a transcription and Japanese translation of the epitaph in his "Shinshutsu no Kataku Jinne tōmei ni tsuite." For a revised summary of Shen-hui's biography, see McRae, "Shen-hui and the Teaching of Sudden Enlightenment," pp. 232–237. See also Yanagida Seizan's "Jinne no shōzō." The dates given in the epitaph, it should be noted, confirm the dates given by Tsung-mi in TSC 277b and LSC 131b-c. In fact, Tsung-mi's account of Shen-hui indicates that he was familiar with the epitaph. Prior to the discovery of Shen-hui's epitaph, scholars had followed Hu Shih's judgment, based largely on the SKSC, that the dates 670–762 should be accepted; see Hu's biographical study, "Ho-tse ta-shih Shen-hui chuan," at the beginning of his *Shen-hui ho-shang i-chi*, esp. pp. 5–12. This is not the only instance in which Hu's rejection of Tsung-mi's information in favor of the SKSC has proven wrong.

796 that established Shen-hui as the rightful seventh patriarch of Ch'an and therefore the legitimate successor to Hui-neng.[26]

In his *Ch'an Chart*, Tsung-mi gives the names of nineteen of Shen-hui's successors.[27] He traces his own particular lineage of Southern Ch'an as running from Shen-hui to Chih-ju, Wei-chung (d. 821), and Tao-yüan (see below). He informs us that Chih-ju was surnamed Wang and was associated with the Fa-kuan ssu in Tzu-chou.[28] His successor, Wei-chung, was surnamed Chang and was associated with the Sheng-shou ssu in Ch'eng-tu. Tsung-mi notes that Wei-chung was also known as I-chou Nan-yin; in other places he refers to him as Ching-nan Chang. Tsung-mi's own master, Tao-yüan, was surnamed Ch'eng and, when Tsung-mi met him, was associated with the Ta-yün ssu in Sui-chou. Tsung-mi adds that in 821 (i.e., after Wei-chung's death) Tao-yüan succeeded to the abbotship of Sheng-shou ssu in Ch'eng-tu.[29] Wei-chung also had another successor, Shen-chao (776–838), with whom Tsung-mi had several encounters. In his *Ch'an Chart*, Tsung-mi also lists I-chou Ju-i and Chien-yüan Hsüan-ya as disciples of I-chou Nan-yin.[30] Tsung-mi thus portrayed himself as the rightful heir to the teaching of Shen-hui, the figure who he maintained correctly transmitted the authentic Southern Ch'an of Hui-neng.

There is much evidence that complicates the picture Tsung-mi gives of his lineage.[31] The problem centers around the identity of Wei-chung/Nan-yin and the fact that there are two different monks named Shen-hui. In addition to the famous Ho-tse Shen-hui, from

[26] TSC 277c2–3; LSC 131c8–9; *Ch'an Chart*, 434b11–14 (K 282).

[27] 435a–b; K 290; see Ui Hakujū's discussion of Shen-hui's disciples in *Zenshūshi kenkyū*, 1:238–255. Although I have not been able to trace the reference, Ui claims that Tsung-mi's LSC notes that Shen-hui had twenty-two successors (p. 238).

[28] It is unclear who this person was. Ui has conjectured that Chih-ju may be Fa-ju, whose biography can be found in SKSC 893c (see *Zenshūshi kenkyū*, 1:239–240).

[29] LSC 131c15–d2.

[30] 435a–b; K 292.

[31] Hu Shih has raised the most serious questions about Tsung-mi's lineage. In his "Pa P'ei Hsiu ti T'ang ku Kuei-feng ting-hui ch'an-shih ch'uan-fa-pei," Hu argued that Wei-chung did not belong to the Ho-tse lineage but was instead a successor of Ching-chung Shen-hui, a separate figure with no lineal relation to the more famous Ho-tse Shen-hui. Hu went on to contend that Tsung-mi deliberately manipulated the confusion over the two Shen-huis in order to align himself falsely with Ho-tse Shen-hui for his own advantage. Hu's conclusions have found wide acceptance among Japanese scholars, most prominently including Yanagida Seizan. Based on the recent discovery of Shen-hui's epitaph and a consideration of a long scroll of Buddhist images from Nan-chao, Yanagida has recently reassessed his opinion in his "Jinne no shōzō." This article has been an important catalyst in the development of the conclusions I present below. Although much of the material and many of the arguments I present in what follows are original, my thoughts on the matter would never have come together in the way that they did without the stimulus of Yanagida's article.

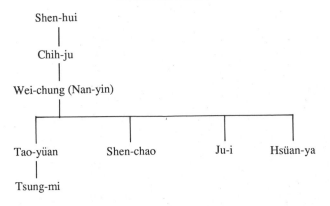

Shen-hui

|

Chih-ju

|

Wei-chung (Nan-yin)

Tao-yüan   Shen-chao   Ju-i   Hsüan-ya

|

Tsung-mi

whom Tsung-mi claimed descent, there was also a Shen-hui (720–794) associated with the lineage of Szechwanese Ch'an affiliated with the Ching-chung ssu (temple of the pure assembly) in Ch'eng-tu. This Ching-chung tradition was not descended from the sixth patriarch Hui-neng—who, by the end of the eighth century, had been established as the main channel through which Ch'an orthodoxy flowed—but rather traced itself back to the fifth patriarch Hung-jen (601–674) through his disciple Chih-shen (609–702).[32]

The issue of the two Shen-huis is related to the identity of Wei-chung/Nan-yin, whom other sources indicate may not have been one person known by two different names but rather two wholly unrelated figures. The *Sung kao-seng chuan* gives separate biographies for Wei-chung (705–782) and Nan-yin (d. 821).[33] According to its account, both men belonged to different generations, had different surnames, completed their training under different masters, and led entirely different kinds of lives. The *Sung kao-seng chuan* says that Wei-chung was surnamed T'ung and died in 782 in his seventy-eighth year, and that Nan-yin was surnamed Chang and died in 821. Whereas Wei-chung studied with Ho-tse Shen-hui, Nan-yin studied with Ching-chung Shen-hui.[34] Other than the fact that Wei-chung came from Ch'eng-tu, there is nothing in his biography to associate

[32] Often romanized as Chih-hsien. For his biography see LTFPC 184b–c (*Shoki II*, p. 137) and SKSC 764a–b. Cf. Ui, *Zenshūshi kenkyū*, 1:148–149.

[33] See SKSC 763c8–20 and 772b2–12 for their respective biographies. The SKSC also contains the biography of another Wei-chung, active during the T'ien-pao period (742–756) and associated with the Fa-ting ssu in Ch'eng-tu; see 835c16–836a20. There is nothing in the latter biography, however, indicating any connection with either Shen-hui.

[34] The situation is actually somewhat more complicated. As will be seen later, Nan-yin first briefly studied under Ho-tse Shen-hui, or one of his immediate disciples, before going to Szechwan.

him with the Ching-chung ssu. The Sheng-shou ssu, with which Nan-yin was so closely affiliated, was not built until twenty-five years after Wei-chung's death. In contrast to the world of metropolitan Buddhism and political power in which Nan-yin moved, Wei-chung is portrayed as leading the eremitic life of a mountain ascetic wielding thaumaturgical powers.[35]

It is clear that the figure Tsung-mi identifies as Wei-chung/Nan-yin corresponds to the Nan-yin of the Sheng-shou ssu in Ch'eng-tu in the *Sung kao-seng chuan* biography. This means that Tsung-mi's lineage was connected with the Ching-chung tradition of Szechwanese Ch'an. The connection of Nan-yin with the Ching-chung tradition is corroborated by other sources as well. The *Pei-shan lu*, for instance, names Nan-yin as a disciple of Ching-chung Shen-hui.[36] Since the author of this text, Shen-ch'ing (d. during the Yüan-ho reign period, 806–820), identified himself as belonging to the Ching-chung tradition, his opinion on the matter bears a certain weight of authority. To understand the Ch'an milieu in which Tsung-mi trained, it is thus necessary to digress briefly and discuss the Ching-chung tradition.[37]

The Ching-chung Tradition

According to Tsung-mi's account, the Ching-chung line was founded by Chih-shen, who was a native of Tzu-chou. Tsung-mi tells us that, after completing his training with the fifth patriarch Hung-jen, Chih-

---

[35] According to its account, Wei-chung was surnamed T'ung and came from Ch'eng-tu. After first studying under the Ch'an master Tao-yüan of Ta-kuang shan, Wei-chung went to see Ho-tse Shen-hui, who cleared away his doubts. He then spent a period of time traveling to various sacred sites before settling down at Huang-lung (yellow dragon) mountain, where he built a grass hut and took up the eremitic life of a mountain ascetic. Although the location of this mountain is unclear, it is clear that it had no association with the Ching-chung ssu in Ch'eng-tu. The biography goes on to recount the miraculous effect of Wei-chung's numinous presence. It tells us that people living on the mountain had been plagued by the pestilent breath of a dragon. Soon after Wei-chung took up residence on the mountain, the people ceased suffering from the dragon's noxious miasmas. Then one day they heard the dragon's voice in the sky proclaiming that it had been liberated by the master dwelling on the mountain. Thereafter the people called the mountain "quelling dragon," claiming that Wei-chung had pacified the leader of the scaly brood (763c8–20).

[36] T 52.611b9–11.

[37] In addition to Yanagida's "Jinne no shōzō," other useful studies of the Ching-chung tradition and Szechwanese Ch'an include Yanagida Seizan, *Shoki zenshū shisho no kenkyū*, pp. 335–349; Yanagida, "The *Li-tai fa-pao chi* and the Ch'an Doctrine of Sudden Awakening," pp. 13–49; Jeffrey Broughton, "Early Ch'an Schools in Tibet," pp. 1–68; and Jan Yün-hua, "Tung-hai ta-shih Wu-hsiang chuan yen-chiu," pp. 47–60. As an appendix to his article "Tsung-mi," Jan has translated the major portions of Tsung-mi's account of the three Szechwanese lines of Ch'an enumerated in TSC.

shen returned to Szechwan, where he took up residence in the Te-ch'un ssu in Tzu-chou. His successor Ch'u-chi (669–736)[38] had four disciples, one of whom was the Korean monk Wu-hsiang (K. Musang, 694–762), often referred to as Priest Kim.[39] Elsewhere Tsung-mi names I-chou Shih as the successor of Wu-hsiang,[40] and from the *Sung kao-seng chuan* we know that I-chou Shih was none other than Ching-chung Shen-hui, who was surnamed Shih.[41]

Although the sources are limited and fragmentary, a general picture of the Ching-chung tradition can still be reconstructed. Located in the northwestern quarter of the provincial capital of Ch'eng-tu, the Ching-chung ssu seems to have played an important role in the Buddhist world of Szechwan during the second half of the eighth century. It was closely associated with the state and was officially licensed to grant ordination certificates. It was built sometime around the middle of the eighth century for Wu-hsiang, who had close ties with the regional political and military magnates of the time.

Wu-hsiang, the main figure in this tradition, was a Korean prince, being the third son of the ruler of the kingdom of Silla.[42] He arrived in Ch'ang-an in 728 and had an audience with the emperor Hsüan-tsung.[43] He later traveled to Tzu-chou in Szechwan, where he studied with Ch'u-chi at the Te-ch'un ssu.[44] After receiving Ch'u-chi's sanc-

[38] For his biography see LTFPC 184c; (*Shoki II*, p. 140) and SKSC 836b. Philip Yampolsky has pointed out the discrepancies in the date of death given for Ch'u-chi in different sources (*The Platform Sutra of the Sixth Patriarch*, p. 43, n. 153). The Taishō version of LTFPC (based on the Pelliot manuscript) gives his date of death as 732 whereas the Stein manuscript gives it as 736 (see T 51.184c10, n. 21). I have followed Yanagida, who follows the Stein version. His biography in the SKSC not only gives yet another date of death (734) but also claims that he died at a different age (in his eighty-seventh year) (836b27–28).

[39] TSC 278b15–18. Other biographical sources for Wu-hsiang are *Pei-shan lu*, T 52.611b9–11; LTFPC 184c17ff (*Shoki II*, pp. 142–144); SKSC 732b10–733a6; and Li Shang-yin's *T'ang Tzu-chou Hui-i Ching-she Nan-ch'an-yüan ssu cheng-t'ang pei-ming*, CTW 780.1a–3a.

[40] *Ch'an Chart*, 435d; K 289.

[41] SKSC 764a24. Would it be trying to read too much out of the sources to find significance in the fact that Tsung-mi refers to this monk as I-chou Shih rather than (Ching-chung) Shen-hui? Might not this indicate an attempt on Tsung-mi's part to conceal his connections with the Ching-chung tradition? Such a suspicion is largely allayed by the observation that there is nothing unusual in Tsung-mi's reference to this monk by his surname and place of origin. Other contemporary sources also refer to monks by their surname and place of origin. I-chou was the former name of the region that, in 758, became promoted to the superior prefecture of Ch'eng-tu.

[42] *Pei-shan lu*, T 52.611b9–10 and SKSC 832b11.

[43] SKSC 831b13–14.

[44] LTFPC 184c22–24 and SKSC 832b14–15. The LTFPC passage relates an incident

tion in 736,[45] he withdrew into the mountains and for a period of time led an ascetic life devoted to meditation.[46] He eventually came to Ch'eng-tu sometime around 740,[47] where his reputation as a meditation master attracted the attention of Chang-ch'iu Chien-ch'iung,[48] military governor of Chien-nan West from 739 to 746. Later he was welcomed by Hsüan-tsung to his court in exile during his residence in Ch'eng-tu (from the seventh month of 756 until the tenth month of 757) after the rebellious army of An Lu-shan had forced him to flee the capital. The *Sung kao-seng chuan* says that the Ching-chung ssu was built for him by the district magistrate Yang I, although it does not indicate when.[49] All that one can say with any confidence is

---

in which Wu-hsiang burned off one of his figures to gain the attention of Ch'u-chi. This incident is also alluded to in Li Shang-yin's inscription.

[45] The date depends on which version of Ch'u-chi's date of death one accepts; see note 38 above. According to the LTFPC this event took place during the fourth month, when Ch'u-chi passed on Bodhidharma's robe to Wu-hsiang as a token of the transmission. Ch'u-chi told Wu-hsiang that Empress Wu had given the patriarchal robe to Chih-shen, who had given it to Ch'u-chi, who in turn was now passing it on to Wu-hsiang (184c10–13; *Shoki II*, p. 140). The story of how Empress Wu obtained the robe that had originally been passed on to Hui-neng is elaborated in detail in an earlier passage (see 184a6–b17; *Shoki II*, pp. 129–130). The SKSC also alludes to the story of Ch'u-chi's transmission of the robe to Wu-hsiang (832b15–19). The story of the transmission of the patriarchal robe originated with Ho-tse Shen-hui, who claimed that the fifth patriarch passed it on to Hui-neng. The LTFPC goes on to claim that Wu-hsiang secretly transmitted the robe to Pao-t'ang Wu-chu. Yanagida sees the elaboration of this story in a Szechwanese Ch'an text as an indication of the widespread influence of Shen-hui in Szechwan during the second part of the eighth century ("The *Li-tai fa-pao chi* and the Ch'an Doctrine of Sudden Awakening," p. 22).

[46] Whereas the LTFPC merely alludes to his meditative prowess, the SKSC places his biography in the section reserved for thaumaturges and relates a number of anecdotes testifying to the extraordinary effects of his meditative power, especially its effect on wild beasts.

[47] It is unclear whether the LTFPC's statement that "he dwelt in the Ching-chung ssu and instructed beings for over twenty years" (185a1–2; *Shoki II*, p. 142) means that he dwelt in Ching-chung ssu for over twenty years or whether the "for over twenty years" merely applies to his teaching activities and not his residence in the Ching-chung ssu. The statement does, in any case, suggest that he probably came to Ch'eng-tu sometime around 740 (if 762 can be accepted as the year of his death).

[48] SKSC 728b28–29. Wu-hsiang's connection with Chang-ch'iu Chien-ch'iung is also mentioned in the LTFPC (184c29–185a1; *Shoki II*, p. 142) as well as the inscription by Li Shang-yin, which notes that none of his followers could equal Chang-ch'iu (see CTW 780.2a). Chang-ch'iu Chien-ch'iung's accomplishments in Szechwan are mentioned in the chapter on Tibet in CTS 196.5234–5235 and HTS 216.6086. It was through Chang-ch'iu's patronage that Yang Kuo-chung was sent to the court, and Yang Kuo-chung's influence there helped to win Chang-ch'iu a position in the capital in 746. See the following note.

[49] Given the patterns of political patronage, it is tempting to speculate that Yang I must have been related to Yang Kuo-chung, the figure who played such an important

that it must have been built sometime during the 740s or 750s.[50] Other sources hint at Wu-hsiang's connection with Yen Li (743–809), a figure remembered in history as the subject of Yüan Chen's (779–831) investigation of corruption in Szechwan.[51]

Ching-chung ssu's official favor was reflected in its status as a tem-

---

role in the events at court leading up to An Lu-shan's rebellion. The appointment of a relative to the position of magistrate of the district of Ch'eng-tu would have helped Yang Kuo-chung maintain a base of power in the provinces while he jockeyed for power with Li Lin-fu and An Lu-shan in the capital. Yang Kuo-chung's political career began with the backing of two of the most powerful figures in Szechwanese politics before the rebellion, Hsien-yü Chung-t'ung and Chang-ch'iu Chien-ch'iung. Yang Kuo-chung also had the good fortune to be a second cousin of Yang Kuei-fei. Shortly after Yang Kuei-fei became the emperor's favorite, Yang Kuo-chung was sent to the capital by Chang-ch'iu and Hsien-yü to secure their position. Yang Kuo-chung quickly succeeded in rivaling, and then superseding, Li Lin-fu in power and, from 752 until the end of Hsüan-tsung's reign, was the dominant figure at court. His official biography can be found in CTS 106.3241–3247 and HTS 206.5846–5852. For his involvement in the events leading up to the An Lu-shan rebellion, see Edwin Pulleyblank, *The Background of the Rebellion of An Lu-shan*, pp. 92–103, and Denis Twitchett, "Hsüan-tsung (reign 712–56)," pp. 428–430 and 447–453.

In keeping with its portrayal of Wu-hsiang as a thaumaturge, the SKSC ascribes the construction of the Ching-chung ssu to Wu-hsiang's wonder-working powers. It says that Yang I was suspicious of Wu-hsiang's powers and sent a group of over twenty men to arrest him. As the men approached Wu-hsiang, they all began trembling with fear and fell into a swoon. Just then a great wind suddenly blew a hail of pebbles into the yamen office, rattling its blinds with great fury. Yang I prostrated himself in fear and dared not speak. Only after he repented did the wind stop. As a result of this episode, Yang I became a benefactor of Buddhism and had four temples constructed in Ch'eng-tu (832c1–6).

[50] Just because the SKSC relates the episode that led to the construction of the Ching-chung ssu after mentioning Wu-hsiang's second audience with Hsüan-tsung does not necessarily mean that the temple was built after Hsüan-tsung's retreat to Ch'eng-tu. If, in fact, Yang I were actually related to Yang Kuo-chung, this would make it more likely that the temple was built sometime after Yang Kuo-chung began to gain influence at the court (i.e., after 746) but before the An Lu-shan rebellion. It is unlikely, moreover, that Yang I would have dared treat Wu-hsiang in the manner described after Wu-hsiang had been received by Hsün-tsung. See the previous note.

[51] His official biography can be found in CTS 117.3407–3408 and HTS 144.4709. See also Charles A. Petersen, "Corruption Unmasked: Yüan Chen's Investigations in Szechwan," which includes a translation of Yüan Chen's memorial (pp. 72–78). Yüan's memorial contributed to his banishment to a minor provincial post. For Po Chü-i's defense of his friend, see Eugene Feifel, *Po Chü-i as a Censor*, pp. 156–163, and Waley, *Po Chü-i*, pp. 65, 70–72.

Ch'üan Te-yü's epitaph for Yen Li notes that for a time during his youth he trained as a novice (śrāmaṇera) under Wu-hsiang (CTW 497.17a). Sometime during the early 760s Yen Li was recruited by a local official. He gradually worked his way up through the provincial government and military administration to become governor of Shan-nan West in 799. Yen's forces played a part in the successful suppression of the revolt by Liu P'i in 807, as a result of which he was appointed governor of Chien-nan East in

ple licensed to confer ordination certificates, a matter the T'ang government endeavored to control strictly. Both Tsung-mi's account and that of the *Li-tai fa-pao chi* indicate that large public ordination ceremonies were a vital part of the temple's life. According to Tsung-mi, its ordination ceremony conformed to the standard practice of the time. A public announcement calling the fourfold sangha together would be posted a month or two before the date set for the ceremony.[52] The *Li-tai fa-pao chi* states that these ceremonies were held annually over the twelfth and first months.[53] Tsung-mi, writing somewhat later, indicates that such ceremonies were not always held every year but were sometimes held every other or every third year.[54] These ceremonies included monks, nuns, and laypeople who, according to the *Li-tai fa-pao chi*, numbered in the thousands.[55]

As a major temple under the leadership of a famous master and located in the most important city in the Szechwan basin, the Ching-chung ssu was able to attract multitudes of aspirants for its ordination ceremonies. The sheer number of participants alone meant that these ceremonies were necessarily protracted affairs. The *Li-tai fa-pao chi* notes that one such ceremony in 859 lasted for three days and nights.[56] Beyond the length of time needed to conduct the ceremony proper, the ordinands were required to participate in a period of ritual preparation lasting for approximately a month, and after the ceremony they would be further required to remain in the monastery for another week or two devoted to seated meditation. Altogether these ceremonies must have engaged the full resources of the temple for a good two or three months, during which time it needed facilities to domicile and feed the ordinands. Overall the Ching-chung ssu must have been an imposing complex.

Tsung-mi provides some further details about these ceremonies:

> Their ceremony (*i-shih*) for [dharma] transmission (*ch'uan-shou*) is, in general, similar to the procedures (*fang-pien*) for receiving the full precepts (*chü-tsu-chieh*) currently followed at the official [ordination] platforms (*kuan-t'an*) in this country. That is to say, one or two months in advance, they first fix a time [for holding the ceremony] and send out a circular inviting monks, nuns, and laymen and laywomen to assemble.

807. In that year the Pao-ying ssu was refurbished as the Sheng-shou ssu to mark the reassertion of imperial authority in Szechwan. Is it possible that Yen Li may have had a hand in the installation of one of Wu-hsiang's successors as its abbot?

[52] TSC 278c5–7.
[53] 185a11; *Shoki II*, p. 143.
[54] TSC 278c12–13.
[55] 185a11–12; *Shoki II*, p. 143.
[56] 185c2–6; *Shoki II*, p. 169.

They establish a "Mahāyāna" (fang-teng)[57] ritual site (tao-ch'ang). The worship and repentence services (li ch'an) go on for three or five seven-day periods, after which they give the dharma (shou-fa). This takes place entirely at night, in order to cut off contact with the outside [world] and avoid noise and confusion. The dharma having been given, [the ordinands] are ordered immediately to sit in meditation (tso-ch'an) and prac-

---

[57] Fang-teng (Skt. vaipulya), meaning "broad" or "extensive," is a term that appears in the title of many Mahāyāna sūtras and was frequently used by Chinese Buddhists to mean Mahāyāna. In the present context fang-teng seems to mean that the Ching-chung ordination ceremonies were open to everyone, including laymen and laywomen. Fang-teng thus seems to be equivalent to the term fang-teng chieh-t'an as explained in the Buddhist encyclopedia, Ta-Sung seng-shih lüeh, compiled by Tsan-ning (919–1002) at the end of the tenth century: "The reason it is called a fang-teng platform is probably because the platform procedures originally derive from the various vinayas, and the vinayas are Hīnayāna teachings. In the Hīnayāna teaching, it is necessary that every single thing be in accord with the rules. With even the slightest deviation, one is far off the mark. Thus, honorable [would-be] ordinands cannot receive the precepts, and those who do mount the [ordination] platform commit an offense. Thus we call it the teaching of 'restriction' (lü). If [on the other hand] it is the 'broadly inclusive' (fang-teng) teaching of the Mahāyāna, then we do not seize on fundamental deficiencies or circumstantial discrepancies, so everyone can receive the precepts. To receive them, one need only give rise to a great thought of enlightenment. Fang-teng means 'encompassing.' The Chih-kuan lun says: 'Fang-teng, in other words, means extensive (kuang) and equal (p'ing).' " (T 54.250b29–c6; as translated by Griffith Foulk, personal communication.)

The Chih-kuan lun referred to at the end of this passage is, of course, Chih-i's monumental Mo-ho chih-kuan, and the quotation (T 46.13c2–3) comes from the section of that work discussing the fang-teng samādhi, which Chih-i classifies as a "partly walking and partly sitting" practice; see Neal Donner's "The Great Calming and Contemplation of Chih-i," pp. 250–257, for a translation of the entire section. See also Daniel Stevenson's "The Four Kinds of Samādhi in Early T'ien-t'ai Buddhism," pp. 61–67, for a comprehensive discussion of this practice. This practice was based on the Fang-teng to-lo-ni ching (Vaipulya dhāraṇi sūtra) and constituted a complex set of procedures governing the construction of an altar, making offerings, ritual purification, circumambulation, worship, repentance, recitation of dhāraṇi, and seated meditation. According to Chih-i, the practice is to be carried out in a specially consecrated sanctuary, must be undertaken for at least one seven-day period, and can include as many as ten people. The procedures for the fang-teng repentance that Chih-i details in his Mo-ho chih-kuan and other works were certainly too restrictive to have been carried out by the large number of ordinands at the Ching-chung ssu. Nevertheless, they may still have provided the basic model for the structure of the ritual repentance practiced under Wu-hsiang. A passage at the end of Chih-i's discussion of the fang-teng samādhi citing the Fang-teng to-lo-ni ching ties in well with Tsan-ning's explanation quoted above: "[If one] breaks [any of] the rules of conduct (chieh), from those for novices (śrāmaṇera) to those for great monks (bhikṣu), then [by this repentance] he cannot fail to be restored to life as a monk [in the assembly of monks]" (Donner, "The Great Calming and Contemplation," pp. 255–256). Many of those partaking in the ceremony would thus have already received the precepts, for whom the ceremony would thus function as a rite of renewal.

tice mindfulness of breathing (*hsi-nien*).[58] Everyone, even those who cannot remain for long—such as persons who have come from a great distance and those belonging to the classes of nuns and laity—must remain for one or two seven-day periods of sitting meditation before dispersing in accord with [their individual] circumstances. As in the case with the rules (*fa*) for mounting the platform (*lin-t'an*) [explained in] the vinaya tradition, it is necessary for those in the assembly [who are planning to "mount the platform" for full ordination] to present their ordination licenses (*yu-chuang*). The government office grants ordination certificates (*wen-tieh*); this is called "establishing a connection" (*k'ai-yüan*).[59]

The *Li-tai fa-pao chi* adds that at the end of the ordination ceremony the master would ascend the high seat and expound the dharma. He would begin by leading the congregation in a form of the recitation of the Buddha's name (*nien-fo*) in which the sound of the Buddha's name seems to have been gradually stretched out with the breath. The final expiration of the breath with the stretching out of the sound of the Buddha's name was used as a way of exhausting thought.[60] The master would then set forth his teaching, which, as both the *Li-tai fa-pao chi* and Tsung-mi indicate, was based on an explanation of Buddhist practice in terms of Ho-tse Shen-hui's teaching of no-thought (*wu-nien*). This teaching was encapsulated in three phrases—not remembering (*wu-i*), not thinking (*wu-nien*), and not forgetting (*mo-wang*)—which were correlated with the threefold discipline of maintaining the precepts (śīla), developing concentration (samādhi), and opening up wisdom (prajñā).[61] According to the *Li-tai fa-pao chi*, Wu-hsiang claimed that these three phrases were not the innovation of his immediate teachers but a comprehensive method of practice handed down from Bodhidharma. "Thoughts not arising is the gate of śīla; thoughts not arising is the gate of samādhi; and thoughts not arising is the gate of prajñā. No-thought itself is the complete fulfillment of the śīla, samādhi, and prajñā. All of the infinite Buddhas of the past, present, and future enter through this

---

[58] Although technically the term *hsi-nien* is a translation of *ānāpāna-smṛti* (mindfulness of breathing), it could also be understood as a verb-object construction meaning "to put a stop to thought" (as Broughton and Jan interpret it). This later interpretation gains plausibility in light of the LTFPC's discussion of the type of *nien-fo* practice Wu-hsiang taught, as discussed below.

[59] TSC 278c5–12. I would like to thank Griffith Foulk for his translation of this passage as well as the passage from the *Ta-Sung seng-shih lüeh* quoted in note 57. Cf. the translations by Jan, "Tsung-mi," p. 43, and Broughton, "Early Ch'an," pp. 32–33.

[60] 185a12–13; *Shoki II*, p. 143. Cf. the translation by Broughton, "Early Ch'an," p. 37. See note 58.

[61] LTFPC 185a13–15; TSC 278c4.

gate."[62] Tsung-mi explains these three phrases as meaning not dwelling on the past, not thinking about the future, and "always conforming to this knowledge without confusion or mistake."[63] Other passages in the *Li-tai fa-pao chi* indicate that Wu-hsiang understood the practice of no-thought in terms of the *Awakening of Faith*: being without thought corresponds to the mind as suchness whereas having thoughts corresponds to the mind subject to birth-and-death.[64]

Ching-chung Shen-hui followed Wu-hsiang as abbot of the Ching-chung ssu. The only source for Ching-chung Shen-hui's life is the *Sung kao-seng chuan*, which says that Shen-hui came to Szechwan in his thirtieth year (i.e., 749 or 750). It goes on to say that, since his aptitude was acute, he was suddenly awakened and received Wu-hsiang's sanction, although it does not indicate when. It notes that his dharma age was thirty-six when he died, which means that he must have received full ordination around 759. It also says that from the time he first received the teaching of his master as a novice until he passed it on to future generations was twelve years, two months, and twenty-two days, suggesting that he first became a teacher in his own right sometime around 772, some ten years after the death of Wu-hsiang.[65]

Like his master, Ching-chung Shen-hui had connections with the regional power-holders of his time. The most important of these was Wei Kao (d. 805), who wrote Shen-hui's epitaph (which unfortunately has not survived). Wei Kao dominated the politics of the region in and around Ch'eng-tu as military governor of Chien-nan West from 785 to 805.[66] The major accomplishment for which he is remembered was his pacification of the kingdom of Nan-chao (present Yunnan Province). Throughout the second half of the eighth century, T'ang rule was continually challenged by both internal and external threats. The An Lu-shan rebellion had been brought to an end not so much by a vigorous reassertion of imperial authority as by a grudging accommodation to the very process of political fragmentation that had been its cause. Not only was T'ang suzerainty repeatedly challenged

---

[62] 185b11–14; *Shoki II*, p. 144.

[63] TSC 278c2–3.

[64] 185a24–26; *Shoki II*, p. 143.

[65] SKSC 764a23–b12. The LTFPC notes that when Tu Hung-chien first arrived in Ch'eng-tu in 766, Wu-hsiang had no clear successor (187c7–13; *Shoki II*, p. 189; cf. Broughton, "Early Ch'an," p. 26).

[66] For his official biography see CTS 140.3821–3826 and HTS 158.3933–3937. The SKSC's entry for the Indian monk Wu-ming, a strange figure whose sole purpose is to predict Wei Kao's ascendency in Szechwan, serves as pretext for introducing a biography of Wei Kao; see 830b17–c16. See also Charles Backus, *The Nan-chao Kingdom and T'ang China's Southwestern Frontier*, pp. 90–99.

internally by the northeastern provinces, but it was also continually threatened externally by Tibetan forces along the western frontier. The tension with Tibet was especially felt in Szechwan. By the middle of the eighth century the Nan-chao kingdom had become firmly allied with Tibet, and its troops often supported Tibetan forces in various incursions into T'ang territory. In 779, for example, a large-scale combined force from Tibet and Nan-chao attacked Szechwan. Even though the invasion was eventually repulsed by Chinese forces, it demonstrated the vulnerability of southwestern frontier to Tibetan incursion.[67]

Through a skillful combination of military action and diplomatic maneuvering, Wei Kao succeeded in gradually wooing Nan-chao away from Tibet and allying it with the T'ang. Wei Kao's efforts to bring Nan-chao into the Chinese political sphere also involved winning it over to Chinese ways, and Buddhism seems to have played an important part in this process. The kind of Buddhism that was introduced into Nan-chao under Wei Kao's influence was the Ching-chung tradition, as suggested by the long scroll of Buddhist images from Nan-chao.[68] Among its host of scenes, it depicts the transmission of Buddhism from Śākyamuni Buddha through a series of Chinese patriarchs to Nan-chao. What is especially interesting is that the transmission is depicted as passing from Hui-neng through Shen-hui to Chang Wei-chung (i.e., Nan-yin), the same line of succession Tsung-mi claims for himself, a point whose significance will soon become clear.

In addition to the use of Buddhism in his sinification of Nan-chao, Wei Kao also seems to have been a devout lay Buddhist. The *Sung kao-seng chuan* notes that he became particularly religious in his later years. "He always carried a rosary and recited the Buddha's name."[69] A curious testament to his piety has survived in an epitaph he wrote for a stūpa containing the relics of a parrot. Apparently a certain Mr.

---

[67] In addition to Backus's *The Nan-chao Kingdom*, for general background see Charles A. Peterson, "The Restoration Completed: Emperor Hsien-tsung and the Provinces," pp. 151–191; Peterson, "Court and Province in Mid- and Late T'ang," pp. 464–560; Michael T. Dalby, "Court Politics in Late T'ang Times," pp. 561–681; Matsui Shūichi, "Tōdai zenpanki no Shisen," pp. 1178–1214; and Edwin G. Pulleyblank, "The An Lu-shan Rebellion and the Origins of Chronic Militarism in Late T'ang China," pp. 32–60.

[68] See Yanagida, "Jinne no shōzō," pp. 238–240. This scroll, painted under the direction of Chang Sheng-wen for the ruler of Ta-li (i.e., Nan-chao) during the early 1170s, belongs to the collection of the National Palace Museum in Taipei. See Helen Chapin and Alexander Soper, *A Long Roll of Buddhist Images*, and Li Lin-ts'an's monograph, *Nan-chao Ta-li kuo hsin tz'u-liao ti tsung-ho yen-chiu*.

[69] 830c12–13.

P'ei had trained this remarkable bird to recite the Buddha's name, as a result of which it attained Buddhahood. After it died its body was cremated, and more than ten relics were found. Hearing of this, the monk Hui-kuan had the relics enshrined, and Wei Kao wrote his commemoration in 803.[70]

Shortly after Wei Kao died in the summer of 805, one of his subordinate generals, Liu P'i, seized control of the province and demanded confirmation from the court. Hesitant to provoke a confrontation, the new emperor Hsien-tsung reluctantly agreed to appoint Liu P'i assistant governor. When Liu P'i then moved to annex Chiennan East, however, Hsien-tsung sent troops to Szechwan, and Liu's insurrection was quickly suppressed by the fall of 806.[71] In the following year, to celebrate the restoration of imperial authority, the Pao-ying ssu in the southwestern quarter of Ch'eng-tu was renamed Sheng-shou ssu (temple for the longevity of the sage [emperor]), and Nan-yin was installed as abbot.[72]

Nan-yin was one of Ching-chung Shen-hui's main disciples. The sources are mute on Wei Kao's relationship with Nan-yin. Yet, given his relationship to Shen-hui, and the increasing fervor of his piety as he grew old, it is difficult to imagine Wei Kao not transferring to Nan-yin his devotion to Shen-hui (who died in 794, over a decade before Wei Kao's death). The *Sung kao-seng chuan* notes that Wei Kao put his faith in the Southern tradition of Ch'an and studied the teaching of mind with Ching-chung Shen-hui.[73] The long scroll of Buddhist images from Nan-chao also suggests Wei Kao's connection with Nan-yin (see fig. 2.2). This scroll is particularly interesting because Nan-yin is referred to as Chang Wei-chung and is depicted as the direct successor of Ho-tse Shen-hui, suggesting that Nan-yin himself adopted the name Wei-chung and protrayed himself as the successor of Ho-tse Shen-hui. In this regard, several otherwise unobtrusive details in Nan-yin's *Sung kao-seng chuan* biography are especially noteworthy. It says that he first studied "the profound teaching of Ts'ao-ch'i (i.e., the sixth patriarch Hui-neng), but, since he did not fully understand it, he went to see Shen-hui of the Ching-chung ssu."[74] A few lines later, the biography states that "he entered Shu (i.e., Sze-

[70] See SKSC 830c13–14; the epitaph can be found in CTW 453.11b-13a.

[71] For Liu P'i's standard biography see CTS 140.3826–3828 and 158.3938–3939. For a brief discussion of his insurrection see Peterson, "The Restoration Completed," pp. 157–160, and Dalby, "Court Politics in Late T'ang Times," pp. 612–613.

[72] The date is given in *T'ang hui yao* 48.853.

[73] 830c14–15.

[74] 772b3–4.

Ho-shang Chang Wei-chung   Shen-hui Ta-shih   Hui-neng Ta-shih

Figure 2.2. The Long Scroll of Buddhist Images from Nan-chao. National Palace Museum,

chwan) from Chiang-ling."[75] Chiang-ling is another name for Ching-chou, where Ho-tse Shen-hui died in 758. The *Sung kao-seng chuan* thus indicates that Nan-yin studied briefly with Ho-tse Shen-hui or one of his immediate disciples (perhaps Chih-ju, whom Tsung-mi places between Shen-hui and Nan-yin in the line of succession) before going to Szechwan. Nan-yin could therefore legitimately claim some lineal connection with Ho-tse Shen-hui.

There is no indication that the practice or teaching of the Nan-yin tradition in any way significantly differed from that of Ching-chung. Even though Nan-yin's teaching seems to have been nothing more than an extension of Ching-chung Ch'an, in claiming a direct filiation with Ho-tse Shen-hui his tradition asserted its institutional independence. To distinguish this tradition from the Ching-chung, I propose that it be referred to as the Sheng-shou tradition (after the name of the temple in Ch'eng-tu where Nan-yin resided), while keeping in mind that, in terms of its teaching and practice, it should be seen as a subtradition of Ching-chung Ch'an. Its lineal filiation can be diagrammed as follows on the next page.

There were several factors that would have induced Nan-yin to stress his connection with Ho-tse Shen-hui. First of all, I have already noted the importance of Ho-tse Shen-hui's teaching of no-thought within the Ching-chung tradition. Second, an imperial commission in 796 established Ho-tse Shen-hui as the seventh patriarch, thus reaffirming that Ch'an orthodoxy flowed through Ho-tse Shen-hui.[76] Third, Nan-yin's installation as abbot in the Sheng-shou ssu gave his tradition an institutional base separate from the Ching-chung ssu and would thus have provided a perfect opportunity for him to emphasize a different source for his tradition. The coincidence of both of his teachers having the same name made such a shift all the more easy. Lastly, Nan-yin's identification with Ho-tse Shen-hui bolstered his claims to orthodoxy over rival Szechwanese traditions, especially the Pao-t'ang line based in Tzu-chou, which used Shen-hui's teaching of no-thought and its corollary subitist doctrine to deny the need for the kind of conventional Buddhist practices that were at the heart of Ching-chung religious life.

Hu Shih's judgment that Tsung-mi capitalized on the confusion over the two Shen-huis to ally himself falsely with Ho-tse Shen-hui must therefore be substantially qualified on several counts. To begin with, Nan-yin could indeed claim some connection with Ho-tse Shen-hui. Furthermore, the identification of the Sheng-shou tradition with Ho-tse Shen-hui did not originate with Tsung-mi. As I have argued,

[75] 772b5.
[76] See note 26 above.

CHING-CHUNG   SHENG-SHOU

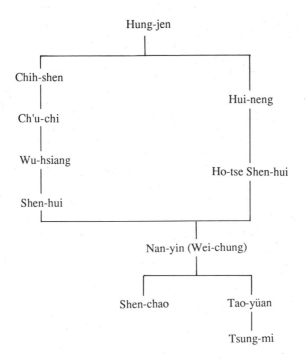

Hung-jen

Chih-shen

Ch'u-chi

Wu-hsiang

Shen-hui

Hui-neng

Ho-tse Shen-hui

Nan-yin (Wei-chung)

Shen-chao   Tao-yüan

Tsung-mi

the long scroll of Buddhist images from Nan-chao, which was independent of any influence from Tsung-mi, suggests that it was Nan-yin himself who first made this connection. The connection of Nan-yin with Ho-tse Shen-hui is also corroborated by Po Chü-i's biography of Nan-yin's disciple Shen-chao; Po writes that Shen-chao studied the teaching of the mind with Wei-chung (who he notes was also known as I-chou Nan-yin), who succeeded to the dharma of the sixth patriarch.[77] These sources also suggest that it was Nan-yin who first identified himself as Wei-chung.

[77] Po Chü-i's epitaph for Shen-chao can be found in *Po-shih Ch'ang-ch'ing chi* 70.13b–15a and CTW 678.21b–22b. In his "Jinne no shōzō," Yanagida suggests that Po Chü-i must have gotten this version of Shen-chao's lineage from Tsung-mi or vice versa (p. 241). The most obvious explanation for the fact that the same version of the lineage appears in works by both Tsung-mi and Po Chü-i is not the supposition that one must have influenced the other but that this version of the lineage had already become independently established before the third decade of the ninth century. Here one should note that Tsung-mi's LSC was written around 824, some three years before he probably met Po for the first time. During his tenure as governor of Lo-yang, Po Chü-i was on close terms with Shen-chao, and it is much more likely that he would have heard

The question of Nan-yin's filiation raises the complex issue of how the notion of lineage was understood in eighth- and ninth-century Ch'an, and here one should be extremely cautious not to read back into late T'ang sources notions that were only clearly articulated and codified in the Sung. The Chinese term in question is *tsung* (lineage, tradition, essential teaching, source of inspiration). While tsung was a central term within Ch'an polemics of the eighth century, its meaning was often ambiguous. It could be and frequently was used to mean "lineage." But it could also mean the "essential teaching" in terms of which a specific tradition defined itself.[78] Such use in the *Platform Sūtra*, for example, is reflected in Yampolsky's translation of tsung as "cardinal principle."[79] The two meanings of tsung were not clearly demarcated and often overlapped in usage. Tsung-mi uses tsung in both senses in his *Ch'an Preface*.[80] Sometimes it means simply lineage, but more often it is used in a broader sense related to its general meaning of essential teaching.[81]

The particular tsung to which a teacher belonged was not merely a matter of lineal filiation but also had to do with the source of inspiration to which his tradition turned. It was the essential teaching emphasized within a given tradition that defined it as a tsung as much as the lineal filiation of a succession of teachers. A tsung was, as it were, the "progenitive idea" around which a tradition crystallized. Even though the personal bond of the master-disciple relationship linked the tradition together, the character of that relationship was not fixed. If someone claimed that he carried on the tsung of a particular teacher, he may have been inspired by him during a brief period of study in his youth, he may have received ordination from him, or he may have succeeded to the abbotship of his temple.

In the late eighth and early ninth centuries, there were no fixed

---

this version of Shen-chao's lineage from Shen-chao himself than from Tsung-mi. In its biography of Tsung-mi, the *Chodang chip* gives the same version of his lineage found in the LSC (i.e., Ho-tse Shen-hui, Tz'u-chou Ju, I-chou Wei-chung, Sui-chou Yüan), although it is probable that it is simply following Tsung-mi and cannot therefore be taken as an independent source of corroboration.

[78] For an insightful discussion of the meaning of *tsung* in the T'ang see Foulk, "The 'Ch'an School,'" part 1. See also Yoshizu Yoshihide's discussion of the meaning of *tsung* in eighth-century Ch'an in his *Kegonzen no shisōshi-teki kenkyū*, chap. 3, and Stanley Weinstein's article on Chinese Buddhist Schools in *The Encyclopedia of Religion*, 2:482–487.

[79] See *The Platform Sutra of the Sixth Patriarch*.

[80] See discussion in B 96, n. 1.

[81] In this second sense Tsung-mi lists three different types of Ch'an *tsung*, which he correlates with three different types of Mahāyāna teaching (*chiao*). According to this latter usage, a single *tsung* can include several unrelated lineages (*tsung* in the first sense). The first of *tsung* Tsung-mi's enumerates includes the Northern line of Ch'an as well as three unrelated Szechwanese lineages. See chapter 7.

ceremonies according to which a disciple's understanding was sanctioned by his master, thereby authorizing him to carry on his master's tradition.[82] At that time the notion of the transmission and succession of the dharma was not clearly defined, and the attendant notion of lineage was fluid. What particular tsung a given teacher chose to identify with might be decided by a range of factors, including his relationship with his own teachers, the nature of his understanding, and his own teaching personality—all of which would be inextricably connected in his own experience. The issue of tsung was also influenced by the changing trends within the Chinese Buddhist world. That factors directly related to a teacher's own self-interest were often involved in such matters does not mean that there was anything inherently "dishonest" about it. It was simply a matter of putting one's best foot forward. Patronage, after all, was related to the influence and prestige of one's tsung. Given Nan-yin's youthful contact with Ho-tse Shen-hui (or one of his immediate disciples), as well as the importance of Ho-tse Shen-hui's interpretation of Ch'an practice within the Ching-chung tradition, there was nothing disingenuous in making the best of his filiation with Ho-tse Shen-hui. Certainly he could look back to Ho-tse Shen-hui as the source of inspiration for his teaching. By the time Tsung-mi met Tao-yüan in Sui-chou in 804, the issue of the identity of his tradition had most likely already been settled.

Let me conclude this discussion of the Ching-chung tradition by summarizing those characteristics that have most bearing on understanding Tsung-mi as a Ch'an figure.

First, both the Ching-chung tradition and its Sheng-shou subtradition were powerful institutions within the world of Szechwanese Buddhism during the second half of the eighth century and the beginning of the ninth. Wu-hsiang, Shen-hui, and Nan-yin were closely associated with the political and military power-holders of the time, and the Ching-chung ssu and Sheng-shou ssu were connected with the state. Tsung-mi's subsequent association with prominent literary and political figures in and around Ch'ang-an was fully consonant with the patterns of behavior set by his Szechwanese forebears.

Second, there was nothing distinctively "Ch'an" about either the practice or institutional life of the Ching-chung ssu or the Sheng-shou ssu, and in this regard both temples seem to have been conventional establishments. We have seen that the Ching-chung ssu's ordination ceremonies were conducted according to the vinaya, and its

---

[82] The artificiality of the story of the transmission of the patriarchal robe begun by Shen-hui and repeated in the LTFPC and *Platform Sūtra* underlines the fact that there was no commonly accepted procedure for transmitting the dharma.

preparatory ritual repentance followed standard Chinese Buddhist practice of the time. Wu-hsiang also taught a peculiar version of *nien-fo*. The basically conservative stance toward Buddhist practice within the Ching-chung tradition can be seen in its criticism of the Pao-t'ang line of Ch'an for applying the radical implications of Ho-tse Shen-hui's message literally. Shen-ch'ing, for instance, criticizes Pao-t'ang as heretical.[83] Even the *Li-tai fa-pao chi*, written to substantiate Pao-t'ang's claims to legitimacy, gives clear evidence that its iconoclastic interpretation of Shen-hui met stout opposition on the part of Wu-hsiang's followers.[84] As I shall discuss in detail later, Tsung-mi was also sharply critical of the Pao-t'ang tradition. His general opposition to antinominian interpretations of Ch'an reflects the attitudes toward practice within the Ching-chung and Sheng-shou traditions. Despite his commitment to the sudden teaching of Ch'an, Tsung-mi affirmed the full range of conventional Buddhist practice. He himself composed an abridged guidebook on vinaya practice. He sponsored a Yü-lan-p'en ceremony, a popular Buddhist festival for feeding the hungry ghosts, and, as noted, wrote a commentary on the *Yü-lan-p'en ching*. Most noteworthy, he also wrote a massive commentary on ritual practice according to the *Scripture of Perfect Enlightenment*, a work that remains a veritable encyclopedia of T'ang Buddhist ritual.

Third, Shen-hui's teaching of no-thought exerted a powerful influence on Szechwanese Ch'an, as seen in the fragments of Wu-hsiang's teaching preserved in the *Li-tai fa-pao chi* and as acknowledged by Nan-yin's affiliation with Ho-tse Shen-hui's lineage. Within both the Ching-chung and Sheng-shou traditions, Shen-hui's teaching of no-thought provided an interpretative context for conventional Buddhist practices. It is only here that we can discern anything distinctively "Ch'an" about them—but what is especially important to note is that their adoption of Shen-hui's message did not entail calling these practices into question (as it did, or at least was alleged to do, within Pao-t'ang Ch'an). Given the centrality of the *Awakening of Faith* in Tsung-mi's thought, this text seems to have provided a philosophical framework for understanding Shen-hui's teaching within the Ching-chung tradition.

· · ·

Such was the context of Tsung-mi's Ch'an training. His autobiographical account goes on to describe his first enlightenment experi-

---

[83] *Pei-shan lu*, T 52.612c11ff.

[84] See 186c29–187a12; *Shoki II*, p. 170; cf. Broughton, "Early Ch'an," pp. 22–23.

ence. Shortly after having become a novice monk under Tao-yüan in Sui-chou, he participated in a maigre gathering (*chai*) at the home of a local official, Jen Kuan. There, when the sūtra chanting was over, he came across a copy of the *Scripture of Perfect Enlightenment* for the first time. After only reading two or three pages, he had an awakening, an experience whose intensity so overwhelmed him that he found himself spontaneously dancing for joy.[85] Later, when he reported back to Tao-yüan, the latter is said to have remarked: "You will greatly propagate the perfect-sudden teaching. This scripture has been especially entrusted to you by all the Buddhas."[86]

This experience was the biographical model for Tsung-mi's understanding of sudden enlightenment, as suggested by the fact that he entitles this section in his subcommentary "suddenly awakening to the principle of the teachings" (*tun-wu chiao-li*). In light of Tsung-mi's subsequent scholarly career, and especially his contention that the scriptures provided a necessary counterbalance to Ch'an experience, it is significant that his initial enlightenment did not occur while he was absorbed in meditation. Nor, as in the case of so many well-known Ch'an enlightenment stories, did it occur as a sudden burst of insight at the turning words or dramatic action of a master. Rather, it came about as a result of reading several lines of scripture.

The text that precipitated this experience was to dominant Tsung-mi's life for the next two decades. During the next several years, Tsung-mi launched into an intensive study of the *Scripture of Perfect Enlightenment*, searching out and pouring through the available commentaries. He mentions four, none of which has survived: those by Wei-ch'üeh fa-shih of Pao-kuo ssu (in one fascicle), Wu-shih ch'an-shih of Hsien-t'ien ssu (in two fascicles), Chien-chih fa-shih of Chien-fu ssu (in four fascicles), and Tao-ch'üan of Tsang-hai ssu (in three fascicles).[87]

After receiving full ordination in 807 from the vinaya master Cheng,[88] Tsung-mi took leave of Tao-yüan and departed Sui-chou in 808 to visit Tao-yüan's master, Wei-chung, who was then abbot of Sheng-shou ssu in Ch'eng-tu. Wei-chung was quick to recognize Tsung-mi's ability and is supposed to have praised him as "someone fit to transmit the teachings."[89] He accordingly urged him to proceed

---

[85] TSC 223a1–3; LSC 106d12–14.

[86] P'ei Hsiu's preface to LS, T 39.523c7; the CTL elaborates Tao-yüan's admonition by adding: "You must practice and never become stuck in a single corner" (205c18).

[87] TSC 223a4–8; LSC 106d16–107a1. Kamata has listed all the fragments Tsung-mi quotes from Wei-ch'üeh's commentary; see his *Shūmitsu*, pp. 108–110.

[88] SKSC 741c26–27.

[89] Kamata, *Shūmitsu*, p. 50.5; cf. SKSC 741c27–28 and CTL 205c19.

to the imperial capital to promote the teachings there. Before leaving Ch'eng-tu, Tsung-mi also met Wei-chung's disciple Shen-chao, who was later to gain renown in Lo-yang. Shen-chao also seems to have been duly impressed with the young monk, allegedly referring to him as a bodhisattva.[90]

Scripture of Perfect Enlightenment

Before considering the next phase of Tsung-mi's life, I shall pause briefly to discuss the scripture that played such a central role in his spiritual development and scholarly career. Indeed, it would be difficult to overestimate the importance of this text for Tsung-mi. Despite his appropriation into the fold of Hua-yen patriarchs, he saw it as superior to even the *Hua-yen Sūtra*, claiming that its straightforwardness was better suited to the needs of the times than the gargantuan scale of the *Hua-yen Sūtra*.

> If you want to propagate the truth, single out its quintessence, and thoroughly penetrate the ultimate meaning, do not revere the *Hua-yen Sūtra* above all others. Ancient and modern worthies and masters of the tripiṭaka in both the western regions and this land have all classified it as supreme, as fully related in [Ch'eng-kuan's] introduction to his commentary. Yet its principles become so confused within its voluminous size that beginners become distraught and have difficulty entering into it. . . . It is not as good as this scripture, whose single fascicle can be entered immediately.[91]

In fact, as later chapters will discuss in detail, Tsung-mi went so far as to revise traditional Hua-yen classification categories in order to establish the supremacy of this text over the *Hua-yen Sūtra*.

Although it purports to have been translated into Chinese by Buddhatrāta in 693, the *Scripture of Perfect Enlightenment* has been shown by modern scholarship to be an "apocryphal" text composed in China sometime around the end of the seventh or beginning of the eighth century. Its teaching was based on two other apocryphal works, the *Śūraṅgama Sūtra* and *Awakening of Faith*.[92]

The first catalogue to mention the *Scripture of Perfect Enlightenment*

---

[90] Kamata, *Shūmitsu*, p. 50.5; cf. SKSC 741c28–29 and CTL 205c20–21.

[91] TSC 226a10–14.

[92] Mochizuki Shinkō, *Bukkyō kyōten seiritsu shiron*, pp. 509–519; Kamata, *Shūmitsu*, pp. 102–105; and Yanagida Seizan, *Chūgoku senjutsu kyōten*, pp. 268–272. By "apocryphal" I mean a text that purports to be a translation but was originally composed in Chinese. For an authoritative discussion of this term in regard to Chinese Buddhism see Robert Buswell's introduction to his *Chinese Buddhist Apocrypha*.

is the *K'ai-yüan shih-chiao lu*, compiled in 730 by Chih-sheng, which lists Buddhatrāta (Fo-t'o-to-lo; Chüeh-chiu) as the translator. It says that Buddhatrāta came from Kashmir (Chi-tsung) and claims that he translated the scripture at the Pai-ma ssu in Lo-yang. Chih-sheng notes that, even though the text "appeared recently," its year of translation is not recorded. He goes on to raise the question of authenticity only to conclude that the fact the date of translation is unknown does not necessarily mean that the text is apocryphal.[93] Both the *Hsü ku-chin i-ching t'u-chi* (also compiled by Chih-sheng in 730)[94] and *Chen-yüan shih-chiao mu-lu* (compiled by Yüan-chao c. 800)[95] repeat the *K'ai-yüan shih-chiao lu* entry verbatim. Buddhatrāta's brief biography in the *Sung kao-seng chuan* only slightly varies the wording of the *K'ai-yüan shih-chiao lu* account without adding any new information.[96] The fact that Buddhatrāta is not listed as the translator or author of any other text and that nothing is known of his life and activities in China are only the first of the many indications that the *Scripture of Perfect Enlightenment* was apocryphal.

Tsung-mi's discussion of the translation of the *Scripture of Perfect Enlightenment* quotes the no longer extant commentary by Tao-ch'üan, which says that the translation was completed by the Kashmiri (Chieh-shih-mi-lo) tripiṭaka master Buddhatrāta at the Pai-ma ssu on the eighth day of the fourth month of 693. Tao-ch'üan ends by cryptically commenting that the details of Buddhatrāta's life are recorded elsewhere.[97] In his subcommentary, Tsung-mi introduces evidence that further complicates the picture. He mentions that among the miscellaneous scriptures in the library at Feng-te ssu on Mount Chung-nan he came across a copy of the *Scripture of Perfect Enlightenment* that was so badly worm-eaten that only the last two or three pages were barely legible. The postface claimed that the translation

[93] T 55.565a1–4.

[94] T 55.369a3–6.

[95] T 55.865a10–15.

[96] See 717c6–14.

[97] TS 119d13–120a4. Mochizuki notes that the *Scripture of Perfect Enlightenment* is not listed in the *Ta-chou k'an-ting chung-ching mu-lu*, compiled under imperial auspices only two years after Tao-ch'üan claims the *Scripture of Perfect Enlightenment* was translated, and goes on to suggest that Tao-ch'üan made up this date to suit his own purposes (*Bukkyō kyōten seiritsu shiron*, p. 511). That the text was not known to Ming-ch'üan and the other compilers of the *Ta-chou k'an-ting chung-ching mu-lu* in 795 does not necessarily mean that it was not in existence at that time. However, the *Ta-chou k'an-ting chung-ching mu-lu*, as perhaps the most comprehensive catalogue compiled to date, indiscriminately mixed any and all listings of a text, from both extant and nonextant listings. If the *Scripture of Perfect Enlightenment* were extant at the time of its compilation, it would be surprising that it was overlooked by its assiduous cataloguers.

was completed on the fifteenth day of the seventh month of 647 at Pao-yün tao-ch'ang in T'an-chou (Ch'ang-sha, Hunan) and listed Lo-hou-t'an-chien as the translator. Noting that he has not been able to corroborate the information on this postface, Tsung-mi concludes that one still cannot rule out the possibility that the text's circulation may have first been restricted to the south and that its existence would thus not have been known to later cataloguers.[98] Lo-hou-t'an-chien, whom the postface names as translator, is a mysterious figure who, as far as I have been able to determine, is not mentioned any-where else.[99] Whatever the truth of the contents of this postface, Tsung-mi's story of the copy of the *Scripture of Perfect Enlightenment* that he discovered at the Feng-te ssu is important as another piece of evidence pointing to the apocryphal origin of the text. That there were widely discrepant versions of its date of translation, as well as the name of the translator, only raises further suspicions about the circumstances of its composition.

Tsung-mi's subsequent discussion of the four commentators con-tains some clues as to the context in which the text circulated. Per-haps because Wei-ch'üeh was well known, Tsung-mi merely refers to him as the commentator to the *Śūraṅgama Sūtra*,[100] a fact of some significance given the connection between the *Scripture of Perfect En-lightenment* and the *Śūraṅgama Sūtra* and the popularity of the *Śūraṅgama Sūtra* in Ch'an circles at the end of the seventh and beginning of the eighth centuries. Although the *Sung kao-seng chuan* biography of Wei-ch'üeh says nothing directly about the *Scripture of Perfect En-lightenment*, it is still valuable for indicating that one of the principal figures with whom the text was first associated was in Lo-yang during the end of Empress Wu's reign and may have had some connection with Shen-hsiu, the famous leader of the Northern line of Ch'an.[101]

[98] TSC 282b13–18.

[99] His name is not listed in the indexes for the Taishō volumes containing biogra-phies and catalogues; nor can it be found in Makita's *Kōsōden* index to the SKSC.

[100] TSC 282c8–9.S

[101] It says nothing about the *Scripture of Perfect Enlightenment* but does mention his commentary to the *Śūraṅgama Sūtra*. It recounts two different versions of how he came into contact with the text, the second of which is particularly noteworthy because it claims that he first came across the *Śūraṅgama Sūtra* at the Tu-men ssu in Ching-chou while Shen-hsiu was there (i.e., sometimes during the last quarter of the seventh cen-tury) (SKSC 738c4–5). The first version, which claims that he encountered the text at the home of the ex–chief minister, Fang Jung, is important because it locates Wei-chih in Lo-yang at the end of Empress Wu's reign (705) (738b22–27). Shen-hsiu resided at the Tu-men ssu throughout the last quarter of the seventh century; see McRae, *The Northern School*, pp. 50–51. Fang Jung was appointed chief minister in the tenth month of 704 and held the post for three months; he was exiled in 705 with Empress Wu's fall from power and died shortly thereafter. Wei-chih's meeting with him must there-

Aside from Wei-ch'üeh, the other three commentators are obscure figures about whom nothing is known other than the meager information Tsung-mi provides. Here it is significant that two of the other commentators also had Ch'an connections. Tsung-mi notes that Tao-shih "received the teaching of Ho-tse"[102] and that Chien-chih was Tao-shih's disciple.[103] Unfortunately, Tsung-mi says nothing about the fourth figure, Tao-ch'üan.

Although the sources do not permit one to determine either where or when the text was first composed, what circumstantial evidence they do present suggests that the *Scripture of Perfect Enlightenment* was current in Ch'an circles in or around Lo-yang during the reign of Empress Wu (690–705). This conclusion is strengthened by the fact that the first text to mention the *Scripture of Perfect Enlightenment* is the *Ch'uan fa-pao chi*, an early Ch'an record of the transmission of the dharma down through Shen-hsiu.[104]

As Robert Buswell has shown in his study of the *Vajrasamādhi Sūtra*, apocryphal texts played an important role in the process of sinification, by which Indian Buddhist concepts were adapted to Chinese cultural presuppositions.

> Apocryphal texts often satisfied East Asian religious presumptions and needs in ways that translated Indian scriptures, which targeted Indian or Central Asian audiences, simply could not. Like the indigenous learned schools of Buddhism [such as T'ien-t'ai and Hua-yen], indigenous sūtras also sought to fashion new, uniquely East Asian forms of Buddhism, without precise analogues within the Indian tradition. In such scriptures, motifs and concepts drawn from translated texts were combined with beliefs and practices deriving from the native culture. These components were then arranged in a familiar sūtra narrative structure: the scripture is spoken by the Buddha at an Indian site, to an audience of Indians (or at least persons with pseudo-Indian names).[105]

Despite Ch'an's much-touted claim not to depend on words or letters, apocryphal texts such as the *Śūraṅgama Sūtra*, *Vajrasamādhi Sūtra*, *Scripture of Perfect Enlightenment*, and *Awakening of Faith* lent legiti-

---

fore have taken place in 705. See Richard Guisso, *Wu Tse-t'ien and the Politics of Legitimation in T'ang China*, p. 198. Fang Jung's official biography can be found in CTS 111 and HTS 139.

[102] TSC 282c9–11.

[103] TSC 282c11–12.

[104] See Yanagida, *Shoki no zenshi I*, p. 408; for a translation see McRae, *The Northern School*, p. 267.

[105] *The Formation of Ch'an Ideology*, p. 16. It is noteworthy that the *Scripture of Perfect Enlightenment* does not specify where it was preached.

macy to the new Ch'an teachings that were taking form at the end of the seventh and beginning of the eighth centuries.

Indeed, there is much in the *Scripture of Perfect Enlightenment* that relates to the theory and practice of Ch'an. Tsung-mi interpreted the main body of the text, what he referred to as the true teaching (*cheng-tsung*), as exemplifying the theory of sudden enlightenment followed by gradual cultivation (*tun-wu chien-hsiu*), which he advocated as the essence of Ho-tse Shen-hui's teaching. Whereas the first chapter set forth "sudden faith and understanding" (*tun hsin chieh*), the next ten chapters dealt with "gradual cultivation and realization" (*chien hsiu cheng*).[106] Tsung-mi claimed that practice must be founded on faith in and understanding of the perfectly enlightened mind with which all beings are endowed—hence sudden enlightenment must precede gradual cultivation. The mind of perfect enlightenment is, of course, what in more technical terms is referred to as the tathāgatagarbha, the Indian Buddhist doctrine that was central to the sinified forms of Buddhism that assumed their mature form in the Sui and T'ang dynasties. This doctrine is at the very core of Tsung-mi's understanding of Buddhism and will be dealt with in detail in subsequent chapters. For now it should be noted that it is the *Awakening of Faith's* highly sinified appropriation of the tathāgatagarbha doctrine that provides the context in which Tsung-mi interprets the *Scripture of Perfect Enlightenment*. That the central scripture for Tsung-mi was apocryphal, and that his interpretation of it was based on yet another apocryphal text, is a good index of how thoroughly sinified his understanding of Buddhism was.

CH'ENG-KUAN AND HUA-YEN (810–816)

Tsung-mi experienced the second major turning point in his life in 810 at the age of thirty. He details his experience, and the events following it, in a letter written to Ch'eng-kuan on October 4, 811. In 810, while staying at Hui-chüeh monastery in Hsiang-yang (Hupei), Tsung-mi happened to meet the ācārya Ling-feng, a disciple of the preeminent Hua-yen master Ch'eng-kuan (738–839). Ling-feng had been seriously ill for several months and was on the verge of death when Tsung-mi met him. Nevertheless, the two monks quickly formed an intimate bond, and Ling-feng gave Tsung-mi a copy of Ch'eng-kuan's commentary and subcommentary to the *Hua-yen Sūtra*. Unfortunately, Ling-feng died before Tsung-mi could finish discussing this new teaching with him. Still, this brief but intense encounter had a profound effect on Tsung-mi, who was convinced that Ling-

---

[106] TS 127c18.

feng had been able to stave off his death solely so that they could meet, and he thus concluded that the way in which he came into contact with the Hua-yen teachings could only have been the result of the ripening of good karmic conditions sown in a previous life.[107] Indeed, much of the numinous quality that this experience had for Tsung-mi must have been related to his conviction that it was karmically predestined, for it is the context in which an experience is interpreted that imbues it with meaning. Tsung-mi thus gave his encounter with these texts a significance that transcended his own personal history; his life was but a part of the historical unfolding of the eternal dharma.

It was in such charged conditions that Tsung-mi began his study of Hua-yen thought in earnest. He compared the significance of his encounter with Ch'eng-kuan's commentary and subcommentary to his earlier meeting of Tao-yüan, which he likewise regarded as karmically fated.[108] In his initial letter to Ch'eng-kuan, he likened it to "coming across sweet dew when thirsty or finding a wish-fulfilling gem when impoverished." His "heart leapt with joy" and he "held [the books] up reverently in both hands and danced." He then sequestered himself in the monastery for a period of intense study and meditation, forgetting to eat and sleep while he read through the two works, "using the commentary to understand the sūtra and the subcommentary to understand the commentary."[109] As a result of this effort his "remaining doubts were completely washed away."[110] Drawing on a well-known Hua-yen image for enlightenment, he compared his experience to "the myriad reflections being brightly manifested when the great ocean has become tranquil."[111] Displaying his mastery of the new Hua-yen idiom, Tsung-mi's letter continues in ornate prose to detail the new and deepened understanding that he had gained from his study of Ch'eng-kuan's commentary and subcommentary. Even factoring out the hyperbole incumbent in such epistolary style, the intensity of Tsung-mi's experience is still apparent. Once again, it is important to note the crucial role that the discovery of a text played in Tsung-mi's religious development.

Tsung-mi's experience must have made a vivid impression on the other monks as well, for he was asked to lecture on the *Hua-yen Sūtra* before leaving Hui-chüeh ssu.[112] From subsequent events one can

[107] T 39.577a7–11.
[108] TSC 225a.
[109] T 39.577a12–24.
[110] T 39.577a16.
[111] T 39.577a18. For the significance of this metaphor, see chapter 4.
[112] The only scripture Tsung-mi mentions in his letter to Ch'eng-kuan is the *Hua-yen*

only suppose that his lecture must have been stirring. Tsung-mi left
Hsiang-yang in 811 for the eastern capital of Lo-yang, intending to
stay there for a short while to pay his respects at Shen-hui's stūpa
before proceeding on to the imperial capital of Ch'ang-an to entreat
Ch'eng-kuan to take him on as a disciple. With the summer retreat
period drawing near, however, he decided to stay on at the Yung-mu
ssu in Lo-yang. Later, in the fall, a group of followers from the Hui-
chüeh ssu in Hsiang-yang sought him out and requested that he lecture on the *Hua-yen Sūtra* once again,[113] saying that only then would
they allow him to proceed on to Ch'ang-an. His lecture must have
been inspiring, for he learned that before that very day (September
28) was over a monk named T'ai-kung, who had been a student of
Ch'eng-kuan's, was so impressed by what he had heard that he cut
off his arm to express his good fortune "at the inconceivable marvel-
ousness" of the dharma he had just encountered.[114] Although the
contents of Tsung-mi's lecture are unknown, it seems reasonable to
assume that it contained a dramatic recounting of the circumstances
of his encounter with Ch'eng-kuan's commentary and subcommentary at Hui-chüeh ssu. Here one sees a side of Tsung-mi that one
would not infer merely from an acquaintance with his scholastic writings: his ability as a public speaker to rouse a powerful emotional
reaction in his audience. His fervent belief that his own religious experience was the consummation of past karma was most likely a
strong ingredient in his effectiveness as a lecturer. Tales of the marvelous workings of karma have always been a staple of popular Buddhism, and it is important to note that they were not neglected even
in Tsung-mi's more philosophical writings.

Tsung-mi went on to comment that the earnestness of the monk's
resolve reflected the power of Ch'eng-kuan's teaching. He added that
there was none who did not marvel at T'ai-kung's composure and
absence of anxiety in carrying out his extraordinary deed of self-am-
putation. An official investigation into the affair awarded T'ai-kung
an imperial citation of merit. Since his wound did not heal, however,
Tsung-mi was charged with responsibility for overseeing his return
to health, thus further delaying his departure for Ch'ang-an.[115]

Sūtra. When he thus says that he lectured on the sūtra, it can only refer to the *Hua-
yen.*

[113] Kamata is in error when he claims that Tsung-mi lectured on the *Scripture of Perfect Enlightenment* (p. 61), as is made clear by P'ei Hsiu's epitaph, Kamata, *Shūmitsu*, p.
50.7; see previous note.

[114] T 39.577b20–24. The model for T'ai-kung's act may have been suggested by the
famous story of the second Chinese Ch'an patriarch, Hui-k'o, who cut off his arm to
demonstrate the seriousness of his resolve to Bodhidharma.

[115] T 39.577b24–c7.

On October 4, 811, Tsung-mi dispatched Hsüan-kuei and Chih-hui to Ch'ang-an. They bore his first letter to Ch'eng-kuan, begging the eminent Hua-yen master for instruction and relating the impact of Tsung-mi's dramatic encounter with his commentary and subcommentary to the *Hua-yen Sūtra* and the ensuing sequence of events at the Yung-mu ssu in Lo-yang. In his reply of November 1, Ch'eng-kuan asks Tsung-mi to admonish T'ai-kung so that others will not be led to follow his example. He points out that the meaning of canonical passages extolling various types of bodily sacrifice is metaphorical: one should cut off one's deluded thoughts, not one's limbs.[116] In his second letter to Ch'eng-kuan, written on November 12, Tsung-mi reports that T'ai-kung's arm had still not healed and that he was thus not free to leave.[117] This distressing affair must have kept Tsung-mi tied up in Lo-yang for another few months, for he did not reach Ch'ang-an until 812.

Tsung-mi studied closely with Ch'eng-kuan for the next two years (812–813), and he remarks that the two were "never apart day and night." Later, even though he dwelt at other temples in Ch'ang-an, he remained in close communication with Ch'eng-kuan and was always free to consult him about any questions that he had.[118] Ch'eng-kuan seems to have had a great respect for Tsung-mi. P'ei Hsiu records that he is supposed to have said: "Aside from you who is able to wander with me in the lotus womb [world] of Vairocana?"[119] P'ei Hsiu's epitaph for Ch'eng-kuan notes that of his thirty-eight disciples, Tsung-mi alone understood the deepest meaning of his teaching.[120]

Ch'eng-kuan was already seventy-four years old when Tsung-mi began his study under him.[121] At that time he was one of the most

[116] T 39.577c10–24.

[117] T 39.577c26–578a5.

[118] TSC 224c8–10; LSC 108b11–13.

[119] Kamata, *Shūmitsu*, p. 50.6. The lotus womb world is the abode of Vairocana Buddha. Rebirth therein was the object of religious aspiration among devotees of the *Hua-yen Sūtra*. Its description in the fifth chapter of Śikṣānanda's translation of the *Hua-yen Sūtra* (T 10.39a–53c) so inspired the monk Nan-ts'ao that he formed a Hua-yen society dedicated to seeking rebirth in Vairocana's lotus womb realm (see *Po-shih Ch'ang-ch'ing-chi* 59.7a–8b). According to Fa-tsang's biography of Chih-yen, after the master had a premonition of his own death he gathered his disciples together and told them that, after he is reborn in a pure land, he vows to journey to the lotus womb world. He then bade them to resolve to join him there (see T 51.163c27–28; cf. Gimello, "Chih-yen," p. 344). See Kimura, *Shoki chūgoku kegon*, pp. 58–59, for an example from the early seventh century. Vairocana was the cosmic Buddha who preached the "eternal" version of the *Hua-yen Sūtra* in the ocean of the lotus womb while in the samādhi of oceanic reflection (see *Hua-yen ching chuan-chi*, T 51.153a15–16).

[120] P. 158.8. All citations to P'ei Hsiu's epitaph will be to the page and line number of the text in Kamata Shigeo, *Chūgoku kegon shisōshi no kenkyū*, pp. 157–158.

[121] The most comprehensive study of Ch'eng-kuan's life and thought is contained in

esteemed prelates in China. In 795 he had been invited to the court
by Te-tsung on the occasion of the emperor's birthday. Because his
lectures on the essentials of Buddhism "cleared" and "cooled" the
emperor's mind, Te-tsung conferred on him the title of Ch'ing-liang
fa-shih[122] and, in 796, awarded him the purple robe.[123] He collaborated with Prajña on the new translation of the *Gaṇḍavyūha* done under imperial auspices between 796 and 798 and lectured the emperor
after its completion.[124] As a result, he was honored as national
teacher (*kuo-shih*) and grand recorder of the clergy (*ta seng-lu*) in
799.[125] In 796 he had responded to the questions of the imperial
prince (who later became the emperor Shun-tsung) with a pithy piece
explaining the essentials of the mind known as the *Ta Shun-tsung hsin-
yao fa-men*.[126] In 810 the emperor Hsien-tsung appointed him con-
troller of monks (*seng-t'ung*).[127] Altogether Ch'eng-kuan served under
seven emperors.

He also had close connections with a number prominent scholar-
officials and military governors. His biography in the *Sung kao-seng*

Kamata's *Chūgoku kegon*. The main primary sources for Ch'eng-kuan's life are P'ei
Hsiu's epitaph, *Ch'ing-liang kuo-shih miao-chüeh t'a-chi*, in CTW 743.21a–b; Tsan-ning's
SKSC 737a–c; Chih-p'an's *Fo-tsu t'ung-chi*, T 49.293b–c; Tsung-chien's *Shih-men cheng-
t'ung*, HTC 130.456a–c; Tsu-hsiu's *Lung-hsing fo-chiao pien-nien t'ung-lun*, HTC
130.335d–336b; Yen-i's *Kuang Ch'ing-liang chuan*, T 51.1120a–b; and Hsü-fa's *Fa-chieh
tsung wu-tsu lüeh-chi*, HTC 134.275b–277a. For a discussion of the biographical sources,
see Kamata, *Chūgoku kegon*, pp. 151–156.

[122] *Fo-tsu t'ung-chi*, T 49.380a6–8; the *Hua-yen hsüan-t'an hui-hsüan chi*, compiled by
P'u-shui in the Yüan, records the words that Te-tsung is supposed to have spoken on
the occasion (see HTC 12.4d3–4). "Ch'ing-liang" was also a name for Mount Wu-t'ai,
where Ch'eng-kuan resided for some fifteen years.

[123] Kamata, *Chūgoku kegon*, p. 158.3; there are discrepancies among the sources as to
when Ch'eng-kuan received various imperial honors; I have followed Kamata's reconstruction; see *Chūgoku kegon*, pp. 222–227.

[124] See the postface to Prajña's translation, *Ta-fang-kuang fo hua-yen ching*, T 10.848c.
The translation was begun on the fifth day of the sixth month of 796 and completed
on the twenty-fourth day of the second month of 798. Although the *Gaṇḍavyūha* originally circulated as an independent text, it was incorporated into the *Hua-yen Sūtra*
corpus. For an English translation from Śikṣānanda's translation of the *Hua-yen Sūtra*,
see Thomas Cleary, *The Flower Ornament Scripture*, vol. 3. See also Fontein, *The Pilgrimage of Sudhana*, and Gomez, "Selected Verses from the *Gaṇḍavyūha*."

[125] Kamata, *Chūgoku kegon*, p. 158.3, and *Fo-tsu li-tai t'ung-tsai*, T 49 609c. Weinstein
notes that the title of *ta seng-lu* "was probably more honorific than substantive" (*Buddhism under the T'ang*, p. 171, n. 11).

[126] See SKSC 737b28–29. This work is contained in CTL 459b22–c22; the text is also
included, with Tsung-mi's commentary, in HTC 103.303c–304a.

[127] Kamata, *Chūgoku kegon*, p. 158.4; see also *Fo-tsu t'ung-chi*, T 49.831a5–8, and Kamata, *Chūgoku kegon*, pp. 223–225. According to Yamazaki Hiroshi's *Shina chūsei bukkyō
no tenkai*, pp. 631–632, this position was largely honorary and conferred little real
power over the sangha.

chuan notes that he was particularly intimate with Ch'i Hang (730–804)[128] and Wei Chü-mou (749–801),[129] who respectively were a grand councilor and head of the Ministry of Justice under Te-tsung. It goes on to name ten other powerful figures with whom Ch'eng-kuan was associated. Of these, Wu Yüan-heng (758–815),[130] Cheng Yen (752–829),[131] Li Chi-fu (758–814),[132] Ch'üan Te-yü (759–818),[133] and Li Feng-chi (758–835)[134] all served as grand councilors under Hsien-tsung. Ch'ien Hui (755–829)[135] held the post of secretariat drafter, and Kuei Teng (754–820)[136] was vice-director of the Ministry of War. Wei Shou (d. 823)[137] was military governor of Hsiang-yang, Meng Chien (d. 824)[138] was surveillance commissioner in Yüeh-chou, and Wei Tan (d.u.)[139] surveillance commissioner in Chiang-hsi. Ch'eng-kuan was also connected with Li Tzu-liang (733–795), military governor of Ho-tung, who invited him to lecture at the Ch'ung-fu ssu in 791.[140] P'ei Hsiu's epitaph adds that Ch'eng-kuan wrote works in response to queries by Cheng Yü-ch'ing (746–820),[141] Wei Kao, Meng Chien, and Po Chü-i.[142] Ch'eng-kuan's prestige and connections with the court must have facilitated Tsung-mi's later recognition.

Ch'eng-kuan's eminence was based on his extensive command of Buddhist learning. In addition to his undisputed authority in Hua-yen, his biography notes that he had also studied vinaya, T'ien-t'ai, San-lun, and Ch'an.[143] According to P'ei Hsiu's epitaph, Ch'eng-kuan "left the household" in 746 at the age of eight and was ordained as a novice two years later.[144] His early studies encompassed a broad spec-

---

[128] For his official biography see CTS 136.3756–3757 and HTS 128.4471–4472.

[129] For his official biography see CTS 135.3728–3729 and HTS 167.5109–5110.

[130] For his official biography see CTS 158.4159–4162 and HTS 152.4833–4835.

[131] For his official biography see CTS 159.4180–4181 and HTS 165.5074–5076.

[132] For his official biography see CTS 148.3992–3997 and HTS 146.4735–4737.

[133] For his official biography see CTS 148.4001–4005 and HTS 165.5076–5080.

[134] For his official biography see CTS 167.4365–4368 and HTS 174.5221–5223.

[135] For his official biography see CTS 168.4382–4386 and HTS 177.5271–5273.

[136] For his official biography see CTS 149.4019–4020 and HTS 164.5038–5039.

[137] For his official biography see CTS 162.4244–4245 and HTS 160.4976–4977.

[138] For his official biography see CTS 163.4257–4258 and HTS 160.4968–4969.

[139] For his official biography see HTS 197.5629–5630.

[140] SKSC 737b13–14. For Li Tzu-liang's official biography see CTS 146.3957–3958 and HTS 159.4950.

[141] For his official biography see CTS 158.4163–4167 and HTS 165.5059–5061.

[142] Kamata, *Chūgoku kegon*, p. 157.13–158.1.

[143] See SKSC 737a9–20.

[144] The SKSC (737a5–6) and other sources claim that Ch'eng-kuan "left the household" at the age of ten (i.e., in 748); see Kamata's discussion, *Chūgoku kegon*, pp. 159–160.

trum of Buddhist scriptures and treatises, whose scope intimates the eclectic spirit seen in his mature writings. As part of his youthful curriculum, P'ei Hsiu singles out for special mention the *Prajñāpāramitā*, *Nirvāṇa*, *Vimalakīrti*, and *Perfect Enlightenment* sūtras, the *Awakening of Faith*, *Yogācārabhūmi*, and *Ch'eng wei-shih lun*, as well as Seng-chao's treatises, Tao-sheng's writings, Tu-shun's *Fa-chieh kuan-men*, Chih-i's *Chih-kuan*, and Fa-tsang's (*sic*) *Hui-yüan kuan*.[145] In 757 he received full ordination and became a disciple of T'an-i of the Nan-shan branch of the vinaya tradition.[146] Chan-jan (711–782), the great reviver of T'ien-t'ai studies in the second half of the eighth century, was also a fellow student of T'an-i, and Ch'eng-kuan later studied under him between 775 and 776.[147]

Ch'eng-kuan studied Ch'an sometime during his twenties and thirties (after 757 but before 775). Tsung-mi and P'ei Hsiu's epitaph both claim that he studied under the Ho-tse master Wu-ming (722–793).[148] The *Sung kao-seng chuan* makes broader claims for the extent of his Ch'an training, maintaining that Ch'eng-kuan studied under masters in three different traditions: he studied Ox-head Ch'an under Hui-chung (683–769) and Fa-ch'in (714–792), Ho-tse Ch'an under Wu-ming, and Northern Ch'an under Hui-yün (d.u.).[149] While these claims are open to serious question,[150] there is no doubt that Ch'eng-

---

[145] Kamata, *Chūgoku kegon*, p. 157.2–3.

[146] For a discussion of Ch'eng-kuan's vinaya studies see Kamata, *Chūgoku kegon*, pp. 170–172.

[147] For a discussion of the influence of T'ien-t'ai on Ch'eng-kuan see Kamata, *Chūgoku kegon*, part 2, chap. 4.

[148] *Ch'an Chart* 435a–b; K 290; and Kamata, *Chūgoku kegon*, p. 157.4. The claim is repeated in the CTL and *Fa-chieh tsung wu-tsu lüeh-chi*.

[149] 737a18–20.

[150] Kamata has argued that the particular form of Ch'an teaching that had the greatest impact on Ch'eng-kuan was that of the Ox-head tradition. He also points out that, aside from Tsan-ning's assertion in the SKSC (compiled a century and a half after Ch'eng-kuan's death), there is no documentary evidence that Ch'eng-kuan studied Northern Ch'an under Hui-yüan. Kamata nevertheless concludes that the possibility cannot be ruled out, given the knowledge of Northern Ch'an teachings displayed in Ch'eng-kuan's writings (*Chūgoku kegon*, pp. 176–181). Elsewhere in the same work, Kamata disputes the generally accepted opinion that Ch'eng-kuan received sanction from Wu-ming in the Ho-tse line of Southern Ch'an, contending that Ch'eng-kuan exhibits a critical attitude toward both the Northern and Southern lines of Ch'an. Kamata contends, moreover, that the claim that Ch'eng-kuan received sanction from Wu-ming derives from Tsung-mi, who, in his desire to unify the teachings and practices of Hua-yen and Ch'an, grafted Ch'eng-kuan onto his own Ho-tse lineage (see pp. 475–484).

While Kamata's cautions are well taken, it seems to me that they are based on a mistaken assumption about the degree of ideological unity within traditions (see the discussion of *tsung* in the previous section). For Ch'eng-kuan to have "studied" under a given teacher at a particular point in his career does not mean that he necessarily

kuan was familiar with the different Ch'an teachings current in the latter part of the eighth century. Indeed, one of the significant points of difference that distinguishes his Hua-yen writings from those of Fa-tsang is his infusion of Ch'an ideas and perspectives. Ch'eng-kuan's work shows an interest in practice that is not seen in Fa-tsang's more strictly philosophical approach.[151] His familiarity with Ch'an must have been one of the factors that drew Tsung-mi to him. Yet there is an important difference between Ch'ang-kuan's and Tsung-mi's attitude toward Ch'an: whereas Ch'eng-kuan appropriated Ch'an from the perspective of Hua-yen, Tsung-mi appropriated Hua-yen from the perspective of Ch'an.[152] Here it is important to note that Tsung-mi was thirty years old when he first encountered Ch'eng-kuan's writings; he had already reached a degree of intellectual maturity, having completed his Ch'an training under Tao-yüan and been sent off to the capital with his teacher's blessings to begin a career as a promising teacher. Despite the enormous impact that Ch'eng-kuan had on Tsung-mi, the significance that Tsung-mi found in Ch'eng-kuan's Hua-yen was determined by an agenda that had been set by his Ch'an training in Szechwan. Tsung-mi actually invoked Ch'eng-kuan's authority to put forward his own original interpretations, which were often at odds with Ch'eng-kuan.

All sources agree that Ch'eng-kuan studied Hua-yen under Fa-shen (718–778).[153] Fa-shen was a disciple of Hui-yüan (ca. 673–743),[154] the disciple of Fa-tsang whom Ch'eng-kuan was later to castigate as a heretic. One of the charges Ch'eng-kuan brought against Hui-yüan was that he failed to remain faithful to Fa-tsang's vision because he was not versed in Ch'an.[155] Fa-shen wrote a commentary to the *Hua-yen Sūtra* and a subcommentary to Hui-yüan's *K'an-ting chi*, neither of which has survived.[156]

---

fully adopted that teacher's point of view. In other words, we cannot use ideological consistency as a criterion for evaluating claims about whether someone "studied under" a particular teacher. Ch'eng-kuan's repudiation of Hui-yüan demonstrates the fallacy of this assumption. So too does the case of Tsung-mi, who was greatly influenced by Ch'eng-kuan and yet departed from his teachings on any number of significant points.

[151] This is a point emphasized by Kamata; see part 2, chap. 6 of his *Chūgoku kegon*, in which he assesses the characteristics of Ch'eng-kuan's Hua-yen.

[152] Yoshizu, *Kegonzen*.

[153] See Kamata, *Chūgoku kegon*, pp. 181–187; his standard biography can be found in SKSC 736a20–b13.

[154] For a reassessment of Hui-yüan's importance see part 1 of Sakamoto Yukio's *Kegon kyōgaku no kenkyū*.

[155] See chapter 3.

[156] He also wrote commentaries to the *Vimalakīrti*, *Fan-wang ching*, and *Ni-chiai pen*. See Kamata, *Chūgoku kegon*, pp. 184–185.

In 776 Ch'eng-kuan traveled to Mount Wu-t'ai, where he resided for the next fifteen years.[157] Believed to be the earthly abode of Mañjuśrī bodhisattva, the mountain had become a flourishing center of cultic activity by the middle of the eighth century.[158] The Hua-yen tradition had a special association with Mount Wu-t'ai as a passage in the *Hua-yen Sūtra* was used to help authenticate Mañjuśrī's presence on the mountain.[159] Ch'eng-kuan spent part of his earlier years there studying non-Buddhist literature. His subsequent incorporation of Confucian and Taoist allusions (especially from the *Lao-tzu, Chuang-tzu,* and *I ching*) in his Buddhist writings gives his work an eclectic stamp not seen in Fa-tsang. But he was also different from Tsung-mi. Ch'eng-kuan claimed that he used "secular" references merely as expedients, "borrowing their words but not adopting their meaning."[160] He excoriated those who held the "three religions" (of Buddhism, Taoism, and Confucianism) were essentially the same. Tsung-mi, by contrast, was a staunch proponent of the essential harmony of the three religions. In comparison with Tsung-mi, Ch'eng-kuan's adaptation of Confucian and Taoist elements within his thought remained on a fairly superficial level. In this context, it is worth noting that Ch'eng-kuan had come to the Chinese classics only after he had gained a thorough grounding in Buddhist literature, whereas Tsung-mi had received a solid classical education before he began to study Buddhism.

During 784–787 Ch'eng-kuan composed his commentary to the "new" eighty-fascicle translation of the *Hua-yen Sūtra* that had been completed by Śikṣānanda in 699.[161] He went on to compose his sub-commentary in the years immediately following.[162] These two works, which had such a momentous effect on Tsung-mi, represent a truly prodigious feat of scholarship.[163] Ch'eng-kuan's commentary and

---

[157] See Raoul Birnbaum's article, "The Manifestations of a Monastery," p. 119, for Ch'eng-kuan's description of Mount Wu-t'ai.

[158] See Raoul Birnbaum, *Studies on the Mysteries of Mañjuśrī,* pp. 9–25.

[159] See the chapter on the dwelling places of the bodhisattvas (P'u-sa chu-ch'u p'in), T 9.589c–590b, especially 590a3–4, which says: "In the northeast there is bodhisattva dwelling place called Mount Ch'ing-liang" (another name for Mount Wu-t'ai).

[160] See T 36.2b9. Ch'eng-kuan's statement occurs after his citation and explanation of a series of allusions from the *Lao-tzu.*

[161] *Ta-fang-kuang fo hua-yen ching shu,* T no. 1735, 35.503a–963a.

[162] *Ta-fang-kuang fo hua-yen ching sui-shu yen-i ch'ao,* T no. 1736, 36.1a–701a.

[163] The Taishō text of Śikṣānanda's translation alone comes to a total of 444 pages. Ch'eng-kuan's commentary, which does not include the original text, is 460 Taishō pages, and his subcommentary is 700 Taishō pages. Considering that Thomas Cleary's three-volume English translation of the Śikṣānanda text comes to a total of 1,472 pages, Ch'eng-kuan's commentary and subcommentary would add up to a total of about 3,850 pages in straight translation.

subcommentary displaced Fa-tsang's earlier commentary, the *T'an-hsüan chi*,[164] which, because it was based on the earlier sixty-fascicle translation of Buddhabhadra of 420, was seen as obsolete (the presumption being that the shorter version of the sūtra was incomplete). It also superseded the *K'an-ting chi*, an abbreviated commentary on Śikṣānanda's new translation begun by Fa-tsang and taken over by Hui-yüan upon his death,[165] as well as Fa-shen's commentary. With his commentary and subcommentary, Ch'eng-kuan established himself as the preeminent authority on Hua-yen. As noted, Ch'eng-kuan took part in the translation of the *Gaṇḍavyūha* done at the very end of the eighth century. This text was a somewhat expanded and independent version of what had appeared as the concluding section of the two earlier translations of the *Hua-yen Sūtra*. Ch'eng-kuan later wrote a commentary to this text (*Hua-yen ching hsing-yüan p'in shu*).[166]

One of Ch'eng-kuan's chief contributions to Hua-yen lay in his theory of the fourfold dharmadhātu,[167] which he elaborated in his commentary to Tu-shun's *Fa-chieh kuan-men* (Discernments of the dharmadhātu)[168] and Prajñā's translation of the *Gaṇḍavyūha*.[169] Ch'eng-kuan's theory adapts the polarity of *li* and *shih* to elaborate four different perspectives in terms of which the dharmadhātu can be understood. In the first (*shih fa-chieh*), the dharmadhātu is viewed in terms of differentiated phenomena (*shih*), whereas in the second (*li fa-chieh*), it is viewed in terms of the true nature (*hsing*) that is com-

[164] *Hua-yen ching t'an-hsüan chi*, T no. 1733, 35.107a–492b.

[165] HTC 5.12a; cf. Sakamoto, *Kegon kyōgaku*, pp. 248–250. The full title of this work is *Hsü hua-yen ching lüeh-shu k'an-ting chi*. It was begun by Fa-tsang as his synoptic commentary to Śikṣānanda's new translation of the *Hua-yen Sūtra*. According to Hui-yüan's account of its composition, Fa-tsang wrote the commentary to the first through nineteenth fascicles of the sūtra (occupying the second through sixth fascicles of the present *Hsü tsang ching* version of the *K'an-ting chi*). Then, perhaps sensing that his death was near, he turned to the "Shih-ting p'in," a chapter that did not occur in the earlier translation of the sūtra, but only finished his commentary on the first nine concentrations (*ting*) (which can be found in the twelfth fascicle of the present text) before he died. Except for these sections, the remainder of the text, including the introduction, was written by Hui-yüan. The fact that Fa-tsang entrusted the completion of this work to Hui-yüan indicates the esteem with which he regarded him. Unfortunately, the *Hsü tsang ching* text is incomplete. See Sakamoto, *Kegon kyōgaku*, pp. 18–19.

[166] Contained in HTC 7.236a–386d.

[167] Sakamoto Yukio has pointed out that Ch'eng-kuan adopted the terminology for the fourfold dharmadhātu theory from Hui-yüan, although Ch'eng-kuan's explanation of its meaning differed from that of Hui-yüan; see his "Hokkai engi no rekishi teki keisei," pp. 902–903.

[168] *Hua-yen fa-chieh hsüan-ching*, T no. 1883, 45.672a–683a, which has been translated by Cleary in his *Entry into the Inconceivable*, pp. 71–124.

[169] In particular see HTC 7.249c10–250c16.

mon to all dharmas.[170] The two most important perspectives are the
third and fourth dharmadhātu: what Ch'eng-kuan refers to as the
unobstructed interpenetration of the absolute and phenomenal (*li-
shih wu-ai*) and the unobstructed interpenetration of each and every
phenomenon (*shih-shih wu-ai*). I shall later show how these two final
perspectives represent different religious paradigms within the Hua-
yen tradition. For now I shall merely note that, although Ch'eng-
kuan upheld the supremacy of the perfect teaching of the *Hua-yen
Sūtra* as the paradigmatic expression of the unobstructed interpenetration of phenomena (*shih-shih wu-ai*), his writings nevertheless emphasize the importance of the unobstructed interpenetration of the
absolute and phenomenal (*li-shih wu-ai*) as the foundation on which
this vision is established. In this regard, his thought anticipates the
shift in the valence of Hua-yen metaphysics that was only fully realized with Tsung-mi, who displaces the unobstructed interpenetration
of phenomena in favor of the one true dharmadhātu on which all
phenomena are based.

EARLY SCHOLARSHIP (816–828)

In the first month of 816 Tsung-mi withdrew to Chih-chü ssu on
Mount Chung-nan. Part of the Ch'in-ling range, which, running east-
west, separated the Wei and Han river valleys, Mount Chung-nan
was situated some fifty miles southwest of Ch'ang-an, and its "blue-
shadowed" peaks could be plainly seen from the imperial capital on
a clear day.[171] By the ninth century Mount Chung-nan already had a
rich history as a flourishing center of Buddhist activity. It was the
center of the tradition of vinaya study begun by the great scholar
Tao-hsüan (596–667) at the beginning of the T'ang. Based on the
Dharmagupta Vinaya, the *Ssu-fen lü*, this tradition took its name
(Nan-tsung) from Mount Chung-nan, the seat of Tao-hsüan's activity.
Tsung-mi later studied at the Feng-te ssu, the temple with which Tao-
hsüan was primarily affiliated, where he compiled an abridged handbook on the vinaya. Mount Chung-nan also had a long association
with the Hua-yen tradition. From at least the last quarter of the sixth
century, when P'u-an (530–609)[172] retired there to escape the ravages

---

[170] Here one might note the shift in the meaning of *li*: whereas for Tu-shun *li* had
the primary meaning of the principle that all dharmas were empty, for Ch'eng-kuan it
has a more ontological connotation of the underlying nature.

[171] Edward Schafer, "The Last Years of Ch'ang-an," p. 141.

[172] See my "The Teaching of Men and Gods," pp. 284–288, for an account of this
monk's activities on Mount Chung-nan. The Northern Chou persecution of Buddhism
(574–577) seems to have been a major impetus in Mount Chung-nan's becoming a

of the Northern Chou persecution of Buddhism, Mount Chung-nan was one of the early cradles in which the Hua-yen cult developed. From the end of the Sui and into the early T'ang, Hua-yen studies on Mount Chung-nan flourished at the Chih-hsiang ssu. Both Tu-shun and Chih-yen, the two figures later honored as the first and second patriarchs of the tradition, resided there, and the remains of many figures associated with the tradition were buried there.[173] Mount Chung-nan was also the home of the Ts'ao-t'ang ssu, the temple with which Tsung-mi came to be most closely affiliated and the place where his memorial stele was later erected. This temple was situated near Kuei Peak (Kuei-feng), by whose name Tsung-mi came to be known. The Ts'ao-t'ang ssu had also enjoyed a prior association with the Hua-yen tradition, as it was there that Ch'eng-kuan had composed his commentary to the new translation of the *Gandhavyūha*.

It was during his initial stay on Mount Chung-nan that Tsung-mi composed his first two works, *Yüan-chüeh ching k'o-wen* and *Yüan-chüeh ching tsuan-yao*, the former being an annotated outline of the *Scripture of Perfect Enlightenment* and the latter, a two-fascicle compilation of essential passages from its four commentaries by Wei-ch'üeh, Wu-shih, Chien-chih, and Tao-ch'üan. These two preliminary works were the beginning of the almost ten years of further research that would culminate in Tsung-mi's series of definitive commentaries and sub-commentaries composed between 823 and 824. While at Chih-chü ssu he vowed not to leave the mountain for three years in order to read through the canon, and for the next three and a half years he carried out his research at various temples on Mount Chung-nan (he names Yün-chü ssu, Ts'ao-t'ang ssu, and Feng-te ssu).[174]

Tsung-mi returned to Ch'ang-an sometime in the latter part of 819 and continued his research. While staying at the Hsing-fu ssu he took detailed notes on works by Asaṅga, Vasubandhu, and Seng-chao in order to interpret the *Diamond Sūtra*. This work resulted in a commentary (*shu*) and subcommentary (*ch'ao*) to that scripture, both in one fascicle, which he probably completed toward the end of the year.[175] From the winter of 819 to the spring of 820, while staying at the Hsing-fu ssu and Pao-shou ssu, he drew from the *Ch'eng wei-shih lun* and K'uei-chi's commentary to compose his own two-fascicle commentary to the thirty verses of Vasubandhu in order, he said, "to elu-

---

major center of Buddhist activity. The HKSC, for example, records that Ching-ai, along with over thirty disciples, fled there to escape the persecution and built twenty-seven temples (T 50.626c18–20).

[173] Gimello, "Chih-yen," p. 58, n. 3.

[174] TSC 223a14–17, 224b14–18, 226b6–8; LSC 107a8–10, 108a17–b3, 110a1–3.

[175] TSC 225c16–18; LSC 109b12–15.

cidate the fundamental meaning of representation-only and enable
people easily to perceive its principle that all dharmas are one's own
mind."[176]

The opportunity to avail himself of the monastic libraries in the
imperial capital apparently accomplished its purpose: after a year
and a half of careful study, Tsung-mi finally felt confident enough to
undertake the fulfillment of the vow he had made some years earlier
to compose his own commentary to the *Scripture of Perfect Enlightenment*.[177] Accordingly, he returned to Ts'ao-t'ang ssu on Mount
Chung-nan in the first month of 821. He says nothing of his activities
during this year other than "I cut off traces and got rid of involve-
ments in order to nourish my spirit and polish my understanding."[178]
Presumably he spent much of his time in meditation. In his *Ch'an
Preface*, he cryptically remarks of this period of his life that he "left
the multitudes behind and entered the mountains to develop my concentration (*ting*; samādhi) and harmonize my wisdom (*hui*;
prajñā)."[179]

Tsung-mi resumed his scholarly efforts in the following year. In
the spring of 822 he made use of his previously composed *K'o-wen*
and *Tsüan-yao*, together with the notes that he had compiled from his
sedulous study of Buddhist texts over the past several years, to begin
his commentary to the *Scripture of Perfect Enlightenment*, a task that he
finally finished at the end of the summer in 823.[180] These years were
productive, and Tsung-mi engaged in a number of other projects as
well. While staying at the Feng-te ssu in 822, he completed the *Hua-
yen lun-kuan*, a five-fascicle work that, as its name implies, tried to tie
together the various threads running through the *Hua-yen Sūtra*,
something he hoped would serve as a ready handbook for lecturers.
Tsung-mi feared that the vast scope of the *Hua-yen Sūtra* made it difficult for people of his time to grasp its essential meaning,[181] one of
the prime reasons he recommended the *Scripture of Perfect Enlightenment* as a more suitable text.[182] The same motivation to render complex material intelligible led Tsung-mi in the summer of 823, while
also at the Feng-te ssu, to compile a three-fascicle selection of key
passages from the vinaya texts and their commentaries to serve as a
guide for practitioners.[183]

---

[176] TSC 225b14–18; LSC 109c11–14.
[177] TSC 223a17–b1; LSC 107a10–12.
[178] TSC 223b1–2; cf. LSC 1–7a12–13.
[179] 399c12; K 30.
[180] TSC 223b2–5; LSC 107a13–16.
[181] TSC 225d1–6; LSC 109b15–c3.
[182] See TSC 226a1–b4; LSC 109c15–d18.
[183] TSC 225d9–11; LSC 109c6–9.

Tsung-mi's autobiographical comments stop in 823, the year in which he completed his *Commentary to the Scripture of Perfect Enlightenment*. Although he does not furnish the dates, it must not have been long afterward that he composed his subcommentary (*ta-shu ch'ao*), a work the *Fa-chieh wu-tsu lüeh-chi* places in 823. It is most likely that he then went on to compose his abridged commentary (*lüeh-shu*) and subcommentary (*lüeh-shu ch'ao*), after which he probably wrote his *Yüan-chüeh ching tao-t'ang hsiu-cheng i*, works that can be assigned to 823–824.

Tsung-mi says that his completion of his *Commentary to the Scripture of Perfect Enlightenment* was the culmination of a wish he had formed some fifteen or more years earlier, sometime, that is, before he left Sui-chou. It is clear that he saw the various scriptures, treatises, and commentarial works that he had studied in the meantime as all being preparatory to this task.[184] Indeed, the breadth of erudition displayed throughout his commentary bears witness to the thoroughness with which he had carried out his research. Some of the more influential of these texts, which Tsung-mi singles out for mention, were the *Awakening of Faith*, *Ch'eng wei-shih lun*, *Ratnagotravibāga* (*Pao-hsing lun*), *Fo-hsing lun*, *Mūlamadhyamaka-kārikā* (*Chung-kuan lun*), *Mahā-yāna-saṃgraha* (*She ta-sheng lun*), *Ta-chih-tu lun*, and *Yogācārabhūmi-śāstra* (*Yu-ch'ieh shih-ti lun*).[185] As this list suggests, the predominant doctrinal influence came from works of the Yogācāra and tathāgata-garbha variety, and, as will become clear in the course of this study, among these texts the one of paramount importance was undeniably the *Awakening of Faith*, the text that provided the structure in terms of which he interpreted the *Scripure of Perfect Enlightenment* and was the basis on which he developed his systematic exposition of Buddhist thought. It is also significant to note that nowhere in his autobiographical comments does Tsung-mi ever mention having read anything written by Fa-tsang, the figure customarily regarded as having systematized Hua-yen thought in its classical form. Indeed, the only work of Fa-tsang that Tsung-mi shows clear evidence of having read was his commentary to the *Awakening of Faith*, to which he composed his own abridged commentary.[186] Aside from the works of Ch'eng-kuan, which had such an impact on Tsung-mi, the only other Hua-yen work that he mentions having studied is the *Fa-chieh kuan-men* attributed to Tu-shun, a work he read in Sui-chou in what was clearly more of a Ch'an than a Hua-yen context. Tsung-mi later wrote his own commentary to this text.[187]

[184] See TSC 226b18–c1; LSC 110a13–14.

[185] TSC 226b10–11; LSC 110a5–6.

[186] Contained in *Dai Nippon kōtei daizōkyō*, case 31, vol. 8, division 5, part 2.

[187] Contained in T 45.683b–699c.

Tsung-mi remained on Mount Chung-nan until 828, when he was invited to court by an imperial edict. Wen-tsung (r. 827–840) had ascended the throne in the beginning of the previous year and had already attracted a number of luminaries to court. P'ei Hsiu's epitaph notes that Tsung-mi congratulated the emperor on his birthday. It goes on to say that, after questioning him on the essentials of the dharma, Wen-tsung bestowed the purple robe on him and granted him title of "Great Worthy" (ta-te; bhadanta).[188] It is possible that Tsung-mi received these honors as a result of having participated in the debate among the three religions traditionally held on the emperor's birthday. Since the time of Tai-tsung (r. 762–779), it was customary for the emperor to reward participants in the debates with the purple robe.[189] Po Chü-i, despite his strong Buddhist sympathies, had represented the Confucian side in the debate the previous year.[190] Since the emperor's birthday occurred in the tenth lunar month, Tsung-mi probably arrived in the capital sometime in late October or early November 828. He remained in the capital for two years, after which he requested to return to the mountains. He thus would have returned to Mount Chung-nan in 829 or early 830 and remained there until 832 or 833. Elsewhere he notes that, aside from his two years in the capital, he stayed on Mount Chung-nan for a total of ten years from the time he moved to Ts'ao-t'ang ssu in 821.[191] The year 833 finds him in Lo-yang.

Tsung-mi's two years in the capital must have been enormously significant ones in terms of both his own sense of personal accomplishment and the course of his subsequent career. Coming shortly after he had finished his various commentaries on the Scripture of Perfect Enlightenment, the culmination of a religious vow and two decades of effort, it must have marked a time of personal completion. Tsung-mi was no longer a promising young Buddhist scholar working in isolation but a nationally honored master who could speak for Buddhism to the court and literati. The recognition he received at court, and the contacts that he made there, must have instilled a new confidence in him. They must also have altered his sense of mission, for the character of his writings changes. From this time on, Tsung-mi turns from primarily exegetical works aimed at a learned Buddhist audience to works of broader appeal; he moves beyond the confines of

[188] Kamata, Shūmitsu, p. 51.8–9.

[189] See Weinstein, Buddhism under the T'ang, p. 117; see p. 192, n. 21, for the significance of the purple robe. See also the entries on the birthday debates and purple robe in Ta-Sung seng-shih lüeh, T 54.248a24–b17 and 248c3–249a29.

[190] See Waley, Po Chü-i, pp. 169–171, for an account of the debate.

[191] Ch'an Preface, 399c12–13; K 30.

Buddhist scholastic concerns to address more encompassing intellectual issues of his day. It is after this point, for instance, that he wrote
his two major works on Ch'an as well as his more popular essay, *Inquiry into the Origin of Man*.

LITERATI CONNECTIONS (828–835)

A number of Tsung-mi's subsequent works were written in response
to requests by various literati of the day. His presence in the court
and the prestige his imperially bestowed honors brought afforded
him the opportunity to meet a number of important scholar-officials
serving in Ch'ang-an at that time. Indeed, many of the prominent
figures with whom we know Tsung-mi was later associated were in
the imperial capital during his stay there in 828–829. A brief look at
who these figures were sheds light on the circles in which Tsung-mi
operated in the years 828–835.

By far the most important of these was P'ei Hsiu (787?–860).[192] P'ei
Hsiu hailed from an illustrious family of scholar-officials from Ho-
nei. His father, P'ei Hsiao, had held a number of important posts. P'ei
Hsiu and his two brothers received a solid classical education, and all
three were successful in the imperial examinations. He came from a
family of devout Buddhists, and his official biography recounts an
anecdote to dramatize his life-long refusal to eat meat. P'ei passed the
chin-shih exam in the Ch'ang-ch'ing era (821–824). From the beginning of the T'ai-ho era (827–836) he held a series of posts in Ch'ang-
an within the Secretariat, advancing from investigating censor, to rectifier of omissions of the right (see below), to senior compiler of the
Historiography Institute. His appointment as investigating censor
would have corresponded with Tsung-mi's two years in the capital.

P'ei Hsiu's relationship with Tsung-mi was intimate. He wrote prefaces to a number of Tsung-mi's works, such as his *Ch'an Preface*, his
commentary to the *Fa-chieh kuan-men*, his abridged commentary to
the *Scripture of Perfect Enlightenment*, and the *Tao-su ch'ou-ta wen-chi*, a
collection of short works, mostly written in response to questions submitted by Tsung-mi's lay and clerical followers, compiled by Tsung-
mi's disciples after his death.[193] P'ei Hsiu was probably responsible

---

[192] For his official biography see CTS 177.4592–4593 and HTS 182.5371–5372; see
also Yamazaki Hiroshi, "Tōdai kōki no koji Hai Kyū ni tsuite," pp. 1–16, and Henri
Maspero, "Sur Quelques Textes Anciens de Chinois Parlé," pp. 4–6.

[193] All four prefaces are contained in CTW 734, which lists the last as that to the
Inquiry into the Origin of Man. As Jan Yün-hua has recently shown, this last piece was
originally written as the preface to the *Tao-su ch'ou-ta wen-chi*, which includes the *Inquiry
into the Origin of Man*, as well as the *Ch'an Chart* and Tsung-mi's responses to Hsiao

for the honorary titles that were posthumously bestowed upon
Tsung-mi as part of the restoration of Buddhism during Hsüan-
tsung's reign (846–859). P'ei also wrote Tsung-mi's epitaph in 853.
As he comments on his relationship to the master at the end of that
piece: "We were brothers in the dharma and close friends in righteousness, I was indebted to him as my spiritual guide, and we were
protectors of the teaching from within and without. I can therefore
talk about him in detail in a way that others cannot."[194]

It was at P'ei Hsiu's request that Tsung-mi wrote his *Ch'an Chart*, a
work with which subsequent chapters will be much concerned. This
work seeks to clarify the historical filiations and essential teachings of
four of the major Ch'an traditions of the day. It thus contains detailed critiques of the Northern line, the Ox-head line, and, within
the Southern line, the Hung-chou and Ho-tse branches. Not only
does the *Ch'an Chart* contain Tsung-mi's most sustained treatment of
these four Ch'an traditions, it is also the only work in which he clearly
differentiates between the Ho-tse and Hung-chou lines, and, as I
shall argue, it is his effort to distinguish the teaching of his own Ho-
tse lineage from that of the Hung-chou that holds the key to his
thought.

Although this work has come to be known as *Chung-hua ch'uan-hsin-
ti ch'an-men shih-tzu ch'eng-hsi t'u* (Chart of the master-disciple succession of the Ch'an gate that has transmitted the mind-ground in
China), it is known from an earlier version of the text discovered at
Shinpuku-ji in Japan that its original title was *P'ei Hsiu shih-i wen*.[195]
Jan Yün-hua has accordingly suggested that the *Chiu T'ang shu*'s reference to P'ei Hsiu's post of rectifier of omissions (*pu-ch'üeh*) is a mistake for reminder (*shih-i*).[196] Given that the rank of investigating censor (8a) was lower than that of rectifier of omissions (7b1) but higher
than that of reminder (8b), it is more likely, in view of the succession
in which P'ei's posts are listed, that it is the title of the *P'ei Hsiu shih-i
wen* that is in error.[197] In any case, the two posts were almost identical

---

Mien, Shih Shan-jan, and Wen Tsao. See Jan, "*Fa-chi* and Chinul's Understanding of
Tsung-mi," pp. 162–163. Jan cites Ch'ing-yüan's preface to his commentary to Tsung-
mi's *Inquiry into the Origin of Man*, which, after citing P'ei Hsiu's preface, comments that
it has mistakenly been placed before the *Inquiry* but was originally written to the *Fa-chi*
(i.e., *Tao-su ch'ou-ta wen-chi*).

[194] Kamata, *Shūmitsu*, p. 51.16–17.

[195] See Ishii Shūdō, "Shinpuku-ji bunko shozō no *Hai Kyū shūi mon* no honkoku."
This text was originally included in the *Tao-su ch'ou-ta wen-chi*.

[196] See his "*Fa-chi* and Chinul's Understanding of Tsung-mi," pp. 163–164.

[197] See Charles O. Hucker, *A Dictionary of Official Titles in Imperial China*, no. 795 (pp.
145b–146a), no. 4777 (pp. 391b-392b), and no. 5256 (p. 452b).

in function and could have easily been confused.[198] Given the standard three-year tenure of office, P'ei Hsiu would have served as either rectifier of omissions or reminder from 830 to 833. This would date Tsung-mi's *Ch'an Chart* to the years he was at Ts'ao-t'ang ssu after his return from the capital but before his visit to Lo-yang in 833.

After Tsung-mi's death during the vehemently anti-Buddhist Hui-ch'ang era (841–846), P'ei Hsiu was transferred from the Secretariat in the capital to a series of provincial posts. It was during this time that he first met Huang-po Hsi-yün (d. 850) in Hung-chou (in north central Kiangsi south of Lake P'o-yang) in 842. Six years later, while serving as prefect of Hsüan-chou[199] (in the southeastern corner of Anhwei), he again met with Huang-po. P'ei Hsiu took detailed notes on both occasions and eventually wrote them up in October 857.[200] Known as *Huang-po-shan Tuan-chi ch'an-shih ch'üan-hsin fa-yao* and *Huang-po Tuan-chi ch'an-shih Wan-ling lu*, these two texts remain one of the most important sources for reconstructing the teachings of the type of Ch'an that Tsung-mi referred to as the Hung-chou line.[201] Despite Tsung-mi's severe criticism of the radical character of this type of Ch'an, its bold and iconoclastic rhetoric emerged as the official Ch'an ideology during the Sung.

Not long after the succession of Hsüan-tsung, P'ei Hsiu was recalled to Ch'ang-an, where he was appointed the vice-director of the Ministry of Revenue. P'ei distinguished himself in a series of increas-

---

[198] Both rectifier of omissions (*pu-ch'üeh*) and reminder (*shih-i*) were remonstrance officials (*chien-kuan*). Both ranks were staffed by twelve officials, with six (those designated to the left) under the Chancellery (*men-hsia sheng*) and six (those designated to the right) under the Secretariat (*chung-shu sheng*). Both ranks were created in 685. The position of reminder was of slightly lower rank than that of rectifier of omissions: the former being a mandarin of the eighth degree, second class (8b), and the latter being a mandarin of the seventh degree, second class, upper grade (7b1). The duties of both positions were similar. According to Hucker's *Dictionary of Official Titles*, the reminder was "responsible for catching and correcting errors of substance or style in state documents" (no. 5256, p. 425b), whereas the rectifier of omissions was "responsible for checking drafts of proclamations and other documents flowing from the throne so as to return for reconsideration any that they considered inappropriate in form or substance, or to propose corrections" (no. 4777, pp. 391b–392b). Po Chü-i held the position of reminder during 808–810. Feifel's *Po Chü-i as a Censor* is devoted to a detailed study of this phase of Po's career.

[199] According to an entry in Chih-p'an's *Fo-tsu t'ung-chi*, P'ei Hsiu held this post in 848; see T 49.387a10. This entry relates P'ei Hsiu's successful petition to the emperor that government officials desist from using Buddhist and Taoist monasteries as guest houses.

[200] See P'ei Hsiu's preface, T 48.379c.

[201] Both texts are contained in T no. 2012. For Iriya Yoshitaka's critically edited version, with an annotated translation into modern Japanese, see *Zen no goroku*, vol. 8. John Blofeld has translated both texts in his *The Zen Teaching of Huang Po*.

ingly important posts,[202] serving as a grand councilor for five years
under Hsüan-tsung. From 856 he held a number of critical appointments within the provincial administration. Throughout Hsüan-
tsung's reign, P'ei Hsiu played an active role in the revival of Buddhism after the disastrous persecutions carried out under Wu-tsung.
Shortly after the ascension of I-tsung, P'ei was recalled to the capital,
where he died in 860.

In addition to his distinguished record of service, P'ei Hsiu found
time to act the part of the devout Buddhist layman. In his later years
he maintained a strict Buddhist diet, constantly exercised restraint,
and practiced continence. He revered the Buddhist scriptures and
delighted in singing hymns.[203] The *Pei-meng so-yen*, a Sung-dynasty
collection of anecdotes about literati in the T'ang and Five Dynasties
period, says that he was in the habit of wearing a priest's robe made
of silk, instead of the usual official dress, and would take his bowl
begging to the houses of singers. The same source alleges that he
made a vow to be reborn as a king in successive lives so as to protect
the dharma.[204] The *Chiu T'ang shu* notes that he took advantage of
the opportunity afforded by his provincial appointments to visit famous monasteries and seek out learned monks and engage them in
serious discussions of Buddhist teaching.[205] Indeed, his various intro-
ductions to Tsung-mi's works bear ample testimony to his sophisticated command of Buddhist doctrine.

Aside from his close association with Tsung-mi, P'ei Hsiu also had
links to a number of other eminent Buddhist figures.[206] Several of
these were nationally honored, learned monks, such as Ch'eng-kuan,
Tuan-fu (770–836),[207] and Chih-hsüan (809–881),[208] all of whom he
would have associated with in the capital. His tours of service in the

---

[202] During the early 850s, for example, as transport commissioner of salt and iron,
he instituted a set of new procedures that overcame the severe breakdown in the transport of tax grain from the lower Yangtze region that had come about through widespread corruption and official negligence. Over a period of three years, P'ei Hsiu tri-
pled the amount of tax grain reaching the storage granaries in the North. See Dalby,
"Court Politics in Late T'ang Times," p. 674.

[203] CTS 177.4594.

[204] *Pei-meng so-yen* 6.45.

[205] CTS 177.4594.

[206] See Yamazaki, "Tōdai kōki no koji Hai Kyū ni tsuite," pp. 7–13, for further discussion of the various figures mentioned below. Yamazaki also discusses P'ei Hsiu's
connection with Shen-chih (819–886), a monk noted for his medical knowledge and
healing powers (see SKSC 869c15–870a3 for his standard biography).

[207] P'ei Hsiu wrote Tuan-fu's epitaph, which can be found in CTW 743; for his standard biography, see SKSC 741a26–c21; see also Weinstein, *Buddhism under the T'ang*,
pp. 99, 101.

[208] SKSC 743b5–744c15; see also Weinstein, *Buddhism under the T'ang*, pp. 140–141.

provincial administration brought him into contact with various Ch'an teachers. In addition to Huang-po, P'ei also had connections with two other Hung-chou figures, Wei-shan Ling-yu (771–853),[209] a disciple of Pai-chang Huai-hai (720–841), and Ch'u-nan (813–888),[210] a disciple of Huang-po. In his last years he came to know Yüan-shao (811–895),[211] a Ch'an monk belonging to the same Ho-tse lineage as Tsung-mi.

The most famous literary figure with whom Tsung-mi was associated was undoubtedly the celebrated poet Po Chü-i (772–846), well known to Western readers through Arthur Waley's engaging biography.[212] Tsung-mi probably came to know Po Chü-i between 828 and 829, when both were in Ch'ang-an at the same time. Po's keen interest in Buddhism, his position at court, and Tsung-mi's evident honor all make it likely that the two would have met then. Po had come to the capital in 827 to become president of the palace library. In the following year he was appointed vice-minister of the Ministry of Justice, where he remained until 829. Worried over becoming implicated in the dangerous and unpredictable swirl of factional politics, Po used the excuse of ill health to gain release from his post and returned to Lo-yang in 829. Tsung-mi visited Po in Lo-yang in 833, where he was living in semiretirement away from the political imbroglios of the capital, spending much of his time cultivating his relationship with various monks in the area. One of these was Shen-chao, with whom Po seems to have been on close terms. He composed at least two poems for him[213] and wrote his epitaph in 839.[214] Shen-chao, it will be recalled, was the disciple of Tao-yüan's teacher, Wei-chung, whom the youthful Tsung-mi had impressed before leaving Ch'eng-tu in 808. Shen-chao's connection to both men must have been one more factor bringing Tsung-mi and Po together. Tsung-mi

[209] SKSC 777b17–c11.

[210] SKSC 817c7–818a3.

[211] SKSC 784b21–785a2. According to the lineal filiations listed in the beginning of fascicle 13 of the CTL (301c), Yüan-shao was a disciple of Chih-yüan, who in turn was a disciple of Shen-chao.

[212] See Po Chü-i. Po's standard biography can be found in CTS 166.4340–4358 and HTS 119.4300–4305. The former has been translated by Eugene Feifel, "Biography of Po Chü-i." See also Feifel, Po Chü-i as a Censor, which covers Po's service in the court from 808 to 810. The role of Buddhism in Po's literary career is discussed by Ch'en in The Chinese Transformation of Buddhism, pp. 184–239; see also Hirano Kenshō, "Haku Kyoi no bungaku to bukkyō"; Shinohara Hisao, "Tōdai zenshisō to Haku Kyoi"; Burton Watson, "Buddhism in the Poetry of Po Chü-i"; and Hachiya Kunio, "Haku Kyoi no shi to bukkyō."

[213] Po-shih Ch'ang-ch'ing-chi 57.23a and 62.9b–10a, the second of which is translated by Ch'en, The Chinese Transformation of Buddhism, p. 219.

[214] Po-shih Ch'ang-ch'ing-chi 70.13b–14a and CTW 678.

participated in a gathering with Po Chü-i, Shen-chao, and two of
Shen-chao's disciples in 833, and Po wrote a poem commemorating
the occasion.

> A white haired old man, wearing purple robes,
> I do not mix with the world but consort with the Tao.
> Three times I have been assigned to Lo-yang on special duty as an official,
> Half of my friends are among the monks.
> One must eventually withdraw from this wealth-conscious world,
> Long have I yearned for my karmic friends of the incense.
> After the vegetarian feasts what can I offer you in return?
> Only the springs, rocks, and the north wind in the western pavillion.[215]

Po also wrote a poem for Tsung-mi in 833 ("Tseng Ts'ao-t'ang
Tsung-mi shang-jen"):

> The way of my master and the Buddha correspond perfectly:
> Successive thoughts being unconditioned, each thing is able [to reveal the
>   dharma].
> The mouth treasury spreads the twelve divisions [of the canon] abroad;
> The mind tower lights thousands of lamps.
> Utterly abandoning the written word is not the middle way;
> Forever abiding in empty vacuity is [the practice of] the lesser vehicle.
> Rare indeed is one who understands the practice of the bodhisattva;
> In the world he alone is to be esteemed as an eminent monk.[216]

Po Chü-i's poem, composed around the time Tsung-mi wrote his
Ch'an Preface, echoes one of the central themes in that work: counter-
ing Ch'an's iconoclastic repudiation of the written word (*wen-tzu*).
Ch'an, of course, was famous for its claim to embody a special mind-
to-mind transmission whose authority did not depend on the textual
tradition. In his *Ch'an Preface*, Tsung-mi contends that, since both the
scriptural corpus and the Ch'an tradition equally derive from the
Buddha's enlightenment, each complements the other, and neither
can be disregarded. Indeed, he argues that the canonical writings are
necessary to validate Ch'an insight.[217] Po Chü-i's reference to the
"mouth treasury" alludes to the canonical tradition, which is customarily classified into twelve divisions. The "mind tower" refers to the
Ch'an transmission, which is frequently compared to a lamp whose
light is passed on from generation to generation. Their parallelism in
the poem clearly indicates that Po, like Tsung-mi, regards both as

---

[215] *Po-shih Ch'ang-ch'ing-chi* 64.7b–8a, as translated by Ch'en, *The Chinese Transformation of Buddhism*, p. 219. See B 59 for another rendition.

[216] *Po-shih Ch'ang-ch'ing-chi* 64.7b.

[217] See chapter 7.

complementary aspects of a singular tradition. Po's choice of terms recalls Tsung-mi's statement in the *Ch'an Preface* that "the scriptures are the Buddha's words, and Ch'an is the Buddha's intent. The minds and mouths of the Buddhas certainly cannot contradict one another."[218] Tsung-mi's emphasis on the indispensability of the canonical teachings for Ch'an must have had great appeal to a poet such as Po. In an earlier poem Po had aired his anxiety that his attachment to literature was an impediment to his progress in Buddhism.[219] Po's present poem concludes by suggesting that the reason Tsung-mi is one of the few to understand the practice of the bodhisattva is precisely that his middle way does not reject literature.

Po's poem also suggests how Tsung-mi's Ch'an writings found a ready audience among the scholar-officials of his day, figures who would have appreciated his classical education and his defense of the written word. It is significant that the *Ch'an Chart*, the one work in which Tsung-mi delivers a sustained critique of Hung-chou Ch'an, was written at the request of P'ei Hsiu—a fact that suggests that his criticism of the radical currents within the Ch'an of his day was directed not so much toward his fellow Ch'an Buddhists as toward the literati audience he addressed in many of his post-828 works.

It was most likely through his connection with Po Chü-i that Tsung-mi came to know another famous statesman and literatus of his day, Liu Yü-hsi (772–842).[220] Liu had passed his *chin-shih* in 793. He became Po Chü-i's poetic confidant during Po's later years in Lo-yang, and many of the poems Po wrote in the last fourteen years of his life are addressed to him.[221] Liu also had a close relationship with two of the other great literary figures of the time: Liu Tsung-yüan (773–819) and Han Yü. Liu Yü-hsi's career well illustrates the unpredictability of the shifting currents of factional politics in the early ninth century. While serving in the Censorate with Liu Tsung-yüan, he became associated with the reform faction centered around Wang Shu-wen (735–806) and Wang P'i (d.u.), which came to power during the brief reign of Shun-tsung (February 28–August 31, 805).[222] In

[218] 400b10–11; K 44; cf. B 111.

[219] See his 817 poem in *Po-shih Ch'ang-ch'ing-chi* 16.27b, translated by Ch'en, *The Chinese Transformation of Buddhism*, p. 202.

[220] For his standard biography see CTS 160.4210–4213 and HTS 168.5128–5132; for an autobiographical sketch see CTW 610. See also Wolfgang Kubin, "Liu Yü-hsi." For a discussion of Liu's involvement with Buddhism, see Ch'en Tsu-lung's "Liu Yü-hsi yü fo-chiao."

[221] Howard Levy, *Translations from Po Chü-i's Collected Works*, 4:xxxiv. Liu seems to have taken over the role of Po's great friend, Yüan Chen, who died in 831.

[222] See *The Veritable Record of the T'ang Emperor Shun-tsung*, translated by Bernard Solomon.

light of Tsung-mi's subsequent implication in the Sweet Dew Incident
of 835, it is worth noting that an important part of the Wangs' reform
program was aimed at curtailing the inordinate power that the eunuchs had come to wield over court politics. When Shun-tsung abdi-
cated in favor of his son, who became the emperor Hsien-tsung, the
faction immediately fell from power, and Liu Yü-hsi was banished to
a minor provincial post. Although he was pardoned in 815, he did
not regain a post in the imperial capital until 828, when he was appointed director of the Bureau of Receptions, one of the four top-
echelon units of the Ministry of Rites. He was banished shortly thereafter, however, for the political criticism voiced in a poem describing
his visit to a Taoist temple.[223] In 831 he was appointed governor of
Su-chou, and in 834 he was appointed governer of Ju-chou, some
fifty miles southeast of Lo-yang.

Liu Yü-hsi would have had occasion to meet Tsung-mi in 828,
when both were in the capital at the same time, or later in 833, when
Tsung-mi visited Lo-yang. Unfortunately, nothing is known of his relationship with Tsung-mi aside from what can be gleaned from the
following poem that Liu wrote for him on the occasion of his return
to Ts'ao-t'ang ssu, during which time Liu also paid a visit to Po Chü-
i. The title ("Tseng Tsung-mi shang-jen kuei Chung-nan Ts'ao-t'ang
ssu yin i Ho-nan yin Po shih-lang") refers to Po as vice-minister, governor of Ho-nan. Since Po Chü-i was governor of Ho-nan from the
very end of 830 to the fourth month (April–May) of 833, Liu's poem
dates Tsung-mi's return to Mount Chung-nan to the early part of
833. The poem presents Liu traveling eastward along the Yangtze
back to Su-chou while Tsung-mi journeys westward back to the lofty
heights of his mountain retreat.

> The root of wisdom has been gained from practice in previous lives;
> Well-versed in ultimate truth, words are utterly transcended.
> From the time when the seventh patriarch transmitted the mind seal,
> The expedient teaching of the three vehicles has no longer been
>   necessary.
> Eastward, I drift along the river searching for ancient traces;
> Westward, you return to purple tower peak escaping the worldly clamor.
> The munificent Governor Po of Ho-nan
> Was fond of leafing through the true scriptures with you.[224]

---

[223] Kubin notes that this poem, entitled "For Presentation to Flower-Viewing Gentle-
man," "describes the peach trees which were planted by a Taoist priest in the Hsüan-
tu Temple after Liu's first banishment (805), which are now being enjoyed by those in
power" (see his entry on Liu Yü-hsi in *The Indiana Companion to Traditional Chinese
Literature*, p. 593a).

[224] *Liu Meng-te wen-chi* 7.55a.

Tsung-mi was also acquainted with two other figures associated with Po Chü-i: Wen Tsao and Hsiao Mien. Wen Tsao (767–836) came from an illustrious family with close ties to the imperial line.[225] He was the fifth-generation descendant of Wen Ta-ya, the famous seventh-century minister who was closely associated with Li Shih-min during his rise to power and whose diary gives an eyewitness account of the early stages of the founding of the T'ang.[226] He was also related to the imperial line by blood, being descended from a fifth-generation female descendant of Li Shih-min. Both his grandfather and father had served as officials. Although he received a classical education as a youth, Wen Tsao spurned the examinations and, instead of seeking employment in the regular bureaucracy, served on the provincial staff of Chang Chien-feng (735–800) while the latter was prefect of Shou-chou in the 780s.[227] He was later employed by Wu Ch'ung-yin, military governor of the Ho-yang army.[228] Wen's demonstrated loyalty to the T'ang cause against the centrifugal pull of the military governors won him the confidence of both Hsien-tsung and Wen-tsung. At the end of his life he was appointed minister in charge of the Ministry of Rites.

Although Wen Tsao must have been one of Tsung-mi's lay disciples, nothing is known about their relationship other than the fact that Tsung-mi wrote an essay in response to a question that Wen Tsao had submitted to him. Given that the enlightened person is freed from karma, Wen inquired about what the numinous nature (*ling-hsing*) of such a person depends on after he dies. Tsung-mi's answer draws on the *Awakening of Faith* to explain how, even though all beings are intrinsically endowed with the enlightened nature of the Buddha, because they are not aware of it, they form attachments and transmigrate according to their karma. Yet their enlightened nature neither is born nor dies. Even after one suddenly realizes that his nature is the unborn dharmakāya, which does not depend on anything, he must still continue to practice in order to get rid of the effects of his deluded attachments. Wen Tsao's question and Tsung-mi's response were included in the *Tao-su ch'ou-ta wen-chi* compiled by Tsung-mi's disciples after his death.[229] ·

[225] His official biography can be found in CTS 165.4314–4318 and HTS 91.3784–3786.

[226] See Howard Wechsler, *Mirror to the Son of Heaven*, pp. 16–17, 19–20.

[227] For Chang Chien-feng's biography see CTS 140.3828–3832 and HTS 158.4939–4941. Chang had literary pretensions of his own and patronized a number of leading literary figures, including Han Yü, Meng Chiao, Li Ao, and Li Ho.

[228] Margaret Tudor South, *Li Ho*, p. 188.

[229] Their exchange can also be found at the end of Tsung-mi's biography in CTL 307c29–308b16; cf. *P'ei Hsiu shih-i wen*, pp. 101–104.

Hsiao Mien (d. 837) was the most highly placed of all Tsung-mi's
lay disciples.[230] He came from a distinguished aristocratic family
boasting descent from the Liang imperial line. Both his great grandfather, Hsiao Sung, and grandfather, Hsiao Hua, served as grand
councilors and were honored with the title of Duke of Hsü. His father, Hsiao Heng, served in the Ministry of Personnel within the Department of State Affairs. Hsiao Mien passed his *chin-shih* in 791. His
bureaucratic career began with two lower-level appointments within
the Censorate in the beginning of the Yüan-ho period (806–821). In
811 he was made a Han-lin scholar, in 812 he was promoted to vice-
director of Bureau of Honors, and in 814 he was appointed director
of the Bureau of Equipment, a top-echelon unit in the Ministry of
War, and also collaborated in the drafting of policy proposals. His
career subsequently suffered a temporary eclipse, but his influential
connection with Huang-fu Po, who was appointed grand councilor in
818, won him an appointment as vice-censor in chief in that year.
Hsiao Mien's political fortunes continued to rise, and he received various honors, including the title of Duke of Hsü. With the ascension
of Mu-tsung in 820, he was made vice-director of the Secretariat; several months later he was appointed vice-director of the Chancellery.
Both positions carried with them the status of grand councillor.
Shortly thereafter Hsiao Mien thrice tried to resign in protest over
the emperor's failure to respond to a case of blatant corruption. Instead he was promoted to vice-director of the Department of State
Affairs and, in the beginning of the following year (821), was elevated to the nobility. Hsiao continued to petition Mu-tsung to allow
him to resign, but the emperor only had him assigned to other posts,
finally appointing him junior guardian of the heir apparent in 822.
He was subsequently made prefect of T'ung-chou and in 826 was
transferred to the branch office of the junior guardian in Lo-yang.
With the ascension of Wen-tsung in 827, Hsiao Men was appointed
junior preceptor of the heir apparent with the authority also to act as
vice-minister of the Department of State Affairs. Wen-tsung gave in
to his continued entreaties, letting Hsiao retire with the rank of vice-
minister of the Department of State Affairs.

Hsiao Mien submitted a request to Tsung-mi asking him to comment on a question about a statement by Ho-tse Shen-hui having to
do with the functioning of the eye of wisdom. Hsiao Mien's query and
Tsung-mi's comments were included in the *Tao-su ch'ou-ta wen-chi*.[231]

[230] His official biography can be found in CTS 172.4476–4479 and HTS 101.3957–
3959.

[231] Their exchange is also appended to Tsung-mi's biography in CTL 307a22–b2; cf.
P'ei Hsiu shih-i wen, pp. 98–99.

In addition to his connection with Wen Tsao and Hsiao Mien, Tsung-mi's biography in the *Ching-te ch'üan-teng lu* also mentions a certain Shih Shan-jen, about whom nothing is known. Tsung-mi's response to ten questions submitted by Shih Shan-jen is appended to his biography in that work;[232] their interchange was also included in the *Tao-su ch'ou-ta wen-chi* as well as Tsung-mi's biography in the *Cho-dang chip*. The questions center around various problems related to cultivation, and Tsung-mi's responses repeat many ideas familiar in his other works.

Many of the themes Tsung-mi broaches in his answers to Wen Tsao, Hsiao Mien, and Shih Shan-jen are given systematic expression in his *Inquiry into the Origin of Man*. Although this work is undated, it must have been composed sometime between 828 and 835. That it was included in the *Tao-su ch'ou-ta wen-chi* suggests that it was written for a literati audience. Its elegant style and adroit use of classical allusions would not have been lost on figures like P'ei Hsiu, Po Chü-i, Wen Tsao, or Hsiao Mien.

As has been frequently noted,[233] the title of this work (*Yüan jen lun*) probably derives from an essay by Han Yü. Han Yü had earlier written a series of five essays whose titles all began with *yüan* ("inquiry into the origin of"); one of these was the *Yüan jen*; another was the *Yüan hsing*, which discussed human nature.[234] The topic of human nature was also the subject of Li Ao's famous *Fu-hsing shu* (Returning to one's true nature).[235] The fact that Tsung-mi's essay took its title from Han Yü also suggests that it was written in part as a response to Han Yü's attacks on Buddhism. Han Yü's criticisms of Buddhism can be found in many places, but the best known are contained in his *Yüan tao*,[236] written around 805, and *Memorial on the Buddha's Bone*,[237]

---

[232] See 307b3–c29; cf. *P'ei Hsiu shih-i wen*, pp. 99–101.

[233] See, for example, Kamata Shigeo's introduction to his translation of the *Yüan jen lun*, *Gennin-ron*, p. 19, or Yanagida Seizan's comments in his study and translation of the *Lin-chi lu*, *Rinzai-roku*, p. 291.

[234] Both works can be found in *Han Ch'ang-li ch'üan-chi* 11.5–7b and CTW 558.558.14a–15a and 17a–b. The *Yüan hsing* has been translated by Wing-tsit Chan in his *A Source Book of Chinese Philosophy*, pp. 451–453. The other three are *Yüan kuei* (. . . Ghosts), *Yüan hui* (. . . Slander), and *Yüan Tao* (. . . the Way). *Yüan hui* has been translated by J. K. Rideout in Cyril Birch, ed., *Anthology of Chinese Literature*, pp. 255–257.

[235] For the definitive study and translation of this text see Timothy Barrett, "Buddhism, Taoism and Confucianism in the Thought of Li Ao."

[236] This work can be found in *Han Ch'ang-li ch'üan-chi* 11.1a–4b and CTW 558.10a–13b; it has been frequently translated; see Chan, *A Source Book of Chinese Philosophy*, pp. 454–456. For a discussion of this work see Hartman, *Han Yü*, pp. 145–162.

[237] This piece can be found in *Han Ch'ang-li ch'üan-chi* 39 and CTW 558.6a–8b. It too has been frequently translated; see that by James R. Hightower in Edwin O. Reis-

presented in 819. Even though Han Yü's strident brand of Confucianism was an anomaly within T'ang intellectual life, there is evidence that his anti-Buddhist sentiments increasingly found favor at
court in the late 820s and early 830s. In 830, for example, officials
within the Ministry of Sacrifices presented a memorial criticizing the
church and calling for reimposition of strict government control.[238]
In 833 the customary practice of inviting eminent Buddhists and
Taoists to court for a banquet on the occasion of the emperor's birthday was abolished.[239]

As a response to renewed attacks against Buddhism, Tsung-mi's
Inquiry into the Origin of Man can be seen as the product of a long
history of Buddhist polemical literature extending back to the introduction of Buddhism in China. Yet, unlike earlier polemics, Tsung-
mi's essay is no mere apology for the faith seeking to refute the traditional array of Chinese objections to Buddhism. Rather, viewed
from the perspective of the subsequent development of Neo-Confucianism in the Sung, Tsung-mi's essay gains importance because it
goes beyond the polemical intent of earlier works and, in so doing,
shifts the field of controversy to a new and more philosophical level
of debate, putting Buddhism, for the first time, in the position of
determining the intellectual context in terms of which Confucianism
was called upon to respond.

Tsung-mi's essay discusses, evaluates, and ranks five of the major
forms of Buddhist teaching, as well as the teachings of Confucianism
and Taoism, in terms of how they answer the question of the ultimate
origin of man. Having progressively and systematically analyzed
these teachings in order to arrive at the ultimate answer, Tsung-mi
then reincorporates their various explanations into an overarching
theory of how the human condition, characterized by suffering and
delusion, comes into being. In so doing, Tsung-mi not only shows
how Confucian and Taoist teachings are inferior to those of Buddhism but also locates Confucianism and Taoism within a Buddhist
discourse. Tsung-mi's discussion of Buddhist teachings in the *Inquiry*
was simple and straightforward and could be understood without a
detailed knowledge of the intricacies of Buddhist doctrine. Indeed, it
could be read as a primer of Buddhist thought written for nonspe-
cialists. Furthermore, the style and content, as well as the overall

---

chauer's *Ennin's Travels in T'ang China*, pp. 221–224. See also Homer H. Dubs, "Han
Yü and the Buddha Relic."

[238] See *Ch'ing shen-chin seng-ni tsou*, in CTW 966; summary by Weinstein, *Buddhism
under the T'ang*, pp. 108–109.

[239] See *Ta-Sung seng-shih lüeh*, T 54.248b, and Weinstein, *Buddhism under the T'ang*, p.
110.

thrust, of the essay suggest that Tsung-mi intended it as a popular tract addressed to a broad intellectual audience. The vocabulary and allusions with which Tsung-mi defines the central focus of the essay in his preface, for example, would have struck a resonant chord with the scholar-officials of his day steeped in the Confucian and Taoist classics.

THE SWEET DEW INCIDENT (835)

While Tsung-mi's connection with various powerful literati was a palpable measure of his success, it also contributed to the political eclipse he suffered during the last years of his life. In 835, through his acquaintance with Li Hsün (d. 835), Tsung-mi became implicated in an abortive attempt to oust the eunuchs from power known as the "Sweet Dew Incident" (kan-lu chih pien).[240]

Li Hsün came from a distinguished family. He was related to Li Feng-chi (758–835), chief minister and leader of the faction in power during Ching-tsung's brief but inept reign (824–827). After receiving his chin-shih in 823, Li Hsün became an active member of Li Feng-chi's faction within the bureaucracy. When this faction fell from power with the ascension of Wen-tsung, Li Hsün was banished to Hsiang-chou. The subsequent death of his mother brought him to Lo-yang, where in 833 he began to plot against the eunuchs. It is possible that it was at this time that Tsung-mi first met him.[241] Li Hsün's reputation as a classical scholar helped secure his appointment as a Han-lin academician in 834. This post gave him ready access to the emperor, who encouraged his conspiracy against the eunuchs. In 835 Wen-tsung had Li Hsün promoted to vice-director of the Ministry of Rites and jointly manager of affairs with the Secretariat-Chancellery, which carried with it status as a grand councilor.

The Sweet Dew Incident must be seen against the backdrop of the rise of eunuchs during the late T'ang. The unprecedented heights that eunuch power reached in the 820s and 830s was part of the po-

---

[240] The incident is recounted in Li Hsün's official biography in CTS 169.4395–4398 and HTS 179.5309–5314. Tsung-mi's involvement in this incident is discussed in his SKSC biography, 742a22–b5, which is clearly modeled on the CTS account. The relevant portion of Li Hsün's CTS biography is translated by Broughton, B 61–62. For other accounts of the Sweet Dew Incident see Dalby, "Court Politics in Late T'ang Times," pp. 654–659; Weinstein, Buddhism under the T'ang, p. 113; and Waley, Po Chü-i, pp. 187–188.

[241] As Waley has suggested in his Po Chü-i, p. 188. Waley points out that Po Chü-i was friends with Shu Yüan-yü, one of Li Hsün's coconspirators in Lo-yang (pp. 180–181).

litical legacy of the An Lu-shan rebellion.[242] Eunuchs proved to be an effective tool in the hands of autocratic emperors set on regaining as much personal power as possible. Both Te-tsung (r. 779–805) and Hsien-tsung (r. 805–820) relied heavily on eunuchs as a direct arm of imperial authority in their efforts to reestablish the central power of the throne. Under both of these emperors, eunuchs came to play an increasingly important role as army supervisors (chien-chün shih), in which capacity they exercised influence over political and military policy within the provinces and, even more important, were in a position to effect the appointment of new governors.[243] From 783 on, eunuchs came to control the palace armies (shen-ts'e chün), which gave them an independent base of power that was the foundation of the dominance they came to exert over the imperial government during the third and fourth decades of the ninth century. In the last decade of Te-tsung's reign, eunuchs not only assumed charge of the imperial treasury (nei-k'u) but also "assumed key positions within the palace handling the transmission of official documents."[244]

Eunuch control of access to the emperor, the transmission of official documents, palace finances, and the palace armies became further institutionalized under the reign of Hsien-tsung. Nevertheless, under the autocratic leadership of Te-tsung and Hsien-tsung, the eunuchs' power was exercised as an instrument of the emperor's will—a situation that was no longer the case with subsequent rulers. With the death of Hsien-tsung, who may have been murdered by eunuchs,[245] eunuchs came to extend their influence over the emperor, as seen most clearly in their control over the process of imperial succession. The ascensions of Hsien-tsung (805), Mu-tsung (820), Ching-tsung (824), and Wen-tsung (827) were all determined by rival eunuch factions. Eunuchs, in fact, conspired to have Ching-tsung murdered.

Perhaps the very circumstances of his ascension made Wen-tsung especially aware of the precariousness of his position. In any case, by 830 Wen-tsung had become sufficiently frustrated over his inability to control some of the more powerful eunuchs that he began to con-

[242] See Peterson, "Court and Province in Mid- and Late T'ang," passim, and Dalby, "Court Politics in Late T'ang Times," passim. For a discussion of eunuchs during the first part of the T'ang, see J. K. Rideout's two-part article, "The Rise of the Eunuchs during the T'ang Dynasty."

[243] See Peterson, "Court and Province in Mid- and Late T'ang," pp. 512–513, 535, and Dalby, "Court Politics in Late T'ang Times," p. 599.

[244] Dalby, "Court Politics in Late T'ang Times," p. 600.

[245] See ibid., pp. 634–635, for a discussion of the inconclusive evidence concerning whether or not Hsien-tsung was murdered by eunuchs.

spire to put an end to their dominance over the court. After the emperor failed in his first attempt to strike at the eunuchs' power,[246] he began to intrigue with Li Hsün. The final plan devised by the conspirators called for massacring the eunuchs in an ambush set for December 15, 835. Accordingly, at the dawn audience on the designated day the chamberlain reported that sweet dew had descended on a pomegranate tree in one of the palace courtyards during the night. The emperor sent the chief eunuchs to investigate this auspicious event. Unfortunately for the conspirators, a sudden gust of wind blew aside a flap in the tent where Li Hsün's men lay in wait, and the clanking of their weapons alerted the eunuchs to the plot. Most of the eunuchs were able to escape unharmed back into the palace, where they held the emperor captive in the harem, preventing his contact with the other conspirators. The eunuchs called in the palace army, which quickly set about systematically slaughtering all those suspected of involvement in the affair.

Li Hsün managed to escape and fled to Mount Chung-nan, where he sought refuge with Tsung-mi, entreating him to shave his head and conceal him. Tsung-mi's followers intervened, however, and Li Hsün was forced to flee Ts'ao-t'ang ssu. He was soon apprehended and executed. Because Tsung-mi had given Li temporary sanctuary, the powerful eunuch Ch'iu Shih-liang (781–843) had him arrested and tried for treason. Under interrogation Tsung-mi admitted that he was aware of the plot but went on to defend his actions by claiming that the teaching of the Buddha enjoined him to save all who suffer no matter what their circumstances. He added that he did not care for his own life and would die with a clean heart. Tsung-mi's courage in the face of almost-certain execution apparently so impressed the eunuch generals that he was pardoned.[247]

Tsung-mi confessed that he had known Li for several years; yet nothing is known about the nature of their relationship. Given his literati connections, one can certainly suppose Tsung-mi to have been sympathetic to the conspirators' goals, although perhaps not with their violent means. Yet there were other aspects of Wen-tsung's and Li Hsün's anti-eunuch agenda that Tsung-mi might not have approved. These involved attempting to curtail the power and wealth of the Buddhist church. Since the supervision of the sangha had been placed under eunuch control by Hsien-tsung in 807, eunuchs had

---

[246] See ibid., p. 655.

[247] Tsung-mi's SKSC biography (742b3–4) quotes the dialogue recorded in Li Hsün's CTS biography (169.4398), which is clearly the basis for its entire account of this episode. The HTS (179.5313–5314) gives an abbreviated account of Tsung-mi's involvement.

been able to use this position as another vehicle for accumulating wealth and augmenting their influence. One way to undermine eunuch power was therefore to weaken the Buddhist church. Thus, in the fourth and seventh months of 835, Li Hsün submitted proposals for purging the sangha, as a result of which Wen-tsung issued an edict announcing a large-scale purge of the church in language that recalled the chauvinistic critique sounded in Han Yü's famous anti-Buddhist memorial some sixteen years earlier.[248]

Li Hsün's anti-Buddhist sentiment seems to have been more than a mere stratagem to subvert eunuch power, a consideration that should give one pause in assessing the degree of his intimacy with Tsung-mi. Still, the nature of Tsung-mi's personal relation to Li Hsün is something about which one can only guess. Nevertheless, the fact that Tsung-mi was privy to the conspiracy indicates the extent to which he had the confidence of highly placed and powerful figures within bureaucracy.

Tsung-mi's association with the great and powerful was the source of criticism. Tsan-ning notes that "there are some who censure Tsung-mi, saying that he should not have received nobles and officials and paid frequent visits to the emperor." He goes on to defend Tsung-mi:

> The [care of the] dharma is entrusted to kings and ministers. If we made no connection with kings and ministers, how could the religion be made to prosper? Or are the Buddha's words about the influence of kings and ministers not true? The sentiment of men today is critical of anyone who is closely associated with kings and ministers. [This is because] they do not fully understand the purpose of those who are close to kings and ministers. If it were for profit and fame, then we should be grateful for their criticism. However, if the association is solely for the sake of the religion, how could that not be noble? Should one rather try to avoid petty criticism? Those who denounce him are merely jealous.[249]

LATER YEARS AND DEATH (835–841)

Tsung-mi passed the last years of his life under the shadow of disgrace cast by his involvement in the Sweet Dew Incident. Nothing is known of his activity after 835. The failure of the coup seems to have broken the emperor's spirit. Wen-tsung became increasingly discon-

---

[248] See Weinstein, *Buddhism under the T'ang*, pp. 110–111. The edict can be found in CTW 74.

[249] SKSC 743a10–17; I have adapted portions of Jan's translation, "Tsung-mi," p. 19.

solate and withdrawn in the remaining few years of his reign, and Ch'iu Shih-liang, the eunuch who had Tsung-mi arrested and brought to trial, emerged as the most powerful figure at court. Despite his disenchantment with court politics, the emperor did, however, take a number of restrictive actions against Buddhism. In 836, for instance, Wen-tsung repeated his earlier ban on monks traveling about to lecture on Buddhism.[250] The atmosphere at court after the Sweet Dew Incident was not one in which Tsung-mi would have been welcome. Tsung-mi suffered other disappointments as well. On April 23, 839, Ch'eng-kuan died. Wen-tsung died at the beginning of the following year and was succeeded by the emperor Wu-tsung (r. 840–846), under whose brief rule one of the most severe persecutions of Buddhism in all of Chinese history was carried out. Wu-tsung quickly made his anti-Buddhist sentiments known by publicly affirming his favoritism of Taoism.[251]

Although it is impossible to date with certainty, it seems likely that Tsung-mi wrote his commentary to the *Yü-lan-p'en ching* sometime between 835 and 840.[252] As he notes in the beginning of his introduction to that work, after having both participated in various celebrations of the *yü-lan-p'en* festival and lectured on the scripture for a number of years, he returned to his native home, where he conducted a *yü-lan-p'en* festival on the fifteenth day of the seventh month. Some of the senior laity and clergy thereupon requested that he write a commentary to the text, and, not daring to offend them, he agreed to comply.[253] Tsung-mi's commentary was thus written in Szechwan[254] after he had established his reputation as an authority on Buddhism. It is known that he spent the years 812–832 either in Ch'ang-an or Mount Chung-nan. He visited Lo-yang in 833, but Liu Yü-hsi's poem has him returning to Mount Chung-nan in the spring of that year. It is thus possible that he could have returned to Szechwan in 834. But it is far more probable that he returned to his native region after the Sweet Dew Incident, when he would have had good reason to want to leave the area in and around the capital.

Tsung-mi died in the meditation posture on February 1, 841, at the

[250] *Fo-tsu t'ung-chi*, T 49.385b; Weinstein, *Buddhism under the T'ang*, p. 144.

[251] See Weinstein, *Buddhism under the T'ang*, pp. 115–116.

[252] In his subcommentary to Tsung-mi's commentary, Yüan-chao claims that Tsung-mi returned to Szechwan sometime after he had returned to Mount Chung-nan after he had been summoned to court in 828 (HTC 35.102a–b).

[253] T 39.505a13–16; see also Jan's "A Study of *Ta-ch'eng ch'an-men yao-lu*," p. 543.

[254] Tsung-mi refers to himself in this work as a śramaṇa of Ch'ung-kuo, which Yüan-chao points out is an ancient name for Kuo-chou (HTC 35.100c); see also Jan, "A Study of *Ta-ch'eng ch'an-men yao-lu*," p. 543.

Hsing-fu yüan in Ch'ang-an. His final injunction enjoined his followers to expose his body to be eaten by birds and beasts, after which his
bones were to be burned and their ashes scattered; they were not to
be enshrined in a stūpa. Nor were his disciples to disturb their meditation by grieving over his passing. They could pay their respects by
visiting his grave during the *ch'ing-ming* festival[255] in the spring and
holding lectures on Buddhism for a seven-day period, after which
they were to disperse.[256]

Seven days after his death his body was placed in a coffin. On February 17 his clerical and lay followers had his body removed to Kuei-
feng, where it was cremated on March 4. P'ei Hsiu reports that several dozen relics (*she-li*) were subsequently collected.[257]

Sometime shortly after Tsung-mi's death, Chia Tao (779–843),[258] a
noted poet who had earlier been closely associated with Han Yü and
Meng Chiao, visited Ts'ao-t'ang ssu and composed the following la-
ment.

> Bird tracks among towering snow-clad peaks;
> With the master's passing away, who will body forth Ch'an?
> Dust on the table has gathered since he entered nirvāṇa;
> The color of the trees is different from the time when he was alive.
> The storied pagoda faces the wind blowing through the pines;
> Traces of his presence linger by the deserted spring.
> I sigh only for the tiger listening for the sūtras,
> As time and again it comes by the side of the dilapidated hermitage.[259]

In 853, twelve years after Tsung-mi's death, he received the posthumous title of Ting-hui Ch'an-shih, and a stūpa, on which was conferred the name "blue lotus," was erected to house his remains.[260]

---

[255] The *ch'ing-ming* festival was a time for visiting graves.

[256] Kamata, *Shūmitsu*, p. 51.11–13; cf. SKSC 742a19–22 and CTL 307a18–21.

[257] Kamata, *Shūmitsu*, p. 51.9–10.

[258] See C. Witzling's entry on Chia Tao in *The Indiana Companion to Traditional Chinese
Literature*, pp. 257–259. Chia Tao's relationship with Han Yü and Meng Chiao is discussed in Stephen Owen, *The Poetry of Han Yü and Meng Chiao*.

[259] *Ch'ang-chiang chi* 8.59–60. I would like to thank my colleague, Wai-yee Li, for her
felicitous translation.

[260] Kamata, *Shūmitsu*, p. 51.13–14; cf. SKSC 742c26–27 and CTL 307a21–22.

PART TWO

Doctrinal Classification

Chapter Three

DOCTRINAL CLASSIFICATION

DOCTRINAL classification (*p'an-chiao*) has often been said to be the hallmark of Chinese Buddhism. Although this judgment is surely one-sided—ignoring as it does many rich areas of more "popular" developments—it is certainly no exaggeration when applied to Chinese Buddhist scholastic writing. Doctrinal classification is one of the most striking features of Chinese Buddhist scholasticism, and it is impossible to understand how medieval Chinese Buddhist scholars thought without understanding p'an-chiao. Before going on to examine Tsung-mi's system of doctrinal classification, or that of the Hua-yen tradition with which he was associated, it is first necessary to place p'an-chiao within the overall context of the development of Buddhism by giving a broad overview of the hermeneutical problem to which it can be seen as a response.[1]

THE HERMENEUTICAL PROBLEM IN BUDDHISM

Although p'an-chiao is a term that, strictly speaking, applies to Chinese Buddhism (or those traditions that derive from it), the hermeneutical problem to which it is a response can be traced back to the earliest stages of Buddhism's development as a religion. The Buddha's teaching career spanned half a century, during which he taught many thousands of people. Those whom he taught were men and women of all ages, both world renouncers and householders, coming from different regions and social classes, all of whom had their own particular point of view and concerns, as well as varying in their receptivity to what the Buddha had to say. The Buddha taught all impartially and, as a keenly perceptive teacher, is portrayed as having an almost uncanny ability to gauge the capacity of his audience and address it in terms that it could most readily understand. One may also presume, against what the tradition might claim, that the Buddha's skill as a teacher matured with experience.

What the Buddha said on one occasion might thus differ markedly from what he said on another. While such a situation was fraught

---

[1] This chapter has adapted portions of my article, "Chinese Buddhist Hermeneutics," which appeared in the *Journal of the American Academy of Religion.*

with potential for misunderstanding and conflicting interpretations, it is unlikely that such problems proved disruptive while the Buddha was alive, since he could always be called on for an explanation. After the Buddha's death, however, there was no one in a position to settle such disputes. In the *Mahāparinirvāṇa-sūtra*, which claims to narrate the Buddha's last days and passing away, the Buddha explicitly declines to designate a successor, telling Ānanda that the dharma should serve as the guide for his community of followers after his death.[2]

But determining what the dharma was turned out to be not such a simple matter. Even in its most restricted sense of the teaching of the Buddha, there were, from the very outset, disagreements as to what the Buddha had said, not to mention what he might have meant when he said it. The first Buddhist council, which Buddhist historiography claims was held in Rājagṛha during the rainy season in the year after the Buddha's death, was allegedly convened to establish what the Buddha had taught. The traditional account relates that Ānanda, as the Buddha's lifelong attendant, was called on to repeat all of the discourses he had heard the Buddha deliver, while Upāli recited the disciplinary code the Buddha had laid down. Despite the attempt of the assembly to codify the Buddha's teachings, there was at least one monk, Purāṇa, who refused to accept as authoritative the teachings established by the council, preferring, instead, to follow the dharma as he remembered it. The council, significantly, did not censure Purāṇa, evidently not feeling itself invested with the authority to dispute what a fellow monk claimed to have heard from the Buddha.[3] This account probably says more about the needs and perceptions of the developing Buddhist community in the early centuries after the Buddha's death than it does about the actual "historical" events of the supposed "council" itself. Nevertheless, the fact that the case of Purāṇa was preserved in the collective memory of the early community reveals its own awareness of the lack of any centralized authority to speak *ex cathedra* for Buddhists as a whole. It also suggests that there were, from the very beginning, varying versions of what the Buddha had taught. While this situation contributed to the many schisms that have divided Buddhists throughout the course of the religion's long

[2] See *Dīgha-nikāya* 2.100, translated by T. W. Rhys Davids, *Dialogues of the Buddha*, 2:107–108; see also *Chang a-han ching*, T 1.15a–b. The version of the text in question is, of course, that of the so-called Hīnayāna; the Mahāyāna version will be referred to throughout as the "*Nirvāṇa Sūtra*."

[3] The accounts of the First Council are substantially identical in the six surviving vinaya. For the Pāli version see I. B. Horner, trans., *The Book of Discipline*, 5:393ff.

history, it also allowed for a diversity of teachings that enabled Buddhism creatively to adapt to changing historical and cultural realities.

Of course, Buddhists were not only confronted with the problem of determining what the Buddha had said on various occasions; they also had the far more difficult problem of interpreting what the Buddha had meant, a problem that became more serious and, at the same time, more intractable as Buddhism grew and developed. As the living memory of the Buddha faded, it is likely that the context of many of his sermons, which would have been self-evident to his immediate disciples, gradually was forgotten. Moreover, as Buddhism spread geographically, different communities formed, each marked by its own set of regional characteristics and preserving its own version of what the Buddha taught in its local dialect. Meanwhile, as the various communities of monks continued to expand in numbers, monastic life became institutionalized; problems unanticipated in the "original" teachings came to the fore and shaped the context in which the teachings were gradually codified into a canon. Since there was no authority outside of the teachings (dharma) and monastic regulations (vinaya), schisms occurred, and different sects began to define themselves in terms of different versions and interpretations of the Buddha's teachings.

One of the earliest hermeneutical devices to which Buddhists resorted to explain apparently conflicting statements in the Buddha's teaching was to distinguish between those teachings whose meaning was explicitly stated (Skt. *nītārtha*; Pāli *nītattha*) and those whose meaning required interpretation (Skt. *neyārtha*; Pāli *neyattha*).[4] This distinction, which may have been in use before the first open schism,[5] is stated explicitly in *Aṅguttara-nikāya* 1.60:

> Monks, these two misrepresent the Tathāgata. What two?
>
> He who proclaims as already explained [*nītattha*] a discourse which needs explanation [*neyattha*]; and he who proclaims as needing explanation a discourse already explained. These are the two.[6]

---

[4] *Nītārtha* consists of two elements: *nīta* and *artha* (meaning). *Nīta* is the past participle of *nī*, "to lead." The compound thus literally means "the meaning that has been led to." *Neyārtha* also consists of two elements: *neya* and *artha*. *Neya* is the future passive participle of *nī*. The compound thus literally means "the meaning that is to be led to." See Franklin Edgerton, *Buddhist Hybrid Sanskrit Grammar and Dictionary*, pp. 310b, 311b; and Sir Monier-Williams, *A Sanskrit-English Dictionary*, pp. 565a, 596b. The Pāli terms can be analyzed in the same way; see T. W. Rhys Davids and William Stede, *Pāli-English Dictionary*, pp. 310b, 311b.

[5] See A. K. Warder, *Indian Buddhism*, p. 151.

[6] F. L. Woodward, trans., *The Book of Gradual Sayings*, 1:54.

The scholastic tradition goes on to explain *nītattha* as designating those teachings whose meaning corresponds to their literal expression and *neyattha* as designating those teachings whose meaning needs to be determined by further interpretation.[7] As here defined, a *nītattha* teaching is one whose meaning is explicitly stated, and a *neyattha* teaching is one that needs clarification in order to be properly understood.

To take the example that is used in the Pāli commentary to the *Aṅguttara* passage just quoted, one of the Buddha's primary teachings consisted in his insight that there was no abiding substantial entity that could be grasped as the self (*ātman*). Nevertheless, he at times spoke as if there were something that transmigrated from one life to another. Since the latter statement seemed to contradict his teaching of no-self (*anātman*), Buddhists were compelled to devise an explanation of how both statements could in some sense be true, if the Buddha's teachings were not to be dismissed as self-contradictory. Such a problem was easily resolved by introducing a distinction between levels of teaching. The Buddha's teaching regarding the illusory character of the self could thus be taken at face value, and was accordingly to be deemed *nītattha*. His teaching that beings transmigrate, however, called for further explanation and was accordingly to be deemed *neyattha*. In other words, when the Buddha spoke of a "being" that transmigrated, he was merely speaking in accordance with linguistic convention; he did not mean to imply that there really was such a "being." His meaning, therefore, demanded further interpretation, because there are no beings in the ultimate sense (*paramatthato*).[8]

The distinction between these two levels of teaching, as the scholastic commentary suggests, intimates a distinction that proved enormously important for the development of Mahāyāna Buddhism, that between two levels of truth, ultimate and conventional, *paramārtha-* and *saṃvṛti-satya*. This distinction, in turn, presupposes the doctrine of expedient means (upāya), which also assumed cardinal importance with the rise of Mahāyāna Buddhism. The Buddha, after all, taught thousands of people in a variety of different circumstances throughout the course of his long ministry, and his statements could only be properly understood by taking their context into consideration.[9]

---

[7] These definitions can be found in the *Nettippakaraṇa*, as cited by Louis de La Vallée Poussin, *L'Abhidharmakośa de Vasubandhu*, tome 5, p. 247.

[8] See K. N. Jayatilleke, *Early Buddhist Theory of Knowledge*, pp. 361–362. Jayatilleke notes that the Pāli commentary elsewhere connects *nitattha* and *neyattha* with *paramattha* (Skt. *paramārtha*) and *sammuti* (Skt. *saṃvṛti*) (p. 363).

[9] In all but name, the Pāli commentary on the *Aṅguttara-nikāya* states the doctrine of

The hermeneutical problem of correctly interpreting what the Buddha said was further exacerbated by the fact that what was preserved by Buddhists as his teachings was never a static corpus of scripture. The canon continually grew and changed as old texts were expanded and new ones added. As different sects arose and articulated their points of controversy, a whole new category of texts appeared—those of the Abhidharma, which sought to systematize the Buddha's teachings into a coherent body of doctrine. As the "higher" (*abhi*) dharma,[10] Abhidharma can be seen as a thorough attempt to translate the conventional speech (*vyavahāra-vacana*) often used in the sūtras into ultimate speech (*paramārtha-vacana*), to devise an entirely impersonal language whereby it would be possible to account for experience without recourse to the notion of self presupposed in conventional discourse.[11]

Sometime around the beginning of the common era, an altogether new Buddhist movement, calling itself the "Mahāyāna" or great vehicle, began to proclaim its own message in a variety of new scriptures claiming to have been preached by the Buddha. One of the primary hermeneutical strategies by which this nascent form of Buddhism asserted its supremacy over the earlier organized forms of the religion, to which it gave the pejorative appellation "Hīnayāna" or "lesser vehicle," lay in its use of the doctrine of expedient means. On its most basic level, this doctrine was simply the articulation of the insight that

expedient means: "The exalted One preaches the conventional teaching to those who are capable of listening to this conventional teaching and penetrating the meaning, discarding ignorance and acquiring eminence. But to those who are capable of listening to the absolute teaching and penetrating the truth, discarding ignorance and attaining distinction, he preaches the absolute truth" (Jayatilleke, *Early Buddhist Theory of Knowledge*, p. 364).

[10] Such, at least, is the traditional gloss cited in Abhidharma literature. There are also places in the *Nikāyas* where the term is used in the locative to mean "pertaining to the dharma." See Leo Pruden's introduction to his translation of the *Abhidharmakośa-bhāṣyam by Louis de la Vallée Poussin*, 1:xxx–xxxvi.

[11] See, for example, Nyanaponika Thera, *Abhidhamma Studies*, p. 5, or Nyanatiloka Mahathera, *Guide Through the Abhidhamma-piṭaka*, pp. 2–3. In his "Mysticism in Its Contexts," Robert Gimello has given a not altogether humorless example of what this kind of linguistic enterprise would sound like: "The sort of experience which one might report in ordinary language by saying simply, 'I hear beautiful music,' would in the language of *abhidharma* be described in something like the following manner: 'There arises in an aural perception (*saṃjñā*) an impulse of auditory consciousness (*vijñāna*) which is produced in dependence upon contact (*sparśa*) between the auditory faculty (*indriya*) and certain palpable vibrations from a material (*rūpa*) instrument; this impulse of consciousness, in concert with certain morally conditioned mental predispositions (*saṃskāra*), occasions a feeling or hedonic tone (*vedanā*) of pleasure which in turn can produce attachment (*upādana*)', and so on" (pp. 74–75).

the Buddha's teachings had to be understood in terms of the context in which they were delivered.

In the hands of those who proclaimed this new form of Buddhism, however, the doctrine of expedient means took on revolutionary significance. It combined within itself a double function. On the one hand, it was used to relegate the earlier teachings to an inferior status and thereby furthered the sectarian ends of Mahāyāna in establishing its superiority as the ultimate teaching of the Buddha. On the other hand, it also offered a means by which those earlier teachings could be subsumed within the more comprehensive framework of the greater vehicle. According to this doctrine, the Buddha, realizing that his disciples lacked the spiritual maturity to understand his ultimate message, provisionally taught them an expedient teaching as a "lesser vehicle" to prepare them for his ultimate revelation, propounded openly for the first time in the teaching of the great vehicle. In the earlier teachings, the Buddha had to compromise the truth in order to reach the relatively unsophisticated level of his followers. The teachings of the lesser vehicle were therefore nothing more than clever devices invented by the Buddha out of his compassionate concern to alleviate the suffering of beings of "lesser" capacity.

Because such expedient teachings involved an accommodation with conventional understanding, they were not ultimately true. Nevertheless, they played a necessary role in preparing the way for the Buddha's ultimate revelation and therefore could be seen as contributing toward the final goal. The doctrine of expedient means thus not only reflects the fundamental ambivalence at the core of Mahāyāna—its simultaneously sectarian and universalist ethos—but also reveals how those two seemingly opposite tendencies were inseparably related.

For East Asian Buddhists, the most influential expression of this doctrine was undoubtedly made in the *Lotus Sūtra*, a relatively early Indian Mahāyāna scripture.[12] The second or "Expedient Means" chapter of that text explains how, during the period immediately following his enlightenment, the Buddha first despaired of ever communicating the breadth and profundity of his insight. He realized that if he directly taught the ultimate truth that all beings were destined to achieve Buddhahood, beings would reject it in disbelief and

---

[12] The scripture was supposedly first translated into Chinese in 225. The oldest surviving translation is that of Dharmarakṣa done in 290 (T no. 263). Kumārajīva's translation, *Miao-fa lien-hua ching* (T no. 262), has remained the standard version of the text in East Asia from the time it was completed in 406. For an English translation of this text see Leon Hurvitz, *Scripture of the Lotus Blossom of the Fine Dharma*. For a discussion of upāya in the *Lotus* see Michael Pye's *Skilful Means*.

thereby bring spiritual harm to themselves. He then recalled the example of the Buddhas of the past, who devised expedient teachings to guide beings on the path, and decided that he too should have recourse to expedients and teach the three vehicles.[13]

In addition to clarifying the rationale for using expedient means, this passage is also important for introducing the teaching of the three vehicles, a rubric that was to play an important role in Chinese Buddhist hermeneutical schemes. The relationship between the three vehicles and expedient means is further clarified in the famous parable of the burning house that occurs in the third chapter of the *Lotus Sūtra*.[14] According to this parable, a wealthy head of a household one day discovers that the great old mansion in which his family lives is being consumed by a raging fire. Although he desperately tries to warn his children of their imminent danger, they heedlessly continue to play their childish games. He then devises a ruse to lure them out of the house. Knowing what each child likes best, he tells them that there are goat-drawn, deer-drawn, and bullock-drawn carts waiting for them outside. The children immediately drop what they are doing and rush out of the house. When they demand that he make good on his promise, he decides to give each of them a great white bullock-drawn cart, thinking, "My wealth being limitless, I may not give small, inferior carriages to my children. Now these little boys are all my sons. I love them without distinction. I have carriages such as these, made of the seven jewels, in incalculable numbers. I must give one to each with undiscriminating thought."[15]

The Buddha then explains that he, like the wealthy and wise head of the household in the parable, devises expedients to lead suffering beings from the burning house of the three worlds. He accordingly teaches three vehicles. The goat-, deer-, and bullock-drawn carts represent the vehicles of the śrāvaka, pratyekabuddha, and bodhisattva. Just as the great man in the parable had ultimately given each of his children the best cart of all, so the Buddha, "being the father of all living beings," decides that he cannot reward his followers with inferior vehicles but must confer the one great Buddha vehicle equally on them all.[16]

According to Fujita Kōtatsu, the notion of the three vehicles was current in the thought of the various pre-Mahāyāna schools—indeed, the basis for the idea can be traced back to passages in the early "Hīna-

---

[13] T 9.9c13–18; Hurvitz, *Scripture*, p. 43.

[14] 12b13ff; Hurvitz, *Scripture*, p. 58ff.

[15] 12c18–23; Hurvitz, *Scripture*, p. 60.

[16] 13b4–c17; Hurvitz, *Scripture*, pp. 62–64.

yāna" canon.[17] As it was developed in the pre-Mahāyāna schools, it referred to three discrete spiritual paths leading to different goals. The first of these was the śrāvaka-vehicle. Translated as *sheng-wen* (voice-hearers) in Kumārajīva's Chinese, the term designates those disciples of the Buddha who "heard his voice" and, by following his instruction, were able to attain the release of arhatship. Even though the śrāvakas may have attained the same liberation as the Buddha, there was still a qualitative difference between them. The Buddha, after all, had attained his liberation alone, without a teacher, and had, moreover, opened up the way of deliverance to others to follow. Although the epithet of "arhat" (meaning "worthy of offerings") was originally applied equally to the Buddha and his disciples who had succeeded in obtaining release, it eventually came to stand for an attainment qualitatively inferior to the supreme perfect enlightenment attained exclusively by the Buddha.[18]

The origin of the notion of pratyekabuddha is somewhat more problematical. It seems to have had a pre-Buddhist origin, originally referring to legendary non-Buddhist recluses who had gained liberation on their own. As it became assimilated within Buddhist doctrine, it was reinterpreted in terms of the Buddha's own enlightenment. After his enlightenment, the Buddha is often portrayed as hesitating to preach. It is only after the intercession of the chief of the gods, who reminds the Buddha of his original vow to seek liberation for the benefit of all beings, that the Buddha is stirred by compassion to teach. "Pratyekabuddha" thus came to be understood to refer to those beings who succeeded in achieving nirvāṇa on their own, without recourse to the Buddha's instruction, but who, unlike the Buddha, did not remain in the world to preach the way to liberation. Their attainment was thus higher than that of the śrāvakas but still qualitatively inferior to that of the Buddha.[19]

A further twist was added to the notion of pratyekabuddha as it was incorporated into Mahāyāna. The *pratyeka* in pratyekabuddha eventually became confused with the *pratītya* in *pratītyasamutpāda* (Ch. *yüan-ch'i*; "conditioned origination"), the central early Buddhist doctrine that the cycle of rebirth is based on a catenation of conditions

---

[17] In what follows I have drawn heavily from Fujita Kōtatsu's excellent article, "One Vehicle or Three?" translated by Leon Hurvitz, who has added much valuable supplementary material in his notes. The original article appeared in Ōchō Enichi, ed., *Hokke shisō*.

[18] See Fujita, "One Vehicle or Three?" pp. 95–98.

[19] See ibid., pp. 98–104. See also Ria Kloppenborg, *The Paccekabuddha*, and the review by J. W. de Jong reprinted in Gregory Schopen, ed., *Buddhist Studies*, pp. 223–225.

and that release can be attained by successively eliminating in reverse order the prior condition on which each condition depends. A tradition accordingly grew up, reflected in its Chinese translation as *yüan-chüeh* (condition-enlightened), that pratyekabuddhas were really those disciples of the Buddha who achieved release by discerning the truth of *pratītyasamutpāda*. Śrāvakas, then, were taken to be those disciples who attained liberation by contemplating the four noble truths, the other central early Buddhist formulation of how salvation could be achieved. This interpretation of the two terms is found in the *Lotus* and generally followed by Chinese Buddhists. Both the path of the śrāvaka and pratyekabuddha constituted separate "vehicles" leading to liberation. But the liberation they achieved was arhatship, a spiritual state clearly inferior to the supreme perfect enlightenment of the Buddha.

Against these two inferior vehicles, both of which together constituted the lesser vehicle, the great vehicle was originally counterposed as a separate and superior spiritual path, the path of the bodhisattva who took supreme Buddhahood as his goal. The third vehicle in its pre-Mahāyāna usage referred to the Buddha-vehicle and served to accentuate the distance the early generations of disciples felt between themselves and the Buddha, as represented by the difference between the supreme perfect enlightenment achieved solely by the Buddha and the arhatship achieved by his followers. As the three-vehicle scheme was adapted by Mahāyāna, the third Buddha vehicle came more commonly to be referred to as the bodhisattva vehicle, which made the goal of Buddhahood available to all those who truly aspired to it and not merely to the Buddha alone.[20]

The third vehicle of the bodhisattva seems to have been originally put forward as a separate vehicle leading to a more exalted goal and can thus be taken to reflect the early Mahāyāna sectarian attempt to establish itself as a unique and "greater" vehicle in contrast to the lesser vehicle that had preceded it. The word "great" in the great vehicle connotes not only the relative sense of superior as contrasted with inferior but also the sense of more comprehensive. The great vehicle is the great vehicle precisely because it makes the highest goal universally available to all. It is therefore superior to the lesser vehicle, which can only ferry a limited number of beings to the other shore of liberation.

In contrast to the understanding of the three vehicles as providing separate paths leading to different religious goals, the *Lotus Sūtra* ad-

[20] See Fujita, "One Vehicle or Three?" p. 93. In the Hīnayāna version of the three vehicles, there could only be one Buddha in any given world cycle.

vances its central teaching of the one vehicle. The *Lotus* proclaims the universal message that all beings are ultimately destined to attain supreme Buddhahood. It was only because he was afraid that the exalted character of this goal would have daunted his followers that the Buddha expediently distinguished among the three vehicles. The *Lotus* declares that all Buddhas appear in the world for one great matter, to make clear the inconceivable insight and vision of the Buddhas.[21] All beings are destined for ultimate Buddhahood, even if they are unaware of it and follow a lesser vehicle, because such vehicles are nothing but expedients devised by the Buddha to lead them to the ultimate goal. Arhatship is merely a provisional and intermediary resting place that the Buddha conjures up to bolster his followers' spirits on the long and treacherous trek to the jewelled treasure of Buddhahood.[22]

The one vehicle, like the very notion of Mahāyāna itself, contained both a sectarian and a universalist claim. It was the one vehicle in the sense that it was the one and only vehicle that could convey beings to the final spiritual goal, something absolutely unique and separate from the expedient teaching of the three vehicles. At the same time, "one" also connoted its all-inclusive character, which enabled it to subsume the three vehicles within itself so that all teachings of the Buddha were understood to lead ultimately to full Buddhahood, the three vehicles being only expedient versions of the truth revealed completely in the one vehicle. The two seemingly opposed functions combined by the rubric of the one vehicle lie behind the distinction that was made by Chinese exegetes between the separate and common teaching of the one vehicle. As will be seen in the following chapter, one of the major points of disagreement between Chih-yen and Fa-tsang had to do with their different understanding of the relationship between these two categories.

The *Lotus*'s account of the one vehicle and three vehicles gave rise to the question of the relationship between the great vehicle of the bodhisattva that is included in the three vehicles and the one great vehicle that the Buddha ultimately confers on all his followers once they have escaped from the burning house of the three worlds to the safety of the open ground outside. That is, is the great vehicle among the three vehicles the same as the one vehicle or not? This question particularly vexed Chinese interpreters of the scripture. Since the *Lotus* itself does not furnish a clear-cut answer, two major interpretive

[21] 7a21–28; Hurvitz, *Scripture*, p. 30.

[22] See the parable of the conjured city in chapter 7, 25c26–26a24 (prose) and 26c29–27b8 (verse); Hurvitz, *Scripture*, pp. 148–149 and 153–155.

positions evolved: the so-called three-vehicle and four-vehicle interpretations. The former held that the two were really one and the
same, and that the *Lotus* therefore only preached three vehicles. The
latter, however, maintained that the one vehicle was a wholly separate
and special vehicle different from the great vehicle preached as part
of the three vehicles, and that the scripture accordingly taught that
there were really four vehicles.[23] The Hua-yen tradition, as will be
seen, opted for the four-vehicle interpretation.

The question was not only important for Chinese exegetes but also
serves to focus a problematic central to understanding the discourse
of Chinese Buddhist hermeneutics. That is, what is the relationship
between expedient means and the goal toward which they lead? Are
expedients necessary, or should they be rejected as ultimately false
once the true teaching has been revealed? Why, after all, would any-
one choose to follow a lesser and expedient vehicle when one could
use the great and ultimate one instead? If the one vehicle is indeed
unique and distinct, then why cannot the three vehicles simply be rejected altogether? What need is there for such expedient—that is, ultimately false—vehicles now that the true vehicle has been made
available to all? Does not the revelation of the one vehicle render the
three vehicles obsolete?

This question can be rephrased in terms of the relationship between conventional (*saṃvṛti-*) and ultimate truth (*paramārtha-satya*)
and related to the different treatment of *saṃvṛti* in Indian Buddhism.
As Nagao Gadjin has shown, the two main traditions of Indian Mahāyāna each take a different stand on the issue.[24] The Madhyamaka
tradition (particularly the Prāsaṅgika tradition based on the interpretation of Candrakīrti) emphasized the primary meaning of *saṃvṛti* as
concealing the truth, whereas the Yogācāra tradition of Sthiramati (as
well as the Svātantrika tradition within Madhyamaka) emphasized the
primary meaning of *saṃvṛti* as manifesting the truth. Thus for the
Madhyamakas, *saṃvṛti* was a negative concept associated with the
realm of falsehood and delusion. For the Yogācārins, however, it was
a positive concept associated with the realm of truth.

The Madhyamaka position assumes that there is an absolute disjunction between *saṃvṛti* and *paramārtha*, that one can only arrive at
paramārtha by transcending *saṃvṛti*. The Yogācāra position assumes
that there is a necessary continuum leading from *saṃvṛti* to
paramārtha, that *saṃvṛti* is the means by which *paramārtha* is rendered

---

[23] See Fujita, "One Vehicle or Three?" pp. 109ff.; see also Sakamoto Yukio, "Chūgoku bukkyō to Hokke shisō no renkan," pp. 520–529.

[24] See "An Interpretation of the Term 'Saṃvṛti' (Convention) in Buddhism."

accessible, that there is a necessary relationship between *saṃvṛti* and *paramārtha*. These two interpretations had very different implications for the understanding of expedients. The first position implied that all expedients must ultimately be rejected in order to arrive at the truth, that all expedients are, from the point of view of *paramārtha*, inextricably tainted with falsehood, and that to get from the realm of falsehood to that of truth involved a leap over the chasm between the two. The second position, by contrast, assigns a more positive role to expedients, which serve as the necessary bridge by which truth can be reached.

Such an understanding of the two truths clarifies how the question of expedients was connected with the problematic of "sudden" (*tun*) and "gradual" (*chien*), one of the central polarities in Chinese p'an-chiao discourse. Although Chinese scholiasts cite the *Laṅkāvatāra-sūtra* as the locus classicus of these terms,[25] they do not seem to have been part of the Indian Buddhist hermeneutical vocabulary. As the terms were used by Chinese Buddhists, the sudden teaching rejected all expedients to reveal ultimate truth directly, whereas the gradual teaching made use of expedients to arrive at ultimate truth by means of a graduated progress. The category of "sudden" became connected with the *Hua-yen Sūtra*, from which the Hua-yen tradition took its name and on which it based its claim to represent the paramount teaching of the Buddha. The *Lotus Sūtra*, with its panoply of expedients, was therefore a gradual teaching—at least within the polemics of Hua-yen thinkers. The Hua-yen tradition could thus argue its superiority over T'ien-t'ai, which looked to the *Lotus* for its scriptural authority, by claiming that it represented a direct and unmediated revelation of ultimate truth. T'ien-t'ai, on the other hand, could argue that it was precisely the fact that the *Hua-yen Sūtra* made no recourse to expedients that its message was lost on all but the most advanced spiritual beings. The *Lotus* was truly superior because its arsenal of upāya made the Buddha's ultimate message accessible to all beings.

THE CHINESE CONTEXT

The doctrine of expedient means provided the main hermeneutical device by which Chinese Buddhists systematically ordered the Buddha's teachings in their classificatory schemes. It enabled them to ar-

[25] See, for example, Ch'eng-kuan's reference to the four different examples of sudden and gradual in the *Laṅkāvatāra* in his *Yen-i ch'ao*, T 36.164b11–c2. The original passage can be found at T 16.485c–486a18 (cf. T 16.525a20–b15 and T 16.596a23–b14); for a translation, see D. T. Suzuki, *The Laṅkāvatāra Sūtra*, pp. 49–50.

range the teachings in such a way that each teaching served as an expedient measure to overcome the particular shortcoming of the teaching that preceded it while, at the same time, pointing to the teaching that was to supersede it. In this fashion a hierarchical progression of teachings could be constructed, starting with the most elementary and leading to the most profound.

While the enterprise of doctrinal classification never had the importance in Indian Buddhism that it was to assume in China, the methodology used in Chinese p'an-chiao was, nevertheless, clearly anticipated in a few Indian Buddhist scriptures. One of the most important examples was the *Saṃdhinirmocana-sūtra*'s teaching of the three turnings of the dharma wheel. According to this early Yogācāra text, the Buddha's teachings could be divided into three successive periods, the order of which represented an ever more profound revelation of the truth. The first of these was contained in the teaching of the lesser vehicle, which taught that there was no substantial self. Yet, because it failed to teach the emptiness of all things (dharmas), it was not ultimate. It was therefore superseded by a second teaching, that contained in the Perfection of Wisdom scriptures, which taught the emptiness of all things. This teaching, however, was also not ultimate, and a third and final teaching, which elucidated (*nirmocana*) the hidden meaning (*saṃdhi*) of the Perfection of Wisdom, accordingly had to be taught. This was, of course, the teaching of the *Saṃdhinirmocana* itself.[26]

The *Saṃdhinirmocana* applies the notion of expedient means within a chronological framework to account for the succession of teachings according to different stages in the Buddha's teaching career. Another important Indian Buddhist example, which was to play a significant role in the doctrinal classification system used in the T'ient'ai tradition, was the parable of the five flavors found in the *Nirvāṇa Sūtra*. This second example could also be interpreted in chronological terms, as it was under the later T'ien-t'ai rubric of the "five periods." It had a less restricted application, however, as it was originally used by Chih-i (538–597). It suggested that the dharma could be understood in terms of successive stages of refinement analogous to the stages by which ghee (liberation) is derived from milk. Just as milk derives from a cow, cream derives from milk, butter derives from cream, melted butter derives from butter, and ghee derives from melted butter, so "the twelve divisions of the canon derive from the Buddha, the sūtras derive from the twelve divisions of the canon, the

---

[26] See T 16.697a23–b9; cf. Étienne Lamotte, trans., *Saṃdhinirmocana-sūtra*, pp. 206–207.

extended [vaipulya, i.e., Mahāyāna] sūtras derive from the sūtras, the Perfection of Wisdom derives from the extended sūtras, and nirvāṇa, which is like ghee, derives from the Perfection of Wisdom."[27]

Even though the examples from these two Indian Buddhist scriptures served as prototypes for Chinese Buddhist p'an-chiao schemes, doctrinal classification itself never played the crucial role in Indian Buddhism that it did in China. Although Indian Buddhism splintered into many sects, each sect was still part of an unbroken religious evolution. Nor were Indian Buddhists called on to justify their existence as a social group whose presence threatened the values and sociopolitical structures of Indian society. Even though the different sects disputed with one another, they could all claim some form of linkage to the historical Buddha. And this consciousness of historical linkage made it unnecessary for them to account for the teachings of other sects in a systematic fashion.

In China, however, the situation was entirely different. First of all, Buddhism was very much an alien tradition that violated some of the most cherished values of Chinese civilization. From the time that Buddhism first began to make its presence felt within Chinese society, it was subjected to an unrelenting stream of objections from its Confucian-minded critics. Many of the aspects of the new religion that the Chinese found most objectionable were more a reflection of the general Indian world view of which Buddhism was a part than particular teachings and practices specific to Buddhism among the religious traditions of India. Many of the most pressing issues with which Chinese Buddhist apologists had to deal thus never arose in the Indian cultural context.

Celibacy, for example, was already an established custom among Indian ascetics when the Buddha enjoined its practice on his monks and nuns. In China, however, not only did celibacy play no role in its indigenous religious practices, it also transgressed the familialism at the heart of Chinese cultural values. The continuation of the family line was a duty made sacred by the need to ensure the proper maintenance of ancestor worship. The emphasis placed on producing progeny was duly stated by Mencius: "There are three things which are unfilial, and to have no posterity is the greatest of them."[28] A celibate son, renouncing his sacred duty for a life as a Buddhist monk, thus seemed to threaten the very cohesiveness of Chinese society.

Celibacy became institutionalized in the cenobitic lifestyle followed

[27] T 12.690c28–691a6, adapting the translation of Neal Donner, "Sudden and Gradual Intimately Conjoined," p. 209.

[28] 4A26; James Legge, *The Chinese Classics*, 3:313.

by Buddhist monks in India, where the monastic institution existed as an autonomous social body outside of secular authority. In China, however, the extraterritorial claims of the monastic institution not only infringed on the prerogatives of the state but also challenged the sacred character of the emperor in both his moral and sacerdotal capacity, invested in him by heaven, of maintaining the proper harmony between the sociopolitical realm and the way of heaven. The existence of a class of nonproductive monks, moreover, offended the Chinese work ethic. It was also decried on purely pragmatic grounds by generations of government officials who saw in it a loss of vital sources of tax revenue and manpower. In India, on the other hand, far from being seen as an economic drain on society, nonproductive religious seekers of all denominations were revered by pious laymen as an all-important means for gaining religious merit by providing a field in which they could sow the seeds of good karma and so improve their spiritual prospects in a life to come.

Chinese critics were never at a loss for articulating other, and in their context equally persuasive, objections to Buddhism. Most of these, however, focused on the impact that Buddhism had as a corporate institution on Chinese society. Aside from the traditional array of social, political, economic, and moral objections leveled against Buddhism, the very values to which Buddhists often appealed in justifying their existence as a distinct and privileged group within Chinese society went against the this-worldly orientation of Chinese civilization, in which there was little distinction between sacred and profane. In India, however, the renunciation of worldly life by religious seekers intent on breaking the shackles of existence was a hallowed, if socially ambivalent, ideal. Rather than viewing the religious life as a separate and higher norm, the Chinese have tended, instead, to invest the secular with religious meaning.

While the objections that Chinese Buddhists had to address in justifying their existence as a distinct group within Chinese society were not, strictly speaking, part of the hermeneutical problem of correctly interpreting the Buddha's teachings, they nevertheless formed the background against which Chinese Buddhists addressed the problem. It was, after all, necessary for Buddhism to reach some form of accommodation with Chinese values and sociopolitical structures in order for it to take root and grow in Chinese cultural soil. Buddhism had to divest itself of its Indian trappings and become Chinese. Thus, whether or not they attempted to answer their Confucian-minded critics, Chinese Buddhists, by the very fact of being Chinese, approached Buddhism with a problem consciousness (in most cases all the more powerful because unconscious) very different from that of their Indian counterparts.

In addition to the unique perspective from which Chinese Buddhists approached the task of interpreting the Buddha's teachings, the hermeneutical problem was for them a more urgent one than it was for their Indian brethren, for whom all the different manifestations of Buddhism were an organic part of the evolving Indian cultural matrix out of which Buddhism originally developed. To Chinese Buddhists, however, not only did Buddhism itself demand justification, but the further problem of interpreting the confusing array of teachings they inherited as the sacred word of the Buddha also proved to be equally vexatious. Chinese Buddhists were, as their Indian counterparts were not, called on to make sense out of Buddhism as a totality.

The problem was exacerbated by the fact that the Chinese never received Buddhism as a complete and coherently wrought system. Rather, the transmission of Buddhism to China took place over a period of centuries—centuries in which Indian Buddhism itself continued to develop and change in profound ways. The process of transmission occurred in a fragmented and haphazard fashion. The order in which texts were translated into Chinese bore no relation to the chronology of their composition. Later texts were often made available before the earlier texts on which they were based or to which they were a response. This situation meant that teachings were introduced divorced from both their historical and doctrinal context, thus making it even more difficult for the Chinese to arrive at an accurate understanding of them. Moreover, the Indian and Central Asian missionaries, who served as the vital link in this process of transmission, hailed from different Buddhist traditions and were often at odds in their interpretation of the various teachings that the Chinese were groping to comprehend.

A particularly apt case in point is the Chinese Buddhists' initial efforts to understand the concept of the ālayavijñāna ("store-consciousness"), a concept that figures heavily in Tsung-mi's thought. Discussion of the meaning of this term formed one of the principal issues of scholastic debate in learned Buddhist circles of the sixth century.[29] The ālayavijñāna is one of the cardinal doctrines of the Yogācāra school of Buddhism, in which it is defined as containing the "seeds" of the mental and physical elements out of which the phenomenal

---

[29] For a more detailed treatment of this complex issue, see Stanley Weinstein, "The Concept of the Ālaya-vijñāna in Pre-T'ang Chinese Buddhism," pp. 33–50, and Gimello, "Chih-yen," pp. 277–337.

world evolves, functioning as the repository of all experience, and serving as the underlying continuum in sentient beings.

While this complex doctrine presents difficulties even when systematically formulated, the problem of reaching an accurate understanding of it was compounded for Chinese Buddhists by the fact that there were no such systematic formulations available to them in the sixth century. The work that brought the concept to the attention of the learned Buddhists of that time was the *Shih-ti ching lun*, Bodhiruci's translation of Vasubandhu's commentary to the *Daśabhūmika-sūtra*, a scripture that had already enjoyed widespread popularity among Chinese Buddhists in the preceding century. Although the *Daśabhūmika* originated as an independent text, it was eventually incorporated into the *Hua-yen Sūtra*. The *Daśabhūmika* itself elucidates the ten stages of the bodhisattva path. It bears no particular relation to Yogācāra teachings and does not mention the ālayavijñāna. Nevertheless, Vasubandhu, as one of the chief systematizers of Yogācāra thought, makes five passing references to this concept in his commentary on the sūtra. His comments on the ālayavijñāna, however, presuppose a familiarity with the Yogācāra works in which this doctrine is systematically explained. Without such a prior understanding, Vasubandhu's references seem to present two conflicting interpretations of the ālayavijñāna. Whereas two of his references imply that the ālayavijñāna is the source of delusion,[30] three imply that it is the source of enlightenment.[31] The fourth reference, in particular, associates the ālayavijñāna with suchness (*chen-ju; tathatā*, i.e., ultimate reality, the absolute).[32] The question, then, as it was formulated by Chinese Buddhists in the sixth century, was this: Is the ālayavijñāna identical with suchness, in which case it must be intrinsically pure, or not, in which case it must be defiled? Since the *Daśabhūmika* had already gained notoriety among Chinese Buddhists for its assertion that the phenomenal world was created by the one mind,[33] the question was rephrased as follows: Is the ultimate basis of the phenomenal world, the realm of suffering and delusion, pure or defiled?

The scholastic tradition that grew up around the study of this text

---

[30] See T 26.142b13 and 188b15–17; cf. Gimello, "Chih-yen," pp. 287, 289, for translations.

[31] See T 26.170c21–22, 172b16–18, and 180a18–20; cf. Gimello, "Chih-yen," pp. 288–289, for translations.

[32] This is the passage at 180a18–20.

[33] See, for instance, Kumārajīva's translation of the *Daśabhūmika, Shih-chu ching,* T 10.514c26. For a discussion of the original passage, its meaning in Vasubandhu's commentary, and its interpretation within the Hua-yen tradition, see Tamaki Kōshirō, "Yuishin no tsuikyū."

was divided on precisely this issue. The "southern" branch of the Ti-lun tradition, represented by Hui-kuan (363–443), held that the phenomenal world was based on suchness (*chen-ju*), whereas the "northern" branch, represented by Tao-ch'ung, maintained that it was based on the ālayavijñāna. While the debate waged between the two sides may strike one today as a highly recondite and even pedantic matter, the whole issue was germane to the process of accommodating Buddhism with Chinese values, and its implications consequently had enormous significance for the development of the uniquely Chinese form of Buddhism that was to assume its mature form in the Sui–T'ang period. For if Buddhism taught that the defiled phenomenal world were ultimately nothing but a manifestation of an intrinsically pure ground, then it would be possible for Chinese Buddhists to fashion an ontology that would affirm the phenomenal world of human endeavor that had been the primary focus of the this-worldly and humanistic concerns of traditional Chinese thought. Such was the tack taken by Hua-yen. On the other hand, the Fa-hsiang tradition of Yogācāra, introduced to China by Hsüan-tsang, held that there was an unbridgeable gap between the defiled world of delusion and the pure mind of enlightenment. As will be seen more fully in later chapters, it was primarily around this issue that Hua-yen rejected Fa-hsiang as representing only a quasi-Mahāyāna teaching.

As this example demonstrates, the historical process by which Buddhism was transmitted to China generated its own set of problems that framed the context in which the Chinese had to operate in their attempt to gain an understanding of the tradition as a whole. Although this situation certainly made the task more difficult, it also opened up the field for speculation, in which Chinese Buddhists could exercise their own genius in defining their own unique form of Buddhism that was at once thoroughly Chinese and authentically Buddhist.

Indeed, the history of Chinese Buddhism can be represented in terms of the development of the increasingly sophisticated hermeneutical frameworks that were devised to understand a religion that was in its origin as foreign conceptually as it was distant geographically. This hermeneutical process, by which Chinese Buddhists gradually came to assimilate Buddhism into their own cultural modalities, could also be characterized in terms of successive phases of "sinification."

The first phase, covering the third and fourth centuries, is masterfully documented in Erik Zürcher's classic study, *The Buddhist Conquest of China*. It represents the period in which Chinese Buddhists tried to understand their newly imported religion in terms of their own cultural and intellectual frames of reference, especially so-called Neo-Taoism (*hsüan-hsüeh*). It is only at the end of the fourth century, with figures like Tao-an (312–385) and Hui-yüan (344–416), that Chinese Buddhists begin to become aware of the distorting lens through which they had come to understand their tradition. At the same time, it was only toward the end of the fourth century that enough texts had been translated for Chinese Buddhists to become aware of the diversity of teachings to which they were heir.

The fifth century, with the arrival of Kumārajīva in Ch'ang-an in 401, begins the second phase of the Chinese attempt to understand Buddhism. Chinese Buddhists, aware of the limitations of earlier efforts to understand the tradition, turned to foreign authorities and sources in order to understand Buddhism on its own terms, shorn of the cultural filters that had characterized the previous period. This period, which extends on through most of the sixth century, is marked by an increasingly scholastic turn. It is the period of the exegetical "schools," which attempt to master the various scholastic traditions of Indian Buddhism. In addition to Kumārajīva's authoritative translations of a number of critically important Mahāyāna texts (especially those associated with the Perfection of Wisdom), this period witnessed the rendering into Chinese of a number of major Yogācāra scriptures and treatises, which became the central focus of Chinese scholastic thought. The gradual assimilation of Yogācāra thought over the sixth century laid the doctrinal ground on which was constructed the new Buddhism of the Sui and T'ang period, which of course represents the third phase in this threefold typology of the process of sinification.

It was during this second period that the Chinese first began to grapple with the hermeneutical problem of rendering intelligible the variegated expanse of Buddhist teachings, and accordingly it was during the early part of the fifth century that the first doctrinal classification schemes were articulated. One of the earliest p'an-chiao systems was devised by Hui-kuan, a figure associated with the exegetical tradition centering on the *Nirvāṇa Sūtra* and best known for his opposition to Tao-sheng's theory of sudden enlightenment.[34] In his preface to the *Nirvāṇa Sūtra*, Hui-kuan divided the Buddha's teachings into two general types: the sudden (*tun*) and gradual (*chien*). The sudden teaching corresponded to the *Hua-yen Sūtra*, which fully revealed the truth and was taught for only the most advanced bodhisattvas. Hui-kuan then divided the gradual teachings into five periods. The first period was one in which the three vehicles were taught

---

[34] His biography can be found in KSC, T 50.368b8–c1.

separately (san-sheng pieh-chiao): that is, the Buddha taught the four noble truths to śrāvakas, the twelvefold chain of conditioned origination to pratyekabuddhas, and the six perfections to bodhisattvas. Because the cause of practice for the followers of each vehicle was not the same, the result that they attained was different. The second period was characterized by the teaching that runs through the three vehicles (san-sheng t'ung-chiao) and corresponds to the Perfection of Wisdom. The third period, in which the Buddha denegrated the śrāvakas and praised the bodhisattvas (i-yang-chiao)—the teaching, that is, in which he made clear the inferiority of Hīnayāna and proclaimed the superiority of Mahāyāna—is represented by the Viśeṣacintā-brahmaparipṛccha and Vimalakīrti sūtras. The fourth period corresponds to the universal teaching (t'ung-kuei-chiao) of the Lotus Sūtra, according to which the three vehicles were all subsumed into the one vehicle. The fifth and final period corresponds to the Nirvāṇa Sūtra's teaching of the eternality of the Buddha (ch'ang-chu-chiao).[35]

Hui-kuan's p'an-chiao is surprisingly sophisticated and anticipates the taxonomical differentiations in the ways of classifying the teachings only made explicit in the eighth-century formulation of the five periods and eight teachings of Chan-jan (711–782).[36] As this later T'ien-t'ai scholar makes clear, Buddhist teachings could be classified according to three different rubrics: method of exposition, content, and chronology. These different classificatory rubrics were necessitated, at least in part, by some of the problems posed by the Hua-yen Sūtra. This scripture was generally acknowledged as containing one of the most profound, if not the most profound, revelations of Mahāyāna. At the same time, it was also generally regarded by Chinese Buddhists as being the first preaching of the Buddha. A simple chronological arrangement, such as the Saṃdhinirmocana's three turn-

[35] San-lun hsüan-i, T 45.5b4–14. See also Ōchō Enichi, "The Beginnings of Tenet Classification in China," pp. 91–94 (originally published as "Kyōsō hanjaku no genshi keitei" in Ōchō, Chūgoku bukkyō no kenkyū, vol. 2).

[36] Sekiguchi Shindai has demonstrated that Chih-i, the great systematizer of T'ien-t'ai thought, never formulated the system of the five periods and eight teachings that, beginning with the authorship of the T'ien-t'ai ssu-chiao i (T no. 1931) by the Korean monk Chegwan in the tenth century, has been attributed to him and has been generally regarded as representing the essence of T'ien-t'ai doctrine. While it is true that the various elements that were later brought together to form the five periods and eight teachings scheme all appear separately in different contexts throughout Chih-i's writings, they were never brought together systematically by Chih-i himself. This task was first accomplished by Chan-jan. A good summary of Sekiguchi's views can be found in his "Goji hakkyō kyōhanron no kigen." An excellent restatement and assessment of Sekiguchi's arguments can be found in David Chappell's "Introduction to the T'ien-t'ai ssu-chiao-i," which appears in a somewhat abridged form as the introduction to T'ien-t'ai Buddhism.

ings of the dharma wheel, which assumed that the order in which the Buddha preached his different teachings represented a progression beginning with the most elementary and advancing to the most profound, therefore could not account for the *Hua-yen Sūtra*.[37] A chronological arrangement of the teachings did not match their arrangement according to their content. Thus, whereas the *Hua-yen Sūtra* would have to be placed first in a chronological arrangement, it could be ranked last—i.e., highest—in terms of an arrangement according to content. The sudden–gradual distinction circumvented this problem by suggesting that the *Hua-yen Sūtra* differed from the other teachings of the Buddha not so much in terms of its ultimate content as in the way that content was revealed. The distinction between sudden and gradual teachings thus had to do with their method of exposition. The sudden teaching differed from the gradual in that it directly proclaimed the ultimate truth without recourse to expedients. The truth that it revealed was the same as that to which the gradual teachings led by a graduated progress. Its content, therefore, did not differ from that of the highest of the gradual teachings.

As far as the later development of the Hua-yen tradition is concerned, Hui-kuan's p'an-chiao is important for introducing "sudden" and "gradual" as classificatory terms. It is also important for identifying the *Hua-yen Sūtra* with the sudden teaching, an identification that was adopted in the subsequent classificatory schemes of Liu Ch'iu (438–495), Master I, Tsung-ai, Seng-jou, Hui-kuang (468–537), Paramārtha (499–569), Chih-i, Hui-tan (Sui dynasty), and the Hua-yen "patriarch" Chih-yen.[38]

Another early classification scheme important for the development of Hua-yen was that of Hui-kuang (468–537), a figure associated with the southern branch of the Ti-lun tradition.[39] Fa-tsang's *Hua-yen ching chuan chi* attributes a four-fascicle commentary on the *Hua-yen Sūtra* to Hui-kuang, claiming that "he established the three teachings of gradual, sudden, and perfect in order to classify the scriptures." Fa-tsang goes on to comment that "the taking of the *Hua-yen* [*Sūtra*] as the perfect teaching began with him."[40] Hui-kuang apparently identified the *Hua-yen Sūtra* with the sudden teaching as well,[41] as

[37] See, for instance, *Wu-chiao chang*, T 45.481a13–23 (Francis Cook, "Fa-tsang's Treatise on the Five Doctrines," pp. 170–171), where Fa-tsang rejects Hsüan-tsang's threefold classification based on the *Saṃdhinirmocana* on precisely these grounds.

[38] See Kimura, *Shoki chūgoku kegon*, pp. 76–78.

[39] His biography can be found in HKSC, T 50.607b18–608b29.

[40] T 51.159b1–3.

[41] In his *Wu-chiao chang*, Fa-tsang claims that Hui-kuang identified the *Hua-yen Sūtra* with the perfect teaching (T 45.480b28). His *T'an-hsüan chi* gives virtually the same

later reflected in Chih-yen's classification of it as both a sudden and perfect teaching, a topic that will be considered in the next chapter.

In the fifth and sixth centuries Chinese Buddhists like Hui-kuan and Hui-kuang employed p'an-chiao as a hermeneutical strategy to reconcile the discrepancies among the different teachings believed to have been taught by the Buddha. By resorting to the doctrine of expedient means, they were able to create a hierarchical framework within which the entire range of Buddhist teachings could be systematically organized into a coherent doctrinal whole. But p'an-chiao was not a neutral methodology. Nor did the rubric of expedient means offer any basis on which to decide the order in which the various teachings were to be classified. The order in which the teachings were ranked was a matter of interpretation that called for value judgments in regard to which scripture or scriptural corpus was to be taken as authoritative. Thus, in addition to providing a hermeneutical method by which the diverse teachings put forward in different scriptures could be harmonized, p'an-chiao also furnished the structure according to which the different traditions of Chinese Buddhism advanced their own sectarian claims for being recognized as the true, ultimate, or most relevant teaching of Buddhism.

Because p'an-chiao was the primary means by which the different traditions of Chinese Buddhism legitimated their sectarian claims, its hierarchical arrangement reveals what each tradition valued as most essential to its own identity as a distinct tradition. A comparative analysis of the changes within the classificatory schemes devised within a particular tradition can thus be used as a gauge to assess the process of doctrinal change within that tradition. The following chapters will therefore examine the changes within the classification schemes within the Hua-yen tradition as a means of evaluating shifts within Hua-yen doctrine. Such an approach will highlight most clearly the character and scope of Tsung-mi's revision of Hua-yen; it should also clarify what it was that Tsung-mi found of value in Hua-yen thought. To clarify Tsung-mi's place within the Hua-yen tradition, it is appropriate to begin by focusing on those categories that are associated with the *Hua-yen Sūtra*.

---

account of Hui-kuang's p'an-chiao, except that it concludes: "he took this [*Hua-yen*] scripture to be included within the perfect and sudden [teachings]" (T 35.111a7). For a full discussion of Hui-kuang's p'an-chiao and the various problems associated with it, see Sakamoto, *Kegon kyōgaku*, pp. 197–205.

Chapter Four

DOCTRINAL CLASSIFICATION IN THE
HUA-YEN TRADITION

DOCTRINAL classification provided a broad and flexible methodology for dealing with a wide range of interrelated issues and was used by Chinese Buddhists to serve a number of different purposes. The hermeneutical and sectarian functions of p'an-chiao have frequently been noted in discussions of Chinese Buddhism, but there is also a third function of p'an-chiao that is often overlooked—what one might call its soteriological function. It is only by taking this soteriological aspect into account that one can understand the distinctive character of Tsung-mi's p'an-chiao. As will be seen in later chapters, Tsung-mi's systematic classification of Buddhist doctrine is itself a theory of the Buddhist path (mārga).

Chinese Buddhists thus used p'an-chiao for what could be characterized as hermeneutical, sectarian, and soteriological purposes. That is, it organized into a coherent and internally consistent doctrinal framework the diverse corpus of sacred scriptures to which Chinese Buddhists were heir; it legitimated the claims of different Chinese Buddhist traditions to represent the supreme, orthodox, or most relevant teaching of the Buddha; and it provided a map of the Buddhist path. These three major functions of p'an-chiao overlap and, in practice, are often hard to distinguish from one another. Because the framework in which the Buddhist teachings were organized was hierarchical—and because it was possible, given the diversity of Buddhist teachings, to justify a number of different classificatory schemes—any given p'an-chiao arrangement involved critical value judgments as to what constituted the most authoritative teaching. Such judgments, of course, provided the basis on which different traditions of Chinese Buddhism put forward their own sectarian claims. The arrangement of Buddhist teachings as a graded progress moving from the most elementary to the most profound, moreover, mirrored the deepening stages of understanding through which the Buddhist adept moved in his advancement along the path.

Although these three functions of p'an-chiao are thus interrelated and, to varying degrees, present in different classification schemes, it is still useful to distinguish among them. For the different aspects of

Buddhist thought that predominate at different points in the development of T'ang Buddhism are reflected in the different functions of p'an-chiao that are emphasized. These different functions of p'an-chiao thus provide a convenient rubric for characterizing the shifting emphases in Hua-yen thought over the course of the T'ang dynasty.

For instance, Chih-yen, whom the Hua-yen tradition was to honor as its second patriarch, used a variety of p'an-chiao schemes in different contexts to organize into an intelligible framework the complex legacy of Buddhist thought of his day. While it would certainly be wrong to imply that Chih-yen was not concerned with soteriology, his primary interest in p'an-chiao was hermeneutical: to provide a rational structure in which Buddhism could be understood. In the case of Chih-yen's disciple Fa-tsang, however, other elements come to the fore. In his selective adaptation of only one of the various rubrics used by his teacher, Fa-tsang gave exclusive prominence to the *Hua-yen Sūtra*, thereby providing a firmer basis for establishing the sectarian claim of the Hua-yen tradition to represent the supreme teaching of the Buddha. For Tsung-mi, however, such hermeneutical and sectarian concerns take second and third place to a greater emphasis on soteriology. In Tsung-mi's p'an-chiao, the logic by which teachings are arranged directly reflects the levels of understanding through which a Buddhist practitioner progresses toward Buddhahood.

The different functions that are emphasized in the classification schemes of these Hua-yen masters reflect the changing historical, social, political, and intellectual realities of T'ang Buddhism. Chih-yen, writing at the beginning of the T'ang, was concerned to rephrase the complex heritage of Six Dynasties scholastic thought in terms of the new religious agenda set by Tu-shun. Fa-tsang's emphasis on the uniqueness of the *Hua-yen Sūtra* as the separate teaching of the one vehicle underlined the superiority of his "school" of interpretation and may well have been influenced by imperial patronage, as Stanley Weinstein has argued.[1] Tsung-mi's explicitly soteriological concerns reflect the importance of the emergence of Ch'an in the eighth century and the formative influence that it had on his thought.[2]

---

[1] See his "Imperial Patronage."

[2] T'ien-t'ai shows a similar pattern of development. The relationship between Tu-shun and Chih-yen parallels that between Hui-ssu (515–577) and Chih-i (538–597), just as the shift in emphasis from Chih-yen to Fa-tsang parallels that from Chih-i to Chan-jan (711–782). Both Chih-yen and Chih-i drew from the doctrinal repertoire of the learned Buddhism of the fifth and sixth centuries to give shape to the new Buddhism of Tu-shun and Hui-ssu. Moreover, Fa-tsang and Chan-jan both articulated classification schemes that emphasized the unique importance of a single scripture, thus revealing a sectarian consciousness not seen in the thought of either Chih-yen or Chih-

To place Tsung-mi within the overall context of the development of the Hua-yen tradition and establish a basis on which to gauge the extent of his revision of Hua-yen thought, this chapter will examine the classification schemes developed by Chih-yen and Fa-tsang, paying special attention to the categories that they apply to the *Hua-yen Sūtra*. Although the chapter will thus not be able to avoid discussing some of the technicalities of Hua-yen doctrinal categories, it is only by bringing into focus the change in such details of doctrine that the significance of the historical shift that they represent can be seen. The chapter will conclude with a schematic comparison of Fa-tsang's and Tsung-mi's system of doctrinal classification as a way of introducing some of the central issues that will be discussed in detail in the following chapters.

CHIH-YEN'S CLASSIFICATION SCHEMES

The doctrinal classification scheme that is almost invariably taken to represent the Hua-yen tradition as a whole is Fa-tsang's fivefold p'an-chiao of the lesser vehicle, the elementary teaching of the great vehicle, the advanced teaching of the great vehicle, the sudden teaching, and the perfect teaching. Fa-tsang's fivefold scheme clearly derives from Chih-yen's last work, the *K'ung-mu chang* (Hua-yen miscellany). Yet, if Fa-tsang's p'an-chiao is compared with that of his teacher, there are major differences that bring out the different context within and purpose for which each wrote.[3]

Even though Fa-tsang takes the names for his five teachings from Chih-yen, their content differs in significant ways. Moreover, the fivefold classification that Fa-tsang adapts from Chih-yen is only one of several fivefold arrangements he uses in his *K'ung-mu chang*. Nor is it a uniquely prominent one within that work, much less within Chih-yen's thought as a whole. Rather, Chih-yen's major p'an-chiao categories consist of three loosely interlocking rubrics: the gradual teaching, the sudden teaching, and the perfect teaching; the lesser vehicle, the three vehicles, and the one vehicle; and the common teaching and the separate teaching.

Chih-yen's first rubric (that of the gradual, sudden, and perfect

---

i. The comparison breaks down with Tsung-mi, as there is no comparable figure in T'ien-t'ai.

[3] My discussion of Chih-yen's p'an-chiao has relied on the following secondary sources: Gimello, "Chih-yen," pp. 369–392; Kimura, *Shoki chūgoku kegon*, pp. 430–441; Nakajō Dōshō, "Chigen no kyōhansetsu ni tsuite"; Sakamoto, *Kegon kyōgaku*, pp. 397–410; Yoshizu Yoshihide, "Kegon kyōhanron no tenkai"; and Yoshizu, *Kegonzen*, pp. 9–24 and passim.

teachings) derives from Hui-kuang. Although Chih-yen identifies the immediate source for his second set of categories (that of the lesser, three, and one vehicles) as Paramārtha's translation of the *Mahāyānasaṃgrahabhāṣya*,[4] it is clear that the most important context for these categories ultimately derives from the *Lotus Sūtra*. In any case, these two rubrics together reflect Chih-yen's attempt to synthesize the two scholastic legacies of the Ti-lun and She-lun traditions, which had comprised the central focus of his early studies.

Sou-hsüan chi

Almost all of the main features of Chih-yen's p'an-chiao appear, at least in rudimentary form, in his first work, the *Sou-hsüan chi* (Record inquiring into the profundities [of the *Hua-yen Sūtra*]). Nevertheless, the threefold rubric of gradual, sudden, and perfect overshadows the others in importance in that work, which was written in 628 as a commentary to Buddhabhadra's sixty-fascicle translation of the *Avataṃsaka*. Chih-yen's concern in the introductory section of the *Sou-hsüan chi* is thus with the proper classification of the *Hua-yen Sūtra*. The most important point to note is that Chih-yen, presumably following Hui-kuang, classifies the *Hua-yen Sūtra* as both a sudden and perfect teaching.[5]

Chih-yen's account of the sudden teaching begins with a quotation from the chapter of *Hua-yen Sūtra* dealing with the ten stages of the bodhisattva.

> As there are beings of a lower order with minds disdainful [of saṃsāra]
>   and [intent upon] the cessation [of nirvāṇa],
> For them is taught the "disciples' " way that they may escape suffering.
> As there are also beings of somewhat keen faculty who rejoice in the law
>   of causes and conditions,
> For them is taught [the way of] the "self-enlightened."
> As there are men of eminently keen faculty, beneficent to all beings
> And possessed of minds of great compassion, for them is taught the
>   bodhisattva path.

---

[4] *Sou-hsüan chi*, T 35.14b18. The passage in question is located at T 31.212b17–22. See Gimello, "Chih-yen," pp. 372–374, for a discussion and translation.

[5] Chih-yen first explains the gradual teaching by distinguishing between the teachings (*so-ch'üan*) and those to whom they were taught (*so-wei*). The first subdivision refers to the three "baskets" (*piṭaka*) into which the Buddhist canon is traditionally divided: the sūtras (sermons of the Buddha), abhidharma (scholastic philosophy), and vinaya (monastic regulations). The second subdivision refers to the followers of the lesser and greater vehicles. See T 35.13c20–14b12. See Gimello, "Chih-yen," pp. 376–377, for a more ample summary.

[But,] as there are some of unexcelled mind resolutely exultant in the
  great matter,
For them are manifest the [very] bodies of the Buddhas and for them
  are taught the measureless Buddha-dharma.[6]

The first three verses clearly refer to the three vehicles: those for
the disciples (śrāvakas), self-enlightened (pratyekabuddhas), and
bodhisattvas. The fourth verse suggests that there is a fourth, even
more exalted vehicle beyond the first three. Indeed, Chih-yen offers
these verses as canonical proof for the distinction between the one
vehicle and the sudden teaching, on the one hand, and the three vehicles, on the other.[7] Chih-yen's coupling of the one vehicle with the
sudden teaching, in contradistinction to the three vehicles, raises the
question of the relationship between the one vehicle and the sudden
teaching. Chih-yen answers that their relationship is indeterminate.
In some cases they are not distinct, while in other cases they are distinct from one another as insight and doctrine or as one is superficial
and the other profound.[8] Although Chih-yen does not so specify

[6] T 35.14b12–17. The translation is that of Gimello, "Chih-yen," pp. 378–379. The
original sūtra passage occurs at T 9.567c13–20. The same passage is quoted in the *Wu-
chiao chang* (T 45.478b7–12), where, significantly, Fa-tsang makes no mention of the
sudden teaching and uses it as authority for emphasizing the qualitative difference
between the one vehicle and the three vehicles (see Cook "Fa-tsang's Treatise," pp.
129–130).

[7] T 35.14b17–18. There is some disagreement as to the proper interpretation of this
passage. It reads: "*I tz'u wen cheng chih yu i-sheng chi tun-chiao san-sheng ch'a-pieh.*" I have
followed the reading given by Kimura ("*ichijō oyobi tonkyō to sanjō to no kubetsu ga aru*")
(*Shoki chūgoku kegon*, p. 432). Yoshizu has criticized this reading and suggested that the
passage should instead be read as: "*ichijō to oyobi tonkyō-sanjō no sabetsu*" (*Kegonzen*, p.
22, n. 12). Yoshizu's reading, however, is grammatically strained, if not untenable.
"*Chi*" (*oyobi*) serves as a connective. Chih-yen so uses it a few lines later when he writes:
"This scripture is included with the two teachings of sudden and perfect" (*tz'u ching chi
tun chi yüan erh chiao she*) (14b24). Again, the same usage occurs at the end of Chih-
yen's discussion of the ten profound gates when he identifies the ten with "the dharma-
gate of the perfect teaching of the one vehicle and the sudden teaching" (*i-sheng yüan-
chiao chi tun-chiao fa-men*) in contradistinction to the three vehicles (15b20–23). Yoshizu's
claim that Chih-yen uses *tun-chiao san-sheng* (sudden teaching–three vehicles) as a set
phrase is forced. When Chih-yen refers to the three vehicles as the gradual teaching
he says *san-sheng chien-chiao* (the gradual teaching of the three vehicles), not *chien-chiao
san-sheng* (gradual teaching–three vehicles). Had Chih-yen meant to couple the sudden
teaching with the three vehicles, it would have been more natural for him to say *san-
sheng tun-chiao* (the sudden teaching of the three vehicles). Moreover, Yoshizu's reading
of this passage violates the context in which it occurs, where it is cited to elucidate the
meaning of the sudden teaching. Finally, Yoshizu's claim that Chih-yen includes the
sudden teaching as part of the three vehicles is difficult to sustain. Granted that there
are occasions in which Chih-yen does include the sudden teaching within the three
vehicles, he far more typically treats them as distinct.

[8] T 35.14b19–21.

here, it is clear from context, as well as from his consistent usage throughout his various works, that he regards the perfect teaching as synonymous with the one vehicle. In fact, he often combines the two terms together as the perfect teaching of the one vehicle.[9]

The perfect teaching "sets forth the ultimate teaching of liberation for the sake of those beings of highest penetration who had partially advanced toward the realm of Buddhahood."[10] Chih-yen concludes his initial account of the three teachings with the observation that the *Hua-yen Sūtra* is included in both the sudden and perfect teachings.[11]

Chih-yen then goes on to take up the relationship of the *Hua-yen Sūtra* to the three vehicles. He points out that the sūtra, as the teaching of the one vehicle, can also be understood as including two aspects: the common and separate teachings. The separate teaching refers to the fact that the one vehicle exists as an independent teaching separate from the three vehicles, just as in the parable from the *Lotus Sūtra* the father offers his children a great white bullock-drawn cart that is different from and superior to the deer-, goat-, or bullock-drawn carts he had promised them to entice them out of the burning house.[12]

Chih-yen discusses p'an-chiao further in the fifth section of his introduction in the *Sou-hsüan chi*, where he gives the following comprehensive definition of the three teachings:

> In the beginning, while [still] under the bodhi tree, [the Buddha], for the sake of those intent on the practice of the great vehicle, on a single occasion directly set out the utmost expression of the fundamental principle. Since the purport of his extensive turning of the dharma wheel was profoundly subtle and was not predicated on anything at all, [this teaching] is taken as the sudden.[13]

> The "gradual" refers to the fact that [the Buddha] devised [various] expedients for the sake of beginners, opening up the three vehicles as a method of ushering them forward. At first [his intention] was obscure, but later it became clear. He proceeded from the superficial to the profound. Because he progressively conveyed them to the other shore by stages, [this teaching] is called gradual.

[9] As he does later, for example, in the fifth section of his introduction in the *Sou-hsüan chi*, T 35.15b21.

[10] T 35.14b22–24.

[11] T 35.14b24.

[12] T 35.14b27–28. See T 9.12b13ff.; Hurvitz, *Scripture*, p. 58ff. Cf. discussion of *Lotus Sūtra* in chapter 3.

[13] Tanei's *Gokyōshō sanshaku*, written in 1334, quotes a passage on the sudden teaching from Hui-kuang's commentary to the *Hua-yen Sūtra* that is identical to the passage by Chih-yen quoted here from the *Sou-hsüan chi* (see Sakamoto, *Kegon kyōgaku*, p. 198).

The "perfect teaching" refers to the fact that [the Buddha], for the sake of those of highest penetration who had partially advanced toward the realm of Buddhahood, set forth the teaching of the liberation of the Tathāgata that utterly exhausted the practice of the final fruit of the cardinal principle. Because it consummated the Buddha task, [this teaching] is termed perfect.[14]

Chih-yen concludes his p'an-chiao account in the *Sou-hsüan chi* by considering the order of the arrangement of the three categories of gradual, sudden, and perfect. From the perspective of the progression of practice, the gradual is first, the sudden second, and the perfect third. From the perspective of their order of exposition, the sudden is first, the gradual second, and the perfect third. From the perspective of their revelation of the truth, the perfect is first, the sudden second, and the gradual third.[15]

Wu-shih yao wen-ta

Whereas the *Sou-hsüan chi* emphasizes the three teachings of gradual, sudden, and perfect that Chih-yen inherited from Hui-kuang, the *Wu-shih yao wen-ta* (Fifty essential questions and answers [in regard to the *Hua-yen Sūtra*])[16] elaborates the three-vehicle rubric of the lesser vehicle, great vehicle, and one vehicle that Chih-yen adopted from the *Mahāyānasaṃgrahabhāṣya*. What is especially noteworthy about Chih-yen's use of p'an-chiao in the *Wu-shih yao wen-ta* is that he introduces the distinction between the elementary and advanced teachings as an important feature of his treatment of the three vehicles. Although he had used these terms on several occasions in his *Sou-hsüan chi*, his use there had been incidental, and they did not figure in his p'an-chiao in that text in any significant way.[17]

Chih-yen's use of the distinction between the elementary and advanced teachings within the three vehicles is clearly a response to the new Yogācāra teachings that Hsüan-tsang had introduced to China after his return from India in 645. The *Wu-shih yao wen-ta* employs the new terminology used by Hsüan-tsang and quotes from a number of his translations. Since the last of Hsüan-tsang's translations from

---

[14] T 35.15c1–8.

[15] T 35.15c10–23.

[16] T no. 1869; as Gimello points out, this text actually discusses fifty-three questions; see "Chih-yen," pp. 536–537.

[17] Yoshizu cites the following instances: Chih-yen uses "elementary teaching" (*ch'u-chiao*) at T 35.27c5; "mature teaching" (*shu-chiao*) at 27c7, 33c1, 52a21; and "advanced teaching" (*chung-chiao*) at 38a13 (see *Kegonzen*, p. 21, n. 12, and "Kegon kyōhanron no tenkai," p. 221, n. 31).

which Chih-yen quotes is the *Ch'eng wei-shih lun,* which was completed in 659, the *Wu-shih yao wen-ta* must have been finished sometime after then.[18]

Chih-yen places the new brand of Yogācāra introduced by Hsüan-tsang within the elementary teaching of the three vehicles. The advanced teaching consists of the brand of Yogācāra-cum-tathāgata-garbha thought more typical of the earlier translations, particularly of Paramārtha, and the Ti-lun and She-lun traditions. One of the primary points of difference between these two types of Mahāyāna teaching had to do with the accessibility of Buddhahood. In the *Wu-shih yao wen-ta,* for example, Chih-yen writes that "according to the elementary teaching of the three vehicles, half attain Buddhahood and half do not," whereas "according to the advanced teaching of the three vehicles, all sentient beings without exception attain Buddhahood." He concludes with the interesting comment that, whereas insentient things "such as grasses and trees" are excluded from attaining Buddhahood according to the advanced teaching, the one vehicle maintains that sentient beings and insentient things attain Buddhahood altogether as set forth in the *Hua-yen Sūtra.*[19]

Chih-yen refers to the distinction he had made between the common (*t'ung*) and separate (*pieh*) teachings of the one vehicle in the *Sou-hsüan chi* as the shared (*kung*) and unshared (*pu-kung*) teachings of the one vehicle in the *Wu-shih yao wen-ta.* He identifies the teaching of the *Hua-yen Sūtra* with the unshared teaching of the one vehicle and subsumes all the other preachings under the shared teaching.[20]

K'ung-mu chang

Chih-yen's final work, the *K'ung-mu chang,* takes over the *Wu-shih yao wen-ta's* distinction between the elementary and advanced teachings within the three vehicles. It also reintroduces the rubric of the gradual, sudden, and perfect teachings that Chih-yen had used in his *Sou-hsüan chi.* Because this work combines the three-teaching and three-vehicle rubrics together, its use of p'an-chiao categories is the most complex of all of Chih-yen's works.

In this work Chih-yen combines his various p'an-chiao categories together in diverse ways in different contexts.[21] To impose some or-

---

[18] Gimello, "Chih-yen," p. 537.

[19] T 45.519c6–7, 11–12.

[20] See T 45.523b3–6 and 523b7–8.

[21] In his section discussing the meaning of the one and three vehicles, for instance, Chih-yen enumerates three different permutations of the five vehicles: (1) Men and gods, śrāvakas and pratyekabuddhas, the gradual teaching of elementary and advanced [teachings of the great vehicle], the sudden teaching, and the one vehicle; (2)

der on the apparent complexity of Chih-yen's use of p'an-chiao categories throughout the *K'ung-mu chang*, eight main categories may be
discerned, which Chih-yen most often refers to as "vehicles" (*sheng*)
or "levels" (*wei*) rather than "teachings" (*chiao*). Their sequential order is clear and invariable: (1) men, (2) gods, (3) śrāvakas, (4)
pratyekabuddhas, (5) elementary teaching, (6) advanced teaching, (7)
sudden teaching, and (8) perfect teaching or one vehicle. Chih-yen's
p'an-chiao seems so complex because he makes use of various permutations of these categories in different contexts.[22]

Placing all of the subcategories under their main headings, Chih-
yen's various p'an-chiao categories can thus be rearranged in the following way (as he so lists them as "the five teachings" at one point):[23]

men, gods, śrāvakas, pratyekabuddhas, great vehicle; (3) gods, brahmas, śrāvakas,
pratyekabuddhas, Tathāgatas (T 45.537b14–18). Elsewhere, Chih-yen lists as the five
vehicles the categories later adapted by Fa-tsang in his comprehensive fivefold system
of doctrinal classification: the lesser vehicle, the elementary teaching, the advanced (or
mature) teaching, the sudden teaching, and the perfect teaching or the one vehicle
(see, for example, T 45.537a, 542c22–25, 548a1–7, and 548c10–11). But, unlike Fa-
tsang, Chih-yen never puts these five categories forward as a definitive and exclusive
system of classification. Nor is there anything in his treatment of them that makes them
stand out as superior to or more important than the other p'an-chiao arrangements he
uses throughout the *K'ung-mu chang*.

[22] Although he sometimes discusses men and gods as distinct vehicles, he frequently
combines them into a single vehicle. Many enumerations fail to include men and gods
altogether—either as separate vehicles or as a single vehicle. As they are related to the
most rudimentary understanding of Buddhism, these two terms are clearly the least
important and least frequently used of the eight. Again, while Chih-yen sometimes
discusses śrāvakas and pratyekabuddhas as separate vehicles, he more often treats
them together under the rubric of the lesser vehicle. Sometimes Chih-yen treats the
elementary teaching and the advanced teaching as separate categories, sometimes as
subdivisions of either the three vehicles or the great vehicle, and sometimes he merely
discusses the three vehicles or great vehicle without mentioning its two subcategories.
Other times Chih-yen discusses the three vehicles or the elementary and advanced
teachings in terms of the gradual teaching. The gradual teaching, of course, also includes the lesser vehicle and that of men and gods. On occasion he also discusses the
sudden teaching under the category of the three vehicles. In his discussion of suchness
(*chen-ju*), for instance, Chih-yen first distinguishes between what he refers to as "suchness according to the one vehicle" and "suchness according to the three vehicles." He
subdivides the former into that of the common and separate teachings. Chih-yen then
divides the suchness according to the three vehicles into that according to the sudden
teaching and that according to the gradual teachings. He then analyzes the gradual
teachings in terms of three further categories (those of the advanced, elementary, and
worldly teachings), each of which he further divides into an earlier (*shih*) and later
(*chung*) phase (T 45.558c17–559a24; see also diagram in Nakajō, "Chigen no kyōhansetsu," p. 259). However, he more typically treats the sudden teaching as a separate
category in its own right; see, for example, T 45.558c23–559a1, where he identifies
the sudden teaching with Vimalakīrti's silence, the advanced teaching with Mañjuśrī's
reply, and the elementary teaching with the replies of the thirty-one bodhisattvas.

[23] See T 45.556a–c. Fa-tsang's five teachings can be derived by dropping the first

1. Men and gods
   a. Men
   b. Gods
2. Lesser vehicle
   a. Śrāvakas
   b. Pratyekabuddhas
3. Three vehicles
   a. Elementary teaching
   b. Advanced (or mature) teaching
4. Sudden teaching
5. Perfect teaching of the one vehicle
   a. Separate teaching
   b. Common teaching

} Gradual teachings

The fact that Chih-yen's first three categories are also included in the gradual teaching reveals how this fivefold scheme can easily be rearranged in terms of the three categories of gradual, sudden, and perfect.

1. Gradual teachings
   A. Men and gods
      a. Men
      b. Gods
   B. Lesser vehicle
      a. Śrāvakas
      b. Pratyekabuddhas
   C. Three vehicles
      a. Elementary teaching
      b. Advanced (or mature) teaching
2. Sudden teaching
3. Perfect teaching of the one vehicle
   A. Separate teaching
   B. Common teaching

What is important is that Chih-yen's arrangement of the "vehicles" (or, less commonly, "teachings") marks a soteriological progress from those suited to the least spiritually advanced to those suited to the most spiritually advanced. Even though, according to context, he sometimes leaves out or includes various of the vehicles that comprise this course, the overall order of their arrangement does not vary. The underlying idea is a familiar one: even though the ultimate import of the Buddha's teaching is beyond distinctions, the Buddha, out

category of men and gods and treating the two subcategories of the three vehicles as separate categories.

of his deep compassion, used various expedients to express his message in a multitude of ways in response to the diverse needs and capabilities of beings. The difference between the different teachings so-called does not really reflect a difference in the Buddha's teaching per se so much as it does the different levels of the different beings to whom it was addressed.

In addition to the various combinations of the three-teaching and three-vehicle rubrics, the *K'ung-mu chang* amplifies the third major set of p'an-chiao terms introduced by Chih-yen in the *Sou-hsüan chi*—that between the common and separate teachings of the one vehicle. Chih-yen's treatment of these terms is important for assessing how far Fa-tsang's p'an-chiao deviates from his master's. Chih-yen again refers to the parable of the burning house from the *Lotus Sūtra* to establish that the one vehicle exists independently of the three vehicles as a separate teaching. He further calls on the "logic" of the *Lotus Sūtra*, according to which "the three are subsumed into the one" (*hui-san kuei-i*), to explain how the one vehicle is at the same time a common teaching. Because the different teachings are ultimately subsumed within the perfect teaching of the one vehicle, there is a common meaning running through them all despite their apparent differences. As the common teaching, the one vehicle thus includes the three vehicles and the lesser vehicle as well. Since the lesser vehicle and three vehicles lead to the one vehicle, they are ultimately identical (*t'ung*) with it.[24] Chih-yen's discussion suggests that, from the point of view of the one vehicle, the difference among the various vehicles is only provisional. It is only from the perspective of the three vehicles that the difference seems to be real. The one vehicle must therefore be established as a separate teaching in order for its inclusive function as the common teaching to be realized. The common teaching thus represents the expedient aspect of the one vehicle, and the separate teaching, its ultimate aspect.

Elsewhere in the *K'ung-mu chang*, Chih-yen refers to the separate and common teachings as "the true vehicle" (*cheng-sheng*) and "the expedient vehicle" (*fang-pien-sheng*). He identifies the true vehicle (i.e., the separate teaching) with the *Hua-yen Sūtra*[25] and goes on to claim that the other scriptures were all preached in order to reveal the meaning of the teaching of the one vehicle, "the utterly comprehensive, inexhaustible dharma treasury." They use expedients to direct beings toward the one vehicle so that they may enter within by understanding it in terms most comprehensible to their diverse spir-

---

[24] T 45.585c27–586a7.
[25] T 45.538a10–12.

itual capacities. Chih-yen thus maintains that all of the expedient teachings are established on the basis of the ultimate teaching of the one vehicle because they all flow from the one vehicle and, at the same time, lead toward the goal of the one vehicle.[26] Chih-yen concludes by remarking that "the sudden belongs to the meaning of the superior part of the fundamental teaching (*ch'i shang-fen pen-chiao i*) whereas the gradual comes from its derived meaning (*mo-i*)."[27]

Overall, in both his *Wu-shih yao wen-ta* and *K'ung-mu chang*, Chih-yen uses his various p'an-chiao categories as a way of organizing and addressing a series of scholastic issues that he inherited from the earlier exegetical traditions of the Six Dynasties. This point is worth bearing in mind because it partially accounts for the seemingly ad hoc and sometimes inconsistent way in which he employs his repertoire of p'an-chiao terms. Since he uses them to clarify specific doctrinal issues, he applies them somewhat differently according to the nature of the issue at hand without ever abstracting them from their specific context. His interest seems to lie more in employing p'an-chiao as a way of making sense out of a series of complicated doctrinal issues than in developing a comprehensive classification system in its own right. Compared to Fa-tsang's, Chih-yen's classification of Buddhist teachings is presystematic—a fact that helps to explain its overall complexity.

That the details of Chih-yen's p'an-chiao resist unambiguous summary reveals much about how he understood it, and the purposes for which he used it. For the sake of comparing Chih-yen's p'an-chiao with Fa-tsang's, or placing it within the overall context of the Hua-yen tradition, the details are not important. By way of summary, the following points bear emphasizing.

1. Chih-yen uses p'an-chiao as a hermeneutical tool, not so much to organize the diverse collection of holy scripture into a harmonious

---

[26] T 45.538b16–21.

[27] T 45.538b23. Although it is not entirely clear, Chih-yen here seems to associate the sudden teaching with the true vehicle—hence the separate teaching of the one vehicle—and the gradual teaching with the expedient vehicle—hence the common teaching of the one vehicle. This interpretation is in keeping with Chih-yen's overall characterization of the sudden teaching as not having recourse to expedients (he frequently identifies the sudden teaching with Vimalakīrti's silence and characterizes it as not being based on language) but seems to be contradicted by other passages (see, for example, T 45.556c8–12, where Chih-yen discusses the difference between the sudden and gradual teachings under the heading of the three vehicles; see also T 45.558c18–37, where he places the sudden teaching under the heading of the three vehicles in contrast to the one vehicle). In the end, however, the precise meaning of the sudden teaching within Chih-yen's p'an-chiao, especially the question of its relationship to the one vehicle and three vehicles, is problematic.

and coherent framework (as Hui-kuan had done), but to make sense out of the complex assimilation of Indian Buddhist doctrines that had taken place in the Six Dynasties and to refocus them in terms of the new agenda that had been posed by Tu-shun and the "new Buddhism of the Sui and T'ang periods."

2. Chih-yen's p'an-chiao does not culminate in five teachings later elaborated by Fa-tsang, as some scholars have suggested.[28] While Fa-tsang's fivefold scheme does derive from Chih-yen, Chih-yen uses a variety of different fivefold arrangements and never puts one forward as a definitive and comprehensive p'an-chiao system.

3. Chih-yen classifies the *Hua-yen Sūtra* as both a sudden and perfect teaching.

4. For Chih-yen, the one vehicle includes two aspects, which he refers to most often as the common and separate teachings, both of which are intimately and inseparably interrelated. Chih-yen never identifies the one vehicle exclusively with the *Hua-yen Sūtra*. It is only as the separate teaching that he identifies it with the *Hua-yen Sūtra*. As the common teaching, he identifies it explicitly with the *Lotus Sūtra*, which was preached "separately" (*pieh*) to set forth the meaning of the common teaching of the one vehicle, and implicitly with all other scriptures, which, according to the *Lotus*'s "logic" of the three being subsumed into the one (*hui-san kuei-i*), are ultimately included within the one vehicle.

FA-TSANG'S CLASSIFICATION SCHEME

Although Fa-tsang frequently cites Chih-yen's authority throughout his *Treatise on the Five Teachings* (*Wu-chiao chang*), his fivefold classification of Buddhist teachings clearly marks a departure from the central emphases of Chih-yen's p'an-chiao. Even though Fa-tsang takes the names of his five categories from Chih-yen, their arrangement and content are different. As discussed previously, the form of Chih-yen's different versions of the different vehicles (or teachings) varies according to context. By contrast, the names and arrangement of the five teachings in Fa-tsang's p'an-chiao are fixed and used consistently throughout his oeuvre. Fa-tsang thus gives his fivefold scheme a prominence that it never had in Chih-yen's writings. Indeed, p'an-chiao plays a much more central role in Fa-tsang's thought than it ever did in Chih-yen's. Whereas Chih-yen had used p'an-chiao as a hermeneutical tool to organize a series of complex scholastic issues,

---

[28] As, for example, does Sakamoto, *Kegon kyōgaku*, pp. 402–403. See Yoshizu's critique of this position, *Kegonzen*, pp. 11 and 20–21, n. 20.

Fa-tsang uses it as the major framework in which to develop Hua-yen thought systematically. Fa-tsang's most famous work, best known under its abbreviated title of the *Treatise on the Five Teachings*,[29] underlines the importance of the five teachings as his major p'an-chiao rubric, as well as indicating the overall significance of p'an-chiao in his thought.

The major shift in content from Chih-yen's p'an-chiao can be seen in Fa-tsang's understanding of the fifth and final teaching and his classification of the *Hua-yen Sūtra* as belonging exclusively to it. As noted, the five categories Fa-tsang takes over from Chih-yen are the teaching of the lesser vehicle, the elementary teaching of the great vehicle, the advanced teaching of the great vehicle, the sudden teaching, and the perfect teaching. While his treatment of the first three teachings is consistent with Chih-yen's, his treatment of the last two is significantly different. In contrast to Chih-yen, who had included the *Hua-yen Sūtra* under both the sudden and perfect teachings, Fa-tsang disengages the *Hua-yen Sūtra* from the sudden teaching and identifies it solely with the perfect teaching. At the same time he also identifies the perfect teaching exclusively with the *Hua-yen Sūtra*, whereas Chih-yen had also included scriptures other than the *Hua-yen* under the perfect teaching in its capacity as the common teaching of the one vehicle. Like Chih-yen, Fa-tsang identifies the separate teaching with the *Hua-yen Sūtra* and the common teaching with the *Lotus Sūtra*. But, whereas Chih-yen had classified both sūtras, as representing the dual aspect of the one vehicle, together under the perfect teaching, Fa-tsang places the *Lotus* within the advanced teaching of the great vehicle and reserves the perfect teaching for the *Hua-yen* alone. He thus emphasizes the gap between the common and separate teachings of the one vehicle. Unlike Chih-yen, who saw a necessary interrelation between these two aspects of the one vehicle, Fa-tsang identified the perfect teaching solely with the separate teaching.[30] The common teaching accordingly falls within the province of the three vehicles.

---

[29] T no. 1866; full title *Hua-yen i-sheng chiao i fen-ch'i chang* (Treatise analyzing the meaning of the teaching of the one vehicle of the Hua-yen). The *Wu-chiao chang* has been translated and annotated by Francis Cook as part of his 1970 University of Wisconsin Ph.D. dissertation, "Fa-tsang's Treatise on the Five Doctrines." Since Fa-tsang uses his fivefold classification system without change consistently in his various works, I have relied almost entirely on his *Wu-chiao chang* for my exposition here.

[30] See T 45.481b and 507b (Cook, "Fa-tsang's Treatise," pp. 173 and 524). The main line of my argument in this section follows Yoshizu's discussion of Fa-tsang's p'an-chiao in his *Kegonzen*, although much of the evidence I present is my own. For other useful discussions of Fa-tsang's p'an-chiao see Yoshizu, "Kegon kyōhan-ron no tenkai," and Liu Ming-wood, "The *P'an-chiao* System of the Hua-yen School in Chinese Buddhism," pp. 10–47.

Hence, whereas Chih-yen saw the separate and common teachings as being different aspects of the perfect teaching of the one vehicle, Fa-tsang saw them as belonging to qualitatively different orders of teaching.

Fa-tsang's treatment of the separate and common teachings reveals the more elevated status that he assigns to the *Hua-yen Sūtra*. In the first chapter of the *Treatise on the Five Teachings*, for example, Fa-tsang is concerned to establish the one vehicle as a totally unique form of Buddhism. As Chih-yen had done, he discusses the one vehicle in terms of the separate and common teachings. The question of the relationship between the common and separate teachings, of course, has to do with the relationship with the one vehicle and three vehicles. While the separate teaching emphasizes the uniqueness of the one vehicle, the common teaching emphasizes its commonality with the three vehicles. In his treatment of the separate teaching of the one vehicle, Fa-tsang gives ten reasons why the one vehicle is a teaching wholly separate from the three vehicles. The teaching of the three vehicles is provisional (*ch'üan*), for example, whereas that of the one vehicle is true (*shih*).[31] Although the common teaching mediates between the three vehicles and the one vehicle, Fa-tsang does not include it under the perfect teaching but associates it with the three vehicles instead. Fa-tsang's treatment of the common teaching thus emphasizes its difference from the separate teaching. He points out that although the three vehicles contain doctrines common to the one vehicle, they do not exhaust the full scope of their meaning—for instance, even though the three vehicles may talk about the net of Indra, they still do not teach the infinite interrelationship of primary and secondary. Again, while the one vehicle includes doctrines common to the three vehicles, they have a different meaning.[32] Fa-tsang's next examples clearly subordinate the common teaching to the separate teaching by emphasizing its provisional and derivative character. The common teaching can only grasp the one vehicle by expedients.[33] The three vehicles can be said to be the "same" (*t'ung*) as the one vehicle in that they "flow from" it.[34] The common teaching differs from the separate teaching, however, in its understanding of the one vehicle itself. Whereas the separate teaching recognizes the one vehicle as a wholly separate Buddha vehicle different from the great vehicle of the three vehicles, the common teaching takes the great

---

[31] T 45.477a24–b8; 119–121.
[32] T 45.478c13–20; 136.
[33] T 45.478c20–22; 137.
[34] T 45.478c22–479a1; 137–138.

vehicle within the three vehicles to refer to the one vehicle.[35] While the three vehicles can thus be seen to share a number of elements in common with the one vehicle, the very way Fa-tsang couches his discussion highlights their differences. The three vehicles are thus expedient and derivative. Even though they may ultimately lead toward the one vehicle, they still only approximate it.

The derivative and secondary quality of the common teaching is further brought out in the sixth chapter of the *Treatise on the Five Teachings*, which deals with the time and places in which the Buddha taught various doctrines.[36] The main purpose of this chapter is to demonstrate the absolutely unique circumstances under which the *Hua-yen Sūtra* was preached, thereby revealing its supremacy over all other teachings. Fa-tsang begins by distinguishing between two qualitatively different orders of teaching: what he calls the fundamental teaching in accord with the truth (*ch'eng-fa pen-chiao*) and the derivative teaching adapted to the capacity of beings (*chu-chi mo-chiao*).[37] The first refers to the separate teaching of the one vehicle and is identified solely with the *Hua-yen Sūtra*. He claims that this sūtra was preached during the second week after the Buddha's enlightenment while he was still seated under the bodhi tree and immersed in the samādhi of oceanic reflection.[38] For Fa-tsang the samādhi of oceanic reflection symbolizes the Buddha's enlightened vision in which the harmonious interrelationship of all phenomena in the entire universe simultaneously appeared as if reflected on the surface of a vast, tranquil ocean. It is the content of the Buddha's enlightenment, which Fa-tsang elsewhere refers to the conditioned origination of the dharma-dhātu (*fa-chieh yüan-ch'i*). The *Hua-yen Sūtra*, preached while the Buddha was still absorbed in this samādhi, was thus the direct revelation of his enlightened vision as he experienced it under the bodhi tree. The fact that Fa-tsang designates this teaching as the separate teaching indicates that it is qualitatively different from all other teachings of the Buddha, which Fa-tsang characterizes as derivative teachings adapted to the capacity of beings. It is under the heading of the derivative teachings adapted to the capacity of beings that Fa-tsang discusses the common teaching.[39] He says that according to the common teaching, the three vehicles were preached at the same time

[35] T 45.479a1–7; 138.

[36] See T 45.482b18–483a19; Cook, "Fa-tsang's Treatise," pp. 188–196.

[37] Chih-yen used a similar distinction in his *K'ung-mu chang* (T 45.538b16–21), where he identified the sudden teaching with the superior part of the fundamental teaching and the gradual teachings with its derived meaning.

[38] T 45.482b19–21.

[39] See T 45.482c5ff.

as the one vehicle but at a different place. This qualification is important because it provides Fa-tsang with another occasion to subordinate the common teaching to the separate teaching. Since numerous other texts claim that they were taught in Deer Park (Mṛgadāva) during the second week after the Buddha's enlightenment, the question arises as to why the place is different if the time is the same. Fa-tsang answers:

> In order to preach the dharma, sameness and difference were required in regard to time and place [respectively]. Thus the *Ti-lun* says: "It is by comparing such things as time and place that superiority is shown."[40] Hence sameness of time reveals that it is the common teaching, and difference of place indicates that it is not the separate teaching. The case of the one vehicle of the separate teaching having been taught beneath the bodhi tree makes clear that that was the place where bodhi was obtained; that is, it reveals that the dharma the Tathāgata himself acquired was taught in accord with the fundamental (*pen*) [truth] and was therefore taught without [the Buddha] changing his place [from beneath the bodhi tree]. [The case of] the other dharmas, such as the three vehicles and so forth, makes clear that [the place] was changed to accord with the capacity of beings. Thus, that the place was changed and the dharma was taught in the Deer Park to beings according to their capacity reveals that it was not the fundamental [truth].[41]

These points are picked up and expanded in the eighth chapter of Fa-tsang's treatise, which is devoted to clarifying the differences between the one vehicle and three vehicles.[42] In this chapter Fa-tsang enumerates ten ways in which these two types of teaching differ: the one vehicle differs from the three vehicles in terms of time (it was taught during the second week after the Buddha's enlightenment); place (it was taught under the bodhi tree); teacher (it was taught by Vairocana Buddha); assembly (it was taught only to the most advanced bodhisattvas); basis (it was taught on the basis of the samādhi of oceanic reflection); teaching (each part of its teaching contains the totality of its teaching); stages (it teaches that each stage of spiritual progress includes all the others); practice (it teaches that one practice includes all practices); numerical categories (whereas the three vehicles give different numbers for various doctrinal categories, the one vehicle gives ten),[43] and phenomena (*shih*) (it teaches that each phe-

[40] *Shih-ti ching lun*, T 26.124a9.

[41] T 45.483a1–9; adapted from Cook, "Fa-tsang's Treatise," pp. 193–194.

[42] T 45.483c7–484b25; Cook, "Fa-tsang's Treatise," pp. 204–213.

[43] The artificiality of this point illustrates the importance of the number ten (symbolizing perfection or wholeness) in Hua-yen thought.

nomenon contains all other phenomena without obstruction). The last five points Fa-tsang enumerates also serve to emphasize that the unique content that separates the one vehicle from the three vehicles is its teaching of the harmonious interrelation of all phenomena, what Fa-tsang refers to as the conditioned origination of the dharma-dhātu and what the later tradition will refer to as *shih-shih wu-ai*. Fa-tsang's treatment of the content of the perfect teaching thus differs from Chih-yen's. As Yoshizu Yoshihide has demonstrated, not only did the notion of the conditioned origination of the dharmadhātu not occupy such a central place in Chih-yen's thought, but Chih-yen also did not tie it to a specific teaching in the way that Fa-tsang did within his doctrinal classification scheme.[44] In his *Shih-hsüan men*, for example, Chih-yen wrote that the reality of conditioned origination had to be understood from the dual perspective of the common and separate teachings.[45]

These examples should suffice to show that Fa-tsang emphasized the disjunction between the one and three vehicles. In this regard his systematization of Hua-yen thought marks a decided break with Chih-yen. In stressing the connection between the one and the three vehicles, Chih-yen had based himself on the "logic" of subsuming the three into the one (*hui-san kuei-i*) associated with the *Lotus Sūtra*. As has been seen, Fa-tsang relegated the *Lotus* (and its common teaching) to a somewhat less exalted status as the advanced teaching of the great vehicle—he placed it, that is, within the teachings of the three vehicles. By emphasizing the disjunction between the one and three vehicles, Fa-tsang also drove a wedge between the separate and common teachings, which Chih-yen had seen as necessarily interrelated aspects of the one vehicle. Fa-tsang's systematization of Hua-yen thought in terms of his five teachings clearly establishes the preeminence of the *Hua-yen Sūtra* over all other scriptures, at once giving a distinct identity and coherent form to the comparatively inchoate teachings he had inherited from Chih-yen as well as strengthening the basis on which he could claim that the Hua-yen tradition represented the pinnacle of Buddhist thought.

The new importance that Fa-tsang assigns to p'an-chiao as the vehicle through which to assert the supremacy of his own tradition lends his thought a sectarian character not seen in Chih-yen. Fa-tsang's separation of the common and separate teachings of the one vehicle not only subordinates the *Lotus* to the *Hua-yen Sūtra*, it also clearly places the T'ien-t'ai tradition in a qualitatively lower category

[44] See *Kegonzen*, "Hōzō no hokai engi setsu," chap. 1, sec. 4, pp. 49–66.
[45] T 45.585c27–29.

of teaching than Hua-yen. His p'an-chiao, moreover, is noteworthy for relegating the Fa-hsiang brand of Yogācāra introduced into China by Hsüan-tsang to an even more inferior position, one that is also decidedly subordinate to the earlier Chinese understanding of Yogācāra represented by the Ti- and She-lun traditions. Fa-tsang's low assessment of Fa-hsiang may well have been a major factor in attracting the patronage of Empress Wu, who, in her efforts to legitimate her own dynasty, sought to associate her reign with a new form of Buddhism, one that was not connected with the Fa-hsiang teachings patronized by her T'ang predecessors or the T'ien-t'ai sponsored by the previous Sui dynasty.[46] Imperial support, in turn, may also have stimulated the new sectarian consciousness noted in Fa-tsang. However difficult it may be to specify the precise causal relationship between the content and structure of Fa-tsang's p'an-chiao and Empress Wu's political and ideological agenda, the new sectarian consciousness evidenced in Fa-tsang's systematization of Hua-yen seems to go hand in hand with Empress Wu's support. In any case, imperial patronage helped give an institutional identity to Fa-tsang's systematization of Hua-yen thought.

It is also in the context of the emerging sectarian identity of Hua-yen as a self-consciously distinct tradition of Buddhism that Fa-tsang's *Hua-yen ching chuan-chi* (A record of the transmission of the *Hua-yen Sūtra*) should be understood.[47] This work discusses the mythic origins of the text, its primordial version preached by the Buddha Vairocana in the ocean of the lotus-womb world while in the samādhi of oceanic reflection, its being hidden away in the nāga palace under the ocean after the death of the Buddha, and its eventual rescue by Nāgārjuna some six hundred years later.[48] It gives much useful information on the different translations and translators of the text, as well as chapters and sections of the text that had been translated as independent works. It also gives biographies of famous exegetes, reciters, and copyists of the scripture, which contain much fascinating cultic lore. Fa-tsang's stories of miracle-working monks, who took the *Hua-yen Sūtra* as the central focus of their religious devotions, validate the

---

[46] See Weinstein, "Imperial Patronage," pp. 297–306; Weinstein, *Buddhism under the T'ang*, pp. 37–47; Kamata, *Chūgoku kegon*, pp. 107–128; and Kamata, "Chūtō no bukkyō no hendō to kokka kenryoku." For a discussion of Empress Wu's political manipulation of Buddhism as a means of legitimating her rule, see Guisso, *Wu Tse-t'ien*, pp. 26–50, and Antonino Forte, *Political Propaganda and Ideology in China at the End of the Seventh Century*.

[47] T no. 2073.

[48] See T 51.153a–c. See Liu, "The Teaching of Fa-tsang," pp. 36–37, for a more detailed paraphrase.

awesome power of the scripture. His accounts of the ritual and communal practices associated with the early Hua-yen cult as it took form around such charismatics in China help to define the Hua-yen as a historically self-conscious tradition.[49] Fa-tsang's *Hua-yen ching chuan-chi* thus legitimates the sectarian claim of Hua-yen to represent an authentic and historically distinct tradition of Chinese Buddhism with its own special claim to preeminence.

Tsung-mi's Classification Scheme

The difference between Chih-yen's and Fa-tsang's use of p'an-chiao categories reflects the changing historical situation in which the Hua-yen tradition found itself from the early to mid T'ang. A comparison of Tsung-mi's system of doctrinal classification with that of Fa-tsang likewise highlights the changes that took place within the Chinese Buddhist world in the late T'ang. The most important of these was the rise of Ch'an, which, as later chapters will show, accounts for the decidedly soteriological use to which Tsung-mi adapted p'an-chiao.

Tsung-mi's mature system of doctrinal classification is developed in his *Inquiry into the Origin of Man* and *Ch'an Preface*. Like Fa-tsang, he divides the Buddha's teachings into five categories. Yet when one compares their arrangements, there are several striking differences:

Fa-tsang	Tsung-mi
	(1) Men and gods
(1) Hīnayāna ⟶	(2) Hīnayāna
(2) Elementary Mahāyāna	
(a) Fa-hsiang/Yogācāra ⟶	(3) Analysis of phenomenal appearances
(b) Madhyamaka ⟶	(4) Negation of phenomenal appearances
(3) Advanced Mahāyāna ⟶	(5) Reveals the nature
(4) Sudden	
(5) Perfect	

Since subsequent chapters will discuss Tsung-mi's p'an-chiao in detail, it is not necessary to do more here than point out some of the more salient ways in which it differs from Fa-tsang's. The first point to note is that Tsung-mi adds as his first category a teaching not found in Fa-tsang's scheme. The teaching of men and gods, which

---

[49] I have discussed some of these miracle-working monks and their role in the formation of the early Hua-yen cult in "The Teaching of Men and Gods," pp. 278–296. See also Kamata, *Chūgoku kegon*, pp. 42–47 and 235–248.

adumbrates the workings of karmic retribution, is the teaching addressed primarily to the laity. As I have argued elsewhere, Tsung-mi's inclusion of this teaching as his first category in his p'an-chiao scheme reflects the growing importance of lay religious societies as part of the changing patterns of patronage in the post–An Lu-shan era.[50]

The two most significant changes, however, deal with the teachings that Tsung-mi eliminates from his scheme. He omits the sudden and perfect teachings, the highest two categories in Fa-tsang's scheme, and in their stead cedes pride of place to the teaching that Fa-tsang had merely ranked as third. Tsung-mi identified himself with the Ch'an tradition of Ho-tse Shen-hui; Shen-hui was, of course, the figure who denounced the gradualist approach of Northern Ch'an and hailed the teaching of Hui-neng as representing the sudden teaching. Is it not strange that Tsung-mi, a "patriarch" in this tradition, did not include the sudden teaching in his classification scheme? Tsung-mi's displacement of the perfect teaching seems equally surprising given that this teaching is identified as the teaching of the *Hua-yen Sūtra* par excellence. How could Tsung-mi, a Hua-yen "patriarch" no less, omit from his classification of Buddhist teachings the very teaching that his tradition had taken as its chief warrant? What could Tsung-mi have seen in the teaching that reveals the nature that was so crucial that it justified displacing the sudden and perfect teachings altogether?

In seeking to answer these questions, the following chapters will show how Tsung-mi's emphasis on soteriology reveals the impact that Ch'an had in altering the context of Chinese Buddhism in the eighth and early ninth centuries. The changes within the formulation of Hua-yen doctrinal categories surveyed within this chapter also illustrate the dynamic and evolving character of a tradition (*tsung*) such as Hua-yen and thereby serve as a useful caution against the tendency to define Hua-yen in normative terms.

[50] See my "The Teaching of Men and Gods."

Chapter Five

THE SUDDEN TEACHING

So FAR I have discussed the difference between Fa-tsang's and Chih-yen's p'an-chiao schemes in terms of their evaluations of the one vehicle in regard to the common and separate teachings. As has been seen, another significant difference between them had to do with their understanding of the sudden teaching. Whereas Chih-yen had followed the established custom in Chinese p'an-chiao of classifying the *Hua-yen Sūtra* as the sudden teaching, Fa-tsang disengaged the sūtra from the sudden teaching altogether. He thereby also broke the connection that Chih-yen had made (following Hui-kuang) between the perfect and sudden teachings. By so doing he accentuated the wholly unique status of the *Hua-yen Sūtra*, which he identified exclusively with the perfect teaching. His dissociation of the sudden teaching from the *Hua-yen Sūtra* is thus connected with the qualitative distinction he drew between the common and separate teachings.

Fa-tsang's redefinition of the sudden teaching, however, only raised further problems for the subsequent tradition. The status of the sudden teaching remained problematic for Hua-yen scholars throughout the T'ang. Fa-tsang's disciple Hui-yüan criticized Fa-tsang's treatment of the sudden teaching for going against the principles according to which Fa-tsang had classified the other teachings in his fivefold scheme and accordingly devised his own fourfold classification scheme that omitted the sudden teaching. Ch'eng-kuan in turn criticized Hui-yüan's omission of the sudden teaching and defended Fa-tsang's fivefold classification scheme by identifying the sudden teaching with Ch'an. In so doing, however, he gave the sudden teaching a new meaning. Tsung-mi could not accept Ch'eng-kuan's identification of the sudden teaching with Ch'an, which thus subordinated Ch'an to Hua-yen, and went on to argue that "sudden" did not refer to a specific teaching of the Buddha so much as it did a particular way in which the Buddha had taught. His classification scheme accordingly omits the sudden teaching entirely.

Examining the changing status of the sudden teaching within the Hua-yen tradition should help illuminate some of the dynamics at work within the tradition as well as clarify some of the major currents within the Chinese Buddhist world of the eighth century that affected Hua-yen, such as the emergence of Ch'an and the revival of T'ien-t'ai.[1]

THE SUDDEN TEACHING ACCORDING TO FA-TSANG

In dissociating the sudden teaching from the *Hua-yen Sūtra*, Fa-tsang gave the sudden teaching a new content. A good example of what Fa-tsang meant by the sudden teaching can be found in the first definition that he gives it in the *Treatise on the Five Teachings*: "In the sudden teaching all words and explanations are suddenly cut off, the nature of the truth is suddenly revealed, understanding and practice are suddenly perfected, and Buddhahood [is attained] upon the non-production of a single moment of thought."[2]

As canonical authority, Fa-tsang goes on to quote the passage from the *Laṅkāvatāra Sūtra* that says that the purification of beings can be spoken of as sudden "just as images in a mirror are reflected suddenly, not gradually."[3] Moreover, in this definition the sudden teaching is explicitly contrasted with the former two teachings in Fa-tsang's p'an-chiao scheme, those of the elementary and advanced Mahāyāna, which are characterized as gradual because "the understanding and practice within them lie within words and explanations, the stages [of the bodhisattva's path] are sequential, cause and effect follow from one another, and one proceeds from the subtle to the manifest."[4]

While Fa-tsang discusses the sudden teaching in different ways from a variety of perspectives throughout the *Treatise on the Five Teachings*,[5] his overall characterization, as the definition just cited suggests, can be analyzed as having two aspects—the first having to do with its doctrinal content, and the second with its practical application.[6] According to the first, the sudden teaching is described as aban-

---

[1] This chapter adapts my "The Teaching of the Sudden Teaching within the Hua-yen Tradition" previously published in *The Journal of the International Association of Buddhist Studies*. The major difference is that I have revised my assessment of the importance of the T'ien-t'ai influence on Tsung-mi.

[2] T 45.481b16–18; cf. Cook, "Fa-tsang's Treatise," pp. 174–175.

[3] Ibid. Fa-tsang is here paraphrasing the sūtra. The passage in question can be found in T 16.486a8 (Guṇabhadra), 525b2–3 (Bodhiruci), and 596b4–5 (Śikṣānanda); cf. Suzuki's translation, *The Laṅkāvatāra Sūtra*, p. 50.

[4] T 45.481b13–15; cf. Cook, "Fa-tsang's Treatise," p. 174. The teaching of the lesser vehicle would, of course, also be included with the gradual teachings.

[5] Fa-tsang discusses the sudden teaching from ten different points of view in the ninth chapter of his *Treatise on the Five Teachings*; see T 45.485b2–7 (Cook, "Fa-tsang's Treatise," p. 223), 487c24–28 (Cook, p. 255), 489b16–23 (Cook, p. 272), 491a5–7 (Cook, p. 291), 492b1–3 (Cook, p. 308), 495c20–25 (Cook, p. 358), 496c6–7 (Cook, p. 368), 497b4–8 (Cook, p. 378), 498b8–10 (Cook, p. 393), and 498c14 (Cook, p. 399).

[6] See Liu, "The Teaching of Fa-tsang," pp. 195–196.

doning all words and concepts because there can be no dichotomous discrimination in the apprehension of the ultimate nature of reality, which ineluctably defies all attempts to verbalize or conceptualize its essence. The canonical paradigm to which Fa-tsang refers most frequently to illustrate this aspect of the sudden teaching is Vimalakīrti's resounding silence, which marks the climax of the ninth chapter of Kumārajīva's translation of the *Vimalakīrti Sūtra*.[7] The chapter begins with Vimalakīrti's request that all the bodhisattvas present express their understanding of the dharma of nonduality. The responses of each of the first thirty-one bodhisattvas all begin by stating a well-known polarity (such as saṃsāra and nirvāṇa, etc.) and then saying that the truth transcends it. Mañjuśrī, the personification of wisdom, then tells the bodhisattvas that they have all indeed spoken well, but the truth is ultimately ineffable. He then asks the honored layman to express his understanding, whereupon Vimalakīrti remains silent. Mañjuśrī then exclaims: "Excellent! Excellent! To be without words and speech! That is called the true entrance into the dharma of nonduality!"[8]

No matter how profound or eloquent their replies, the answers of all the bodhisattvas still fall within the province of either the elementary or advanced teaching, for they still rely on words to try to express the inexpressible. Only Vimalakīrti succeeds in directly expressing the ineffable nature of ultimate reality by his refusal to enter the realm of dichotomous discourse. Fa-tsang aptly indicates the qualitative difference in their responses by saying that the thirty-two bodhisattvas merely "spoke about" (*shuo*) the dharma of nonduality, whereas Vimalakīrti "revealed" (*hsien*) it.[9]

As this example from the *Vimalakīrti Sūtra* also indicates, what Vimalakīrti succeeds in revealing through his silence and what the other bodhisattvas try, but inevitably fail, to express in words is the same ultimate reality. The difference between their responses lies in the manner in which they express, or try to express, the true nature of this reality. When Mañjuśrī says, "In my opinion, to be without words, without speech, without indication, without knowing, and beyond all questions and answers in regard to all things—that is entering the dharma of nonduality,"[10] he merely says what it is. Only Vimala-

---

[7] See T 14.550b–551c; cf. Charles Luk, trans., *The Vimalakīrti Nirdeśa Sūtra*, pp. 92–100. The same chapter appears as number eight in the Tibetan translation; cf. Étienne Lamotte, trans., *L'Enseignement de Vimalakīrti*, pp. 301–318.

[8] T 14.551c23–24.

[9] See, for example, T 45.485b3–4.

[10] T 14.551c23–24.

kīrti's silence succeeds in directly manifesting the true import of Mañjuśrī's words.

If Vimalakīrti's silence is taken as the paradigm upon which Fa-tsang establishes the sudden teaching, then the sudden teaching does not differ in content from the advanced teaching, which Fa-tsang identifies as the one mind of suchness (chen-ju i-hsin) in another passage in the *Treatise on the Five Teachings*:

> According to the sudden teaching, all things are nothing but the one mind of suchness, wherein all discriminations have utterly ceased. The dharma of nonduality as spoken of by the thirty-two bodhisattvas in the *Vimalakīrti Sūtra* corresponds to the harmonious interfusion of the pure and impure without duality in the previous teaching of the advanced [Mahāyāna], while the nonduality transcending words that was revealed by Vimalakīrti corresponds to this [sudden] teaching. Because all pure and impure characteristics have been utterly brought to an end and there are no longer any two things that can be harmonized with one another, the ineffable is nonduality.[11]

This passage is of further interest in that it makes clear that what Fa-tsang has in mind when he discusses the content of these two teachings is the tathāgatagarbha as expounded in the *Awakening of Faith*. The following passage from the *Treatise on the Five Teachings* makes this connection with the *Awakening of Faith* even more explicit.

> Within the *Awakening of Faith*, it is in connection with the sudden teaching that the suchness transcending words is revealed and in connection with the gradual teaching that the suchness predicated in words is expounded. Within [the suchness] predicated in words, it is in connection with the elementary and advanced teaching that the empty and nonempty [aspects of] suchness are expounded.[12]

Fa-tsang is here basing himself on a passage in the beginning of the *Awakening of Faith* that distinguishes between suchness transcending words (chen-ju li-yen) and suchness predicated in words (chen-ju i-yen).

> What is called the nature of the mind neither is born nor dies. It is only on the basis of deluded thinking that all of the dharmas come to be differentiated. If one frees oneself from deluded thoughts, then there are no longer any phenomenal appearances of external objects. Therefore, from the very beginning all dharmas transcend all forms of verbalization, description, and conceptualization and are ultimately undifferen-

---

[11] T 45.485b2–7; cf. Cook, "Fa-tsang's Treatise," p. 223. Cf. Chih-yen's *K'ung-mu chang*, T 45.558c17–559a2.

[12] T 45.481c6–8; cf. Cook, "Fa-tsang's Treatise," pp. 176–177.

tiated, unchanging, and indestructible. Because they are nothing but the one mind, they are referred to as suchness. Because all verbal explanations are merely provisional designations without any reality* and are merely used in accordance with false thoughts and cannot denote [suchness], the term "suchness" is without any [determinate] characteristics. This means that it is the limit of verbal expression wherein a word is used to put an end to words. . . . Because all things are ineffable and inconceivable, they are referred to as "suchness."[13]

This passage refers to the suchness transcending words, which is suchness in its true (*shih*) aspect, as distinguished from the suchness predicated in words, which is only provisional (*chia*).

The *Awakening of Faith* then introduces the suchness predicated in words, which it says has two aspects. The first is termed "the truly empty (*ju-shih k'ung*) because it is ultimately able to reveal what is real," and the second is termed "the truly non-empty (*ju-shih pu-k'ung*) because it is in its very essence fully endowed with undefiled excellent qualities."[14]

As these various passages make clear, the sudden teaching is represented for Fa-tsang by Vimalakīrti's silence and is based on the *Awakening of Faith's* suchness transcending words, while the gradual teaching—denoting, in this context, both the elementary and advanced teachings—is represented by the replies of the thirty-two bodhisattvas and is based on the *Awakening of Faith's* suchness predicated in words. Moreover, the sudden and gradual teachings do not differ in content, only in the way in which they express that content. Fa-tsang thus makes the following equations:

elementary teaching = empty aspect of suchness predicated in words
advanced teaching = nonempty aspect of suchness predicated in words
sudden teaching = suchness transcending words

As the initial definition of the sudden teaching cited above indicates, however—and as Fa-tsang makes clear in other contexts—there is also another aspect to his characterization of this teaching, one that bears on the nature of religious practice. That is, the sudden teaching is the teaching that it is possible to attain Buddhahood suddenly, in a single moment of thought, without having to progress step-by-step through a long and arduous succession of stages on the path. As Fa-tsang says in the *Treatise on the Five Teachings*, "According to the sudden teaching, all stages of practice are without exception ineffable

[13] T 32.576a8–18; I have adapted the translation of Yoshito S. Hakeda, *The Awakening of Faith*, pp. 32–33.
[14] Ibid., 576a24–26; cf. Hakeda, *The Awakening of Faith*, p. 34.

because they transcend all forms, because Buddhahood [is attained] upon the nonproduction of a single moment of thought, and because, if one perceives forms such as distinctions in the stages of practice, then that is an erroneous view."[15] The three scriptural passages that Fa-tsang quotes as canonical authority for this characterization of the sudden teaching[16] are:

1. *Viśeṣacintābrahmaparipṛcchā*. If someone hears of the true nature of all things and diligently practices accordingly, then he will not advance stage-by-stage, and, if he does not advance stage by stage, then he will not abide in either saṃsāra or nirvāṇa.[17]

2. *Laṅkāvatāra*. The first stage is identical with the eighth stage. . . . Since there are no [stages] that exist, how could there be a sequence [of stages]?[18]

3. *Daśabhūmika*. The ten stages are like the traces of a bird in the sky. How could there be differences that could be attained?[19]

The sudden teaching for Fa-tsang thus not only indicates a superior way of revealing the true nature of reality but also contains a specific teaching about the true nature of religious practice. The second aspect of Fa-tsang's characterization of this teaching grows out of the first, both being based on the *Awakening of Faith*. Just as the true nature of suchness lacks all determinate characteristics and any attempt to express it in words is therefore merely provisionally true at best, so too the distinctions among the various stages of religious practice are only provisional and do not obtain in the realm of suchness. It is therefore possible, by realizing their empty nature, to transcend them. The second aspect can thus be seen as an extension of the first to the realm of practice, and, as such, seems to intimate the teaching of sudden enlightenment that was to become the battle cry of Ch'an Buddhists in the eighth century, although Fa-tsang does not use the term "sudden enlightenment," nor does he refer to the Ch'an tradition.[20]

---

[15] T 45.489b16–19; cf. Cook, "Fa-tsang's Treatise," p. 272. Cf. also *K'ung-mu chang*, T 45.537c9–10.

[16] Fa-tsang refers to all three of the following passages in his *T'an-hsüan chi*, T 35.115c13–17, but only to the first two in his *Treatise on the Five Teachings*, T 45.489b16–23.

[17] See T 15.36c6–8. Fa-tsang has abridged the passage slightly.

[18] T 16.509c22–24; cf. Suzuki, *The Laṅkāvatāra Sūtra*, p. 189.

[19] Fa-tsang seems to be paraphrasing rather than quoting. See T 9.544b18–19. Sakamoto (*Kegon kyōgaku*, p. 260, n. 37) locates the passage as coming from T 26.133c.

[20] See n. 26 below.

THE PROBLEMATICAL NATURE OF THE SUDDEN TEACHING

The first to raise the issue of the problematical nature of the sudden teaching within Fa-tsang's p'an-chiao scheme was Fa-tsang's own favored disciple, Hui-yüan. In his discussion of Fa-tsang's system of doctrinal classification in the *K'an-ting chi*, Hui-yüan delivers the following criticism of the inclusion of the sudden teaching in Fa-tsang's fivefold scheme:

> You should know that this [sudden teaching] abandons the use of language (*wang-ch'üan*) to reveal the truth (*li*). How, then, can it be established as [a teaching that] can be expressed in words (*neng-ch'üan*)? If it is a teaching, then what truth (*li*) does it express? If one were to say that the teaching is not separate from the truth (*li*) because it transcends words, then surely it must be true that the advanced and perfect teachings [also] transcend words. But, if one admits that [teachings that] transcend words must always be called "sudden," then why are there five teachings? If one were to claim that, even though it is [a teaching that] expounds the transcendence of words, it still does not exclude the use of words, then the advanced and perfect teachings should also be called "sudden" because they both transcend words while not excluding the use of words.[21]

Hui-yüan's criticism is twofold. His first point can be restated in the following terms: For something to qualify as a teaching (*chiao*), there must be a certain content (*so-ch'üan, li*) that it is able to express (*neng-ch'üan*). If the "teaching" in question abandons the use of language (*wang-ch'üan*), however, and thereby has no way in which to express itself (*neng-ch'üan*), then there can be no content that it expresses (*so-ch'üan*), and it consequently fails to meet the criterion necessary to qualify as a teaching. Since Fa-tsang's sudden teaching is characterized precisely by its rejection of language to express the truth, it is thus a contradiction in terms to establish it as a teaching. On the other hand, if it is admitted that the sudden teaching does succeed in expressing the truth, then it cannot completely abandon all modes of expression, for the truth (*li*) cannot be expressed (*so-ch'üan*) without some means of expression (*neng-ch'üan*). This conclusion brings one to the second point raised by Hui-yüan's criticism: If the content of the sudden teaching is the truth that transcends words and is ultimately inexpressible, then it hardly differs from either the advanced or perfect teaching. There is therefore no reason to establish it as a separate teaching.

[21] HTC 5.12a; cf. Sakamoto, *Kegon kyōgaku*, pp. 248–250.

Hui-yüan's criticism raises the question of the taxonomical consistency of Fa-tsang's p'an-chiao scheme. The organizing principle according to which Fa-tsang seems to be operating in his classification of Buddhist teachings has to do with ranking the teachings according to their content. Since the sudden teaching has the same content as the advanced teaching, it cannot be set up as a separate category of teaching without doing violence to the taxonomical principle according to which the other teachings are arranged.

The problematic nature of the sudden teaching within Fa-tsang's p'an-chiao scheme becomes even more apparent when viewed in terms of the systematic formulation of the T'ien-t'ai p'an-chiao first articulated by Chan-jan in the middle of the eighth century.[22] Chan-

---

[22] Sekiguchi Shindai has demonstrated that it was Chan-jan, and not Chih-i, who formulated the system of the five periods and eight teachings (wu-shih pa-chiao) that has been generally regarded as representing the essence of T'ien-t'ai thought. It is impossible to do justice to the full scope of Sekiguchi's arguments here. Suffice it to say that he shows that not only does Chih-i never employ the term "five periods and eight teachings" in any of his writings, but also that he never systematically formulated a p'an-chiao scheme corresponding to that of the five periods and eight teachings. In place of the five periods, for example, Chih-i emphasizes the five flavors (wu-wei), a metaphor of far broader range than the more narrowly chronological framework of the five periods. Chih-i only enumerates what were later collectively designated as the "eight teachings" twice within the entirety of his voluminous opera (see T 34.3b3–4 and T 46.97c21). Nor, more significantly in the present context, does Chih-i distinguish between teachings to be classified according to the content of their exposition (hua-fa chiao) and those classified according to the method of their exposition (hua-i chiao). Rather, he separately elaborates in different works the types of teachings that were later included within these two classificatory rubrics. In his Fa-hua hsüan-i, Chih-i discusses the characteristics of the teachings according to the threefold typology— sudden (tun), gradual (chien), and variable (pu-ting)—that later served as the basis for the so-called four teachings according to the method of their exposition (hua-i ssu-chiao). While Chih-i sometimes also mentions a fourth type of teaching—the secret (mi-mi), corresponding to the fourth type of teaching in the four teachings according to the method of their exposition—his use of the threefold typology—corresponding, as it does, to his three types of discernment (san-kuan)—is much more common in his thought. It is only in his Ssu-chiao i (T no. 1929) and his commentary to the Vimalakīrti Sūtra that Chih-i elaborates the four teachings—tripiṭaka (san-tsang), common (t'ung), separate (pieh), and perfect (yüan)—that were later designated as the four teachings according to the content of their exposition (hua-fa ssu-chiao). See Sekiguchi's "Goji hakkyō no kigen" and Chappell's "Introduction to the T'ien-t'ai ssu-chiao-i."

Sekiguchi's findings are corroborated by the evidence that can be gleaned from the Hua-yen tradition. Neither Fa-tsang nor Hui-yüan makes any reference to the five periods and eight teachings in their discussions of T'ien-t'ai p'an-chiao. Both discuss Chih-i's system under the heading of those former scholars who had classified the Buddha's teachings in four categories. The four categories that both Fa-tsang and Hui-yüan enumerate are those of the tripiṭaka, common, separate, and perfect; neither mentions the sudden, gradual, and variable. Ch'eng-kuan, who had studied under Chan-jan, is the first to mention the distinction between the teachings to be classified

jan, reckoned as the sixth patriarch in the T'ien-t'ai tradition, was responsible for the revival of the fortunes of the T'ien-t'ai teachings in the later T'ang after a century or more of almost total eclipse. More important in the present context, Chan-jan also seems to have been the first to make explicit the crucial distinction in the taxonomy of Buddhist teachings between the classification of teachings according to the method of their exposition (*hua-i chiao*) and according to the content of their exposition (*hua-fa chiao*). According to Chan-jan's creative synthesis of the various forms of doctrinal classification variously used by Chih-i in his different works, the sudden teaching falls within the category of teachings that should be classified according to the method of their exposition, whereas all of the other teachings in Fa-tsang's p'an-chiao scheme would have to be categorized as teachings that should be classified according to the content of their exposition. The distinction between these two ways of classifying Buddhist teachings introduced by Chan-jan—and later adopted by Tsung-mi—makes clear the taxonomical confusion entailed by Fa-tsang's inclusion of the sudden teaching within his fivefold classification scheme.

THE SUDDEN TEACHING AND CH'AN

The question of the sudden teaching takes on a new and extra-doctrinal dimension with Ch'eng-kuan. One of the main reasons for Ch'eng-kuan's attack on Hui-yüan had to do with Hui-yüan's exclusion of the sudden teaching from his own fourfold classification scheme and his related criticism of Fa-tsang's scheme for having included it. After quoting Hui-yüan's first point of criticism, Ch'eng-kuan offers his own defense of Fa-tsang's inclusion of the sudden teaching:

> "Because it suddenly expresses the truth, it is called 'the sudden teaching' " means that what is expressed is the truth (*li*). How could it be that the sudden preaching of the truth in this case is not able to express [the truth]? Now, teachings that are able to express [truth] are always established in accordance with [the truth] that they express. For instance, if it expresses [the truth of] the three vehicles, then it is a gradual teaching; if it expresses the unobstructed interrelation of each and every thing, then it is the perfect teaching. How could it be that if that which is expressed is the truth, [Hui-yüan] could not admit that that which is able to express it is a teaching? How could he have criticized [this teaching]

---

according to the method of their exposition and according to the content of their exposition.

by saying, "then what truth [does it express]?" That is the epitome of delusion![23]

In arguing that the sudden teaching must be a teaching because it expresses the truth, Ch'eng-kuan misses the point of Hui-yüan's criticism that, if the sudden teaching by definition discards all means of expressing the truth, then there is nothing that it can be said to express. In fact, Ch'eng-kuan's attempted rebuttal only raises Hui-yüan's second criticism, which Ch'eng-kuan makes no effort to address. Ch'eng-kuan's rather lame response suggests that it is not just a question of doctrine that is at stake. Instead of attempting to show how the truth expressed by the sudden teaching differs from that of the advanced or perfect teachings, Ch'eng-kuan comes to the real substance of his objection when he says:

> Because [Hui-yüan] never penetrated Ch'an, he was utterly deluded about the true meaning of the sudden [teaching]. . . . The mind-to-mind transmission of Bodhidharma truly refers to this [sudden] teaching. If a single word were not used to express directly that this very mind is Buddha, how could the essentials of the mind be transmitted? Therefore, using words that are wordless, the truth that transcends words is directly expressed. . . . The Northern and Southern lines of Ch'an are [both] comprised within the sudden teaching.[24]

What is really at issue for Ch'eng-kuan is the fact that he takes the sudden teaching to refer to Ch'an, and it is important to recall that, in addition to being honored as the fourth Hua-yen patriarch by the later tradition, Ch'eng-kuan was also closely associated with various Ch'an lines of his days. As already noted, the *Sung kao-seng chuan* credits Ch'eng-kuan with having studied under masters in three different Ch'an traditions.[25]

Even though it is highly unlikely that Fa-tsang could have had Ch'an in mind when he discussed the sudden teaching in the *Treatise on the Five Teachings*,[26] Ch'eng-kuan's identification of the sudden

[23] *Yen-i ch'ao*, T36.62a10–15; cf. Sakamoto, *Kegon kyōgaku*, pp. 50–51. The quote at the beginning of the passage is from Ch'eng-kuan's *Hua-yen ching shu*, T 35.512c2, to which this passage is a commentary.

[24] T 36.62a21–22 and b1–4.

[25] See chapter 2, pp. 64–65 and n. 150.

[26] The *Treatise on the Five Teachings* was an early work and seems to have been composed before 684, when Fa-tsang met the Indian monk Divākara (see Liu, "The Teaching of Fa-tsang," pp. 24–26). The Northern Ch'an master Shen-hsiu did not enter the capital until 701, when he was given a lavish reception by Empress Wu. There is little chance that Fa-tsang would have had occasion to become acquainted with Ch'an teachings before this event. Nor is it clear that any of the traditions of the late seventh and

teaching with Ch'an does provide a way in which Fa-tsang's fivefold classification scheme can be salvaged from Hui-yüan's criticism. As noted before, Fa-tsang's characterization of the sudden teaching can be analyzed as having two aspects. While Hui-yüan's critique holds against the first aspect, according to which the sudden teaching differs from the advanced teaching only in its method of exposition but not in its content, it does not fare so well against the second aspect, which has to do with religious practice. That is, even though the sudden teaching does not reveal any new truth about the ultimate nature of reality, it may still have something unique to say about the nature of religious practice, and it is in this context that it can still be considered as a bona fide teaching in its own right.[27] Nevertheless, in so identifying the sudden teaching with Ch'an, Ch'eng-kuan has given to this teaching a totally different valuation from that found in the *Treatise on the Five Teachings*, where the "practical" aspect of this teaching was of secondary importance.

More important, Ch'eng-kuan's identification of the sudden teaching with Ch'an points to the enormous impact that the rise of Ch'an had on other forms of Chinese Buddhism in the eighth century. That century witnessed the transformation of Ch'an from a little-known and isolated phenomenon into a large scale movement whose ramifications affected the course of Chinese Buddhism as a whole. More than anything else it is the presence of Ch'an that gives the Hua-yen writings of Ch'eng-kuan and Tsung-mi an entirely different cast from those of Fa-tsang.

THE SUDDEN TEACHING IN TSUNG-MI'S THOUGHT

Tsung-mi was even more closely identified with Ch'an than was his Hua-yen mentor Ch'eng-kuan. Nevertheless, Tsung-mi did not identify the sudden teaching with Ch'an as Ch'eng-kuan had done. Nor, for a number of reasons, did he establish the sudden teaching as a separate category in his p'an-chiao scheme.

First of all, Tsung-mi could not make the kind of blanket identification that Ch'eng-kuan had made in subsuming different Ch'an lines together under the sudden teaching. When Tsung-mi formulated his p'an-chiao scheme in the *Inquiry into the Origin of Man*, almost half a century had elapsed since Ch'eng-kuan had written his *Yen-i ch'ao*, a period in which Ch'an had become even more influential and the differences among the various Ch'an lines had become even more

---

early eighth centuries that were later identified as Ch'an were seen by their followers as belonging to a "Ch'an School."

[27] The same point is made by Liu, "The Teaching of Fa-tsang," p. 196.

apparent, especially the difference between the Northern and Southern lines. As a successor to the Ho-tse line, whose founder, Shen-hui, had championed Southern Ch'an as teaching sudden enlightenment and had disparaged Northern Ch'an as teaching a gradualistic form of practice, Tsung-mi could not have placed the two lines of Ch'an in the same category. Rather, he makes a point of distinguishing between them. For instance, in the *Ch'an Chart*, a work that seeks to clarify the historical roots and doctrinal characteristics of the major Ch'an lines of his day, Tsung-mi says:

> The Southern line is the true line in which the robe and dharma have been uninterruptedly transmitted over successive generations from the time when the great master Hui-neng of Ts'ao-ch'i received the essence of Bodhidharma's teaching. Later, because Shen-hsiu widely spread the gradual teaching in the north, it was called the Southern line to distinguish it [from the Northern line of Shen-hsiu].[28]
>
> . . . . .
>
> After the priest Hui-neng died, the gradual teaching of the Northern line was greatly practiced and thus became an obstacle to the wide-scale transmission of the sudden teaching. . . . In the beginning of the T'ienpao era [742–756] Ho-tse [Shen-hui] entered Lo-yang and, as soon as he proclaimed this teaching, made it known that the descendants of Shenhsiu were collateral and that their teaching was gradual. Since the two lines were being practiced side by side, people of the time wanted to distinguish between them; therefore the use of the names "Northern" and "Southern" began from that time.[29]

Moreover, as Tsung-mi makes clear elsewhere in the *Ch'an Chart*, the teaching of Ho-tse Shen-hui is referred to as "sudden" because it advocates sudden enlightenment. In contrast to the Southern line of Ch'an, the Northern line founded by Shen-hsiu is referred to as "gradual" because it merely teaches gradual practice, ignoring sudden enlightenment altogether.[30]

Given Tsung-mi's deep personal identification with the Ho-tse line of Southern Ch'an and his characterization of its teaching in terms sharply contrasting with those of the Northern line, it would have been impossible for him to have included both the Southern and Northern lines of Ch'an together in the same category under the rubric of the sudden teaching, as Ch'eng-kuan had done. If, in fact, Ch'eng-kuan was associated with both the Northern and Southern

---

[28] HTC 110.433d11–13; K 277.
[29] HTC 110.434a16–b3; K 282.
[30] HTC 110.438b5; K 341.

lines, as his biography in the *Sung kao-seng chuan* claims, one can assume that he would have wanted to minimize the difference between them. Furthermore, if Ch'eng-kuan's Ch'an allegiance was to the Ox-head lineage, as Kamata has argued,[31] it would only have been natural for him to have minimized the differences between the Northern and Southern lines, especially if the Ox-head line of Ch'an arose as an attempt to bridge the sectarianism that had become rife among Ch'an Buddhists as a result of the rivalry between the Northern and Southern lines in the eighth century.[32]

In identifying the sudden teaching with Ch'an, Ch'eng-kuan also clearly subordinated Ch'an to Hua-yen.[33] Such a move would have been unacceptable to Tsung-mi. Whereas Ch'eng-kuan appropriated Ch'an through his understanding of Hua-yen, Tsung-mi appropriated Hua-yen through his experience of Ch'an. Their primary orientations in regard to Ch'an and Hua-yen were thus reversed: Ch'eng-kuan approached Ch'an from the point of view of doctrine (*chiao*), and Tsung-mi approached doctrine (*chiao*) from the point of view of Ch'an.

Moreover, Tsung-mi did not regard the Ch'an lines as espousing teachings that were separate from the teachings of the more scholastic traditions of Chinese Buddhism.[34] In fact, the efforts of the last years of his career were devoted to overcoming the separation between Ch'an and more scholastic teachings (*chiao*). Tsung-mi went to great pains in the *Ch'an Preface* to link the major lines of Ch'an prevalent in his day with the scholastic traditions that had preceded them. He links the teaching of the Northern line of Ch'an with the Fa-hsiang/Yogācāra tradition; the teaching of the Ox-head line of Ch'an with the San-lun/Madhyamaka tradition; and the teaching of the Southern line of Ch'an with the Hua-yen tradition. It would thus have violated the very intent of this work to have established Ch'an as a separate teaching. Clearly, as far as Tsung-mi was concerned, the various Ch'an lines did not differ from the major scholastic traditions in terms of the content of their teaching; the innovation and contribution of the Ch'an lines lay in the way in which they applied these teachings in the sphere of religious practice.[35]

[31] See chapter 2, n. 150.

[32] See McRae, "The Ox-head School."

[33] This was also a major issue for Chinul. See Robert Buswell, "Ch'an Hermeneutics."

[34] In his *Kegonzen*, Yoshizu has argued that Tsung-mi's thought could be more accurately characterized as *chiao-tsung i-t'i* instead of the more customary *chiao-ch'an i-chih* (pp. 307–308). See chapter 9 below.

[35] As Jeffrey Broughton has pointed out in a personal communication, this point is reflected in the way that Tsung-mi analyzes the different Ch'an lines in the *Ch'an Pref-*

Tsung-mi's thought in regard to the sudden teaching is elaborated most fully in his *Ch'an Preface*, which, with some slight alteration in terminology, employs the same p'an-chiao scheme that he developed in the *Inquiry into the Origin of Man*.[36] In response to the question:

> Previously you said that the Buddha expounded the sudden and gradual teachings and that Ch'an opened up the sudden and gradual gates [of practice]. It is still not clear what is the sudden [teaching] and what is the gradual [teaching] within the three categories of teaching.

Tsung-mi replies:

> It is only because of variations in the style (*i-shih*) of the World Honored One's exposition of the teachings that there are sudden expositions in accordance with the truth (*ch'eng-li tun shuo*) and gradual expositions in accordance with the capacities [of beings] (*sui-chi chien shuo*). Although [these different styles of exposition] are also referred to as the sudden teaching and the gradual teaching, this does not mean that there is a separate sudden and gradual [teaching] outside of the three teachings.[37]

This passage makes clear that Tsung-mi, like Chan-jan, understands the terms "sudden" and "gradual" to refer to methods by which the Buddha taught, not to separate teachings. Since the teachings included within Tsung-mi's p'an-chiao scheme are classified according to their content, it would have entailed a taxonomical confusion for Tsung-mi to have established the sudden teaching as a separate category.

Tsung-mi goes on to distinguish between two types of sudden teaching, what he refers to as *chu-chi tun-chiao*, the sudden teaching that was expounded in response to beings of superior capacity, and *hua-i tun-chiao*, the sudden teaching as a method of exposition. He says that the first type of sudden teaching corresponds to those cases in which the Buddha "directly revealed (*chih-shih*) the true dharma (*chen-fa*)" to "unenlightened persons (*fan-fu*; *pṛthagjana*) of superior capacity (*shang-ken*) and keen insight (*li-chih*)" who "on hearing [the Buddha's words] would be suddenly enlightened (*tun-wu*)." Tsung-mi illustrates their sudden attainment of enlightenment, "which is wholly equal to the fruit of Buddhahood (*ch'üan t'ung fo-kuo*)," by comparing it to the *Hua-yen Sūtra's* teaching that "when one first raises the aspiration for enlightenment, he immediately attains su-

---

ace. In discussing their teachings and practices, Tsung-mi distinguishes between their "idea" (*i*; sometimes he uses the term *chieh* or *fa-i*), which corresponds to the teaching of one of the scholastic traditions, and their "practice" (*hsing*), which is unique.

[36] For a comparison of the classification schemes in these two works, see chapter 8.

[37] T 48.407b13–17; K 184; cf. B 238.

preme perfect enlightenment"[38] and the *Scripture of Perfect Enlightenment's* teaching that "to practice meditation (*kuan-hsing*) is to complete the Buddha way."[39] Tsung-mi then says that only after such a person has suddenly awakened to his true nature does he gradually begin to eliminate the residual effects of his past conditioning, a process that he compares to the ocean that has been stirred up by the wind: even though the wind ceases suddenly, the movement of its waves only subsides gradually. Tsung-mi then identifies this type of sudden teaching with those scriptures that expound the tathāgatagarbha, such as one part of the *Hua-yen Sūtra* and all of the *Perfect Enlightenment, Śūraṅgama, Ghanavyūha, Śrīmālā,* and *Tathāgatagarbha* sūtras. He concludes his discussion by saying that since this type of teaching was expounded in response to beings of superior capacity, it was not taught during a set period in the Buddha's teaching career, adding that it is the same teaching as that found in the third and highest category of Ch'an teaching, that which directly reveals the nature of the mind.[40]

The second type of sudden teaching Tsung-mi discusses in the *Ch'an Preface*, the sudden teaching as a method of exposition, refers exclusively to the *Hua-yen Sūtra*.[41] Whereas the first type of sudden teaching was not taught during a set period of the Buddha's career (*pu-ting ch'u-huo*), the second was "suddenly taught" (*tun shuo*) by the Buddha "on one occasion" (*i-shih*) immediately after he had attained enlightenment. This type of sudden teaching was expounded for the sake of those followers who possessed superior capacities as a result of the ripening of conditions cultivated in past lives. After noting that the second type of sudden teaching is also referred to as the perfect-sudden teaching (*yüan-tun-chiao*), Tsung-mi goes on to catalogue under this heading such cardinal Hua-yen doctrines as the universe being contained within each speck of dust, the unobstructed interpenetration and mutual determination of all phenomena, and the ten

[38] Tsung-mi is quoting the passage found at T 10.89a1–2.

[39] I have been unable to trace this reference. Nor is it clear that it is a direct quotation.

[40] See T 48.407b21–c2; K 185; cf. B 240–241.

[41] See T 48.407c5–7, where Tsung-mi also mentions the *Daśabhūmikabhāṣya* as belonging to this type of sudden teaching. In other places where he mentions this type of sudden teaching (see, for example, TS 166d6 and TSC 218b7–9), Tsung-mi does not mention any text other than the *Hua-yen Sūtra*. Tsung-mi's inclusion of the *Daśabhūmikabhāṣya* in this context in the *Ch'an Preface* seems out of place. It is not a sūtra and makes no pretense to have been preached by the Buddha. The *Daśabhūmikasūtra* was, of course, incorporated into the *Hua-yen Sūtra*, forming chapter 26 in Śikṣānanda's translation.

profundities[42]—all of which fall under the category of what Fa-tsang had designated as the perfect teaching.

Tsung-mi does not draw a distinction between these two types of sudden teaching in his *Inquiry into the Origin of Man*. His explanation of the sudden teaching in the *Inquiry* corresponds to the account that he gives of the first type of this teaching in the *Ch'an Preface*—that is, the sudden teaching expounded to beings of superior capacity. His inclusion of the first type of sudden teaching in the highest category of teaching in his p'an-chiao identifies it with the teaching of Shen-hui, and his exclusion of the second type of sudden teaching from his *Inquiry into the Origin of Man* clearly indicates that the second type is subordinate to the first. In this regard it is especially noteworthy that he identifies the second type of sudden teaching exclusively with the *Hua-yen Sūtra*; his subordination of it to the first type parallels his displacement of the *Hua-yen Sūtra* to the *Awakening of Faith* and the perfect teaching to that of the tathāgatagarbha, a point whose significance will be explored more fully in the next chapter. For now it is necessary only to note that Tsung-mi explicitly says that only one part (*i-fen*) of the *Hua-yen Sūtra* is included in the first type of sudden teaching. As the following chapter will make clear, the part of the *Hua-yen Sūtra* that is not included within this type of sudden teaching is the interpenetration and mutual determination of all phenomena that Fa-tsang had designated as the special content of the perfect teaching, a point further indicated by the fact that Tsung-mi notes that the second type of sudden teaching is also called the sudden-perfect teaching. Not only does Tsung-mi reject Ch'eng-kuan's attempt to preserve the sudden teaching within Fa-tsang's fivefold classification, but in so doing he also reverts back to the earlier p'an-chiao nomenclature of Hui-kuang and Chih-yen that had classified the *Hua-yen Sūtra* as both a sudden and perfect teaching.

The first type of sudden teaching (i.e., that expounded to beings of superior capacity) is correlated with the highest type of Ch'an teaching, that of the Ho-tse tradition of Shen-hui with which Tsung-mi identified. This is the teaching of sudden enlightenment followed by gradual cultivation (*tun-wu chien-hsiu*), as is made clear by Tsung-mi's analogy of the sudden ceasing of the wind and gradual subsiding of the waves (a metaphor derived from the *Awakening of Faith*, and one about which more will be said later). This experience of sudden enlightenment overturns "primordial ignorance" (*ken-pen wu-ming*—the wind that had originally stirred the tranquil surface of the water into waves) but does not abolish the defilements (*fan-nao; kleśa*), which

---

[42] T 48.407c2–12; K 185; cf. B 241–243.

must then be eliminated through a gradual process of continued cultivation. Although the first type of sudden teaching is addressed to beings of superior capacity, it is significant that Tsung-mi explicitly refers to them as *fan-fu*, a term that translates *prthagjana* and indicates an ordinary person who has not as yet made decisive progress on the path. For Tsung-mi it specifically denotes someone who has not yet overcome the defilements.[43] The people to whom the first type of sudden teaching is addressed are clearly in a different category from the advanced bodhisattvas to whom the *Hua-yen Sūtra* was addressed in the second type of sudden teaching. Tsung-mi's emphasis on the ordinary unenlightened people to whom the first type of sudden teaching is addressed reveals his practical concern with the soteriological relevance of the teachings. Such concern is rooted in the overall Ch'an orientation underlying his approach to the teaching, as is also evident in his identification of this type of sudden teaching with Shen-hui.

Tsung-mi's subordination of the second type of sudden teaching also reflects the T'ien-t'ai criticism of the *Hua-yen Sūtra* as being a largely ineffective preaching whose profundity was lost on the overwhelming majority of its audience, who were "as if deaf and dumb" to its meaning. Tsung-mi's choice of terminology is particularly significant in this regard. The term that he uses to designate the second type of sudden teaching, *hua-i*, derives from the terminology developed by Chan-jan in his p'an-chiao scheme of five periods and eight teachings (*wu-shih pa-chiao*). Chan-jan divided the eight teachings into two sets of four, each of the two representing a different perspective according to which the Buddha's teachings could be analyzed: what he referred to as the four teachings according to their method of exposition (*hua-i ssu-chiao*) and the four teachings according to the content of their exposition (*hua-fa ssu-chiao*). The sudden teaching was represented for Chan-jan by the Buddha's preaching of the *Hua-yen Sūtra* immediately after his attainment of enlightenment. The Buddha's preaching of this sūtra was termed "sudden" because it was a direct and unadulterated exposition of the truth that made no recourse to a graduated method of teaching more suited to the still immature capacities of the preponderance of his disciples. Thus, according to Chan-jan's analysis of the different ways in which the Buddha's teaching could be classified, "sudden" referred exclusively to the method the Buddha used when he expounded the *Hua-yen Sūtra*; the sudden teaching was accordingly classified as a *hua-i* type

[43] See TSC 218b9–10.

of teaching, that is, as a teaching to be classified according to the method of its exposition.

As a method by which the Buddha taught, Tsung-mi was able to include the sudden teaching within the highest category of teaching in his p'an-chiao scheme. But it was not identical with the highest teaching, which contained a gradual component as well. Tsung-mi thus envisioned a "two-track" system by which the highest teaching could be approached. It could either be approached gradually, through a series of successive approximations, or suddenly, through a direct revelation of the truth. Whereas the sudden teaching was suited only to those of highest capacity, the gradual teachings were suited to those of average or inferior capacity. The Buddha made use of the gradual teachings as an expedient by which he progressively deepened the capacity of his disciples to understand the truth until they were ready to hear the teaching of ultimate meaning (liao-i; nītārtha), such as that contained in the Lotus and Nirvāṇa sūtras, which represented the gradual method by which the highest teaching was taught. As Tsung-mi writes in the Inquiry into the Origin of Man:

> In the case of [beings of] medium and inferior capacity, [the Buddha] proceeded from the superficial to the profound, gradually leading them forward. He would initially expound the first teaching [of men and gods], enabling them to be free from evil and to abide in virtue; he would then expound the second and third teachings [i.e., those of the small vehicle and the phenomenal appearances of the dharmas], enabling them to be free from impurity and to abide in purity; he would then expound the fourth and fifth [teachings], negating phenomenal appearances and revealing the nature, subsuming the provisional into the true, and, by practicing in reliance upon the ultimate teaching, they attain Buddhahood.[44]

In contrast to the gradual approach, by which the succession of teachings defined the path by which the Buddhist could reach the highest goal, the sudden teaching revealed the truth directly. It was then necessary, however, to go back to the practices contained in the gradual teachings to remove the defilements that prevented one from fully integrating one's insight into one's intrinsically enlightened Buddha-nature into one's actual behavior. In other words, the realization that one was a Buddha was not sufficient to guarantee that one acted like a Buddha. The gradual practices thus played a necessary role in the postenlightenment actualization of the insight afforded by the sudden teaching to beings of superior capacity.

[44] T 45.710b1–2.

Chapter Six

THE PERFECT TEACHING

TSUNG-MI'S revalorization of Hua-yen thought was no mere reshuffling of doctrinal categories. Not only did he exclude the sudden teaching from his classification scheme, but he also omitted the very teaching that had been taken by the Hua-yen tradition to embody the most profound insight of the Buddha, which was believed to have been revealed exclusively in the *Hua-yen Sūtra* and was therefore the basis of the tradition's claim to represent the most exalted teaching of Buddhism. In its stead he raised the teaching represented by the *Awakening of Faith* to the supreme position within his hierarchical arrangement of Buddhist teachings. Tsung-mi's displacement of the perfect teaching reflects a shift in what was deemed to be the most fundamental teaching of the Buddha and so affected the very heart of the tradition's identity. To define the nature of this shift, and thereby begin to clarify what was at stake for Tsung-mi, this chapter will show how the perfect teaching of the *Hua-yen Sūtra* and the teaching based on the *Awakening of Faith* can be seen to represent two distinct paradigms with different implications for religious practice.[1]

THE SAMĀDHI OF OCEANIC REFLECTION

As discussed in the fourth chapter, Fa-tsang used the fact that the *Hua-yen Sūtra* was purported to have been preached while the Buddha was still absorbed in the samādhi of oceanic reflection (*hai-in san-mei*) as the canonical basis for his assertion of its preeminence over all other Buddhist scriptures, thereby establishing its absolutely unique status as the separate teaching of the one vehicle. Although the samādhi of oceanic reflection does not play a consequential role within the sūtra itself, it was taken up by Fa-tsang as a central symbol illustrating the essential meaning of the scripture and hence expressing the quintessence of the perfect teaching. As a metaphor of the Buddha's enlightened awareness, the samādhi of oceanic reflection expresses the totalistic vision in which the harmonious and dynamic interrelation of all phenomena is simultaneously perceived, just as if

---

[1] This chapter adapts and amplifies material that appeared in "What Happened to the Perfect Teaching?"

the entire universe were reflected on the surface of the ocean. As Fa-tsang writes in his *Hua-yen yu-hsin fa-chieh chi* (Reflections on the dharmadhātu):

> It is like the reflection of the four divisions [of a great army] on a vast ocean. Although the reflected images differ in kind, they appear simultaneously on [the surface of] the ocean in their proper order. Even though the appearance of the images is manifold, the water [that reflects them] remains undisturbed. The images are indistinguishable from the water, and yet [the water] is calm and clear; the water is indistinguishable from the images, and yet [the images] are multifarious. . . . It is also described as "oceanic" (*hai*) because its various reflections multiply endlessly and their limit is impossible to fathom. To investigate one of them thoroughly is to pursue the infinite, for, in any one of them, all the rest vividly appear at the same time. For this reason, it is said to be "oceanic." It is called "reflection" (*in*) because all the images appear simultaneously within it without distinction of past and present. The myriad diverse kinds [of images] penetrate each other without obstruction. The one and the many are reflected in one another without opposing each other. . . . [It is called] "samādhi" because, although [the images within it] are many and diverse, it remains one and does not change. Even though myriads of images arise in profusion, it remains empty and unperturbed.[2]

The vision of reality seen in the samādhi of oceanic reflection is that which the subsequent tradition, following Ch'eng-kuan's theory of the fourfold dharmadhātu,[3] characterized as the dharmadhātu of *shih-shih wu-ai*, the realm of the unobstructed interrelation of each and every phenomenon. And for Fa-tsang it is this vision that is the specific hallmark of the perfect teaching.

In the *Treatise on the Five Teachings*, as noted, Fa-tsang defines the perfect teaching as being represented by what he refers to as *fa-chieh yüan-ch'i*, the conditioned origination of the dharmadhātu, which he regards as the crowning insight of the *Hua-yen Sūtra*.[4] As elaborated in the final chapter of the *Treatise on the Five Teachings*, the conditioned origination of the dharmadhātu means that, since all phenomena are devoid of self-nature and arise contingent upon one another, each phenomenon is an organic part of the whole defined by the harmonious interrelation of all of its parts. The character of each phenomenon is thus determined by the whole of which it is an integral part, just as the character of the whole is determined by each of the

---

[2] T 45.646b–c; adapted from Liu, "The Teaching of Fa-tsang," pp. 122–123.

[3] See chapter 2, pp. 67–68.

[4] T 45.485b7–9; Cook, "Fa-tsang's Treatise," p. 223.

phenomena of which it is comprised. Since the whole is nothing but the interrelation of its parts, each phenomenon can therefore be regarded as determining the character of all other phenomena as well as having its own character determined by all other phenomena.

As the culmination of his description of the perfect teaching, Fa-tsang makes use of the ten profundities (shih-hsüan), first formulated by his teacher Chih-yen, to elaborate the implications of the conditioned origination of the dharmadhātu.[5] The infinite interpenetration (hsiang-ju) and mutual determination (hsiang-chi) [6] of all phenomena described in the ten profundities can be illustrated by the metaphor of Indra's net, the fourth profundity Fa-tsang discusses in the Treatise on the Five Teachings. According to this metaphor, the universe is represented as a vast net extending infinitely in all directions; the manifold phenomena of which it is comprised are represented as resplendent jewels suspended at each point of intersection. In this way each jewel both reflects and is reflected by every other jewel. Each jewel, moreover, reflects each and every other jewel's reflection of its simultaneous reflecting of and being reflected by every other jewel on the net. Thus the process of mutual reflection multiplies endlessly (ch'ung-ch'ung wu-chin), just as all phenomena of the universe interrelate without obstruction.[7]

Fa-tsang's biography in the Sung kao-seng chuan relates that, to enable Empress Wu to visualize the endless multiplication of the process of mutual reflection according to the conditioned origination of the dharmadhātu, Fa-tsang arranged ten mirrors, with eight placed at each of the points of the compass and one above and one below, all facing each other. He then placed a Buddha image, illuminated by a bright lamp, in the center. In this way not only was the Buddha image reflected in each mirror, but its reflection in each mirror was also re-

---

[5] The ten profundities (shih-hsüan) were first elaborated by Chih-yen in his Hua-yen shih-hsüan men (Ten profound gates of the Hua-yen [Sūtra]; see translation by Cleary in Entry into the Inconceivable, pp. 126–146). Fa-tsang adopted these in his Treatise on the Five Teachings without modification, other than in their order (see T 45.505a12ff.; Cook, "Fa-tsang's Treatise," pp. 496ff.). Fa-tsang's enumeration of the ten profundities in his T'an-hsüan chi, however, replaces two of Chih-yen's categories with two new ones (see T 35.123a28–b4). Significantly, one of those deleted by Fa-tsang in his "new" version is that of "creation through the transformation of the mind alone." Kamata has suggested that this change marked a shift in Fa-tsang's thought away from the tathā-gatagarbha doctrine of the Awakening of Faith toward a greater emphasis on shih-shih wu-ai; see Chūgoku kegon, p. 553.

[6] The term hsiang-chi is often translated as "mutual identity." I have followed Liu in translating it as "mutual determination." See "The Teaching of Fa-tsang," p. 427, n. 25.

[7] See T 45.506a13–b10; Cook, "Fa-tsang's Treatise," pp. 509–513.

flected in every other mirror, and the reflected images continued to multiple infinitely in all directions.[8]

As these examples show, the regnant imagery by which Fa-tsang illustrates the conditioned origination of the dharmadhātu is related to the mirror—or, more precisely, the capacity of each phenomenon to mirror, and be mirrored by, all other phenomena. Fa-tsang's explanation of Indra's net, as well as his practical demonstration of its meaning for Empress Wu, amplifies the imagery of infinite reflection seen earlier in his account of the samādhi of oceanic reflection, itself a metaphor for the Buddha's enlightened vision. I shall return to the significance of this imagery in chapter 9 when I discuss Tsung-mi's criticism of the Hung-chou line of Ch'an, in which he uses mirror imagery to illustrate a model of enlightenment whose meaning is appreciably different from Fa-tsang's.

TWO PARADIGMS

In addition to defining the perfect teaching in terms of the conditioned origination of the dharmadhātu in his *Treatise on the Five Teachings*, Fa-tsang includes nature origination (*hsing-ch'i*) under its heading as well.[9] Although this term derives from the title of the thirty-second chapter of Buddhabhadra's translation of the *Hua-yen Sūtra*, its meaning in Hua-yen thought owes far more to the *Awakening of Faith*, the primary text upon which Fa-tsang bases his account of the advanced teaching of the Mahāyāna. In his commentary on the *Awakening of Faith*, Fa-tsang characterizes this teaching in terms of the conditioned origination from the tathāgatagarbha (*ju-lai-tsang yüan-ch'i*), a doctrine that he describes as elucidating the "harmonious interaction of the absolute and phenomenal without obstruction" (*li-shih jung-t'ung wu-ai*).[10] This characterization of the tathāgatagarbha echoes throughout his other works as well. In both his *Treatise on the Five Teachings*[11] and *Hua-yen yu-hsin fa-chieh chi*,[12] Fa-tsang explains the unobstructed interpenetration of the absolute and phenomenal in terms of the two aspects of the one mind taught in the *Awakening of Faith*. He identifies the absolute (*li*) with the mind as suchness (*hsin chen-ju*) and the phenomenal (*shih*) with the mind subject to birth-and-death (*hsin sheng-mieh*). Their unobstructed interaction is manifested as the ālayavijñāna, which is but another term for the tathā-

---

[8] T 50.732a26ff.

[9] T 45.485b10–11; Cook, "Fa-tsang's Treatise," pp. 223–224.

[10] T 44.243c1.

[11] T 45.484c29–b2; Cook, "Fa-tsang's Treatise," pp. 218–222.

[12] T 45.644a1–3.

gatagarbha as it responds to conditions (*sui-yüan*) to give rise to all mundane and supermundane dharmas. Just as the ālayavijñāna harbors both the capacity for enlightenment (*chüeh*) and nonenlightenment (*pu-chieh*), so too the tathāgatagarbha is the basis for both saṃsāra and nirvāṇa. Even though the tathāgatagarbha as the ālayavijñāna responds to conditions to generate all phenomena, it is, at the same time, identical with the dharmakāya and therefore remains forever untainted. Fa-tsang characterizes this aspect of the tathāgatagarbha as its immutability (*pu pien*). Moreover, he identifies these two aspects of the tathāgatagarbha—its responding to conditions and its immutability—with the one mind as seen from the point of view of conventional (*su-*) and ultimate truth (*chen-ti*).

Although the terms *li-shih wu-ai* and *shih-shih wu-ai* were established as a set pair after Fa-tsang's death and were generally avoided by Tsung-mi, they nevertheless became a fixed part of the Hua-yen lexicon and can serve as convenient categories for organizing various aspects of Hua-yen doctrine into an intelligible framework. They can also be taken as representing different paradigms for religious practice. *Shih-shih wu-ai* relates to the content of enlightenment, whereas *li-shih wu-ai* pertains to the noetic ground that makes such an experience possible. The first, that is, has to do with the phenomenology of enlightenment, and the second, with its ontological basis. These two categories can be tied to different causal models—*shih-shih wu-ai* corresponding to the conditioned origination of the dharmadhātu, and *li-shih wu-ai* to nature origination. Within Fa-tsang's p'an-chiao categories, *shih-shih wu-ai* would correspond to the perfect teaching, and *li-shih wu-ai* to the advanced teaching. Textually, *shih-shih wu-ai* is represented by the *Hua-yen Sūtra*, while *li-shih wu-ai* is represented by the *Awakening of Faith*.

The difference between these two paradigms of religious practice can be illustrated by considering a different version of the samādhi of oceanic reflection. This version comes from the *Wang-chin huan-yüan kuan* (Contemplation on exhausting delusion and returning to the source). Although this work is often attributed Fa-tsang, Kojima Taizan has argued convincingly against Fa-tsang's authorship.[13] Ko-

---

[13] See his "*Mōjin gengen kan no senja o meguru shomondai*." Kojima points out that the attribution of the *Wang-chin huan-yüan kuan* (WCHYK) to Fa-tsang only begins to gain general acceptance with Ching-yüan's (1011–1088) *Wang-chin huan-yüan kuan chi chung chiao*, which was written in 1066 and is appended to the Taishō version of the text. Before then the dominant opinion had been that the work was written by Tu-shun. Ching-yüan's attribution of the WCHYK to Fa-tsang influenced both Ŭich'ŏn's catalog (1090) and the *Shih-men cheng-t'ung* (1237). Still the attribution to Tu-shun did not die out. The *Tsu-t'ing shih-yüan* (1108) lists Tu-shun as the author. Chih-p'an's *Fo-tsu t'ung-chi* (compiled 1258–1269) combines the accounts of the *Tsu-t'ing shih-yüan* and

jima sees this work as playing a transitional role between Fa-tsang's interpretation of Hua-yen and that of Ch'eng-kuan and Tsung-mi, speculating that it was probably written between 730 and 750. Whereas Fa-tsang's interpretation of this samādhi emphasized the infinite process of mutual reflection, the *Wang-chin huan-yüan kuan* version focuses less on the imagery of reflection than that of the reflec-

---

Shih-men cheng-t'ung and even attributes the WCHYK to Fa-shun (i.e., Tu-shun) while listing Fa-tsang as the author of a *Huan-yüan chi.* The *Fa-chieh tsung wu-tsu lüeh-chi's* claim (1680) that the WCHYK is falsely attributed to Tu-shun testifies to the persistence of that attribution, which remains the majority opinion from the middle of the eighth century down through the Ch'ing. Ching-yüan's attribution, however, became the prevalent opinion in Korea and Japan, two countries in which Tu-shun did not have a cultic following.

Kojima also calls into question the arguments Ching-yüan adduces in support of Fa-tsang's authorship. To Ching-yüan's citation of a passage from Fa-tsang's *I-hai pai-men* (T 45.633a9–10) in the WCHYK (637a7–8), for instance, Kojima points out that the present version of the *I-hai pai-men* has been revised by Ching-yüan (see T 45.636c) and that there is accordingly no way to be sure that he has not interpolated this passage. Kojima goes on to comment that Ching-yüan was concerned to preserve the integrity of Hua-yen lineage and, by attributing the WCHYK to Fa-tsang, helped to patch over the obvious discontinuity that occurred between Fa-tsang, on the one hand, and Ch'eng-kuan and Tsung-mi, on the other.

Kojima concludes by demonstrating how the WCHYK's conception of intrinsic enlightenment is different from that found in Fa-tsang's other works—the basic point being that, whereas the WCHYK links intrinsic enlightenment with the gate suchness, Fa-tsang connects it with the gate of birth-and-death. Interestingly, Kojima argues that the position of the WCHYK is closer to that of Fa-tsang's disciple Wen-ch'ao, who, in his *Hua-yen ching i-ch'ao,* wrote that "ocean" in oceanic reflection samādhi corresponded to suchness, "reflection" to its according with conditions, and "samādhi" to its immutability. Both Wen-ch'ao's and the WCHYK's account of *hai-yin san-mei* emphasize suchness as the fundamental ground of the samādhi of oceanic reflection. Both point to the fundamental shift in emphasis that occurred in Hua-yen thought following the death of Fa-tsang, one that emphasized the one true dharmadhātu (*i-chen fa-chieh*) as the underlying ontological basis for all of the various Hua-yen doctrines. The WCHYK and Wen-ch'ao's *Hua-yen ching i-ch'ao* thus represent a transitional stage pointing to the full-blown ontological emphasis seen in Ch'eng-kuan and Tsung-mi.

Tamura Yoshirō has also noted that the WCHYK's conception of intrinsic enlightenment differs from that of Fa-tsang. In his *Tendai hongaku-ron,* pp. 486–487, Tamura quotes a passage from Fa-tsang's commentary to the *Awakening of Faith* (T 44.256a21ff.) that, in response to a question having to do with the relationship between intrinsic enlightenment (*pen-chüeh*) and suchness, says that *pen* means nature, and *chüeh* means wisdom; because it overturns delusion and defilement, intrinsic enlightenment "is included within the gate of birth-and-death (*sheng-mieh men*)." Fa-tsang goes on to say that it is not included within the gate of suchness because there is no defilement to be overturned in that gate. After citing similar statements in Fa-tsang's *Wu-chiao chang* (see T 45.485c19 [Cook, "Fa-tsang's Treatise," p. 230] and 487b2–4 [Cook, p. 251]), Tamura concludes that, for Fa-tsang, intrinsic enlightenment is the potentiality or cause for attaining enlightenment and therefore is found within the ālayavijñāna. He then points to the discrepancy between Fa-tsang's position and that of the WCHYK as a means of calling into question Fa-tsang's authorship of that text.

tive capacity of the water, an emphasis that clearly reveals the importance of the *Awakening of Faith* as the primary source of inspiration for the *Wang-chin huan-yüan kuan* version of the samādhi of oceanic reflection.

> "Oceanic reflection" refers to the intrinsically enlightened awareness of suchness (*chen-ju pen-chüeh*). When delusion is brought to an end, the mind is clear and the myriad forms are simultaneously reflected. It is like the vast ocean: waves arise because of the wind; once the wind stops, the surface of the ocean becomes clear and still and there is no form that is not reflected upon it. This is what the *Awakening of Faith* refers to as "the treasure store of infinite excellent qualities, the ocean of the suchness of reality (*fa-hsing chen-ju hai*)."[14] That is why it is called the samādhi of oceanic reflection.
>
> A scripture [*Fa-chü ching*] says: "The manifold phenomena of the universe are the reflection of a single dharma."[15] That single dharma is what is meant by the one mind. "That mind embraces all mundane and supramundane dharmas."[16] "It is the one dharmadhātu, which is characterized by its all-inclusiveness and which is the essence of the dharma."[17] "It is only because deluded thoughts come into being that distinctions are made."[18] If one can free oneself from deluded thoughts, then there is just one [undifferentiated] suchness (*wei i chen-ju*). It is therefore called "oceanic reflection samādhi."[19]

As this passage makes clear, this version of the samādhi of oceanic reflection is based on the *Awakening of Faith*. Not only is the text explicitly cited once, it is also quoted without attribution four more times. Moreover, the central image of the water and waves itself derives from the *Awakening of Faith*.[20] The key passage in that text occurs as part of a discussion of intrinsic enlightenment (*pen-chüeh*), a uniquely Chinese elaboration of the Indian Buddhist doctrine of the tathāgatagarbha. According to the *Awakening of Faith*, intrinsic enlightenment is the true nature of the mind. It is present in all states of mind, just as the wet nature of the water is always present whether the surface of the water is calm or broken into waves. The passage in question might be freely rendered as follows:

---

[14] T 32.575b14–15; cf. Hakeda, *The Awakening of Faith*, p. 23.

[15] T 85.1435a23.

[16] T 32.575c21–22; cf. Hakeda *The Awakening of Faith*, p. 28.

[17] T 32.576a8; cf. Hakeda, *The Awakening of Faith*, p. 32.

[18] T 32.576a9–10; cf. Hakeda, *The Awakening of Faith*, pp. 32–33.

[19] T 45.637b21–28.

[20] See T 32.576c and 578a; cf. Hakeda, *The Awakening of Faith*, pp. 41 and 55.

All [defiled] modes of consciousness (*i-ch'ieh hsin-shih chih hsiang*) are manifestations of ignorance. Since the modes of ignorance (*wu-ming chih hsiang*) are not separate from the nature of enlightenment (*chüeh hsing*), they can neither be destroyed nor not destroyed. It is like the water of a vast ocean: when it is stirred into waves by the wind, the motion of the water (*shui hsiang*) and the activity of the wind (*feng hsiang*) are not separate from one another. Yet water is not mobile by nature. If the wind ceases, its motion will also cease, but the wet nature of the water will not thereby be annulled. In the same way, when the intrinsically pure mind of sentient beings is stirred into motion by the wind of ignorance, mind and ignorance, not having distinct characteristics of their own, are not separate from each other. Yet the mind is not mobile by nature. If ignorance ceases, its continuation will also cease, but the wisdom nature of the mind will not thereby be annulled.[21]

The image of the water and waves illustrates the process by which the absolute (*li*), the mind as suchness (*hsin chen-ju*), which is intrinsically pure and enlightened, accords with conditions (*sui-yüan*) to give rise to phenomenal reality (*shih*), the mind subject to birth-and-death (*hsin sheng-mieh*)—a process that Fa-tsang refers to as "the harmonious interaction of the absolute and phenomenal without obstruction." In the version of the samādhi of oceanic reflection exemplified by the passage from the *Wang-chin huan-yüan kuan*, the mind is likened to water. In according with conditions, its originally tranquil surface becomes disturbed by the "wind of ignorance." The resulting waves represent discriminating thought, which breaks up the undifferentiated nature of reality, fragmenting it into a montage of seemingly disconnected and unstable images in which the unitary nature of the whole can no longer be perceived. It is this distorted vision that is delusion. The function of religious practice must therefore be to quell the wind of ignorance so that the waves of discriminating thought can subside and the surface of the water can return to its originally tranquil nature, at which time it will be able to reflect reality truly. All the same, whether the mind is tranquil or disturbed, its reflective quality (i.e., intrinsic enlightenment) is never lost.

Rather than focusing on the harmonious interrelation of the myriad images reflected on the surface of the ocean, as does the first version of the samādhi of oceanic reflection, this version emphasizes the reflective surface of the water. In other words, instead of focusing on the phenomenology of enlightenment, the second paradigm empha-

---

[21] T 32.576c9–16. I have based my translation on Fa-tsang's commentary to this passage (T 44.260a14–b28) and Hirakawa Akira's annotated Japanese translation, *Daijō kishin-ron*, pp. 119–127.

sizes the noetic nature of the mind that makes enlightenment possible. While the perspective of the second paradigm thus differs from the first, the two are nevertheless related. For it is only by bringing the mind back to its originally tranquil state by putting an end to discriminating thought that the mind can reflect phenomenal reality in an undistorted fashion. The second paradigm thus represents the ontological basis of the first, just as in Hua-yen theory the unobstructed interrelation of all phenomena (*shih-shih wu-ai*) is made possible by the unobstructed interpenetration of the absolute and phenomenal (*li-shih wu-ai*). Despite the intimate connection that thus obtains between the two paradigms, Fa-tsang clearly subordinates the second to the first, as indicated by his ranking of the perfect teaching above that of the advanced Mahāyāna within his system of doctrinal classification.

By way of summary, the content of the two paradigms can be schematized as follows:

First Paradigm	Second Paradigm
Shih-shih wu-ai	*Li-shih wu-ai*
Mystical vision in which harmonious interrelation of all things is seen as if reflected on a vast ocean	Mind compared to ocean whose originally tranquil surface is stirred up into waves by the wind of ignorance
Phenomenology of enlightenment	Ontological basis of reality
Conditioned origination of the dharmadhātu	Nature origination
Perfect teaching	Advanced teaching
Hua-yen Sūtra	*Awakening of Faith*
	Tathāgatagarbha

The Shift from *Shih-shih wu-ai* to *Li-shih wu-ai*

For Fa-tsang, nature origination, understood in terms of *li-shih wu-ai*, points to the dynamic functioning of the mind (*li*) in the generation of the phenomenal realm (*shih*). All phenomena are thus manifestations of the mind, and since this mind is intrinsically pure and immutable, the entire realm of phenomena is thereby validated. In this way *li-shih wu-ai* provides the ontological structure in terms of which Fa-tsang articulates his vision of *shih-shih wu-ai*. Nevertheless, the significance of *li-shih wu-ai* becomes eclipsed in his elaboration of the meaning of *shih-shih wu-ai* in the last chapter of the *Treatise on the Five Teachings*.

In his study of Fa-tsang's metaphysics, Liu Ming-Wood has shown that there is a tension between *hsing-ch'i* and *fa-chieh yüan-ch'i*—or *li-shih wu-ai* and *shih-shih wu-ai*—that is represented in Fa-tsang's thought by the presence of elements of the advanced teaching within the perfect teaching. Even though Fa-tsang tends to talk as if the advanced teaching had been wholly transcended in the perfect, he cannot do so without also undermining its ontological base—for the perfect teaching (*shih-shih wu-ai*) cannot be established independent of the advanced teaching (*li-shih wu-ai*). Liu thus contends that there is an inherent instability in Fa-tsang's account of the perfect teaching. He also points out that the advanced teaching of the Mahāyāna plays a far greater role in Fa-tsang's thought than his classification of it as merely the third teaching within his fivefold scheme would suggest.[22]

Although Ch'eng-kuan follows Fa-tsang in regarding *shih-shih wu-ai* as the supreme teaching of the Buddha, he nonetheless emphasizes *li-shih wu-ai* over *shih-shih wu-ai* in his exposition of Hua-yen teachings. Whereas *li-shih wu-ai* tends to vanish into *shih-shih wu-ai* in Fa-tsang's writings, Ch'eng-kuan focuses on the importance of *li-shih wu-ai* in making *shih-shih wu-ai* possible, as the following passage demonstrates.

> The dharmadhātu of the nonobstruction of phenomena and phenomena constitutes the cardinal teaching of the [*Hua-yen*] *Sūtra*. . . . The reason that each phenomenon is different from every other phenomenon and yet is unobstructed by all other phenomena is that the absolute permeates phenomena. . . . Because phenomena are formed on the basis of the absolute, the one and the many arise in dependence upon one another. . . . It is only as a result of the nonobstruction of the phenomenal and the absolute that the nonobstruction of phenomena and phenomena is made possible. . . . Were phenomena not identical with the absolute, they would not be formed from the absolute, and phenomena would then obstruct one another. However, because they are identical with the absolute, they are unobstructed. . . . Since phenomena are formed from the absolute, they are included in one another without obstruction.[23]

Tsung-mi's supplanting of the perfect teaching (i.e., *shih-shih wu-ai*) with that of the tathāgatagarbha (i.e., *li-shih wu-ai*) in his classification of Buddhist teachings can thus be seen as an extension of a trend already evidenced by his teacher Ch'eng-kuan. Moreover, Tsung-mi's primary exposure to Hua-yen thought was through Ch'eng-kuan. Ch'eng-kuan's commentary and subcommentary to the "new" trans-

---

[22] See Liu, "The Teachings of Fa-tsang," especially the concluding chapter.
[23] T 36.9a28–b7.

lation of the *Hua-yen Sūtra* by Śikṣānanda had rendered obsolete Fa-tsang's commentary (*T'an-hsüan chi*) to the "old" translation by Buddhabhadra. The only work of Fa-tsang's that we can say for certain Tsung-mi studied was his commentary on the *Awakening of Faith*, which served as the basis on which Tsung-mi composed his own abridged commentary.[24] Fa-tsang's commentary, however, is concerned with explicating the conditioned origination of the tathāgatagarbha and has nothing to say about *shih-shih wu-ai*.

The legacy of Hua-yen teachings to which Tsung-mi was heir thus did not accord the prominence to the teaching of *shih-shih wu-ai* that it had enjoyed in Fa-tsang's writings. But Tsung-mi also went much further than his teacher Ch'eng-kuan in subordinating *shih-shih wu-ai* to *li-shih wu-ai*, as witnessed most dramatically in his exclusion of the perfect teaching as a category from his p'an-chiao scheme. The difference between Ch'eng-kuan and Tsung-mi in this regard can also be seen by comparing their comments on the last section of Tu-shun's *Fa-chieh kuan-men* (Discernments of the dharmadhātu), that of the discernment of total pervasion and accommodation (*chou-pien han-jung kuan*). Ch'eng-kuan interprets the ten discernments enumerated in this section in terms of the ten profundities, which he characterizes as the paradigmatic expression of *shih-shih wu-ai*.[25] Tsung-mi, by contrast, merely observes that the ten discernments correspond to the ten profundities, which he does not even bother to list.[26] Again, in his subcommentary to Ch'eng-kuan's *Hsing yüan p'in shu*,[27] Tsung-mi only mentions, but does not discuss, the ten profundities, which Ch'eng-kuan had subjected to a detailed analysis in his commentary.[28]

Not only does Tsung-mi give scant attention to the ten profundities in precisely those places where one would expect him to devote sustained discussion to them, he eschews the whole vocabulary of *li* and *shih* in terms of which Ch'eng-kuan had formulated his theory of the fourfold dharmadhātu. Where he does make reference to the fourfold dharmadhātu,[29] he refers to a passage from Ch'eng-kuan's *Hsing yüan p'in shu*[30] that emphasizes the one true dharmadhātu (*i-chen fa-*

---

[24] Tsung-mi's commentary can be found in case 31, vol. 8, division 5, part 2 of the *Dai Nippon kōtei daizōkyō*.

[25] T 45.683a3–11.

[26] T 45.692b4–5.

[27] HTC 7.399c.

[28] *Hsing yüan p'in shu*, HTC 7.246a–d.

[29] See *Chu Hua-yen fa-chieh kuan-men*, T 45.684b24–c1; TS 116d3–6; and *Ta-sheng ch'i-hsin lun shu*, 14b2–3.

[30] HTC 7.249c11–d2.

chieh) as the essential reality from which the fourfold dharmadhātu derives.[31] Most significantly for Tsung-mi, that passage identifies the one true dharmadhātu with the one mind (*i-hsin*) that wholly embraces manifold existence (*tsung-kai wan-yu*). Tsung-mi identifies the one true dharmadhātu with the tathāgatagarbha, the central doctrine of the teaching that he ranks highest in his classification system. As will be discussed in detail in the next chapter, it is also in terms of the one true dharmadhātu that he elaborates his discussion of nature origination in his subcommentary to Ch'eng-kuan's *Hsing yüan p'in shu*.

THE TEACHING THAT REVEALS THE NATURE

Within the doctrinal classification scheme that he outlines in his *Inquiry into the Origin of Man*, Tsung-mi accords pride of place to the teaching of the tathāgatagarbha, which he refers to as "the teaching that reveals the nature" (*hsien-hsing-chiao*).

> The teaching of the one vehicle that reveals the nature holds that all sentient beings without exception have the intrinsically enlightened true mind. From [time] without beginning it is permanently abiding and immaculate. It is shining, unobscured, clear and bright ever-present awareness. It is also called Buddha-nature, and it is also called tathāgatagarbha. From time without beginning deluded thoughts cover it, and [sentient beings] by themselves are not aware of it. Because they only recognize their inferior qualities, they become indulgently attached, enmeshed in karma, and experience the suffering of birth-and-death. The Great Enlightened One took pity upon them and taught that everything without exception is empty. He further revealed that the purity of the numinous enlightened true mind is wholly identical with that of all Buddhas.[32]

Like Fa-tsang, Tsung-mi turns to the *Hua-yen Sūtra* to support his interpretation of the meaning of the Buddha's enlightenment, but in so doing, he chooses a passage with a thrust quite different from Fa-tsang's vision of the unobstructed harmonious interaction of all phenomena. He quotes the following passage from the *Hua-yen Sūtra*, one that was especially valued in the Ch'an tradition as it was believed

[31] The phrase "*t'ung wei i-chen fa-chieh*," which Tsung-mi claims to be quoting from Ch'eng-kuan, does not occur in in Ch'eng-kuan's *Hsing yüan p'in shu*. Ch'eng-kuan does, however, use the phrase "*tsung wei i-chen wu-ai fa-chieh*" in the beginning of his commentary on the "Ju fa-chieh p'in" in his commentary on the *Hua-yen Sūtra* (see T 35.908a16).

[32] T 45.710a11–16.

to have contained the first words uttered by the Buddha after his enlightenment.[33]

> Oh sons of Buddha, there is no place where the wisdom of the Tathāgata does not reach. Why? Because there is not a single sentient being that is not fully endowed with the wisdom of the Tathāgata. It is only on account of their deluded thinking, erroneous views, and attachments that they do not succeed in realizing it. When they become free from deluded thinking, the all-comprehending wisdom, the spontaneous wisdom, and the unobstructed wisdom will then be manifest before them. . . . At that time the Tathāgata with his unobstructed pure eye of wisdom universally beheld all sentient beings throughout the dharmadhātu and said, "How amazing! How amazing! How can it be that these sentient beings are fully endowed with the wisdom of the Tathāgata and yet, being ignorant and confused, do not know it and do not see it? I must teach them the noble path, enabling them to be forever free from deluded thinking and to achieve for themselves the seeing of the broad and vast wisdom of the Tathāgata within themselves and so be no different from the Buddhas."[34]

According to Takasaki Jikidō's reconstruction of the development of the tathāgatagarbha doctrine, this passage served as a model for the *Tathāgatagarbha Sūtra* (*Ju-lai-tsang ching*), the first text to propound the tathāgatagarbha teaching explicitly.[35] It occurs in the chapter of the *Hua-yen Sūtra* that Buddhabhadra had translated as "Ju-lai hsing-ch'i"[36] and within the Hua-yen tradition was connected with the development of the theory of nature origination (*hsing-ch'i*). Its significance for Tsung-mi lay in the fact that it established that the Buddha's enlightenment consisted in his realization that all sentient beings already fully possess the enlightened wisdom of the Buddha and are therefore fundamentally identical with all Buddhas. The defilements that appear to obscure this wisdom are merely adventitious. Buddhist practice should thus be directed toward uncovering the original enlightenment that is the fundamental nature of all beings. Enlightenment is a matter of becoming aware of that which has always been present from the very beginning.

Tsung-mi's account of the teaching that reveals the nature in his

---

[33] See Miura and Sasaki, *Zen Dust*, p. 254.

[34] T 10.272c4–7 and 272c25–273a2.

[35] See *A Study of the Ratnagotravibhāga*, pp. 35–36.

[36] According to Takasaki, this chapter seems to have originally circulated as an independent scripture, *Tathāgatatotpattisambhava-nirdeśa*, which was translated into Chinese as the *Ju-lai hsing-hsien ching* (T no. 291) by Dharmarakṣa in the late third century (see *A Study of the Ratnagotravibhāga*, p. 35).

Ch'an Preface adds that this teaching is exemplifed in those scriptures that expound the tathāgatagarbha, such as the *Hua-yen, Ghanavyūha, Perfect Enlightenment, Śūraṅgama, Śrīmālā, Tathāgatagarbha, Lotus,* and *Nirvāṇa,* as well as in treatises such as the *Awakening of Faith, Buddha Nature (Fo-hsing),* and *Ratnagotravibhāga (Pao-hsing lun).*[37]

As both his quotation of the *Hua-yen Sūtra* as canonical authority for the teaching that reveals the nature and his inclusion of it within his enumeration of scriptures that exemplify that teaching make clear, Tsung-mi regards the principal teaching of this scripture as the tathāgatagarbha, not its vision of the unobstructed interrelation of all phenomena. He also includes the *Hua-yen Sūtra* within the teaching that reveals the nature in the *Ch'an Preface,*[38] although, as noted in the previous chapter, he makes the important qualification that only "one part" (*i-fen*) of its teaching falls within this category.

THE *SCRIPTURE OF PERFECT ENLIGHTENMENT*

One of the scriptures that Tsung-mi lists among those exemplifying the teaching that reveals the nature is the *Scripture of Perfect Enlightenment.* Despite his appropriation within the fold of Hua-yen patriarchs, Tsung-mi's primary exegetical activity was devoted to this text and not the *Hua-yen Sūtra.* Tsung-mi's esteem for this work was a direct result of his personal experience: it was his encounter with this text that precipitated his initial enlightenment experience while still a novice monk under Tao-yüan's tutelage in Sui-chou. Given the fact that Tsung-mi revered this scripture above the *Hua-yen Sūtra* and that he classified it under the teaching that reveals the nature, it should hardly be surprising that he would have been reluctant to posit the perfect teaching, identified exclusively with the *Hua-yen Sūtra,* as a still higher category within his p'an-chiao.

In a passage from his introduction to his commentary to the *Scripture of Perfect Enlightenment* discussing how that scripture, within its brief compass, includes a wide variety of ideas, Tsung-mi comments that, within its single fascicle of only twenty-eight pages, the *Scripture of Perfect Enlightenment* fully embodies the ideas expressed in the advanced and sudden teachings and the teaching traditions of emptiness and the analysis of phenomenal appearances (*k'ung-tsung* and *hsiang-tsung,* i.e., the two subcategories in Fa-tsang's elementary Mahāyāna), as well as containing those of the Hīnayāna and perfect separate teachings.[39] In his subcommentary to this passage, he explains

[37] T 48.405a24–26; K 132.
[38] T 48.407c7–12; K 185.
[39] TS 110c8–11.

that, even though it contains the ideas of the Hīnayāna and perfect teachings, they are still not its cardinal principle (*tsung*).[40] This passage indicates that Tsung-mi regarded the *Scripture of Perfect Enlightenment* as fully expressing the content of the advanced and sudden teachings and only partially that of the perfect teaching. Again, at the end of the section discussing the classification systems of previous scholars in his introduction to his commentary,[41] Tsung-mi indicates how that scripture would be classified according to Fa-tsang's five categories of teaching.

1. It is wholly included within, but only partially includes, the perfect teaching. Tsung-mi goes on to explain that the *Scripture of Perfect Enlightenment* cannot be said to include the entirety of the perfect teaching because it does not teach the unobstructed interpenetration and mutual determination of all things. It does, however, "directly reveal the essence of the one true dharmadhātu" (*i-chen fa-chieh*), which is included within the perfect teaching of the *Hua-yen Sūtra*.

2. It includes, but is not included within, the first two teachings within Fa-tsang's p'an-chiao, those of the Hīnayāna and elementary Mahāyāna, because it includes the two *nairātmya* (i.e., the emptiness of both self and dharmas) whereas they do not include the tathāgatagarbha.

3. It both includes and is included within the advanced teaching of the Mahāyāna "because this scripture is also based on the tathāgatagarbha." Tsung-mi adds that it is also referred to as "the Mahāyāna of the sudden teaching."

This passage is especially significant because it reveals precisely that aspect of the perfect teaching that the *Scripture of Perfect Enlightenment* contains as well as that which it lacks: this scripture contains the *Hua-yen Sūtra's* teaching of the one true dharmadhātu but not its teaching of interpenetration and mutual determination. To put it in terms that Tsung-mi does not use, the *Scripture of Perfect Enlightenment* contains the Hua-yen teaching of *li-shih wu-ai* but not that of *shih-shih wu-ai*.

In addition to identifying the *Scripture of Perfect Enlightenment* with the advanced teaching, Tsung-mi also identified this text with the sudden teaching, and his discussion of how it fits within that latter rubric further reveals the way in which he saw it as differing from the *Hua-yen Sūtra*.[42] In his subcommentary to the *Scripture of Perfect Enlightenment*,[43] Tsung-mi distinguishes between the two types of sudden teaching discussed in the previous chapter: *hua-i-tun* (the sudden

[40] TSC 234d16–17.
[41] TS 116b5–12.
[42] Cf. chapter 5.
[43] TSC 218b7–15.

teaching as a method of exposition) and *chu-chi-tun* (the sudden teaching expounded in response to beings of superior capacity). The first refers solely to the *Hua-yen Sūtra*, which, "in accordance with the nature (*ch'eng-hsing*), was suddenly taught (*tun-shuo*) at one time (*i-shih*)" immediately after the Buddha had attained enlightenment (*ch'u ch'eng-fo shih*). The second type of sudden teaching refers to those scriptures—such as the *Śrīmālā*, *Ghanavyūha*, *Vajrasamādhi*, *Tathāgata-garbha*, and *Perfect Enlightenment*—which, preached to ordinary beings of superior capacity who have not yet eliminated their defilements (*shang-ken chü-tsu fan-nao fan-fu*), "reveal the one true enlightened nature" (*hsien i-chen chüeh-hsing*).

Tsung-mi's account of the two types of sudden teaching in his sub-commentary to the *Scripture of Perfect Enlightenment* agrees with that found in his *Ch'an Preface*, and there is no need to repeat the conclusions reached in the last chapter. Here I would only like to call attention to two of the terms Tsung-mi uses in his account: *ch'eng-hsing*, "in accordance with the nature," and *chu-chi*, "in response to the capacity [of beings]." These terms recall a distinction made by Fa-tsang (see chapter 4), and the different use to which Tsung-mi puts them highlights from yet another angle the wide divergence between their respective evaluations of the *Hua-yen Sūtra*. Fa-tsang had used the terms *ch'eng-fa* (equivalent in meaning to Tsung-mi's *ch'eng-hsing*)[44] and *chu-chi* to emphasize the qualitative distinction between the separate and common teaching—the former being characterized as "the fundamental teaching in accord with the truth" and the latter as "the derivative teaching adapted to the capacity of beings."[45] Tsung-mi not only treats the two as belonging to the same category but also reverses Fa-tsang's valuation by treating the teaching in response to the capacities of beings (*chu-chi*) as being superior to that in accordance with the nature/truth (*ch'eng-hsing/fa*). In contrast to Fa-tsang, who had used this distinction to clarify the difference between the separate and common teachings, Tsung-mi, like Chih-yen, saw the separate and common teachings as both belonging to the one vehicle.[46] It is also worth noting that Tsung-mi regarded the content of the separate teaching of the one vehicle as consisting in nature origination (*hsing-ch'i*), and not the conditioned origination of the dharmadhātu (*fa-chieh yüan-ch'i*), and that of the common teaching as conditioned origination (*yüan-ch'i*)—another indication of how far his revision of Hua-yen thought diverged from Fa-tsang's.

[44] See Nakamura Hajime, *Bukkyōgo daijiten*, 1:730c.

[45] See chapter 4.

[46] *Hsing yüan p'in shu-ch'ao*, HTC 7.100d17.

Tsung-mi's discussion of the sudden teaching shows that its content is identical to that of the advanced teaching. His teaching that reveals the nature thus also includes that which Fa-tsang had listed, under a separate category, as the sudden teaching. His claim that the *Scripture of Perfect Enlightenment* contains part of what was taught in the *Hua-yen Sūtra*, moreover, indicates that the teaching that reveals the nature also partially includes the perfect teaching. Finally, Tsung-mi regarded that aspect of the perfect teaching—*shih-shih wu-ai*—that was not included within the teaching that reveals the nature as of so little significance as not to merit the status of a separate category in his classification system. Since this aspect was that which the previous tradition had claimed epitomized the most profound teaching of the Buddha, Tsung-mi's revalorization of Hua-yen teachings marks a radical shift in Hua-yen hermeneutics, a point that belies the claim of one authority on the dharmadhātu theory in the Hua-yen tradition that "it is difficult to find any new development" in Tsung-mi's idea of the dharmadhātu.[47]

[47] See Oh, "A Study of Chinese Hua-yen Buddhism," p. 199; the same opinion is repeated in Oh, "*Dharmadhātu*," p. 86.

PART THREE

The Ground of Practice

Chapter Seven

A COSMOGONIC MAP FOR BUDDHIST PRACTICE

TSUNG-MI's supplanting of the perfect teaching by the teaching that reveals the nature can be correlated with his displacement of the *Hua-yen Sūtra* by the *Awakening of Faith*. Not only does this shift signal a fundamental alteration in the valence of Hua-yen thought, it also points to the importance of Ch'an in determining the context within which Tsung-mi adapted Hua-yen metaphysics. As I shall argue in the next three chapters, Tsung-mi's revision of Hua-yen doctrine can be best understood as part of his attempt to articulate the ontological basis and philosophical rationale for Ch'an practice, and for this purpose the *Awakening of Faith* provided a far more suitable model than the *Hua-yen Sūtra*. To lay the ground for this argument, the present chapter will give a detailed examination of Tsung-mi's appropriation of the *Awakening of Faith* by showing how he read out of this text a cosmogonic model from which he derived a systematic theory of the path (mārga). It will trace the development of this theory from early works, such as his commentary and subcommentary to the *Scripture of Perfect Enlightenment*, to later works, such as his *Ch'an Preface* and *Inquiry into the Origin of Man*. Not only has this aspect of Tsung-mi's thought not been sufficiently explored before, it is also its very crux, being that from which all others can be seen as derived. As this and the next chapter will demonstrate, the cosmogonic model Tsung-mi constructed from the *Awakening of Faith* provided the basis on which he established his system of doctrinal classification.[1]

THE FIVE STAGES OF PHENOMENAL EVOLUTION

As has already been noted, Tsung-mi regarded the one true dharmadhātu as being that aspect of the teaching of the *Hua-yen Sūtra* contained within the teaching that reveals the nature. He discusses the one true dharmadhātu in the fourth section of his introduction to both his commentary and abridged commentary to the *Scripture of Perfect Enlightenment*, "Analyzing the Mysterious and Profound" (*fen-*

---

[1] Portions of this chapter incorporate and adapt material from "What Happened to the Perfect Teaching?" and "Tsung-mi's Theory of Sudden Enlightenment Followed by Gradual Cultivation."

ch'i yu-shen), in which he outlines his understanding of the central content of the scripture in terms of five stages of phenomenal evolution[2]—a "cosmogony" based on the *Awakening of Faith*. Not only does Tsung-mi consider this cosmogonic process as fundamental to the message of the *Scripture of Perfect Enlightenment*, it is also one of the primary elements within the overall structure of his thought. He discusses it again in the second part of the third section of his introduction to his commentary to the *Awakening of Faith*—a context that emphasizes the crucial role that it played within his understanding of Buddhism, as it is one of the two places wherein his commentary diverges in substance from that of Fa-tsang, on which it is based.[3] This five-stage theory is a more primitive version of the process of phenomenal evolution described in the concluding sections of both his *Inquiry into the Origin of Man* and *Ch'an Preface*. Its importance in these two works again underlines its centrality within Tsung-mi's thought as a whole. Both works are later than his commentaries and reflect a more mature intellectual position. Nor is their form dictated by the conventions of a commentary format, whose set categories and fragmentary nature discourage the innovative expression of systematically developed thought.

Tsung-mi's five-stage theory explains how the world of delusion and defilement, the world in terms of which unenlightened beings experience themselves, evolves out of a unitary ontological ground that is both intrinsically enlightened and pure. Beings' suffering in delusion is a function of the epistemological dualism out of which the world of their experience is constructed. Religious practice thus entails the recovery of a primordial state of perfection before the bifurcation of consciousness into subject and object. While the terms in which Tsung-mi explains his theory are thoroughly Buddhist, his underlying cosmogonic model is one that has deep resonances with indigenous Chinese models. Such models presume that the world is generated through a process by which an originally undifferentiated whole divides into a primordial polarity, through whose interaction the world of differentiated phenomena is then generated.[4]

[2] See TS 116c16–117c4 and LS 526b19–c16; for Tsung-mi's subcommentary, see TSC 264a16–267b5 and LSC 125a18–126d18. This section of this chapter is based primarily on Tsung-mi's account in TS and TSC. The corresponding sections in Ch'eng-kuan's introduction to his commentary and subcommentary to the *Hua-yen Sūtra* (T 35.514a4–517c14 and T 36.70b20–86b18) and his commentary to the *Hsing yüan p'in* (244a16–248d14) discuss the four dharmadhātu and ten profundities—another instance of the difference between Tsung-mi and Ch'eng-kuan noted in the last chapter. See Yoshizu, *Kegonzen*, p. 299.

[3] See Yoshizu Yoshihide, "Shūmitsu no *Daijō kishin ronshū* ni tsuite."

[4] This theme has been most thoroughly explored by Norman Girardot in his *Myth*

Although its content is different, Tsung-mi's theory has the same soteriological function in his thought that the twelve-link chain of conditioned origination (*pratītyasamutpāda*; *yüan-ch'i*) had in early Buddhism. As Frank Reynolds has noted, the twelve-link chain represents a "saṃsāric cosmogony."[5] The cosmos in question, of course, is not the "objective" universe that exists independent of beings' perception of it. Nor is the creation a single act that takes place in the beginning of time. Rather, the "cosmos" is one that is continually generated through beings' construction of it. As it functions in early Buddhist psychology, the twelve-link chain of conditioned origination presents a coherent theory of the process of world construction by which beings ensnare themselves in self-reinforcing patterns of thought and behavior that keep them bound to the relentless wheel of birth-and-death.[6] The twelve-link chain might thus be better characterized as a "psychocosmogony."

Insofar as it offers an etiology of saṃsāric existence, the twelve-link chain correlates with the second noble truth, the origin of suffering (*samudaya*). As the structure of the four noble truths makes clear, the third noble truth, that of cessation (*nirodha*), is made possible by the second noble truth. It is because the process by which beings become bound in saṃsāra is based on a complex pattern of conditioning that liberation is possible. That is, because the process by which this whole mass of suffering comes about is predicated on a series of conditions, it is possible to reverse the process by successively eliminating the conditions on which each link in the chain is predicated. Thus the Buddha's enlightenment is often described in terms of his successive reversal of each link in the twelvefold chain of conditioned origination.[7]

---

and Meaning in Early Taoism. See also chapter 3 ("Cosmogony") of Edward Schafer's *Pacing the Void*, pp. 21–33.

[5] See his "Multiple Cosmogonies," pp. 203–224. I am here using "cosmogony" in the sense of the original Greek terms from which the word is derived, namely, an account of the genesis of the cosmos. This usage is in keeping with the definition Charles Long gives in his entry on "Cosmogony" in vol. 4 of *The Encyclopedia of Religion*: "Cosmogony thus has to do with myths, stories, or theories regarding the birth or creation of the universe as an order or the description of the original order of the universe" (p. 94). I would accordingly distinguish a "cosmogony" from a "cosmology" in the following way: whereas the former has to do with an account of the origin of the universe, the latter has to do with a description of the structure of the universe. Buddhist cosmology thus refers to theories about the three realms of being or the six modes of existence and so forth.

[6] For an interesting psychological interpretation of the twelve-link chain, see Rune Johansson, *The Dynamic Psychology of Early Buddhism*.

[7] For a discussion of early accounts of the Buddha's enlightenment, see L. Schmit-

It is in these terms, for instance, that Aśvaghoṣa describes the Buddha's enlightenment in the *Buddhacarita*.[8] Having seen the coming into existence and passing away of all beings and realized the full scale of the suffering entailed by the unremitting cycle of birth and death in which all beings are trapped, the Buddha reflects on the necessary condition on which old age and death (*jarā-maraṇa*) depend. Realizing that old age and death depend on birth (*jāti*), the Buddha then reflects on the necessary condition on which birth depends. Realizing that birth depends on becoming (*bhava*), the Buddha then reflects on the necessary condition on which becoming depends. The Buddha continues in this fashion, moving backward from becoming to grasping (*upādāna*), craving (*tṛṣṇā*), sensation (*vedanā*), contact (*sparśa*), the six sense modalities (*ṣaḍāyatana*), name and form (*nāmarūpa*), consciousness (*vijñāna*), constructions (*saṃskāra*), all the way back to ignorance (*avidyā*) as the final condition on which this whole mass of suffering depends.[9] Having thus derived the twelve-fold chain of conditioned origination, the Buddha then formulates the chain in its forward direction, beginning with ignorance and ending with old age and death. "When it is thus scorched by death's anguish great pain arises; such verily is the origin of this great trunk of pain."[10]

Having thus discerned the process by which this whole mass of suffering originates, the Buddha then realizes that the entire process can be brought to an end if each of the links of which it is constituted is successively stopped. Thus reflecting that old age and death may be brought to an end if birth is stopped, and that birth may be brought

---

hausen, "On Some Aspects of Descriptions or Theories of 'Liberating Insight' and 'Enlightenment' in Early Buddhism."

[8] In the following account, I have drawn on the translation by E. B. Cowell reprinted in *Buddhist Mahāyāna Texts*. Cowell's translation was based on a corrupt and relatively late Nepalese text. A subsequent translation, based on an earlier and more reliable text, was made by E. H. Johnston in *The Buddhacarita, or Acts of the Buddha*. Although Johnston's translation is to be preferred, I have followed Cowell's translation for the purely expedient reason that its account corresponds more closely to the twelve-link chain. I am here concerned with the general pattern illustrated in the account of the Buddha's enlightenment and not with textual questions concerning the *Buddhacarita*. For an example of the Buddha's enlightenment described in terms of the twelve-link chain of conditioned origination in the Pāli Canon, see *Saṃyutta-nikāya* 2.103, translated by Caroline Rhys Davids in *The Book of the Kindred Sayings*, part 2, pp. 72–73.

[9] In Johnston's translation, the Buddha originally traces the chain back to consciousness (*vijñāna*), leaving out constructions (*saṃskāra*) and ignorance (*avidyā*) (see p. 211 in the reprint edition). The Chinese translation by Dharmakṣema also omits these two terms (see *Fo-so-hsing tsan ching*, T 4.27c26–29).

[10] Cowell, *Buddist Mahāyāna Texts*, pp. 153–154; this verse is missing from both Johnston's and Dharmakṣema's texts.

to an end if becoming is stopped, and so forth, the Buddha moves back through the chain until he realizes that once ignorance has been brought to an end, the constructions will no longer have any power. Thus ignorance is declared to be the root of this great mass of suffering; therefore it is to be stopped by those who seek liberation.[11]

The twelve-link chain could thus be taken as a map for Buddhist practice, and the process of conditioned origination accordingly was bidirectional: it could either move with the flow of saṃsāra (*anuloma*; *shun*) or move against the flow of saṃsāra (*pratiloma*; *ni*), either further enmeshing one in bondage or advancing one toward liberation. The important point to note is the reciprocality that obtains between the two directions. It is because *pratiloma* reverses *anuloma* that the twelve-link chain of conditioned origination provides a map for liberation.

Tsung-mi's five-stage cosmogony stands on the same premise as the twelve-link chain of conditioned origination: that it is only through insight into the complex process of conditioning by which beings become ever more deeply bound in self-reinforcing patterns of thought and behavior that they can begin to deconstruct the process, thereby freeing themselves from bondage. Again, it is the reciprocality of the two directions in the process that enables the five stages in the process of phenomenal evolution to provide a map for Tsung-mi's explanation of the nature and course of Buddhist practice. His theory of sudden enlightenment followed by gradual cultivation, for instance, is derived from the cosmogony he reads out of the *Awakening of Faith*.

In both his discussion of this theory of phenomenal evolution in his commentary and subcommentary to the *Scripture of Perfect Enlightenment*, and his commentary to the *Awakening of Faith*, Tsung-mi elucidates the fundamental basis of this process by linking it to Ch'eng-kuan's description of the one true dharmadhātu. This is a particularly significant hermeneutical move that indicates a marked shift in the principal valence of Hua-yen thought. The fourfold dharmadhātu theory was the primary framework within which Ch'eng-kuan interpreted Hua-yen thought and represented his main contribution to the development of Hua-yen hermeneutics. It established the supremacy of the perfect teaching of the *Hua-yen Sūtra* in terms of the interrelation of all phenomena (*shih-shih wu-ai*). Tsung-mi's recasting of the significance of the dharmadhātu in terms of the *Awakening of Faith* not only pushes Hua-yen thought toward a much more explicitly ontological position but also makes room for traditional Chinese cosmological preoccupations within the field of Buddhist discourse.

---

[11] See ibid., pp. 151–154; cf. Johnston, *The Buddhacarita*, pp. 209–213; T 4.27c–28a.

At the same time, his bending of Ch'eng-kuan's statements on the dharmadhātu to a different purpose both legitimates his reinterpretation and disguises its extent.

The First Stage: The One Mind

The first stage corresponds to the one mind, which, as the ultimate source (*pen-yüan*) of all pure and impure dharmas, constitutes the first principle in Tsung-mi's cosmogonic scheme. Tsung-mi identifies the one mind of the *Awakening of Faith* with the wondrous mind of perfect enlightenment (*yüan-chüeh miao-hsin*) of the *Scripture of Perfect Enlightenment* and the one true dharmadhātu of the *Hua-yen Sūtra*—all of which are thus synonymous with one another, as well as serving as different expressions for the tathāgatagarbha. In his commentary to the *Awakening of Faith*, Tsung-mi writes: "Even though there are four types of dharmadhātu within the *Hua-yen*, [Ch'eng-kuan's] commentary on that scripture says, 'In all there is just one true dharmadhātu. It wholly embraces manifold existence and is identical with the one mind.' "[12] This quotation from Ch'eng-kuan allows Tsung-mi to set aside the four types of dharmadhātu in favor of the one true dharmadhātu. It also enables him to equate the one true dharmadhātu with the mind of sentient beings in the *Awakening of Faith*, quoting the passage from that text that states: " 'Dharma' means the mind of sentient beings. That mind embraces all mundane and supermundane dharmas."[13]

The one mind here is equivalent to the tathāgatagarbha as the basis for both saṃsāra and nirvāṇa.[14] Even though it is the ultimate source of all pure and impure dharmas, the one mind itself transcends all such dualities.[15] As will be seen in the next section, the one mind is the underlying nature (*hsing*) from which all conditioned phenomena (*hsiang*) arise (*ch'i*). It is thus the ontological ground on which conditioned origination (*yüan-ch'i*) takes place. Conditioned origination, moreover, is twofold. The impure or mundane dharmas are those

[12] 14b3; the identical passage occurs in TS 116d3–4; see also *Chu Hua-yen fa-chieh kuan-men*, T 45.684b24–c1. For a discussion of the quotation from Ch'eng-kuan, see chapter 6, n. 29.

[13] TSC 264b6–7; cf. LSC 125b8–9. The quotation from the *Awakening of Faith* comes from T 32.575c21–22; cf. Hakeda, *The Awakening of Faith*, p. 28; Hirakawa, *Daijō kishin-ron*, p. 56.

[14] Cf. *Śrīmālā Sūtra*, T 12.222b4 and b17–20 (Alex and Hideko Wayman, *The Lion's Roar of Queen Śrīmālā*, pp. 104, 105); *Awakening of Faith*, T 32.576b7 (Hakeda, *The Awakening of Faith*, p. 36; Hirakawa, *Daijō kishin-ron*, p. 95).

[15] TSC 264b11–12.

produced through the process of phenomenal evolution, and the pure or supermundane dharmas are those arrived at through the process of religious cultivation, by which one reverses the flow of saṃsāra and returns to the original source.[16] Enlightenment is thus the process by which one returns to the original source, and the one mind is both that into which one has insight and the ontological ground that makes such insight possible.

The Second Stage: The Two Aspects of the One Mind

The second stage in Tsung-mi's cosmogony corresponds to the two aspects of the one mind described in the *Awakening of Faith*. The first is the mind as suchness (*hsin chen-ju men*), which the text defines as that which neither is born nor dies. The second is the mind subject to birth-and-death (*hsin sheng-mieh men*), which refers to the ālaya-vijñāna, in which the tathāgatagarbha and that which is subject to birth-and-death are interfused. Fa-tsang had referred to the first as the unchanging (*pu-pien*) aspect of the one mind and the second as its conditioned (*sui-yüan*) aspect. The two together totally comprehend all dharmas.[17]

In his commentary to the *Awakening of Faith*, Tsung-mi quotes Ch'eng-kuan's statement in regard to the dharmadhātu to characterize the mind as suchness: "Its essence transcends being and nonbeing; its defining characteristic is that it neither is born nor dies. Since none can probe its beginning or end, how could its center or periphery be perceived?"[18] He then quotes Ch'eng-kuan's statement—"One who understands it is greatly enlightened; one who is deluded about it transmigrates without cease"—to characterize the mind subject to birth-and-death,[19] which, as the third stage in the process of phenomenal evolution makes clear, has both an enlightened and unenlightened aspect.

Tsung-mi's explanation of the second stage of phenomenal evolution in his commentary to the *Scripture of Perfect Enlightenment* largely consists of quotations from the *Awakening of Faith*, with his subcommentary frequently supplying the accompanying commentary by Fa-tsang. Tsung-mi begins with the following quotation from the *Awakening of Faith*:

[16] TSC 264a17–b1.

[17] T 32.576a6–7; quoted in TSC 264c7–8 and LSC 125b14. Cf. Hakeda, *The Awakening of Faith*, p. 31; Hirakawa, *Daijō kishin-ron*, p. 69.

[18] 14b3–4, quoting *Hsing-yüan p'in shu*, HTC 7.249c13–14.

[19] 14b4, quoting *Hsing-yüan p'in shu*, HTC 7.249c15.

The mind as suchness is the one dharmadhātu. It is characterized as all-embracing and is the essence of the teachings. What is called the nature of the mind neither is born nor dies. It is only on the basis of deluded thinking (*wang-nien*) that all of the dharmas come to be differentiated. If one frees oneself from deluded thoughts (*li wang-nien*), then there are no longer any phenomenal appearances of external objects (*wu i-ch'ieh ching-chieh chih hsiang*).[20]

Tsung-mi's subcommentary goes on to quote the rest of this passage, which says that since the nature of the mind is ineffable and inconceivable, "all locutions (*yen-shuo*) are provisional designations (*chia-ming*), lack reality (*wu-shih*), and are merely used in accordance with deluded thinking (*wang-nien*)."[21] The text concludes by stating that the term "suchness" (*chen-ju*) does not designate anything at all but is only a device used to put an end to discursive discourse (*yen-shuo chih chi yin yen ch'ien yen*).[22]

The second aspect of the one mind, the mind subject to birth-and-death, exists "on the basis of the tathāgatagarbha."[23] The *Awakening of Faith* identifies this aspect of the one mind with the ālayavijñāna, which it defines as "the interfusion of that which is not subject to birth-and-death [i.e., the mind as suchness] and that which is subject to birth-and-death in such a way that they are neither one nor different."[24]

In his subcommentary to the *Scripture of Perfect Enlightenment*, Tsung-mi cites Fa-tsang's commentary, which adapts the *Awakening of Faith*'s famous metaphor of wind and waves to explain the relationship between the ālayavijñāna and the tathāgatagarbha.

The mind not subject to birth-and-death is stirred by the wind of ignorance to give rise to birth-and-death. Therefore [the text] says that the mind subject to birth-and-death is based on the mind not subject to birth-and-death. Still, even though there are these two [aspects of the one] mind, there are not two [separate] essences. It is only in terms of these two aspects [of the one mind] that [the text] is able to explain the dependence of phenomenal appearances. It is just like [the case of] unmoving water that is blown by the wind to become moving water. Even

[20] T 32.576a8–10; quoted in TS 116d6–9 and LSC 125b16–18. Cf. Hakeda, *The Awakening of Faith*, pp. 32–33; Hirakawa, *Daijō kishin-ron*, pp. 71–72.

[21] T 32.576a10–14; quoted in TSC 264b10–13.

[22] T 32.576a13–14; cf. Hakeda, *The Awakening of Faith*, p. 33; Hirakawa, *Daijō kishin-ron*, p. 72.

[23] T 32.576b8; quoted in TS 116d10 and LSC 125c1–2.

[24] T 32.576b8–9; quoted in TS 116d10–11 and LSC 125c2–3. Cf. Hakeda, *The Awakening of Faith*, p. 36; Hirakawa, *Daijō kishin-ron*, p. 95.

though stillness and motion are different, the essence of the water is one.
. . . The intrinsically pure mind is called the tathāgatagarbha. It is stirred
by the wind of ignorance to give rise to birth-and-death.[25]

The relationship between these two aspects of the one mind, which
are neither one nor different, traces back to a paradox at the core of
the tathāgatagarbha doctrine: the tathāgatagarbha is at once intrinsically pure and identical with the dharmakāya and yet appears to be
defiled. The two aspects of the one mind thus seem to be a matter of
perspective, and their difference can be seen as corresponding to the
point of view of ultimate and conventional truth. The tathāgatagarbha as seen from the enlightened perspective of a Buddha is perfectly pure and undefiled. It is only due to the deluded thinking of
unenlightened beings that it appears to be otherwise.

The relationship between these two aspects of the one mind brings
into focus the central philosophical problem for the tathāgatagarbha
tradition: the origin of ignorance.[26] If the mind is intrinsically enlightened, how can it become deluded? The problem arises because
it is the consistent position of tathāgatagarbha theory that ignorance
is only adventitious.[27] The problem is even more acute for the *Awakening of Faith*, which develops its doctrine of the one mind as a monistic ontology. The *Awakening of Faith*'s metaphor of the wind and
waves is an unsatisfactory resolution of the problem insofar as the
comparison of the wind to ignorance posits a separate origin for ignorance. If ignorance had a separate origin, it would thus have its
own autonomous ontological status placing it on an equal footing
with enlightenment. The resulting dualistic ontology would undermine the axial premise of the tathāgatagarbha tradition that enlightenment is universally accessible to all beings.

In so identifying the ālayavijñāna with the tathāgatagarbha, the
Awakening of Faith stands in the tradition of the *Laṅkāvatāra-sūtra*.[28]
This identification grounds the process of conditioned origination
(*yüan-ch'i*) on an intrinsically pure ontological foundation. This
means that the defilements that appear to obscure the intrinsically
enlightened mind of suchness are merely the manifestation of that
mind as it accords with conditions and have no independent basis of

[25] T 44.254b25–c3; quoted in TSC 265a6–11.

[26] See my "The Problem of Theodicy in the *Awakening of Faith*."

[27] The passage often cited as the locus classicus of this idea occurs in *Aṅguttara-nikāya*
1.10: "This mind, monks, is luminous, but it is defiled by taints that come from without; that mind, monks, is luminous, but it is cleansed of taints that come from without"
(Woodward, *The Book of Gradual Sayings*, 1:8).

[28] For one of the many instances that could be cited, see T 16.556b29–c1: "The
ālayavijñāna is called the tathāgatagarbha."

their own. The relationship between the tathāgatagarbha and ālaya-vijñāna is thus the basis on which the Hua-yen tradition establishes its theory of nature origination (*hsing-ch'i*) and is the central issue in terms of which it distinguishes its type of Yogācāra from that of Fa-hsiang.

The Third Stage: The Two Modes of the Ālayavijñāna

The third stage of phenomenal evolution is concerned with the dynamic ambivalence of the ālayavijñāna. This consciousness has two modes, which embrace (*she*) and give rise to (*sheng*) all dharmas.[29] The first is enlightened (*chüeh*), and the second is unenlightened (*pu-chüeh*). It is in terms of these two modes that Tsung-mi explains conditioned origination. Fa-tsang's commentary points out that the unenlightened mode gives rise to impure dharmas and the enlightened mode gives rise to pure dharmas.[30] Tsung-mi quotes the *Awakening of Faith*:

> "Enlightened" means that the essence of the mind (*hsin-t'i*) is free from thoughts (*li-nien*). The characteristic of being free from thoughts is like the realm of empty space in that there is nowhere it does not pervade. As the single characteristic of the dharmadhātu, it is the undifferentiated dharmakāya of the Tathāgata. Since it is based on the dharmakāya, when it is spoken of it is referred to as "intrinsic enlightenment."[31]

The *Awakening of Faith* goes on to distinguish intrinsic enlightenment (*pen-chüeh*) from experiential enlightenment (*shih-chüeh*). Experiential enlightenment, moreover, is contrasted with unenlightenment (*pu-chüeh*). In fact, the text states that experiential enlightenment can only be spoken of in the context of unenlightenment. Experiential enlightenment constitutes the process by which one awakens to the ultimate source of the mind (*chüeh hsin-yüan*). Intrinsic enlightenment is at once the ontological ground that makes experiential enlightenment possible as well as that which experiential enlightenment realizes.[32]

Under the heading of the unenlightened mode of the ālayavijñāna, Tsung-mi quotes the following sequence of passages from the *Awakening of Faith*, interspersed with bits of Fa-tsang's commentary.

---

[29] T 32.576b10; quoted in TSC 265c8–9.
[30] T 44.256b4–7; quoted in TSC 265c8–10.
[31] T 32.567b11–14; quoted in TS 116d13–14 and LSC 125c5–7. Cf. Hakeda, *The Awakening of Faith*, p. 37; Hirakawa, *Daijō kishin-ron*, p. 102.
[32] T 32.567b11–c4; partially quoted in TSC 265d1–5.

Because of not truly knowing the oneness of the dharma of suchness, the unenlightened mind arises, and thoughts come into being.[33]

Fa-tsang's commentary points out that this unenlightened mind refers to "primordial unenlightenment" (ken-pen pu-chüeh). Thoughts (nien) refer to the three subtle and six coarse phenomenal appearances of mind described in the fourth and fifth stages of the process of phenomenal evolution, which collectively represent "evolved unenlightenment" (chih-mo pu-chüeh). Primordial unenlightenment is the "root" (pen) or "essence" (t'i) of evolved unenlightenment, which represents its "branches" (mo) or "phenomenal appearances" (hsiang).[34]

Since thoughts lack any [distinguishing] characteristic of their own, they are not separate from intrinsic enlightenment.[35]

Fa-tsang's commentary underscores the point that this passage means that thoughts have no separate essence of their own.[36] The Awakening of Faith continues:

It is like a man who has gone astray (mi). His confusion (mi) is based on his sense of his sense of direction. Apart from his sense of direction, there is no confusion (mi). The case of sentient beings is also like this. Their delusion (mi) is based on intrinsic enlightenment. Apart from the nature of enlightenment, there is no unenlightenment.[37]

Tsung-mi notes that Fa-tsang's commentary thus says that ignorance has no essence of its own.[38] The text adds that it is only in the context of unenlightenment that the term "enlightenment" has any meaning. "Apart from the mind that is unenlightened, there is no real enlightenment with a [distinguishing] characteristic of its own that can be set forth."[39]

The Fourth Stage: The Three Subtle Phenomenal Appearances

The fourth stage consists of the three subtle phenomenal appearances (san hsi hsiang) enumerated in the Awakening of Faith—namely, activation (yeh) or the activity of ignorance (wu-ming yeh), the perceiv-

---

[33] T 32.577a1–2; quoted in TSC 265d17–266a1 and LSC 125c9–10. Cf. Hakeda, The Awakening of Faith, p. 43; Hirakawa, Daijō kishin-ron, p. 139.

[34] T 44.262a9–23; partially quoted in TSC 265d18.

[35] T 32.577a2; quoted in TSC 266a1–2.

[36] T 44.262a22; quoted in TSC 266a2.

[37] T 32.577a2–4; quoted in TSC 266a2–3.

[38] TSC 266a3–4.

[39] T 32.577a4–6; quoted in TSC 266a4–5.

ing subject (*neng-chien*), and the perceived object (*ching-chieh*). The activity of ignorance refers to the first subtle movement of thought. Based on the unenlightened mode of the ālayavijñāna, thought stirs the originally tranquil consciousness, which then manifests itself in terms of subject (*neng-chien*) and object (*ching-chieh*).[40] Tsung-mi goes on to correlate the three subtle phenomenal appearances with the *Ch'eng wei-shih lun's* explanation of the transformation (*pien*; *pariṇāma*) of consciousness: the first phenomenal appearance corresponds to the self-essence (*tzu-t'i*) of the ālayavijñāna; the second to its subjective mode (*chien-fen*; *darśanabhāga*); and the third to its objective mode (*hsiang-fen*; *nimittabhāga*).[41] Tsung-mi then criticizes Fa-hsiang, for which the *Ch'eng wei-shih lun* is authoritative, for its failure to realize that the ālayavijñāna is based on suchness.[42]

The Fifth Stage: The Six Coarse Phenomenal Appearances

The fifth stage in the process of phenomenal evolution is comprised of the six coarse phenomenal appearances (*liu ts'u hsiang*) enumerated in the *Awakening of Faith*—namely, discrimination (*chih*), continuation (*hsiang-hsü*), attachment (*chih-ch'ü*), conceptual elaboration (*chi-ming-tzu*), generating karma (*ch'i-yeh*), and the suffering of karmic bondage (*yeh-hsi-ku*). This final stage in the process of phenomenal evolution describes how the epistemological dualism that emerged in the previous stage leads to attachment to objects (*fa-chih*; *dharma-grāha*) and self (*wo-chih*; *ātmagrāha*), which in turn create patterns of association and behavior whose inevitable consequence "entails the ensuance of existentiality."[43]

The *Awakening of Faith* defines these six phenomenal appearances as follows:

1. The phenomenal appearance of discrimination: Based on its perception of objects, the mind thus gives rise to discrimination of likes and dislikes.

2. The phenomenal appearance of continuation: Based on such discriminations, awareness of pleasure and pain is produced, and the mind thus

[40] T 32.577a7–12; quoted in TS 117a1–4 and LSC 125c14–d1. Cf. Hakeda, *The Awakening of Faith*, p. 44; Hirakawa, *Daijō kishin-ron*, p. 142.

[41] TS 117a5–6; for an explanation of these terms, see *Ch'eng wei-shih lun*, T 31.10aff.

[42] TS 117a9ff.

[43] To borrow the concluding catena of James Joyce's parody of the twelve-link chain of conditioned origination: "In the ignorance that implies impression that knits knowledge that finds the nameform that whets the wits that convey contacts that sweeten sensation that drives desire that bitches birth that entails the ensuance of existentiality" (*Finnegans Wake*, p. 18).

gives rise to thoughts in association with [such awareness], and [they con-
tinue] without cease.

3. The phenomenal appearance of attachment: Based on the continuation
   [of such thoughts], one objectifies perceptual objects, fixating on their
   pleasurefulness or painfulness, and the mind thus gives rise to attachment.

4. The phenomenal appearance of conceptual elaboration: Based on such
   deluded attachments, one thus distinguishes among them in terms of
   provisional concepts.

5. The phenomenal appearance of generating karma: Based on such conceptual elaboration, one categorizes [one's experience], forming an attachment to it, and thus commits various actions (*yeh*; *karma*).

6. The phenomenal appearance of the suffering of karmic bondage:
   Based on one's actions (*yeh*; *karma*), one experiences the consequences
   and is thus not free.[44]

The text concludes: "Therefore know that ignorance is able to produce all impure dharmas because all impure dharmas are nothing
but the phenomenal appearances of unenlightenment."[45]

The five-stage process of phenomenal evolution can be represented diagrammatically as shown on the next page:

Tsung-mi's account of the five stages of phenomenal evolution also
links the various stages with different teachings in a way that anticipates the p'an-chiao scheme he develops in the *Inquiry into the Origin
of Man*. Since the five stages represent a cosmogony that serves as a
blueprint for the course of Buddhist practice, the p'an-chiao correspondences suggest the essentially soteriological focus behind Tsung-
mi's arrangement of the teachings.

Tsung-mi correlates the first three stages of phenomenal evolution
with the sudden and advanced teachings, both of which are contained
in the *Scripture of Perfect Enlightenment* and the *Awakening of Faith*.[46]
The fourth stage corresponds to the Fa-hsiang interpretation of
Yogācāra; as seen above, the three subtle phenomenal appearances correspond to the three divisions (*fen*; *bhaga*) of the ālayavijñāna described in the *Ch'eng wei-shih lun*.[47] The first two of the six coarse
phenomenal appearances—those of discrimination and continua-

---

[44] T 32.577a13–20; quoted in TS 117b11–18 and LSC 125d1–12. Cf. Hakeda, *The
Awakening of Faith*, pp. 44–45; Hirakawa, *Daijō kishin-ron*, p. 142.

[45] T 32.577a20–21; quoted in TSC 267a14–16.

[46] LSC 126a13–16. It is worth noting that Tsung-mi here names the *Lotus* and *Nirvāṇa* sūtras to represent the advanced teaching and the *Hua-yen* and *Śrīmālā* sūtras to
represent the sudden teaching—another example of how he sees the highest teaching
as containing both a sudden and a gradual aspect. See also *Ch'i-hsin lun shu*, 14b4–6.

[47] See LSC 126a4–13 and TS 117a5.

DIAGRAM OF THE PROCESS OF PHENOMENAL EVOLUTION

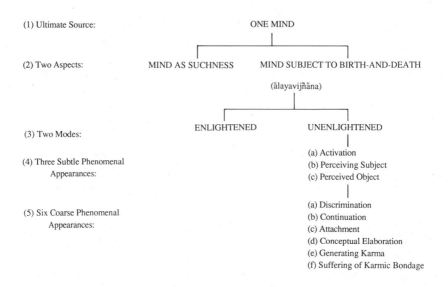

| (1) Ultimate Source: | ONE MIND |
| (2) Two Aspects: | MIND AS SUCHNESS   MIND SUBJECT TO BIRTH-AND-DEATH |

(ālayavijñāna)

(3) Two Modes:
ENLIGHTENED   UNENLIGHTENED

(4) Three Subtle Phenomenal
Appearances:
(a) Activation
(b) Perceiving Subject
(c) Perceived Object

(5) Six Coarse Phenomenal
Appearances:
(a) Discrimination
(b) Continuation
(c) Attachment
(d) Conceptual Elaboration
(e) Generating Karma
(f) Suffering of Karmic Bondage

tion—constitute *dharmagrāha*, attachment to dharmas, and as such are refuted by the Mahāyāna teaching of the emptiness of all dharmas. The third and fourth coarse phenomenal appearances—those of attachment and conceptual elaboration—constitute *ātmagrāha*, attachment to self, and as such are overcome by the Hīnayāna teaching of no-self (*anātman*).[48] The last two coarse phenomenal appearances—those of generating karma and the suffering of karmic bondage—correlate to the teaching of men and gods, which expounds the simple teaching of karma whereby beings can gain knowledge of the karmic effects of their actions and so be led to perform those kinds of actions that will ensure a good birth as a human or god.[49]

Such correspondences reveal how different teachings serve to overcome different stages in the process of phenomenal evolution,

[48] See *Ch'i-hsin lun shu*, 14b11–12, where Tsung-mi abridges the thirteen different items comprising his five-stage scheme into eight stages: (1) the one mind that constitutes the ultimate basis, (2) unenlightenment that forms the phenomenal appearance of activation, (3) the phenomenal appearance of the perceiving subject, (4) the phenomenal appearance of the perceived object, (5) attachment to dharmas (which includes the phenomenal appearances of discrimination and continuation), (6) attachment to self (which includes the phenomenal appearances of attachment and conceptual elaboration), (7) generating karma, and (8) experiencing suffering. See also TS 117b18–c1.

[49] See LSC 125d18–126a1 and TS 117c1.

suggesting how they can be arranged in a hierarchical fashion that reverses the course of phenomenal evolution and so recapitulates the course of progress along the path of enlightenment. By beginning with the most superficial teaching and progressing to the most profound, one can gradually advance from the outermost effects (*hsiang*) of the phenomenal evolution of the one mind—its "branches" (*mo*) in Tsung-mi's metaphor—back to its underlying nature (*hsing*)—its "root" (*pen*). By providing a map of Buddhist practice, Tsung-mi's five-stage cosmogony also serves as the template by which he organizes the teachings. The thrust of Tsung-mi's p'an-chiao is thus thoroughly soteriological. His classification of the teachings is a theory of the path (mārga).

Tsung-mi's soteriological concerns in emphasizing the cosmogonic meaning of the *Awakening of Faith* also reveal how his understanding of the significance of that text differs from Fa-tsang's. For Fa-tsang the *Awakening of Faith* was important because its teaching of the interrelation of the absolute and phenomenal (*li-shih wu-ai*) provided the theoretical basis on which he elaborated the interpenetration (*hsiang-ju*) and mutual determination (*hsiang-chi*) of all phenomena embodied in the perfect teaching. His interest was primarily metaphysical. Tsung-mi's was more "practical."[50] For Tsung-mi the *Awakening of Faith*'s teaching of the interrelationship of the absolute and phenomenal was important because its teaching of how the mind of suchness accorded with conditions provided an ontological basis for Buddhist practice.

NATURE ORIGINATION AND CONDITIONED ORIGINATION

Tsung-mi's adoption of the one true dharmadhātu as the first principle in a five-stage cosmogonic scheme was already suggested by Ch'eng-kuan's opening words in the preface to his *Hsing yüan p'in shu*: "How great the true dhātu (*ta-tsai chen-chieh*)! The myriad dharmas owe their inception to it (*wan-fa tzu-shih*)." This proclamation, as Tsung-mi points out in his subcommentary, derives from the comments on the first hexagram, *ch'ien* (the creative), in the *Classic of Change (I ching)* ("*Ta-tsai ch'ien-yüan. Wan-wu tzu-shih.*").[51] Whatever the underlying intent behind Ch'eng-kuan's allusion,[52] Tsung-mi

[50] As I trust should be obvious in context, by "practical" I mean "practice-oriented" (*jissen-teki*).

[51] See Z. D. Sung, *The Text of the Yi King*, p. 3.

[52] Ch'eng-kuan often claimed to borrow the words from the classics without thereby also adopting their meaning; see, for example, T 36.2b9.

took its implications seriously, and it is in his discussion of these words that he provides his fullest account of nature origination.

After elucidating the allusion, Tsung-mi defines the "true dhātu" as the "dharmadhātu of suchness" (chen-ju fa-chieh). He goes on to say: "Although the varieties of dharmadhātu are of many types, when its overall character is disclosed, there is just the one true dharmadhātu, the pure mind that is the source of Buddhas and sentient beings."[53] The true dhātu refers to the nature of the essence (t'i-hsing) of the mind of the one dharmadhātu (i fa-chieh hsin), whereas the myriad dharmas that owe their inception to it refer to the phenomenal appearance of its essence (t'i-hsiang).[54] Tsung-mi continues: "There is not a single dharma that is not a manifestation of the original mind. Nor is there a single dharma that does not conditionally arise from the true dhātu."[55]

Tsung-mi then invokes the authority of Wen-ch'ao (active first half of the eighth century) to distinguish between two modes of causality according to which "the mind of the one dharmadhātu brings all dharmas to completion."[56] The first of these is nature origination (hsing-ch'i); the second, conditioned origination (yüan-ch'i). In regard to the first, "nature" corresponds to the true dhātu, and "origination" to the myriad dharmas. Tsung-mi says that nature origination thus means that "the entire essence of the dharmadhātu as the nature arises (ch'i) to form all dharmas."[57]

In a parallel passage commenting on his preface to his commentary to the Scripture of Perfect Enlightenment, Tsung-mi introduces his discussion of nature origination by saying: "The nature and its phenomenal appearances are unobstructed because the absolute (li) and the phenomenal (shih) interpenetrate (chiao-ch'e), the phenomenal is no different from the absolute, the absolute is no different from the

[53] Hsing-yüan p'in shu-ch'ao, HTC 7.399b5–6.

[54] Ibid., 399b15–17.

[55] Ibid., 399c1–2.

[56] Ibid., 399c3–4. Wen-ch'ao was a disciple of Fa-tsang about whom little is known. Tsung-mi here alludes to his Hua-yen kuan-chien (The key to the Hua-yen [Sūtra]), a work that is unfortunately not extant. The only writing of Wen-ch'ao's that has survived is the tenth and last fascicle of his Hua-yen ching i-ch'ao, also referred to as Sui-wen yao-k'o tzu-fang i-wang chi (see Takamine Ryōshū, "Monchō hōshi no Kegon-kyō gishō ni tsuite"). Ch'eng-kuan cites ten contemplations (kuan) from Wen-ch'ao's I-wang chi in his Yen-i ch'ao (T 36.271a19ff). Takamine Ryōshū summarizes the contents of the tenth fascicle of the I-wang chi in his discussion of Wen-ch'ao in Kegon shisōshi, pp. 267–270. Takamine concludes that, in his analysis of nature origination and conditioned origination, as well as the structure of his ten contemplations (which move from li-shih wu-ai to shih-shih wu-ai), Wen-ch'ao takes a step in the direction of the doctrinal developments wrought by Ch'eng-kuan and Tsung-mi (p. 269). See chapter 6, n. 13, above.

[57] Hsing-yüan p'in shu-ch'ao, HTC 7.399c5–6; TSC 336d6–7.

phenomenal, and they are interfused."[58] Tsung-mi here clearly identifies nature origination with *li-shih wu-ai*. His wording also makes clear that he uses phenomenal appearances (*hsiang*) and phenomena (*shih*) as interchangeable terms. He then proffers two analogies: "It is like gold: only after it has been extracted from its ore can it be made into various objects. Or it is like a mirror: only after dust has been removed can it reflect myriad images."[59]

He goes on to point out that nature origination distinguishes the Hua-yen tradition from that of the Fa-hsiang: "Because the Fa-hsiang tradition explains suchness as being totally inert (*ning-jan*) and unchanging (*pu-pien*), it lacks the principle of nature origination."[60] Tsung-mi's criticism is based on the two aspects of the one mind described in the *Awakening of Faith*. Although Fa-hsiang recognizes the unchanging (*pu-pien*) aspect of the one mind, it fails to acknowledge its conditioned (*sui-yüan*) aspect. But it is precisely this conditioned aspect of the one mind that allows it to act as a creative principle in the generation of all pure and impure dharmas. According to the Fa-hsiang position, however, impure dharmas are produced by the ālayavijñāna, which is unconnected with suchness. For Hua-yen, of course, the importance of the *Awakening of Faith* lies in the fact that it connects the ālayavijñāna with suchness. Nature origination is thus but another term for the conditioned functioning of the one mind and, as such, centers on the linkage between the phenomenal realm of pure and impure dharmas and the absolute realm of suchness.

In contrast to Fa-hsiang, Tsung-mi points out that in the Hua-yen or *fa-hsing* (dharma-nature) tradition,

the true nature is clear (*chan-jan*) and spiritually luminous (*ling-ming*). Because its entire essence is identical with its functioning, inherently (*fa-erh*) it constantly forms the myriad dharmas. Inherently it is constantly tranquil in and of itself. Because its tranquility is a tranquility that is wholly identical with the myriad dharmas, it is not the same as the obtuse stupidity (*wan-chih*)[61] of a vacuous understanding of emptiness as annihilation (*hsü-k'ung tuan-k'ung*). Because the myriad dharmas are the myriad dharmas that are wholly identical with tranquility, they are not the same as the things that are imputed to have a fixed character due to the projection of inverted views (*p'ien-chi tao-chien ting-hsiang chih wu*).[62]

[58] TSC 214b5–7; LSC 98c6–8.

[59] TSC 214b7–8; LSC 98c8–9.

[60] *Hsing-yüan p'in shu-ch'ao*, HTC 7.399c5–6; TSC 336d6–7.

[61] *Hsing-yüan p'in shu-ch'ao* (HTC 7.399c9) gives *wan-chih*, while TSC (214b14 and 336d10) and LSC (98d15) all give *wan-ning*.

[62] *Hsing-yüan p'in shu-ch'ao*, HTC 7. 399c7–11; TSC 336d8–11; cf. TSC 214b11–15

Since all mundane and supermundane dharmas originate wholly from the nature, there is no other dharma outside of the nature. That is why Buddhas and sentient beings are inextricably interconnected and the pure and defiled lands harmoniously interpenetrate. Each and every dharma mutually includes one another. Every single speck of dust contains [all] worlds. They mutually determine and interpenetrate one another, their unobstructed interfusion is endowed with ten profound gates, and their infinite multiplication is without end. Truly this wholly derives from nature origination.[63]

The mutual determination (*hsiang-chi*), interpenetration (*hsiang-ju*), unobstructed interfusion (*jung-jung*), and infinite multiplication (*ch'ung-ch'ung wu-chin*) of all dharmas, which are detailed in the ten profundities (*shih-hsüan*), all refer to what is otherwise known as *shih-shih wu-ai*. Tsung-mi's concluding comment makes clear in no uncertain terms that *shih-shih wu-ai* derives from and is subordinate to nature origination—that is, *li-shih wu-ai*.

Tsung-mi concludes his account of nature origination by quoting the *Wang-chin huan-yüan kuan*, which defines nature origination as "the arising (*ch'i*) of its functioning (*yung*) based on its essence (*t'i*). Since it responds to myriad differentiated [things] as it arises, it is said to be profuse. Since it is always constant (*ku-chin ch'ang-jan*), it is said to occur inherently (*fa-erh*)."[64]

Whereas nature origination derives from the ālayavijñāna's connection with suchness, conditioned origination derives from its two modes. Conditioned origination thus refers to the process by which both delusion and enlightenment unfold and, accordingly, is discussed in terms of its impure and pure aspects. Tsung-mi explains impure conditioned origination as follows: "Even though sentient beings are fully endowed with the true nature as well as infinite excellent dharmas as explained above, yet, because they are deluded about it and do not realize it for themselves, they thus separately cling to infinite evil dharmas due to the projection of their inverted views."[65]

Tsung-mi divides impure conditioned origination into two further categories, what he here calls "beginningless root" (*wu-shih ken-pen*) and "evolved branches" (*chan-chuan chih-mo*). The first refers to au-

---

and LSC 98d12–16. I would like to thank Robert Buswell for his suggestions on the translation of some particularly thorny parts of this passage.

[63] *Hsing-yüan p'in shu-ch'ao*, HTC 7.399c11–14. Cf. *Ch'an Preface*, 407c9–11; K 185; B 242–243.

[64] *Hsing-yüan p'in shu-ch'ao*, HTC 7.399c15–17; TSC 336d15–17; quoted from T 45.639b20–22; cf. Cleary, *Entry into the Inconceivable*, p. 162.

[65] *Hsing-yüan p'in shu-ch'ao*, HTC 7.399d3–6.

tonomous (*tu-t'ou*) or primordial ignorance (*ken-pen wu-ming*),[66] exists independently of the defilements (*fan-nao*; *kleśa*), and is the root (*pen*) of the evolved branches. It consists in being deluded about the true (*mi-chen*) and clinging to the false (*chih-wang*). The evolved branches comprise the defilements, which arise from autonomous ignorance and serve as the basis for various actions; generating karma; and the karmic result of life-and-death in the six modes of existence.[67]

Tsung-mi also divides pure conditioned origination into two sub-categories—what he calls the partially pure (*fen-ching*) and the perfectly pure (*yüan-ching*). The partially pure refers to the three vehicles of the śrāvaka, pratyekabuddha, and bodhisattva who practices the six perfections of the provisional teaching.[68] These vehicles are said to be partially pure because they have not yet availed themselves of the perfect and sudden true teaching (*yüan tun shih-chiao*) but only have recourse to provisional teachings (*ch'üan-chiao*) that do not result in the true fruit.[69]

Perfectly pure conditioned origination, on the other hand, is only accessible through the true teaching (*shih-chiao*). This category comprises sudden enlightenment (*tun-wu*) and gradual cultivation (*chien-hsiu*). Sudden enlightenment overturns primordial ignorance. Gradual cultivation has two aspects—what Tsung-mi calls removing faults (*li-kuo*) and perfecting virtues (*ch'eng-te*). The first overcomes the effects of primordial ignorance, that is, its evolved branches. The second involves perfecting the subtle functioning of the infinite excellent qualities inherent in the true nature.[70]

Tsung-mi's account of conditioned origination can be outlined as follows:

1. Impure conditioned origination
   A. Beginningless ignorance
      i. Deluded about the true
      ii. Clinging to the false
   B. Evolved branches
      i. Defilements
      ii. Generating karma
      iii. Experiencing the results
2. Pure conditioned origination
   A. Partially pure

[66] Ibid., 399d7; he later refers to it as "primordial ignorance" at 400c5.
[67] Ibid., 399d13–400b2.
[68] Ibid., 400b3–14.
[69] Ibid., 400b14–16.
[70] Ibid., 400c4–d11.

  i. Śrāvaka
 ii. Pratyekabuddha
iii. Novice bodhisattva
B. Perfectly pure
 i. Sudden enlightenment
ii. Gradual cultivation
   a. Removing faults
   b. Perfecting virtues

Tsung-mi's discussion of conditioned origination is interesting in a number of respects. His casting of conditioned origination in terms of the reciprocal processes of delusion and enlightenment—rather than in terms of a realm in which phenomena interpenetrate without obstruction—makes clear his underlying soteriological concern. Compared to the metaphysical character of Fa-tsang's description of the conditioned origination of the dharmadhātu, Tsung-mi's account is more psychological in orientation. That is, it has to do with the process by which beings construct their experience of the world. In this regard it parallels the traditional twelve-link chain of conditioned origination. Nevertheless, there are important differences in content here as well. While the twelve-link chain is couched in terms of Hīnayāna abhidharma, Tsung-mi's version is thoroughly Mahāyāna, being based on a Yogācāra understanding of the mind. Still, as a theory of world construction it is, like the twelve-link chain, a cosmogony. As it is based on nature origination, however, it is cosmogonic in a sense that the twelve-link chain is not: it posits an ultimate ontological ground for the process.

Tsung-mi's explanation of conditioned origination is also important for introducing the notions of sudden enlightenment and gradual cultivation, which he subsumes under the heading of perfectly pure conditioned origination. As such they are contained in the perfect and sudden true teaching, which in his more mature p'an-chiao he refers to as the teaching that reveals the nature. His theory of sudden enlightenment followed by gradual cultivation is developed most fully in the *Ch'an Preface* and *Ch'an Chart* and will be treated in the next section. For now it is sufficient to note that sudden enlightenment is founded on the tathāgatagarbha whereas gradual cultivation is founded on the ālayavijñāna.

Sudden Enlightenment Followed by Gradual Cultivation

Even though Tsung-mi does not include the sudden teaching as a separate category within his classification scheme, his highest teaching—that which reveals the nature—contains a sudden and gradual component. The sudden component of the highest teaching is associated primarily with the *Scripture of Perfect Enlightenment* and *Awakening of Faith*, whereas the gradual component is associated with *Lotus* and *Nirvāṇa* sūtras. The sudden component, furthermore, is identified with the Ch'an tradition of Ho-tse Shen-hui, whose cardinal teaching Tsung-mi characterizes in terms of sudden enlightenment followed by gradual cultivation.

For Tsung-mi, sudden enlightenment did not obviate the need for the cultivation of a graduated series of stages of religious practice. In fact, according to him, the experience of sudden enlightenment was the indispensable foundation upon which such practice had to be carried out. As he says in the *Ch'an Preface*: "If one engages in spiritual cultivation without having first experienced enlightenment, then it is not authentic practice."[71] In other words, it is the experience of sudden enlightenment that authenticates Buddhist practice, an experience that Tsung-mi conceptualized in the *Ch'an Preface* as being only the first stage in a ten-stage process culminating in the attainment of Buddhahood.

Tsung-mi uses three analogies in the *Ch'an Chart* to illustrate what he means by sudden enlightenment followed by gradual cultivation. The first, adapted from the *Awakening of Faith*,[72] is that even though the wind that has stirred the originally tranquil surface of the ocean into movement ceases suddenly, the motion of its waves only subsides gradually.[73] The second is that even though the sun appears suddenly, the morning frost only melts gradually.[74] The last, which Tsung-mi borrows from Shen-hui,[75] is that even though an infant "suddenly" possesses all of its limbs and faculties intact the moment it is born, it only learns to master their use gradually.[76] Doctrinally, Tsung-mi claims that the teaching of sudden enlightenment followed by gradual cultivation is based on the *Awakening of Faith*, *Scripture of Perfect Enlightenment*, and *Hua-yen Sūtra*.[77]

---

[71] T 48.407c21–22; K 191; cf. B 246.

[72] See T 32.576c11–14; cf. Hakeda, *The Awakening of Faith*, p. 41.

[73] T 48.407b26–27; K 185; cf. B 240–241.

[74] T 48.407c19; K 191; cf. B 245.

[75] See *Ting shih-fei lun, Shen-hui ho-shang i-chi*, p. 287: "You should suddenly see your Buddha-nature and then gradually cultivate causal conditions. . . . It is like a mother suddenly giving birth to a child, giving him her breast, and gradually nurturing and rearing him. . . . Suddenly awakening and seeing one's Buddha-nature is also like this—wisdom naturally increases gradually."

[76] T 48.407c19–20.

[77] See *Ch'an Chart*, HTC 110.438b8–9; K p. 341.

Tsung-mi's fullest description of sudden enlightenment occurs in the *Ch'an Chart*, where he says:

> While awakening from delusion is sudden, the transformation of an unenlightened person (*fan*) into an enlightened person (*sheng*) is gradual.[78] Sudden enlightenment means that although [beings] have been deluded [from time] without beginning, recognizing the four elements as their body and deluded thoughts as their mind and taking them both together as constituting their self, when they meet a good friend (*shan-yu; kalyāṇamitra*) who explains to them the meaning of the absolute and conditioned [aspects of suchness], the nature and its phenomenal appearance, the essence and its functioning . . . , then they at once realize that [their own] marvelous awareness and vision is their true mind, that the mind—which is from the beginning empty and tranquil, boundless and formless—is the dharmakāya, that the nonduality of body and mind is their true self, and that they are no different from all Buddhas by even a hair.[79]

Thus, for Tsung-mi, sudden enlightenment is the experience in which one sees that his true nature is, and always has been, wholly identical with that of all Buddhas. Moreover, one realizes that the actual functioning of one's mind is nothing but an expression of the intrinsically enlightened true mind. Although Tsung-mi does not himself make the connection here, his description of sudden enlightenment makes clear that it consists in an insight into nature origination.

The paradigm for this experience is, of course, the Buddha's own enlightenment as described in the passage from the *Hua-yen Sūtra* quoted in the previous chapter.[80] All the same, it must also be pointed out that what Tsung-mi meant by sudden enlightenment differs significantly from the enlightenment experienced by the Buddha, which all Buddhist traditions have characterized as supreme, perfect enlightenment (*anuttarāsamyaksambodhi*). Here it is significant to note a critical distinction Tsung-mi adopts from Ch'eng-kuan between two qualitatively different types of enlightenment—that between *cheng-*

---

[78] Both the HTC and Kamata versions of the text read: "*chuan-fan ch'eng-sheng chi tun-wu yeh.*" I have emended this passage to read "*chuan-fan ch'eng-sheng chi chien yeh*" in light of *P'ei Hsiu shih-i wen*, p. 95, and Chinul's *Chŏryo*, p. 29. According to traditional mārga theory, the transformation from *pṛthagjana* (*fan*) to *ārya* (*sheng*) took place at the stage of *darśana-mārga*. If Tsung-mi's theory of the three stages of religious cultivation can be correlated with traditional mārga theory, then he has the transformation from *pṛthagjana* to *ārya* taking place not at the stage of *darśana-mārga* (i.e., *chieh-wu*), but at the completion of *bhāvanā-mārga* (i.e., *chien-hsiu*).

[79] HTC 110.437d17–438a3; K 340.

[80] T 10.272c4–7 and 272c25–273a2; see p. 166.

wu, the enlightenment of full realization, and *chieh-wu*, the enlightenment of initial insight. As he explains these terms in his subcommentary to the *Scripture of Perfect Enlightenment*: "Because one first has an initial experience of enlightenment (*ch'u yin chieh-wu*), he engages in religious practice based on that experience (*i wu hsiu hsing*), and, as soon as his practice is completed and his task perfected (*hsing man kung yüan*), he realizes the fulfillment of enlightenment (*chi te cheng-wu*)."[81] Tsung-mi's explanation of these two qualitatively different kinds of enlightenment presupposes a three-stage model of the path: (1) initial insight (*chieh-wu*), (2) gradual cultivation (*chien-hsiu*), and (3) final enlightenment (*cheng-wu*). "Sudden enlightenment" in the context of Tsung-mi's theory of sudden enlightenment followed by gradual cultivation refers to *chieh-wu*, initial awakening, only the first stage in his ten-stage process of spiritual cultivation that Tsung-mi elaborates in the *Ch'an Preface*. The Buddha's enlightenment, on the other hand, would correspond to *cheng-wu*, the final culmination of enlightenment that is Buddhahood.

For Tsung-mi the necessity of commencing a process of gradual cultivation following the experience of enlightenment (*chieh-wu*) is based on the sheer tenacity of the karmic residue of past actions (*hsün-hsi*; *vāsanā*), which has thoroughly permeated the ālayavijñāna over the course of incalculable lifetimes. Thus, although the experience of enlightenment (*chieh-wu*) is sudden, one must still engage in a long process of cultivation in order to extirpate the deeply rooted seeds of the false view of a substantial self that has become ingrained over a period of innumerable kalpas. As Tsung-mi says in the *Ch'an Chart*:

> Even though one suddenly realizes that the dharmakāya, the true mind, is wholly identical with Buddha, still, since for numerous kalpas one has deludedly clung to the four elements as constituting one's self [so that this view] has become second nature and is difficult to do away with all at once, one must cultivate oneself on the basis of [this experience of] enlightenment. When one has reduced it and further reduced it until there is nothing left to reduce, then it is called attaining Buddhahood.[82]

Even though the practitioner gains an insight into his own true nature, realizing that he is wholly identical with all Buddhas, he is still not fully liberated, for he has yet to root out the deeply embedded effects of his misperception of himself as a separate, self-existing en-

[81] TSC 280b9–10.

[82] K p. 340. This passage is missing from the HTC text. Kamata has supplied it from Chinul's *Chŏryo*. It can also be found in *P'ei Hsiu shih-i wen*, pp. 96–97. Reducing it and further reducing it (*sun chih yu sun*) is an allusion to *Lao-tzu* 48.

tity. Although he has seen that this view is illusory, his behavior and entire mode of being in the world is still predicated on this false view of self, to which he has become habituated through a process of conditioning tracing back over innumerable lifetimes. It is thus necessary to embark on a process of gradual cultivation in order to eliminate the persistent effects of this misconception so that his original insight into his true nature can be fully and freely manifested in his every action. Gradual cultivation is thus the process by which one's initial insight is integrated into his personality.

TSUNG-MI'S TEN-STAGE MODEL

Tsung-mi's most developed explanation of conditioned origination occurs in his *Ch'an Preface*, where he outlines the process in terms of ten reciprocal stages. The etiology of delusion that he describes there is a modified version of that already seen in his five-stage cosmogony. It is also a more explicitly articulated version of the process of phenomenal evolution described in the concluding section of the *Inquiry into the Origin of Man*. In the ten stages in the process of enlightenment, Tsung-mi specifies how each stage overturns (*fan*) a corresponding stage in the etiology of delusion. The account in the *Inquiry*, moreover, points out how each stage in the process of phenomenal evolution is connected with the different teachings that comprise his p'an-chiao scheme. Tsung-mi's arrangement of the teachings is itself a theory of the path (mārga), and the structure of that path is derived from the cosmogony he adapts from the *Awakening of Faith*. Tsung-mi's interest in cosmogony is thus related to his primarily soteriological approach to the teachings: it provides a solid ontological basis on which to ground his vision of Buddhist practice. This soteriological concern, as will be argued more fully in chapter 9, is itself a reflection of Tsung-mi's ethical reaction against the antinomian danger that he perceived in some of the more radical Ch'an movements in his day.

As graphically illustrated in the diagram that occurs at the end of the *Ch'an Preface*, both the process of delusion and that of enlightenment are based on the dynamic ambivalence of the ālayavijñāna (fig. 7.1). Tsung-mi, furthermore, breaks down both of these processes into ten reciprocal stages, which can best be represented by reproducing the relevant portion of Tsung-mi's diagram.[83]

---

[83] The following diagram is based on the diagram that appears in the Taishō version of the *Ch'an Preface*. Even though the Taishō diagram does not appear in the Tun-huang version of the text (see Tanaka, "Tonkōbon *Zengen shosenshū tojo* zankan kō," pp. 61–63), it nevertheless accurately represents Tsung-mi's explanation of the ten stages and can therefore still be used for illustrative purposes.

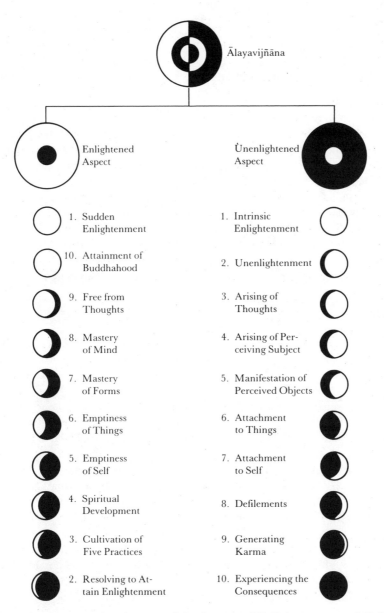

Figure 7.1. Tsung-mi's Diagram of the Process of Enlightenment and Delusion. From *Sudden and Gradual: Approaches to Enlightenment in Chinese Thought*, edited by Peter N. Gregory, (c) 1987 Kuroda Institute. Reprinted by permission of University of Hawaii Press.

The ten stages in the process of the genesis and development of delusion answer the question of how sentient beings come to assume a human form. Basing himself on the *Awakening of Faith*, Tsung-mi gives an account of the ultimate origin from which this process begins in his *Inquiry into the Origin of Man*:

> At first there is only the one true numinous nature (*i-chen-ling-hsing*), which is neither born nor destroyed, neither increases nor decreases, and neither changes nor alters. [Nevertheless,] sentient beings are [from time] without beginning asleep in delusion and are not themselves aware of it. Because it is covered over, it is called the tathāgatagarbha, and the phenomenal appearance of the mind that is subject to birth-and-death comes into existence based on the tathāgatagarbha. The interfusion of the true mind that is not subject to birth-and-death and deluded thoughts that are subject to birth-and-death in such a way that they are neither one nor different is referred to as the ālayavijñāna. This consciousness has the two modes of enlightenment and unenlightenment.[84]

The etiology of delusion, as it is schematically laid out in the *Ch'an Preface*,[85] can be outlined as follows:

1. Intrinsic enlightenment (*pen-chüeh*). This is the ontological ground from which the process evolves. Tsung-mi compares intrinsic enlightenment to a wealthy and respected man, upright and wise, living in his own home.

2. Unenlightenment (*pu-chüeh*). This refers to the unenlightened aspect of the ālayavijñāna. Tsung-mi compares it to the wealthy and respected man falling asleep and forgetting who he is. The metaphor of delusion as a state of being asleep is naturally suggested by the term for enlightenment, *chüeh*, which literally means "to awaken." This stage is what in other contexts Tsung-mi refers to as primordial ignorance (*ken-pen wu-ming*) or autonomous ignorance (*tu-t'ou wu-ming*). It is the "root" (*pen*) of the remaining stages in the process of the evolution of delusion, which, accordingly, are its "branches" (*mo*).

3. Arising of thought (*nien-ch'i*). This is the first subtle movement of thought, which initiates the process of phenomenal evolution by giving rise to the bifurcation of consciousness into subject and object. It corresponds to the first of the three subtle phenomenal appearances (*san hsi hsiang*) enumerated in the *Awakening of Faith*, that of activity (*yeh*) or, more fully, the activity of ignorance (*wu-ming yeh*). Tsung-mi compares it to the dreams that naturally arise in the mind of the sleeping man.

---

[84] T 45.710b8–13.

[85] See Tsung-mi's narrative explanation of the processes of enlightenment and delusion at the end of the *Ch'an Preface* (T 48.407b6–408a3; K 217–18, 222–223; cf. B 269–278) as well as the relevant portion of the diagram itself (410–411).

4. Arising of the perceiving subject (*chien-ch'i*). This corresponds to the second subtle phenomenal appearance of the *Awakening of Faith*, that of perceiving subject (*neng-chien*). Tsung-mi compares it to the dreaming consciousness.

5. Manifestation of perceived objects (*ching-hsien*). This refers to the manifestation of the body of the senses and the receptacle world.[86] It corresponds to the third subtle phenomenal appearance of the *Awakening of Faith*, that of perceived objects (*ching-chieh*). Tsung-mi compares it to the wealthy and respected man who, within his dream, sees himself dwelling in squalor and misery and perceives things that he likes and dislikes.

6. Attachment to dharmas (*fa-chih*). This corresponds to the first and second of the six coarse phenomenal appearances (*liu ts'u hsiang*) enumerated in the *Awakening of Faith*, those of discrimination (*chih*) and continuation (*hsiang-hsü*). Tsung-mi compares this stage to the man clinging to the things that he sees in his dream as real.

7. Attachment to self (*wo-chih*). This corresponds to the third and fourth coarse phenomenal appearance in the *Awakening of Faith*, those of attachment (*chih-ch'ü*) and conceptual elaboration (*chi-ming-tzu*). Tsung-mi compares this stage to the man identifying himself with the person in the dream.

8. Defilements (*fan-nao*). This refers to the three poisons of greed, anger, and folly. Tsung-mi compares it to the man hankering after those things in the dream that accord with his feelings and forming an aversion to those things in the dream that go against his feelings.[87]

9. Generating karma (*tsao-yeh*). This corresponds to the fifth coarse phenomenal appearance in the *Awakening of Faith*, that of giving rise to karma (*ch'i-yeh*). The dreaming man commits various good and bad deeds on the basis of his likes and dislikes.

10. Experiencing the consequences (*shou-pao*). This corresponds to the sixth coarse phenomenal appearance in the *Awakening of Faith*, that of

---

[86] This stage corresponds to the objective mode (*hsiang-fen*; *nimittabhāga*) of the ālaya-vijñāna, which the *Ch'eng wei-shih lun* describes as transforming itself internally into the body of the senses (*ken-shen*; *sendriyakakāya*) and externally into the receptacle world (*ch'i-shih-chien*; *bhājanaloka*). The *Ch'eng wei-shih lun* defines the body of the senses as "the sense organs and the body that serves as their support" and the receptacle world (i.e., what we would call the physical environment) as "the place which serves as the support for all sentient beings" (see T 31.10a13–16).

[87] Since Tsung-mi says in his *Ch'i-hsin lun shu* that the fourth and fifth coarse phenomenal appearances correspond to attachment to self (see 14b12), this stage would seem to have no precise correlate in the *Awakening of Faith*. This and the next two stages, however, correspond to the three stages of the evolved branches that Tsung-mi enumerated in his explanation of conditioned origination in his *Hsing-yüan p'in shu-ch'ao*, as discussed earlier in this chapter.

the suffering of karmic bondage (*yeh-hsi-ku*). The dreaming man thus experiences various good and bad consequences.

The relationship between the ten stages of phenomenal evolution in the *Ch'an Preface* and the five-stage cosmogony derived from the *Awakening of Faith* is represented in the following list, which also shows to which teaching they correspond according to the *Inquiry into the Origin of Man*.

Awakening of Faith	Ch'an Preface	Teaching
One mind		Reveals nature
Ālayavijñāna		
Enlightened mode	1. Intrinsic enlightenment	
Unenlightened mode	2. Unenlightenment	Negation
Activity of ignorance	3. Arising of thoughts	Fa-hsiang
Perceiving subject	4. Arising of perceiving subject	
Perceived objects	5. Manifestation of perceived objects	
Discrimination	6. Attachment to dharmas	
Continuity		
Attachment	7. Attachment to self	Hīnayāna
Conceptual elaboration		
	8. Defilements	
Generating karma	9. Generating karma	Men and gods
Suffering of karmic bondage	10. Experiencing the consequences	

The ten stages of phenomenal evolution that Tsung-mi enumerates in the *Ch'an Preface* serve as a map for liberation. Accordingly, each stage in the process of enlightenment overturns (*fan*) the corresponding stage in the process of delusion. As Tsung-mi explains:

As the meanings of delusion and enlightenment are distinct, the directions of conforming to (*shun*; *anuloma*) and reversing (*ni*; *pratiloma*) [the flow of birth-and-death] are different. The former is being deluded about the true and following after the false. It arises from the fine and subtle and, moving in the direction of conforming to [the flow of birth-and-death], evolves toward the coarse. The latter is being enlightened about the false and returning to the true. It moves from the coarse and heavy in the reverse direction, cuts off [successive stages of delusion], and evolves toward the subtle. The wisdom necessary to overturn [the successive stages of delusion] proceeds from the superficial to the profound. The coarse obstructions are easy to get rid of because a superficial wisdom is able to overturn them. The subtle delusions are difficult to eliminate because only a profound wisdom is able to cut them off. Therefore the latter ten [stages in the process of enlightenment] proceed from the last [stage in the process of delusion] and, in reverse order, overturn the former ten [stages of delusion].[88]

Tsung-mi lists the ten stages in the process of enlightenment as follows:

1. Sudden enlightenment (*tun-wu*). In this stage one meets a good friend (*shan-yu*; *kalyāṇamitra*) whose guidance enables him to gain an insight into the intrinsically enlightened true nature of the mind. He thus comes to have faith in suchness and the three jewels (Buddha, dharma, and sangha).[89] This stage counteracts the second stage in the process of delusion, that of unenlightenment.

2. Resolving to attain enlightenment (*fa-hsin*). In this stage one generates compassion, wisdom, and vows, resolving to attain supreme enlightenment. This stage counteracts the tenth stage in the process of delusion, that of experiencing the consequences of one's actions, according to which one is born in one of the six destinies.

3. Cultivating the five practices (*hsiu wu-hsing*). In this stage one cultivates giving (*dāna*), morality (*śīla*), patience (*kṣānti*), striving (*vīrya*), and meditative insight (*śamatha-vipaśyanā*) and thereby develops the root of one's faith.[90] The five practices are those enumerated in the *Awakening of Faith*,[91] according to which the fifth and sixth perfections (*pāramitā*)—those of dhyāna and prajñā—in the standard scheme of six have been collapsed into one, that of meditative insight. The fifth practice, however, consists of two elements, corresponding to dhyāna and prajñā, which are subsequently treated separately in the *Awakening of Faith*.[92] This stage counteracts the ninth stage in the process of delusion, that of generating karma.

---

[88] T 48.409b22–29; K 222; B 273–274.

[89] Tsung-mi quotes a passage from the *Awakening of Faith* (T 32.578b10) that explains how the process by which suchness permeates ignorance enables one to gain faith in his true nature and understand that the objects to which he has become attached are merely a function of the deluded activity of his mind (see Hakeda, *The Awakening of Faith*, p. 58; Hirakawa, *Daijō kishin-ron*, p. 218). He equates coming to have faith in one's true nature with the first of the four kinds of faith discussed in the *Awakening of Faith* (that is, faith in the ultimate source) and goes on to enumerate the other three (that is, faith in the infinite excellent qualities of the Buddhas, faith in the great benefits of the dharma, and faith in the sangha), which correspond to the three jewels (see T 32.581c8–14; cf. Hakeda, pp. 92–93; Hirakawa, p. 339). Cf. B 275.

[90] Tsung-mi quotes the *Awakening of Faith*: "There are five practices by which one can perfect his faith" (T 32.581c14; cf. Hakeda, *The Awakening of Faith*, p. 93; Hirakawa, *Daijō kishin-ron*, p. 341).

[91] See T 32.581c14ff.; cf. Hakeda, *The Awakening of Faith*, pp. 93–95.

[92] See T 32.582a16ff. and 582c15ff.; cf. Hakeda, *The Awakening of Faith*, pp. 96–102.

4. Spiritual development (*k'ai-fa*). This stage entails the development of the compassion, wisdom, and vows previously generated in the second stage[93] and counteracts the eighth stage in the process of delusion, that of defilements.

5. Emptiness of self (*wo-k'ung*). In this stage one realizes that there is no substantially existing autonomous self. This stage counteracts the ninth stage in the process of delusion, that of attachment to self.

6. Emptiness of dharmas (*fa-k'ung*). In this stage one realizes that all dharmas are devoid of self-nature. This stage counteracts the sixth stage in the process of delusion, that of attachment to dharmas.

7. Mastery of form (*se-tzu-tsai*). Having realized that the objects of perception are nothing but manifestations of one's own mind, one gains mastery over them in this stage. This stage counteracts the fifth stage in the process of delusion, that of manifestation of perceived objects.

8. Mastery of mind (*hsin-tzu-tsai*). In this stage one gains mastery over the perceiving subject. This stage counteracts the fourth stage in the process of delusion, that of arising of perceiving subject.

9. Freedom from thought (*li-nien*). In this stage one becomes fully aware of the ultimate origin of deluded thoughts and sees that the true nature of the mind is eternal. This is the stage of ultimate awakening (*chiu-ching chüeh*) described in the *Awakening of Faith*[94] and counteracts the third stage in the process of delusion, that of arising of thoughts.

10. Attainment of Buddhahood (*ch'eng-fo*). In this stage one returns to the ultimate source of the mind, realizing that, since the mind is of its very essence free from thoughts, there is ultimately no distinction between the various stages in the process of the realization of enlightenment, all of which were from the very beginning undifferentiated and identical with intrinsic enlightenment, which is one and indivisible.

---

[93] Tsung-mi quotes the *Awakening of Faith*: "In generating the aspiration for enlightenment through the perfection of faith . . . there are three types [of mind]: (1) the straightforward mind, which correctly keeps the dharma of suchness in mind, (2) the profound mind, which takes delight in accumulating all of the excellent practices, and (3) the great compassionate mind, which seeks to save all sentient beings from suffering" (T 32.580c6–9; cf. Hakeda, *The Awakening of Faith*, p. 82; Hirakawa, *Daijō kishinron*, p. 305).

[94] The *Awakening of Faith* defines ultimate awakening as "awakening to the source of the mind" (*chüeh hsin-yüan*) (T 32.576b16–17; cf. Hakeda, *The Awakening of Faith*, p. 38). It then goes on to say: "When the bodhisattva stages have been completed and one has fulfilled the expedient [practices], one becomes united [with suchness] in a single moment of thought (*i-nien hsiang-ying*). Having become aware of the first stirrings of the mind, one's mind is without the first phenomenal appearance [of the arising of thoughts]. Because one is far removed from the subtlest thought, one sees the nature of the mind—that the mind is eternal—and that is what is called ultimate awakening" (576b23–26; cf. Hakeda, p. 39).

When this process of the realization of enlightenment is completed and one has attained Buddhahood, it is seen that the genesis and unfolding of delusion and the realization of enlightenment are not two separate but parallel linear processes moving in opposite directions. Rather, one realizes that the two form a continuum. The final stage in the process of the realization of enlightenment brings one back to the fundamental basis from which the process of delusion unfolded. The process taken as a whole thus forms a circle in which intrinsic enlightenment would be represented by 0 degrees, and attainment of Buddhahood by 360 degrees. Tsung-mi symbolizes the circularity of the process by the circles that correspond to each stage, whose relative degree of enlightenment and delusion is represented by the relative degree of white and black, suggesting that the phases of delusion and enlightenment evolve and change like the waxing and waning of the moon. The points between 0 and 180 degrees—that is, the nine stages in the process of the unfolding of delusion beginning with unenlightenment and ending with experiencing the consequences—all involve a movement away from enlightenment, what Tsung-mi refers to as the process of conforming to the flow of birth-and-death (*shun*; *anuloma*). It is during this phase of the process that one gains a human body and, because of good karma generated in previous existences, finally comes to the turning point in the process, located at 180 degrees, when one meets a good friend, whose guidance enables one to gain a sudden insight into his true nature. This is what Tsung-mi refers to as sudden enlightenment (i.e., *chieh-wu*), an experience that reverses the direction of one's karma—what Tsung-mi refers to as the process of going against the flow of birth-and-death (*ni*; *pratiloma*)—and begins one's return back to one's original enlightened nature. The eight stages in the process of the realization of enlightenment—those beginning with resolving to attain enlightenment and ending with freedom from thoughts—describe the process of gradual cultivation (or what the *Awakening of Faith* refers to as *shih-chüeh*, "experiential enlightenment"). With the attainment of Buddhahood (i.e., *cheng-wu*), one returns to the ultimate point of origin, beginning and end are one, the circle is completed, and the process is brought to its natural conclusion. Tsung-mi's diagram can thus be rearranged in the form of a circle (fig. 7.2).

Moreover, one who has attained Buddhahood realizes that all of the stages in the process are equally nothing but a manifestation of the one mind (*i-hsin*), whose fundamental nature is eternally pure and enlightened and can never be tainted by the defilements that appear to cover it over. The defilements are merely accidental, being only the result of sentient beings' delusion. But the true nature of

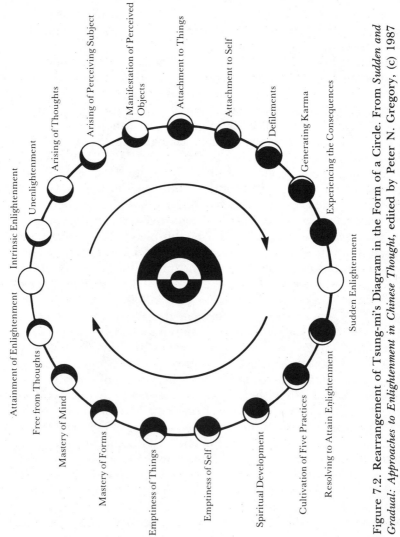

Figure 7.2. Rearrangement of Tsung-mi's Diagram in the Form of a Circle. From *Sudden and Gradual: Approaches to Enlightenment in Chinese Thought*, edited by Peter N. Gregory, (c) 1987 Kuroda Institute. Reprinted by permission of the University of Hawaii Press.

reality is unaffected by sentient beings' failure to see it as it really is. Thus, even though the tathāgatagarbha appears to be defiled, it is forever immaculate and inviolate. When one attains enlightenment, one thus realizes that intrinsic enlightenment is more than a stage in the process of delusion and enlightenment, it is also the fundamental ground upon which the entire process is based. The *pen* in the term "intrinsic enlightenment" (*pen-chüeh*) thus indicates that intrinsic enlightenment is not only ontologically prior to the other phases of the process, which are but epiphenomena (*mo* or *hsiang*), but that it is also the ontological ground (*pen* or *hsing*) that underlies all of them equally.

The relationship between intrinsic enlightenment and the other phases of the process of delusion and enlightenment can best be illustrated by making use of Tsung-mi's adaptation of the famous metaphor of water and waves from the *Awakening of Faith*. The originally tranquil surface of the water in which all things are reflected clearly (i.e., intrinsic enlightenment) becomes stirred up by the action of the wind of ignorance (i.e., unenlightenment) to form waves (i.e., the process of delusion). Even though the wind ceases suddenly (i.e., sudden enlightenment, *chieh-wu*), the motion of the waves only subsides gradually (i.e., the process of the realization of enlightenment, gradual cultivation, *shih-chüeh*) until all movement has stopped and the surface of the water is once again tranquil (i.e., attainment of Buddhahood, *cheng-wu*). Nevertheless, whether the surface of the water is tranquil or agitated, whether its waves are large or small, it is all equally water (i.e., the one mind). Moreover, the changing condition of the surface of the water does not affect its fundamental nature of being able to reflect all things (i.e., intrinsic enlightenment).

Chapter Eight

THE ROLE OF EMPTINESS

TSUNG-MI valued the tathāgatagarbha doctrine because it not only provided an ontological ground for Buddhist practice but also offered a rationale by which the radical apophasis of Madhyamaka could be subordinated to a more kataphatic mode of discourse. In this regard he stood within a long tradition of Chinese Buddhists who sought to overcome the negative conative implications of the teaching of emptiness by using the tathāgatagarbha doctrine to develop a more affirmative religious discourse. In stressing this aspect of the tathāgatagarbha doctrine, Tsung-mi was concerned to counter the antinomian implications of emptiness, particularly as it had been developed within Ch'an doctrines such as no-thought (*wu-nien*), which could be misinterpreted to call for a rejection of all forms of Buddhist practice from reciting sūtras to engaging in seated meditation. This chapter will accordingly focus on the role of emptiness in Tsung-mi's thought by showing how it develops the critique of emptiness found in the tathāgatagarbha literature. Although Tsung-mi's position reflects a general Chinese Buddhist reaction to the teaching of emptiness, the extent to which his system tended to suppress the teaching of emptiness in its emphasis on ontology bordered on what many would consider unorthodox.[1]

A COSMOGONY-DERIVED P'AN-CHIAO

Tsung-mi's discussions of different p'an-chiao categories in his commentarial works are incidental. In none of these works is he primarily concerned with elaborating his own system of doctrinal classification. It is only in two of his later works, the *Inquiry into the Origin of Man* and *Ch'an Preface*, that he sets out explicitly to develop his own system. P'an-chiao plays a central role in both of these works. It provides the governing structure around which the *Inquiry into the Origin of Man* is organized and furnishes the conceptual framework in which the *Ch'an Preface* assesses the various Ch'an traditions and establishes

---

[1] This chapter has adapted a section from my article "Tsung-mi and the Single Word 'Awareness' " as well as a portion of my "Chinese Buddhist Hermeneutics."

its claim that Ch'an does not represent a special teaching distinct from those of the scholastic teachings.

The intimate connection between cosmogony and p'an-chiao within Tsung-mi's soteriological orientation is seen most clearly in his *Inquiry into the Origin of Man*. The whole structure of the work, as the title suggests, is organized around what is an essentially cosmogonic question phrased in terms of the ultimate origin of man. As Tsung-mi glosses the title, his inquiry is not limited to probing the origin of human existence but encompasses all six modes of sentient existence as conceived by Buddhist cosmology.[2] In other words, his investigation takes in the whole of saṃsāra, the world of suffering and delusion in which beings are born and die without cease.

Tsung-mi's inquiry is twofold. In the first three sections of this work, he organizes the various teachings into a hierarchical structure according to the superficiality or profundity with which they address the question of the origin of man. The highest teaching reveals that the ultimate origin is the intrinsically enlightened mind possessed by all sentient beings. Enlightenment is based on and consists in insight into this mind. The initial three sections of the *Inquiry* thus correspond to what in an earlier context Tsung-mi had referred to as the process of pure conditioned origination, which reverses the flow of saṃsāra.

The concluding section of the essay moves in the opposite direction, corresponding to the process of impure conditioned origination, which follows the flow of saṃsāra. The various teachings that Tsung-mi so clearly differentiated from one another in his p'an-chiao sections are here brought back together into an all-encompassing explanation of the process of phenomenal evolution. Since each teaching accounts for different stages in the process, they can all be harmonized together within a unified cosmogonic framework. The superficial teachings only deal with the most outward developments of the process of phenomenal evolution—its "branches" (*mo*). As the teachings become more profound, they come closer to the ultimate source—or "root" (*pen*)—until the highest teaching finally reveals it. The order of the teachings in Tsung-mi's p'an-chiao sections thus re-

---

[2] As Tsung-mi explains in his autocommentary (T 45.708c23–24): "The reason that gods, [hungry] ghosts, and the denizens of hell are not mentioned in the title [of this treatise] is because their realms, being different [from that of man], are beyond ordinary understanding. Since the secular person does not even know the branches, how much less could he presume to investigate the root thoroughly. Therefore, in concession to the secular teaching, I have entitled [this treatise], 'An Inquiry into the Origin of Man.' [However,] in now relating the teachings of the Buddha, it was, as a matter of principle, fitting that I set forth [the other modes of existence] in detail."

verses the stages in the cosmogony he describes in the concluding section. Their arrangement is itself a description of the course of the spiritual path (mārga) leading from the suffering of delusion to the liberation of enlightenment.

The most elementary category of teaching in Tsung-mi's scheme is that of men and gods (jen-t'ien chiao). It consists in the simple moral teaching of karmic retribution, which enables beings to gain a favorable rebirth as either a human or a god. In terms of Tsung-mi's cosmogonic scheme, it overturns the last two stages in the process of phenomenal evolution, those of generating karma and experiencing the consequences.

Since the basic import of the teaching of men and gods hinges on the doctrine of rebirth, it naively assumes that there is, in fact, something that is reborn. It is thus superseded by the teaching of the lesser vehicle (hsiao-sheng chiao), whose doctrine of no-self (anātman) refutes the belief in an unchanging self. This teaching develops a sophisticated psychological vocabulary of dharmas (here designating the basic categories into which all experience can be analyzed) in order to break down the conceit of self into an ever-changing concatenation of impersonal constituents, none of which can be grasped as a substantial entity. It thus overturns the next two stages in Tsung-mi's cosmogonic scheme, those of defilements and attachment to self.

In its psychological analysis, however, the teaching of the lesser vehicle talks as if these dharmas were real. It is accordingly superseded by the third category of teaching, which deconstructs the reality of the dharmas by showing that they, like the conceit of self, are nothing but mental constructions. This category, referred to as the teaching of the phenomenal appearances of the dharmas (fa-hsiang chiao), is represented by the brand of Yogācāra introduced into China by Hsüan-tsang. It demonstrates that since the conceptions of both self and the dharmas are merely the projections of an underlying consciousness (the ālayavijñāna), they are therefore equally unreal. This teaching thus overturns the next stage in the process of phenomenal evolution, that of attachment to dharmas. It also points back to the underlying constructive process on which attachment to both self and dharmas is predicated. This constructive process is detailed in the next three phases of phenomenal evolution (those of the manifestation of perceived objects, the arising of the perceiving subject, and the arising of thought), in which Tsung-mi combines the Awakening of Faith's three subtle phenomenal appearances with the Ch'eng wei-shih lun's account of the transformation of the "self-essence" of consciousness into subject and object.

Yet this teaching is not final. Even though it clarifies how deluded thought arises, it still does not reveal its ultimate basis. Tsung-mi ar-

gues that the teaching of the phenomenal appearances of the dharmas fails to discern that the projecting consciousness and the projected objects are interdependent and hence equally unreal. This
teaching is thus superseded by that which Tsung-mi refers to as the
teaching that negates phenomenal appearances (*p'o-hsiang chiao*),
which demonstrates the emptiness of both the projecting consciousness and the projected objects. Although this teaching offers a clear
rationale for the supersedure of the third teaching, it does not have
any obvious cosmogonic content. Nevertheless, the thrust of Tsung-
mi's scheme impels him to correlate it with the second stage in the
process of phenomenal evolution, that of unenlightenment.

While this fourth level of teaching succeeds in determining what
ultimate reality is not, it still does not reveal what it is and is therefore
superseded by the next and final teaching, that which reveals the nature (*hsien-hsing chiao*). By clarifying that the ālayavijñāna is based on
the intrinsically enlightened pure mind, the tathāgatagarbha, this
teaching reveals the ultimate source on which both delusion and enlightenment are based. It thus corresponds to the first stage in
Tsung-mi's cosmogonic scheme, intrinsic enlightenment.

The correlations between the various teachings and cosmogonic
stages are diagrammed as follows:

	Teaching	Cosmogonic Stage
1.	Men and Gods	
		10. Experiencing the Consequences
		9. Generating Karma
2.	Lesser Vehicle	
		8. Defilements
		7. Attachment to Self
3.	Phenomenal Appearances	
		6. Attachment to Dharmas
		5. Manifestation of Perceived Objects
		4. Arising of Perceiving Subject
		3. Arising of Thoughts
4.	Refutation of Phenomenal Appearances	
		2. Unenlightenment
5.	Revelation of the Nature	
		1. Intrinsic Enlightenment

TSUNG-MI'S THEORY OF RELIGIOUS LANGUAGE

The p'an-chiao scheme that Tsung-mi uses in the *Ch'an Preface* is virtually identical to that of the *Inquiry into the Origin of Man*. Even the
wording in his accounts of the various teachings is largely the same

in both works. The only notable difference between them is that, whereas Tsung-mi uses a fivefold scheme in the *Inquiry*, he uses a threefold one in the *Ch'an Preface*. This difference, however, is more apparent than real, as Tsung-mi includes the first three teachings of the *Inquiry* in the first category of teaching in the *Ch'an Preface*, which thus treats the same five teachings that he deals with in the *Inquiry*. The relationship between the p'an-chiao schemes used in these two works can thus be represented as follows.

Inquiry	*Preface*
	1. Hidden intent that sets forth the phenomenal appearances that are based on the nature
1. Men and gods	A. Causes and effects of men and gods
2. Lesser vehicle	B. Extinction of suffering by cutting off defilements
3. Phenomenal appearances	C. Negation of objects by means of consciousness
4. Negation of phenomenal appearances	2. Hidden intent that negates phenomenal appearances in order to reveal the nature
5. Revelation of the nature	3. Direct revelation that the mind is the nature

Tsung-mi refers to the first and most elementary teaching in the *Ch'an Preface* as "the teaching of hidden intent that sets forth the phenomenal appearances that are based on the nature" (*mi-i i-hsing shuo-hsiang chiao*). He explains this designation as follows:

> The Buddha saw that the three realms [of existence] and six paths [of rebirth] were all phenomenal appearances of the true nature. [Phenomenal appearances] have no separate essence of their own but only arise because sentient beings are deluded about their nature. Hence [the designation of this teaching] says "based on the nature." Because its explanation does not reveal [the nature], it is said to be of "hidden intent."[3]

Tsung-mi subdivides this teaching into three further categories, corresponding to the first three teachings in the *Inquiry into the Origin of Man*. He refers to them as "the teaching of the causes and effects of [being born as] a human or a god" (*jen-t'ien yin-kuo chiao*), "the teaching of extinguishing suffering by cutting off the defilements"

---

[3] T 48.403a16–18; K 103; cf. B 157.

(*tuan-huo mieh-ku chiao*),[4] and "the teaching that negates objects by means of consciousness" (*chiang-shih p'o-ching chiao*).

The third subcategory, of course, refers to the Fa-hsiang brand of Yogācāra. Tsung-mi also refers to it as the tradition that takes phenomenal appearances as its cardinal principle (*hsiang-tsung*). It corresponds to the first type of Ch'an that Tsung-mi distinguishes in the *Ch'an Preface*, the tradition that cultivates the mind by eliminating delusion (*hsi-wang hsiu-hsin tsung*), which is represented primarily by the Northern line identified with Shen-hsiu and his disciples.[5]

Tsung-mi refers to the second category of teaching in the *Ch'an Preface* as "the teaching of hidden intent that negates phenomenal appearances in order to reveal the nature" (*mi-i p'o-hsiang hsien-hsing chiao*). He gives the following explanation of this designation:

> According to the true ultimate meaning, since deluded thoughts are originally empty, there is nothing that can be negated. All dharmas, being without defilement, are originally the true nature, and its marvelous functioning-in-accord-with-conditions is not only never interrupted but also cannot be negated. It is only because a class of sentient beings clings to unreal phenomenal appearances, obscures their true nature, and has difficulty attaining profound enlightenment that the Buddha provisionally negated everything without distinguishing between good and bad, tainted and pure, or the nature and its phenomenal appearances. Although he did not regard the true nature and its marvelous functioning to be nonexistent, because he provisionally said they were nonexistent, [this teaching] is designated as being of "hidden intent." Furthermore, though his intention lay in revealing the nature, because his words thus negated phenomenal appearances and his intent was not expressed in words, they are referred to as "hidden."[6]

This category of teaching corresponds to the teaching of emptiness expounded in the Perfection of Wisdom scriptures and the Madhyamaka treatises that Tsung-mi had classified as the fourth teaching in the *Inquiry into the Origin of Man*. Tsung-mi also refers to it as the tradition that takes emptiness as its cardinal principle (*k'ung-tsung*). It corresponds to the second type of Ch'an Tsung-mi distinguishes in the *Ch'an Preface*, the tradition that holds that all things are utterly

---

[4] *Huo* stands for *kleśa*.

[5] Tsung-mi also includes Chih-shen, Pao-t'ang, and Hsüan-shih in this category of Ch'an. He adds that, although the type of practice advocated by Ox-head, T'ien-t'ai, Hui-ch'ou, Guṇabhadra, and so forth are similar, their understanding (*chien-chieh*) is different. See T 48.402b21–c3; K 86–87; B 147–148.

[6] T 48.404a7–9; K 121; cf. B 176.

without support (min-chüeh wu-chi tsung), which is represented primarily by the Ox-head line identified with Fa-jung and his disciples.[7]

Both of the first two main categories of teaching are characterized as being of "hidden intent" (mi-i) because in neither is the Buddha's ultimate intent revealed. In this way Tsung-mi indicates that the first two levels of teaching are neyārtha (pu-liao), that is, not those of ultimate meaning. The second, however, is the more profound of the two because it does "intimate" (mi-hsien) it.[8]

The third teaching is ultimate (liao; nītārtha) because, in contrast to the previous two, it "directly reveals" (hsien-shih) the essence. Tsung-mi thus refers to it as "the teaching that directly reveals that the true mind is the nature" (hsien-shih chen-hsin chi hsing chiao).

> Because [this category of teaching] directly points (chih-chih) to the fact that one's very own mind is the true nature, revealing (shih) it neither in terms of the appearances of phenomena (shih-hsiang) nor in terms of the negation of phenomenal appearances (p'o-hsiang), it has "is the nature" [in its name]. Because its intent is not hidden (yin-mi) by expedients, it is said to "reveal it directly."[9]

The content of this category of teaching is the tathāgatagarbha. Tsung-mi also refers to it as the tradition that takes the nature as its cardinal principle (hsing-tsung). In terms of Ch'an, it corresponds to the third and highest type, the tradition that directly reveals the mind as the nature (chih-hsien hsin-hsing tsung), represented by the Southern line of the Ho-tse lineage of Shen-hui and the Hung-chou lineage of Ma-tsu Tao-i.

Tsung-mi's explanation of his three categories of teachings in the Ch'an Preface reveals another rationale within his ordering of the teachings, one that parallels and partially overlaps the cosmogony-derived rationale discussed in regard to the Inquiry into the Origin of Man. The progression of the teachings in both works begins with the naive kataphasis of the teaching of men and gods, whose successive negation by each subsequent teaching culminates in the thorough apophasis of the teaching of emptiness, which is then superseded by the new and higher kataphasis of the teaching that reveals the nature. This rationale clarifies the soteriological role that the teaching of emptiness plays within Tsung-mi's p'an-chiao and compensates for its anomalous status in his cosmogony-derived ordering.

---

[7] He also includes Shih-t'ou within this category of Ch'an. See T 48.402c10; K 91; B 150.

[8] See TS 121b and TSC 285b.

[9] T 48.404b26–27; K 131; cf. B 188.

The teaching of emptiness overcomes deluded attachments so that the true nature can be perceived as it is in reality: pure and immutable. The primarily negative function of emptiness thus has tremendous soteriological value, for it is only after attachments to phenomenal appearances have been destroyed that one can realize their ultimate ontological basis. The teaching of emptiness thus serves as the crucial turning point that enables one to move from attachment to phenomenal appearances to a realization of their underlying nature. It can, however, do no more than intimate (*mi-hsien*) the nature and must therefore be superseded by the teaching that is able to reveal it directly.

Elsewhere in the *Ch'an Preface* Tsung-mi explains that both the tradition that takes phenomenal appearances as its cardinal principle (*hsiang-tsung*) and tradition that takes emptiness as its cardinal principle (*k'ung-tsung*) use negative modes of expression because they fear that words will only become a source of further attachment. As such, they are suited for beginners and those of shallow capacity. The tradition that takes the nature as its cardinal principle (*hsing-tsung*), by contrast, is geared to advanced students and those of superior ability. "Because it causes them to forget words and apprehend the essence, a single word directly reveals [the nature]."[10] As I shall discuss more fully later, the single word is *chih*, "awareness," which directly reveals the essence of the mind. Tsung-mi identifies the teaching that reveals the nature with the lineage of Ho-tse Shen-hui, whose central teaching he claims is represented by the expression "the single word awareness is the gate of all mysteries" (*chih chih i-tzu chung-miao chih men*).[11]

Tsung-mi's arrangement of the teachings, insofar as it recapitulates the course of spiritual progress, is predicated on his understanding of the nature and function of religious language. While he does not explicitly articulate a theory of religious language as such, one can, nevertheless, be extrapolated from the passages discussed so far. For the teachings that still only approximate the ultimate, the function of religious language is primarily to overcome the untoward effects arising out of the confusion of words (*ming*) and essences (*t'i*). Language is thus turned against itself as the principal vehicle of reification. Such a misconception of language is inextricably part of the basic dichotomizing mode of awareness that separates beings from their true nature. Apophatic language, by calling attention to the unconscious

[10] T 48.407a1–2; K 170; cf. B 228.

[11] See, for example, T 48.403a1–3 (K 95; B 154) and 405b15 (K 141; B 203). In his *Ch'an Chart*, Tsung-mi uses the expression *chih chi i-tzu chung-miao chih yüan* to characterize Shen-hui's teaching (see 436b18; K 318).

hold that the fundamental structures of language have in determining the forms of experience, thus plays a necessarily therapeutic role in deconstructing the false premises upon which deluded thinking is based. Tsung-mi's ranking of the provisional levels of teaching is accordingly done on a scale of their increasing use of negative modes of discourse, culminating with the thorough apophasis of emptiness. Only after one has recognized the emptiness of words, their provisional and arbitrary character as dependent upon convention, can religious language take on a new and potent function. When words are no longer mistaken for essences, they no longer provide a basis upon which an imaginary reality can be constructed and are thus free to reveal the essence directly. Such positive use of language could be called, playing on Tsung-mi's own terminology, "revelatory" (*hsien-shih*). By such an expression, of course, I do not mean a special kind of language that is sacred because it is revealed by a more exalted spiritual authority, but language that is able to reveal the essence directly (*hsien-shih*). "Revelatory language" thus refers to language that is so efficacious that it is able, with only a single word, to bring about a direct insight into the very essence itself—at least in the case of persons of the highest spiritual caliber. The primary distinguishing characteristic of the teaching that reveals the nature is that it makes use of such revelatory language. And the paradigm of such language, for Tsung-mi, is the single word "awareness" (*chih*).[12]

Unlike those forms of Buddhism, particularly vocal within Ch'an, that held that only negative statements such as "there is nothing whatsoever to be attained" or "neither mind nor Buddha" were ultimately true, Tsung-mi mounts a forceful argument for the ultimate value of positive religious assertions. Indeed, his contention that the exclusive use of apophatic discourse (*che-ch'üan*) is not the final word in Ch'an is one of the major themes running through the *Ch'an Preface*. His most unequivocal statement of his preference for kataphatic over apophatic modes of teaching is found in his discussion of the sixth of ten points of difference between the tradition that takes emptiness as its cardinal principle (*k'ung-tsung*) and that which takes the nature as its cardinal principle (*hsing-tsung*).

[The two traditions] differ from one another in regard to their use of negative discourse (*che-ch'üan*) and affirmative discourse (*piao-ch'üan*). "Negative" means rejecting what is not the case. "Affirmative" means re-

---

[12] If this formulation is indeed a fair extrapolation of Tsung-mi's "theory of religious language," there are, of course, problems; see my "Tsung-mi and the Single Word 'Awareness,'" p. 256.

vealing what is the case. In other words, negation is the denial of every-thing other than [the real], while affirmation is the direct demonstration of the very essence itself. Consider, for example, the true nature of the marvelous principle as expounded in various scriptures. When it is spo-ken of as subject to neither birth nor death, neither tainted nor pure, without cause or effect, without characteristics or conditions, neither or-dinary (*fan*) nor noble (*sheng*), neither self-essence nor external charac-teristics, and so forth, all [such expressions] are [examples of] negative discourse. (In scriptures and treatises the word "is not" (*fei*) is used to negate all things. The word "is not" may appear thirty-five to fifty times in a single passage. The words "not" (*pu*) and "without" (*wu*) are also used in the same way. Thus [the scriptures and treatises] speak of the hundredfold negation.) But when it is spoken of as the enlightened illumination of awareness and vision, the mirror-like radiance of the spirit, brilliant refulgence, clear tranquility, and so forth, all [such ex-pressions] are [examples of] affirmative discourse.

If it were not for such substantial realities as awareness and vision, what could be revealed as the nature, what could be said to be subject to neither birth nor death, and so forth? One must recognize that the awareness that sees things as they are this very moment is the nature of the mind before one can say that this awareness is subject to neither birth nor death, and so forth. For example, in the case of salt, when one says that it is not tasteless, that is negation, and when one says that it is brack-ish, that is affirmation. Or, in the case of water, when one says that it is not dry, that is negation, and when one says that it is wet, that is affir-mation. When the various teachings speak of the hundredfold negation, they are all using negative modes of expression, and when they directly reveal the absolute, they are using affirmative modes of expression. The terminology of the tradition that takes the nature as its cardinal principle uses both negation and affirmation. Nowadays people say that negative speech is profound and affirmative speech is superficial. Therefore they just value expressions such as "neither mind nor Buddha," "without con-ditions or characteristics," "nothing whatsoever to be attained," and so forth. Truly this is because they mistake negative speech for profundity and do not aspire after an intimate personal realization of the essence of the truth.[13]

Tsung-mi makes the same point in his *Ch'an Chart*, where he claims that negative discourse does not reveal the essence of the mind, which he goes on to identify as the "empty tranquil awareness" (*k'ung chi chih*) emphasized by Shen-hui.

[13] T 48.406b17–c5; K 167; cf. B 223–224. I have adapted the translation of Gimello from his "Mysticism in Its Contexts," pp. 76–77.

If I did not point to the direct revelation that this clear and bright, unobscured, ever-present awareness is your own mind at this very moment,
what could I say is without construction and phenomenal appearance,
and so forth? We thus know that the various teachings just say that it is
this awareness that is without birth and destruction, and so forth. Thus
Ho-tse [Shen-hui] directly revealed the awareness and vision within the
empty state of being without phenomenal appearances to enable people
to apprehend it, then they would become aware (*chüeh*) that it is their
own mind that passes through lifetime after lifetime eternally uninter-
rupted until they attain Buddhahood. Moreover, Ho-tse summed up expressions such as unconstructed, nonabiding, inexpressible, and so
forth, by simply speaking of the empty tranquil awareness that includes
them all.[14]

This empty tranquil awareness is but another term for the tathāgatagarbha. The ultimate teaching for Tsung-mi thus combines negation and affirmation, and the term "empty tranquil awareness" expresses both its positive and negative aspects.

"Empty" means empty of all phenomenal appearances and is still a negative term. "Tranquil" just indicates the principle of the immutability of
the true nature and is not the same as nothingness. "Awareness" indicates the revelation of the very essence and is not the same as discrimination. It alone constitutes the intrinsic essence of the true mind.[15]

As the term "awareness" is the paradigmatic example of the positive use of language that characterizes the highest teaching for
Tsung-mi, it is worth examining in more detail.

THE MEANING OF AWARENESS

In both his *Inquiry into the Origin of Man* and *Ch'an Preface*, Tsung-mi
identifies the content of the highest teaching with awareness (*chih*),
one of several synonyms for the tathāgatagarbha.[16] Sometimes he
uses the term "awareness" singly, and at other times he uses it in col-
location with other words, such as "numinous awareness" (*ling-chih*),
"numinous awareness unobscured" (*ling-chih pu-mei*), "ever-present
awareness" (*ch'ang-chih*), and "empty tranquil awareness" (*k'ung chi
[chih] chih*). The following characterization of the teaching that re-

14 HTC 110.437b7–16; K 332–333.
15 HTC 110.437b16–18; K 333.
16 The rendering of *chih* as "awareness" was first proposed by Buswell in his *Korean
Approach to Zen*, p. 165. For further discussion of this term, see Buswell, "Chinul's Systematization of Chinese Meditative Techniques in Korean Sŏn Buddhism," pp. 214–
215.

veals the nature in the *Ch'an Preface* clearly reveals the centrality of awareness in Tsung-mi's thought:

> This teaching propounds that all sentient beings without exception have the empty, tranquil, true mind. From time without beginning it is the intrinsically pure, effulgent, unobscured, clear, and bright ever-present awareness (*ch'ang-chih*). It abides forever and will never perish on into the infinite future. It is termed Buddha-nature; it is also termed tathā-gatagarbha and mind ground.[17]

Tsung-mi goes on to gloss what he means by "ever-present awareness" in a later part of this section.[18] After stating that it is not the awareness of realization (*cheng-chih*), he says that the true nature is nevertheless spoken of as aware to indicate that it is different from insentient nature.[19] However, awareness is neither the mental activity of discrimination (*fen-pieh chih shih*) nor wisdom (*chih*, fourth tone). For canonical authority he then refers to the "Wen-ming" (The bodhisattvas ask for clarification) chapter of the *Hua-yen Sūtra*,[20] which he claims differentiates between awareness (*chih*, first tone) and wisdom (*chih*, fourth tone), pointing out that "wisdom is not shared by the ordinary person (*fan*)," whereas "awareness is possessed by the sage (*sheng*) and ordinary person alike."[21] In his interlinear comments he glosses the "wisdom" in the question as "the wisdom of consummated enlightenment" (*cheng-wu chih chih*) and the "awareness" in the question as "the intrinsically existent true mind" (*pen-yu chen hsin*). He first quotes Mañjuśrī's answer to the bodhisattvas' question, "What is the wisdom of the realm of Buddhas?"

> "The wisdom of all Buddhas freely [penetrates] the three times without obstruction." (Since there is nothing within the past, present, and future that is not utterly penetrated, [it is said to be] free and unobstructed.)[22]

---

[17] T 48.404b27–c3; K 131; cf. B 188–189; I have omitted Tsung-mi's autocommentary.

[18] T 48.404c28–405a12; K 131–132; cf. B 192–194.

[19] T 48.404c29–405a1.

[20] See T 10.69a.

[21] T 48.405a4–5; Tsung-mi makes the same point elsewhere in the *Ch'an Preface*, HTC 110.406b8–9; K 163.

[22] T 48.405a7–8; the question is quoted from the prose section of the scripture at T 10.69a6–7 and its supposed answer from the verse section at 69a19. It is by no means obvious that this line from the verse section is meant as a specific answer to the question in regard to "the wisdom of the realm of Buddhas" stated in the prose section. Nor is it obvious that the *Hua-yen Sūtra* is here concerned with making a distinction between "wisdom" and "awareness." The portion in parentheses is Tsung-mi's interlinear gloss.

He then quotes Mañjuśrī's answer to their question, "What is the awareness of the realm of Buddhas?"

> "It is not something that can be known by consciousness (*fei shih so neng shih*)" (It cannot be known by consciousness. Consciousness falls within the category of discrimination. "Were it discriminated, it would not be true awareness." "True awareness is only seen in no-thought.") "nor is it an object of the mind (*i fei hsin ching chieh*)." (It cannot be known by wisdom. That is to say, if one were to realize it by means of wisdom, then it would fall within the category of an object that is realized, but since true awareness is not an object, it cannot be realized by wisdom.)[23]

What Tsung-mi thus means by "awareness" is not a specific cognitive faculty but the underlying ground of consciousness that is always present in all sentient life. It is not a special state of mind or spiritual insight but the noetic ground of both delusion and enlightenment, ignorance and wisdom, or, as he aptly terms it, the mind ground (*hsin-ti*).

Tsung-mi's use of "*chih*" to designate the tathāgatagarbha, and the specific meaning that it has for him in terms of "revelatory" language, gives a decided Ch'an twist to tathāgatagarbha doctrine. At the same time, it also brings a scholastic dimension back into Ch'an, which the iconoclasm of Shen-hui's attack on the Northern line had temporarily eclipsed. The reconciliation of Ch'an and the canonical teachings (*ch'an-ching i-chih*) was, of course, one of the major objectives to which Tsung-mi devoted the *Ch'an Preface*.

THE TATHĀGATAGARBHA CRITIQUE OF EMPTINESS

For Tsung-mi the content of the highest teaching was the tathāgatagarbha doctrine. In addition to providing an ontological ground for Buddhist practice, this doctrine was also important for Tsung-mi because it furnished a clear rationale for sublating the Madhyamaka teaching of emptiness into a more kataphatic framework. The most important scriptural formulation of this doctrine was made in the *Śrīmālā Sūtra*, which proclaimed that the tathāgatagarbha represented the true meaning of emptiness. The *Śrīmālā Sūtra* thereby implied that the teaching of emptiness as it had been previously expounded in the Perfection of Wisdom scriptures was only provisional (*neyārtha*) because it did not recognize the infinite excellent qualities of the Tathāgata. The former teaching of emptiness was therefore not so

[23] T 48.405a9–13; the question is taken from the prose section at T 10.69a8 and its supposed answer from the verse section at 69a25. The two sentences in quotation marks within Tsung-mi's interlinear gloss are quoted from Ch'eng-kuan's commentary and subcommentary respectively—see T 35.612b27 and T 36.261b22.

much wrong as it was incomplete and one-sided. The tathāgata-garbha was the ultimate (*nītārtha*) teaching because it revealed the full meaning of emptiness. "The wisdom of the tathāgatagarbha is the Tathāgata's wisdom of emptiness."[24]

The Tathāgata's wisdom of emptiness, moreover, is twofold. The tathāgatagarbha can be spoken of as being both empty (*śūnya; k'ung*) and not empty (*aśūnya; pu-k'ung*) in that it is at once empty of all defilements and, at the same time, not empty of all Buddha-dharmas. Or, as the scripture puts it,

> O World Honored One, the tathāgatagarbha as empty is at once free from, dropped off from, and different from the store of defilements. O World Honored One, the tathāgatagarbha as not empty is not free from, not dropped off from, and not different from the inconceivable Buddha-dharmas, which are more numerous than the sands of the Ganges.[25]

The true understanding of emptiness, therefore, entails the recognition that the other side of the tathāgatagarbha's being empty of all defiled dharmas is its being replete with infinite Buddha-dharmas. It is on this basis that the *Śrīmālā Sūtra* represents its teaching as being of ultimate meaning, in implicit contradistinction to the purely negative exposition of emptiness in the Perfection of Wisdom scriptural corpus.

The *Awakening of Faith*, whose adaptation of the tathāgatagarbha doctrine was authoritative for Tsung-mi, follows the *Śrīmālā Sūtra* in distinguishing between the empty and not empty aspects of the absolute: suchness (*chen-ju*) can be said to be both truly empty (*ju-shih k'ung*), "because it is ultimately able to reveal what is real," and truly not empty (*ju-shih pu-k'ung*), "because it has its own essence (*yu tzu t'i*) and is fully endowed with excellent qualities whose nature is undefiled."[26]

Because it is not empty, the tathāgatagarbha is endowed with positive qualities. The *Śrīmālā Sūtra* and affiliated texts apply a stock set of four predicates to the tathāgatagarbha in its true aspect as the dharmakāya: it is said to be permanent (*nitya; ch'ang*), steadfast (*dhruva; heng*), calm (*śiva; ch'ing-liang*), and eternal (*śāśvata; pu-pien*).[27]

---

[24] T 12.221c13.

[25] T 12.221c16–18. Cf. *Pu-tseng pu-chien ching*, T 16.467a17–21.

[26] T 32.576b24; cf. Hakeda, *The Awakening of Faith*, p. 34; Hirakawa, *Daijō kishin-ron*, p. 80.

[27] See Wayman, *The Lion's Roar of Queen Śrīmālā*, p. 98: "Lord, the cessation of suffering is not the destruction of Dharma. Why so? Because the Dharmakāya of the Tathāgata is named 'cessation of suffering,' and it is beginningless, uncreate, unborn, undying, free from death; permanent, steadfast, calm, eternal; and accompanied by

The *Ratnagotravibhāga* (*Pao-hsing lun*), a treatise that drew on the early tathāgatagarbha scriptures to articulate the doctrine systematically in its classical form, glosses these terms by explaining that the perfectly pure state of Buddhahood is said to be permanent because it is not born, steadfast because it does not die, calm because it does not suffer, and eternal because it does not grow old.[28]

The most notable set of positive qualities the *Śrīmālā Sūtra* attributes to the dharmakāya are permanence (*nitya*; *ch'ang*), bliss (*sukha*; *le*), selfhood (*ātman*; *wo*), and purity (*śubha*; *ching*).[29] These four perfected qualities (*guṇapāramitā*) are discussed extensively in the *Nirvāṇa Sūtra* and *Ratnagotravibhāga*. Their importance had, of course, already been established in the pre-Mahāyāna tradition, where they had a wholly opposite meaning. The Hīnayāna texts singled out these qualities as constituting the four inverted views (*viparyāsa*; *tien-tao*). As such they were seen to constitute ignorance. Beings suffered in saṃsāra because they mistakenly grasped after what was impermanent as if it were permanent, what caused suffering as if it could lead to bliss, what lacked any substantial self as if had such a self, and what was impure as if it were pure. The arhat's liberation thus lay in his realization that all existence was characterized by impermanence (*anitya*), suffering (*duḥkha*), lack of self (*anātman*), and impurity (*aśubha*). Any teaching that ascribed permanence, bliss, selfhood, or purity to reality was therefore to be rejected as false.

In attributing these four inverted views to the absolute, the tathāgatagarbha tradition inverted the Hīnayāna teaching. The *Ratnagotravibhāga*, for example, points out that permanence, bliss, self, and purity are inverted views (*viparyāsa*) when applied to constructed

---

Buddha natures more numerous than the sands of the Ganges. . . . This Dharmakāya of the Tathāgata when not free from the store of defilement is referred to as the Tathāgatagarbha." See also Wayman's comments on p. 45. The four terms "permanent" (*nitya*; *ch'ang*), "steadfast" (*dhruva*; *heng*), "calm" (*śiva*; *ch'ing-liang*), and "eternal" (*śāśvata*; *pu-pien*) do not occur in either the Guṇabhadra (T 12.221c7–11) or Bodhiruci (T 11.677a15–19) translation of this passage but can be found in the *Śrīmālā* passage quoted in Ratnamati's translation of the *Ratnagotravibhāga* (T 31.824a16–22; Takasaki, *Ratnagotravibhāga*, p. 167). They also occur in a later passage in the *Śrīmālā* as quoted in the *Ratnagotravibhāga* (T 31.833b20–24; Takasaki, pp. 242–243; cf. Wayman, *The Lion's Roar of Queen Śrīmālā*, pp. 104–105; Guṇabhadra, T 12.222b8–11; Bodhiruci, T 11.677c11–14). This set of terms occurs frequently throughout tathāgatagarbha literature; see, for example, *Ratnagotravibhāga*, T 31.835a14–25 (Takasaki, pp. 256–257), 842a3–4 (Takasaki, p. 319), 842a22–23 (Takasaki, p. 321), 842b10–11 (Takasaki, p. 322), etc. and *Pu-tseng pu-chien ching*, T 16.467b1–5.

[28] T 31.835b19–25 (Takasaki, *Ratnagotravibhāga*, pp. 256–257). See also T 31.842b24–25 (Takasaki, p. 323) and David Seyfort Ruegg, *La Théorie du Tathāgatagarbha et du Gotra*, pp. 362–364.

[29] Wayman, *The Lion's Roar of Queen Śrīmālā*, p. 102.

things, which truly are impermanent, cause suffering, lack self, and are impure. In this context impermanence, suffering, lack of self, and impurity are said to constitute the four noninverted views (*aviparyāsa*; *fei tien-tao fa*). However, attributing impermanence, suffering, lack of self, and impurity to the absolute is itself an inverted view because the dharmakāya represents the perfection of permanence, the perfection of bliss, the perfection of self, and the perfection of purity.[30]

The *Ratnagotravibhāga* goes on to explain that the four perfected qualities are the result (*phala*; *kuo*) of the cultivation of various purifying practices, each of which overcomes the type of obstacle associated with a different class of beings. Thus the perfection of purity is the result of the cultivation of faith in the Mahāyāna, which serves as an antidote to the revilement of Mahāyāna associated with the *icchantika*; the perfection of self is the result of the cultivation of the perfection of wisdom, which serves as an antidote to the concept of self associated with the non-Buddhist; the perfection of bliss is the result of the cultivation of samādhi, which serves as an antidote to the fear of saṃsāra associated with the śrāvaka; and the perfection of permanence is the result of the cultivation of great compassion, which serves as an antidote of the indifference to beings associated with the pratyekabuddha.[31]

The *Awakening of Faith* thus stands solidly in the tathāgatagarbha tradition in attributing positive qualities to the absolute. It says that since suchness (*chen-ju*; *tathatā*)

> was neither born at the beginning of time nor will perish at the end of time, it is utterly permanent (*ch'ang*; *nitya*) and steadfast (*heng*; *dhruva*). In its nature it is itself fully endowed with all excellent qualities (*kung-te*). That is, its essence itself possesses the radiant light of great wisdom; [the capacity of] universally illuminating the dharmadhātu; true cognition; the intrinsically pure mind; permanence (*ch'ang*; *nitya*), bliss (*le*; *sukha*), selfhood (*wo*; *ātman*), and purity (*ching*; *śubha*); and calmness (*ch'ing-liang*; *śiva*), eternality (*pu-pien*; *śāśvata*), and freedom.

[30] Takasaki, *Ratnagotravibhāga*, pp. 208–209; T 31.828b. The *Nirvāṇa Sūtra* strikes a similar note, arguing that the four inverted views are themselves really inverted views. To grasp what is impermanent as permanent is just as much an inverted view as to grasp what is permanent as impermanent. Impermanence, suffering, lack of self, and impurity correspond to a mundane understanding of reality whereas permanence, bliss, selfhood, and purity correspond to the supermundane understanding (T 12.377b15–c14).

[31] T 31.828c10ff. (Takasaki, *Ratnagotravibhāga*, pp. 210–213); see Ruegg, *La Théorie du Tathāgatagarbha*, pp. 364–368.

The text then adds, in language redolent of the *Śrīmālā Sūtra*,

> Therefore it is fully endowed with inconceivable Buddha-dharmas that
> are more numerous than the sands of the Ganges and that are not free
> from, not cut off from, and not different from [the essence of such-
> ness].[32]

Elsewhere the *Awakening of Faith* suggests how the teaching of the
tathāgatagarbha serves to overcome the misunderstanding to which
the apophasis of the teaching of emptiness is liable.

> [Ordinary beings] hear the scriptures proclaim that all dharmas in the
> world are ultimately empty of [any] essence, that even the dharmas of
> nirvāṇa and suchness are also ultimately empty, and that they are from
> the very beginning themselves empty and free from all phenomenal ap-
> pearances. Since they do not understand that [such statements were
> taught] in order to break their attachments, they hold that the nature of
> suchness and nirvāṇa is merely empty. How is [this view] to be counter-
> acted? It must be made clear that the dharmakāya of suchness is in its
> own essence not empty but fully endowed with incalculable excellent
> qualities.[33]

The theme that the kataphasis of the tathāgatagarbha was taught
as an antidote to the psychological dangers inherent in the apophasis
of the teaching of emptiness had already been intimated by the *Ratnagotravibhāga*. Basing itself on passage from the *Śrīmālā Sūtra*, that
text says that among those who cannot gain access to the tathāgatagarbha are those novice bodhisattvas "whose minds have become distracted by emptiness."[34] Since they do not understand the true mean-

---

[32] T 32.579a12–18; cf. Hakeda, *The Awakening of Faith*, p. 65.

[33] T 32.580a8–13; cf. Hakeda, *The Awakening of Faith*, pp. 76–77, and Hirakawa, *Daijō
kishin-ron*, p. 282. This is the second of five biased views enumerated in *The Awakening
of Faith*. Tsung-mi's critique of the Ox-head line of Ch'an echoes this passage; see the
following chapter, pp. 234–236.

[34] *Śūnyatāvikṣiptacitta*: there is disagreement among buddhologists as to whether this
phrase means "distracted by emptiness" or "distracted from emptiness." Ruegg clearly
understands the phrase to mean the former when he translates it as "l'esprit perturbé
par la śūnyatā" (*La Théorie du Tathāgatagarbha*, p. 313). In his review of Ruegg's book,
Hattori argues that the phrase should be translated as "(the bodhisattva) whose mind
is distracted from the [*sic*] śūnyatā" (p. 61). This is also the way the phrase is understood by Takasaki, who translates it as "those whose mind has deviated from the conception of non-substantiality" (*Ratnagotravibhāga*, p. 296). Ratnamati's Chinese translation (*san-luan hsin shih k'ung chung-sheng*) (T 31.839b23–24) clearly supports the
reading of Hattori and Takasaki. The original passage, however, is quoted from the
Śrīmālā Sūtra, Guṇabhadra's Chinese translation of which renders it according to
Ruegg's interpretation (*k'ung luan i chung-sheng*) (T 12.222b21). Both of the English
translations of the *Śrīmālā Sūtra* also interpret the phrase to mean "distracted by emp-

ing of emptiness as the tathāgatagarbha, they are liable to two types of error: whereas some regard emptiness as meaning the annihilation of all things subject to change, believing that nirvāṇa can only be attained when the elements of existence have been extinguished, others hypostatize emptiness, believing it to be something that exists apart from form.[35] The treatise then goes on to explicate the true meaning of emptiness in the following two verses:

> Here there is nothing to be removed
> And absolutely nothing to be added;
> The truth should be perceived as it is,
> And he who sees the truth becomes liberated.

> The essence [of the Buddha] is [by nature]
> Devoid of the accidental [pollutions] which differ from it;
> But it is by no means devoid of the highest properties
> Which are, essentially, indivisible from it.[36]

The *Ratnagotravibhāga* continues, saying that the tathāgatagarbha was taught as an antidote to the defects entailed by the misunderstanding of emptiness as previously taught (i.e., in the Perfection of Wisdom scriptures and the Madhyamaka treatises) and therefore represents the supreme doctrine (*uttaratantra*; *chiu-ching-lun*). It then elaborates on this theme, pointing out that those who have not yet heard of the tathāgatagarbha doctrine are often disheartened when they hear the teaching of emptiness and are consequently unable to resolve to attain enlightenment. On the other hand, there are also those who have resolved to attain enlightenment who regard themselves as superior to those who have not. They deludedly cling to the faults of others, not realizing that they are only adventitious, and that, in their true nature, they are at once devoid of all such faults and fully endowed with infinite excellent qualities. Since this type of person just clings to illusory faults and fails to recognize sentient beings' true excellent qualities, he cannot generate the compassion that regards self and other as equal.[37]

---

tiness" (Wayman, *The Lion's Roar of Queen Śrīmālā*, p. 106; Diana Paul, *The Buddhist Feminine Ideal*, p. 215).

[35] T 31.840a3–7 (Takasaki, *Ratnagotravibhāga*, pp. 299–300).

[36] Takasaki, *Ratnagotravibhāga*, pp. 300–301; the Chinese version of this passage gives quite a different reading (see T 31.840a9–12). The parallel passage in the *Fo-hsing lun* (T 31.812b21–24), however, agrees with the Sanskrit text of the *Ratnagotravibhāga* as translated by Takasaki. Takasaki also notes nine other occurrences of this verse in Mahāyāna literature (p. 300, n. 53).

[37] T 31.840c11–12 (Takasaki, *Ratnagotravibhāga*, pp. 306–308).

Chapter Nine

TSUNG-MI'S CRITIQUE OF CH'AN

TSUNG-MI'S extension of his systematic classification of Buddhist teachings to the different Ch'an traditions with which he was familiar created a framework in which those traditions could be systematically evaluated. This chapter will accordingly discuss Tsung-mi's critical evaluation of the major Ch'an traditions of his day. It will go on to claim that Tsung-mi's critique of the Hung-chou tradition furnishes the key for understanding his revision of Hua-yen and will emphasize the importance of his reaction to the antinomian interpretation of Ch'an practice adopted by the P'ao-t'ang tradition as providing the context for assessing his critique of Hung-chou Ch'an. It will conclude by proposing that Tsung-mi saw in the Hung-chou teaching a parallel to the Hua-yen paradigm represented by the unobstructed interpenetration of phenomena (*shih-shih wu-ai*).[1]

CH'AN AND THE TEACHINGS

As noted in the last chapter, the *Ch'an Preface* correlates the three Mahāyāna teachings with three different types of Ch'an. The teaching that negates objects by means of consciousness (i.e., Fa-hsiang Yogācāra) corresponds to the type of Ch'an that cultivates the mind by eliminating delusion (*hsi-wang hsiu-hsin*); the teaching of hidden intent that negates phenomenal appearances in order to reveal the nature (i.e., the Madhyamaka teaching of emptiness) corresponds to the type of Ch'an that is utterly without support (*min-chüeh wu-chi*); and the teaching that directly reveals that the mind is the nature (i.e., the tathāgatagarbha teaching) corresponds to the type of Ch'an that directly reveals the mind as the nature (*chih-hsien hsin hsing*). Moreover, the first type of Ch'an is represented by the Northern line of Shen-hsiu and his disciples; the second, by the Ox-head line of Fa-jung and his disciples; and the third, by the Southern line of the Ho-tse lineage of Shen-hui and the Hung-chou lineage of Ma-tsu.

[1] This chapter adapts portions of my "Sudden Enlightenment Followed by Gradual Cultivation," "Tsung-mi and the Single Word 'Awareness,'" and "The Integration of Ch'an/Sŏn and the Teachings in Tsung-mi and Chinul."

Teaching	Type of Ch'an	Tradition
Negation of objects by means of consciousness	Cultivates mind by eliminating delusion	Northern line
Hidden intent that negates phenomenal appearances in order to reveal the nature	Utterly without support	Ox-head line
Direct revelation that mind is the nature	Directly reveals mind as nature	Southern line

Tsung-mi's correlation of the different types of Ch'an with the different types of doctrinal teaching is integrally connected to one of the major reasons he gives for writing the *Ch'an Preface*: to overcome the often fractious divisions that rent the Chinese Buddhist world of his day. He delineates the contours of those splits as being drawn along two fronts: the first, and more general, between doctrinal scholars and textual exegetes, on the one hand, and Ch'an practitioners, on the other; and the second, and more narrow, among the various contending traditions of Ch'an themselves. The synthetic approach that Tsung-mi adopts in the *Ch'an Preface* is thus addressed to two complexly interrelated issues that are usually lumped together under the rubric of the correspondence of the teachings and Ch'an (*chiao-ch'an i-chih*), which is often cited as one of the hallmarks of his thought. To understand what is going on in the *Ch'an Preface*, however, it is useful to distinguish between them. In calling attention to this distinction, I am following the lead of Yoshizu Yoshihide, who in his excellent study, *Kegonzen no shisōshi-teki kenkyū*, argues that the rubric of *chiao-ch'an i-chih* oversimplifies the complexity of Tsung-mi's thought.[2]

In the first case (relating to the split between textual exegetes and Ch'an practitioners), Tsung-mi generally avoids the term *chiao* ("teachings") and uses the idea of the teachings in a broad, generic sense to refer to Buddhist scriptures (*ching; sūtra*) and treatises (*lun; śāstra*)—"the word of the Buddha" (*fo-yen; buddhavacana*) as he sometimes terms it. In this case he is concerned to show how Ch'an in general corresponds to the word of the Buddhas (who preached the scriptures) and bodhisattvas (who wrote the treatises) as preserved in the Buddhist canon. Yoshizu suggests that Tsung-mi's approach in this case might be more accurately characterized as *ch'an-ching i-chih* (the correspondence of Ch'an and the canon). It is only in the second case (relating to the intramural divisions within Ch'an) that Tsung-mi

[2] See pp. 307–308.

explicitly and consistently uses the term *chiao*. And in this case *chiao* refers to the specific categories of teaching that occur in his p'an-chiao scheme. Here Tsung-mi is concerned to show how the essential teaching (*tsung*) emphasized by the different Ch'an traditions (*tsung*)[3] of his time corresponds to the different teachings (*chiao*) within his doctrinal classification scheme. Yoshizu accordingly suggests that the approach Tsung-mi adopts in the second case might be more aptly characterized as *tsung-chiao i-chih* (the correspondence of the Ch'an traditions and doctrinal teachings). The two issues are, of course, connected. It is precisely because Ch'an in general can be shown to correspond to the canonical teachings that Tsung-mi is able to link specific teachings with specific Ch'an traditions.

In the beginning of his *Ch'an Preface*, Tsung-mi claims that there is no conflict between the enlightenment transmitted by the Ch'an patriarchs and the contents of the Buddhist scriptures as both the scriptures and patriarchal transmission derive from Śākyamuni Buddha. "The scriptures are the Buddha's words," he writes, "and Ch'an is the Buddha's intent (*i*). The minds and mouths of the Buddhas certainly cannot be contradictory."[4]

Tsung-mi goes on to argue that the original unity of the Buddha's teaching was gradually lost as later generations began to specialize in different aspects of Buddhism. It was only in China, however, that the problem became severe. Realizing that the Chinese were overly attached to words, Bodhidharma "wanted to make them aware that the moon did not lie in the finger that pointed to it." He consequently "just used the mind to transmit the mind (*i-hsin-ch'uan-hsin*) without setting up written words (*pu-li wen-tzu*)." Tsung-mi explains that Bodhidharma used such means "to make the essential meaning clear and break attachments, and that it does not mean that [Bodhidharma] taught that liberation was separate from written words." He maintains, however, that since Buddhists of his day do not understand how this expression came about, "those who cultivate their minds take the scriptures and treatises to be a separate tradition (*tsung*), and

[3] Note the ambiguity of the term *tsung*, which Tsung-mi's uses to mean both "essential teaching" and "tradition." See the discussion of this term in chapter 2, pp. 50–51.

[4] T 48.400b10–11; K 44; cf. B 111. Such a sentiment must have struck a sympathetic chord in Chinul (1158–1210), for we find it echoed in his *Hwaŏmnon chŏryo* (as quoted from Buswell, "Chinul's Systematization of Chinese Meditative Techniques," p. 202): "What the World Honored Ones said with their mouths are the teachings (*kyo*). What the patriarchs transmitted with their minds is Sŏn. The mouths of the Buddhas and the minds of the patriarchs certainly cannot be contradictory. How can [students of Sŏn and *kyo*] not plumb the fundamental source but, instead, complacent in their own training, wrongly foment disputes and waste their time?" See my "The Integration of Ch'an/Sŏn and the Teaching (*chiao/kyo*) in Tsung-mi and Chinul," p. 10.

those who elucidate [the texts] take Ch'an to be a separate teaching (*fa*)." Even though the terminology used by textual scholars and Ch'an masters is quite distinct, they must both be understood in terms of the same fundamental concerns. Exegetes "do not realize that the cultivation and realization [that they discuss] are truly the fundamental concerns of Ch'an," just as Ch'an practitioners "do not realize that the mind and Buddha [that they emphasize] are truly the fundamental meaning of the scriptures and treatises."[5]

This passage from the *Ch'an Preface* is often cited as the basis for Tsung-mi's theory of the correspondence of the teachings and Ch'an (*chiao-ch'an i-chih*).[6] In a passage just before this one, Tsung-mi had defined the "teachings" (*chiao*) as "the scriptures (*ching*; *sūtra*) and treatises (*lun*; *śāstra*) left behind by the Buddhas and bodhisattvas," and "Ch'an" as "the sayings and verses passed down by the good friends (*shan-chih-shih*; *kalyāṇamitra*, i.e., Ch'an masters)."[7] What is important to note, however, is that the term "teachings" is here used in the generic sense of the canonical texts and not in the sense of the specific p'an-chiao categories that Tsung-mi later connects with the different Ch'an traditions.

It is because the mind transmitted by the Ch'an patriarchs corresponds to the meaning of the canonical texts that Tsung-mi is able to defend Ch'an against its scholastic critics who denied that it was a valid form of Buddhism because it was extra-canonical. At the same time he also establishes the importance of scripture against Ch'an iconoclasts who claimed that Ch'an enlightenment was independent of any textual authority. In fact, Tsung-mi goes on to argue that the scriptures provide a standard by which to gauge the genuineness of Ch'an enlightenment. He writes: "The scriptures are like a marking-line to be used as a standard to determine true and false." Just as a marking-line must be applied by a skilled craftsman, so "those who transmit Ch'an must use the scriptures and treatises as a standard."[8]

Tsung-mi develops this point further in his discussion of the three sources of valid knowledge (*liang*; *pramāṇa*): inference (*pi-liang*; *anumāna*), direct perception (*hsien-liang*; *pratyakṣa*), and the word of the Buddha (*fo-yen*; *buddhavacana*). He contends that all three sources must coincide.

---

[5] See T 48.400b10–26; K 44; B 111–114.

[6] In his annotated, modern Japanese translation of the *Ch'an Preface*, for example, Kamata entitles this section "kyōzen itchi no seitōsei" (the legitimacy of the correspondence of Ch'an and the teachings).

[7] T 48.399c18–20; K 33; B 102.

[8] T 48.400c25–27; K 54; B 121.

If one just depends on the sayings of the Buddha and does not infer for himself, his realization will be no more than a matter of baseless faith. If one just holds on to direct perception, taking what he perceives for himself to be authoritative without comparing it to the sayings of the Buddha, then how can he know whether it is true or false? Non-Buddhists also directly perceive the principles to which they adhere and, practicing according to them, obtain results. Since they maintain that they are correct, how else would we know they were false [without the word of the Buddha]?[9]

Tsung-mi concludes that, since the various Ch'an traditions for the most part only make use of inference and direct perception, they must be verified by the scriptures and treatises in order to fulfill the requirements of the three sources of knowledge.

Tsung-mi's insistence on the correspondence of Ch'an and the canonical texts implies an approach to Buddhist cultivation that calls for both textual study and meditation practice. Such an approach parallels his emphasis on the inseparability of prajñā and samādhi. That the inseparability of prajñā and samādhi clearly connoted the integration of doctrinal study and meditation practice for Tsung-mi is borne out in an autobiographical comment from the *Ch'an Preface*. There he notes that he "left the multitudes behind to enter the mountains" for a ten-year period "to develop my concentration (samādhi) and harmonize my wisdom (prajñā)."[10] The passage goes on to contrast his balanced approach of textual study and meditation practice, prajñā and samādhi, to the one-sided approach of "the ignorant Ch'an of those who vainly maintain silence or the mad wisdom of those who merely follow texts."[11] It is on this basis that Tsung-mi establishes his own personal authority to bridge the gap that divided exegetes and Ch'an practitioners.

It is because Tsung-mi is able to demonstrate the correspondence of Ch'an and the canonical texts that he is able to link the different Ch'an traditions of his time with the different categories of teaching within his classification scheme. In addition to the general issue of the relationship of Ch'an practice to textual study, the *Ch'an Preface* is also concerned to reconcile the conflict between different Ch'an traditions. Tsung-mi points out that the various traditions of Ch'an all put a premium on different principles (*tsung*).

---

[9] T 48.401a14–18; K 57; B 123–124.

[10] T 48.399c12; K 30; B 100–101. See chapter 2 above.

[11] T 48.399c16–17; Chinul repeats this phrase in his *Kwŏn su chŏnghye kyŏlsa mun*, translated by Buswell in *The Korean Approach to Zen*, p. 104.

Some take emptiness as the true basis of reality, while others take awareness (chih) as the ultimate source. Some say that tranquility and silence
alone are true, while others say that [ordinary activities such as] walking
and sitting are what it is all about (shih). Some say that all everyday discriminative activities are illusory, while others say that all such discriminative activities are real. Some carry out all the myriad practices, while
others reject even the Buddha. Some give free reign to their impulses,
while others restrain their minds. Some take the sūtras and vinaya as
authoritative, while others take them to be a hindrance to the Way.[12]

Tsung-mi goes on to point out that such differences are not merely
a matter of words. Each "adamantly spreads its own tradition and
adamantly disparages the others. Since later students cling to their
words and are deluded about their meaning, in their emotional views
they obstinately contend with one another and cannot reach agree-
ment."[13] It is not that the different teachings emphasized by the different Ch'an traditions are wrong or heretical. The problem is that
each takes itself to be the party in exclusive possession of what is right
and criticizes the others as wrong, a situation Tsung-mi likens to the
famous parable of the blind men and the elephant.[14] He concludes
that the views of the different traditions must be brought into harmony, something that can only be done by uncovering a more comprehensive framework in which such apparently conflicting views can
all be validated as integral parts of a manifold whole—in which the
trunk, tail, leg, side, and so forth are all seen to belong to the same
elephant. "Since the supreme Way is not an extreme and the ultimate
meaning does not lean to one side, one must not grasp onto a single
biased viewpoint. Thus we must bring them back together as one,
making them all perfectly concordant."[15]

The underlying assumption behind Tsung-mi's synthetic approach
is that the various Ch'an traditions, when viewed in isolation from
one another and outside of their overall context within the Buddha's
teachings, are wrong in their self-absolutization. When understood
within that context, however, each will be seen to be true. As Tsung-
mi comments, "If taken in isolation, each of them is wrong. But if

[12] T 48.400c3–7; K 48; B 117–118. Cf. TS 119c7–12.

[13] T 48.400c7–9.

[14] Ch'an Preface, T 48.402b4; K 81; B 143. Tsung-mi also alludes to the parable of
the blind men and the elephant in the TS passage referred to in note 3 above. The
parable can be found in Udāna: Verses of Uplift, trans. F. L. Woodward in The Minor
Anthologies of the Pali Canon, pp. 82–83.

[15] T 48.400c13–15. Tsung-mi strikes a similar note at the end of his preface to the
Inquiry into the Origin of Man, T 45.708a13–18.

taken together, each of them is valid."[16] This statement succinctly encapsulates Tsung-mi's basic methodology for dealing with discrepancies within Buddhism. Whether they lie in the formulation of scholastic dogma or the divergent approaches to practice advocated by the different Ch'an traditions of his day, Tsung-mi's characteristic tendency is always to articulate a comprehensive framework in which such discrepant perspectives can be harmoniously subsumed. Such a comprehensive framework not only provides a larger context in which the divergent perspectives can be validated as parts of a whole, it also provides a new and higher perspective that is superior to the others because it succeeds in sublating them within itself.

The doctrinal correspondences that Tsung-mi establishes thus enable him to place the various types of Ch'an in a hierarchical order. His use of p'an-chiao in the *Ch'an Preface* is not so much concerned with providing a hermeneutical framework in which the different teachings can be systematically integrated as it is concerned with developing a framework in which the different types of Ch'an can all be included. The doctrinal apparatus Tsung-mi presents in the *Ch'an Preface* might thus more accurately be described as a *p'an-ch'an*.[17]

The different teaching with which each Ch'an tradition is connected provides a critical context for evaluating it on a hierarchical scale. While the professed attempt of Tsung-mi's *p'an-ch'an* is to resolve the schisms that split Ch'an into contending factions and pitted Ch'an adepts against doctrinal exegetes, it also serves to elevate his own version of Ch'an to the supreme position. The criticisms that Tsung-mi levels against various doctrinal teachings are extended to their corresponding type of Ch'an, and the other types of Ch'an are accordingly revealed to be inferior to that of his own Ho-tse tradition.

CRITIQUE OF THE DIFFERENT TYPES OF CH'AN

Tsung-mi's most extensive discussion of the differences between the major Ch'an lines of his day is contained in the *Ch'an Chart*. As noted, this work was written around 831 at the request of Tsung-mi's influential lay disciple P'ei Hsiu to clarify the historical filiations and essential teachings of four of the major Ch'an traditions of the day. It thus contains detailed critiques of the Northern line, the Ox-head line, and the Hung-chou and Ho-tse branches of the Southern line. The *Ch'an Chart* is the only work in which he clearly differentiates between the Ho-tse and Hung-chou traditions, and it is in his effort to distin-

---

[16] T 48.400c21–22; K 49; B 119; a virtually identical statement occurs at the beginning of the *Ch'an Chart*, HTC 110433c10–11; K 267.

[17] As Jeffrey Broughton suggested in the preface to his dissertation (p. iii).

guish the teaching of these two traditions that the key to Tsung-mi's thought is to be found.

Critique of the Northern Line

Tsung-mi's clearest criticism of Northern Ch'an occurs in his *Ch'an Chart*, where he gives the following characterization of its major tenets:

> Sentient beings originally have an enlightened nature just as a mirror has a luminous nature, but defilements cover it from view just as a mirror is darkened by dust. If we rely on the teachings of a master and extinguish our deluded thoughts, then, when those thoughts are gotten rid of, the nature of the mind will be enlightened and there will be nothing that is not known. It is like wiping away dust: when the dust is gotten rid of, the essence of the mirror is luminous and clear and there is nothing that is not reflected in it. Therefore, the founder of this lineage, Shen-hsiu, presented the following verse to the fifth patriarch:

> > The body is the bodhi tree,
> > The mind is like a luminous mirror.
> > We must always wipe it clean
> > And never let dust collect.[18]

Tsung-mi then goes on to deliver the following critique:

> This [teaching] merely consists in the method of going against the flow [of birth-and-death] and opposing residual conditioning (*hsi*; *vāsanā*) [based on] the phenomenal appearances of pure and impure conditioned origination (*ching-jan yüan-ch'i chih hsiang*) and has not yet awakened to the fact that deluded thoughts are intrinsically empty and that the nature of the mind is intrinsically pure. When enlightenment is not yet deeply penetrating, how can cultivation be in conformity with the true?[19]

[18] HTC 110.435c13–18; K 298. The verse by Shen-hsiu that Tsung-mi here quotes is that made famous by the *Platform Sūtra*'s story of the exchange of "mind-verses" that decided the issue of the sixth patriarch. It is especially curious that Tsung-mi, who identified so strongly with Shen-hui's lineage, never cites or refers to Hui-neng's matching verse. To the best of my knowledge, Tsung-mi never refers to the *Platform Sūtra* in any of his writings. Ch'eng-kuan quotes half of Shen-hsiu's verse, but also fails to refer to Hui-neng's, in his *Yen-i ch'ao* (see T 36.164c5).

[19] HTC 110.435d1–2; K 298. The summary and critique of the Northern Ch'an teachings that Tsung-mi gives in TSC 277c8–14 is substantially the same as that of the *Ch'an Chart*. The *Ch'an Chart* can thus be used as a corrective to the TSC passage. The *yen* ("smoke") in the TSC passage "*tz'u tan shih jan-ching yüan-ch'i chih yen*" (277c12–13) should therefore obviously be emended to read *hsiang* ("phenomenal appearances").

Tsung-mi's characterization of Northern Ch'an emphasizes the importance of the tathāgatagarbha (i.e., the intrinsically enlightened nature possessed by all sentient beings). His criticism also shows that he sees its understanding of the tathāgatagarbha as being different from his own in a profoundly significant way. To see precisely wherein this difference lies, and what it means for Tsung-mi, it is necessary to place Tsung-mi's critique of Northern Ch'an into the larger doctrinal context that he articulates in his *Ch'an Preface*, where he identifies its teaching with that of the Fa-hsiang brand of Yogācāra. As has been seen, Tsung-mi's major critique of Fa-hsiang is that there is an unbridgeable gap between the ālayavijñāna and suchness (*chen-ju*; *tathatā*). He charges that in the Fa-hsiang teaching "dharmas subject to birth-and-death are not connected with suchness" (*sheng-mieh teng fa pu-kuan chen-ju*).[20] In terms of the two aspects of the mind outlined in the *Awakening of Faith*, this means that there is no connection between the mind as suchness (*hsin chen-ju*) and the mind subject to birth-and-death (*hsin sheng-mieh*); in other words, there is no connection between the tathāgatagarbha and ālayavijñāna. Suchness is seen to be static (*ning-jan*, "inert," and *pu-pien*, "unchanging"), that is, it is not involved in the production of all pure and impure phenomenal appearances (*hsiang*). Where the Fa-hsiang teaching falls short is in its recognizing of only one aspect of the absolute mind (*i-hsin*): while it acknowledges its "unchanging" (*pu-pien*) character, it wholly ignores its "conditioned" (*sui-yüan*) character. In other words, it does not realize that the phenomenal appearances (*hsiang*) that it purports to analyze are the functioning (*yung*) of the mind as suchness as it accords with conditions (*sui-yüan*). But it is just the conditioned aspect of suchness that is of vital importance for Tsung-mi because it links the tathāgatagarbha with the ālayavijñāna and thereby accounts for how suchness accords with conditions to form all pure and impure states. It is this conditioned aspect of suchness that Tsung-mi refers to as nature origination (*hsing-ch'i*), a term that emphasizes the dynamic quality of his understanding of the fundamental nature of the mind.

In Tsung-mi's view, it is because the Fa-hsiang teaching lacks the principle of nature origination that there is nothing to mediate be-

---

Tsung-mi's TSC account goes on to give a detailed summary of the five expedient means (*wu fang-pien*, see 177c14–178b14). The "five expedient means" were a characteristic feature of Northern Ch'an teaching, and there are a variety of surviving Northern Ch'an texts all featuring *wu fang-pien* in their titles. For a composite translation, see McRae, *The Northern School*, pp. 171–196. Kamata has conveniently collated the *Ch'an Chart* and TSC accounts of the Northern line with that of the *Ch'an Preface* in his *Shū-mitsu*, pp. 316–321. Note, however, that Kamata has mistakenly placed the critique appearing in the *Ch'an Chart* in his column for the *Ch'an Preface* (p. 321).

[20] T 48.403b26–27; K 104; B 164.

tween the ālayavijñāna and suchness, the realm of defiled activity and that of unconditioned purity. It is thus guilty of a fundamental dualism. Nature origination, on the other hand, bridges this gap by affirming that all phenomenal appearances (*hsiang*) are nothing but a manifestation (*yung*) of the nature (*hsing*) that is their very essence (*t'i*). Nature origination overcomes this dualism by making use of the conceptual paradigm of essence and function (*t'i-yung*). This paradigm, which had played a dominant role in Chinese metaphysical vocabulary since at least the "Neo-Taoist" speculations of the third century, provides the basic conceptual framework in terms of which Tsung-mi structures his thought. The various polarities that Tsung-mi employs—such as nature and phenomenal appearance(s) or root (*pen*) and branch(es) (*mo*)—all conform to this paradigm. Essence, nature, and root, on the one hand, and function, phenomenal appearance(s), and branch(es), on the other, are all interchangeable. The equation of the essence/function paradigm with that of root/branch also reveals toward which side the polarity is weighted in value. Moreover, since we have seen that nature origination is connected with *li-shih wu-ai*, the following correspondences can thus be established:

Essence (*t'i*)	Function (*yung*)
Nature (*hsing*)	Phenomenal appearance(s) (*hsiang*)
Root (*pen*)	Branch(es) (*mo*)
Absolute (*li*)	Phenomenal (*shih*)

As Tsung-mi's criticism of Fa-hsiang applies to Northern Ch'an, the fault lies with its practice directed toward removing the impurities that obscure the intrinsic purity of the mind. Such a practice is based on a fundamental misconception because it does not realize that the impurities themselves are empty (*k'ung*; *śūnya*)—and by "empty" Tsung-mi means that they lack any independent reality of their own because they are nothing but a manifestation of the intrinsically pure mind as it accords with conditions. The "impurities" are thus not impure in themselves. Rather, their impurity lies in the dualistic misapprehension of them as impure—in other words, the failure to see through them to the intrinsically pure nature that is their essence and of which they are an expression.

This dualism, or fundamental misconception, which Tsung-mi sees as informing Northern Ch'an teaching, is based on the absence of an initial, sudden experience of insight (*chieh-wu*). Such an insight consists in recognizing the fundamental identity of sentient beings and Buddhas, saṃsāra and nirvāṇa, hence it also entails the recognition that deluded thought (i.e., dust) lacks any reality of its own (*wang-nien pen wu*) because it is merely the functioning of the essence of the mind as it accords with conditions. To put it in other terms, *chieh-wu* is an insight into nature origination as the fundamental unifying principle behind the apparent multiplicity of phenomenal appearances. This insight validates the mundane world of phenomenal appearances as the manifestation of the nature. Phenomenal appearances are therefore "empty" and so are not really impure.

Within his scheme of the various permutations of the terms "sudden" and "gradual" as they apply to enlightenment and cultivation, Tsung-mi categorizes the teaching and practice of the Northern line as falling under gradual cultivation followed by sudden enlightenment.[21] Since the Northern line lacks sudden enlightenment, its "gradual cultivation" is qualitatively different from the gradual cultivation that follows sudden enlightenment. Nature is not only the basis of phenomenal appearances, it is also the ground of practice. This failure to recognize the essential nature of all phenomenal appearances lies behind Tsung-mi's charge that the practice taught by Northern Ch'an is "inauthentic" (*fei-chen*). As Tsung-mi adds in his account of this teaching in his subcommentary to the *Scripture of Perfect Enlightenment*, "If cultivation is not in conformity with the true, how can one attain realization even after many kalpas?"[22] Thus, when Tsung-mi says that Northern Ch'an "merely consists in the method of going against the flow and opposing residual conditioning [based on] the phenomenal appearances of pure and defiled conditioned origination," he is implicitly criticizing it for not teaching nature origination.

Critique of the Ox-head Line

In his *Ch'an Chart*, Tsung-mi characterizes the Ox-head line as holding:

> In essence all dharmas are like a dream, and from the very beginning nothing is of any concern; mind and its objects are intrinsically tranquil,

---

[21] In both his subcommentary to his commentary and abridged commentary to the *Scripture of Perfect Enlightenment*, Tsung-mi points out that this case can be interpreted in two ways (TSC 280b17–c8 and LSC 132a10–b1). The first presumes a prior sudden insight (i.e., *chieh-wu*), thus conforming to his threefold model of religious practice and so differing only in emphasis, but not substance, from the case of sudden enlightenment followed by gradual cultivation (which presumes a subsequent realization of enlightenment [*cheng-wu*] as its unstated third term). The second interpretation of gradual cultivation followed by sudden enlightenment does not presume a prior experience of insight, and it is within this framework that Tsung-mi places, and criticizes, Northern Ch'an.

[22] TSC 277c14.

and it is not that they are now for the first time empty. It is because we are deluded about this fact and take [dharmas] to exist that we perceive matters such as prosperity and decay or high and low status. Because such matters may be agreeable or disagreeable, they give rise to feelings such as love and hate. Once feelings arise, we become bound in all sorts of suffering. But when these are created and experienced in a dream, what gain or loss could there be? If one had the wisdom that was able to understand this, it would still be like a dreaming mind. Even if there were a dharma that surpassed nirvāṇa, it would still be like a dream or hallucination. If we penetrate the principle that originally nothing is of any concern, that should enable us to do away with the self and forget the feelings. When the feelings are forgotten, we cut off the cause of suffering, thereupon transcending all suffering and distress. This [Ch'an line] takes forgetting the feelings to constitute cultivation.[23]

Tsung-mi's criticism of Ox-head Ch'an is based on the tathāgata-garbha critique of a one-sided understanding of emptiness. The basic point is that it does not recognize the nonempty aspect of the mind. Elsewhere in the *Ch'an Chart*, Tsung-mi writes that when the followers of the Ox-head tradition "hear . . . the exposition of emptiness in the various Perfection of Wisdom scriptures, . . . they assume that the intrinsically enlightened nature is likewise empty and that there is nothing to be cognized. . . . When they hear it taught that the place where all dharmas are empty and tranquil can be thoroughly known, they say that, on the contrary, the nonemptiness of the essence of mind can neither be penetrated nor known." Tsung-mi goes on to

[23] HTC 110.436a14–b3; K 313; cf. TSC 279b9–c8. Tsung-mi follows the traditional claim that the Ox-head line was founded by Fa-jung (594–657), a supposed disciple of the fourth patriarch, Tao-hsin (580–651). He traces the lineage as running from Fa-jung to Chih-yen (577–654) in the second generation, Hui-fang (627–695) in the third generation, Fa-ch'ih (635–702) in the fourth generation, Chih-wei (646–722) in the fifth generation, and Hui-chung (683–769) and Ma-su (i.e., Hsüan-su, 688–752) in the sixth generation. Tsung-mi further lists Ching-shan Tao-ch'in (i.e., Ching-shan Fa-ch'in, 714–792) as a disciple of Hsüan-su (see TSC 279c9–18; cf. *Chan Chart*, HTC 110.433c14–d4; K 270). Modern scholarship has shown that the Ox-head line originated in the eighth century and had no historical connection to Fa-jung, who in turn had no connection with Tao-hsin. See McRae, "The Ox-head School of Chinese Ch'an Buddhism," pp. 169–252. For an attempt to describe the context and content of Fa-jung's actual teaching (apart from his later appropriation within the Ox-head line), see Albert Dalia, "Social Change and the New Buddhism in South China." The major text associated with the Ox-head line is the *Chüeh-kuan lun*. Although traditionally attributed to Fa-jung, Yanagida Seizan has argued that this work was probably written during the third quarter of the eighth century (*Shoki zenshū shisho no kenkyū*, p. 143). The authoritative version of the text, including an English translation by Tokiwa Gishin, was published by the Institute for Zen Studies at Hanazono in 1973 as *A Dialogue on the Contemplation-Extinguished*.

explain the meaning of nonemptiness by referring to the *Nirvāṇa Sūtra*,[24] which says that "when there is nothing in a jar, the jar is said to be empty—it does not mean that there is no jar." In the same way, "when there are no discriminating thoughts such as desire or anger in the mind, the mind is said to be empty—it does not mean that there is no mind. 'No mind' (*wu-hsin*)[25] only means that the defilements (*fan-nao*; *kleśa*) have been eliminated from the mind."[26]

Tsung-mi's criticism of Ox-head Ch'an draws on the standard tathāgatagarbha understanding of emptiness as meaning that the absolute is empty of defilements. His critique of the teaching that negates phenomenal appearances in the *Inquiry into the Origin of Man* expands on this point.

> If the mind and its objects are both nonexistent, then who is it that knows that they do not exist? Again, if there are no real things whatsoever, then on the basis of what are illusions made to appear? Moreover, there has never been a case of the illusory things in the world before us being able to arise without being based on something real. If there were no water whose wet nature were unchanging, how could there be the waves of illusory, provisional phenomenal appearances? If there were no mirror whose pure luminosity was unchanging, how could there be the reflections of a variety of unreal phenomena? Again, . . . the dream that is illusory must still be based on someone who is sleeping. Now, granted that the mind and its objects are both empty, it is still not clear on what the illusory manifestations are based. Therefore we know that this teaching merely destroys our attachment to feelings but does not yet reveal the nature that is true and numinous.[27]

Critique of the Hung-chou Line

Tsung-mi characterizes the teaching of the Hung-chou line as being diametrically opposed to that of the Northern line. He contrasts the two by remarking that the Northern line regards "everything as altogether false (*wang*)" whereas the Hung-chou line regards "everything as altogether true (*chen*)." Their approach to cultivation is accordingly opposite: the Northern line advocates "subjugating the mind so as to extinguish the false (*fu-hsin mieh-wang*)," whereas the

[24] See T 12.395b.

[25] Supplied from *P'ei Hsiu shih-i wen*, p. 91, and *Chŏryo*, p. 21; both the HTC and Kamata editions give *wu*.

[26] HTC 110.337a8–10; K 329; the Chinul passage is considerably abbreviated (see 156b; Buswell, *The Korean Approach to Zen*, p. 274).

[27] T 45.709c26–710a5.

Hung-chou line advocates "entrusting oneself to act freely according to the nature of one's feelings (*hsin-jen ch'ing-hsing*)."[28] Whereas the Northern line falls into dualism, the position of the Hung-chou line leads to a radical nondualism by collapsing essence (*t'i*) into function (*yung*). As Tsung-mi characterizes its stance in the *Ch'an Chart*:

> The arising of mental activity, the movement of thought, snapping the fingers, or moving the eyes, all actions and activities are the functioning of the entire essence of the Buddha-nature. Since there is no other kind of functioning, greed, anger, and folly, the performance of good and bad actions and the experiencing of their pleasurable and painful consequences are all, in their entirety, Buddha-nature.[29]

Because all activities—whether good or bad, enlightened or deluded—are "the functioning of the entire essence of the Buddha-nature," there is no essence outside of its functioning.

> If one examines the nature of its essence thoroughly, he will see that ultimately it can neither be perceived nor realized just as the eye cannot see itself, and so forth. If one considers its responsive functioning, he will see that everything that he does is the Buddha-nature and that there is nothing else that can either realize it or be realized.[30]

The ethically dangerous implication of this teaching for Tsung-mi is that, if the essence can only be perceived through its functioning and, moreover, everything is equally the functioning of the essence in its entirety, then the essence becomes totally eclipsed by its functioning. Tsung-mi, however, insists that while the essence and its functioning are different aspects of the same reality, they are nevertheless still different, and that their difference is important because the essence, as what is most fundamental (*pen*), is the basis on which the experience of enlightenment (*chieh-wu*) is validated. His assimilation of the essence/function (*t'i-yung*) paradigm into that of root/branch (*pen-mo*) entails a notion of religious practice as a return to a more basic state, the primordial condition of the mind before its bifurcation into subject and object attendant upon the first subtle movement of thought. It is only through a direct experience of the essence that its functioning can be validated as true.

It is because the Hung-chou line collapses essence into function

---

[28] *Ch'an Chart*, HTC 110.436b3–5; K 315.

[29] HTC 110.435d4–6; K 307.

[30] HTC 110.435d17–18; K 307. Neither the HTC nor Kamata version of the text has "Buddha-nature" (*fo-hsing*). This has been supplied from *P'ei Hsiu shih-i wen*, p. 85, and *Chŏryo*, p. 7.

that Tsung-mi regards its attitude toward cultivation as antinomian. He holds that its proponents thus maintain that

> One should rouse the mind neither to cut off evil nor to cultivate the Way. Since the Way itself is the mind, one cannot use the mind to cultivate the mind. Since evil is also the mind, one cannot use the mind to cut off the mind. One who neither cuts off [evil] nor does [good] but freely accepts things as they come is called a liberated person. There is no dharma that can be clung to nor any Buddhahood that can be attained. . . . Simply allowing the mind to act spontaneously is cultivation.[31]

Although on one level Tsung-mi would not gainsay the Hung-chou position that there is ultimately no Buddhahood to attain, he would also insist that that realization is precisely what Buddhahood consists in, and that such a statement can only be meaningfully made from the position of one who has attained Buddhahood. For one who has not yet reached such a state facilely to conclude that there is therefore no reason to cultivate Buddhahood is a grave error. Tsung-mi insists that while ultimately the nature transcends all dualistic categories, there is nevertheless a difference between enlightenment and delusion as far as sentient beings are concerned. And it is the tension between the difference between enlightenment and delusion that vivifies practice.

> Hung-chou constantly says: "Since greed, anger, compassion, and good deeds are all the Buddha-nature, how could there be any difference between them?" This is like someone seeing that there is never any difference in the wet nature [of the water] and not realizing that there is an enormous difference between the success of a boat that crosses over it and the failure of a boat that capsizes in it. Therefore, as far as this line's approach toward sudden enlightenment is concerned, even though it comes close, it still does not hit the mark, and, as far as its approach toward gradual cultivation is concerned, it is mistaken and completely backward.[32]

Tsung-mi's criticism of the Hung-chou line reveals that his use of the essence/function paradigm is more complex than might at first be apparent. While he emphasizes the inseparability of essence and function as but different aspects of the same reality, he also stresses their difference: they are neither one nor different (*pu-i pu-i*) (just as the true mind that is not subject to birth-and-death interfuses with deluded thoughts in such a way that they are neither one nor different). Their inseparability is what makes religious cultivation possible,

---

[31] HTC 110.436a4–9; K 308.
[32] HTC 110.438a18–b4; K 341.

and their difference is what makes religious cultivation necessary. Tsung-mi thus uses the essence/function paradigm to preserve an ethically critical duality within a larger ontological unity. While this paradigm overcomes the dualism of Northern Ch'an on the one hand, it serves to avoid the radical nondualism of Hung-chou on the other.

As part of his criticism of the Hung-chou line, Tsung-mi introduces a critical distinction between two levels of functioning: what he calls the "intrinsic functioning of the self-nature" (*tzu-hsing pen-yung*) and its "responsive functioning in accord with conditions" (*sui-yüan ying-yung*). "The intrinsic essence of the true mind (*chen-hsin tzu-t'i*) has two kinds of functioning: the first is the intrinsic functioning of the self-nature and the second is its responsive functioning-in-accord-with-conditions."[33] Tsung-mi then proceeds to illustrate this statement with an analogy of a bronze mirror.

> The material substance of the bronze [mirror] is the essence of self-nature; the luminous reflectivity (*ming*) of the bronze is the functioning of the self-nature; and the images reflected by its luminous reflectivity are its functioning-in-accord-with-conditions. The images are reflected in direct response to conditions. While the reflections may have thousands of variations, the luminous reflectivity is the ever-present luminous reflectivity of the self-nature.[34]

Tsung-mi goes on to explain this analogy: "The ever-present tranquility of the mind is the essence of the self-nature, and the ever-present awareness of the mind is the functioning of the self-nature." The functioning of self-nature, of course, is none other than intrinsic enlightenment. The functioning-in-accord-with-conditions refers to the psycho-physical functions of "speech, discrimination, bodily movement, and so forth."[35] The analogy can be schematized as follows:

Mirror	Ontology	Mind
Bronze	Essence of self-nature	Ever-present tranquility
Luminous reflectivity	Functioning of self-nature	Ever-present awareness
Reflected images	Functioning-in-accord-with-conditions	Psycho-physical functions

[33] HTC 110.437d4–5; K 336.
[34] HTC 110.437d5–7; K 336.
[35] HTC 110.437d7–8; K 336.

The relationship between these two different orders of functioning, furthermore, can be characterized in terms of the essence/func-
tion-root/branch paradigm: the functioning of the self-nature is the
essence or root of the functioning-in-accord-with-conditions.

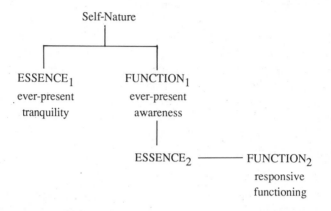

Tsung-mi uses this distinction to point out that the Hung-chou
line, in overemphasizing the "responsive functioning" of the Buddha-nature, altogether misses the functioning of its self-nature. Its
practice therefore lacks ontological grounding and is apt to veer off
in ethically dangerous directions. In drawing this distinction as crucial for differentiating between the Hung-chou and Ho-tse teachings,
Tsung-mi reaffirms his emphasis on essence in contradistinction to
function. By calling attention to the importance of the intrinsic functioning of the self-nature, Tsung-mi effectively drives a wedge between essence and function to insure that they cannot be collapsed in
the way in which he understands the Hung-chou teaching to have
done.

The analysis of the structure of the mind upon which Tsung-mi's
use of this metaphor is based derives from the *Awakening of Faith*,
which, as has been seen, discusses the mind in terms of two aspects:
the mind as suchness (*hsin chen-ju*) and the mind subject to birth-and-
death (*hsin sheng-mieh*). Following Fa-tsang, Tsung-mi characterizes
these two aspects of the mind as absolute (*pu-pien*) and conditioned
(*sui-yüan*). These two aspects of the mind, in turn, trace back to the
two different perspectives in terms of which the tathāgatagarbha was
traditionally discussed: seen in its true form, the tathāgatagarbha is
none other than the dharmakāya that is intrinsically pure and devoid
of all defilements; seen, however, through the deluded perception of
sentient beings, it appears to be defiled.

The absolute and conditioned aspects of the mind, as Tsung-mi understands them, conform to the conceptual paradigm of essence (*t'i*) and function (*yung*). What is interesting and unique about Tsung-mi's analysis, however, is that he also views the absolute aspect of the mind in terms of its essence and function. Accordingly, tranquility (*chi*) in the term "empty tranquil awareness" refers to the essence of the self-nature of the mind, and awareness, to its functioning. As Tsung-mi writes, " 'Tranquil' refers to the invariable steadfastness of the real essence, the principle of immovability and immutability. . . . Were there no essence of the true mind, what could be said to be tranquil and what could be said to be immovable and immutable?"[36] Awareness is a "direct manifestation of the very essence itself (*t'ang-t'i piao-hsien*)."[37] "Tranquility is the awareness that is tranquil, and awareness is the tranquility that is aware. Tranquility is the essence of the self-nature that is aware, and awareness is the functioning of the self-nature that is tranquil."[38] Tsung-mi then invokes the authority of Shen-hui to clinch the point that the essence of the mind and its functioning are only different modes of one another: "Ho-tse said, 'The functioning of the essence is aware in and of itself, and the essence of this awareness is tranquil in and of itself. Although the terms are different, essence and function form a unity.' "[39]

The importance of Tsung-mi's application of the essence/function paradigm to the absolute aspect of the mind is that it allows him to distinguish between two different orders of functioning: the intrinsic functioning of the self-nature and its responsive functioning-in-accord-with-conditions. The functioning of the self-nature, like the luminous reflectivity of a mirror, is absolute in that it is ever-present and not contingent upon conditions: it exists in and of itself. It is in this sense that it is characterized as *pen*, "intrinsic," in contrast to the functioning-in-accord-with-conditions, which is causally contingent and hence characterized as *ying*, "responsive." Moreover, just as the luminous reflectivity of the mirror is able to reflect both pure and impure images without its intrinsically pure and luminous nature being affected, so too the mind is able to respond to pure and impure conditioning without its intrinsically pure and enlightened nature being affected. The functioning-in-accord-with-conditions, on the other hand, is what could be called a second order functioning. It involves two levels of contingency. Not only do the pyscho-physical functions, like the reflected images in a mirror, only become activated in response to stimuli, they are also dependent upon the mind as their

[36] LSC 97b8–10.
[37] Ibid. 97b11.
[38] Ibid. 97b12–14.
[39] Ibid. 97b18–c1.

ontological ground, just as images could not be reflected in the absence of a mirror. The psycho-physical functions are thus, in an important sense, epiphenomena (*hsiang, mo*) of ever-present awareness. The difference between these two kinds of functioning could thus be represented as follows:

Functioning of self-nature	Functioning-in-accord-with-conditions
Eternal	Transient
Unchanging	Variable
Unconditioned	Conditioned
Absolute	Relative
Primary (*pen*)	Derivative (*mo*)

These two different orders of functioning also reflect two different levels of "causality." The first has to do with the sequence of causes and conditions whereby each thing or event arises or occurs contingent upon a series of other things or events, which, in turn, are contingent upon yet other things or events. In terms of Tsung-mi's analogy, the various images that are reflected in the mirror are contingent upon the different objects that appear before it, those objects themselves ultimately being contingent upon an infinite series of causes and conditions. It is just this order of contingency that is accounted for in the doctrine of conditioned origination (*yüan-ch'i; pratītyasamutpāda*). As the analogy has already suggested, however, there is another kind of causality, one that makes the first possible. This second kind of causality is, of course, nature origination (*hsing-ch'i*). It has already been seen that Tsung-mi draws from the *Wang-chin huan-yüan kuan*[40] to define nature origination as "the arising of functioning (*yung*) based on the essence (*t'i*)."[41] "Nature," it will be recalled, refers to the one mind of the *Awakening of Faith*, "the pure mind that is the ultimate source of Buddhas and sentient beings,"[42] and "origination" refers to the manifestation of the manifold phenomena of the universe from the nature, the process of phenomenal appearance.[43] Whereas nature origination means that all phenomenal appearances are ultimately based on the nature, conditioned origination connotes the relative interdependency of all phenomenal appearances. While each and every phenomenal appearance is conditioned by every other phenomenal appearance, it is simultaneously also grounded upon the nature, which is its ultimate source.

The two different levels of causality could be visualized as a cone.

[40] See T 45.639b20–22, quoted in chapter 7 p. 190.
[41] HTC 7.399c16–17.
[42] Ibid. 399b6 and c5.
[43] Ibid. 399c5–6.

The circular surface of the cone (the directrix) would represent the dimension of conditioned origination (*yüan-ch'i*), in which every point is connected with every other point in a causal series. Since the position of each point is conditioned by that of every other point, each point could be said to be infinitely contingent. The individual points, moreover, represent the infinite variety of phenomenal appearances (*hsiang*). Each phenomenal appearance, however, in addition to being conditioned by all others, is also a manifestation of the nature (*hsing*), which, in the image of the cone, would be represented by the vertex. Not only is each point on the directrix serially linked with every other point on the directrix, it is at the same time also linked with the vertex, just as all phenomenal appearances are simultaneously interdependent and a manifestation of the nature, which is their ultimate ground. The direct and simultaneous linkage of each point of the directrix with the vertex represents the dimension of nature origination (*hsing-ch'i*)—what, in the geometrical terminology of this image, is aptly termed the generatrix.

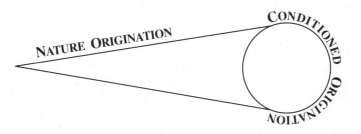

The significance of nature origination as a causal model is that phenomenal appearances only have reality insofar as they are manifestations of the nature. When they are taken as real in themselves, they become the basis for deluded attachment. Only when they are seen as empty, as lacking any intrinsic reality, can they be seen as manifestations of the nature and their ultimate reality be understood. The import of nature origination is thus both ontological and soteriological: the ontological structure of reality that it describes is at once a soteriological map. And awareness (*chih*), as the functioning of self-nature, occupies the nodal point in this model. Awareness is the ontological ground of phenomenal appearances, which only have reality as manifestations of the nature. It is the underlying basis of all mental states. In this way enlightenment and delusion are only changing reflections on the surface of awareness. In the terms of the *Awakening of Faith*, from which Tsung-mi's interpretation of nature origination derives, awareness would correspond to intrinsic enlightenment (*pen-chüeh*). The "luminous reflectivity" in Tsung-mi's use of the analogy of the mirror translates *ming*, a word that doctrinally plays on *wu-ming*, ignorance (Skt., *avidyā*), and hence serves as an appropriate metaphorical expression for intrinsic enlightenment.

Awareness, as the functioning of the self-nature, thus represents the dynamic, creative aspect of the nature. It is therefore important to note that the word *chih* is primarily verbal, meaning "to know." Even when it is used nominally, as it is by Tsung-mi, its verbal force is still retained. What *chih* refers to, then, is an activity rather than a thing. For this reason it is preferable to the word "mind" (*hsin*), which, as a noun, is more apt to be reified. The English word "knowing," accordingly, might seem to be a better translation of *chih*, as it more faithfully represents both the literal meaning and verbal character of the Chinese word. The problem with "knowing," however, is that the verb "to know" is transitive and demands an object. But Tsung-mi emphasizes the fact that *chih* is intransitive and does not demand an object. And "awareness," insofar as it is possible to be aware without necessarily being aware of anything, better expresses the intransitive character of *chih*.

Historical Context

Tsung-mi introduced the metaphor of the mirror in the *Ch'an Chart* to make explicit the differences between the Ho-tse and Hung-chou lines of Southern Ch'an and to demonstrate the superiority of the former. Even though this work discusses the Northern and Ox-head lines of Ch'an, it is most concerned with that of Hung-chou as representing the most serious challenge to the Ho-tse tradition with which Tsung-mi identified himself. Since both the Northern and Ox-head lineages claimed descent from the fifth and fourth patriarchs respectively and, by the 830s when he composed the *Ch'an Chart*, it had been generally accepted that Hui-neng had succeeded to the title of sixth patriarch, they represented collateral lines and thus, in terms of their historical filiation, did not pose a threat to the orthodoxy of the Southern Ch'an to which the Ho-tse lineage belonged. Hung-chou, however, also claimed descent from Hui-neng and thus boasted better credentials. Moreover, by the fourth decade of the ninth century, the Northern and Ox-head lines were no longer vital traditions within Ch'an. The Hung-chou line, however, inspired by the dynamic personality and teaching style of Ma-tsu Tao-i (709–788), had come to represent a new and ascendent force within Ch'an. Nor, in terms of their teachings, did the Northern and Ox-head lines represent the same danger for Tsung-mi as did Hung-chou. In terms of the doctrinal analysis elaborated in the *Ch'an Preface*, the teaching of the

Northern line of Ch'an was identified with the Fa-hsiang brand of Yogācāra, and that of the Ox-head line with Madhyamaka. The criticism that Tsung-mi had leveled against the first and second categories of Mahāyāna teachings in that work consequently applied to them as well. He had, however, placed the Hung-chou line together with that of Ho-tse under the rubric of the third and highest category of teaching.

Tsung-mi's emphasis on the single word "awareness" as the hallmark of Shen-hui's teaching singled out precisely that which for him most clearly distinguished the teaching of the Ho-tse line from those of the contending Ch'an lines which he considers in the *Ch'an Chart*. Moreover, the fact that his most detailed analysis of this crucial term occurs within a metaphor whose explicit purpose is to contrast the Ho-tse and the Hung-chou understanding of Ch'an suggests that one of the reasons that Tsung-mi fixed on this term was that it served not only to differentiate his brand of Ch'an from that of Hung-chou but also to clarify exactly wherein it was superior.

In terms of the analysis of empty tranquil awareness that Tsung-mi develops in his use of the metaphor of the mirror, the fault of the Hung-chou line is that it does not apprehend the functioning of the self-nature but merely that of its responsive functioning-in-accord-with-conditions.[44] This is tantamount to saying that the Hung-chou teaching mistakes the reflections in the mirror for its luminous reflectivity. To put it in other terms, it mistakes the variegated and ever-changing phenomenal appearances of the nature for the nature itself. As far as Tsung-mi is concerned, this is a dangerously antinomian view, for it does away with any basis for drawing moral distinctions between good and bad courses of action. Since it validates all the different activities that one engages in every day,[45] it can be seen as undermining the purpose of religious practice. If the three poisons of greed, anger, and folly are nothing but the expression of Buddha-nature, what need is there to uproot them?

The force of this criticism is brought out in Tsung-mi's use of a variation of the metaphor of the mirror that he also employs in the *Ch'an Chart*. Here he uses a maṇi jewel to represent the one numinous mind (*i-ling-hsin*); its perfectly pure luminous reflectivity, empty tranquil awareness; and its complete lack of coloration, the fact that this awareness is intrinsically without any differentiated manifestations. "Because the essence [of the jewel] is luminously reflective, whenever it comes into contact with external objects, it is able to re-

[44] HTC 110.437d10–11; K 336.
[45] HTC 110.436a11; K 308.

flect all of their different colors." Likewise, "because the essence [of the mind] is aware, whenever it comes into contact with conditions, it is able to differentiate them all into good and bad, pleasurable and unpleasurable, as well as produce the manifold variety of mundane and supermundane phenomena. This is its conditioned aspect (sui-yüan-i)." Tsung-mi continues, "Even though the [reflected] colors are themselves distinct, the luminously reflective jewel never changes." And he comments, in his interpolated note, "Even though ignorance and wisdom, good and bad, are themselves distinct, and anguish and joy, love and hate, arise and perish of themselves, the mind that is capable of awareness is never interrupted. This is its absolute aspect (pu-pien-i)."[46]

Tsung-mi then considers the case of when the maṇi jewel comes into contact with something black: its entire surface appears black, just as the intrinsically enlightened nature of the mind appears totally obscured by the presence of ignorance.[47] Tsung-mi claims that proponents of the Hung-chou line would maintain that the very blackness itself is the jewel, and that its essence can never be seen. Because such people do not apprehend the luminously reflective jewel, when they see something black of similar size and shape, they misidentify it as the maṇi jewel. If, however, they were to see the maṇi jewel as it is in itself when it is not reflecting any colors at all, they would not be able to recognize it. Tsung-mi goes on to explain that the state in which the jewel is not reflecting any colors means "being without thoughts (wu so-nien)." When only its luminous reflectivity is in evidence, furthermore, refers to "the absence of thought which is thoroughly aware in and of itself (liao-liao tzu-chih wu-nien)."[48]

Tsung-mi's case rests upon his claim that the luminously reflective jewel can be seen in itself when it is not reflecting any colors. While it is unclear in phenomenological terms precisely in what such a direct perception of the nature might consist, it is important to note that Tsung-mi connects such a perception with no-thought (wu-nien). In his quotation from the "Wen-ming" chapter of the Hua-yen Sūtra in his explication of ever-present awareness in the Ch'an Preface, he quotes Ch'eng-kuan's comment that "true awareness can only be seen in no-thought" (chen-chih wei wu-nien fang chien).[49] In addition to representing the method by which the nature is directly apprehended, no-thought also represents the intrinsic condition of the nature, which is devoid (k'ung) of all phenomenal appearances (hsiang), just

[46] HTC 110.436c17– d3; K 322.
[47] HTC 110.436d3–7; K 322.
[48] HTC 110.436d13–437a4; K 326.
[49] See chapter 8, p. 218.

as the *Awakening of Faith* characterizes the intrinsically enlightened mind as being without thoughts. It is this ontological dimension of no-thought that is behind Tsung-mi's characterization of awareness as being "empty" in the phrase "empty tranquil awareness." Although Tsung-mi does not clarify further what he means by the practice of no-thought, what is important to note here is that it is his claim that a direct perception of the nature is not only possible but necessary that distinguishes the Ho-tse line from that of Hung-chou—and such a direct perception of the nature is what, for Tsung-mi, sudden enlightenment (*tun-wu*) is all about. Elsewhere he claims that the Hung-chou line, in contradistinction to that of Ho-tse, only has inferential knowledge (*pi-liang*; *anumāna*) but not direct perception (*hsien-liang*; *pratyakṣa*) of the nature.[50] And it is because it does not have a direct perception of it that it can mistake something else for the nature. This means, for Tsung-mi, that followers of the Hung-chou line have no clear assurance that their insight is true and, accordingly, their practice of "simply allowing the mind to act spontaneously" can become a rationalization for deluded activity. Tsung-mi thus charges them not only with failing to understand the meaning of sudden enlightenment, but also with not recognizing the necessity of the subsequent gradual cultivation, in which the deeply rooted habitual conditioning that keeps one from integrating his insight into the nature throughout all dimensions of his personality and behavior is progressively extirpated.[51]

If Tsung-mi's emphasis on awareness can be seen, at least in part, as a reaction against what he perceived as the overly radical character of other forms of Ch'an, then, given the centrality of awareness within his thought as a whole, it further suggests that his revaluation of some of the basic tenets of Hua-yen thought also had its impetus in his response to developments within the Ch'an of his day. While Tsung-mi is noted for his infusion of Ch'an into Hua-yen, it might be more accurate to characterize him as a conserative Ch'an figure who adapted Hua-yen thought as a hedge against more extreme Ch'an movements of the late eighth and early ninth centuries. Certainly one of the reasons Hua-yen appealed to Tsung-mi was that it provided an ontological rationale for Ch'an practice, and that was precisely wherein he perceived the Hung-chou teaching to be lacking.

The primary exponent of the Hung-chou lineage, Ma-tsu, like Tsung-mi, hailed from Szechwan. Tsung-mi points out that Ma-tsu first studied Ch'an under Wu-hsiang in the Ching-chung tradition be-

[50] HTC 110.437d11–12; K 336.
[51] See HTC 110.438a18–b3; K 341.

fore meeting and eventually succeeding Nan-yüeh Huai-hai (677–744).[52] As Yanagida Seizan has suggested in his perceptive study of the background of the *Li-tai fa-pao chi*, just as Ma-tsu's teaching can be seen as a development out of trends within the Szechwanese Buddhist milieu from which he came, so Tsung-mi's can be seen as a reaction against them. In either case, it was the Ch'an movements in Szechwan that formed the context out of which, or against which, each later articulated his own teaching. The most radical of these movements was that of Pao-t'ang, whose fabrication of its own history is preserved in the *Li-tai fa-pao chi*. According to Tsung-mi,[53] the Pao-t'ang line derived from Lao-an (584?–708).[54] One of Lao-an's disciples was the layman Ch'en Ch'u-chang (sometimes known as Vimalakīrti Ch'en), who transmitted the teaching to Wu-chu (714–774), under whom it flourished in Szechwan. Tsung-mi notes Wu-chu's association with Wu-hsiang, claiming that, although he attended Wu-hsiang's assembly and questioned him, it did not alter his understanding. Nevertheless, since Wu-chu thought it improper to have received the teachings from a layman (i.e., Ch'en Ch'u-chang), he tried to align himself with Wu-chu. Tsung-mi goes on to point out the ways in which Wu-chu's teaching differed from Wu-hsiang's. Thus, despite Wu-chu's attempt to affiliate himself with Wu-hsiang, Tsung-mi evidently believed his approach to be distinctive enough to count as a separate tradition.[55] Tsung-mi characterizes the teaching of this line as "extinguishing consciousness by not adhering to the teachings and practices" (*chiao hsing pu-chü erh mieh-shih*).

This school of Ch'an extended Shen-hui's teaching of no-thought (*wu-nien*)[56] to its logical conclusion by discarding all forms of traditional Buddhist ethical practice and ritual observance. As Tsung-mi notes, followers of this type of Ch'an "did not follow any of the ob-

---

[52] See *Ch'an Chart*, HTC 110.434b15–c3.

[53] See TSC 278c14–d5.

[54] Literally "Old An"; also known as Hui-an. Tsung-mi claims that he lived to the age of 120. Later sources put his age at 128. See McRae, *The Northern School*, pp. 57–58, for a discussion of his life, and p. 290, n. 137, for biographical sources.

[55] Yanagida shares Tsung-mi's suspicions, concluding that, despite its attempt to connect Wu-chu with Wu-hsiang, "a careful reading of the LTFPC [*Li-tai fa-pao chi*] reveals that Wu-chu never actually met his supposed master Wu-hsiang" ("The *Li-tai fa-pao chi* and the Ch'an Doctrine of Sudden Awakening," p. 23). Yanagida also notes that Shen-ch'ing (d. 806-820), the author of the *Pei-shan lu*, "represents himself as a disciple of Wu-hsiang, and is sharply critical of Wu-chu's school" (p. 24), further calling into question the *Li-tai fa-pao chi's* claim that Wu-chu was the sole legitimate heir of Wu-hsiang's teaching. See T 52.611b.

[56] For a discussion of the importance of *wu-nien* in Wu-chu's thought, see Suzuki Tetsuo, *Tō-godai zenshūshi*, pp. 356–359.

servances of the Buddhist tradition." Not only was there nothing comparable to the large ordination ceremonies that were such a central feature of the Ching-chung line, there was no ordination ceremony in which the precepts were conferred; to become a monk was simply a matter of shaving one's head and donning the robes. "Worship, repentance, reciting scriptures, painting Buddhist images, and copying sūtras are all rejected as deluded ideas, and no Buddhist services are given in the cloister where the monks live."[57]

Tsung-mi goes on to explain that the rationale for such antinomian behavior is an extension of their attempt to "extinguish discriminative consciousness" (mieh-shih).

> Their idea is that the cycle of birth-and-death is entirely due to the arousal of mind (ch'i-hsin). Since the arousal of mind is delusion (wang), they are not concerned with good and evil; and since its nonarousal is truth (chen), they also do not imitate the practice of religious observances (shih-hsiang). They take discrimination (fen-pieh) as the enemy and non-discrimination as the marvelous way.[58]

Tsung-mi explains that they adapted the three phrases of Wu-hsiang by interpreting the third, not forgetting (mo-wang), as meaning being without delusion (mo-wang). Since remembering (i) and thinking (nien) are deluded activities (wang), one must not let delusion arise by practicing not remembering (wu-i) and not thinking (wu-nien).[59]

> Their abolition of religious works is aimed at extinguishing discrimination and preserving the true. Therefore, wherever they stay, they do not concern themselves about clothing and food but trust that others will present them as offerings. If they are given, they have warm clothing and enough to eat. If they are not given, they bear hunger and cold, neither seeking donations nor begging for food. When visitors come to the monastery, they do not greet them, nor do they see them off, regardless of whether they are of high or low status. Whatever praise or offerings, blame or harm, come their way, they simply resign themselves to them.[60]

Tsung-mi concludes his account by remarking that since this tradition "advocates nondiscrimination as its essential point, it takes its

[57] TSC 278d6–7, as translated by Carl Bielefeldt, "The Li-tai fa-pao chi and the Ch'an Doctrine of Sudden Awakening," p. 33.
[58] Ibid. 278d8–10.
[59] Ibid. 278d10–13.
[60] Ibid. 278d13–16. I have freely incorporated portions of Jan's and Broughton's translations; cf. "Tsung-mi's Analysis," p. 45, and "Early Ch'an," p. 40.

method of practice to be beyond [distinctions of] right or wrong. It just values no mind (*wu-hsin*) as the ultimate."[61]

Wu-chu, the "founder" of this school, seems to have been a persuasive speaker who often held large public meetings in which he proselytized his radical message. The *Li-tai fao-pao chi* emphasizes his close ties with a number of the regional military and political power holders of the time. Most notable among these was the minister Tu Hung-chien (709–769), vice director of the Chancellory.[62] According to the *Li-tai fa-pao chi*, when Tu first arrived in Szechwan in 766 he sought out Wu-chu, invited him to come down from the mountains, and later had his Pao-tang monastery designated as an official government temple.[63]

In any case, it is likely that it was Tsung-mi's acquaintance with this school that shaped his perception of the Hung-chou line of Ch'an represented by Ma-tsu and his successors, as well as sensitizing him to the antinomian dangers inherent in some of the more radical Mahā-yāna doctrines preached in Ch'an. The ethical thrust of Tsung-mi's critique of the Hung-chou line and its emphasis on spontaneity (*tzu-jan*) can also be seen in the philosophical critique that he gives of the Taoist teaching of spontaneity, which (as will be seen in the next chapter) he interprets as an acausal principle that undermines the efficacy of religious and ethical cultivation.

Although Tsung-mi does not make the explicit connection, it is tempting to speculate that he may have felt a similarity in the ethical import of the teachings of the Hung-chou line of Ch'an and the Hua-yen teaching of *shih-shih wu-ai* (i.e., the unobstructed interrelation of all phenomena). This suggestion gains plausibility when one recalls the imagery of infinite mutual reflection that Fa-tsang used to illustrate the interpenetration and mutual determination of all phenom-

---

[61] Ibid. 278d16–18.

[62] For his biography see CTS 108.3282–3284 and HTS 126.4422–4424; his funerary inscription can be found in CTW 369. Tu first distinguished himself during the An Lu-shan Rebellion. After emperor Hsüan-tsung fled to Szechwan in 756, Tu helped support Su-tsung in Ling-wu. In 766 he was sent to Szechwan as military governor (*chieh-tu shih*) to subjugate the insurrection of Ts'ui Ning. Ts'ui had become a local military hero by leading a campaign that had been successful in driving the Tibetans out of the Hsi-shan region northwest of Ch'eng-tu. Ts'ui later came into conflict with the military governor Kuo Ying-i, who was killed in the ensuing struggle. Wary of suffering a similar fate, Tu brought the affair to a peaceable conclusion by having Ts'ui appointed as military governor in 767 (see Yanagida, *Shoki II*, p. 197, and Backus, *The Nan-chao Kingdom*, pp. 82–83). The *Li-tai fa-pao chi* also notes Wu-chu's connection with Ts'ui Ning and Chang-ch'iu Chien-ch'iung, another figure who had rendered distinguished service against the Tibetans (see Yanagida, *Shoki II*, pp. 151–152).

[63] See Yanagida, "The *Li-tai fa-pao chi* and the Ch'an Doctrine of Sudden Awakening," p. 25.

ena in the perfect teaching. As discussed in chapter 6, two of the most representative examples by which Fa-tsang elucidated the perfect teaching were the samādhi of oceanic reflection and Indra's net. The point that is particularly significant to recall here is that the regnant imagery in both of these examples was based on the ability of each phenomenon to reflect, and be reflected by, all other phenomena. If Fa-tsang's examples are rephrased in the terms used by Tsung-mi in his examples of the bronze mirror or maṇi jewel, shih-shih wu-ai would correspond to what Tsung-mi refers to as the functioning-in-accord-with-conditions.

There is also a striking parallelism in the status of the Hua-yen teaching of shih-shih wu-ai and the Hung-chou teaching within Tsung-mi's p'an-chiao. In the Ch'an Preface, Tsung-mi places the Hung-chou line together with his own Ho-tse line under the teaching of the direct revelation that the mind is the nature. Its placement within the highest type of Ch'an parallels the Hua-yen Sūtra's ambiguous status within the highest teaching in Tsung-mi's classification scheme. It should be recalled here that Tsung-mi made a point of specifying that only "one part" (i-fen) of the Hua-yen Sūtra's teaching properly fell under the heading of the teaching that reveals the nature,[64] and this part was its teaching of the one true dharmadhātu, not its teaching of interpenetration.

There are good reasons for supposing that Tsung-mi may well have felt that the Hung-chou line of Ch'an expressed the antinomian danger implicit in the Hua-yen teaching of shih-shih wu-ai. Behind Tsung-mi's discussion and evaluation of various teachings, whether Buddhist or non-Buddhist, there is always a keen sensitivity to their ethical implications at work. One of the reasons Tsung-mi valued the tathāgatagarbha so highly was that it provided a firm ontological ground for Buddhist practice. As expressed in his interpretation of nature origination (hsing-ch'i), this doctrine meant that all phenomenal appearances (hsiang) only had reality insofar as they were seen to be manifestations (ch'i) of the nature (hsing). Taken as real in and of themselves, however, phenomenal appearances are the basis of deluded attachment. Only when they are seen to be empty can their true reality be grasped. The doctrine of nature origination can be seen as an elaboration of the meaning of li-shih wu-ai (i.e., the interpenetration of the absolute and phenomenal). As has been seen, Tsung-mi equates shih (phenomena) with hsiang (phenomenal appearances). The Hua-yen teaching of shih-shih wu-ai thus refers to the intricate web of interconnections that obtain among phenomenal ap-

---

[64] See chapter 5, p. 151, and chapter 6, pp. 167–168.

pearances. They are that which—in the context of his criticism of the
Hung-chou line of Ch'an—he refers to the functioning-in-accord-
with-conditions, merely the ever-changing images reflected on the
surface of the mind, nothing more than the epiphenomena (*mo*) of
the intrinsically enlightened true mind.

If the criticism that Tsung-mi levels against the Hung-chou teaching can thus be applied against *shih-shih wu-ai*, it further clarifies why,
to employ the traditional Hua-yen categories used throughout this
book, he valued *li-shih wu-ai* over *shih-shih wu-ai*, and therefore also
why he omitted the perfect teaching from his doctrinal classification
system, ceding its place to that of the tathāgatagarbha.

Despite Tsung-mi's efforts to uphold the orthodoxy of Shen-hui's
line of Ch'an, it was the teaching and style of the Hung-chou line that
triumphed historically. Tsung-mi was the fifth and last patriarch
within the Ho-tse tradition. Shortly after his death in 841, the Hui-
ch'ang persecution sealed the demise of the Ho-tse line of Ch'an once
and for all. After the persecution, his devoted disciple P'ei Hsiu became grand councilor and labored to resurrect the fortunes of Buddhism. He also became a disciple of Huang-po Hsi-yün (d. 850), a
forceful master in the Hung-chou line and teacher of Lin-chi I-hsüan
(d. 866). Huang-po's collected sermons and dialogues were recorded
by none other than Tsung-mi's former lay disciple, P'ei Hsiu,[65] a fact
that can be taken as symbolizing the failure of the Ho-tse line to per-
petuate itself as a living Ch'an tradition and the attendent shift toward a more radical form of Ch'an teaching. While Tsung-mi's more
ontological point of view did not prevail within Ch'an, it did, ironi-
cally, survive within Neo-Confucianism. Chu Hsi's criticism of the
Buddhist understanding of "nature" (*hsing*), for instance, merely recapitulates Tsung-mi's criticism of the Hung-chou line,[66] a point to
which I shall return in the final chapter.

[65] *Ch'üan-hsin fa-yao* (T 48.379b–384a) and *Wan-ling lu* (T 48.384a–387b), originally
compiled by P'ei Hsiu in 842 and 848. See the annotated translation by Iriya, *Denshin
hōyō*. See also Blofeld's translation in his *The Zen Teaching of Huang Po*.

[66] For Yanagida's comment on how Tsung-mi's criticism of Hung-chou anticipates
Chu Hsi's criticism of Buddhism, see his postscript to Iriya, *Denshin hōyō*, p. 162.

PART FOUR

The Broader Intellectual Tradition

Chapter Ten

CONFUCIANISM AND TAOISM IN
TSUNG-MI'S THOUGHT

TSUNG-MI found in Hua-yen doctrine an ontological rationale with which to justify Ch'an practice and buttress it against the antinomian implications of the more radical Ch'an movements of his day. For this purpose the Hua-yen doctrine of *li-shih wu-ai*, based on the *Awakening of Faith*'s adaptation of tathāgatagarbha doctrine, provided a far more suitable model than *shih-shih wu-ai*, which could be seen as opening up the very ethical dilemma that he saw in the Pao-t'ang and Hung-chou lines of Ch'an against which he was reacting. The ethical tenor of Tsung-mi's Ch'an points not only to his Ching-chung and Sheng-shou training but also to the lasting influence of the Confucian moral vision that he had absorbed in his youth.

This chapter will accordingly assess the role of Confucianism in Tsung-mi's thought by focusing on his *Inquiry into the Origin of Man*. The importance that Confucianism had for Tsung-mi is far more extensive than his formal ranking of it in that work would suggest. In the *Inquiry into the Origin of Man*, Tsung-mi extends the Buddhist rubric of p'an-chiao to Confucianism and Taoism in order to appraise them, together with various Buddhist teachings, in terms of the degree to which they succeed in revealing the ultimate ontological basis of human experience and ethical action. Within this hierarchical framework, the Confucian answer is ranked below that of even the most superficial explanation found in Buddhism, the fundamental moral teaching of karma. But such a low ranking is deceptive. In analyzing the criticism that Tsung-mi raises against Confucianism in that essay, it is important to note that he does not reject its moral vision; rather, what he rejects is its ability to rationalize that vision. Tsung-mi, in fact, goes on to argue that the Buddhist teaching of karma, represented in the teaching of men and gods, is superior to Confucianism precisely because it succeeds in justifying the moral order inherent in the cosmos. As I shall set forth in more detail below, Tsung-mi makes a point of showing how the five Buddhist precepts that form the substance of the teaching of men and gods correspond to the five Confucian virtues. Given the workings of karma, the practice of Confucian moral teachings is therefore just as effective in ensuring a desirable human rebirth as the practice of Buddhist moral teachings. Tsung-mi thus uses the Buddhist teaching of karma to validate Confucian moral values. Indeed, it seems likely that one of the reasons that Tsung-mi was originally drawn to Buddhism was that it offered a more coherent and persuasive justification of the Confucian moral order.[1]

Tsung-mi's Extension of P'an-chiao to the Two Teachings

Tsung-mi's most important discussion of Confucianism and Taoism appears in his *Inquiry into the Origin of Man (Yüan jen lun)*. Considered within the general context of Chinese Buddhist p'an-chiao literature, Tsung-mi's *Inquiry* is remarkable in that it extends the problematic of p'an-chiao to Confucianism and Taoism. Whatever the particular scheme by which the teachings were classified, p'an-chiao was typically an enterprise that applied exclusively to the Buddha's teachings. Among Tsung-mi's predecessors within the Hua-yen tradition, for instance, neither Chih-yen, Fa-tsang, nor Ch'eng-kuan had included Confucianism and Taoism within the scope of his classification of the teachings. Indeed, one of the principal objections that Ch'eng-kuan leveled against the fourfold classification scheme developed by Hui-yüan, Fa-tsang's unjustly maligned disciple, was that his first category comprised non-Buddhist teachings, thus confusing Buddhism with falsehood.[2] The charge was serious and was one of the prime reasons for which Hui-yüan was posthumously excised from the Hua-yen lineage and branded as a heretic.

The case of Hui-yüan highlights the innovative character of Tsung-mi's *Inquiry into the Origin of Man*. Even though, as "outer" teachings (*wai-chiao*), Tsung-mi does not include Confucianism and Taoism within his fivefold categorization—which only applies to the "inner" teachings (*nei-chiao*) of Buddhism—he does, nonetheless, extend the problematic of p'an-chiao to the two teachings, something

---

[1] This chapter adapts portions of my "The Teaching of Men and Gods."

[2] See *Yen-i ch'ao*, T 36.17a26. Elsewhere in the same work, Ch'eng-kuan says that Hui-yüan's inclusion of non-Buddhist teachings within his p'an-chiao scheme constitutes "the error of confusing the true and the false. . . . If one does not know what is false, then how can one understand what is true?" (51c23–24). Altogether Ch'eng-kuan levels ten criticisms against Hui-yüan in the beginning of the *Yen-i ch'ao* (see T 36.16b15–18c7; for a discussion of these, see Sakamoto, *Kegon kyōgaku*, pp. 58–91).

Hui-yüan's fourfold classification scheme, it should be said in his defense, was based on solid canonical authority, deriving from a passage in the *Ratnagotravibhāga* (T 31.839b18–21), itself based on a passage from the *Śrīmālā Sūtra* (T 12.222b19–21), categorizing the different types of sentient beings who do not have access to the tathāgatagarbha (see *K'an-ting chi*, HTC 5.12a18–12b2).

that is only possible because he places Confucius and Lao-tzu on a par with the Buddha. As he writes in his preface: "Confucius, Lao-tzu, and Śākyamuni were consummate sages, who, in accord with the times and in response to beings, made different paths in setting up their teachings."[3] Tsung-mi here uses the Buddhist rubric of expedient means to account for the differences among the three teachings.[4] The three sages should all be regarded as equally enlightened. The differences among their teachings are due to the limitations set by the particular historical circumstances in which they lived and taught rather than to any qualitative difference in their understanding. Tsung-mi continues:

> The inner and outer [teachings] complement one another, together benefiting the people. As for promoting the myriad practices, clarifying cause and effect from beginning to end, exhaustively investigating the myriad phenomena, and elucidating the full scope of birth and arising— even though these are all the intention of the sages, there are still provisional (ch'üan) and ultimate (shih) [explanations]. The two teachings [of Confucianism and Taoism] are just provisional, [whereas] Buddhism includes both provisional and ultimate. Since encouraging the myriad practices, admonishing against evil, and promoting good contribute in common to order, the three teachings should all be followed and practiced. [However,] if it be a matter of investigating the myriad phenomena, exhausting principle, realizing the nature, and reaching the original source, then Buddhism alone is the ultimate judgment.[5]

[3] T 45.708a8.

[4] In his commentary to the *Inquiry into the Origin of Man*, Yüan-chüeh illustrates how this doctrine works (HTC 104.111b). He writes that since men's roots had not yet ripened in the time of Confucius and Lao-tzu, and they were thus not yet ready to hear even the most elementary teaching of cause and effect, how much less were they prepared to hear the ultimate teaching of Buddha-nature. Therefore Confucius and Lao-tzu first used the moral teaching of humanity (jen) and righteousness (i) to lead them gradually forward and pointed to the primal pneuma as the origin. Yüan-chüeh goes on to say that even during the first part of the Buddha's teaching career the roots of his disciples were not yet ripened, and they were also not yet ready to hear the ultimate teaching of Buddha-nature. Only after forty years of preparing them by expounding provisional teachings, such as karma and the law of cause and effect, was the Buddha able to deliver the ultimate message.

Tsung-mi, of course, was not the first to extend the rubric of expedient means to Chinese sages. It was a ploy that had long been used by Buddhist apologists in China. See, for example, Arthur Link and Tim Lee, "Sun Ch'o's *Yü-tao-lun*," and Eric Zürcher, *The Buddhist Conquest of China*, 1:133.

[5] T 45.708a8–13. This passage is of particular interest because it reveals the ease and skill with which Tsung-mi was able to draw from his early education in the Confucian classics. The phrase "exhausting principle, realizing the nature, and reaching the ultimate source," for instance, is based on an almost identical passage from the *I ching*,

While it should be no surprise that Tsung-mi regards Buddhism as a higher level of teaching than either Confucianism or Taoism, what is especially noteworthy is that his attitude toward the "two teachings" is sympathetic and inclusive. Even though his designation of them as exclusively provisional places them in a category inferior to the Buddhist teachings, it also—and far more significantly—places them within the same realm of discourse. Although its concrete forms of expression differ, the truth realized by the three sages is universal. Tsung-mi's originality thus does not lie in the mere reshuffling of the traditional repertoire of Buddhist teachings to devise a new p'an-chiao arrangement; it lies in extending the scope p'an-chiao itself.

Tsung-mi's synthetic approach stands in sharp contrast to that of Ch'eng-kuan and Hui-yüan. Not only was Ch'eng-kuan critical of Hui-yüan for incorporating non-Buddhist teachings into his p'an-chiao scheme, he also excoriated those who maintained that the three teachings were one. He said: "Those who go too far and equate [false teachings] with Buddhism are all outside the Buddhadharma."[6] He goes on to liken the Buddha's teaching to cow's milk, from which the ghee of liberation can be obtained; the teachings of non-Buddhists,

which James Legge translates as: "They (thus) made an exhaustive discrimination of what was right, and effected the complete development of (every) nature, till they arrived ... at what was appointed for it (by heaven)" (Sung, *Yi King*, pp. 338–339). Tsung-mi's phrase "contribute in common to order" (*t'ung kuei yü chih*) is drawn from the *Shu ching* passage that Legge translates as: "Acts of goodness are different, but they contribute in common to government. Acts of evil are different, but they contribute in common to disorder" (*Chinese Classics*, 3:490). Tsung-mi's use of the phrase *t'ung kuei*, moreover, recalls another pasage from the *I ching*, which Legge renders as: "In all (the processes taking place) under heaven, what is there of thinking? What is there of anxious scheming? They all come to the same (successful) issue, though by different paths; there is one result, though there might be a hundred anxious schemes" (Sung, *Yi King*, p. 316). The *I ching* passage is of further importance in that it connects Tsung-mi's use of the phrase *t'ung kuei* with the phrase *shu t'u*, which he used in the previous quotation when he said that the three sages "made different paths in setting up their teachings." Taken together, the phrase *shu t'u t'ung kuei*—which could be freely rendered as "the different paths ultimately lead to the same goal"—was used by Chinese Buddhists to characterize the universal teaching of the one vehicle (*i-sheng*; *ekayāna*) associated with the *Lotus Sūtra*, according to which the teachings of the three vehicles (i.e., those of the śrāvaka, pratyekabuddha, and bodhisattva) were all subsumed into one all-inclusive vehicle of salvation. The phrase "the different paths ultimately lead to the same goal" thus provided Chinese Buddhists with a convenient formula for establishing the ultimate identity of not only all the different teachings of the Buddha but also the three teachings of Buddhism, Confucianism, and Taoism. For Tsung-mi's explanation of the phrase, see TSC 240b16–c2 (see TS 112b6) (which he quotes from Ch'eng-kuan's *Yen-i ch'ao*, T 36.39b2–8; see T 35.508a10).

[6] *Hua-yen ching shu*, T 35.521b15–16. Ch'eng-kuan goes on at length in his subcommentary to elaborate ten major points of difference that distinguish Buddhism from Confucianism and Taoism (see *Yen-i ch'ao*, T 36.106a27–107a13).

however, are likened to donkey's milk, from which ghee can never be obtained: they lack the taste of liberation and can only be made into urine and ordure.[7] Further, he says that the gap between Buddhism and the two teachings is "so vast that even a thousand leagues would not seem far."[8] He concludes his invective with the following admonition:

> Do not seek after the trivial reputation of a single age and confuse the three teachings as one. Studying the poisonous seeds of false views is a deep cause for being born in hell, opens up the wellspring of ignorance, and blocks of the road to omniscience. Take heed! Take heed![9]

Ch'eng-kuan's charge against Hui-yüan is apt to give the misleading impression that Hui-yüan had a generally accommodating attitude toward non-Buddhist teachings. But such is far from the case. Although the first category of Hui-yüan's fourfold classification comprises non-Buddhist teachings (i.e., the ninety-five heretical views of the Indian philosophers), he uses his discussion of them as an opportunity to criticize those who identify Buddhist teachings with Confucianism and Taoism. He says that those who claim that the Buddhist tathāgatagarbha is the same as the Taoist nonbeing's engendering of the manifold universe, for instance, "not only do not understand the *garbha* [i.e., embryo, womb, matrix] of the Tathāgata, but have also not yet even discerned the true meaning of nothingness."[10] Hui-yüan,

---

[7] *Yen-i ch'ao*, T 36.106a7–12. Ch'eng-kuan's remark is based on a parable from the *Nirvāṇa Sūtra* (see T 12.381c–382b), which he cites in full in the preceding passage (see 105b17–106a5). In this parable, which is related to illustrate the difference between the Buddha's teaching and the worldly teachings, the Buddha recounts the story of a man who had a herd of cows. He kept them and saw that they were well tended in order to have ghee made out of their milk. When the man died, the whole herd was stolen by a band of thieves, who also wanted to make ghee from the milk. Since they did not know how to churn the milk to make cream, however, they could not make it thicken. They then added water to it, hoping thereby to make ghee, but only ruined the milk. The Buddha explains that even though the common man has access to the Buddha's most excellent teaching, he does not know how to use it to attain liberation, just as the thieves did not know how to use the cow's milk to make ghee. Ch'eng-kuan's remark also recalls the well-known analogy of the five flavors, which is also found in the *Nirvāṇa Sūtra* (see T 12.690c27–691a6). The Buddha uses this analogy to compare the different levels of his teaching to milk, cream, butter, melted butter, and ghee—all of which are made from cow's milk (see chapter 3 above). By likening the teachings of Confucianism and Taoism to donkey's milk, Ch'eng-kuan puts them in an entirely different soteriological class from the teachings of Buddhism.

[8] T 45.107a7–8.

[9] T 45.107a11–13.

[10] *K'an-ting chi* HTC 5.13a9–10. In his comment on this passage, Sakamoto (*Kegon kyōgaku*, p. 273) has speculated that Hui-yüan might here be referring to Ch'eng Hsüan-ying (active early to middle seventh century), whom Ch'eng-kuan singles out

in other words, charges those who try to explain Taoist ideas by drawing from the doctrinal repertoire of Buddhism not only with demonstrating their failure to understand Buddhism, but also, more damagingly, with revealing their ignorance of the meaning of the principal ideas of their own tradition, which they only distort in such misguided attempts at elucidation.

Tsung-mi's extension of p'an-chiao to Confucianism and Taoism thus stands in marked contrast to his Hua-yen predecessors. Before going on to consider Tsung-mi's critical assessment of the two teachings, we might pause here briefly to note the particular "logic" by which p'an-chiao manages to accomplish two apparently opposed tasks. P'an-chiao served as a critical tool by which different teachings could be evaluated and put in their place, thereby establishing a hierarchical grading of teachings. In this way it was used for polemical purposes to justify the sectarian claims of different traditions. But the important point to notice is that the very means that p'an-chiao used to subordinate other teachings at the same time created a framework in which those teachings could be subsumed, and thereby validated, within a broader vision of the dharma. P'an-chiao thus also had a synthetic function built into its critical framework. The "logic" by which these two functions worked together as different aspects of one another was "dialectical" and is most accurately denoted by the term "sublation" (*aufheben*; *shiyō*). The hermeneutical value of such logic was that it provided an approach to conflicting points of view that avoided absolute judgments of right and wrong. Different teachings are not so much wrong as they are limited or partial. There is thus a gradient of truth along which all teachings can be arranged. And the

---

for censure for confusing the three teachings (see *Yen-i ch'ao*, T 36.105b13–16). Ch'eng-kuan comments that Ch'eng Hsüan-ying, in using Buddhist ideas to elucidate the meaning of the *Lao-tzu* and *Chuang-tzu* in his commentaries to those two works, merely saw that there was some similarity in their expression without recognizing that their meaning differed greatly. Tao-hsüan, in discussing an imperial edict ordering Hsüan-tsang to translate the *Lao-tzu* into Sanskrit, names Ts'ai Hung and Ch'eng Hsüan-ying as two of the Taoists directed to collaborate with Hsüan-tsang. He remarks that it was their custom to quote Buddhist works (such as the *Middle Treatise* and the *Hundred Treatise*) to explain the meaning of Taoist ideas (see *Chi ku-chin fa-tao lun-heng*, T 52.386c2–7). Yoshioka Yoshitoyo has shown that Ch'eng Hsüan-ying made use of Buddhist methodology (especially the Madhyamaka logic of negation) in his interpretation of the *Lao-tzu* (see *Dōkyō to bukkyō*, 1:109–115). For further discussion of Ch'eng Hsüan-ying's use of Buddhism, see Kamata, *Chūgoku kegon*, pp. 274–276; see also Kamata, *Chūgoku bukkyō shisōshi kenkyū*, p. 182. Ch'eng Hsüan-ying's commentary to the *Chuang-tzu* can be found in the Taoist Canon (Harvard-Yenching no. 507). His commentary to the *Lao-tzu* was among the works discovered at Tun-huang (Pelliot no. 2353), and its preface has been published by Yoshioka in his *Dōkyō to bukkyō*, 1:110–115.

way in which one supersedes the other is dialectical, each teaching overcoming in turn the particular limitation or partiality of the one that preceded it. The supreme teaching, of course, is the one that succeeds in offering the most comprehensive point of view in which all other teachings can be harmoniously sublated. The highest teaching was therefore often referred to as *yüan* (literally, "round," that is, having no sides or partiality, not leaning in any direction), the perfect teaching in which all the others were consummated.[11]

Tsung-mi's inclusion of the two teachings within his p'an-chiao scheme thus enabled him at once both to demonstrate their inferiority to Buddhism and to integrate them within a Buddhist vision. Nowhere is Tsung-mi's synthetic approach more apparent than in the concluding section of the *Inquiry into the Origin of Man*, where he incorporates Confucianism and Taoism, together with the five levels of Buddhist teaching, into an overarching explanation of the origin of man. By creating a framework in which Confucianism, Taoism, and Buddhism could be synthesized, Tsung-mi not only transcended the polemical intent of the earlier debates between the three teachings but also laid out a methodology by which Confucian terms—infused with Buddhist meaning—were later to be resurrected in the Confucian revival of the Sung dynasty.

TSUNG-MI'S CRITIQUE OF CONFUCIANISM AND TAOISM

The first main section of the *Inquiry into the Origin of Man*, entitled "Exposing Deluded Attachments" (*ch'ih mi chih*), is addressed to "those who practice Confucianism and Taoism." This section is divided into two main parts. The first consists of a brief synopsis of the gist of Confucianism and Taoism, followed by a general critique. The second singles out four major concepts to subject to more detailed scrutiny and criticism: the Way (*tao*), spontaneity (*tzu-jan*), the primal pneuma (*yüan-ch'i*), and the mandate of heaven (*t'ien-ming*). This section is modeled after an earlier discussion of the two teachings that had appeared in Tsung-mi's *Commentary to the Scripture of Perfect Enlightenment*.[12] The close correspondence of the two versions enables one to use the corresponding sections of Tsung-mi's *Subcommentary to the Scripture of Perfect Enlightenment* as "footnotes" to amplify his discussion of Confucianism and Taoism in the *Inquiry into the Origin of Man*.

[11] Fa-tsang's emphasis on the exclusive character (*pieh*) of the Hua-yen teaching thus goes against his characterization of it as "perfect" (*yüan*).

[12] Kamata has conveniently collated the two versions of Tsung-mi's discussion of Confucianism and Taoism in his *Shūmitsu*, pp. 115–117.

General Critique

Tsung-mi's general summary and critique of the two teachings introduces the themes that he examines in more detail in the second part
of this section and intimates some of the criticisms developed there.
He begins by summarizing the cosmogonic basis of Confucianism and
Taoism:

> The two teachings of Confucianism and Taoism hold that men, beasts,
> and the like are all produced and nourished by the great Way of noth-
> ingness (hsü-wu ta-tao). They maintain that the Way, conforming to what
> is naturally so (tao fa tzu-jan), engenders the primal pneuma. The primal
> pneuma engenders heaven and earth, and heaven and earth engender
> the myriad things.[13]

Tsung-mi's account draws on a series of allusions to the Lao-tzu.[14]
In his note to this passage in his Subcommentary to the Scripture of Perfect
Enlightenment,[15] he links the process of cosmogony here described
with that found in chapter 42 of the Lao-tzu: "The Way engenders
the one; the one engenders the two; the two engender the three; and
the three engender the myriad things."[16] The Way's engendering of
the primal pneuma[17] thus corresponds to the Way's engendering of

---

[13] T 45.708a26–28; cf. TS 163a6–9 and TSC 430d9ff.

[14] See, for example, Lao-tzu 51: "The Way gives them life and rears them; brings
them up and nurses them; brings them to fruition and maturity; feeds and shelters
them" (Lau, Lao Tzu, p. 112); Lao-tzu 25: "There is a thing confusedly formed, born
before heaven and earth. Silent and void it stands alone and does not change, goes
round and does not weary. It is capable of being the mother of the world. I know not
its name so I style it 'the Way.' I give it the makeshift name of 'the great' " (Lau, p. 82);
and Lao-tzu 25: "Man models himself on earth, earth on heaven, heaven on the Way,
and the Way on that which is naturally so" (Lau, p. 82). Tsung-mi's own note to this
last passage makes it clear that he understands fa in the phrase "tao fa tzu-jan" to be
functioning as a verb (see TSC 413d–414a).

[15] TSC 414a.

[16] Cf. Lau, Lao Tzu, p. 103. Tsung-mi had already alluded to this passage in his preface to the Inquiry. See T 45.708a3–5: "The one pneuma (i-ch'i) of the primordial chaos
(hun-tun) divided into the dyad of yin and yang, the two engendered the triad of
heaven, earth, and man, and the three engendered the myriad things."

[17] Ch'i is a notoriously difficult term to translate. As a philosophical concept, it has
been variously rendered as "vital force" (Bodde), "material force" (Chan), "ether of
materialization" (Metzger), "pneuma" (Needham, Schafer), "ether" (Graham),
"breath" (Watson), and so forth. Bernhard Karlgren defines it as "breath, air, vapour,
steam; vital fluid, temperament, energy; anger" in his Analytic Dictionary of Chinese and
Sino-Japanese and traces its etymology to the pictograph representing "breath, air, vapour" (p. 120). In his Two Chinese Philosophers, A. C. Graham indicates the range of
meaning encompassed by this term: "Ch'i, a common and elusive word in ordinary
Chinese speech as well as in philosophy, covers a number of concepts for which we

the one; the primal pneuma's engendering of heaven and earth, to the one's engendering of the two; and so forth. He goes on to identify the primal pneuma's engendering of heaven and earth with the great ultimate's (*t'ai-chi*) engendering of the two elementary forms (*liang i*) as recounted in the Great Appendix of the *I ching*.[18] In so doing, Tsung-mi is following the tradition of K'ung Ying-ta (574–648), who, in his subcommentary to this line, linked the cosmogonic process described in the *I ching* passage with that given in *Lao-tzu* 42.[19] Elsewhere in his *Subcommentary to the Scripture of Perfect Enlightenment*,[20] Tsung-mi quotes a lengthy passage from Ch'eng-kuan's *Yen-i ch'ao*[21] that cites both Han K'ang-po's (332–380) commentary and K'ung Ying-ta's subcommentary to the *I ching*. The *Yen-i ch'ao* passage goes on to cite the *I kou-ming chüeh*, which further connects the cosmogonic process found in the Great Appendix with that given in the first chapter of the *Lieh-tzu*.[22] That work analyzes the cosmogonic process

---

have different names in English or none at all. Unlike the abstract *li* [Principle] . . . , *ch'i* is quite concrete; it really is, among other things, the breath in our throats. It is the source of life, dispersing into the air at death; we breathe it in and out, and feel it rising and ebbing in our bodies as physical energy, swelling when we are angry, failing in a limb which grows numb; we smell it as odours, feel it as heat or cold, sense it as the air or atmosphere of a person or a place, as the vitality of a poem, or as the breath of spring which quickens and the breath of autumn which withers; we even see it condensing as vapour or mist" (p. 31).

Wing-tsit Chan writes in *A Source Book in Chinese Philosophy*: "*ch'i* as opposed to *li* (Principle) means both energy and matter. . . . In many cases, especially before the Neo-Confucian doctrine of *li* developed, *ch'i* denotes the psycho-physiological power associated with blood and breath. As such it is translated as 'vital force' or 'vital powers' " (p. 784).

When *ch'i* is used to designate a cosmogonic force (i.e., *yüan-ch'i* or *i-ch'i*), I have followed Edward Schafer, who translates *yüan-ch'i* as "primal pneuma." "Pneuma" is at once faithful to the etymological meaning of *ch'i* as well as being sufficiently vague to intimate the elusive and metaphysical character of *ch'i* as a cosmogonic term. When Tsung-mi uses *ch'i* to refer to an individual's endowment of life, however, it is translated as "vital force."

[18] See Sung, *Yi King*, p. 299.

[19] See *Chou-i chu-shu* 7.17a.

[20] TSC 352c.

[21] See T 36.104b. Jan Yün-hua discusses this passage at length in "Tsung-mi's Questions Regarding the Confucian Absolute" but fails to note that it is quoted in its entirety from Ch'eng-kuan.

[22] In answer to the question: "From what were heaven and earth born?" Lieh-tzu answers: "There was the great interchangeability (*t'ai-i*), there was the great antecedence (*t'ai-ch'u*), there was the great initiation (*t'ai-shih*), and there was the great simplicity (*t'ai-su*). The great interchangeability refers to the time when the pneuma was not yet visible (*wei chien ch'i*). The great antecedence refers to the beginning of the pneuma (*ch'i chih shih*). The great initiation refers to the beginning of form (*hsing chih chih*). The great simplicity refers to the beginning of material substance (*chih chih shih*)" (*Lieh-tzu* 1.6–7; cf. Graham, *The Book of Lieh-tzu*, pp. 18–19).

into five phases, the first four corresponding to those enumerated in the first chapter of the *Lieh-tzu* (i.e., the great interchangeability, the great antecedence, the great initiation, and the great simplicity) and the fifth referring to the great ultimate of the Great Appendix. Such a five-phase theory must have enjoyed wide currency in the T'ang, for it is referred to in other works as well.[23] Tsung-mi evidently had this scheme in mind when, in the conclusion to the *Inquiry into the Origin of Man*, he wrote: "The beginning for them starts with the great interchangeability and evolves in five phases to the great ultimate."[24]

Tsung-mi's synopsis of the two teachings continues, pointing out the consequences of such a cosmogony:

> Thus dullness and intelligence, high and low station, poverty and wealth, suffering and happiness are all endowed by heaven and proceed according to time and destiny. Therefore, after death one again returns to heaven and earth and reverts to nothingness.[25]

Tsung-mi here makes two points that will prove central for his critique of Confucianism and Taoism. The first has to do with the relationship of the Way or heaven, as the ultimate basis of phenomenal reality, to the evident inequalities that pertain in the world. This point is connected with what could be broadly characterized as the problem of theodicy, which Tsung-mi raises as part of his more pointed criticism of the Way and the mandate of heaven in the second part of this section. It is significant because it reveals that as far as Tsung-mi is concerned, the standard by which cosmogonic theories are to be measured has to do with their ability to clarify the ontological basis of ethical action. The second point has to do with the dispersion of the vital force (*ch'i*) after death. In his note to this passage in his *Subcommentary to the Scripture of Perfect Enlightenment*, Tsung-mi quotes a passage from the *Li chi* that says that at death "the intelligent spirit (*hun-ch'i*) returns to heaven, and the bodily soul (*p'o*) returns to the earth."[26] Tsung-mi focuses on the implications of this point in his critique of the primal pneuma, where he mounts a force-

[23] For example, both the *Pien-cheng lun* by Fa-lin (572–640) (see T 52.490b19–22) and the *Pei-shan lu* (see T 52.573b24–26) quote the *I kou-ming chüeh* passage detailing this five-phase cosmogony. Other works, such as the *T'ai-p'ing yü-lan*, divide the cosmogonic process into a series of six phases by designating the primal pneuma as the first phase, which is even prior to the grand initiation. For a discussion of these terms see Schafer, *Pacing the Void*, pp. 25–29.

[24] T 45.710c15.

[25] Ibid., 708a28–29; cf. TS 163a9–10.

[26] See *Li chi* 8.11b; adapted from Legge's translation, *Book of Rites*, 1:444. Tsung-mi quotes this passage in his TSC 414b2–3.

ful defense of the Buddhist theory of rebirth. This point, then, is related to Tsung-mi's general criticism of the two teachings for their ignorance of the process of rebirth. These two points, moreover, are connected by the Buddhist teaching of karma, which, as embodied in the teaching of men and gods, supersedes Confucianism and Taoism in Tsung-mi's scheme of things. The teaching of karma both clarifies the relationship between cause and effect, on which ethical action must depend, and explains how the process of rebirth operates.

Tsung-mi gives the following general critique of the two teachings:

> This being so, the essential meaning of the outer teachings merely lies in establishing [virtuous] conduct based on this bodily existence and does not lie in thoroughly investigating the ultimate source of this bodily existence. The myriad things that they talk about do not have to do with that which is beyond tangible form. Even though they point to the great Way as the origin, they still do not fully illuminate the pure and impure causes and conditions of conforming to and going against [the flow of] origination and extinction (*shun-ni ch'i-mieh jan-ching yin-yüan*). Thus, those who study [the outer teachings] do not realize that they are provisional (*ch'üan*) and cling to them as ultimate (*liao*).[27]

Here there are several points to note. The first and second sentences are related to the short-sightedness of Confucianism and Taoism for their failure to understand human existence in terms that go beyond this single bodily existence (*shen*). Elsewhere Tsung-mi characterizes the essential meaning of Confucianism as lying in its moral teaching of loyalty, filial piety, humanity, and righteousness (*chung, hsiao, jen, i*) and that of Taoism, in its life-nurturing practices (*yang-hsing pao-shen*).[28] In either case, the religious purview of the two teachings does not extend beyond the present existence. As Tsung-mi states in the preface to the *Inquiry into the Origin of Man*, followers of the two teachings merely know that "they have received this body from their ancestors and fathers having passed down the bodily essence in a continuous series."[29] The two teachings are thus inferior to

---

[27] T 45.708a29–b4.

[28] See TSC 352a17–b1.

[29] T 45.708a2–3. The expression *nai tsu nai fu* comes from the *Shu ching*, where Legge translates it as "your ancestors and fathers" (*Chinese Classics*, 3:239, 240). In his commentary on this passage (91c), Ching-yüan cites the following passage from Tsung-mi's *Yü-lan-p'en ching shu*: "What the outer teachings take as their cardinal principle (*tsung*) is that man has material form as his basis and passes down his bodily essence in a continuous series" (T 39.508a11). The idea is echoed in the *Hsiao ching*: "The son derives his life from his parents and no greater gift could possibly be transmitted" (Legge, *The Sacred Books of China*, 1:479; HY 4/9/5). The two Chinese commentaries

even the most superficial Buddhist teaching, whose theory of karma presupposes a series of lifetimes in which the retribution for good and bad actions can be worked out. Furthermore, just as the two teachings are unaware that this life is but a single moment in an innumerable series of lives, so Taoism is ignorant of the fact that this cosmos is but a momentary pulse in a beginningless and endless series of cosmic cycles.

> Taoism merely knows of the single kalpa of emptiness when the present world had not yet been formed. It calls it nothingness, the one pneuma of the primordial chaos, and so forth, and designates it as the primeval beginning. It does not know that before [the kalpa of] empty space there had already passed thousands upon thousands and ten thousands upon ten thousands of [kalpas of] formation, continuation, destruction, and emptiness, which, on coming to an end, began again. Therefore we know that within the teaching of Buddhism even the most superficial teaching of the lesser vehicle already surpasses the most profound theories of the outer [i.e., non-Buddhist] canon.[30]

"The pure and impure causes and conditions of conforming to and going against [the flow of] origination and extinction" refers to the reciprocal processes of pure and impure conditioned origination that were discussed in detail in chapter 7. *Shun* and *ni* (Skt., *anuloma* and *pratiloma*), of course, refer to the processes of conforming to and going against the flow of birth-and-death. *Shun* designates the process by which beings become increasingly enmeshed in the continuous cycle of suffering that is saṃsāra, while *ni* designates the process by which beings reverse the momentum of their karma and move toward nirvāṇa. "Origination" (*ch'i*) refers to the process by which the suffering attendant upon birth, sickness, old age, and death comes into existence, while "extinction" (*mieh*) refers to the process by which it is eliminated. Pure causes and conditions lead to extinction, and impure causes and conditions lead to further involvement in the process of origination. The process of conforming to birth-and-death is a case of impure causes and conditions, whereas that of going against birth-and-death is a case of pure causes and conditions.[31]

As has been seen, the importance of the reciprocality of the processes of conforming to and going against the flow of birth-and-death lies in their soteriological implications. Understanding the cosmo-

---

cite passages from the *Ta-hsüeh, Mencius, Hsiao-ching,* and *Lao-tzu* in support of Tsung-mi's characterization of the two teachings.

[30] T 45.709b3–5.

[31] See Ching-yüan's comment on this passage (93a).

gonic process by which beings become enmeshed in saṃsāra provides a map for reversing the process and attaining liberation. Tsung-mi is here pointing to the ethical failure of the Confucian and Taoist cosmogonic theory to articulate such a map. Once again one sees that for Tsung-mi it is the coherence and profundity of such a map by which different teachings are to be judged.

Critique of the Mandate of Heaven and the Way

The moral thrust behind Tsung-mi's critique of Confucianism and Taoism can most clearly be seen in his raising, *mutatis mutandis*, the issue of theodicy. Whereas in a Christian context the question of theodicy asks how there can be evil in a world where God is at once omnibenevolent and omnipotent, the question in a Confucian context devolves around the existence of social inequity and injustice in a universe that functions in accord with the Confucian moral order. According to Confucian mythology tracing back to the *Shu ching* (Classic of history) and the *Shih ching* (Classic of poetry), heaven—whether conceived as a personal godlike agency or as an impersonal natural force—is that which monitors the sociopolitical world of human endeavor to ensure that it resonates with the larger rhythms of a universe functioning in natural harmony with Confucian moral principles.[32] Heaven is thus a providential moral force that intervenes in human history, as it did paradigmatically in the founding of the Chou dynasty. As it became translated into a theory of dynastic cycles, this myth held that whenever a ruler became tyrannical or otherwise morally unfit to exercise rule, heaven would display its disfavor by manifesting ominous portents and natural disasters. If the situation became critical enough, heaven would withdraw its mandate, disorder would increase, and the political order would fall into chaos. Out of the ensuing turmoil and strife, heaven would select the most worthy upon whom to confer a new mandate to rule, and peace and order would once again be restored.

Thus, according to this myth, heaven was seen as a cosmic moral force, or, as stated in the more straightforward words of the *Shu ching*: "The Way of heaven is to bless the good and punish the bad."[33] At the same time, other Confucian texts of equally hallowed provenance maintained that the individual's lot in life was determined by

[32] See Herrlee Creel, *The Origins of Statecraft in China*, chap. 5, "The Mandate of Heaven," 1:81–100.

[33] Legge, *Chinese Classics*, 3:186. Tsung-mi cites this passage in his notes to his critique of the decree of heaven; see TSC 415d1–2.

heaven. Tsung-mi cites the *Lun-yü* (Analects), which quotes Confucius as saying: "Death and life have their determined appointment, riches and honor depend upon heaven."[34] If this is so, Tsung-mi reasons, then heaven must also be responsible for the manifold examples of injustice so apparent in the world. How then, he asks, can it be moral? As he puts the case in his critique of the mandate of heaven in the *Inquiry into the Origin of Man*:

> Again, as for their claim that poverty and wealth, high and low station, sageliness and ignorance, good and evil, good and bad fortune, disaster and bounty all proceed from the mandate of heaven, then, in heaven's endowment of destiny, why are the impoverished many and the wealthy few, those of low station many and those of high station few, and so on to those suffering disaster many and those enjoying bounty few? If the apportionment of many and few lies in heaven, why is heaven not fair? How much more unjust is it in cases of those who lack moral conduct and yet are honored, those who maintain moral conduct and yet remain debased, those who lack virtue and yet enjoy wealth, those who are virtuous and yet suffer poverty, or the refractory enjoying good fortune, the righteous suffering misfortune, the humane dying young, the cruel living to an old age, and so on to the moral being brought down and the immoral being raised to eminence. Since all these proceed from heaven, heaven thus makes the immoral prosper while bringing the moral to grief. How can there be the reward of blessing the good and augmenting the humble, and the punishment of bringing disaster down upon the wicked and affliction upon the full? Furthermore, since disaster, disorder, rebellion, and mutiny all proceed from heaven's mandate, the teachings established by the sages are not right in holding man and not heaven responsible and in blaming people and not destiny. Nevertheless, the [*Classic of*] *Poetry* censures chaotic rule, the [*Classic of*] *History* extols the kingly Way, the [*Classic of*] *Rites* praises making superiors secure, and the [*Classic of*] *Music* proclaims changing [the people's] manners. How could that be upholding the intention of heaven above and conforming to the mind of creation?[35]

[34] Legge, *Chinese Classics*, 1:253. Tsung-mi cites this passage in the corresponding section of his TS 163b3–4.

[35] T 45.708b28–c9. In his notes to the corresponding passage in the TS (see TSC 415d), Tsung-mi also quotes the following passage from the *I ching*: "It is the way of heaven to diminish the full and augment the humble" (Sung, *Yi king*, p. 71). For Tsung-mi's reference to the morally transforming power of the rites and music, see *Hsiao ching* 4/12/1: "For changing [the people's] manners and altering their customs there is nothing better than music; for securing the repose of superiors and good order of the people there is nothing better than the rules of propriety" (Legge, *The Sacred Books of China*, 1:481–482).

He makes the same point in regard to the Way:

> Their claim that the myriad things are all engendered by the great Way of nothingness means that the great Way itself is the origin of life and death, sageliness and ignorance, the basis of fortune and misfortune, bounty and disaster. Since the origin and basis are permanently existent, disaster, disorder, misfortune, and ignorance cannot be decreased, and bounty, blessings, sageliness, and goodness cannot be increased. What use, then, are the teachings of Lao-tzu and Chuang-tzu? Furthermore, since the Way nurtures tigers and wolves, conceived Chieh and Chou, brought Yen Hui and Jan Ch'iu to a premature end, and brought disaster upon Po I and Shu Ch'i, why deem it worthy of respect?[36]

Tsung-mi concludes this passage on a rhetorical note with a series of historical references that would have been well-known to his readers. Chieh and Chou were the last rulers of the Hsia and Shang. They became archetypes of the wicked last ruler whose crimes against heaven and tyranny against the people caused the downfall of their dynasties.[37] Yen Hui and Jan Ch'iu were two of Confucius's disciples who died at an early age;[38] Yen Hui, in particular, was held up as a paragon of moral virtue. Po I and Shu Ch'i were upright and loyal followers of the Shang who, in protest over what they regarded as the unjust usurpation by King Wu, refused to eat the grain of the new Chou dynasty and withdrew to Mount Shou-yang, where they starved to death.[39]

Critique of Spontaneity

Tsung-mi's critique of spontaneity (*tzu-jan*) is based on a more complex series of arguments, which also have implications for his critique of the Way. Nevertheless, like his critique of the Way, the thrust of

---

[36] Ibid., 708b9–13. In the corresponding section of the TS (163a), Tsung-mi cites passages from the *Lao-tzu*, *Chuang-tzu*, and *Lieh-tzu* that, he claims, mean that there is nothing anywhere that is not the Way of nothingness.

[37] For Chieh see *Shih-chi* 2; for Chou see *Shih-chi* 3 and *Shu ching*, chap. 5, "The Books of Chou" (*Chinese Classics*, 3:284–285).

[38] Their biographies may be found in *Shih-chi* 67.

[39] See *Shih-chi* 61; cf. Watson, *Records of the Historian*, pp. 11–15. After relating the story of Po I and Shu Ch'i, Ssu-ma Ch'ien mentions the fate of Yen Hui, who, although virtuous in deed, suffered severe hardship throughout his short life. He then tells of Robber Chih, who, although he terrorized the world and ate the flesh of the innocent people he killed, lived to a ripe old age. These flagrant examples of injustice prompt Ssu-ma Ch'ien to ask the same question that Tsung-mi here raises: how can the way of heaven be just in the face of such obvious instances of injustice in the world?

his criticism of spontaneity focuses on its moral implications. His critique in the *Inquiry into the Origin of Man* is as follows:

> Again, their claim that the myriad things are all spontaneously engendered and transformed and that it is not a matter of causes and conditions means that everything should be engendered and transformed [even] where there are no causes and conditions. That is to say, stones might engender grass, grass might engender men, men engender beasts, and so forth. Further, since they might engender without regard to temporal sequence and arise without regard to due season, the immortal would not depend on an elixir, the great peace would not depend on the sage and the virtuous, and humanity and righteousness would not depend on learning and practice. For what use, then, did Lao-tzu, Chuang-tzu, the Duke of Chou, and Confucius establish their teachings as invariable norms? (T 45.708b9–13)

Tsung-mi interprets the cosmogonic significance of spontaneity as meaning that all things come into existence in a haphazard way in total disregard of any causal process.[40] Spontaneity is thus an acausal (*wu-yin*) cosmogonic principle. Tsung-mi develops this theme in the corresponding section of his *Commentary to the Perfect Enlightenment Sūtra*.[41] There he explains spontaneity by making reference to the *Chuang-tzu* passage that says: "The snow goose needs no daily bath to stay white; the crow needs no daily inking to stay black."[42] In his notes to this passage in his *Subcommentary*,[43] he elaborates his interpretation of spontaneity by piecing together a wide selection of passages from the *Chuang-tzu*.[44] He concludes that what these passages all add up to is that

[40] See TS 145a.

[41] TS 163b.

[42] 39/14/58–59; Watson, *Records of the Historian*, p. 163.

[43] TSC 416c–d.

[44] He writes: "Birth and death, rising and falling, all emerge from nothingness and are completed by nonaction. Therefore their emerging without a place from which they come forth is called indistinct and shadowy; their being engendered without a place from where they are born is called mysterious and obscure." He then quotes the following passage from the *Chuang-tzu*: "There is no trace of its coming, no limit to its going. Gateless, roomless, it is airy and open as the highways of the four directions. . . . Heaven cannot help but be high, earth cannot help but be broad, the sun and moon cannot help but revolve, the ten thousand things cannot help but flourish. Is this not the Way?" (58/22/31–33; Watson, *The Complete Works of Chuang Tzu*, p. 239)." "Therefore," Tsung-mi continues, quoting again from the *Chuang-tzu*, " 'it comes out from no source, it goes back in through no aperture' [63/23/54–55; Watson, p. 256]. It is born of itself without a source; it dies of itself without an aperture. That which is without a source or aperture is nothingness. Nothingness does not act and yet is born

what is spontaneously so (*tzu-jan*) does not depend on being made, and what is transformed of itself does not depend on causes and conditions (*yin-yüan*), but always emerges forth from nothingness (*hsü-wu*) and is engendered by nonaction (*wu-wei*). Being completed by nonaction, it does not labor with compass and square, and emerging forth from nothingness, it does not avail itself of curve and plumb line.[45]

Tsung-mi is here alluding to another passage from the *Chuang-tzu*:

If we must use curve and plumb line, compass and square to make something right, this means cutting away its inborn nature; if we must use cords and knots, glue and lacquer to make something firm, this means violating its natural virtue. . . . Where there is constant naturalness (*ch'ang tzu-jan*), things are arced not by the use of the curve, straight not by the use of the plumb line, rounded not by compass, squared not by T squares, joined not by glue and lacquer, bound not by ropes and lines.[46]

The soteriological implication of such passages is in Tsung-mi's opinion clear and damning:

If the principle of heaven is spontaneity and does not depend upon cultivation and study, then, if one were to cultivate and study it, it would be the action of man and not the action of heaven. It would be like using a plumb line to make something straight, using a curve to make an arc, using glue to join, or using ropes to bind—there would be no difference. . . . Since one violates heaven by using a plumb line, one should not use a plumb line. One who does not use a plumb line trusts in its being straight of itself in accord with the condition of heaven.[47]

---

of itself, does nothing and yet comes forth of itself. Therefore [the *Chuang-tzu*] says: '[Wonderfully, mysteriously, there is no place they come up out of . . .]. Each thing minds its business and all grow out up [out of inaction. So I say, heaven and earth do nothing and there is nothing that is not done]' [46/18/13–14; Watson, p. 191]. Since this is so, nonaction is the activity of heaven and nothingness is the gate of heaven."

"The gate of heaven" is an allusion to another passage from the *Chuang-tzu*: "In the coming out and going back its form is never seen. This is called the heavenly gate. The heavenly gate is nonbeing. The ten thousand things come forth from nonbeing" (63/23/56–57; Watson, pp. 256–257). Tsung-mi continues: "The heavenly gate is nonbeing and cannot be sought for in being; the heavenly activity is nonaction and cannot be looked for in action. Because it does not act, there is nothing that is not done; because it is without being, there is nothing that does not exist. Therefore 'it transports and weighs the ten thousand things without ever failing them' " (59/22/35; Watson, p. 239).

[45] TSC 416d2–4

[46] 21/8/13–16; Watson, *The Complete Works of Chuang Tzu*, pp. 100–101.

[47] TSC 416d7–12. For the phrase translated as "grass might engender man" both the Taishō text and that followed by Ching-yüan read: *ts'ao huo sheng jen*. I am here following the reading found in the Yüan-chüeh commentary and the corresponding pas-

According to such a rationale, the effortful cultivation of moral virtues such as humanity (*jen*) and righteousness (*i*) is fundamentally misguided. Tsung-mi concludes by saying that this is why the *Lao-tzu* contends that "in pursuit of the Way one does less every day"[48] and admonishes men to "exterminate the sage" and "discard the wise."[49] Tsung-mi never questions that moral and spiritual endeavor is meaningful and necessary. Since such a conclusion cannot be countenanced, the premises that lead to it must be rejected as false.

Against such an acausal theory, Tsung-mi argues that, if the existence of things did not depend on causes and conditions, anything could be produced anywhere and anytime. In his *Subcommentary*, he points out that everything's being engendered and transformed where there are no causes and conditions is a case of what he refers to as "the error of universally engendering" (*pien-sheng chih kuo*). He likens it to grain's growing without either a seed (its cause) or water, soil, and human cultivation (its conditions). He goes on to draw out the absurd consequences entailed by such a theory: everything from the physical environment throughout the entire universe to the thousands of varieties of animate and inanimate things within it should all be spontaneously engendered at once without any causes or conditions. He concludes that, since nothing can be engendered or transfomed without causes and conditions, the principle of spontaneity is thereby refuted.[50]

Tsung-mi continues, claiming that the example of stones engendering grass, which he employs to illustrate the implications of such a theory, goes against the principle that the causes and conditions of one thing do not also engender another thing and that the causal process does not act wantonly (*pu tsa luan*).[51] The example of things engendering one another without regard to temporal sequence is a case of what Tsung-mi refers to as "the error of constant engendering" (*ch'ang-sheng chih kuo*), which has consequences equally absurd as

---

sage in the TS, which both have *ying* in place of *huo*. In any case, either reading hardly affects the meaning of the passage.

[48] Chapter 48; cf. Lau, *Lao Tzu*, p. 109.

[49] Chapter 19; cf. Lau, *Lao Tzu*, p. 75.

[50] TSC 417a2–9. See T. R. V. Murti, *The Central Philosophy of Buddhism*, p. 172, n. 4, for an example of a stone producing a plant.

[51] See TSC 417c9–15. This passage throws light on the reasoning behind Tsung-mi's statement elsewhere (TS 145a and TSC 353a) that a single cause cannot engender various different effects. A specific set of causes and conditions is necessary for the engendering of each individual thing. Since this set of causes and conditions is specific to each individiual thing, it is thus impossible for one universal cause to engender the variegated and ever-changing phenomena of the manifold universe.

the error of universally engendering. It would mean, for instance, that grain, wheat, hemp, beans, and other crops might all come up at the same time on the first of the year and that there would be no need to wait until the third or fourth month for grain, the sixth of seventh month for beans, or the ninth or tenth month for wheat.[52]

Elsewhere Tsung-mi goes on to point out that spontaneity can also be interpreted as an underlying ontological principle—"a separately existing self so." If such an interpretation were adopted, spontaneity would then be a case of erroneous causality (*hsieh yin*), and the same argument that is used against an eternal and universal Way would apply. In charging that the Confucian and Taoist cosmogonic theories are examples of either acausality or erroneous causality,[53] Tsung-mi is following Ch'eng-kuan, who made the same charge in his *Hua-yen ching shu* and *Yen-i ch'ao*.[54] In either case—whether spontaneity be interpreted as a case of acausality or erroneous causality—there is no scope for moral and spiritual striving.[55]

[52] See TSC 417a15–d1.

[53] See TS 145a.

[54] See T 35.521b and T 36.104b.

[55] This latter argument ultimately derives from the *Ch'eng wei-shih lun*, as Tsung-mi clearly states in his *Subcommentary* (TSC 353a). The argument in the *Ch'eng wei-shih lun* is directed against the Jains, who believe that the manifold universe is created by a single god, Maheśvara, whose substance is real (*shih*), universal (*pien*), eternal (*ch'ang*), and capable of engendering all things (*neng-sheng*). This theory is in error because something that is capable of engendering other things cannot be eternal. Following K'uei-chi's commentary, Tsung-mi here points out that the four great elements of earth, water, fire, and wind, although they are not eternal, are capable of engendering everything (TSC 352d). He then quotes K'uei-chi's comment that things that are capable of engendering other things must themselves be engendered by other things (T 43.262b3–4). The *Ch'eng wei-shih lun* argument continues: what is not eternal cannot be universal, and what is not universal is not truly real. If Maheśvara's substance were eternal and universal, then he should have all the energies and capacities necessary to engender all things all at once in all places and times (T 31.3b7–11; cf. La Vallée Poussin, *Vijñaptimātratāsiddhi*, 1.30 and Wei Tat, *Ch'eng Wei-Shih Lun*, pp. 38–39). The argument is an old one as La Vallée Poussin notes.

Tsung-mi was not the first to see the applicability of this argument to Confucian and Taoist cosmogonic theories—it had already been pointed out by K'uei-chi in his commentary on the *Ch'eng wei-shih lun* (see T 43.262c9–11). In the *Inquiry into the Origin of Man* passage, however, Tsung-mi has shifted the context of the *Ch'eng wei-shih lun* argument from one directed against a theory of erroneous causality to one of acausality.

Although Tsung-mi's analysis of such mistaken causal theories derives from the *Ch'eng wei-shih lun* and K'uei-chi's commentary, the arguments on which it is based have a long history in Buddhist polemics. As these earlier examples demonstrate, Buddhists have traditionally criticized the causal theories of their opponents on moral grounds. For all of the ways in which his highly sinified interpretation of Buddhism

Critique of the Primal Pneuma

Tsung-mi's main objection to the primal pneuma (*yüan-ch'i*) is that it cannot account, on the one hand, for the predispositions inherited at birth, nor, on the other hand, for the existence of spirits of the dead (*kuei-shen*). In the corresponding sections of his *Commentary* and *Sub-commentary to the Scripture of Perfect Enlightenment*, Tsung-mi adduces a number of examples of the existence of spirits of the dead, drawing from a body of largely Confucian historical literature, to support his contention that death is not a mere cessation of existence. Again, the thrust of his critique is ethical. After all, without the mechanism of rebirth supplied by the teaching of karmic retribution, there would be no impelling reason for men to behave morally. Ample cases of wicked men prospering with impunity and good men suffering unjustly could be cited from both history and the contemporary world. If, upon death, their "spirits" simply dispersed into nothingness and there were no punishment or reward in a future state, then why should men behave morally, especially in cases where moral behavior demanded that they act contrary to their own immediate interests?

Tsung-mi's detailed critique of the primal pneuma in the *Inquiry into the Origin of Man* begins:

> Again, since their claim that [the myriad things] are engendered and formed from the primal pneuma means that a spirit, which is suddenly born out of nowhere (*hu*), has not yet learned and deliberated, then how, upon gaining [the body of] an infant, does it like, dislike, and act willfully? If they were to say that he suddenly comes into existence from out of nowhere and is thereupon able to like, dislike, and so forth in accordance with his thoughts (*sui i*), then it would mean that the five virtues and six arts can all be understood by according with one's thoughts. Why then, depending on causes and conditions, do we study to gain proficiency?[56]

In this passage Tsung-mi raises the same general objection that he had raised against spontaneity as an acausal principle. In the corresponding section of his *Commentary to the Scripture of Perfect Enlightenment*, he alludes to a series of passages from the *Chuang-tzu*, *Huai-nan-tzu*, and *I ching* that claim that life consists in a coming together of the

---

differs from that of India, Tsung-mi's emphasis on soteriology is part of a continuous concern that goes back as far as we can trace Buddhist teachings.

[56] T 45.708b13–17. In his TSC (417c13), Tsung-mi defines *hu* as "to come into existence suddenly *ex nihilo*."

vital force (*ch'i*), and that death consists in its dispersion.[57] He goes on to argue that feelings such as attraction and aversion do not suddenly arise out of nowhere but are the result of the reactivation of residual conditioning acquired in previous lives. Such residual conditioning lies latent within the ālayavijñāna as seeds lie in the ground awaiting the proper set of conditions to germinate. Only when the proper set of conditions occurs do feelings such as attraction and aversion become manifested.[58] The five constant virtues, of course, refer to humanity (*jen*), righteousness (*i*), propriety (*li*), wisdom (*chih*), and trustworthiness (*hsin*), and the six arts refer to the rites, music, archery, charioteering, composition, and arithmetic.

In the corresponding section of his *Commentary*,[59] Tsung-mi gives two further arguments that do not appear in the *Inquiry into the Origin of Man*. Both are directed against the view that one is born upon receiving his endowment of vital force (*ch'i*), and that one's nature is originally quiescent and only changes from its original state of quiescence when it is stimulated by external things (*kan wu*). Tsung-mi contends that the alarm and fear of a one-month old infant gives rise, in turn, to the greed, anger, and willfulness of the infant in his first, second, and third years without these emotions ever having been learned from another person. How then, he asks, can such emotions arise in response to external stimulation? His point is that such feelings develop out of an internal causal process within the ālayavijñāna. Whereas his first argument is based on a Yogācāra understanding of mind and mental processes, the second is based on a Chinese understanding of the meaning of the nature (*hsing*) of a thing as referring to its inherent potential or tendency. The second argument runs as follows: since it is the nature of falcons and dogs to seize their prey, it is possible to train them to hunt. If it were the case that they were

---

[57] See *Chuang-tzu* 58/22/11: "Man's life is a coming together of breath (*ch'i*). If it comes together, there is life; if it scatters, there is death" (Watson, *The Complete Works of Chuang Tzu*, p. 235); *Chuang-tzu* 46/18/18: "In the midst of the jumble of wonder and mystery a change took place and she had a spirit (*ch'i*). Another change and she had a body. Another change and she was born" (Watson, p. 192); *Chuang-tzu* 58/22/12–13: "The ten thousand things are really one. . . . You have only to comprehend the one breath (*i-ch'i*) that is the world. The sage never ceases to value oneness" (Watson, p. 236); *Huai-nan-tzu*: "The heavenly pneuma (*t'ien-ch'i*) constitutes the spiritual soul (*hun*) and the earthly pneuma (*ti-ch'i*) constitutes the bodily soul (*p'o*)" (9.1b); and *I ching*: "[The sage] traces things to their beginning and follows them to their end—thus he knows what can be said about death and life. (He perceives how the union of) essence and breath form things, and the (disapperance or) wandering away of the soul produces the change (of their constitution)—thus he knows the characteristics of the anima and animus" (Sung, *Yi King*, p. 278).

[58] TSC 417c.

[59] TS 163c.

originally without this nature and only learned to hunt and seize their prey by being taught to do so, then why cannot doves and sheep be trained to hunt and seize prey?

Tsung-mi continues his critique in the *Inquiry*:

Furthermore, if birth were a sudden coming into existence upon receiving the endowment of the vital force and death were a sudden going out of existence upon the dispersion of the vital force, then who would become a spirit of the dead (*kuei-shen*)? Moreover, since there are those in the world who see their previous births as clearly as if they were looking in a mirror and who recollect the events of past lives, then we know that there is a continuity from before birth and that it is not a matter of suddenly coming into existence upon receiving the endowment of the vital force. Further, since it has been verified that the consciousness (*chih*) of the spirit (*ling*) is not cut off, then we know that after death it is not a matter of suddenly going out of existence upon the dispersion of the vital force. This is why the classics contain passages about sacrificing to the dead and beseeching them in prayer, to say nothing of cases, in both present and ancient times, of those who have died and come back to life and told of matters in the dark paths or those who, after death, have influenced their wives and children or have redressed a wrong and requited a kindness.[60]

The corresponding sections of Tsung-mi's *Commentary* and *Subcommentary to the Scripture of Perfect Enlightenment* contain a wealth of fascinating material culled from a variety of historical sources (the *Chin shu* being prominent among them) as "proof" for the existence of the spirits of the dead and their effect on the living.[61] We need only cite

[60] T 45.708b20–23.

[61] As examples of people who have recollected their past lives, Tsung-mi recounts the cases Yang Hu, T'an-ti, and Pao Ching, which can be found in *Chin shu* 34.1023–1024, KSC, T 50.370c24–371a16, and *Chin shu* 95.2482 (see TSC 418b). As examples of cases proving that the consciousness of the spirit is not cut off after death, Tsung-mi recounts those of Chiang Chi, Su Shao, and the favorite concubine (see TSC 418b–d). The story of Chiang Chi can be found in *San-kuo chih* 14.454–455. (The account that Tsung-mi gives in the TSC is a somewhat abridged version of one that appears in a biographical collection of marvelous tales, the *Lieh-i chüan*, which is quoted by Pei Sung-chih in his commentary on Chiang Chi's biography in the *San-kuo chih*.) Although Tsung-mi claims that the story of Su Shao comes from the *Chin shu*, I have not been able to locate it in that source; a different version of this story can be found in the *Meng-ch'iu* 1.41a, a popular collection of supernatural tales, which were grouped together by category with rhyming four-character headings, compiled during the T'ang by Li Han. The story of the favorite concubine occurs in the *Tso-chüan*, the fifteenth year of Duke Hsüan (see Legge, *Chinese Classics*, 5:328b). Tsung-mi recounts the details of Liu Ts'ung's son's journey to the realm of the dead, derived from the biography of Liu Ts'ung in *Chin shu* 102.2673–2677, in TSC 419a–b. His reference to sacrifices to

one example here to indicate the flavor of such evidence. This is the case of Tou Ying, who distinguished himself as the general in charge of suppressing the revolt of Wu and Ch'u in 154 B.C.[62] His character, however, was inflexible, and he was apt to offend others by his self-righteous behavior. Tou Ying's tragic demise grew out of his rivalry with T'ien Fen, who was a generation younger than Tou Ying and was related to the imperial house by marriage. With the death of Emperor Ching, T'ien Fen's influence began to rival, and then eclipse, that of Tou Ying. As his political fortunes waxed, T'ien Fen's behavior is depicted as becoming increasingly arrogant and ostentatious. While out of favor in retirement at his villa, Tou Ying befriended Kuan Fu, a general who had earlier distinguished himself by his daring feats of bravery during the suppression of the Wu-ch'u revolt. Kuan Fu is described as stubborn and outspoken, especially when in his cups. Through a series of increasingly acrimonious encounters, the rivalry between Tou Ying and T'ien Fen finally reached its crescendo at a banquet celebrating the marrige of T'ien Fen in 131, when Kuan Fu brazenly insulted one of T'ien Fen's guests and was arrested for his outburst of disrespect. Tou Ying tried to intercede with the emperor in behalf of Kuan Fu, but the empress favored T'ien Fen, who succeeded in having charges trumped up that implicated Tou Ying in the affair and led to his execution following that of Kuan Fu. Shortly thereafter, T'ien Fen fell ill and spent his time crying out that he was at fault and begging for forgiveness. When the emperor summoned a shaman who could see ghosts, he reported that he saw Tou Ying and Kuan Fu watching over the bed, preparing to kill T'ien Fen. T'ien Fen died soon thereafter.

A few pages later, Tsung-mi's subcommentary refutes the objections against the existence of the spirits of the dead raised by Wang Ch'ung's first-century treatise, Lun heng, famous for the skeptical attitude it takes toward many traditional beliefs. There he cites two passages in which Wang Ch'ung offers a psychological explanation for

---

the dead is based on the Li chi; see chapters 23, 24, and 25 of the Li-chi (chapters 20, "The Law of Sacrifices"; 21, "The Meaning of Sacrifices"; and 22, "A Summary Account of Sacrifices," in Legge's translation). His allusion to beseeching them in prayer is drawn from the Shu ching; see "The Metal-Bound Coffer" chapter of the Shu ching (Chinese Classics, 3:351ff.). Tsung-mi gives seven different examples of people who either redressed a wrong or requited a kindness after they died (see TSC 419b–420d), the most noteworthy of which is the case of Tou Ying.

[62] Tou Ying's biography can be found in Han shu 52 and Shih chi 107, the latter of which has been translated by Burton Watson in Records of the Grand Historian of China, 2:109–129. The particular episode concerning Tou Ying's ghost occurs at Han shu 52.10a and Shih chi 107.10a–b (see Watson, pp. 127–128).

the belief in the existence of ghosts. In the first passage,[63] Wang Ch'ung refers to Tou Ying, contending that T'ien Fen's mind had become so deranged by animosity that he hallucinated, and did not actually see, the ghosts of Tou Ying and Kuan Fu. In the second passage,[64] Wang Ch'ung gives a generic explanation for such phenomena, arguing that ghosts are products of a deranged imagination: when people become seriously ill, they become anxious and afraid, and their anxiety and fear work on their imagination to produce hallucinations. In response, Tsung-mi asks how, if the apparition of Tou Ying and Kuan Fu were merely a hallucination, could the shaman also have seen their ghosts? Was his mind similarly deranged by fever? If the shaman's mind were also deranged, Tsung-mi continues, then he surely would not have seen the same apparition as the ailing T'ien Fen.[65]

Tsung-mi's critique in the *Inquiry* also implicitly takes aim at Wang Ch'ung.

> An outsider [i.e., a non-Buddhist] may object, saying: If men become ghosts when they die, then the ghosts from ancient times would crowd the roads and there should be those who see them—why is it not so? I reply: When men die, there are six paths; they do not all necessarily become ghosts. When ghosts die, they become men or other forms of life again. How could it be that the ghosts accumulated from ancient times exist forever? Moreover, the vital force of heaven and earth is originally without consciousness. If men receive vital force that is without consciousness, how are they then able suddenly to wake up and be conscious? Grasses and trees also all receive vital force, why are they not conscious?[66]

In his *Subcommentary*,[67] Tsung-mi quotes the original passage from the *Lun-heng*:

> If everyone who dies becomes a ghost, there should be a ghost at every pace of the road. If men see ghosts when they are about to die, they should see millions and millions filling the hall and crowding the road instead of only one or two.[68]

To this objection, Tsung-mi gives the Buddhist answer that not everyone who dies becomes a ghost. There are six possible paths of re-

---

[63] 21.10a; see Alfred Forke, trans., *Lun-Heng*, 1:217–218.

[64] 22.10a; see Forke, *Lun-Heng*, 1:239.

[65] See TSC 420d18–421a10.

[66] T 45.708b23–28.

[67] TSC 421a.

[68] 20.10b; Chan, *Source Book*, p. 301.

birth: one may be reborn as a god (*deva*), human (*manuṣya*), animal (*tiryagyoni*), titan (*asura*), hungry ghost (*preta*), or denizen of hell (*naraka*). Moreover, even those who are reborn as ghosts do not remain ghosts forever. When the particular karma that has caused them to be reborn as ghosts is exhausted, they reenter the cycle to be reborn in another form.

Underlying the different arguments he employs, the thrust of Tsung-mi's critique of the two teachings focuses on their ethical implications. What is especially significant about Tsung-mi's critique of Confucianism and Taoism is that it is carried out within the framework of the moral vision of Confucianism. This moral vision itself is not challenged; it is only the ability of Confucianism and Taoism to provide a coherent ontological basis for that vision that is disputed. It is in this context that the teaching of men and gods takes on importance as its teaching of karmic retribution provides a way in which the Confucian moral vision can be preserved, for it is precisely the teaching of karmic retribution that is needed to explain the apparent cases of injustice in the world. If the good suffer hardship and die young, it is because they are reaping the consequences of evil committed in a former life. If the wicked prosper with impunity, it is because they are enjoying the rewards of good deeds done in a former life.

THE TEACHING OF MEN AND GODS

In terms of the overall structure of the *Inquiry into the Origin of Man*, the teaching of men and gods serves as the crucial link relating the teachings of Confucianism and Taoism to those of Buddhism. On the one hand, it serves a polemical purpose by subordinating the two teachings to even the most elementary and superficial teaching of Buddhism. On the other hand, it serves a broader and more synthetic purpose. The teaching of karmic retribution, by resolving the dilemma of theodicy,[69] preserves the Confucian belief in a moral universe. It also opens the way for Confucian moral practices to be in-

[69] The ability of karma theory to resolve the problem of theodicy has frequently been noted. Max Weber, for one, has argued that the Buddhist teaching of karma represents "the most complete formal solution of the problem of theodicy." See his "Theodicy, Salvation, and Rebirth," p. 145. Peter Berger, who uses Weber's discussion as the starting point for his own treatment of theodicy in *The Sacred Canopy*, regards "the *karma-samsara* complex" as "the most rational" theodicy (p. 65), claiming that "Buddhism probably represents the most radical rationalization of the theoretical foundations of the *karma-samsara* complex" (p. 67). See also Gananath Obeyesekere, "Theodicy, Sin and Salvation in a Sociology of Buddhism," and Arthur Herman, *The Problem of Evil and Indian Thought*.

corporated into Buddhism by assimilating the five constant virtues of Confucianism into the five precepts of Buddhism. Even though Confucianism cannot provide a convincing metaphysical rationale for the moral functioning of the universe, the moral practices that it advocates—no different, in essence, from those advocated in Buddhism—are still meritorious and can lead to a good future birth in the human realm.

The teaching of men and gods consists in the simple moral teaching of karmic retribution. It is so called because it teaches men how they can gain a propitious birth as a man or a god by maintaining the five precepts prescribed for laymen and by practicing the ten good deeds.[70] The teaching of men and gods generally corresponds to the teaching for laymen as propounded in such early Indian Buddhist scriptures as the *Discourse on the Lesser Analysis of Deeds* (*Cūlakamma-vibhaṅgasutta*) and *Discourse on the Greater Analysis of Deeds* (*Mahākamma-vibhaṅgasutta*).[71] While the teaching of karma was basic to all forms of Buddhism, it seems to have formed the central focus of the teaching directed to laymen, especially as it dealt with the causal link between various actions or types of action and specific forms of rebirth. While lay practice centered around the maintenance of the five precepts, it was always justified in terms of the good consequences to be experienced in the future, either later in one's present lifetime or in a subsequent rebirth.[72] One finds the Buddha in numerous other early

---

[70] The ten good deeds are not to commit the ten evil deeds (*daśakuśala*), namely, killing, stealing, adultery, lying, slander, harsh speech, frivolous chatter, covetousness, malice, and false views.

[71] *Majjhima-nikāya* 3.202–206 and 207–215, translated by I. B. Horner, *The Middle Length Sayings*, 3:248–253 and 254–262; cf. *Ying-wu ching* and *Fen-pieh ta-yeh ching*, nos. 170 and 171 of the *Chung a-han*, T 1.703c23–706b10 and 706b14–708c28. In the first of these scriptures, for example, a young brahmin asks the Buddha why human beings live in such a variety of circumstances, some being short lived while others are long lived, some suffering many illnesses while others enjoy good health, some being impoverished while others are wealthy, some being born into families of low station while others are born into families of high station, and so on. The Buddha answers that the discrepancies seen in human life are all due to karma. The Buddha then elaborates, saying that those who kill other living creatures, if they are reborn as humans in their next life, will be short lived, and those who abstain from killing other living creatures, if they are reborn as humans in their next life, will be long lived. Similarly, in their next life, those who mistreat living creatures will suffer many illnesses, those who are kind to living creatures will enjoy good health, those who are stingy will be impoverished, those who are generous will be wealthy, those who are arrogant will be born into families of low station, and those who are humble will be born into families of high station.

[72] In his *Indian Buddhism* (p. 187), Warder notes that the standard course of instruction for lay disciples comprised discourses on giving (*dāna*), morality (*śīla*), and heaven (*svarga*); the disadvantage, vanity, and depravity of sense pleasures; and the advantage

scriptures exhorting laymen to practice almsgiving (*dāna*) with the promise that their generosity will lead to a desirable rebirth in a heavenly realm.

Although the teaching of men and gods thus seems to correspond to the teaching for laymen in the Indian Buddhist tradition, it was not referred to as a particular category of teaching by this name in Indian Buddhism. Rather, the term "the teaching of men and gods" seems to have been coined by Chinese Buddhists during the second half of the fifth century in an effort to accommodate Buddhism to the needs of its growing number of lay adherents by adapting it to the more socially oriented concerns of Confucianism. The first mention of the teaching of men and gods occurs in the doctrinal classification scheme of Liu Ch'iu (438–495), a lay Buddhist recluse in the South. As seen in chapter 3, he divided the Buddha's teachings into two general types, the sudden and gradual. Liu went on to divide the gradual teachings into five, the first of which was that of men and gods, as taught in the *T'i-wei Po-li ching* (The sūtra of Trapuśa and Bhallika).

The *T'i-wei Po-li ching*,[73] the scripture on which the teaching of men and gods is based, was composed in northern China around 460 by T'an-ching.[74] It fit in well with the widespread ideological use of Bud-

---

of renunciation (see, for instance, *Dīgha-nikāya* 1.110, trans. by T. W. Rhys-Davids, *Dialogues of the Buddha*, 1:134–135, and *Majjhima-nikāya* 1.379, trans. by I. B. Horner, *The Middle Length Sayings*, 2:45).

[73] Tsukamoto Zenryū has gathered together the various fragments of the *T'i-wei Po-li ching* that are quoted in other sources and has published them in his *Shina bukkyōshi kenkyū, Hokugi hen*, pp. 293–353; reprinted in *Tsukamoto Zenryō chosaku shū*, 2:189–240. The second fascicle of this text (Stein no. 2051) was among the works found at Tun-huang and has been published by Makita Tairyō in his "Tonkōbon *Daiikyō* no kenkyū," pp. 137–185. See also Whalen Lai, "The Earliest Folk Buddhist Religion in China." While there is nothing, in terms of content, comparable to the *T'i-wei Po-li ching* in Indian Buddhist literature, the *Aṅguttara-nikāya* does contain a *Tapussasutta* (see Hare, *The Book of Gradual Sayings*, 4:293–295), whose resemblance to the *T'i-wei Po-li ching*, however, does not go beyond its title. The earliest account of Trapuśa and Bhallika occurs in the vinaya section of the tripiṭaka, where they offer the Buddha his first meal after his enlightenment, take refuge in the Buddha and dharma (the sangha still not having been formed), and become the Buddha's first lay disciples (see Horner, *The Book of Discipline*, 1:5–6; cf. *Ssu-fen lü*, T 22.103a; *Jui-ying pen-ch'i ching*, T 3.479a; *Pen-hsing chi ching*, T 3.801a; and *P'u-yao ching*, T 3.526b.

[74] At the end of the biography of T'an-yao, the famous superintendent of monks who set the course for the revival of Buddhism after the Northern Wei persecution of 446, Tao-hsüan adds a brief note on T'an-ching, which links the composition of the *T'i-wei Po-li ching* with the restoration of Buddhism (see HKSC 428a10–12). He writes that since the former translations had been burned up during the persecution, some basis for guiding the people was urgently needed, and that T'an-ching thus composed the *T'i-wei Po-li ching* to make up for this deficiency.

dhism on the part of the Northern Wei state in its efforts both to control a people of mixed ethnic stock, for whom Confucian moral teachings had not yet been deeply ingrained, and to mobilize the general population for the restoration of Buddhism on a massive scale. This text is purported to have been taught on the seventh day after the Buddha's enlightenment to a group of five hundred merchants led by Trapuśa (T'i-wei) and Bhallika (Po-li). It exhorts them to take the triple refuge in the Buddha, dharma, and sangha, to maintain the five precepts, and to practice the ten good deeds so as to ensure a good future birth as a man or a god. The five precepts are given special emphasis and are even accorded cosmological significance. They are said to be "the root of heaven and earth and the source of all spiritual beings. When heaven observes them, yin and yang are harmonized; when earth observes them, the myriad creatures are engendered. They are the mother of the myriad creatures and the father of the myriad spirits, the origin of the great Way and the fundamental basis of nirvāṇa."[75]

The five precepts are homologized with other sets of five in Chinese cosmology—such as the five phases, five planets, five emperors, five sacred peaks, five internal organs, five colors, and five virtues[76]—and the failure to maintain them consequently has cosmic reverberations throughout the various spheres with which they correspond. Most significantly for Chinese lay Buddhist practice, the Buddha matches the five Buddhist precepts for laymen with the five constant virtues of Confucianism. Thus, the Buddhist precept not to take life is paired with the Confucian virtue of humanity (*jen*); not to take what is not given, with righteousness (*i*); not to engage in illicit sexual activity, with propriety (*li*); not to drink intoxicating beverages, with wisdom (*chih*); and not to lie, with trustworthiness (*hsin*).[77]

Whereas the *T'i-wei Po-li ching* couches Buddhist moral injunctions within the framework of Chinese cosmological thought, Tsung-mi's version of the teaching of men and gods in the *Inquiry into the Origin of Man* rationalizes the teaching of karmic retribution with Buddhist cosmology as systematically developed in the abhidharma literature. In Tsung-mi's account, all of the practices whose karmic fruits still involve beings in the various realms of birth are encompassed within the purview of the teaching of men and gods. Thus, while the teach-

---

[75] Fragment 6, quoted in *Tsukamoto chosaku shū*, 2:203.

[76] See fragment 8, in ibid., p. 204.

[77] See fragment 9, ibid., p. 204. The way in which the five precepts are paired with the five constant virtues differs in different fragments of the text quoted by Tsukamoto. For a discussion of these, see Ch'en, *The Chinese Transformation of Buddhism*, pp. 57–59.

ing of men and gods generally refers to the lay teaching within Buddhism, the more advanced stages of meditation included within Tsung-mi's version of this teaching go beyond the usual sphere of lay Buddhist practice.

Tsung-mi gives a condensed account of this teaching in his *Ch'an Preface*:

> The teaching of the causes and effects of men and gods, teaching the karmic retribution of good and bad, enables [beings] to know that there is no discrepancy between cause and effect, to dread the suffering of the three [evil] destinies, to seek the joy of [being reborn as] men and gods, to cultivate all good practices—such as giving, maintaining the precepts, and practicing meditation—and thereby gain birth in the realm of men and gods and even the realm of form and the realm of formlessness.[78]

In the *Inquiry into the Origin of Man*, Tsung-mi gives a more detailed explanation of the workings of karmic retribution, connecting various types of moral and spiritual action with birth in specific realms described in Buddhist cosmology. Accordingly, the commission of the ten evils leads to birth in the three evil destinies. The commission of the ten evils in their highest degree leads to birth in hell; in their lesser degree, to birth as a hungry ghost; and in their lowest degree, to birth as a beast. The maintenance of the five precepts, on the other hand, enables men to avoid birth in the three evil destinies and to gain birth as a man, and the practice of the ten good deeds leads to birth as a god in one of the six heavens of desire. All of the destinies enumerated so far fall within the realm of desire (*kāmadhātu; yü-chieh*), the first and lowest of the three realms of birth. Birth into the next two realms is only possible through the practice of meditation. While the early Indian Buddhist scriptures do contain examples of laymen who succeeded in being born into these higher realms through the practice of meditation,[79] such cases are the exception rather than the rule. In general, the moral practices usually taught to laymen would only lead to birth in the higher spheres of the realm

[78] T 48.403a18–21; K 103; cf. B 157–158.

[79] In the *Dhānañjānisutta* of the *Majjhima-nikāya* (trans. Horner, *The Middle Length Sayings*, 2:372–379), the brahmin Dhānañjāni succeeds in gaining birth in the heaven of Brahma as a result of having practiced the meditation of suffusing the universe with friendliness, compassion, sympathic joy, and equanimity. In the *Anāthapiṇḍikovādasutta* (trans. Horner, 3:309–315), the pious layman and dānapati Anāthapiṇḍika succeeds in being born in the Tuṣita heaven as a result of having heard Sāriputta discourse on the course of mental discipline usually taught to monks. As a final example, Ānanda, following instructions of the Buddha, explains the four stages of meditation to a group of laymen in the *Sekhasutta* (trans. Horner, 2:18–25), concluding his sermon with the assertion that even householders can achieve nirvāṇa.

of desire. Birth into the next realm, the realm of form (*rūpadhātu*; *se-chieh*), is attained through the mastery of the four stages of meditation, and birth into the highest realm, the realm of formlessness (*arūpadhātu*; *wu-se-chieh*), is attained through the mastery of the four formless attainments. Tsung-mi's scheme of karmic retribution can be diagrammed as follows:

Action (*karma*)	Destiny (*gati*)		Realm (*dhātu*)
Four formless attainments	God	Four formless heavens	Realm of form-lessness (*arūpadhātu*)
Four stages of meditation	God	Four meditation heavens	Realm of form (*rūpadhātu*)
Ten good deeds	God	Six heavens of desire	
Five precepts	Human		Realm of desire (*kāmadhātu*)
Ten evils {	Beast Hungry ghost } Hell	Three evil destinies	

A point that is especially noteworthy in Tsung-mi's account of the teaching of men and gods in the *Inquiry* is his claim that the Buddha matched the five Buddhist precepts with the five Confucian constant virtues in order to encourage beginners to maintain the five precepts and so succeed in gaining birth as a human. In his own note to this passage, Tsung-mi pairs the five precepts with the five constant virtues in the same manner in which they had been paired with one another in the *T'i-wei Po-li ching* passage referred to before:

> Not killing is humanity, not stealing is righteousness, not committing adultery is propriety, not lying is trustworthiness, and, by neither drinking wine nor eating meat, the spirit is purified and one increases in wisdom.[80]

As a final comment on the teaching of men and gods in the *Ch'an Preface*, Tsung-mi adds a critical note on this teaching that points to the way in which it is superseded by the next level of Buddhist teaching, that of the lesser vehicle. He says that the teaching of men and gods only explains "worldly causes and effects" and not "the causes and effects of transcending the world."

[80] T 45.708b19–20.

It merely causes [beings] to have an aversion for the lower [realms] and to take delight in the higher [realms], not yet teaching that the three realms are all afflictions which should be renounced. It also has not yet destroyed [the belief in] the self.[81]

TSUNG-MI'S SYNTHESIS OF CONFUCIANISM AND TAOISM

In addition to matching the five Buddhist precepts with the five Confucian virtues, there are other places in the *Inquiry into the Origin of Man* where Tsung-mi goes out of his way to point out the correspondences between Buddhism, on the one hand, and Confucianism and Taoism, on the other. For instance, as part of his discussion of the teaching of the lesser vehicle, Tsung-mi draws from the systematic account of the *Abhidharmakośabhāṣya* to summarize the well-known cosmogony found with minor variations in numerous Buddhist sources. He begins by commenting on his statement that just as in the case of individual bodily existence there are the four stages of birth, old age, sickness, and death, and that after death one is born again, so in the case of worlds there are also four stages in each cosmic cycle: formation (*ch'eng*; *vivartakalpa*), continuation (*chu*; *vivartasthāyikalpa*), destruction (*huai*; *saṃvartakalpa*), and emptiness (*k'ung*; *saṃvartasthāyikalpa*). In his autocommentary, Tsung-mi details how, after the end of one cosmic cycle when the universe has been totally destroyed, the receptacle world (*ch'i-shih-chien*; *bhājanaloka*) is created again at the end of the kalpa of emptiness. The receptacle world is composed of three concentric circles. The first is the circle of wind, which contains the second circle, that of water. The third circle, that of gold, arises out of the circle of water. The process begins when "a great wind arises in empty space" and forms the circle of wind. Next "a golden treasury cloud spreads throughout the great chiliocosm" and pours down "raindrops [as large as] cart hubs," thus forming the circle of water, which is held in check by the wind that circles around it and keeps it from flowing out. After the circle of gold is formed,[82]

the golden treasury cloud then pours down rain and fills it up, first forming the Brahma [heavens, and then going on to form all the other heavens] down to the Yāma [heaven]. The wind stirs up the pure water, forming Mount Sumeru, the seven gold mountains, and so on. When the

---

[81] T 48.403b7; K 104; cf. B 161.

[82] Following Ching-yüan 's gloss (100a); Tsung-mi has "diamond world" (*chin-kang-chieh*). See *Abhidharmakośabhāṣya*, T 29.57b2–c18, and La Vallée Poussin, *L'Abhidharma-kośa de Vasubandhu*, 2:141–145.

sediment forms the mountains, earth, four continents, and hell, and a salty sea flows around their circumference, then it is called the establishment of the receptacle world.[83]

Tsung-mi goes on to describe the creation of human beings:

Finally, when the merit of [beings in] the second meditation [heaven] is exhausted, they descend to be born as humans. They first eat earth cakes and forest creepers; later the coarse rice is undigested and excreted as waste, and the figures of male and female become differentiated. They divide the fields, set up a ruler, search for ministers, and make distinctions as to the various classes.[84]

The meaning of the details in this account need not be pursued here.[85] What is important are the correspondences that Tsung-mi establishes:

[83] T 45.709a20–22.

[84] T 45.709a22–23. Tsung-mi's account condenses that found in the *Abhidharma-kośabhāṣya*. At the end of the kalpa of destruction all beings, except those whose root of merit is destroyed, are reborn in the *ābhāsvara* heaven, the second meditation (*dhyāna*) heaven, where they reside throughout the duration of the kalpa of emptiness. Those beings whose root of merit is destroyed are reborn in the hells of other universes. When the merit of the beings in the *ābhāsvara* heaven is exhausted, they descend to be reborn as men. They still have all the characteristics of the radiant gods of the *ābhāsvara* heaven: they are made of mind, feed on joy, radiate light, traverse the air, and continue in glory. Gradually, the earth appears as a kind of foam on the surface of the primeval waters. It is a savory earth (*ti-wei*; *pṛthivīrasa*), which tastes as sweet as honey. One being of greedy disposition smells its fragrance and eats of it; other beings follow suit. With the eating of the savory earth, their bodies become grosser and heavy, and their radiance disappears. Thus are born the sun, moon, and stars. As the savory earth disappears with beings' attachment to it, earth cakes (*ti-ping*; *pṛthivīparpaṭaka*) appear. As beings become attached to their taste, they too begin to disappear, and forest creepers (*lin-t'eng*; *vanalatā*) appear in their stead. These also disappear with beings' attachment to them, and rice spontaneously begins to grow. Being a still grosser form of food, when beings eat this rice, some of it remains undigested and their bodies produce wastes. It is at this juncture in the process of materialization that beings first become differentiated sexually. One being of a lazy nature begins to store up rice for future consumption, and others, fearing that there will not be enough to go around, follow his example. With this, the rice begins to disappear and cultivation becomes necessary. The people then divide the land up into fields, but since some steal rice from others' fields, they elect a ruler to protect the fields. Thus, the process of social differentiation begins. See T 29.65b18–19c and La Vallée Poussin, *L'Abhidharmakośa de Vasubandhu*, 2:204–206; see also La Vallée Poussin, "Cosmogeny and Cosmology," p. 190. The oldest form of this legend is found in the *Aggaññasutta*, trans. Rhys Davids as "A Book of Genesis," in *Dialogues of the Buddha*, 3:77–94. This version is repeated in the *Mahāvastu* (Jones, *The Mahāvastu*, 1:285–293). A parallel account in the Chinese Āgamas can be found in T 1.37b28ff. A somewhat different version appears in the *Visuddhimagga* 13 (Ñāṇamoli, *The Path of Purification*, pp. 458–459).

[85] See Stanley Tambiah's *World Conqueror*, pp. 11–16, for an interesting analysis.

[The period of time] during the kalpa of empty space is what the Taoists designate as the Way of nothingness. However, since the essence of the Way is tranquilly illuminating and marvelously pervasive, it is not nothingness. Lao-tzu either was deluded about this or postulated it provisionally to encourage [people] to cut off their human desires. Therefore he designated empty space as the Way. The great wind [that arises] in empty space corresponds to their one pneuma of the primordial chaos; therefore they say that the Way engenders the one. The golden treasury cloud, being the beginning of the pneuma's taking form, is the great ultimate. The rain coming down and not flowing out refers to the congealing of the yin pneuma. As soon as yin and yang blend together, they are able to engender and bring [all things] to completion. From the Brahma Kings' realm down to Mount Sumeru corresponds to their heaven, and the sediment corresponds to the earth, and that is the one engendering the two. The merits [of those in] the second meditation [heaven] being exhausted and their descending to be born refers to man, and that is the two engendering the three, and the three powers (san-ts'ai) thus being complete. From the earth cakes to the various classes is the three engendering the myriad things. This corresponds to [the time] before the three kings when men lived in caves, ate in the wilderness, did not yet have the transforming power of fire, and so on.[86]

The care with which Tsung-mi spells out the correspondences between this Buddhist cosmogony and Taoist theory is precisely the kind of effort so stridently criticized by Ch'eng-kuan and Hui-yüan. Not only are specific items in the Buddhist account made to correspond to specific items in Taoist cosmogony, but what is even more interesting is the fundamental assumption that underlies Tsung-mi's approach: that both must be describing the same process. He seems never to have seriously entertained the possibility that both might reflect fundamentally irreconcilable conceptions. Tsung-mi does not dismiss the Taoist account as false. It is only a less perfect version of what is recorded in Buddhist texts. It must therefore be taken seriously, and Tsung-mi takes pains to account for the discrepancies between the two versions.

It is only because there were no written records at the time that the legendary accounts of people of later times were not clear; they became

---

[86] T 45.709a23–27. Tsung-mi's reference to the time when men lived in caves is drawn from Li chi 7.3a–b: "Formerly the ancient kings had no houses. In winter they lived in caves which they had excavated, and in summer in nests which they had framed. They knew not yet the transforming power of fire, but ate the fruits of plants and trees, and the flesh of birds and beasts, drinking their blood, and swallowing (also) the hair and feathers" (Legge, 1:369).

increasingly confused, and different traditions wrote up diverse theories of sundry kinds. Moreover, because Buddhism penetrates and illuminates the great chiliocosm and is not confined to China, the writings of the inner and outer teachings are not entirely uniform.[87]

The best example of Tsung-mi's synthetic approach is to be seen in the concluding section of his *Inquiry into the Origin of Man*, which he entitles "Reconciling Root and Branch" (*hui-t'ung pen-mo*).[88] In this section, Tsung-mi integrates Confucianism and Taoism, together with the five Buddhist teachings that he evaluated within his p'an-chiao, into his final cosmogonic vision. As he states: "When [the teachings that] have been refuted previously are subsumed together into the one source, they all become true." Since this section masterfully synthesizes many of the themes discussed within the last several chapters of this book, it will be translated in full below.

In the previous sections of the *Inquiry into the Origin of Man*, Tsung-mi demonstrated the partial nature of the provisional teachings (i.e., those of Confucianism, Taoism, and the first four Buddhist teachings) by showing that they all fail to discern the ultimate origin of man, which is only accomplished by the fifth and final teaching, that which reveals the nature. The arrangement of teachings in the previous sections thus describes a process of the return to the ontological ground of phenomenal existence—what Tsung-mi refers to as the "root" (*pen*). Tsung-mi's arrangement of the teachings thus also describes the path of soteriological progress and answers the first side of the question posed by his inquiry by revealing the ontological ground of enlightenment, which is the ultimate origin of man. The concluding section of the essay turns to the other side of the question posed by his inquiry, attempting to show how the process of phenomenal evolution, whose end product is the sentient condition marked by suffering and delusion, emerges from the intrinsically pure and enlightened nature. The concluding section thus describes a process that moves from the ontological ground or root to its phenomenal manifestation or branch (*mo*) and is at once a cosmogony and an etiology of delusion.

Although the true nature constitutes the [ultimate] source of bodily existence, its arising must surely have a causal origin, for the phenomenal appearance of bodily existence cannot be suddenly formed from out of nowhere. It is only because the previous traditions had not yet fully dis-

[87] T 45.709a27–b1.
[88] See T 45.710b4–c25.

cerned [the matter] that I have refuted them one by one. Now I will reconcile root and branch, including even Confucianism and Taoism.

Tsung-mi begins with the true nature, which is the ultimate source from which phenomenal evolution proceeds. He points out in his autocommentary (represented below in small type) how the successive stages in this process can be correlated with the different teachings, each of which accounts for different phases. In my own comments, I will point out how these different stages correspond to Tsung-mi's mature ten-stage cosmogony discussed in chapter 7.

At first there is only the one true numinous nature, which is neither born nor destroyed, neither increases nor decreases, and neither changes nor alters. [Nevertheless,] sentient beings are [from time] without beginning asleep in delusion and are not themselves aware of it. Because it is covered over, it is called the tathāgatagarbha, and the phenomenal appearance of the mind that is subject to birth-and-death comes into existence based on the tathāgatagarbha.

The next phase corresponds to unenlightenment. As noted in chapter 8, Tsung-mi's claim that this stage is accounted for by the fourth teaching, that of emptiness, is forced.

The interfusion of the true mind that is not subject to birth-and-death and deluded thoughts that are subject to birth-and-death in such a way that they are neither one nor different is referred to as the ālayavijñāna. This consciousness has the aspects of both enlightenment and unenlightenment.

The next phase corresponds to the third through sixth stages in Tsung-mi's ten-stage scheme (i.e., arising of thoughts, arising of perceiving subject, manifestation of perceived objects, and attachment to dharmas). It is accounted for by the teaching of the phenomenal appearances of the dharmas (fa-hsiang chiao). Given the general antipathy toward Fa-hsiang within the Hua-yen tradition, Tsung-mi's ready incorporation of its teachings here is noteworthy.

When thoughts first begin to stir because of the unenlightened aspect [of the ālayavijñāna], it is referred to as the phenomenal appearance of activity. Because [sentient beings] are also unaware that these thoughts are from the beginning nonexistent, [the ālayavijñāna] evolves into the manifestation of the phenomenal appearance of a perceiving subject and its perceived objects. Moreover, being unaware that these objects are deludedly manifested from their own mind, [sentient beings] cling to them as fixed existents, and that is referred to as attachment to things.

The following phase is accounted for by the teaching of the lesser vehicle, which enables beings to overcome their attachment to self and defilements (i.e., stages seven and eight).

> Because they cling to these, [sentient beings] then perceive a difference between self and others and immediately form an attachment to the self. Because they cling to the phenomenal appearance of a self, they hanker after things that accord with their feelings, hoping thereby to enhance themselves, and have an aversion to things that go against their feelings, fearing that they will bring harm to themselves. Their foolish feelings thus continue to escalate ever further.

The next phase corresponds to the last two stages (i.e., generating karma and experiencing the consequences) and is accounted for by the teaching of men and gods. Note that it is at the point in the process of rebirth when consciousness first enters a womb that Tsung-mi introduces the Confucian and Taoist notion of vital force (*ch'i*). He thus clearly accepts this concept as contributing an integral part to the overall understanding of phenomenal evolution. The two teachings are not wrong; they only err in taking their explanation to be the ultimate answer.

> Therefore, when one commits [evil deeds] such as murder or theft, his spirit (*hsin-shen*), impelled by this bad karma, is born among the denizens of hell, hungry ghosts, or beasts. Again, when one who dreads suffering or is virtuous by nature practices [good deeds] such as bestowing alms or maintaining the precepts, his spirit, impelled by this good karma, is transported through the intermediate existence (*chung-yu; antarābhava*) into the mother's womb (from here on corresponds to that which was taught in the two teachings of Confucianism and Taoism) and receives an endowment of vital force and material substance. ([This] incorporates their statement that the vital force constitutes the origin.) The moment there is vital force, the four elements are fully present and gradually form the sense organs; the moment there is mind, the four [mental] aggregates are fully present and form consciousness. When ten [lunar] months have come to fruition and one is born, he is called a human being. This refers to our present body-and-mind. Therefore, we know that the body and mind each has its origin and that as soon as the two interfuse, they form a single human. It is virtually the same as this in the case of gods, titans, and so forth.

Tsung-mi goes on to show how karma determines the particular circumstances within which one is reborn. "Directive karma" (*yin-yeh*) is that which draws (*yin*) beings toward the destiny (*gati*) in which they are to be reborn; that is, it determines their mode of existence as a god, human, beast, and so forth. "Particularizing karma" (*man-yeh*) is that which fills out (*man*) the specific details of their existence.[89] Tsung-mi's explanation shows how karma operates as a moral principle to account for the injustices and inequalities experienced in life. Note that Tsung-mi uses his explanation of karma to reject spontaneity (*tzu-jan*). Moral action can only have meaning and be effective within the causal framework established by the Buddhist theory of karma.

> While one receives this bodily existence as a result of his directive karma, one is in addition honored or demeaned, impoverished or wealthy, long or short lived, ill or healthy, flourishes or declines, suffers or is happy, because of his particularizing karma. That is to say, when the respect or contempt shown [to others] in a previous existence serves as the cause, it determines the result of one's being honored or demeaned in the present, and so on and so forth to the humane being long lived, the murderous short lived, the generous wealthy, and the miserly impoverished. The various types of individual retribution [are so diverse that they] could not be fully enumerated. Therefore, in this bodily existence, while there may be cases of those who are without evil and even so suffer disaster, or those who are without virtue and even so enjoy bounty, or who are cruel and yet are long lived, or who do not kill and yet are short lived, all have been determined by the particularizing karma of a previous lifetime. Therefore, the way things are in present lifetime does not come about from what is done spontaneously. Scholars of the outer teachings do not know of previous existences, but relying on [only] what is visible, just adhere to their belief in spontaneity. ([This] incorporates their statement that spontaneity constitutes the origin.) Moreover, there are those who in a previous life cultivated virtue when young and perpetuated evil when old, or else were evil in their youth and virtuous in their old age; and who hence in their present lifetime enjoy moderate wealth and honor when young and suffer great impoverishment and debasement when old, or else experience the suffering of impoverishment in youth and enjoy wealth and honor in old age. Thus, scholars of the outer teachings just adhere to their belief that success and failure are due to the sway of fortune. ([This] incorporates their statement that everything is due to the mandate of heaven.)

The following passage, more than anywhere else in the *Inquiry into the Origin of Man*, is remarkable for showing the extent to which Tsung-mi applies his synthetic approach. Not only does he assimilate

---

[89] See *Abhidharmakośabhāṣya*, T 29.92b10–11, which compares directive karma to the broad brushstrokes by which a painter delineates the outline of a figure and particularizing karma to his use of various colors to flesh out the image (cf. La Vallée Poussin, *L'Abhidharmakośa de Vasubandhu*, 3:200). For a discussion of these two types of karma, see Mochizuki, *Bukkyō daijiten*, 1:178b–c and 5:4754a–b.

Confucian and Taoist terminology into a Buddhist frame of reference, he also incorporates the Fa-hsiang scheme of the division of the
ālayavijñāna into subjective and objective modes into the process of
phenomenal evolution derived from the *Awakening of Faith*. The evolution of the mind and objects refers to the subjective and objective
transformation of the ālayavijñāna as set forth in the *Ch'eng wei-shih
lun*. The primal pneuma is thus nothing but the objective transformation of the ālayavijñāna internally into the body of the senses
(*ken-shen*; *sendriyakakāya*), and heaven and earth are its objective transformation externally into the receptacle world. The various correspondences Tsung-mi establishes prove for him that the concepts put
forward by the two teachings as an explanation for the ultimate
ground of existence, when thoroughly examined, turn out to refer to
epiphenomena in the process of phenomenal evolution. They are
thus clearly subordinated to his own Buddhist vision; but, more significantly, they are also shown to make their own essential, albeit limited, contribution to that vision.

> Nevertheless, the vital force with which we are endowed, when it is
> traced all the way back to its origin, is the primal pneuma of the undif-
> ferentiated oneness; and the mind which arises, when it is thoroughly
> investigated all the way back to its source, is the numinous mind of the
> absolute. Speaking in ultimate terms, there is nothing outside of mind.
> The primal pneuma also comes from the transformation of mind, be-
> longs to the category of the objects that were manifested by the previ-
> ously evolved consciousness, and is included within the objective aspect
> of the ālaya[vijñāna]. From the phenomenal appearance of the activation
> of the very first thought, [the ālayavijñāna] divides into the dichotomy of
> mind and objects. The mind, having developed from the subtle to the
> coarse, continues to evolve from false speculation to the generation of
> karma (as previously set forth). Objects likewise develop from the fine to
> the crude, continuing to evolve from the transformation [of the ālaya-
> vijñāna] into heaven and earth. (The beginning for them starts with the grand
> interchangeability and evolves in five phases to the great ultimate. The great ul-
> timate [then] produces the two elementary forms. Even though they speak of
> spontaneity and the great Way as we here speak of the true nature, they are ac-
> tually nothing but the subjective aspect of the transformation [of the ālayavijñāna]
> in a single moment of thought; even though they talk of the primal pneuma as
> we here speak of the initial movement of a single moment of thought, it is actually
> nothing but the phenomenal appearance of the objective world.) When karma
> has ripened, then one receives his endowment of the two vital forces
> from his father and mother, and, when it has interfused with activated
> consciousness, the human body is completely formed. According to this,
> the objects that are transformed from consciousness immediately form

two divisions: one division is that which interfuses with consciousness to form man, while the other division does not interfuse with consciousness and is that which forms heaven and earth, mountains and rivers, and states and towns. The fact that only man among the three powers [of heaven, earth, and man] is spiritual (*ling*) is due to his being fused with spirit. This is precisely what the Buddha meant when he said that the internal four elements and the external four elements are not the same.

Tsung-mi concludes with the following exhortation:

How pitiable the confusion of the false attachments of shallow scholars! Followers of the Way heed my words: If you want to attain Buddhahood, you must thoroughly discern the coarse and the subtle, the root and the branch. Only then will you be able to cast aside the branch, return to the root, and turn your light back upon the mind source. When the coarse has been exhausted and the subtle done away with, the numinous nature is clearly manifest and there is nothing that is not penetrated. That is called the dharmakāya and sambhogakāya. Freely manifesting oneself in response to beings without any bounds is called the nirmāṇakāya Buddha.

TSUNG-MI'S INTELLECTUAL PERSONALITY

Tsung-mi's attempt to elaborate a synthetic framework in which Confucian moral teachings could be integrated within Buddhism, his effort to clarify the underlying ontological basis for moral and religious action, and the ethical thrust of his criticism of the Hung-chou line of Ch'an all reveal his preoccupation with moral order. One could use Levensonian terms to say that Tsung-mi's writings demonstrate his life-long effort to justify the values that he had learned as a youth in terms of the discrepant claims of the intellectual tradition to which he had converted as an adult. Here it is important to note that his actual conversion to Buddhism occurred at the age of twenty-four. Even though Tsung-mi interrupted his concentration on Confucian classics to read Buddhist texts for a few years in his late adolescence, he did not take up the practice of Buddhism until after his conversion in 804. That is, Tsung-mi began Buddhist practice at a time after which one can suppose that his basic values would have already been formed—and the core of those values were heavily influenced by the moral vision found in the Confucian classics. What is significant in Tsung-mi's case is that his conversion to Buddhism did not entail a rejection of his early Confucian training. Rather, it seems to have been impelled, at least in part, by concerns growing out of his early study of Confucian texts.

Tsung-mi's effort to integrate Confucian moral values with Buddhist teachings reveals what I would see to be the most fundamental characteristic of his thought—his consistent attempt to articulate a framework in which discordant systems of value can be integrated. This tendency can be seen in every important aspect of his thought. It is revealed, most obviously, in his system of doctrinal classification. It can also be found in his effort to harmonize Ch'an practice and scholastic thought or in his attempt to define a coherent vision of the path in which the conflicting claims on the nature of enlightenment and the role of practice put forth by different Ch'an traditions can be reconciled. This characteristic also suggests how Tsung-mi's thought is different from that typical of either Ch'an or Hua-yen.

To clarify this last point, I would like to conclude this chapter by proposing a threefold typology. One can think of different systems of thought, just as one can think of different personality types, as involving strategies for reconciling the tension between the discordant claims of different systems of value. One way to deal with this problem is to adopt an exclusivistic approach that holds that there is only one true teaching. Conflicting traditions can thus be either rejected or ignored. This kind of approach is often seen in Ch'an, with its special claim to represent an exclusive and privileged transmission. Ch'an's championing of itself as the sudden teaching, for instance, meant that it had direct access to the ultimate and thereby rendered the gradualistic approaches of the other traditions irrelevant.

A second approach would be to compartmentalize the conflicting values and claims of different traditions. This kind of approach is more characteristic of the scholastic solution of p'an-chiao, in which the tension between different doctrines is managed by assigning each to its proper category. Even though this approach reconciles conflicting doctrinal traditions within a larger framework, it does not truly integrate them with one another. Rather, it succeeds to the extent that it can keep them separate. This compartmentalizing approach tends to be the one most characteristically employed by Tsung-mi's Hua-yen predecessors Fa-tsang, Hui-yüan, and Ch'eng-kuan. Fa-tsang's classification system, as seen in chapter 4, was explicitly devised to assert the peerless supremacy of the *Hua-yen Sūtra*.

The third approach is one in which conflicting traditions are genuinely integrated with one another, in which they actually inform one another, and in which they are interpreted in terms of one another. This last approach, of course, is most characteristic of Tsung-mi and sets him off from both his Ch'an and Hua-yen forebears.

Chapter Eleven

TSUNG-MI AND NEO-CONFUCIANISM

ANALYSIS of Tsung-mi's thought has shown that its different aspects are all integrally interwoven in such a way that it is impossible to elucidate any one of them in isolation from the others. Tsung-mi's soteriological concern with articulating the nature and structure of the path of liberation, for instance, is inseparable from his ethics, which has to do with clarifying the kind of moral and religious actions that are meaningful and effective within the context of such a path. Both, in turn, are related to Tsung-mi's cosmogonic theory, which articulates the structure of the path at the same time that it grounds ethical action on a solid ontological foundation. His cosmogony, moreover, provides a comprehensive soteriological framework in which the various teachings can all be harmoniously integrated and thus well serves his synthetic approach to the various teachings, Buddhist and non-Buddhist alike.

As has been seen, the revisions that Tsung-mi makes in Hua-yen theory (such as his deletion of the perfect teaching as a separate category in his p'an-chiao, his displacement of the *Hua-yen Sūtra* in favor of the *Awakening of Faith*, his emphasis on nature origination over conditioned origination, or his preference for *li-shih wu-ai* over *shih-shih wu-ai*) can all be understood as part of his effort to provide an ontological basis for Buddhist practice. His revalorization of Hua-yen thought, in turn, points back to his involvement with, and reaction to, various developments that had taken place within Ch'an. The iconoclastic rhetoric of the radical movements that had gained currency within Chinese Ch'an during the latter part of the T'ang could easily be misinterpreted in antinomian ways that denied the need for spiritual cultivation and moral discipline. Having grown up and received his early Ch'an training in Szechwan, an area in which the most extreme of these movements flourished in the late eighth and early ninth centuries, Tsung-mi was particularly sensitive to such ethical dangers. As I have argued, he was drawn to Hua-yen because it provided him with a solid ontological rationale for Ch'an practice, and he accordingly adapted its theory as a buttress against the antinomian implications of these radical interpretations of Ch'an teaching. His critique of Hung-chou Ch'an, in particular, is important for establishing the ethical thrust behind his adaptation of Hua-yen metaphysics. The ethical tenor animating Tsung-mi's systematic classification of the teachings, moreover, reveals the importance of the Confucian moral vision that he had internalized in his youthful study of the classics. The centrality of such ethical concern helps to locate Tsung-mi's significance within the broader field of Chinese intellectual history.

Tsung-mi's preoccupation with articulating the ontological basis of religious and ethical action reflects a persisting preoccupation in Chinese thought that can be traced back to Mencius. As A. C. Graham has shown,[1] Mencius's theory, which locates the sources of morality within human nature, arose as a response to the "proto-Taoist" claim that human nature lacked any inherent moral direction. Such concern with the fundamental basis of human nature and the sources of moral behavior exerted a lasting influence on the ways in which the Chinese appropriated Buddhism. The doctrine of the tathāgata-garbha, which occupies the nodal point in Tsung-mi's system, is a prime example. While this doctrine played a minor role in the development of Indian Buddhism, Chinese Buddhists were quick to see its resonance with their own concerns and, in texts such as the *Awakening of Faith*, adapted it as the framework in which they developed their own uniquely "sinitic" systems of Mahāyāna Buddhist thought and practice. The new direction that Tsung-mi gave to Hua-yen thought thus helps to clarify one of the dominant themes in the process of the sinification of Buddhism. And it was this sinified version of Buddhism that served as the doctrinal matrix for East Asian Buddhism as a whole.

At the same time, Buddhist theories about an intrinsically enlightened Buddha-nature, with which all men were endowed, provided a more sophisticated conceptual framework in which earlier Chinese speculations on human nature were given greater philosophical latitude. In this way the kind of theory articulated in Tsung-mi's adaptation of the *Awakening of Faith* refined the set of issues in terms of which Neo-Confucian thinkers formulated their response. Not only does the specifically ethical thrust of Tsung-mi's critique of Hung-chou Ch'an parallel Chu Hsi's (1130–1200) subsequent Neo-Confucian critique of Buddhism, but the very form that Tsung-mi's defense takes anticipates in fascinating ways Chu Hsi's theory of human nature. Tsung-mi's thought thus stands at a critical juncture in Chinese intellectual history. It both brings into focus a central theme in the sinification of Buddhism and reveals how the sinified forms of Bud-

---

[1] See his "The Background of the Mencian Theory of Human Nature."

dhism transformed the indigenous tradition. This chapter will develop this broad theme by focusing on Chu Hsi's critique of the Buddhist understanding of human nature.[2]

CHU HSI'S CRITIQUE OF THE BUDDHIST UNDERSTANDING OF NATURE

In its attempt to reestablish the true way of the ancient sages, the Confucian revival that culminated with Chu Hsi in the Southern Sung (1127–1279) can be seen in part as a reaction against the pervasive impact that Buddhism had had on Chinese culture. The philosophical context in which the revival occurred was thus itself conditioned by the very phenomenon against which it was reacting. Buddhism called into question and made relative the traditional norms enshrined in the Confucian classics, making it incumbent upon Neo-Confucian thinkers to articulate a coherent metaphysic that would provide an ontological basis for reaffirming the traditional moral values that had been challenged by Buddhism. Chu Hsi's response to this challenge can be seen most readily in his theory of human nature (*hsing*), for it is here that ontology and ethics converge in his thought: human nature is the locus of moral principle as it is instantiated in human beings. Ethical norms are thus not the arbitrary product of human culture but an integral part of the cosmic order. It is also in regard to human nature that Chu Hsi profers his most philosophically serious critique of Buddhism. Although Chu Hsi advances his theory as a superior Confucian alternative to Buddhism, his explanation of human nature builds on Buddhist paradigms and so offers one perspective in terms of which one can discern the way in which Buddhism helped to frame Neo-Confucian philosophical discourse.

One of the most significant criticisms that Chu Hsi levels against

---

[2] The best single source for Chu Hsi's critique of Buddhism is fascicle 126 of the *Chu-tzu yü-lei*, which appears in slightly abbreviated form in fascicle 60 of *Chu-tzu ch'üan-shu*. Some of the more important passages are translated by Wing-tsit Chan in his *A Source Book of Chinese Philosophy*. Galen Eugene Sargent has translated fascicle 60 of *Chu-tzu ch'üan-shu* in his "Tchou Hi contre le Bouddhisme." For discussions of Chu Hsi's critique of Buddhism, see also Charles Wei-hsun Fu, "Morality or Beyond"; Fu, "Chu Hsi on Buddhism," pp. 377–407; and Edward T. Ch'ien, "The Neo-Confucian Confrontation with Buddhism." I have also consulted the following studies in Japanese: Araki Kengo, *Bukkyō to jukyō*; Kubota Ryōon, *Shina ju dō butsu kōshō-shi*; Kubota, *Shina ju dō butsu sankyō shiron*; and Tokiwa Daijō, *Shina ni okeru bukkyō to jukyō dōkyō*. Other useful sources that touch on the Neo-Confucian critique of Buddhism are Wing-tsit Chan, trans., *Reflections on Things Near at Hand*; Graham, *Two Chinese Philosophers*; and Ira E. Kasoff, *The Thought of Chang Tsai*.

Buddhism lies in his claim that what the Buddhists call the nature (*hsing*) is really only what the Confucians mean by mind (*hsin*)—a criticism he traces back to Hsieh Shang-ts'ai (Liang-tso) (1050–1103), one of the leading disciples of the Ch'eng brothers. In response to Hsü Tzu-jung's theory that there is a sense in which dry and withered things can be said both to have and not to have the nature, Chu Hsi remarked:

> The nature is just principle (*li*). . . . Where Tzu-jung is wrong is to have recognized the mind as the nature. This is just like the Buddhists, except that the Buddhists polish the mind to the highest degree of refinement. It is as if it were a lump of something. They peel off one layer of skin and then peel off another until they have reached the point where there is nothing left to peel away. In this way they attain the mind's purity and radiance, which they then recognize as the nature. They do not at all realize that this is just what the sages called the mind. Therefore [Hsieh] Shang-ts'ai said: "What the Buddhists call the nature is just what the sages call the mind, and what the Buddhists call the mind is just what the sages call the intentions."[3]

This is a crucial point for Chu Hsi to make. By stripping the mind bare in order to arrive at its purity and radiance, Chu Hsi describes what he takes to be the Ch'an experience of "seeing the nature" (*chien-hsing*). The Ch'an claim to point directly to the mind of man, thereby causing him to see his true nature and suddenly realize Buddhahood, went against the grain of the moral task of self-cultivation as Chu Hsi conceived it, making nugatory the life-long process of "investigating things" and "extending knowledge." By maintaining that the Buddhists mistake the mind for nature, Chu Hsi discredits what the Buddhists claim to achieve in *chien-hsing* as nothing but seeing into their own minds. Chu Hsi's criticism, of course, is based on his own understanding of the mind; that his charge wholly misrepresents the Buddhist understanding of mind is not the issue here.

[3] *Yü-lei* 126.11b; I have adapted Chan's translation from his *Source Book*, p. 649; cf. *Ch'üan-shu* 60.15b–16a, and Sargent, "Tchou Hi contre le Bouddhisme," pp. 91–98. In his *Recorded Conversations*, Hsieh said: "The Buddhists' discussion of the nature is like the Confucians' discussion of the mind, and the Buddhists' discussion of the mind is like the Confucians' discussion of the intentions (*i*)" (*Shang-ts'ai yü-lu* 2.7a). A virtually identical statement occurs on the next page: "What the Buddhists call the nature is like what we Confucians call the mind, and what the Buddhists call the mind is like what we Confucians call the intentions" (ibid., 2.7b).

Note that whereas I have earlier translated *li* as "the absolute" or, less frequently, "truth," in this section I follow the standard convention among scholars of Neo-Confucianism and render it as "principle"; see Wing-tsit Chan, "The Evolution of the Neo-Confucian Concept of *Li* as Principle."

Chu Hsi continues:

The mind is just [that which] embraces principle. . . . The Buddhists have never understood this part about principle and recognize consciousness (*chih-chüeh*) and movement (*yün-tung*) as the nature. For example, in regard to seeing, hearing, speaking, and acting, when the sage sees, there is the principle of seeing; when he hears, there is the principle of hearing; when he speaks, there is the principle of speaking; when he acts, there is the principle of acting; and when he thinks, there is the principle of thinking. It is like what the Viscount of Chi [in the "Hung fan" chapter of the *Shu ching*] called clearness [in seeing], distinctness [in hearing], reasonableness [in speaking], respectfulness [in acting], and perspicacity [in thinking]. The Buddhists merely recognize what enables us to see, what enables us to hear, what enables us to speak, what enables us to think, and what enables us to move and regard that as the nature. Whether seeing is clear or not, whether hearing is distinct or not, whether speaking is reasonable or not, or whether thinking is perspicacious or not—they do not care in the least. No matter whether it goes this way or that way, they always recognize it as the nature. . . . This, indeed, is Kao Tzu's theory that "the life force (*sheng*) is what is meant by the nature."[4]

Chu Hsi's allusion to Kao Tzu is telling. In the *Mencius*, Kao Tzu is said to maintain that the nature is morally neutral, a position connected with his identification of the nature with the natural appetites for food and sex.[5] Mencius, of course, argues that such appetites are what humans have in common with animals. What makes nature distinctly human nature for Mencius are our incipient moral propensities, the so-called four sprouts (*ssu tuan*)—i.e., the heart/mind (*hsin*) of compassion (*ts'e-yin*), shame (*hsiu-wu*), courtesy and modesty (*kung-ching*), and right and wrong (*shih-fei*)—which, if properly nourished, will ripen into the four cardinal virtues of humanity (*jen*), righteousness (*i*), propriety (*li*), and wisdom (*chih*). Mencius's theory of human nature thus locates the sources of morality within the heart/mind (*hsin*).

Within Chu Hsi's own philosophical anthropology, the mind belongs to the realm of "material force" (*ch'i*),[6] which is "below form" (*hsing-erh-hsia*), and is accordingly qualitatively different from the

[4] *Yü-lei* 126.11b; *Ch'üan-shu* 60.16a–b.

[5] 6A1–4.

[6] Note that whereas I have previously rendered *ch'i* as "pneuma" or "vital force," I here follow what seems to be the standard translation used by scholars of Neo-Confucianism. Benjamin Schwartz has suggested that, in the context of Chu Hsi's thought, this term might best be understood as meaning "psycho-physical stuff."

realm of principle (*li*), which belongs to the realm of moral value and truth "above form" (*hsing-erh-shang*). The nature is associated with heavenly principle (*t'ien-li*), which is impartial (*kung*) and never evil, whereas *ch'i* is associated with human desire, which is self-centered (*wo*) and sometimes evil.[7] It is because the nature is embedded in *ch'i* that it can become warped when it moves in response to things and feelings (*ch'ing*), and hence the potentiality for good and evil arises with the feelings. Chu Hsi defines the nature as the mind's principles, the feelings as the movement of the nature, and the mind as the master of the nature and feelings.[8] As that which governs both the nature and feelings, the mind is charged with the moral task of overcoming the self-centeredness of human desire so that man may act in accord with his heaven-endowed nature with the impartiality of heavenly principle. Since the mind is the locus of moral responsibility in man, it has a double valence and can accordingly be characterized as either the human mind (*jen-hsin*) or the moral mind (*tao-hsin*).

Chu Hsi's use of the two terms *jen-hsin* and *tao-hsin* derives from the *Shu ching*: "The human mind is precarious (*wei*), and the moral mind is subtle (*wei*). Be discriminating (*ching*), be one (*i*), that you may sincerely hold fast the mean."[9] In his preface to the *Chung yung*, he cites these words, saying that while the mind is one,

> it can be considered as having the distinction of the human mind and the moral mind because sometimes it is generated by the self-centeredness of material form (*hsing-ch'i*) and sometimes it springs from the righteousness (*cheng*) of the heaven-conferred nature (*hsing-ming*), and this is why consciousness is not the same. Therefore it is sometimes precarious and insecure and sometimes subtle and difficult to discern. However, since there is no one who does not have form, no matter how wise he may be, he cannot but have a human mind; likewise, since there is no one who does not have the nature, no matter how foolish he may be, he cannot but have the moral mind. These two are mixed together in the heart, and if one does not know how to regulate them, then what is precarious will be even more precarious and what is subtle will be even more subtle, and the impartiality of heavenly principle will consequently not be able to overcome the self-centeredness of human desire. "Discrimi-

[7] *Wen chi* 44.1b; see Araki, *Jukyō to bukkyō*, p. 288.

[8] *Yü-lei* 5.7b; see Araki, *Jukyō to bukkyō*, p. 294.

[9] Legge translates this passage as: "The mind of man is restless—prone (to err); its affinity for the (right) way is small. Be discriminating, be undivided, that you may sincerely hold fast to the Mean" (*Chinese Classics*, 3:61–62). Chu Hsi, however, clearly understands *jen-hsin* and *tao-hsin* as two contrasting terms. For a discussion of this passage see Benjamin Elman, "Philosophy (*i-li*) versus Philology (*k'ao-cheng*)," pp. 192–211. See also Donald Munro, *Images of Human Nature*, p. 159.

nating" means examining the difference between the two and not mixing them together. "One" means maintaining the righteousness of the original nature and not becoming separate from it. If one accords with affairs in this regard without interruption, then he will surely cause the moral mind to be the master of the self and the human mind always to heed its command. Then what is precarious will be secure and what is subtle will be manifest.[10]

Chu Hsi, of course, claims that the Buddhists only acknowledge the human mind without knowing about the moral mind.

The Buddhists abandon the moral mind but hold on to the precarious human mind. . . . While they regard humanity, righteousness, propriety, and wisdom as not being the nature, they regard the psycho-physical functions before their eyes as the nature. This just indicates that they are mistaken in regard to the ultimate source.[11]

The mind, according to Chu Hsi's philosophical anthropology, is thus morally indeterminate: it can follow moral principles or be led astray by human desires. It therefore cannot provide a stable foundation for morality. Such a foundation can only be found in the nature, the locus of moral principle in man. In claiming that what the Buddhists take to be nature is only what the Confucians take to be mind, Chu Hsi is charging that the Buddhist notion of nature lacks any inner moral standard.[12] Chu Hsi makes the same point in a different way with his oft-repeated remark that, for the Buddhists, the nature is "empty" (k'ung), whereas for the Confucians it is "full" (shih), and precisely what the nature is either empty or full of are the concrete moral principles of humanity, righteousness, propriety, and wisdom.[13]

Hence, for Chu Hsi the nature cannot be described as function (yung). Rather, he characterizes the nature as the essence (t'i) and the feelings as its functioning (yung). He brings out these points in his commentary to Mencius 6A3, where he writes that " 'the life force (sheng)' indicates the means by which humans and creatures have consciousness and movement," commenting that Kao Tzu's theory is similar to the Buddhists' taking the psycho-physical functions (tso-yung) to be the nature. At the end of this section Chu Hsi further comments:

[10] Wen-chi 65.21b.

[11] Yü-lei 126.13a; cf. Fu, "Chu Hsi on Buddhism," p. 388.

[12] See Yü-lei 126.8b: "For us Confucians, while the mind is vacuous (hsü), principle is full (shih)."

[13] See, for example, Yü-lei 126.8b: "The nature consists of full principles; humanity, righteousness, propriety, and wisdom are all fully possessed." Cf. Ch'üan-shu 42.6b.

The nature is that which man obtains from the principle of heaven. The life force is that which man obtains from the *ch'i* of heaven. The nature is what is above form, and the *ch'i* is what is below form. As for the life force in humans and creatures, there are none who do not have the nature, and also there are none who do not have *ch'i*. However, if we speak about it in terms of *ch'i*, then consciousness and movement do not seem to be different in humans and creatures. If we speak of it in terms of principle, then how can humanity, righteousness, propriety, and wisdom be that which is obtained and perfected by creatures?[14]

This passage brings us to Chu Hsi's next criticism: that the Buddhists take the nature to be the psycho-physical functions (*tso-yung*). When asked about this, Chu Hsi admits that the psycho-physical functions are in some sense what is meant by the nature, quoting *Mencius* 7A38: "The bodily organs with their functions belong to our heaven conferred nature. But a man must be a sage before he can satisfy the design of his bodily organization."[15] Chu Hsi explains the implications of this passage as follows:

This, then, is the nature. For example, the mouth can talk, but who is it who talks? The eyes are able to see, but who is it who sees? The ears are able to hear, but who is it who hears? This, then, is that [i.e., the nature]. They [the Buddhists] say: "In regard to the eyes, it is called seeing; in regard to the ears, hearing; in regard to the nose, smelling; in regard to the mouth, speaking; in regard to the hands, grasping; and in regard to the feet, walking. When it is manifested universally, it encompasses the dharmadhātu [*sic*]; when it is concentrated together, it exists within a single mote of dust. Those who understand know that it is the Buddha-nature; those who do not understand call it the spirit."[16]

Chu Hsi then comments that the Buddhists' error lies in what they nourish.

That which we Confucians nourish is humanity, righteousness, propriety, and wisdom, whereas that which they nourish is merely seeing, hearing, speaking, and moving. For us Confucians, there are within the entirety [of our nature] many moral principles, each different from the

---

[14] *Meng-tzu chi-chu* 6.1b–2a.

[15] Legge, *Chinese Classics*, 2:396.

[16] Chu is here quoting from the *Ching-te ch'uan-teng lu*, T 51.218b. The text of both the *Yü-lei* (13b5) and *Ch'üan-shu* (17b2) mistakeningly give *fa-chieh* (dharmadhātu) for *sha-chieh*, an expression meaning "worlds as numerous as the sands of the Ganges." See below. Despite Fu's laudable attempt to redress the excesses of Chu Hsi's misunderstandings of Buddhism, he goes too far when he says that no "Sinitic Mahāyānist" ever held the view that "the natural functioning of the mind is itself the nature" (p. 391).

others and having a right and wrong [application]. . . . They [the Buddhists] just see something wholly undifferentiated, without distinctions and right and wrong [applications]. Whether it is this way or that way, straight or crooked, makes no difference. Whether one perceives [things] contrary to principle or in accordance with principle, they still take that to be the nature. Due to this slight discrepancy, there is a great difference in application [between Confucians and Buddhists]. They are totally confused and [their understanding of nature] is unsupportable. . . . They just speak of one side [of the matter]. They merely recognize the human mind but do not speak of the moral mind.[17]

The quotation by which Chu Hsi substantiates his claim that the Buddhists equate the nature with the psycho-physical functions derives from the *Ching-te ch'uan-teng lu*, a Ch'an "transmission of the lamp" text compiled by Tao-yüan in 1004. His quote is taken from the section dealing with Bodhidharma's alleged teacher, Prajñātāra, in which the following dialogue between Prajñātāra and a non-Buddhist king occurs:

The king asked: "What is Buddha?"
Prajñātāra said: "Seeing the nature is Buddha."
The king said: "Master, have you seen the nature?"
He answered: "I have seen the Buddha-nature."
The king said: "Where is the nature?"
Prajñātāra answered: "The nature resides in the psycho-physical functions (*hsing tsai tso-yung*)."[18]

Prajñātāra then uttered the following verse (part of which was quoted by Chu Hsi above):

In the womb, it becomes a body;
In the world, it becomes a man.
In regard to the eyes, it is called seeing;
In regard to the ears, it is called hearing;
In regard to the nose, smelling;
In regard to the mouth, speaking;
In regard to the hands, grasping;
In regard to the feet, walking.
When manifested universally, it encompasses worlds as numerous as the
     sands of the Ganges;
When concentrated together, it exists within a single mote of dust.

[17] *Yü-lei* 126.13b; *Ch'üan-shu* 60.18a–b; Sargent, "Tchou Hi contrele Bouddhisme," pp. 99–108; cf. Fu, "Chu Hsi on Buddhism," p. 388.
[18] Chu Hsi quotes this dialogue in *Yü-lei* 126.13a.

Those who understand know that it is the Buddha-nature;
Those who do not understand call it the spirit (shen).[19]

A COMMON PROBLEMATIC

Chu Hsi's charge that the Buddhists mistake the pyscho-physical functions for the nature, and his argument that the nature is the essence (t'i) and the feelings (ch'ing) are its function (yung), recall Tsung-mi's critique of the Hung-chou line of Ch'an. As seen in chapter 9, Tsung-mi characterized the Hung-chou line in terms of its teaching that the Buddha-nature is manifested in the psycho-physical functions. He went on to criticize it for overemphasizing function (yung) to the point of totally eclipsing its underlying essence (t'i). Tsung-mi developed his critique with his analogy of a bronze mirror, which he used to introduce a critical distinction between two levels of functioning to ensure that essence and function could not be collapsed in the way in which he believed Hung-chou to have done. Tsung-mi used his explanation of the two levels of functioning to clarify precisely wherein his understanding of Ch'an was different from, and superior to, that of the Hung-chou line.

By Chu Hsi's time the style and approach typified by the Hung-chou line had clearly emerged as the dominant form of Ch'an practiced in China, and it is largely the sayings and doings attributed to the great eighth- and ninth-century masters within that tradition that are celebrated within the transmission of the lamp records, recorded sayings (yü-lu), and kung-an anthologies compiled during the Sung. It is toward this brand of Ch'an that Chu Hsi directs his criticism of Buddhism.

Nevertheless, in the early ninth century when Tsung-mi wrote, Hung-chou was only one among several contending traditions of Ch'an then current. The Ch'an of that period was marked by its lively variety, as Tsung-mi's own accounts testify. The late T'ang was a time of great experimentation within Ch'an, before it assumed the classical guise in which it presented itself in the Sung. There is thus a pronounced difference in the way in which Ch'an is represented in the T'ang and Sung. Its actual practice and institutional structure may have changed little during this time, but the way in which it is depicted in the Ch'an literature of these two periods presents a sharp contrast.

The Ho-tse line of Ch'an, with which Tsung-mi identified, did not

---

[19] T 51.218b (the identical passage also occurs in Ch'uan-fa cheng-tsung chi, T 51.741c). Note the discrepancy pointed out in note 16 above.

survive the T'ang. The Northern and Ox-head lines, as well as the different Szechwan lineages, whose various teachings and practices Tsung-mi documented and analyzed, also did not continue on into the Sung. The two T'ang lineages to which all of the Sung traditions traced back their descent are those founded by Ma-tsu Tao-i and Ch'ing-yüan Hsing-ssu (d. 740), a figure whom Tsung-mi never mentions in the *Ch'an Preface*.[20] Of the "five houses" (*wu-chia*) into which Sung Ch'an organized itself, only one, the Ts'ao-tung (Sōtō), traced its lineage back to Ch'ing-yüan Hsing-ssu. The other four—i.e., Lin-chi (Rinzai), Yün-men, Fa-yen, and Kuei-yang—all derived from the Hung-chou line of Ma-tsu. Compared to the diversity among the Ch'an traditions at the end of the T'ang, the Sung traditions present a uniform picture. It is the virtuosity with which the different masters compose variations within a common repertoire that is celebrated. The differences among the various lineages are appreciated in terms of the distinctive styles of teaching displayed within them and not in terms of any substantial difference in the content of their teachings.

The various genres of Sung Ch'an literature all depict the sayings and doings of the great T'ang dynasty masters to which they look back for legitimation in terms that are broadly consonant with Tsung-mi's description of Hung-chou Ch'an. What is emphasized is the dynamic activity of these masters in their direct encounter with students. This literature is concerned to demonstrate the concrete functioning (*yung*) of the Buddha-nature in the course of everyday life situations. There is little or no concern with articulating its theoretical basis or clarifying the kinds of practices that are necessary for its realization.

As has been seen, Tsung-mi was highly critical of the antinomian implications of Hung-chou Ch'an's radical rhetoric, and the kind of revalorization of Hua-yen theory that he made can be seen as part of his effort to clarify the underlying ontological foundation of Ch'an practice. Chu Hsi's reaction to Buddhism likewise seems to have sprung from a similar ethical concern to clarify the ultimate basis of morality. Like Tsung-mi, he is pushed to elaborate his metaphysics of principle in order to provide an ontological basis for Confucian moral cultivation. Not only do both figures seem to operate out of the same ethical problematic, but they both also seem to have evolved "solutions" that are remarkably similar in important respects. But, before turning to a consideration of some of the structural similarities

[20] Tsung-mi twice in passing mentions Shih-t'ou Hsi-ch'ien (700–790), the supposed successor of Ch'ing-yüan Hsi-ch'ien. See *Ch'an Preface*, T 48.400c2 (K 49; B 116) and 402c10 (K 91; B 150).

in their respective theories of the nature, I shall first take up the related issue of the predicability of the absolute.

THE PROBLEM OF PREDICATION

Tsung-mi's criticism of the Hung-chou line of Ch'an was connected with his general critique of apophatic language, and both were based on his understanding of the tathāgatagarbha as derived from the *Awakening of Faith*. As seen in chapter 8, this doctrine qualified the thorough apophasis of the Madhyamaka teaching of emptiness, holding that Buddha-nature was both empty of all defilement and at the same time not empty of the infinite qualities of Buddhahood. It thus provided Buddhists like Tsung-mi with a philosophical rationale for asserting the value of positive religious statements about the ultimate ground of reality in the face of the more typical Ch'an claims that only negative statements—such as "there is nothing whatsoever to be attained" or "there is neither mind nor Buddha"—were ultimately true. Tsung-mi characterized the highest teaching of Buddhism as that which reveals the nature (*hsien-hsing chiao*). It superseded the teaching of emptiness precisely because it directly revealed the essence of the nature. The fact that a series of positive predicates could be ascribed to the nature ensured that it could serve as basis of religious and ethical practice. The issue of the predicability of the absolute was thus integrally related to Tsung-mi's soteriological imperative to uncover the fundamental ontological ground of ethical and religious cultivation. Chu Hsi's attempt to establish the ontological basis of morality was linked to a similar claim that the nature was not beyond all predication—such as good and evil.

Among the Confucian scholars of his own day, there was a school of thought that maintained that the nature transcended good and evil and accordingly claimed that when Mencius said that the nature was good, he was not using the word "good" in the relative sense of good as contrasted with evil but rather was expressing admiration. Chu Hsi traces this theory from Hu Chi-sui, Hu Hung (1106–1161), and Hu An-kuo (1074–1138) back through Yang Shih (1053–1135) to the Ch'an monk Ch'ang-tsung (1025–1091).[21] According to Chu Hsi,

[21] Hu Hung was the leading master in the "Hunan School" founded by his father, Hu An-kuo. This school was one of the major traditions of Confucian learning during Chu Hsi's youth, and Chu was, for a time, influenced by it. For a discussion of this school and Chu Hsi's reaction to it, see Conrad Schirokauer, "Chu Hsi and Hu Hung," pp. 480–502. Schirokauer notes that this school shared Chu Hsi's hostility toward Buddhism and goes on to point out that, even though Chu Hsi traced Hu's theory that the

when Yang Shih asked Ch'ang-tsung whether Mencius's theory that the nature was good was true or not, Ch'ang-tsung said that it was. When he further asked how the nature could be spoken of in terms of good and evil, Ch'ang-tsung replied: "The original nature is not contrasted with evil."[22] Chu Hsi approves of Ch'ang-tsung's statement, saying that his words are fundamentally without fault and agreeing that "the original nature is fundamentally without evil."[23] Hu An-kuo learned this theory from Yang Shih but interpreted it to mean that since the word "good" in Mencius's statement that the nature was good was not contrasted with evil, it must have been uttered as an exclamation of admiration. It is to this that Chu Hsi strenuously objects. In his *Classified Sayings* he is recorded to have said:

> [Hu] Chi-sui, as spokesman for his family's school of learning, says that the nature cannot be spoken of as good since the original nature itself fundamentally has no opposite. As soon as it is spoken of in terms of good and evil, then it is not the original nature. The original nature is transcendent (*shang-men*), absolute, and beyond comparison, whereas goodness is mundane (*hsia-men*). . . . As far as Mencius's saying that the nature is good is concerned, it is not that he meant that the nature was good, but rather that he used words of admiration as if to say "How fine the nature!" just as the Buddha said "How good!" I have criticized this theory and said that the original nature is an all-pervading perfection not contrasted with evil. This is true of what heaven has conferred in the self. However, when it operates in man, there are good and evil. When man acts in accord with it there is good, and when he acts out of accord with it there is evil. How can it be said that the good is not the original nature? It is only in its operation in man that there is the distinction between the two. . . . If, as they say, there is original goodness [that is not contrasted with evil] and also relative goodness as contrasted with evil, then there are two natures. Now, what is received from heaven is this nature, and conduct in accord with goodness is also this nature. It is just that as soon as there is good, there is not-good. Therefore good and evil must be spoken of as contrasting.[24]

nature transcended good and evil back to the Ch'an monk Ch'ang-tsung, "Hu Hung would, of course, have been deeply dismayed by the suggestion that his teachings were tinged by the Buddhism he so heartily opposed" (p. 488).

[22] *Yü-lei* 101.30a.

[23] Ibid.

[24] Ibid., 101.29a–b; *Ch'üan-shu* 42.9b–10a; I have adapted Chan's translation from his *Source Book*, pp. 616–617. See Tokiwa, *Shina ni okeru bukkyō to jukyō dōkyō*, pp. 346–351, for a discussion of this issue.

"If the good is not the original nature," Chu Hsi asks rhetorically, "then where does goodness come from?"[25] Chu Hsi makes the same point in a letter to Hu Hung's cousin Hu Shih (1136–1173): "We can say that we cannot speak of the nature as evil, but if we consider goodness as inadequate to characterize the nature, we will not understand where goodness comes from."[26] The success of Chu Hsi's attempt to establish an ontological basis for his moral philosophy is at issue in his refuting the theory of the Hu family. If, in fact, characterizing the nature as good were merely a means of indicating its ultimate transcendence, and, due to the inadequacy of language to describe the absolute, the word "good" were used as an exclamation in a special sense divorced from its ordinary usage as a moral term, then Chu Hsi would not be able to establish the nature as the ontological source of human morality. Chu Hsi must therefore maintain that the word "good" cannot be used in these two different senses. For Chu Hsi the goodness of the nature has to be moral goodness. Ontology and ethics cannot be separated. The nature is principle as it is embedded in man by heaven, and, as principle, it is at once that which links man ontologically with the great ultimate as well as the concrete moral principles of humanity, righteousness, propriety, and wisdom. Thus for Chu Hsi the moral principles contained in man's mind are part of the very fabric of the cosmic order. In this way Chu Hsi is also able to reassert Confucian moral values with a sense of philosophical confidence in the face of the Buddhist challenge.

Chu Hsi's insistence on the goodness of human nature is also related to his rejection of Buddhism for its teaching of emptiness. He frequently contrasts Confucianism and Buddhism in terms of their respective emphases on principle (*li*) and emptiness (*k'ung*). Chu Hsi's understanding of the Buddhist notion of emptiness is certainly superficial, if not wholly misguided, as others have argued.[27] But what is interesting here is that Chu Hsi seems to be unaware of the complex ways in which Chinese Buddhists reacted to, adapted, and qualified the teaching of emptiness in their development of the tathā-

[25] Ibid., 30a.

[26] Quoted from Schirokauer, "Chu Hsi and Hu Hung," p. 494. Schirokauer points out that earlier in the same letter Chu Hsi had written: "At first there is goodness and there is no evil; there is the Mandate of Heaven and there are no human desires." In a subsequent letter to Hu Shih he added: "The nature is called good in order to distinguish the Principle of Heaven from human desires" (ibid.).

[27] See, for example, Fu, "Morality and Beyond," pp. 390–391; Ch'ien, "The Neo-Confucian Confrontation with Buddhism," pp. 312–313; and Fu, "Chu Hsi on Buddhism," pp. 383–386.

gatagarbha doctrine. As seen in regard to Tsung-mi, this doctrine was of paramount importance because it enabled him to go beyond the apophatic stance of emptiness and attach a series of positive predicates to the absolute. In fact, Chu Hsi's critique follows the same tack as Tsung-mi's.

The Structural Parallels

While the nature, for Chu Hsi, is one and indivisible, it can be spoken of from two different perspectives. When Chu Hsi discusses it as the principle endowed by heaven, he refers to it as either the heaven-conferred nature (*t'ien-ming chih hsing*) or original nature (*pen-jan chih hsing*), and it is from this perspective that he can agree with Ch'ang-tsung's statement that the original nature is not contrasted with evil. When he discusses it as it is actually instantiated in an individual, however, he refers to it as *ch'i-chih chih hsing*, a term Wing-tsit Chan renders as the "physical nature." *Ch'i-chih chih hsing* refers to the nature as it is eclipsed by the varying degrees of turbidity of an individual's endowment of *ch'i*. While in actuality the nature can only exist as it is embedded in the mind of an individual, it nevertheless derives its value from transcendent principle and thus, in a metaphysical sense, eternally "exists" independent of and unaffected by its concrete instantiation in an individual. While the *t'ien-ming chih hsing* is the ultimate metaphysical ground for the individual's moral endeavor, the *ch'i-chih chih hsing* is the actual existential ground along which he must proceed.[28]

Chu Hsi's distinction between these two different aspects of the nature is the ontological correlate to his moral distinction between the moral mind (*tao-hsin*) and the human mind (*jen-hsin*). More interestingly, it also parallels a distinction at the crux of the tathāgatagarbha tradition in Buddhism. Within tathāgatagarbha literature, the tathāgatagarbha is always spoken of in terms of two perspectives. From the ultimate perspective of an enlightened Buddha, the tathāgatagarbha is no other than the dharmakāya, which is fully endowed with all the infinite, excellent qualities of Buddhahood. As it is actually instantiated within sentient beings, however, it appears covered over by their defilements (*fan-nao; kleśa*), just as pure gold is hidden by the gangue in which it is found. It is because the tathāgatagarbha is ultimately identical with the dharmakāya that all beings are fully endowed with the perfect wisdom of the Buddha and hence are able to

---

[28] See Araki, *Jukyō to bukkyō*, pp. 287–301, for a discussion of these terms.

realize their inherent Buddha-nature. On the other hand, it is precisely because the tathāgatagarbha is covered over by their defilements that they must engage in religious practice to uncover its true nature. The following parallels can thus be drawn:

heaven-conferred nature (*t'ien-ming chih hsing*)	tathāgatagarbha as the dharmakāya
physical nature (*ch'i-chih chih hsing*)	tathāgatagarbha as it exists within the sentient condition

Such correlations also indicate the way in which Chu Hsi's thought takes over a philosophical stance that had been worked out earlier within the Chinese Buddhist tradition. The dual perspective in which the tathāgatagarbha was understood made it possible for Chinese Buddhists like Tsung-mi to make a crucial philosophical move. The fact that the *Awakening of Faith* identified the tathāgatagarbha in its true nature with the one mind meant that there was a singular ontological principle on which religious and moral cultivation could be based. On the other hand, the fact that this immutable one mind also accorded with conditions allowed for its operation in a less than perfect mode. In other words, the dual aspect of the tathāgatagarbha enabled Chinese Buddhists to preserve an ethical dualism within the monistic ontology of the *Awakening of Faith*. Both sides were necessary. The fact that a certain course of action was believed to be in accord with the very structure of reality gave the practitioner a sense of confidence in the face of the apparently disconfirming experiences of life. Conversely, without his awareness of his own imperfection, he would have no motivation to follow a religious or moral path. Without such critical distinctions of enlightened and unenlightened (or good and evil), the system would collapse into a static monism that admitted no scope for ethical or religious action. Chu Hsi's distinction between the two aspects of human nature likewise allowed him to preserve a fundamental ethical duality within a monistic ontology. Such a move was surely purchased at the price of a heightened philosophical tension, but the practical payoff made it a worthwhile compromise for figures like Tsung-mi and Chu Hsi.

Chu Hsi's related distinction between the moral mind and the human mind parallels the *Awakening of Faith's* theory of the ālayavijñāna. Just as the mind is inherently undependable in Chu Hsi's theory of human nature, so too the ālayavijñāna is marked by a fundamental ambivalence: it has both an enlightened (*chüeh*) and unenlightened (*pu-chüeh*) aspect. Just as the moral mind embraces principle, so too the enlightened aspect of the ālayavijñāna is tathāgatagarbha as the pure seed of Buddhahood within all sentient beings. In the same way, just as the human mind is self-centered and under the sway of desire, so too the unenlightened aspect of the ālayavijñāna is characterized by the ignorance that is based on the false conceit of self out of which attachment arises. The following set of correlations can thus be made:

moral mind (*tao-hsin*)   enlightened aspect of the ālayavijñāna
human mind (*jen-hsin*)   unenlightened aspect of the ālayavijñāna

Both Tsung-mi and Chu Hsi, in responding to similar types of issues, advance the same kind of argument. Although I do not mean to suggest that Chu Hsi consciously borrowed from Buddhist theory in developing his philosophy of human nature, he did nevertheless draw on a tradition of reflection that had been enriched by the type of Buddhist developments discussed in regard to Tsung-mi. Such Buddhist developments, moreover, were related to an earlier problematic in Chinese thought that colored the way in which the Chinese adapted Buddhism to their own philosophical concerns.

In pointing out the ethical problematic common to both Tsung-mi and Chu Hsi, or in suggesting the structural parallels in their theories of the nature, I do not mean to reduce Chu Hsi to a crypto-Buddhist or Tsung-mi to a crypto-Confucian. The similarities in their respective theories of the fundamental nature of man operate on the level of structure. They differ in the content that they ascribe to that nature. For Tsung-mi the nature is Buddha-nature and so contains the infinite excellent qualities of Buddhahood; for Chu Hsi it is the locus of the cardinal Confucian moral principles of humanity, righteousness, propriety, and wisdom. Nevertheless, whereas Chu Hsi insisted on the uniquely Confucian content of the nature, Tsung-mi held that the Buddhist understanding of nature subsumed the Confucian moral virtues. And it was just the kind of accommodating approach that Tsung-mi adopted toward Confucianism that enabled Confucian terms to become suffused with Buddhist connotations. Thus, one of the ways in which Buddhism was able to survive in Chinese thought was by becoming invisible. Having so thoroughly permeated Chinese associations and modes of thought, it was no longer necessary for it to maintain its pretense as a separate intellectual tradition.

A NOTE ON BIOGRAPHICAL SOURCES

THE TWO most important sources for Tsung-mi's life are his own auto-biographical comments and P'ei Hsiu's epitaph—both of which contain much of the primary material from which the subsequent biographies draw. Also important as a supplement to these is Tsung-mi's biography in the *Sung kao-seng chuan*. Of these sources, Tsung-mi's autobiographical comments provide the most detail, as well as furnishing an insight into the character of his religious experience. Aside from the few autobiographical references that appear in other works, the most important sources among Tsung-mi's writings are: (1) his preface to his·commentary (*Ta-shu*, HTC 14.109a–b) and abridged commentary (*Lüeh-shu*, T 39.524b–c) to the *Scripture of Perfect Enlightenment* along with his corresponding notes in their two subcommentaries (*Ta-shu ch'ao*, HTC 14.222a–226d, and *Lüeh-shu ch'ao*, HTC 15.105d–110b; and (2) his initial letter to Ch'eng-kuan written on October 4, 811, and appended to his *Abridged Commentary to the Scripture of Perfect Enlightenment* (T 39.576c577c and HTC15.88b–89b). The first covers his life up to the age of forty-three; the second, while giving a cursory summary of his early studies and training, presents the most detailed account of his experiences during the period 810–811.

P'ei Hsiu's epitaph was composed in 853 and erected at Ts'ao-t'ang ssu on Mount Chung-nan in 855. Useful biographical information is also contained in some of the prefaces that P'ei Hsiu wrote to Tsung-mi's works. P'ei Hsiu was Tsung-mi's most intimate lay disciple. Besides Tsung-mi's own statements, P'ei Hsiu's epitaph, composed only a dozen years after the master's death, bears the authority of being the oldest biographical source. Both its date and P'ei Hsiu's close relationship with Tsung-mi make it one of the most valuable sources. Of course, the very factors that recommend it also suggest its limitations. P'ei Hsiu's evident partiality was probably responsible for his having passed over events that might have raised questions about Tsung-mi's political entanglements, such as his involvement in the Sweet Dew Incident of 835.

P'ei Hsiu's epitaph is contained in *Ch'üan T'ang wen* 743 and *Chin-shih ts'ui-pien* 114. Kamata Shigeo has conveniently listed the variations in his reproduction of the *Ch'üan T'ang wen* text on pp. 49–52 of his *Shūmitsu kyōgaku no shisōshi-teki kenkyū*. I would like to thank Prof. Jeffrey Broughton of California State University at Long Beach for kindly giving me a copy of the rubbing from the original stele at Ts'ao-t'ang ssu published in

Taipei by Hsin-shih-lin ch'u-pan-she in 1981. A small, poor-quality photograph of the stele is reproduced in plate 1608 of vol. 8 of Mochizuki's *Bukkyō daijiten*. A photograph of a rubbing from the stele can be seen in plate 79 of vol. 9 of Tokiwa Daijō's *Shina bunka shiseki*.

The chief value of the biography of Tsung-mi in the *Sung kao-seng chuan*, compiled by Tsan-ning in 988, is its inclusion of an account of his involvement in the Sweet Dew Incident. It is thus an indispensable supplement of Tsung-mi's autobiographical statements and P'ei Hsiu's epitaph. Tsan-ning's account of the incident is based on Li Hsün's biography in the *Chiu T'ang shu* 169.4395–4398.

Although Tsung-mi's biography in the *Chodang-chip* is relatively early (952), it is the shortest and least informative of any of the sources. Its primary interest is its inclusion of a short text by Tsung-mi, his reply to ten questions submitted by Shih Shan-jen (*Shih Shan-jen shih-wen Ts'ao-t'ang Ho-shang*).

Tsung-mi's biography in the *Ching-te ch'uan-teng lu*, compiled in 1004 by Tao-yüan, contains no new information. It paraphrases portions of his *Ch'an Preface* and includes three short works by Tsung-mi—his exchanges with Hsiao Mien, Wen Tsao, and Shih Shan-jan—all of which were originally included in the *Tao-su ch'ou-ta wen-chi*.

Other traditional sources include *Ch'uan-fa cheng-tsung chi* (T 51.753b), compiled by Ch'i-sung in 1061; *Lung-hsing fo-chiao pien-nien t'ung-lun* (HTC 130.336b–337b), compiled by Tsu-hsiu in 1164; *Shih-men cheng-t'ung* (HTC 130.456c457a), compiled by Tsung-chien in 1237; *Fo-tsu t'ung-chi* (T 49.293c), compiled by Chih-p'an in 1269; *Fo-tsu li-tai t'ung-tsai* (T 49.635b–636a), compiled by Nien-ch'ang in 1341; and *Fa-chieh wu-tsu lüeh-chi* (HTC 134.277a–278a), compiled by Hsü-fa in 1680. Despite its late date, the last of these is especially valuable for its judicious synthesis of earlier sources. For a critical evaluation of these sources, see Kamata Shigeo, *Shūmitsu kyōgaku no shisōshi-teki kenkyū*, pp. 10–20. Kamata has also collated P'ei Hsiu's epitaph with the corresponding sections of the *Sung kao-seng chuan*, *Chodang-chip*, *Ch'uan-teng lu*, and *Wu-tsu lüeh-chi* biographies on pp. 21–35.

The most useful modern studies of Tsung-mi's life have been done by Jan Yün-hua in his "Tsung-mi: His Analysis of Ch'an Buddhism" and more recent monograph in Chinese, *Tsung-mi*, pp. 1–42; Jeffrey Broughton in his 1975 Columbia University dissertation, "Kuei-feng Tsung-mi," pp. 39–64; and Kamata Shigeo in his *Shūmitsu kyōgaku no shisōshi-teki kenkyū*, pp. 52–72. These have largely rendered the earlier studies by Furuta Shō-kin ("Keihō Shūmitsu no kenkyū"), Hu Shih ("Pa P'ei Hsiu ti T'ang ku Kuei-feng Ting-hui ch'an-shih ch'uan-fa pei"), and Yamazaki Hiroshi ("Keihō Shūmitsu ni tsuite" and "Keihō Shūmitsu kō") to have little more than bibliographic interest.

A NOTE ON TSUNG-MI'S WRITINGS

By any reckoning, Tsung-mi's oeuvre was extensive. P'ei Hsiu's epitaph states that his writings came to over ninety fascicles,[1] whereas Tsan-ning's biography of Tsung-mi in the *Sung kao-seng chuan* claims that they totaled more than two hundred fascicles.[2] The list of Tsung-mi's works appended to the Tun-huang text of the *Ch'an Preface* names twenty-six works (not counting charts [*tu* 圖] and outlines [*k'o-wen* 科文]).[3] Kamata Shigeo's study of Tsung-mi lists thirty-seven works,[4] whereas Jan Yün-hua's more recent critical list contains forty-one.[5] The way in which one counts the works written by Tsung-mi is, of course, to some extent arbitrary. Many works both circulated as independent texts and were included as parts of various collections. Any list is therefore bound to contain a certain degree of redundancy. In the following enumeration, I have included all extant works of Tsung-mi and all nonextant works about which I can be relatively certain. Some texts are thus listed twice under different titles (6 and 9, for example) as well as being included as parts of other works (27). I have not included charts or outlines.

Tsung-mi's Extant Works

1. *Ch'an-yüan chu-ch'üan-chi tu-hsü* 禪源諸詮集都序 (T no. 2015, 48.397b–413c; HTC 103.304c–320d), in two fascicles, composed around 833. Tsung-mi's preface to his *Collected Writings on the Source of Ch'an* (see entry 21 below). Based on a Korean edition of 1576, Kamata Shigeo has published a critically edited, annotated version of the text with a modern Japanese translation, *Zengen shosenshū tojo*, in vol. 9 of the Zen no goroku series under the general editorship of Iriya Yoshitaka.[6] An earlier Japanese translation by Ui Hakuji was published by Iwanami bunko in

---

[1] Kamata, *Shūmitsu*, p. 50.9–10.

[2] SKSC 742a9–10. Part of the discrepancy may be due to the fact that different editions counted the number of fascicles differently. In one work, for instance, each fascicle might be divided into two parts (*shang* and *hsia*), whereas in another edition of the same text each part might be numbered as a separate fascicle, thus making the text seem twice as long.

[3] See Tanaka, "Tonkōbon *Zengen shosenshū tojo* zankan kō," p. 68.

[4] See his *Shūmitsu*, pp. 85–101.

[5] See his *Tsung-mi*, pp. 44–54.

[6] See K 370–374 for a discussion of the different versions of the *Ch'an Preface*.

1939. A Tun-huang version of the second fascicle of the text, under the title *Ta-sheng ch'an-men yao-lu* 大乘禪門要錄, is listed as catalogue no. 133 of the Tun-huang collection in the National Central Library in Taipei, a photographic reprint of which has been published by P'an Chung-kuei.[7] The Tun-huang text has also been published and discussed by Tanaka Ryōshō in his "Tonkōbon *Zengen shosenshū tojo* zankan kō."[8] A colophon at the end of the text states that it was copied on April 7, 952, from the manuscript of Chih-ch'ing.[9] Tanaka notes the places where the Tun-huang text differs from the version of the *Ch'an Preface* published by Kamata. Overall the discrepancies between these two versions of the *Ch'an Preface* are minor. The most significant difference between these two versions of the text and that published in the Taishō canon has to do with the chart that appears at the end of the text. Jeffrey Broughton has translated Tsung-mi's *Ch'an Preface* as part of his 1975 Columbia University Ph.D. dissertation, "Kuei-feng Tsung-mi: The Convergence of Ch'an and the Teachings." Alan Fox's 1988 Temple University dissertation, "Elements of Omnicontextual Thought in Chinese Buddhism: Annotated Translations of Gui Feng Zong Mi's *Preface to Collection of Various Writings on the Chan Source* and his *Commentary on Meditative Approaches to the Hua Yen Dharmadhātu*," also includes a translation of the text.

2. *Ch'i-hsin lun shu* 起信論疏 (*Dainippon kōtei daizōkyō*, case 31, vol. 8, division 5, part 2, pp. 14a–39a; *Chung-hua ta-tsang-ching*, section 2, vol. 27, pp. 2251–2301), in four fascicles, undated. Tsung-mi's commentary to the *Awakening of Faith*. Since Tsung-mi does not mention this text in his introduction to his subcommentary to the *Scripture of Perfect Enlightenment*, it was probably written after 823. Nevertheless, its straight commentary format and derivative character mark it as an early work, and my guess is that it must have been written sometime between 823 and 828. Tsung-mi's text abridges Fa'tsang's commentary to the *Awakening of Faith*, *Ta-sheng ch'i-hsin lun i-chi*, T no. 1846, 44.240c–287b. Yoshizu Yoshihide has discussed the differences between Tsung-mi's and Fa-tsang's commentaries, which on the whole are relatively minor.[10] The only noteworthy discrepancy, for our purposes, occurs in the second part of the third section of Tsung-mi's introduction.[11] Whereas the corresponding section of Fa-tsang's text contained an enumeration of four doctrinal principles (*tsung*), Tsung-mi used this section to introduce his five stages of phenomenal evolution. The list

---

[7] See his "Kuo-li Chung-yang-t'u-shu-kuan so-t'sang Tun-huang chüan-tzu t'i-chi," *Tun-huang hsüeh-pao* (1975), 2:1–55; see also Jan Yün-hua's "A Study of *Ta-ch'eng ch'an-men yao-lu*."

[8] The original article, published in *Komazawa daigaku bukkyōgakubu kenkyū kiyō* (1979), has been reprinted in Tanaka's *Tonkō zenshū bunken no kenkyū*.

[9] Tanaka, "Tonkōbon *Zengen shosenshū tojo* zankan kō," p. 70 (of original article).

[10] See his "Shūmitsu no *Daijōkishinronshū* ni tsuite."

[11] See the first section of chapter 7 above.

of Tsung-mi's writings appended to the version of the *Ch'an Preface* discovered at Tun-huang mentions a nine-fascicle subcommentary (*ch'ao*), which is no longer extant and is unmentioned in other sources.

3. *Chin-kang po-jo ching shu lun tsuan-yao* 金剛般若經疏論纂要 (T no. 1701, 33.154c–170a), in two fascicles, written in 819 and redacted by Tzu-hsüan (d. 1038) in the Sung. A commentary on Kumārajīva's translation of the *Diamond Sūtra* drawing on key passages (*tsuan-yao*) from works (*lun*; *śāstra*) by Vasubandhu and Asaṅga,[12] commentaries (*shu*) by Ta-yün and others,[13] and the treatises of Seng-chou.[14] Tsung-mi notes that he thus composed a commentary (*shu*) and subcommentary (*ch'ao*), each in one fascicle.[15] It seems likely that the present redaction by Tzu-hsüan combines Tsung-mi's commentary and subcommentary into one work.

4. *Chu hua-yen fa-chieh kuan-men* 注華嚴法界觀門 (T no. 1884, 45.683b–692b), in one fascicle, undated. Tsung-mi's commentary to the *Fa-chieh kuan-men* attributed to Tu-shun. Tsung-mi's commentary is shorter than Ch'eng-kuan's *Hua-yen fa-chieh hsüan-ching* (T no. 1885, 45.672a–683a). Although the discrepancies between Tsung-mi's and Ch'eng-kuan's versions of the *Kuan-men* are slight, they are enough to suggest that the two used different versions of the text.[16] As noted in chapter 6 above, one significant point of difference between Tsung-mi's and Ch'eng-kuan's commentaries is that, whereas Ch'eng-kuan used his discussion of the third discernment to elaborate the ten profundities (*shih-hsüan*) as the paradigmatic expression of *shih-shih wu-ai*, Tsung-mi merely notes that the ten discernments included in this section correspond to the ten profundities, which he does not even bother to list. Sallie King translated Tsung-mi's commentary, with an introduction and notes, as her 1975 master's thesis for the Department of Religious Studies at the University of British Columbia ("Commentary to the Hua-yan Dharma-Realm Meditation"). A more recent translation is included in Alan Fox's dissertation.

5. *Ch'üan fa-p'u-t'i-hsin wen hsü* 勸發菩提心文序 (HTC 103.350a–353d), in one fascicle. Tsung-mi's preface to P'ei Hsiu's "Essay Exhorting the Generation of the Aspiration for Enlightenment"; P'ei Hsiu's essay is

---

[12] There are several commentaries (*lun*; *śāstra*) on the *Diamond Sūtra* attributed to Asaṅga and/or Vasubandhu, all of which could have had the Sanskrit title of *Vajracchedikāprajñā-pāramitsāsūtraśātra*: *Chin-kang po-jo lun* by Asaṅga (T no. 1510; translated by Dharmagupta in 613); *Chin-kang po-jo po-lo-mi ching lun* by Vasubandu (T no. 1511; translated by Bodhiruci in 509); *Neng-tuan chin-kang po-jo po-lo-mi-to ching lun shih* by Asaṅga and Vasubandhu (T no. 1513; translated by I-ching in 711); and *Neng-tuan chin-kang po-jo po-lo-mi-to ching sun lun* by Asaṅga and Vasubandhu (T no. 1514; translated by I-chung in 711).

[13] Kamata quotes the *Zensekishi*, which specifies the commentaries by Ch'ing-lung, Ta-yün, Tzu-sheng, and Ch'en-wai (*Shūmitsu*, p. 93).

[14] *Chao-lun*, T no. 1858.

[15] See TSC 225c16–18; LSC 109b12–15.

[16] See Gimello, "Chih-yen," p. 455.

dated October 5, 836. This is probably the work referred to as *Chu fa-p'u-t'i-hsin chieh* 注發菩提心戒 in the list of Tsung-mi's writings appended to the end of the Tun-huang text of the *Ch'an Preface*. Probably included in *Tai-su ch'ou-ta wen-chi* (see entry 27 below).

   6. *Chung-hua ch'uan-hsin-ti ch'an-men shih-tzu ch'eng-hsi t'u* 中華傳心地禪門師資承襲圖 (HTC 110.433c–438c), in one fascicle, written between 830 and 833 in reply to P'ei Hsiu's questions about the teachings and lineal filiations of four of the major Ch'an traditions of the time. A critically edited, annotated version of the *Ch'an Chart* with a modern Japanese translation is contained in Kamata's *Zengen shosenshū tojo*. Based on a comparison with the quotations from this text that appear in Chinul's *Pŏpchip pyŏrhaeng nok chŏryo pyŏngip sagi*, Ui Hakuju has pointed out that the HTC edition is missing some 288 characters.[17] Kamata has accordingly incorporated the missing section into his edition. The text seems to have originally borne the title of *P'ei Hsiu shih-i wen*, as a 1241 copy with that title was recently discovered in Shinpuku-ji in Japan and has been published by Ishii Shūdō in *Zengaku kenkyū* 60 (1981): 71–104 (see entry 9 below). The Shinpuku-ji text contains the missing section quoted by Chinul as well as three other short essays by Tsung-mi (namely, his replies to Hsiao Mien, Wen Tsao, and Shih Shan-jen). These were all originally published together as part of a collection of short pieces Tsung-mi had written in response to questions from his lay and clerical followers that his disciples compiled shortly after his death under the title of *Tao-su ch'ou-ta wen-chi* (also referred to as *Fa-chi*; see entries 27 and 28 below). At some point the *Ch'an Chart* came to circulate in a separate edition (*pieh-hsing* 別行; K. *pyŏrhaeng*) of the *Fa-chi* 法集 (K. *Pŏpchip*). As Jan Yün-hua has shown,[18] it was that edition that formed the basis of Chinul's *Pŏpchip pyŏrhaeng nok chŏryo pyŏngip sagi* (Excerpts from the separately circulated record of the dharma collection [of Tsung-mi] with personal notes).[19] Chinul's work omits the first part of Tsung-mi's text, which discusses the lineal filiations of the Northern, Ox-head, Hung-chou, and Ho-tse lineages, but otherwise includes the major portion of Tsung-mi's text. An authoritative translation of Chinul's *Chŏryo* has been done by Robert Buswell in his *The Korean Approach to Zen*, pp. 262–374.

---

[17] *Zenshūshi kenkyū*, 3:477–510.

[18] See his "*Fa-chi* and Chinul's Understanding of Tsung-mi."

[19] Unaware of the meaning of *Fa-chi pieh-hsing* (K. *Pŏpchip pyŏrhaeng*), Korean commentators have interpreted the reference to Tsung-mi's work included in Chinul's title to mean "Dharma Collection and Special Practice Record"—a reading that makes sense given that Tsung-mi's text not only gives a synopsis of the four Ch'an traditions but also evaluates them according to their approach to Ch'an practice. See Buswell's "The Identity of the *Dharma Collection and Special Practice Record*" included as an appendix to his *The Korean Approach to Zen*, pp. 375–384.

7. *Hua-yen ching hsing-yüan p'in shu ch'ao* 華嚴經行願品疏鈔 (HTC 7.387a–506b), in six fascicles, undated. Tsung-mi's subcommentary to Ch'eng-kuan's commentary to Prajña's translation of the *Gaṇḍ havyūha*, *Hua-yen ching hsing-yüan p'in shu* (HTC 7.236a–386b). As noted in chapter 6 above, Tsung-mi's subcommentary only mentions, but does not discuss, the ten profundities that Ch'eng-kuan had subjected to a detailed exposition in his commentary.

8. *Hua-yen hsin-yao fa-men chu* 華嚴心要法門注 (HTC 103.303c–304a), in one fascicle, undated. Tsung-mi's commentary to Ch'eng-kuan's brief essay on the essentials of mind written in 796 in response to the questions of Li Sung (who later became Emperor Shun-tsung).[20]

9. *P'ei Hsiu shih-i wen* 裴休拾遺問 (*Zengaku kenkyū* 60 [1981]: 71–104). Original title of work that has come to be known as *Chung-hua ch'uan-hsin-ti ch'an-men shih-tzu ch'eng-hsi t'u* (Chart of the master-disciple succession of the Ch'an gate that transmits the mind ground in China) (see entry 6 above). The Shinpuku-ji version of the text also includes Tsung-mi's replies to Hsiao Mien, Wen Tsao, and Shih Shan-jen. The title of that text also refers to three other works as appended that, however, are not included in the Shinpuku-ji text. The *P'ei Hsiu shih-i wen* and appended pieces were originally collected in *Tao-su ch'ou-ta wen-chi* (see entry 27 below).

10. *Shen-ming Fu-li fa-shih wen* 申明復禮法師問 (contained in *Yüan-tsung wen-lei*, HTC 103.420b–420d). In this short piece Tsung-mi responds to a question that had been raised in a verse by Fu-li (late seventh century) about how what is false can originate from what is true.[21] The title of the Shinpuku-ji copy of the *P'ei Hsiu shih-i wen* refers to this work as appended,

---

[20] I.e., *Ta Shun-tsung hsin-yao fa-men* contained in Ch'eng-kuan's biography in CTL 459b22–c22.

[21] Fu-li's biography can be found in SKSC 812c3–813al. He was active during the reign of Empress Wu and collaborated in a number of major Buddhist projects carried out under her sponsorship. His *Shih-men pien-huo lun* (T no. 2111, 52.551a–559a), written in 681, responds to a series of ten doubtful points about Buddhism that had been raised by Ch'üan Wu-erh's *Shih-tien chi-i*. Slightly different versions of Fu-li's verse, to which Tsung-mi responds, can be found in *Yüan-tsung wen-lei* (HTC 103.419d8–12) and *Fo-tsu t'ung-chi* (T 49.213a25–28)—see Kamata, *Chūgoku kegon*, pp. 526–531. Fu-li's verse reads:

> The true dharma nature is intrinsically pure;
> how can false thoughts arise therefrom?
> If what is false arises from what is true,
> then how can what is false ever be made to cease?
> What is without beginning must be without end,
> and what has an end must have a beginning.
> Being without a beginning and yet having an end—
> long have I harbored confusion over this principle.
> I vow to open its secret,
> to resolve it and escape birth-and-death.

although it is not included at the end of the text. Originally collected in *Tao-su ch'ou-ta wen-chi* (see entry 27 below).

11. *Shih Hsiao hsiang-kung chien-chieh* 釋蕭相公見解 (appended to Tsung-mi's biography in *Ching-te ch'uan-te lu*, T 51.307a22–b2), probably written sometime between 828 and 835. Tsung-mi's reply to a question by Hsiao Mien regarding a statement by Ho-tse Shen-hui having to do with the functioning of the eye of wisdom. Originally collected in *Tao-su ch'ou-ta wen-chi* (see entry 27 below).

12. *Ta Shih Shan-jen shih-wen* 答史山人十問 (appended to Tsung-mi's biography in *Ching-te ch'uan-te lu*, T 51.703b2–c29; also included in Tsung-mi's biography in *Chodang-chip*, pp. 43–47), probably written sometime between 828 and 835. Tsung-mi's reply to a set of ten questions submitted by Shih Shan-jen. Originally collected in *Tao-su ch'ou-ta wen-chi* (see entry 27 below).

13. *Ta Wen Shang-shu so-wen* 答溫尚書所問 (appended to Tsung-mi's biography in *Ching-te ch'uan-te lu*, T51.307d29–308b16), probably written sometime between 828 and 835. Tsung-mi's reply to a question by Wen Tsao on what the numinous nature of an enlightened person depends on after he dies. Originally collected in *Tao-su ch'ou-ta wen-chi* (see entry 27 below).

14. *Yüan-chüeh ching lüeh-shu* 圓覺經略疏 (T no. 1795, 39.523b–578a; HTC 15.57c–89c), in four fascicles, written in 823 or 824. Tsung-mi's abridged commentary to the *Scripture of Perfect Enlightenment*.

15. *Yüan-chüeh ching lüeh-shu ch'ao* 圓覺經略疏鈔 (HTC 15.90a–277b), in twelve fascicles, written in 823 or 824. Tsung-mi's subcommentary to his abridged commentary to the *Scripture of Perfect Enlightenment*.

16. *Yüan-chüeh ching tao-ch'ang hsiu-cheng i* 圓覺經道場修證儀 (HTC 128.361a–498c), in eighteen fascicles, probably written in 824. A Manual of Procedures for the Cultivation and Realization of Ritual Practice according to the *Scripture of Perfect Enlightenment*. Listed as *Yüan-chüeh shu-li wen* 圓覺庶禮文 in eighteen fascicles at the end of the Tun-huang text of the *Ch'an Preface*. This is a major work that has not yet received the scholarly attention it deserves. It is divided into three main parts: the first discusses the conditions for practice (fascicle 1); the second, various methods of worship (*li-ch'an*) (fascicles 2–16); and the third, the method of seated meditation (*tso-ch'an*) (fascicles 17 and 18). In his *Tendai shō shikan no kenkyū*, Sekiguchi Shindai has shown that the discussions of meditation found in the first and last two fascicles of Tsung-mi's text consist almost entirely of excerpts from Chih-i's *Hsiao chih-kuan* (T no. 1915) reassembled in a different order.[22] Ikeda Rosan has further pointed out that Tsung-

---

[22] See pp. 29–32 and 285–302, where Sekiguchi provides a chart collating corresponding sections of the *Hsiao chih-kuan*, Tsung-mi's *Hsiu-cheng i*, Chih-i's *Ch'an-men yao-lu*, and TSC.

mi's discussion of preparatory practices found in the first two fascicles draws heavily from Chih-i's *Fa-hua san-mei ch'an-i* (T no. 1941).[23] Kamata Shigeo has summarized the content of the first two parts of this text (fascicles 1–16) and provided a chart collating the last part of this text discussing the method of seated meditation with the corresponding sections of Chih-i's *Hsiao chih-kuan* in his *Shūmitsu kyōgaku no shisōshi-teki kenkyū*.[24] Various sections of this text seem to have also circulated as independent works (see entry 24 below) or been abridged as ritual guides (see entry 30 below). Carl Bielefeldt has discussed the influence of Tsung-mi's text on Tsung-tse's twelfth-century manual of seated meditation.[25]

17. *Yüan-chüeh ching ta-shu* 圓覺經大疏 (HTC 14.108a–203b), in twelve fascicles, written in 823. Tsung-mi's commentary to the *Scripture of Perfect Enlightenment*.

18. *Yüan-chüeh ching ta-shu ch'ao* 圓覺經大疏鈔 (HTC 14.204a–15.41b), in twenty-six fascicles, written in 823 or 824. Tsung-mi's subcommentary to his commentary to the *Scripture of Perfect Enlightenment*.

19. *Yüan-jen lun* 原人論 (T no. 1886, 45.707c–710c), in one fascicle, written between 828 and 835. Although Tsung-mi's *Inquiry into the Origin of Man* was originally included in the *Tao-su ch'ou-ta wen-chi*, it also circulated as an independent text and in that form came to be one of his best-known works. The two most valuable commentaries are those by Ching-yüan (1011–1088), *Hua-yen yüan-jen lun fa-wei lu* (HTC 104.90a–107d), and Yüan-chüeh (Yüan dynasty), *Hua-yen yüan-jen lun chieh* (HTC 104.108a–143b). There are also a large number of commentaries available in Japanese, many of them dating from the Meiji period (1866–1912), when the text became especially popular. Some of the more useful of these are Ōtomo Tōsu, *Genninron shōkai*; Kimura Yoshiyuki, *Genninron shinkō*; Yusugi Ryōei, *Kanwa taishō genninro shinyaku*; and Kamata Shigeo, *Genninron*. There are also six translations of Tsung-mi's text into Western languages: two into German,[26] one into French,[27] and three into English.[28]

20. *Yü-lan-p'en ching shu* 盂蘭盆經疏 (T no. 1792, 39.505a–512c), in two

[23] See his "*Engakukyō dōjō shushōgi* no reizanhō," especially the chart on pp. 398–399.

[24] See pp. 499–608.

[25] See his "Ch'ang-lu Tsang-tse's *Tso-ch'an i* and the 'Secret' of Zen Meditation."

[26] Hans Haas, "Tsungmi's *Yuen-zan-lun*, eine Abhandlung über den Ursprung des Menschen aus dem Kanon des chinesischen Buddhismus"; and Heinrich Dumoulin, "*Genninron*: Tsung-mi's Traktat vom Ursprung des Menschen."

[27] Paul Masson-Oursel, "Le *Yuan Jen Louen*."

[28] Those by Nukariya Kaiten, included as an appendix to his *The Religion of the Samurai*, pp. 219–253; by Yoshito S. Hakeda, in *The Buddhist Tradition in India, China, and Japan*, ed. William Theodore deBary, pp. 179–196; and by myself as part of my 1981 Harvard University doctoral dissertation, "Tsung-mi's *Inquiry into the Origin of Man*: A Study of Chinese Buddhist Hermeneutics," pp. 217–313.

fascicles, probably written sometime between 835 and 840. Tsung-mi's commentary to the *Yü-lan-p'en* sūtra.

No Longer Extant Works

21. *Ch'an-yüan chu-ch'üan-chi* 禪源諸詮集. Collected Writings on the Source of Ch'an. Tsung-mi's preface subtitles this work *Ch'an-na li-hsing chu ch'üan-chi* 禪那理行諸詮集 (Collected writings on the principle and practice of dhyāna). He explains the title of this work in the beginning of his preface:

> *The Collected Writings on the Source of Ch'an* records the prose and verse expressing the truth of the fundamental source of the Ch'an gate as passed down by the various [Ch'an] houses. I have collected them together into a single "basket" (*tsang; piṭaka*) in order to pass them on to future generations. . . . "Ch'an" is an Indian term fully transliterated as *ch'an-na*. In Chinese it is translated as "contemplative practice" (*ssu-wei hsiu*) or "silent reflection" (*ching-lü*). Both are inclusive designations for prajñā and samādhi. "Source" refers to the intrinsically enlightened true nature of all sentient beings, Buddha-nature, or the mind ground. To awaken to it is called prajñā; to cultivate it is called samādhi. Prajñā and samādhi together are termed "Ch'an." Since this nature is the ultimate source of Ch'an, I have used "the Source of Ch'an" [in the title].[29]

Elsewhere in the *Ch'an Preface*, Tsung-mi hints at the contents of his collection. He says that he has assembled the various Ch'an teachings into ten houses: (1) the Kiangsi (i.e., Hung-chou) tradition, (2) the Ho-tse tradition, (3) the Northern tradition of Shen-hsiu, (4) the Southern tradition of Chih-shen, (5) the Ox-head tradition, (6) the tradition of Shih-t'ou (700–790),[30] (7) the Pao-t'ang tradition, (8) the tradition of Hsüan-shih, (9) the tradition of Seng-ch'ou (480–560)[31] and Guṇabhadra (394–429),[32] and (10) the T'ien-t'ai tradition.

There has been much speculation as to whether Tsung-mi ever compiled this collection. Both P'ei Hsiu and Tsan-ning state that Tsung-mi collected the various Ch'an teachings into a separate piṭaka,[33] and the work is accordingly often referred to as the *Ch'an-tsang* 禪藏. While Tsan-ning's reference may be no more than a repetition of P'ei Hsiu's, and

---

[29] T 48.399a16–22; K 13; cf. B 86–87.

[30] A successor of Hsing-ssu (d. 740), who is alleged to have been a successor of the sixth patriarch; his standard biography can be found in SKSC 763c–764a.

[31] See Jan Yün-hua's "Seng-ch'ou's Method of *Dhyāna*."

[32] The *Leng-ch'ieh shih-tzu chi* considered Guṇabhadra the first Ch'an patriarch (see T 85.1283c–1284c).

[33] See both P'ei Hsiu's preface to the *Ch'an Preface* (T 48.398b10; K3; b 79) and his epitaph for Tsung-mi (50.8) as well as SKSC (742a7).

hence carries little independent weight as evidence, P'ei Hsiu's statement should be taken seriously given his close relationship with Tsung-mi. The most important piece of evidence for the existence of Tsung-mi's collection is the reference to it at the end of the Tun-huang text of the *Ch'an Preface* as *Chi ch'an-yüan chu-lun k'ai-yao* 集禪源諸論開要 in 130 fascicles. Of course, the big question is: if Tsung-mi actually compiled such an important collection, what happened to it? Although it is impossible to answer such a question with any certitude, the most plausible hypothesis has been put forward by Jan Yün-hua (and supported by Robert Buswell), who has suggested that major portions of Tsung-mi's collection were incorporated into Yen-shou's *Tsung-ching lu* (T no. 2016).[34] Even though the discovery of Tsung-mi's collection would be of inestimable value for reconstructing the history of T'ang-dynasty Ch'an, it would probably add little to what we already know about Tsung-mi's thought.

22. *Chu pien-tsung-lun* 注辯宗論. Commentary to the *Pien-tsung lun*, Hsieh Lung-yün's (385–433) treatise in defense of Tao-sheng's (ca. 360–434) theory of sudden enlightenment.[35] The only reference to this work occurs at the end of the Tun-huang text of the *Ch'an Preface*.

23. *Hua-yen lun-kuan* 華嚴綸貫. A five-fascicle work that, as its name implies, tried to tie together the various threads running through the *Hua-yen Sūtra*; composed at Feng-te ssu in 822.[36] Also listed at the end of the Tun-huang text of the *Ch'an Preface*.

24. *Ming tso-ch'an hsiu-cheng i-shih* 明座禪修證儀式. This work, listed at the end of the Tun-huang text of the *Ch'an Preface*, is almost certainly the third and last section of Tsung-mi's *Yüan-chüeh ching hsiu-cheng i* (fascicles 17 and 18) circulated as an independent work. This section (entitled *Tso-ch'an fa* 坐禪法) discussed the procedures for seated meditation under eight headings. As Sekiguchi has shown, Tsung-mi's discussion of seated meditation consists in large part of a rearrangement of passages from Chih-i's *Hsiao chih-kuan*.

25. *Nieh-p'an ching shu* 涅槃經疏. Both P'ei Hsiu and Tsan-ning mention that Tsung-mi wrote a commentary to the *Nirvāṇa Sūtra*.[37] The Tun-huang text of the *Ch'an Preface* lists this work as *Nieh-p'an kang-yao* 涅槃綱要 in three fascicles.

26. *Ssu-fen lü shu* 四分律疏. Commentary to the Dharmagupta Vinaya. Tsung-mi notes that while at Feng-te ssu (the center of the tradition of

[34] See Jan's "Two Problems Concerning Tsung-mi's Compilation of *Ch'an-tsang*" and the appendix to Buswell's *The Korean Approach to Zen*. Jan points out that Sekiguchi was the first to suggest that Tsung-mi's compilation had been absorbed into Yen-shou's *Tsung-ching lu* (p. 46).

[35] The *Pien-tsung lun* is collected in the *Kuang hung-ming chi*, T 52.224c–226c.

[36] See TSC 225d1–6; LSC 109b15–c3.

[37] See epitaph (50.7–8) and SKSC 742a5–6.

vinaya studies begun by Tao-hsüan) on Mount Chung-nan in 823 he compiled a three-fascicle selection of key pasages from the vinaya texts and their commentaries to serve as a guide for practitioners.[38] Both the Tun-huang text of the *Ch'an Preface* and the *Sung kao-seng chuan* (742a8) list a *Ssu-fen lü-tsang shu* 四分律藏疏 in five fascicles and a *Lü ch'ao hsüan-t'an* 律鈔玄談 in two fascicles.

27. *Tao-su ch'ou-ta wen-chi* 道俗酬答文集. Collected Correspondence with Laity and Clergy. A ten-fascicle posthumous collection of Tsung-mi's correspondence with lay and clerical followers with a preface by P'ei Hsiu.[39] Some of the short works for which Tsung-mi is best known (such as his *Ch'an Chart* and *Inquiry into the Origin of Man*) were originally written as responses to queries by different followers. Even though they were collected together by his disciples after his death, many of them later also circulated as independent works. The *Tao-su ch'ou-ta wen-chi* originally contained, among other works whose titles are not even known, *P'ei Hsiu shih-i wen* (9), *Shih Hsiao hsiang-kung chien-chieh* (11), *Ta Shih Shan-jen shih-wen* (12), *Ta Wen shang-shu so-wen* (13), *Shen-ming Fu-li fa-shih wen* (10), *Ta-mo ssu-hsing kuan* 達磨四行觀, *Wei-ching chüeh-ti sung* 惟頸覺地頌, and *Yüan-jen lun* (19). Jan Yün-hua has discussed this work in a number of articles.[40]

28. *Tsa-shu chan-ta fa-i chi* 雜述膽答法義集. Collection of Miscellaneous Correspondence on the Meaning of the Dharma. Although this title is listed as a separate twelve-fascicle work at the end of the Tun-huang text of the *Ch'an Preface* right next to the *Tao-su ch'ou-ta wen-chi*, it seems reasonable to assume that it was a different edition of the latter. Both were collections of Tsung-mi's correspondence. In his preface to the *Yüan-jen lun*, Ching-yüan quotes what he cites as P'ei Hsiu's preface to Tsung-mi's *Fa-chi* (which he notes was often mistakenly placed as the preface to the *Yüan-jen lun*).[41] Ching-yüan's reference to the *Fa-chi* is tantalizingly close to the *Fa-i chi* in the title of this work. The problem, of course, as Jan Yün-hua has pointed out,[42] is that P'ei Hsiu's preface to the *Fa-chi* specifically states that Tsung-mi's correspondence was collected in ten fascicles, and this work is listed as comprising twelve fascicles. Nevertheless, one should not forget that many of Tsung-mi's works circulated under different titles, and that various editions of the same work were often divided into a differ-

---

[38] See TSC 225d10–12; LSC 109c6–9.

[39] The preface is often misidentified as P'ei Hsiu's preface to the *Yüan-jen lun*, as it is in CTW 743.4b–5b. See following entry.

[40] See his "Tsung-mi chu *Tao-su ch'ou-ta wen-chi* te yen-chiu," "A Study of *Ta-ch'eng ch'an-men yao-lu*," and "*Fa-chi* and Chinul's Understanding of Tsung-mi."

[41] See HTC 104d14–16; see also Jan Yün-hua's discussion of P'ei Hsiu's preface and Ching-yüan's comments in his "A Study of *Ta-ch'eng ch'an-men yao-lu*," p. 541, and "*Fa-chi* and Chinul's Understanding of Tsung-mi," pp. 162–163.

[42] See "*Fa-chi*," p. 163, where Jan seems to reject the possibility that the *Tao-su ch'ou-ta wen-chi* and *Tsa-shu chan-ta fa-i chi* were different versions of the same work.

ent number of fascicles. The two collections may well have contained slightly different compilations of basically the same works. Or the *Tsa-shu chan-ta fa-i chi* may have been the same compilation as the *Tao-su ch'ou-ta wen-chi* with the addition of a few short works.

29. *Yüan-chüeh ching tsuan-yao* 圓覺經纂要. A two-fascicle compilation of essential passages from the commentaries to the *Scripture of Perfect Enlightenment* by Wei-ch'üeh, Wu-shih, Chien-chih, and Tao-ch'üan done sometime during Tsung-mi's initial stay at Mount Chung-nan between 816 and 819.[43]

30. *Yüan-chüeh li-ch'an wen* 圓覺禮懺文. Listed at the end of the Tun-huang text of the *Ch'an Preface* as comprising four fascicles. This text is probably the same as that which Ŭich'ŏn lists as the *Li-ch'an lüeh-pen* 禮懺略本 in four fascicles.[44] As such it was probably an abridgment of the second section of Tsung-mi's *Yüan-chüeh ching tao-ch'ang hsiu-cheng i* (fascicles 2–16).

31. *Wei-shih sung shu* 唯識頌疏 and *ch'ao* 鈔. Tsung-mi notes that, while staying at the Hsing-fu ssu and Pao-shou ssu in Ch'ang-an during the winter of 819 and spring of 820, he drew from the *Ch'eng wei-shih lun* (T no. 1830) and K'uei-chi's commentary (T no. 1585) to compose his own commentary to the original thirty verses by Vasubandhu.[45] The Tun-huang text of the *Ch'an Preface* lists a *Wei-shih sung shu* in two fascicles and a subcommentary (*ch'ao*) in nine fascicles.

[43] See TSC 223a15–17; LSC 107a9–10.
[44] See *Sinp'yŏn chejong kyojang ch'ongnok*, T 55.1169c22.
[45] See TSC 225b14–18d; LSC 109c11–14.

GLOSSARY

An Lu-shan　安祿山

chai　齋
Ch'an　禪
ch'an-chiao i-chih　禪教一致
ch'an-ching i-chih　禪經一致
ch'an-chuan chih-mo　展轉枝末
ch'ang　常
Chang Chien-feng　張建封
ch'ang tzu-jan　常自然
Chang Wei-chung　張惟忠
Ch'ang-an　長安
ch'ang-chih　常知
Chang-ch'iu Chien-ch'iung　章仇兼瓊
ch'ang-chu-chiao　常住教
ch'ang-sheng chih kuo　常生之過
Ch'ang-tsung　常總
Chan-jan　湛然
che-ch'üan　遮詮
chen　真
Ch'en Ch'u-chang　陳楚章
chen-chih wei wu-nien fang chien
　真知唯無念方見
chen-fa　真法
cheng　正
ch'eng　成
Cheng Yen　鄭絪
Cheng Yü-ch'ing　鄭餘慶
cheng-chih　證知
ch'eng-fa pen-chiao　稱法本教
ch'eng-hsing　稱性
Ch'eng-kuan　澄觀
ch'eng-li tun shuo　稱理頓說
cheng-sheng　正乘
ch'eng-te　成德
cheng-tsung　正宗
Ch'eng-tu　成都
cheng-wu　證悟
cheng-wu chih chih　證悟之智
chen-hsin pen-t'i　真心本體
chen-ju　真如
chen-ju fa-chieh　真如法界
chen-ju i-hsin　真如一心
chen-ju i-yen　真如依言
chen-ju li-yen　真如離言

chen-ju pen-chüeh　真如本覺
chen-k'ung kuan-fa　真空觀法
chen-ti　真諦
chi　及
ch'i (vital force, pneuma, material force)
　氣
ch'i (origination)　起
Ch'i Hang　齊抗
ch'i shang-fen pen-chiao i　其上分本教義
chi te cheng-wu　即得證悟
chia　假
Chia Tao　賈島
chia-ming　假名
Chiang Chi　蔣濟
chiang-shih p'o-ching chiao　將識破境教
chiao　教
chiao hsing pu-chü erh mieh-shih
　教行不拘而滅識
chiao-ch'an i-chih　教禪一致
chiao-che　交徹
chiao-tsung i-ti　教宗一體
chiao-wai pieh-ch'uan　教外別傳
ch'i-chih chih hsing　氣質之性
chieh　解
Chieh　桀
chieh-wu　解悟
ch'ien　乾
chien hsiu cheng　漸修證
Ch'ien Hui　錢徽
chien-ch'i　見起
chien-chiao san-sheng　漸教三乘
Chien-chih　堅志
chien-chün shih　監軍使
chien-fen　見分
chien-hsing　見性
chien-hsing ch'eng-fo　見性成佛
chien-hsiu　漸修
Chien-nan　劍南
chih (awareness)　知
chih (wisdom)　智
chih chih i-tzu chung-miao chih men
　知之一字衆妙之門
chih chih i-tzu chung-miao chih yüan
　知之一字衆妙之源
ch'ih mi chih　斥迷執

chih-chih　直指

chih-chih jen-hsin　直指人心

chih-ch'ü　執取

Chih-chü ssu　智炬寺

chih-chüeh　知覺

Chih-hsiang ssu　至相寺

chih-hsien hsin-hsing　直顯心性

chih-hsien hsin-hsing tsung　直顯心性宗

Chih-hsüan　知玄

Chih-hui　智輝

Chih-i　智顗

Chih-ju　智如

chih-mo pu-chüeh　枝末不覺

Chih-p'an　志磐

Chih-shen　智詵

Chih-sheng　智昇

chih-shih　直示

chih-wang　執妄

Chih-yen　智儼

chi-ming-tzu　計名字

ching (discriminating)　精

ching (purity)　淨

ching (sūtra)　經

ch'ing (feelings)　情

ching-chieh　境界

Ching-chung Shen-hui　淨衆神會

Ching-chung ssu　淨衆寺

Ching-chung tsung　淨衆宗

ch'ing-liang　清涼

Ching-tsung　敬宗

Ch'ing-yüan Hsing-ssu　青原行思

chin-kang-chieh　金剛界

chin-shih　進士

Chinul　知訥

ch'i-shih-chien　器世間

Ch'i-sung　契嵩

Ch'iu Shih-liang　仇士良

chiu-ching chüeh　究竟覺

chiu-ching-lun　究竟論

ch'i-yeh　起業

Chou　紂

chou-pien han-jung kuan　周遍含容觀

chu　住

ch'u ch'eng-fo shih　初成佛時

Chu Hsi　朱熹

ch'u yin chieh-wu　初因解悟

ch'üan　權

Ch'üan Te-yü　權德輿

ch'üan t'ung fo-kuo　全同佛果

ch'üan-chiao　權教

chuan-fan ch'eng-sheng chi chien yeh　轉凡成聖即漸也

chuan-fan ch'eng-sheng chi tun-wu yeh　轉凡成聖即頓悟也

chuang chu　莊居

ch'uan-shou　傳授

chu-chi　逐機

Ch'u-chi　處寂

chu-chi mo-chiao　逐機末教

chu-chi tun-chiao　逐機頓教

ch'u-chiao　初教

chüeh　覺

chüeh hsing　覺性

chüeh hsin-yao　覺心要

Chüeh-chiu　覺救

Ch'u-nan　楚南

chung (late)　終

chung (loyalty)　忠

chung-chiao　終教

ch'ung-ch'ung wu-chin　重重無盡

chung-yu　中有

chü-tsu chieh　具足戒

fa　法

fa-chieh　法界

fa-chieh yüan-ch'i　法界緣起

fa-chih　法執

Fa-ch'in　法欽

fa-erh　法爾

Fa-hsiang　法相

fa-hsiang-chiao　法相教

fa-hsin　發心

fa-hsing　法性

fa-hsing chen-ju hai　法性眞如海

fa-i　法意

fa-k'ung　法空

fan (ordinary)　凡

fan (overturn)　翻

fan-fu　凡夫

fang-pien　方便

fang-pien-sheng　方便乘

fang-teng　方等

fan-nao　煩惱

Fa-shen　法詵

fa-shen　法身

Fa-shun　法順

Fa-tsang　法藏

Fa-yen　法眼

fei shih so neng shih　非識所能識

fei tien-tao fa　非顛倒法

fen　分

fen-ch'i yu-shen　分齊幽深

feng-hsiang　風相

fen-pieh　分別

fen-pieh chih shih　分別之識

Feng-te ssu　豐德寺

fo-hsing　佛性

Fo-t'o-to-lo　佛陀多羅

fo-yen　佛言

fu-hsin mieh-wang　伏心滅妄

hai-in san-mei　海印三昧

hai-in ting　海印定

Han K'ang-po　韓康伯

Han Yü　韓愈

hao chia　豪家

heng　恒

Ho-tse Shen-hui　荷澤神會

Ho-tse tsung　荷澤宗

hsi　習

hsia-men　下門

hsiang　相

hsiang-chi　相即

hsiang-fen　相分

hsiang-hsü　相續

hsiang-ju　相入

hsiang-tsung　相宗

Hsiang-yang　襄陽

hsiao　孝

Hsiao Mien　蕭俛

hsiao-sheng　小乘

hsiao-sheng-chiao　小乘教

Hsi-ch'ung　西充

Hsieh Ling-yün　謝靈運

Hsieh Shang-ts'ai (Liang-tso)

　謝上蔡(良佐)

hsieh yin　邪因

hsien　顯

hsien i-chen chüeh-hsing　顯一眞覺性

hsien-hsing-chiao　顯性教

hsien-liang　顯量

hsien-shih　顯示

hsien-shih chen-hsin chi hsing chiao

　顯示眞心即性教

Hsien-tsung　憲宗

hsin (mind)　心

hsin (trustworthiness)　信

hsin chen-ju　心眞如

hsin chen-ju men　心眞如門

hsin sheng-mieh　心生滅

hsin sheng-mieh men　心生滅門

hsin-fa　心法

hsing　性

hsing man kung yüan　行滿功圓

hsing tsai tso-yung　性在作用

hsing-ch'i (nature origination)　性起

hsing-ch'i (material form)　形氣

Hsing-ch'i p'in　性起品

hsing-erh-hsia　形而下

hsing-erh-shang　形而上

Hsing-fu ssu　興福寺

Hsing-fu yüan　興福院

hsing-ming　性命

hsi-nien　息念

hsin-nien ch'ing-hsing　信念情性

hsin-shen　心神

hsin-t'i　心體

hsin-tzu-tsai　心自在

hsiu wu-hsing　修五行

hsiu-wu　羞惡

hsi-wang hsiu-hsin　息妄修心

hsi-wang hsiu-hsin tsung　息忘修心宗

Hsü Tzu-jung　徐子融

Hsüan-kuei　玄珪

Hsüan-tsang　玄奘

Hsüan-tsung (r. 712–756)　玄宗

Hsüan-tsung (r. 846–859)　宣宗

Hsüan-ya　玄雅

Hsü-fa　續法

hsü-k'ung tuan-k'ung　虛空斷空

hsün-hsi　熏習

hsü-wu　虛無

hsü-wu ta-tao　虛無大道

hsüan-hsüeh　玄學

hu　欲

Hu An-kuo　胡安國

Hu Chi-sui　胡季隨

Hu Hung　胡宏

Hu Shih (1136–1173)　胡實

hua-fa chiao　化法教

hua-fa ssu-chiao　化法四教

hua-i chiao　化儀教

hua-i ssu-chiao　化儀四教

hua-i tun-chiao　化儀頓教

huai　壞

Hua-yen　華嚴

Huang-po Hsi-yün　黃檗希運

Hui-ch'ang　會昌

Hui-chung　慧忠

Hui-chüeh ssu　恢覺寺

Hui-kuan　慧觀

Hui-kuang　慧光

Hui-neng　慧能

hui-san kuei-i　會三歸一

hui-t'ung pen-mo　會通本末

Hui-yüan (c. 673–743)　慧苑

Hui-yüan (334–417)　慧遠

Hui-yün　慧雲

hun-ch'i　魂氣
Hung-chou tsung　洪州宗
Hung-jen　弘忍
hun-tun　渾沌
huo　或

i (righteousness)　義
i (idea, intent)　意
i fa-chieh hsin　一法界心
i fei hsin ching-chieh　亦非心境界
i shen li hsing　依身立行
I tz'u wen cheng chih yu i-sheng chi
　tun-chiao san-sheng ch'a-pieh
　以此文證知有一乘及頓教三乘差別
i wu hsiu hsing　依悟修行
i-chen fa-chieh　一眞法界
i-chen-ling-hsing　一眞靈性
i-ch'i　一氣
i-chieh　義解
i-ch'ieh hsin-shih chih hsiang
　一切心識之相
ichijō oyobi tonkyō to sanjō to no kubetsu ga
　aru　一乘および頓教と三乘との区
　別がある
ichijō to oyobi tonkyō-sanjō no sabetsu
　一乘と及び頓教三乘の差別
I-chou Shih　益州石
i-fen　一分
i-hsin　一心
i-hsin-ch'uan-hsin　以心傳心
I-hsüeh yüan　義學院
i-ling-hsin　一靈心
i-nien hsiang-ying　一念相應
i-sheng　一乘
i-sheng yüan-chiao chi tun-chiao fa-men
　一乘圓教及頓教法門
i-shih (one time)　一時
i-shih (ceremony, style)　儀式
I-tsung　懿宗
i-yang-chiao　抑揚教

Jan Ch'iu　冉耕
jan-ching yüan-ch'i chih hsiang
　染淨緣起之相
jen　仁
Jen Kuan　任灌
jen-hsin　人心
jen-t'ien-chiao　人天教
jen-t'ien yin-kuo chiao　人天因果教
jissen-teki　実践的
Ju fa-chieh p'in　入法界品
ju-hsüeh　儒學

Ju-i　如一
ju-lai-tsang　如來藏
ju-lai-tsang yüan-ch'i　如來藏緣起
jung-jung　鎔融
ju-shih k'ung　如實空
ju-shih pu-k'ung　如實不空

k'ai-fa　開發
k'ai-yüan　開緣
kan wu　感物
kan-lu chih pien　甘露之變
kan-t'ung　感通
Kao Tzu　告子
ken-pen wu-ming　根本無明
ken-shen　根身
King Wu　武王
Kuan Fu　灌夫
kuan-hsing　觀行
kuan-t'an　官壇
ku-chin ch'ang-jan　古今常然
Kuei Teng　歸登
K'uei-chi　窺基
kuei-feng　圭峯
Kuei-feng Tsung-mi　圭峯宗密
kuei-shen　鬼神
Kuei-yang　溈仰
kung (impartial)　公
kung (common)　共
k'ung　空
K'ung Ying-ta　孔穎達
kung-an　公案
k'ung-chi-chih　空寂知
kung-chiao　共教
kung-ching　恭敬
k'ung luan i chung-sheng　空亂意眾生
kung-te　功德
k'ung-tsung　空宗
kuo　果
Kuo-chou　果州
kuo-shih　國師

Lao-an　老安
le　樂
li (principle, absolute, truth)　理
li (propriety)　禮
Li Ao　李翱
li ch'an　禮懺
Li chi-fu　李吉甫
li fa-chieh　理法界
Li Feng-chi　李逢吉
Li Hsün　李訓
Li Lin-fu　李林甫

Li Shih-min 李世民
Li T'ung-hsüan 李通玄
Li Tzu-liang 李自良
li wang-nien 離妄念
liang 量
liao 了
liao-i 了義
liao-liao tzu-chih wu-nien 了了自知無念
li-chih 利智
li-kuo 離過
Lin-chi 臨濟
ling 靈
ling-chih 靈知
ling-chih pu-mei 靈知不昧
Ling-feng 靈峯
ling-hsing 靈性
ling-ming 靈明
li-nien 離念
lin-t'an 臨壇
lin-t'eng 林藤
li-pu shih-lang 禮部侍郎
li-shih jung-t'ung wu-ai 理事融通無礙
li-shih wu-ai 理事無礙
li-shih wu-ai kuan 理事無礙觀
Liu Ch'iu 劉虬
Liu P'i 劉闢
Liu Ts'ung 劉聰
Liu Tsung-yüan 柳宗元
Liu Yü-hsi 劉禹錫
liu-hsiang 六相
liu-ts'u-hsiang 六麤相
Lo-hou-t'an-chien 羅睺曇捷
Lo-yang 洛陽
lun 論

man-yeh 滿業
Ma-tsu Tao-i 馬祖道一
mei lu hsüeh-shuang chih pei
    每履雪霜之悲
Meng Chiao 孟郊
Meng Chien 孟簡
mi 迷
miao-yu 妙有
mi-chen 迷眞
mieh 滅
mieh-shih 滅識
mi-hsien 密顯
mi-i 密意
mi-i i-hsing shuo-hsiang chiao
    密意依性說相教
mi-i p'o-hsiang hsien-hsing chiao
    密意破相顯性教

mi-mi 秘密
min-chüeh wu-chi 泯絕無寄
min-chüeh wu-chi tsung 泯絕無寄宗
ming (luminous reflectivity) 明
ming (name) 名
ming-ching 明經
mo 末
mo-fa 末法
mo-i 末義
Mount Chung-nan 終南山
Mount Wu-t'ai 五臺山
mo-wang (not forgetting) 莫忘
mo-wang (being without delusion) 莫妄
Mu-tsung 穆宗

nai tsu nai fu 乃祖乃父
Nan-chao 南詔
Nan-tsung 南宗
Nan-yin 南印
Nan-yüeh Huai-hai 南嶽懷讓
nei-chiao 內教
nei-k'u 南庫
neng-chien 能見
neng-ch'üan 能詮
neng-sheng 能生
ni 逆
Nien-ch'ang 念常
nien-ch'i 念起
nien-fo 念佛
ning-jan 凝然
Niu-t'ou tsung 牛頭宗

Pai-chang Huai-hai 百丈懷海
Pai-ma ssu 白馬寺
p'an-chiao 判教
Pao Ching 鮑靚
Pao-shou ssu 保壽寺
Pao-t'ang tsung 保唐宗
P'ei Hsiu 裴休
pen 本
pen-chüeh 本覺
pen-jan chih hsing 本然之性
pen-yu chen hsin 本有眞心
pen-yüan 本源
piao-ch'üan 表詮
pieh 別
pieh-chiao 別教
pien 變
pien-chi tao-chien ting-hsiang chih wu
    遍計倒見定相之物
pien-sheng chih kuo 偏生之過
pi-liang 比量

p'o   魄
Po Chü-i   白居易
Po I   伯夷
p'o-hsiang-chiao   破相教
Po-li   波利
pu tsa luan   不雜亂
P'u-an   普安
pu-chüeh   不覺
pu-ch'üeh   補闕
pu-i pu-i   不一不異
pu-kung   不共
pu-k'ung   不空
pu-kung-chiao   不共教
pu-li wen-tzu   不立文字
pu-liao   不了
pu-pien   不變
pu-pien-i   不變義
pu-ting   不定
pu-ting ch'u-huo   不定初後

san-chiao i-chih   三教一致
san-hsi-hsiang   三細相
san-kuan   三觀
san-luan hsin shih k'ung chung-sheng
    散亂心失空衆生
san-sheng   三乘
san-sheng chien-chiao   三乘漸教
san-sheng pieh-chiao   三乘別教
san-sheng tun-chiao   三乘頓教
san-sheng t'ung-chiao   三乘通教
san-ts'ai   三才
san-tsang   三藏
se   色
se-chieh   色界
Seng-chao   僧肇
seng-t'ung   僧統
se-tzu-tsai   色自在
sha-chieh   沙界
shan-chih-shih   善知識
shang-fen   上分
shang-ken chü-tsu fan-nao fan-fu
    上根具足煩惱凡夫
shang-men   上門
shan-yu   善友
she   攝
she-li   舍利
She-lun tsung   攝論宗
shen (body)   身
shen (spirit)   神
Shen-chao   神照
Shen-ch'ing   神清

sheng (life force)   生
sheng (sage)   聖
sheng (vehicle)   乘
sheng-mieh teng fa pu-kuan chen-ju
    生滅等法不關眞如
Sheng-shou ssu   聖壽寺
Sheng-shou tsung   聖壽宗
sheng-wen   聲聞
Shen-hsiu   神秀
Shen-hui   神會
shen-ts'e chün   神策軍
shih (phenomenon)   事
shih (true, ultimate, full)   實
shih (early)   始
shih (reveal)   示
shih (to be the case, hit the mark)   是
shih fa-chieh   事法界
Shih Shan-jen   史山人
shih-chiao   始教
shih-chüeh   始覺
shih-fei   是非
shih-hsiang   事相
shih-hsüan   十玄
shih-i   拾遺
shih-shih wu-ai   事事無礙
Shinpuku-ji   眞福寺
shiyō (sublation; aufheben)   止揚
shou-fa   授法
shou-pao   受報
Shu Ch'i   叔齊
shu-chiao   熟教
shui hsiang   水相
shun   順
shun-ni ch'i-mieh jan-ching yin-yüan
    順逆起滅染淨因緣
Shun-tsung   順宗
shuo   說
shu-t'u   殊塗
shu-t'u t'ung-kuei   殊塗周歸
so-ch'üan   所詮
so-wei   所謂
ssu-tuan   四端
su-fu   素服
sui-chi chien shuo   隨機漸說
Sui-chou   遂州
sui-i   隨意
sui-yüan   隨緣
sui-yüan ying-yung   隨緣應用
sui-yüan-i   隨緣義
sun chih yu sun   損之又損
su-ti   俗諦

ta seng-lu 大僧錄

t'ai-chi 太極

t'ai-ch'u 太初

t'ai-i 太易

T'ai-kung 太泰

t'ai-shih 太始

t'ai-su 太素

T'ai-tsung 太宗

T'ai-yüan ssu 太原寺

T'an-ching 曇靖

t'ang-t'i piao-hsien 當體表顯

T'an-i 曇一

T'an-ti 曇諦

Tao 道

tao fa tzu-jan 道法自然

Tan-an 道安

tao-ch'ang 道場

Tao-ch'üan 道詮

tao-hsin 道心

Tao-hsüan 道宣

Tao-sheng 道生

Tao-yüan 道圓

ta-sheng 大乘

ta-te 大德

ta-tsai chen-chieh 大哉眞界

Ta-tsai ch'ien-yüan. Wan-wu tzu-shih
  大哉乾元．萬物資始

Ta-yün ssu 大雲寺

Te-ch'un ssu 德純寺

Te-tsung 德宗

t'i 體

t'ien 天

T'ien Fen 田蚡

t'ien-li 天理

t'ien-ming 天命

t'ien-ming chih hsing 天命之性

T'ien-t'ai 天台

tien-tao 顛倒

t'i-hsiang 體相

t'i-hsing 體性

Ti-lun tsung 地論宗

ti-ping 地餅

ti-wei 地味

T'i-wei 提謂

t'i-yung 體用

Tou Ying 竇嬰

ts'ao huo sheng jen 草或生人

Tsan-ning 贊寧

Ts'ao-t'ang ssu 草堂寺

Ts'ao-tung 曹洞

tsao-yeh 造業

ts'e-yin 惻隱

tso-ch'an 坐禪

tso-yung 作用

Tsu-hsiu 祖琇

Ts'ui Ning 崔寧

tsung 宗

tsung wei i-chen wu-ai fa-chieh
  總唯一眞無礙法界

tsung-chi 宗旨

tsung-chiao i-chih 宗教一致

tsung-kai wan-yu 總該萬有

Tsung-mi 宗密

Tu Hung-chien 杜鴻漸

Tuan-fu 端甫

tuan-huo mieh-ku chiao 斷惑滅苦教

tun 頓

tun hsin chieh 頓信解

tun-chiao 頓教

tun-chiao san-sheng 頓教三乘

t'ung (common) 通

t'ung (identical) 同

t'ung wei i-chen fa-chieh 統唯一眞法界

t'ung-chiao 同教

t'ung-kuei 同歸

t'ung-kuei yü chih 同歸於治

t'ung-kuei-chiao 同歸教

tun-shuo 頓說

tun-wu 頓悟

tun-wu chiao-li 頓悟教理

tun-wu chien-hsiu 頓悟漸修

Tu-shun 杜順

tu-t'ou 獨頭

tu-t'ou wu-ming 獨頭無明

tz'u ching chi tun chi yüan erh chiao she
  此經即頓及圓二教攝

tz'u tan shih jan-ching yüan-ch'i chih yen
  此但是染淨緣起之烟

Tzu-chou 資州

Tz'u-en 慈恩

tzu-hsing pen-yung 自性本用

tzu-jan 自然

tzu-t'i 自體

wai-chiao 外教

wan-chih 頑癡

wan-fa tzu-shih 萬法資始

wang (false, delusion) 妄

wang (forget) 忘

Wang Ch'ung 王充

Wang Pi 王弼

Wang P'i 王伾

Wang Shu-wen　王叔文
wang-ch'üan　亡詮
wang-nien　妄念
wang-nien pen wu　妄念本無
wan-ning　頑凝
wei (level)　位
wei (precarious)　危
wei (subtle)　微
Wei Chü-mou　韋渠牟
wei i chen-ju　唯一眞如
Wei Kao　韋皐
Wei Shou　韋綬
Wei Tan　韋丹
Wei-ch'üeh　惟慤
Wei-chung　惟忠
Wei-shan Ling-yu　潙山靈祐
Wen Ta-ya　溫大雅
Wen Tsao　溫造
Wen-ch'ao　文超
wen-tieh　文牒
Wen-tsung　文宗
wen-tzu　文字
wo　我
wo-chih　我執
wo-k'ung　我空
Wu (empress)　武后
Wu Ch'ü-mou
Wu Ch'ung-yin　烏重胤
wu i-ch'ieh ching-chieh chih hsiang
　　無一切境界之相
wu fang-pien　五方便
wu so-nien　無所念
Wu Yüan-heng　武元衡
wu-chia　五家
Wu-chu　無住
Wu-hsiang　無相
wu-i　五位
wu-ming　無明
Wu-ming　無名
wu-ming chih hsiang　無明之相
wu-ming yeh　無明業
wu-nien　無念
wu-se-chieh　無色界
wu-shih　五時
Wu-shih　悟實
wu-shih ken-pen　無始根本

wu-shih pa-chiao　五時八教
Wu-tsung　武宗
wu-wei　無為
wu-wo　無我
wu-yin　無因

Yang Hu　羊祜
Yang I　楊翌
Yang Kuei-fei　楊貴妃
Yang Kuo-chung　楊國忠
Yang Shih　楊時
yang-hsing pao-shen　養性保身
yeh　業
yeh-hsi-ku　業繫苦
yen　烟
Yen Hui　顏回
Yen Li　嚴礪
yen-shuo　言說
yen-shuo chih chi yin yen ch'ien yen
　　言說之極因言遣言
ying　應
yin-hsin　印心
yin-mi　隱密
yin-yeh　引業
yin-yüan　因緣
yu tzu t'i　有自體
yüan　圓
Yüan Chen　元稹
yüan-ch'i　元氣
yüan-chiao　圓教
yüan-ching　圓淨
yüan-chüeh　圓覺
yüan-chüeh miao-hsin　圓覺妙心
yüan-miao　圓妙
Yüan-shao　圓紹
yüan-tun shih-chiao　圓頓實教
yüan-tun-chiao　圓頓教
yü-chieh　欲界
yu-chuang　由狀
yü-lan-p'en　盂蘭盆
yü-lu　語錄
Yün-chü ssu　雲居寺
yung　用
Yung-mu ssu　永穆寺
Yün-men　雲門
yün-tung　運動

BIBLIOGRAPHY

Primary Sources: Buddhist

A-p'i-ta-mo chü-she lun 阿毘達磨俱舍論 (*Abhidharmakośabhāṣya*), by Vasubandhu. Translated by Hsüan-tsang 玄奘. T vol. 29, no. 1558.

Ch'an-yüan chu ch'üan-chi tu-hsü 禪源諸詮集都序, by Tsung-mi 宗密. T vol. 48, no. 2015.

Ch'eng wei-shih lun 成唯識論. Translated by Hsüan-tsang 玄奘. T vol. 31, no. 1585.

Ch'eng wei-shih lun shu-chi 成唯識論述記, by K'uei-chi 窺基. T vol. 43, no. 1830.

Chen-yüan hsin-ting shih-chiao mu-lu 貞元新定釋教目錄, by Yüan-chao 圓照. T vol. 55, no. 2157.

Chi ku-chin fa-tao lun-heng 集古今佛道論衡, by Tao-hsüan 道宣. T vol. 52, no. 2104.

Chih-kuan fu-hsing chuan hung-chüeh 止觀輔行傳弘決, by Chan-jan 湛然. T vol. 46, no. 1912.

Ching-te ch'uan-teng lu 景德傳燈錄, by Tao-yüan 道原. T vol. 51, no. 2076.

Chin-kang po-jo ching shu lun tsuan-yao 金剛般若經疏論纂要, by Tsung-mi 宗密. Redacted by Tzu-hsüan 子璿. T vol. 33, no. 1701.

Chiu-ching i-sheng pao-hsing lun 究竟一乘寶性論 (*Ratnagotravibhāga*). Translated by Ratnamati. T vol. 31, no. 1611.

Chodang chip 祖堂集. Taipei: Kuang-wen shu-chü, 1971.

Chu hua-yen fa-chieh kuan-men 註華嚴法界觀門, by Tsung-mi 宗密. T vol. 45, no. 1884.

Ch'uan-fa cheng-tsung chi 傳法正宗記, by Ch'i-sung 契嵩. T vol. 51, no. 2078.

Ch'üan fa-pao chi 傳法寶紀, by Tu Fei 杜胐. T vol. 85, no. 2838.

Chung-hua ch'uan-hsin-ti ch'an-men shih-tzu ch'eng-hsi t'u 中華傳心地禪門師資承襲圖, by Tsung-mi 宗密. HTC vol. 110.

Fa-chieh tsung wu-tsu lüeh-chi 法界宗五祖略記, by Hsü-fa 續法. HTC vol. 134.

Fa-chü ching 法句經. T vol. 85, no. 2901.

Fo-hsing lun 佛性論. T vol. 31, no. 1610.

Fo-shuo pu-tseng pu-chien ching 佛說不增不減經. Translated by Paramārtha. T vol. 16, no. 668.

Fo-shuo yü-lan-p'en ching shu 佛說盂蘭盆經疏, by Tsung-mi 宗密. T vol. 39, no. 1792.

Fo-tsu li-tai t'ung-tsai 佛祖歷代通載, by Nien-ch'ang 念常. T vol. 49, no. 2036.

Fo-tsu t'ung-chi 佛祖統紀, by Chih-p'an 志磐. T vol. 49, no. 2035.

Hsiu hua-yen ao-chih wang-chin huan-yüan kuan 修華嚴奧旨妄盡還源觀. T vol. 45, no. 1876.

Hsü hua-yen ching lüeh-shu k'an-ting chi 續華嚴經略疏刊定記, by Hui-yüan 慧苑. HTC vol. 5.

Hsü kao-seng chuan 續高僧傳, by Tao-hsüan 道宣. T vol. 50, no. 2060.

Hsü ku-chin i-ching t'u-chi 續古今譯經圖紀, by Chih-sheng 智昇. T vol. 55, no. 2152.

Hua-yen ching chuan-chi 華嚴經傳記, by Fa-tsang 法藏. T vol. 51, no. 2073.

Hua-yen ching hsing-yüan p'in shu 華嚴經行願品疏, by Ch'eng-kuan 澄觀. HTC vol. 7.

Hua-yen ching hsing-yüan p'in shu ch'ao 華嚴經行願品疏鈔, by Tsung-mi 宗密. HTC vol. 7.

Hua-yen ching-nei chang-men teng-tsa k'ung-mu chang 華嚴經內章門等雜孔目章, by Chih-yen 智儼. T vol. 45, no. 1870.

Hua-yen ching t'an-hsüan chi 華嚴經探玄記, by Fa-tsang 法藏. T vol. 35, no. 1733.

Hua-yen fa-chieh hsüan-ching 華嚴法界玄鏡, by Ch'eng-kuan 澄觀. T vol. 45, no. 1883.

Hua-yen i-sheng chiao-i fen-ch'i chang 華嚴一乘教義分齊章, by Fa-tsang 法藏. T vol. 45, no. 1866.

Hua-yen wu-shih yao wen-ta 華嚴五十要問答, by Chih-yen 智儼. T vol. 45, no. 1869.

Hua-yen yu-hsin fa-chieh chi 華嚴遊心法界記, by Fa-tsang 法藏. T vol. 45, no. 1877.

Huang-po-shan Tuan-chi ch'an-shih ch'üan-hsin fa-yao 黃檗山斷際禪師傳心法要. Compiled by P'ei Hsiu 裴休. T vol. 48, no. 2012A.

Huang-po Tuan-chi ch'an-shih Wan-ling lu 黃檗斷際禪師宛陵錄. Compiled by P'ei Hsiu 裴休. T vol. 48, no. 2012B.

Hung-ming chi 弘明集. Compiled by Seng-yu 僧祐. T vol. 52, no. 2102.

Ju leng-ch'ieh ching 入楞伽經 (*Laṅkāvatāra Sūtra*). Translated by Bodhiruci. T vol. 16, no. 671.

K'ai-yüan shih-chiao lu 開元釋教錄, by Chih-sheng 智昇. T vol. 55, no. 2154.

Kao-seng chuan 高僧傳, by Hui-chiao 慧皎. T vol. 50, no. 2059.

Kuang Ch'ing-liang chuan 廣清涼傳, by Yen-i 延一. T vol. 51, no. 2099.

Kuang hung-ming chi 廣弘明宗, by Tao-hsüan 道宣. T vol. 52, no. 2103.

Leng-ch'ieh a-pa-to-lo pao ching 楞伽阿跋多羅寶經 (*Laṅkāvatāra Sūtra*). Translated by Guṇabhadra. T. vol. 16, no. 670.

Leng-ch'ieh shih-tzu chi 楞伽師資記, by Ching-chüeh 淨覺. T vol. 85, no. 2837.

Li-tai fa-pao chi 歷代法寶記. T vol. 51, no. 2075.

Lung-hsing fo-chiao pien-nien t'ung-lun 隆興佛教編年通論, by Tsu-hsiu 祖琇. HTC vol. 130.

Miao-fa lien-hua ching 妙法蓮華經. Translated by Kumārajīva. T vol. 9, no. 261.

Mo-ho chih-kuan 摩訶止觀, by Chih-i 智顗. T vol. 46, no. 1911.

Pei-shan lu 北山錄, by Shen-ch'ing 神清. T vol. 52, no. 2113.

Pien-cheng lun 辯正論, by Fa-lin 法琳. T vol. 52, no. 2110.

Pŏpchip pyŏrhaeng nok chŏryo pyŏngip sagi 法集別行錄節要並入私記, by Chinul 知訥. Edited by An Chin-ho. Seoul: Pŏmnyun-sa, 1976.

Sheng-man shih-tzu-hou i-sheng ta-fang-pien fang-kuang ching 勝鬘師子吼一乘大方便方廣經 (*Śrīmālā Sūtra*). Translated by Guṇabhadra. T vol. 12, no. 353.

Shih-men cheng-t'ung 釋門正統, by Tsung-chien 宗鑑. HTC vol. 130.

Shih-men pien-huo lun 十門辯惑論, by Fu-li 復禮. T vol. 52, no. 2111.

Shih-ti ching lun 十地經論 (*Daśabhūmikabhāṣya*), by Vasubandhu. Translated by Bodhiruci. T vol. 26, no. 1522.

Sinp'yŏn chejong kyojang ch'ongnok 新編諸宗教藏總錄, by Ŭich'ŏn 義天. T vol. 55, no. 2184.

Ssu-chiao i 四教義, by Chih-i 智顗. T vol. 46, no. 1929.

Sung kao-seng chuan 宋高僧傳, by Tsan-ning 贊寧. T vol. 50, no. 2061.

Ta-chih-tu lun 大智度論. Translated by Kumārajīva. T vol. 25, no. 1509.

Ta-fang-kuang fo hua-yen ching 大方廣佛華嚴經 (*Avataṃsaka Sūtra*). Translated by Buddhabhadra. T vol. 9, no. 278.

Ta-fang-kuang fo hua-yen ching 大方廣佛華嚴經 (*Avataṃsaka Sūtra*). Translated by Śikṣānanda. T vol. 10, no. 279.

Ta-fang-kuang fo hua-yen ching 大方廣佛華嚴經 (*Gaṇḍavyūha*). Translated by Prajña. T vol. 10, no. 293.

Ta-fang-kuang fo hua-yen ching sou-hsüan fen-ch'i t'ung-chih fang-kuei 大方廣佛華嚴經搜玄分齊通智方軌, by Chih-yen 智儼. T vol. 35, no. 1732.

Ta-fang-kuang fo hua-yen ching shu 大方廣佛華嚴經疏, by Ch'eng-kuan 澄觀. T vol. 35, no. 1735.

Ta-fang-kuang fo hua-yen ching sui-shu yen-i ch'ao 大方廣佛華嚴經隨疏演義鈔, by Ch'eng-kuan 澄觀. T vol. 36, no. 1736.

Ta-fang-kuang yüan-chüeh hsiu-to-lo liao-i ching 大方廣圓覺修多羅了義經. T vol. 17, no. 842.

Ta-fang-kuang yüan-chüeh hsiu-to-lo liao-i ching lüeh-shu 大方廣圓覺修多羅了義經略疏, by Tsung-mi 宗密. T vol. 39, no. 1795.

Ta-feng-teng t'o-lo-ni ching 大方等陀羅尼經. Translated by Fa-chung 法衆. T vol. 21, no. 1339.

Ta-fo-ting shou-leng-yen ching 大佛頂首楞嚴經 (*Śūraṅgama Sūtra*). T vol. 19, no. 945.

Ta-pao-chi ching 大寶積經. Translated by Bodhiruci. T vol. 11, no. 310.

Ta-sheng ch'i-hsin lun 大乘起信論. T vol. 32, no. 1666.

Ta-sheng ch'i-hsin lun i-chi 大乘起信論義記, by Fa-tsang 法藏. T vol. 44, no. 1846.

Ta-sheng ch'i-hsin lun shu 大乘起信論疏, by Tsung-mi 宗密. *Dainippon kōtei daizōkyō*, case 31, vol. 8, div. 5, part 2.

Ta-sheng ju leng-ch'ieh ching 大乘入楞伽經 (*Laṅkāvatāra Sūtra*). Translated by Śikṣānanda. T vol. 16, no. 672.

Ta-sheng she lun 攝大乘論 (*Mahāyānasaṃgraha*). Translated by Pramārtha. T vol. 31, no. 1595.

Ta-Sung seng-shih lüeh 大宋僧史略, by Tsan-ning 贊寧. T vol. 54, no. 2126.

T'ien-t'ai su-chiao i 天台四教儀, by Chegwan 諦觀. T 46, no. 1931.

Wei-mo-chieh so-shuo ching 維摩詰所說經 (*Vimalakīrti-nirdeśa Sūtra*). Translated by Kumārajīva. T vol. 14, no. 475.

Yüan jen lun 原人論, by Tsung-mi 宗密. T vol. 45, no. 1886.

Yüan jen lun chieh 原人論解, by Yüan-chüeh 圓覺. HTC vol. 104.

Yüan jen lun fa-wei lu 原人論發微錄, by Ching-yüan 淨源. HTC vol. 104.

Yüan-chüeh ching lüeh-shu ch'ao 圓覺經略疏鈔, by Tsung-mi 宗密. HTC vol. 15.

Yüan-chüeh ching tao-ch'ang hsiu-cheng i 圓覺經道場修證儀, by Tsung-mi 宗密. HTC vol. 128.

Yüan-chüeh ching ta-shu 圓覺經大疏, by Tsung-mi 宗密. HTC vol. 14.

Yüan-chüeh ching ta-shu ch'ao 圓覺經大疏鈔, by Tsung-mi 宗密. HTC vols. 14–15.

Yüan-tsung wen-lei 圓宗文類. HTC vol. 103.

Yü-lan-p'en ching shu hsin-chi 盂蘭盆經疏新記, by Yüan-chao 元照. HTC vol. 35.

PRIMARY SOURCES: NON-BUDDHIST

Ch'ang-chiang chi 長江集. Ts'ung-shu chi-ch'eng ch'u-pien, vol. 2237.

Chin shu 晉書. 5 vols. Peking: Chung-hua shu-chü, 1974.

Chin-shih ts'ui-pien 金石萃編, by Wang Ch'ang 王昶. 24 vols. Shanghai: Sao-yeh san-fang, 1921.

Chiu T'ang shu 舊唐書. 16 vols. Peking: Chung-hua shu-chü, 1975.

Chou-i chu-shu 周易注疏. SPPY, vol. 54.

Chu Tzu ch'üan-shu 朱子全書. Facsimile reprint of 1885 reprint of 1715 edition. 2 vols. Taipei: Kuang-hsüeh she, 1977.

Chu Tzu yü-lei 朱子語類. Edited by Li Ching-te 黎靖德. 1880 edition.

Ch'uan T'ang wen 全唐文. Imperial edition, 1814. Reprint. Taipei: Hua-wen shu-chü, 1961.

Chuang-tzu 莊子. Harvard-Yenching Sinological Index Series, Supplement no. 20. Cambridge: Harvard University Press, 1956.

Han Ch'ang-li ch'üan-chi 韓昌黎全集. SPPY, vols. 533–534.

Han shu 漢書. SPPY, vols. 209–216.

Hsiao ching 孝經. Harvard-Yenching Sinological Index Series, Supplement no. 23. Taipei: Ch'eng-wen Publishing Co., 1966.

Hsin T'ang shu 新唐書. 20 vols. Peking: Chung-hua shu-chü, 1975.

Huai-nan-tzu 淮南子. SPTK, vol. 85.

Hui-an hsien-sheng Chu Wen-kung wen-chi 晦庵先生朱文公文集. SPPY, vols. 395–406.

Lao-tzu 老子. Taipei: Chung-hua shu-chü, 1973.

Li chi 禮記. SPPY, vols. 29–30.

Lieh-tzu 列子. Taipei: I-wen yin-shu-kuan, 1971.

Liu Meng-te wen-chi 劉夢得文集. SPTK, vol. 694.

Lun heng 論衡, by Wang Ch'ung 王充. SPPY, vols. 389–390.

Meng-ch'iu 蒙求, by Li Han 李瀚. I-ts'un ts'ung-shu, vols. 16–17.

Meng-tzu chi-chu 孟子集注, by Chu Hsi 朱熹. SPPY, vol. 24.

Pei-meng so-yen 北夢瑣言, by Sun Kuang-hsien 孫光憲. Ts'ung-shu chi-ch'eng ch'u-pien, vols. 2841–2842.

Po-shih Ch'ang-ch'ing-chi 白氏長慶集. SPPY, vols. 724–747.

San-kuo chih 三國志. 3 vols. Peking: Chung-hua shu-chü, 1973.

Shang-ts'ai yü-lu 上蔡語錄. Ying-yin wen-yüan ko ssu-k'u ch'üan-shu, vol. 698. Taipei, 1983.

Shih chi 史記, by Ssu-ma Ch'ien 司馬遷. SPPY, vols. 201–208.

T'ang hui-yao 唐會要, by Wang P'u 王溥. Ts'ung-shu chi-ch'eng ch'u-pien, vols. 813–828.

Secondary Sources

Araki, Kengo 荒木見悟. *Bukkyō to jukyō* 仏教と儒教. Kyoto: Heirakuji shoten, 1963.

Backus, Charles. *The Nan-chao Kingdom and T'ang China's Southwestern Frontier.* Cambridge: Cambridge University Press, 1981.

Barrett, Timothy Hugh. "Buddhism, Taoism and Confucianism in the Thought of Li Ao." Ph.D. dissertation, Yale University, 1978.

Becker, Carl B. "The Importance of the Concept of Nature (*hsing*) in the Philosophy of Chu Hsi." *Ming Studies* 15 (1982): 36–44.

Berger, Peter. *The Sacred Canopy*. Garden City: Doubleday, 1969.

Berling, Judith A. *The Syncretic Religion of Lin Chao-en*. New York: Columbia University Press, 1980.

Bielefeldt, Carl. "Ch'ang-lu Tsung-tse's *Tso-ch'an i* and the 'Secret' of Zen Meditation." In *Traditions of Meditation in Chiese Buddhism*. Edited by Peter N. Gregory. Studies in East Asian Buddhism, no. 4. Honolulu: University of Hawaii Press, 1986.

Birch, Cyril, ed. *Anthology of Chinese Literature*. New York: Grove Press, 1965.

Birnbaum, Raoul. "The Manifestations of a Monastery: Shen-ying's Experiences on Mount Wu-t'ai in T'ang Context." *Journal of the American Oriental Society* 106, 1 (1986): 119–137.

———. *Studies on the Mysteries of Mañjuśrī*. Society for the Study of Chinese Religion Monograph no. 2 (1983).

Blofeld, John. *The Zen Teaching of Huang Po: On the Transmission of the Mind*. New York: Grove Press, 1958.

Broughton, Jeffrey L. "Early Ch'an Schools in Tibet." In *Studies in Ch'an and Hua-yen*. Edited by Robert M. Gimello and Peter N. Gregory. Studies in East Asian Buddhism, no. 1. Honolulu: University of Hawaii Press, 1983.

———. "Kuei-feng Tsung-mi: The Convergence of Ch'an and the Teachings." Ph.D. dissertation, Columbia University, 1975.

Buswell, Robert E., Jr., ed. *Chinese Buddhist Apocrypha*. Honolulu: University of Hawaii Press, 1990.

———. "Ch'an Hermeneutics." In *Buddhist Hermeneutics*. Edited by Donald S. Lopez, Jr. Studies in East Asian Buddhism, no. 6. Honolulu: University of Hawaii Press, 1988.

———. "Chinul's Systematization of Chinese Meditative Techniques in Korean Sŏn Buddhism." In *Traditions of Meditation in Chinese Buddhism*. Edited by Peter N. Gregory. Studies in East Asian Buddhism, no. 4. Honolulu: University of Hawaii Press, 1987.

———. *The Formation of Ch'an Ideology in China and Korea*. Princeton: Princeton University Press, 1989.

———. *The Korean Approach to Zen: The Collected Works of Chinul*. Honolulu: University of Hawaii Press, 1983.

Chaffee, John W. *The Thorny Gates of Learning in Sung China*. Cambridge: Cambridge University Press, 1985.

Chan, Wing-tsit, ed. *Chu Hsi and Neo-Confucianism*. Honolulu: University of Hawaii Press, 1986.

———. "The Evolution of the Neo-Confucian Concept of *Li* as Principle." *Tsing-hua Journal of Chinese Studies* 4 (1964): 123–149.

———, trans. *Reflections on Things Near at Hand: The Neo-Confucian Anthology*. New York: Columbia University Press, 1967.

———. *A Source Book in Chinese Philosophy*. Princeton: Princeton University Press, 1963.

Chang, Garma C. C. *The Buddhist Teaching of Totality: The Philosophy of Hwa Yen Buddhism*. University Park: Pennsylvania State University Press, 1971.

Chapin, Helen, and Alexander Soper. *A Long Roll of Buddhist Images*. Ascona: Artibus Asiae, 1971.

Chappell, David, ed. *Buddhist and Taoist Practice in Medieval Chinese Society.* Buddhist and Taoist Studies II. Honolulu: University of Hawaii Press, 1987.

———. "From Dispute to Dual Cultivation: Pure Land Responses to Ch'an Critics." In *Traditions of Meditation in Chinese Buddhism.* Edited by Peter N. Gregory. Studies in East Asian Buddhism, no. 4. Honolulu: University of Hawaii Press, 1986.

———. "Introduction to the *T'ien-t'ai ssu-chiao-i.*" *The Eastern Buddhist* 9, 1 (1976): 72–86.

———. "The Teachings of the Fourth Ch'an Patriarch Tao-hsin (580–651)." In *Early Ch'an in China and Tibet.* Edited by Whalen Lai and Lewis R. Lancaster. Berkeley: Berkeley Buddhist Studies Series, 1983.

———, ed. *T'ien-t'ai Buddhism: An Outline of the Fourfold Teachings.* Tokyo: Daiichi shobō, 1983.

Chen, Jo-shui. "The Dawn of Neo-Confucianism: Liu Tsung-yüan and the Intellectual Changes in T'ang China, 773–819." Ph.D. dissertation, Yale University, 1987.

Ch'en, Kenneth K. S. *Buddhism in China: A Historical Survey.* Princeton: Princeton University Press, 1964.

———. *The Chinese Transformation of Buddhism.* Princeton: Princeton University Press, 1973.

Ch'en, Tsu-lung 陳祚龍. "Liu Yü-hsi yü fo-chiao" 劉禹錫與佛教. In *Chung-hua fo-chiao wen-hua shih san-ts'e ch'u-chi* 中華佛教文化史散策初集, by Ch'en Tsu-lung. Taipei: Shin-wen-feng, 1978.

Ch'ien, Edward T. "The Neo-Confucian Confrontation with Buddhism: A Structural and Historical Analysis." *Journal of Chinese Philosophy* 9, 4 (1982): 307–328.

Cleary, J. C. *Zen Dawn: Early Zen Texts from Tun Huang.* Boston: Shambala, 1986.

Cleary, Thomas. *Entry into the Inconceivable: An Introduction to Hua-yen Buddhism.* Honolulu: University of Hawaii Press, 1983.

———, trans. *The Flower Ornament Scripture.* 3 vols. Boulder: Shambala, 1984–1987.

Cook, Francis H. "Fa-tsang's Treatise on the Five Doctrines: An Annotated Translation." Ph.D. dissertation, University of Wisconsin, 1970.

———. *Hua-yen Buddhism: The Jewel Net of Indra.* University Park: Pennsylvania State University Press, 1977.

Cowell, E. B., trans. *The Buddha-karita of Asvaghosha.* In *Buddhist Mahāyāna Texts.* New York: Dover Publications, 1969.

Creel, Herrlee G. *The Origins of Statecraft in China*, vol. 1. *The Western Chou Empire.* Chicago: University of Chicago Press, 1970.

Dalby, Michael T. "Court Politics in Late T'ang Times." In *The Cambridge History of China*, vol. 3, *Sui and T'ang China (589–906)*, part 1. Edited by Denis Twitchett. Cambridge: Cambridge University press, 1979.

Dalia, Albert A. "Social Change and the New Buddhism in South China: Fa-jung (A.D. 594–657)." Ph.D. dissertation, University of Hawaii, 1985.

deBary, William Theodore, ed. *The Buddhist Tradition in India, China, and Japan.* New York: Random House, 1969.

Donner, Neal. "The Great Calming and Contemplation of Chih-i. Chapter One: The Synopsis." Ph.D. dissertation, University of British Columbia, 1976.

———. "Sudden and Gradual Intimately Conjoined: Chih-i's T'ien-t'ai View." In *Sudden and Gradual: Approaches to Enlightenment in Chinese Thought*. Edited by Peter N. Gregory. Studies in East Asian Buddhism, no. 5. Honolulu: University of Hawaii Press, 1987.

Dubs, Homer H. "Han Yü and the Buddha Relic: An Episode in Medieval Chinese Religion." *The Review of Religion* 11, 1 (1946): 5–17.

Dumoulin, Heinrich. "*Genninron*: Tsung-mi's Traktat vom Ursprung des Menschen." *Mounmenta Nipponica* 1, 1 (1938): 178–221.

Edgerton, Franklin. *Buddhist Hybrid Sanskrit Grammar and Dictionary*. 2 vols. New Haven: Yale University Press, 1953.

Elman, Benjamin A. "Philosophy (*i-li*) versus Philology (*k'ao-cheng*): The *Jen-hsin tao-hsin* Debate." *T'oung Pao* 69, 4–5 (1983): 175–222.

Endo, Kōjirō 遠藤孝次郎. "Kegon shōki ronkō" 華厳性起論考. *Indogaku bukkyōgaku kenkyū* 14, 1 (1965): 214–216 and 15, 2 (1967): 523–528.

Faure, Bernard. *La volonté d'orthodoxie dans le bouddhisme chinois*. Paris: Centre National de la Recherche Scientifique, 1988.

Feifel, Eugene. "Biography of Po Chü-i." *Monumenta Serica* 17 (1958): 255–311.

———. *Po Chü-i as a Censor*. The Hague: Mouton, 1961.

Fontein, Jan. *The Pilgrimage of Sudhana: A Study of Gaṇḍavyūha illustrations in China, Japan and Java*. The Hague: Mouton, 1967.

Forke, Alfred. *Lun-Heng: Philosophical Essays of Wang Ch'ung*. 2 vols. 2d edition. New York: Paragon Book Gallery, 1962.

Forte, Antonino. *Political Propaganda and Ideology in China at the End of the Seventh Century: Inquiry into the Nature, Author, and Function of the Tunhuang Document S. 6502. Followed by an Annotated Translation*. Napoli: Istituto Universitario Orientale, Seminario di Studi Asiatici, 1976.

Foulk, Theodore Griffith. "The 'Ch'an School' and Its Place in the Buddhist Monastic Tradition." Ph.D. dissertation, University of Michigan, 1987.

Fox, Alan. "Elements of Omnicontextual Thought in Chinese Buddhism: Annotated Translations of Gui Feng Zong Mi's *Preface to Collection of Various Writings on the Chan Source* and His *Commentary on Meditative Approaches to the Hua Yan Dharmadhātu*." Ph.D. dissertation, Temple University, 1988.

Fu, Charles Wei-hsun. "Chu Hsi on Buddhism." In *Chu Hsi and Neo-Confucianism*. Edited by Wing-tsit Chan. Honolulu: University of Hawaii Press, 1986.

———. "Morality of Beyond: The Neo-Confucian Confrontation with Mahāyāna Buddhism." *Philosophy East and West* 23, 3 (1973): 375–396.

Fujita, Kōtatsu. "One Vehicle or Three?" Translated by Leon Hurvitz. *Journal of Indian Philosophy* 3 (1975): 79–166.

Fung, Yu-lan 馮友蘭. *Chung-kuo che-hsüeh shih* 中國哲學史. 1931–34. Reprint. Hong Kong: T'ai-p'ing yang t'u-shu, 1975.

Furuta, Shōkin 古田紹欽. "Keihō Shūmitsu no kenkyū" 圭峯宗密の研究. *Shina bukkyō shigaku* 2, 2 (1983): 83–97.

Gimello, Robert M. "Apophatic and Kataphatic Discourse in Mahāyāna: A Chinese View." *Philosophy East and West* 26, 2 (1976): 117–136.

————. "Chih-yen (602–668) and the Foundations of Hua-yen Buddhism." Ph.D. dissertation, Columbia University, 1976.

————. "The Doctrine of 'Nature-Origination' (hsing-ch'i) in Early Hua-yen Buddhism." Paper presented at Regional Seminar in Chinese Studies, University of California, Berkeley, February, 1977.

———— "Mysticism in Its Contexts." In Mysticism and Religious Traditions. Edited by Steven T. Katz. New York: Oxford University Press, 1983.

Gimello, Robert M., and Peter N. Gregory, eds. Studies in Ch'an and Hua-yen. Studies in East Asian Buddhism, no. 1. Honolulu: University of Hawaii Press, 1983.

Girardot, Norman J. Myth and Meaning in Early Taoism. Berkeley: University of California Press, 1983.

Gomez, Luis O. "Observations on the Role of the Gaṇḍavyūha in the Design of Barabuḍur." In Barabuḍur: History and Significance of a Buddhist Monument. Edited by Luis O. Gomez and Hiram W. Woodward, Jr. Berkeley: Berkeley Buddhist Studies Series, 1981.

————. "Selected Verses from the Gaṇḍavyūha: Text, Critical Apparatus and Translation." Ph.D. dissertation, Yale University, 1967.

Graham, Angus C. "The Background of the Mencian Theory of Human Nature." Tsing Hua Journal of Chinese Studies, n.s., 6 (1967): 215–271.

————, trans. The Book of Lieh Tzu. London: John Murray, 1960.

————. Two Chinese Philosophers: Ch'eng Ming-tao and Ch'eng Yi-ch'uan. London: Lund Humphries, 1958.

Gregory, Peter N. "Chinese Buddhist Hermeneutics: The Case of Hua-yen." Journal of the American Academy of Religion 51, 2 (1983): 231–249.

————. "The Integration of Ch'an/Sŏn and the Teachings (chiao/kyo) in Tsung-mi and Chinul." Journal of the International Association of Buddhist Studies 12, 2 (1989): 7–19.

————. "The Place of the Sudden Teaching Within the Hua-yen Tradition: An Investigation of the Process of Doctrinal Change." Journal of the International Association of Buddhist Studies 6, 1 (1983): 31–60.

————. "The Problem of Theodicy in the Awakening of Faith." Religious Studies 22, 1 (1986): 63–78.

————. "Sudden Enlightenment Followed by Gradual Cultivation: Tsung-mi's Analysis of Mind." In Sudden and Gradual: Approaches to Enlightenment in Chinese Thought. Edited by Peter N. Gregory. Studies in East Asian Buddhism, no. 5. Honolulu: University of Hawaii Press, 1987.

————. "The Teaching of Men and Gods: The Doctrinal and Social Basis of Lay Buddhist Practice in the Hua-yen Tradition." In Studies in Ch'an and Hua-yen. Edited by Robert M. Gimello and Peter N. Gregory. Studies in East Asian Buddhism, no. 1. Honolulu: University of Hawaii Press, 1983.

————. "Tsung-mi and the Single Word 'Awareness' (chih)." Philosophy East and West 35, 3 (1985): 249–269.

————. "What Happened to the Perfect Teaching?—Another Look at Hua-yen Buddhist Hermeneutics." In Buddhist Hermeneutics. Edited by Donald S. Lopez, Jr. Studies in East Asian Buddhism, no. 6. Honolulu: University of Hawaii Press, 1988.

——, ed. *Sudden and Gradual: Approaches to Enlightenment in Chinese Thought.* Studies in East Asian Buddhism, no. 5. Honolulu: University of Hawaii Press, 1983.

——, ed. *Traditions of Meditation in Chinese Buddhism.* Studies in East Asian Buddhism, no. 4. Honolulu: University of Hawaii Press, 1986.

Guisso, Richard W. L. "The Reigns of the Empress Wu, Chung-tsung and Jui-tsung (684–712)." In *The Cambridge History of China,* vol. 3, *Sui and T'ang China (589–906),* part 1. Edited by Denis Twitchett. Cambridge: Cambridge University Press, 1979.

——. *Wu Tse-t'ien and the Politics of Legitimation in T'ang China.* Bellingham: Western Washington University, 1978.

Hachiya, Kunio 蜂屋邦夫. "Haka Kyoi no shi to bukkyō" 白居易の詩と仏教 *Chūgoku no bukkyō to bunka* 中国の仏教と文化. Tokyo: Daizō shuppan, 1988.

Hakeda, Yoshito S. *The Awakening of Faith Attributed to Aśvaghosha.* New York: Columbia University Press, 1967.

Hartman, Charles. *Han Yü and the T'ang Search for Unity.* Princeton: Princeton University Press, 1986.

Hass, Hans. "Tsungmi's *Yuen-zan-lun,* eine Abhandlung über den Ursprung des Menschen aus dem Kanon des chinesischen Buddhismus." *Archiv für Religionswissenschaft* 12 (1909): 491–532.

Hattori, Masaaki. Review of *La Théorie du Tathāgatagarbha et du Gotra. Journal of Indian Philosophy* 2 (1972): 53–64.

Herman, Arthur. *The Problem of Evil and Indian Thought.* Delhi, Varanasi, Patna: Motilal Banarsidass, 1976.

Hervouet, Yves, ed. *A Sung Bibliography (Bibliographie des Sung).* Hong Kong: Chinese University Press, 1978.

Hibi, Nobumasa 日比宣正. *Tōdai tendaigaku josetsu* 唐代天台学序説. Tokyo: Sankibō busshorin, 1975.

——. *Tōdai tendaigaku kenkyū* 唐代天台学研究. Tokyo: Sankibō busshorin, 1975.

Hightower, James R., trans. *Han shih wai chuan: Han Ying's Illustrations of the Didactic Application of the Classic of Songs.* Cambridge: Harvard University Press, 1952.

Hirai, Shun'ei 平井俊栄. "Mujū no gainen no keisei to tenkai" 無住の概念の形成と展開. *Komazawa daigaku bukkyō gakubu kenkyū kiyō* 34 (1976): 48–63.

Hirakawa, Akira 平川彰, trans. *Daijō kishin-ron* 大乗起信論. Button kōza 22. Tokyo: Daizō shuppan, 1973.

Hirano, Kenshō 平野顕照. "Haku Kyoi no bungaku to bukkyō" 白居易の文学と仏教. *Ōtani daigaku kenkyū nempō* (1964): 119–187.

Horner, Isaline B., trans. *The Book of the Discipline (Vinaya-Pitaka).* 6 vols. Sacred Books of the Buddhists, vols. 10, 11, 13, 14, 20, 25. London: Luzac & Co., 1949–1966.

——, trans. *The Collection of the Middle Length Sayings (Majjhima-Nikāya).* 3 vols. London: Luzac & Co., 1975–77.

Hu, Shih 胡適. "Pa P'ei Hsiu ti T'ang ku Kuei-feng ting-hui ch'an-shih ch'uan-fa-pei" 跋裴休的唐故圭峯定慧禪師傳法碑. *Bulletin of the Institute of History and Philology, Academia Sinica* 34 (1962): 5–26.

——. *Shen-hui ho-shang i-chi* 神會和尚遺集. 1930. Reprint. Tapei: Hu Shih chi-nien kuan, 1970.

Hucker, Charles O. *A Dictionary of Official Titles in Imperial China.* Stanford: Stanford University Press, 1985.

Hung, William. *Tu Fu: China's Greatest Poet.* New York: Russell & Russell, 1952.

Hurvitz, Leon, trans. *Scripture of the Lotus Blossom of the Fine Dharma (The Lotus Sūtra). Translated from the Chinese of Kumārajīva.* New York: Columbia University Press, 1976.

Ikeda, Rosan 池田魯参. "*Engakukyō dōjō shūshōgi* no reizanhō" 「円覚経道場修証儀」の礼懺法. *Chūgoku no bukkyō to bunka* 中国の仏教と文化. Tokyo: Daizō shuppan, 1988.

———. "*Shūmitsu Engakukyō dōjō shūshōgi* no reizanhō" 宗密「円覚経道場修証儀」の礼懺法. *Indogaku bukkyōgaku kenkyū* 35, 1 (1986): 118–121.

———. "Tannen ni seiritsu suru goji hakkyō-ron" 湛然に成立する五時八教論. *Indogaku bukkyōgaku kenkyū* 24, 1 (1975): 268–271.

———. "Tendaigaku kara enton no kannen ni tsuite" 天台学から円頓の観念について. *Indogaku bukkyōgaku kenkyū* 21, 1 (1973): 307–310.

Iriya, Yoshitaka 入矢義高. *Denshin hōyō* 伝心法要. Zen no goroku, vol. 8. Tokyo: Chikuma shobō, 1969.

Ishibashi, Shinkai 石橋真誠. "Kegon kyōgaku ni okeru nyoraizō shisō" 華厳教学に於ける如来蔵思想. *Indogaku bukkyōgaku kenkyū* 35, 2 (1987): 636–640.

Ishii, Shūdō 石井修道. "Keihō Shūmitsu nikukotsuzui tokuhō setsu no seiritsu hakei ni tsuite" 圭峯宗密肉骨髄得法説の成立背景について. *Indogaku bukkyōgaku kenkyū* 30, 2 (1982): 791–794.

———. "Shinpuku-ji bunko shozō no *Hai Kyū shūi mon* no honkoku" 真福寺文庫所蔵の「裴休拾遺問」の翻刻. *Zengaku kenkyū* 60 (1981): 71–104.

———. "Tongo zenshū ni tsuite: *Hai Kyū shūi mon* o chūshin to shite" 頓悟漸修について「裴休拾遺問」を中心として. *Indogaku bukkyōgaku kenkyū* 29, 2 (1981): 586–591.

———: "Zen no bunrui ni tsuite: Keihō Shūmitsu no goshuzen no minaoshi" 禅の分類について―圭峯宗密の五種禅の見直し *Zenbunka kenkūjo kiyō* 15 (1988): 297–336.

Jan, Yün-hua 冉雲華. "Conflict and Harmony in Ch'an and Buddhism." *Journal of Chinese Philosophy* 4, 3 (1977): 360–381.

———. "*Fa-chi* and Chinul's Understanding of Tsung-mi." *Pojo sasang* 2. Songgwang-sa, Korea: Pojo sasang yŏn'guwŏn, 1988.

———. "*K'an Hui* or the 'Comparative Investigation': The Key Concept in Tsung-mi's Thought." In *Korean and Asian Religious Tradition.* Edited by Chia-Shin Yu. Toronto: Korean and Related Studies Press, University of Toronto, 1977.

———. "Seng-ch'ou's Method of *Dhyāna.*" In *Early Ch'an in China and Tibet.* Edited by Whalen Lai and Lewis Lancaster. Berkeley Buddhist Studies Series, 1983.

———. "A Study of *Ta-ch'eng ch'an-men yao-lu*: Its Significance and Problems." *Chinese Studies* 8 (1986): 533–547.

———. *Tsung-mi* 宗密. Taipei: Tung ta t'u-shu kung-ssu yin-hsing, 1988.

———. "Tsung-mi chu *Tao-su ch'ou-ta wen-chi* ti yen-chiu" 宗密著「道俗酬答文集」的研究. *Hwakang Buddhist Journal* 4 (1980): 132–166.

———. "Tsung-mi: His Analysis of Ch'an Buddhism." *T'oung Pao* 58 (1972): 1–54.

———. "Tsung-mi's Questions Regarding the Confucian Absolute." *Philosophy East and West* 30, 4 (1980): 495–504.

———. "Tung-hai ta-shih Wu-hsiang chuan yen-chiu" 東海大師無相傳研究. *Tun-huang hsüeh* 4 (1979): 47–60.

———. "Two Problems Concerning Tsung-mi's Compilation of *Ch'an-tsang*." *Transactions of the International Conference of Orientalists in Japan* 19 (1974): 37–47.

Jayatilleke, K. N. *Early Buddhist Theory of Knowledge*. London: George Allen and Unwin, 1963.

Johansson, Rune E. A. *The Dynamic Psychology of Early Buddhism*. London: Curzon Press, 1979.

Johnston, E. H. *The Buddhacarita, or Acts of the Buddha*. Calcutta: Baptist Mission Press, 1936. Reprint. New Delhi: Oriental Books Reprint Corporation, 1972.

Jones, J. J., trans. *The Mahāvastu*. 3 vols. London: The Pali Text Society, 1952–1973.

Joyce, James. *Finnegans Wake*. New York: Viking Press, 1969.

Kachi, Tettei 加地哲定. "Shūmitsu no *Genninron* ni tsuite" 宗密の「原人論」について. *Mikkyō bunka* 13 (1951): 22–32.

Kaginushi, Ryōkei 鍵主良敬. "Kegon no shōki ni tsuite" 華厳の性起について. *Ōtani gakuhō* 51, 4 (1972): 93–96.

———. "*Kegon-kyō* shōki-hin no kenkyū" 華厳経性起品の研究. *Ōtani daigaku kenkyū nenpō* 25 (1972): 71–153.

Kamata, Shigeo 鎌田茂雄. *Chūgoku bukkyō shisōshi kenkyū* 中国仏教思想研究. Tokyo: Shunjūsha, 1967.

———. *Chūgoku kegon no shisōshi no kenkyū* 中国華厳の思想史の研究. Tokyo: Tōkyō daigaku shuppankai, 1965.

———. "Chūtō no bukkyō no hendō to kokka kenryoku" 中唐の仏教の変動と国家権力. *Tōyō bunka kenkyūjo kiyō* 25 (1961): 201–245.

———, trans. *Gennin-ron* 原人論. Tokyo: Meitoku shuppansha, 1973.

———. *Shūmitsu kyōgaku no shisōshi-teki kenkyū* 宗密教学の思想史的研究. Tokyo: Tōkyō daigaku shuppansha, 1975.

———, trans. *Zengen shosenshū tojo* 禅源諸詮集都序. Zen no goroku, vol. 9. Tokyo: Chukuma shobō, 1971.

Kamekawa, Kyōshin 亀川教信. *Engi no kōzō* 縁起の構造. Kyoto: Zenjinsha, 1944.

———. *Kegongaku* 華厳学. Kyoto: Hyakkaen, 1949.

Karlgren, Bernhard. *Analytic Dictionary of Chinese and Sino-Japanese*. Paris: Librairie Orientaliste Paul Geuthner, 1923.

Kasoff, Ira E. *The Thought of Chang Tsai*. Cambridge: Cambridge University Press, 1984.

Kawada, Kumatarō 川田熊太郎. "Engi to hokkai" 縁起と法界. *Komazawa daigaku bungakubu kenkyū* 21 (1962): 21–41.

Kimura, Kiyotaka 木村清孝. *Shoki chūgoku kegon shisō no kenkyū* 初期中国華厳思想の研究. Tokyo: Shunjūsha, 1977.

Kimura, Yoshiyuki 木村義之. *Genninron shinkō* 原人論新講. Tokyo: Kōshisha shuppansha, 1931.

King, Sallie. "Commentary to the Hua-yan Dharma-Realm Meditation." M.A. thesis, University of British Columbia, 1975.

Kloppenborg, Ria. *The Paccekabuddha: A Buddhist Ascteic*. Leiden: E. J. Brill, 1974.

Kobayashi, Jitsugen 小林実玄. "Chōkan kyōgaku no kenkyū: Kegon kanmon no tenkai to kyōgaku no hensen" 澄観教学の研究—華厳観門の展開と教学の変遷. *Ryūkoku daigaku ronshū* 377 (1964): 83–136.

———. "Hokkai engi no kenkyū josetsu" 法界縁起の研究序説. *Nanto bukkyō* 19 (1966): 16–33.

———. "Jijimuge to jirimuge: shōki to no kanren ni oite" 事事無礙と事理無礙—性起との関連に於て. *Bukkyōgaku kenkyū* 16–17 (1959): 105–118.

———. "Kegon no shinshō ron: genshi kegon ni okeru kyōgaku no keisei to yuishin no tachiba" 華厳の心性論—原始華厳における教学の形成と唯心の立場. *Nanto bukkyō* 7 (1959): 29–51.

———. "Kegonshū kangyō no tenkai ni tsuite" 華厳宗観行の展開について. *Indogaku bukkyōgaku kenkyū* 15, 2 (1967): 653–655.

———. "Keihō Shūmitsu no 'chi' no shisō ni tsuite" 圭峯宗密の「知」の思想について. *Zengaku kenkyū* 49 (1959): 110–127.

———. "Shūmitsu no engaku no kyōgaku ni tsuite" 宗密の円学の教学について. *Indogaku bukkyōgaku kenkyū* 17, 2 (1969): 782–785.

———. "Shūmitsu no sōgō kyōgaku no ronsei ni tsuite" 宗密の綜合教学の論成について. *Indogaku bukkyōgaku kenkyū* 16, 2 (1968): 760–764.

Kojima, Taizan 小島岱山. "*Mōjin gengen kan* no senja o meguru shomondai" 「妄盡還源観」の撰者をめぐる諸問題. *Nanto bukkyō* 49 (1982): 13–31.

Kubin, Wolgang. "Liu Yü-hsi." In *The Indiana Companion to Traditional Chinese Literature*. Edited by William H. Nienhauser, Jr. Bloomington: Indiana University Press. 1986.

Kubota, Ryōon 久保田量遠. *Shina ju dō butsu kōshō-shi* 支那儒道仏交渉史. Tokyo: Daitō shuppansha, 1943.

———. *Shina ju dō butsu sankyō shiron* 支那儒道仏三教史論. Tokyo: Tōhō shoin, 1931.

La Vallée Poussin, Louis de, trans. *L'Abhidharmakośa de Vasubandhu*. 6 vols. Edited by Étienne Lamotte. *Mélanges chinois et bouddhiques*, vol. 16. Brussels: Institut Belge des Hautes Études Chinoises, 1971.

———. "Cosmogony and Cosmology (Buddhist)." In *Encyclopedia of Religion and Ethics*, vol. 4. Edited by James Hastings. Edinburgh: T. and T. Clark, 1912.

———, trans. *Vijñaptimātratāsiddhi: La Siddhi de Hiuan-tsang*. 2 vols. Paris: Librairie Orientaliste Paul Geuthner, 1928–1929.

Lai, Whalen. "The Earliest Folk Buddhist Religion in China: *T'i-wei Po-li Ching* and Its Historical Significance." In *Buddhist and Taoist Practice in Medieval Chinese Society*. Edited by David W. Chappell. Honolulu: University of Hawaii Press, 1987.

Lamont, H. G. "An Early Ninth Century Debate on Heaven: Liu Tsung-yüan's *T'ien Shuo* and Liu Yü-hsi's *T'ien Lun*." *Asia Major* 18, 2 (1973): 181–208 and 19, 1 (1973): 37–85.

Lamotte, Étienne, trans. *L'Enseignement de Vimakakīrti (Vimalakīrtinirdeśa)*. Louvain: Publications Universitaires and Leuven: Institut Orientaliste, 1962.

———, trans. *Saṃdhinirmocana-sūtra: L'Explication des mystères*. Louvain: Université de Louvain, 1935.

Lau, D. C., trans. *Lao Tzu, Tao Te Ching*. Harmondsworth: Penguin Books, 1963.

Legge, James, trans. *The Chinese Classics*. 5 vols. Oxford: Clarendon Press, 1893.

———, trans. *Li Chi: The Book of Rites*. 2 vols. Edited by Ch'u and Winberg Chai. Reprint. New York: University Books, 1967.

———, trans. *The Sacred Books of China: The Texts of Confucianism*, vol. 1. *The Sacred Books of the East*, vol. 5. New York: Charles Scribner's Sons, 1899.

Levering, Miriam L. "Ch'an Enlightenment for Laymen: Ta-hui and the New Religious Culture of the Sung." Ph.D. dissertation, Harvard University, 1978.

Levy, Howard, trans. *Translations from Po Chü-i's Collected Works*, vol. 4. San Francisco: Chinese Materials Center, 1978.

Li, Lin-ts'an 李霖燦. *Nan-chao Ta-li kuo hsin tz'u-liao ti tsung-ho yen-chiu* 南詔大理國新資料的綜合研究. Taipei: National Palace Museum, 1982.

Link, Arthur, and Tim Lee. "Sun Ch'o's *Yü-tao-lun: A Clarification of the Way*," *Monumenta Serica* 25 (1966): 169–196.

Liu, Ming-Wood. "The *P'an-chiao* System of the Hua-yen School in Chinese Buddhism." *T'oung Pao* 67, 1–2 (1981): 10–47.

———. "The Teaching of Fa-tsang: An Examination of Buddhist Metaphysics." Ph.D. dissertation, University of California, Los Angeles, 1979.

Long, Charles. "Cosmogony." In *The Encyclopedia of Religion*. Edited by Mircea Eliade et al. New York: Macmillan, 1987.

Lopez, Danald S., Ju., ed. *Buddhist Hermeneutics*. Studies in East Asian Buddhism, no. 6. Honolulu: University of Hawaii Press, 1988.

Luk, Charles. *Ch'an and Zen Teaching. Third Series*. Berkeley: Shambala, 1973.

———, trans. *The Vimalakīrti Nirdeśa Sūtra*. Berkeley: Shambala, 1972.

McMullen, David. *State and Scholars in T'ang China*. Cambridge: Cambridge University Press, 1988.

McRae, John R. *The Northern School and the Formation of Early Ch'an Buddhism*. Studies in East Asian Buddhism, no. 3. Honolulu: University of Hawaii Press, 1986.

———. "The Ox-head School of Chinese Ch'an Buddhism." In *Studies in Ch'an and Hua-yen*. Edited by Robert M. Gimello and Peter N. Gregory. Studies in East Asian Buddhism, no. 1. Honolulu: University of Hawaii Press, 1983.

———. Review of *Zen Dawn*. *The Eastern Buddhist* 19, 2 (1986): 138–146.

———. "Shen-hui and the Teaching of Sudden Enlightenment in Early Ch'an Buddhism." In *Sudden and Gradual: Approaches to Enlightenment in Chinese Thought*. Edited by Peter N. Gregory. Studies in East Asian Buddhism, no. 5. Honolulu: University of Hawaii Press, 1987.

Makita, Tairyō 牧田諦亮. "Tonkōbon *Daiikyō* no kenkyū" 敦煌本提謂経の研究. *Bukkyō daigaku daigakuin kenkyū kiyo* (1968): 137–185 and (1971): 165–197.

———, trans. *Sōkōsōden* 宋高僧伝. Kokuyaku issaikyō, part 4, vols. 12–13. 1959. Reprint. Tokyo: Daitō shuppansha, 1980.

Makita, Tairyō, et al. *Chūgoku kōsōden sakuin* 中国高僧伝索引. 7 vols. Kyoto: Heirakuji shoten, 1972–1978.

Maspero, Henri. "Sur Quelques Textes Anciens de Chinois Parlé." *Bulletin de l'École Francaise d'Etrême-Orient* 14, 4 (1914): 1–36.

Masson-Oursel, Paul. "Le *Yuan Jen Louen*." *Journal Asiatique* (1915): 299–354.

Matsui, Shūichi 松井秀一. "Tōdai zenpanki no shisen" 唐代前半期の四川. *Shigaku zasshi* 71 (1962): 1178–1214.

Michihata, Ryōshū 道端良秀. *Tōdai bukkyō-shi no kenkyū* 唐代仏教史の研究. Kyoto: Hōzōkan, 1957.

Miura, Isshū, and Ruth Fuller Sasaki. *Zen Dust: The History of the Koan and Koan Study in Rinzai (Lin-chi) Zen*. New York: Harcourt, Brace and World, 1966.

Mochizuki, Shinkō 望月信享. *Bukkyō daijiten* 仏教大事典. 10 vols. Tokyo: Sekai seiten kankō kyōkai, 1958–1963.

———. *Bukkyō kyōten seiritsu shiron* 仏教経典成立史論. Kyoto: Hōzōkan, 1946.

Monier-Williams, Monier. *A Sanskrit-English Dictionary*. Oxford: Clarendon Press, 1899.

Morohashi, Tetsuji 諸橋轍次. *Daikanwa jiten* 大漢和辞典. 13 vols. Tokyo: Taishū-kan shoten, 1957–60.

Munro, Donald J. *Images of Human Nature*. Princeton: Princeton University Press, 1988.

Murti, T. R. V. *The Central Philosophy of Buddhism*. London: George Allen and Unwin, 1960.

Nagao, Gadjin. "An Interpretation of the Term 'Samvṛti' (Convention) in Buddhism." In *Silver Jubilee Volume of the Zinbun-Kagaku-kenkyusyo*. Kyoto: Institute for Humanistic Studies, 1954.

Nakajō, Dōshō 中條道照. "Chigen no kyōhansetsu ni tsuite" 智儼の教判説について. *Komazawa daigaku bukkyō gakubu ronshū* 9 (1978): 245–259.

Nakamura, Hajime 中村元. *Bukkyōgo daijiten* 仏教語大辞典. 3 vols. Tokyo: Tōkyō shoseki, 1975.

Nakasone, Ronald Yukio. "The *Huan-yüan kuan*: A Study of the Hua-yen Interpretation of *Pratītyasamutpāda*." Ph.d. dissertation, University of Wisconsin, 1980.

Ñāṇamoli, Bhikkhu, trans. *The Path of Purification (Visuddhimagga)*. Kandy: Buddhist Publication Society, 1979.

Nienhauser, William H., Jr., ed. *The Indiana Companion to Traditional Chinese Literature*. Bloomington: University of Indiana Press, 1986.

Nishi, Giyū 西義雄. "Zen to nyoraizō shisō ni tsuite" 禅と如来蔵思想に就いて. *Zen bunka kenkyū kiyō* 3 (1971): 1–20.

Nukariya, Kaiten. *The Religion of the Samurai: A Study of Zen Philosophy and Discipline in China and Japan*. London, 1919. Reprint. London: Luzac and Co., 1973.

Nyanaponika Thera. *Abhidamma Studies: Researches in Buddhist Psychology*. Kandy: Buddhist Publication Society, 1976.

Nyanatiloka Mahathera. *Guide Through the Abhidhamma-piṭaka*. Kandy: Buddhist Publication Society, 1971.

Obeyesekere, Gananath. "Theodicy, Sin and Salvation in a Sociology of Buddhism." In *Dialectic in Practical Religion*. Edited by Edmund Leach. Cambridge: Cambridge University Press, 1968.

Ōchō Enichi 横超慧日. "The Beginnings of Tenet Classification in China." Translated by Robert Rhoades. *The Eastern Buddhist* 14, 2 (1981): 71–94.

———, ed. *Hokke shisō* 法華思想. Kyoto: Heirakuji shoten, 1969.

Oda, Tokunō 織田得能. *Bukkyō daijiten* 仏教大辞典. Revised ed., Tokyo: Daitō shuppansha, 1977.

Oh, Kang Nam. "A Study of Chinese Hua-yen Buddhism with special Reference to the *Dharmadhātu* (*fa-chieh*) Doctrine." Ph.D. dissertation, McMaster University, 1976.

———. "*Dharmadhātu*: An Introduction to Hua-yen Buddhism." *The Eastern Buddhist* 12, 2 (1979): 72–91.

Okabe, Kazuo 岡部和雄. "Shūmitsu ni okeru kōron no tenkai to sono hōhō" 宗密における孝論の展開とその方法. *Indogaku bukkyōgaku kenkyū* 15, 2 (1967): 574–578.

Ono, Gemmyō 小野玄妙, ed. *Bussho kaisetsu daijiten* 仏書解説大辞典. 13 vols. Tokyo: Daitō shuppansha, 1933–36.

Ōtomo, Tōsu 大友洞達. *Genninron shōkai* 原人論詳解. Tokyo: Nihon zensho kankōkai, 1921.

Owen, Stephen. *The Poetry of Han Yü and Meng Chiao*. New Haven: Yale University Press, 1975.

P'an, Chung-kuei 潘重規. "Kuo-li Chung-yang-t'u-shu-kuan so-ts'ang Tun-huang chüan-tzu t'i-chi" 國立中央圖書館所藏敦煌卷子題記. *Tun-huang hsüeh-pao* 2 (1975): 1–55.

Paul, Diana Mary. *The Buddhist Feminine Ideal: Queen Śrīmālā and the Tathāgatagarbha*. Missoula, Montana: Scholars Press, 1980.

Perry, John Curtis, and Bardwell L. Smith, eds. *Essays on T'ang Society*. Leiden: E. J. Brill, 1976.

Peterson, Charles A. "Corruption Unmasked: Yüan Chen's Investigations in Szechwan." *Asia Major* 18 (1973): 34–78.

———. "Court and Province in Mid- and Late T'ang." In *The Cambridge History of China*, vol. 3, *Sui and T'ang China (589–906)*, part 1. Edited by Denis Twitchett. Cambridge: Cambridge University Press, 1979.

———. "The Restoration Completed: Emperor Hsien-tsung and the Provinces." In *Perspectives on the T'ang*. Edited by Arthur F. Wright and Denis Twittchett. New Haven: Yale University Press, 1973.

Peterson, Willard J. "Making Connections: Commentary on the Attached Verbalizations of the *Book of Change*." *Harvard Journal of Asiatic Studies* 42, 2 (1982): 67–116.

Pruden, Leo, trans. *Abhidharmakośabhāṣyam by Louis de la Vallée Poussin*. 5 vols. Berkeley: Asian Humanities Press, 1988–.

Pulleyblank, Edwin G. "The An Lu-shan Rebellion and the Origins of Chronic Militarism in Late T'ang China." In *Essays on T'ang Society*. Edited by John Curtis Perry and Bardwell Smith. Leiden: E. J. Brill, 1976.

———. *The Background of the Rebellion of An Lu-shan*. London: Oxford University Press, 1955.

———. "Neo-Confucianism and Neo-Legalism in T'ang Intellectual Life, 755–805." In *The Confucian Persuasion*. Edited by Arthur F. Wright. Stanford: Stanford University Press, 1969.

Pye, Michael. *Skilful Means: A Concept in Mahayana Buddhism*. London: Duckworth, 1978.

Reischauer, Edwin O., trans. *Ennin's Diary: The Record of a Pilgrimage to China in Search of the Law*. New York: Ronald Press Co., 1955.

———. *Ennin's Travels in T'ang China*. New York: Ronald Press Co., 1955.

Retours, Robert des. *Le Traité des examens*. Paris: Leroux, 1932.

Reynolds, Frank E. "Multiple Cosmogonies: The Case of Theravāda Buddhism." In *Cosmogony and the Ethical Order: New Studies in Comparative Ethics.* Edited by Robin W. Lovin and Frank E. Reynolds. Chicago: University of Chicago Press, 1985.

Rhys Davids, Caroline A. F., and F. L. Woodward, trans. *The Book of Kindred Sayings (Sanyutta-Nikāya) or Grouped Suttas.* 5 vols. London: Luzac & Co., 1950–1965.

Rhys Davids, T. W., trans. *Dialogues of the Buddha (Dīgha-Nikāya).* 3 vols. Sacred Books of the Buddhists, vols. 2–4. London: The Pali Text Society, 1977

Rhys Davids, T. W., and William Stede. *Pāli-English Dictionary.* London: Pali Text Society, 1959.

Rideout, J. K. "The Context of the *Yüan Tao* and the *Yüan Hsing." Bulletin of the School of Oriental and African Studies, University of London* 12 (1947–48): 403–408.

———. "The Rise of the Eunuchs during the T'ang Dynasty. Part I (618–705)." *Asia Major* 1, 1 (1949): 53–72.

———. "The Rise of the Eunuchs during the T'ang Dynasty. Part II." *Asia Major* 3, 1 (1952): 42–58.

Ruegg, David Seyfort. *La Théorie du Tathāgatagarbha et du Gotra: Étude sur la Sotériologie et la Gnoséologie du Bouddhisme.* Paris: École Française d'Extrême-Orient, 1969.

Sakamoto, Yukio 坂本幸男. "Chūgoku bukkyō to Hokke shisō no renkan" 中国仏教と法華思想の連関. In *Hokekyō no shisō to bunka* 法華経の思想と文化. Kyoto: Heirakuji shoten, 1965.

———. "Hokkai engi no rekishi teki keisei" 法界縁起の歴史的形成. In *Bukkyō no konpon shinri* 仏教の根本真理. Edited by Miyamoto Shōson 宮本正尊. Tokyo: Sanseidō, 1957.

———. *Kegon kyōgaku no kenkyū* 華厳教学の研究. Tokyo: Heirakuji, 1964.

Sankyō kōshōshi kenkyūhan 三教交渉史研究班. "*Hokuzanroku* yakuchū" 「北山録」訳注. *Tōyō bunka kenkyūjo kiyō* 81 (1980): 179–257; 84 (1981): 245–278; 89 (1982): 171–250.

Sargent, Galen Eugene. "Tchou Hi contre le Bouddhisme." *Mélanges Publies par l'Instiute des Hautes Études Chinoises* 1 (1957): 1–157.

Schafer, Edward H. "The Last Years of Ch'ang-an." *Oriens Extremus* 2 (1963): 133–179.

———. *Pacing the Void: T'ang Approaches to the Stars.* Berkeley: University of California Press, 1977.

Schirokauer, Conrad. "Chu Hsi and Hu Hung." In *Chu Hsi and Neo-Confucianism.* Edited by Wing-tsit Chan. Honolulu: University of Hawaii Press, 1986.

Schmithausen, L. "On Some Aspects of Descriptions or Theories of 'Liberating Insight' and 'Enlightenment' in Early Buddhism." *Alt- und Neu-Indische Studien* 12 (1981): 199–250.

Schopen, Gregory, ed. *Buddhist Studies: Selected Essays of J. W. Jong.* Berkeley: Asian Humanities Press, 1979.

Sekiguchi, Shindai 関口真大. "Goji hakkyō kyōhanron no kigen" 五時八教の起元. Taishō daigaku kiyō 61(1975):1–15.

———. *Tendai shō shikan no kenkyū* 天台小止観の研究. 1954. Reprint. Tokyo: Sankibō busshorin, 1961.

Shiina, Kōyū 椎名宏雄. "*Hokuzanroku* ni tsuite" 「北山録」について. *Indogaku bukkyōgaku kenkyū* 19, 2 (1971): 919–923.

Shinohara, Hisao 篠原壽雄. "Tōdai zenshisō to Haku Kyoi" 唐代禅思想と白居易. *Indogaku bukkyōgaku kenkyū* 7, 2 (1959): 610–615.

Solomon, Bernard S. *The Veritable Record of the T'ang Emperor Shun-tsung (February 28, 805–August 31, 805): Han Yü's Shun-tsung shih-lu.* Harvard-Yenching Institute Studies XIII. Cambridge: Harvard University Press, 1955.

South, Margaret Tudor. *Li Ho: A Scholar-official of the Yüan-ho period (806–821).* Adelaide: Libraries Board of South Australia, 1967.

Stevenson, Daniel. "The Four Kinds of Samādhi in Early T'ien-t'ai Buddhism." In *Traditions of Meditation in Chinese Buddhism.* Edited by Peter N. Gregory. Studies in East Asian Buddhism, no. 4. Honolulu: University of Hawaii Press, 1986.

Sung, Z. D. *The Text of the Yi King.* Reprint. Taipei: Ch'eng Wen Publishing Co., 1971.

Suzuki, D. T., trans. *The Laṅkāvatāra Sūtra.* London: Routledge Kegan & Paul, 1973.

Suzuki, Tetsuo 鈴木哲雄. *Tō-godai zenshūshi* 唐五代の禅宗史. Tokyo: Sankibō busshorin, 1985.

Takamine, Ryōshū 高峯了州. *Kegon shisō shi* 華厳思想史. 2d ed. Tokyo: Hyakkaen, 1963.

———. *Kegon to zen no tsuro* 華厳と禅の通路. Nara: Nanbu bukkyō kenkyūkai, 1956.

———. "Monchō hōshi no *Kegon-kyō gishō* ni tsuite" 文超法師の華厳経義鈔について. *Ryūtani gakuhō* 315 (1936): 251–283.

Takasaki, Jikidō 高崎直道. *Nyoraizō shisō no keisei* 如来蔵思想の形成. Tokyo: Shunjūsha, 1974.

———. "Nyoraizō to engi: *Hōshō-ron* o tegakari to shite" 如来蔵と縁起—宝性論を手がかりとして. *Indogaku bukkyōgaku kenkyū* 2, 1 (1953): 244–247.

———. *A Study on the Ratnagotravibhāga (Utttaratantra): Being a Treatise on the Tathāgatagarbha Theory of Mahāyāna Buddhism.* Serie Orientale Roma 33 (1966).

Takeuchi, Kōdō 竹内弘道. "Jinne to Shūmitsu" 神会と宗密. *Indogaku bukkyōgaku kenkyū* 34, 2 (1986): 481–485.

———. "Shinshutsu no Kataku Jinne tōmei ni tsuite" 新出の荷沢神会塔銘について. *Shūgaku kenkyū* 27 (1985): 313–325.

Tamaki, Kōshirō 玉城康四郎. "Kegon no shōki ni tsuite" 華厳の性起について. *Indo tetsugaku to bukkyō* 印度哲学と仏教. Edited by Miyamoto Shōsan 宮本正尊. Tokyo: Iwanami shoten, 1951.

———. "Yuishin no tsuikyū" 唯心の追究. In *Kegon shisō* 華厳思想. Edited by Kawada Kumatarō 川田熊太郎 and Nakamura Hajime 中村元. Kyoto: Hōzōkan, 1960.

Tambiah, Stanley J. *World Conqueror and World Renouncer.* Cambridge: Cambridge University Press, 1976.

Tamura, Yoshirō 田村芳朗. *Tendai hongaku-ron* 天台本覚論. Nihon shisō taikei, vol 9. Tokyo: Iwanami shoten, 1973.

Tanaka, Ryoshō 田中良昭. "Tonkōbon *Zengen shosenshū tojo* zankan kō" 敦煌本「禅源諸詮集都序」残巻考. *Komazawa daigaku bukkyō gakubu kenkyū kiyō* 37 (1979): 51–71.

———. *Tonkō zenshū bunken no kenkyū* 敦煌禅宗文献の研究. Tokyo: Daitō shuppansha, 1983.

Teiser, Stephen F. *The Ghost Festival in Medieval China*. Princeton: Princeton University Press, 1988.

Thurman, Robert. "Buddhist Hermeneutics." *Journal of the American Academy of Religion* 46 (1978): 19–39.

Tokiwa, Daijō 常盤大定. *Shina bunka shiseki* 支那文化史蹟. 12 vols. Tokyo: Hōzōkan, 1939–1941.

———. *Shina ni okeru bukkyō to jukyō dōkyō* 支那における仏教と儒教道教. Tokyo: Tōyō bunko, 1937.

Tokiwa, Gishin, trans. *A Dialogue on the Contemplation-Extinguished*. Kyoto: Hanazono University, Institute for Zen Studies, 1973.

Tsukamoto, Zenryū 塚本善隆. *Shina bukkyōshi kenkyū, Hokugi hen* 支那仏教史研究・北魏篇. Tokyo, 1942. Reprinted in *Tsukamoto Zenryū chosaku shū* 塚本善隆著作集. vol. 2. Tokyo: Daitō shuppansha, 1974.

Twitchett, Denis. "Hsüan-tsung (reign 712–56)." In *The Cambridge History of China*, vol. 3, *Sui and T'ang China, 589–906*, part 1. Edited by Denis Twitchett. Cambridge: Cambridge University Press, 1979.

———, ed. *Sui and T'ang China, 589–906*, part I. Vol. 3 of *The Cambridge History of China*. Cambridge: Cambridge University Press, 1979.

Ueyama, Daishun 上山大峻. "Tonkō shutsudo *Jōdo hosshin san* ni tsuite" 敦煌出土「浄土法身讃」について, *Shinshū kenkyū* 21 (1976): 62–71.

Ui, Hakuju 宇井伯壽. *Bukkyō hanron* 仏教汎論. Vol. 2. Tokyo: Iwanami shoten, 1948.

———. *Zenshūshi kenkyū* 禅宗史研究. 3 vols. Tokyo: Iwanami shoten, 1939–1943.

———, trans. *Zengen shosenshū tojo* 禅源諸詮集都序. Tokyo: Iwanami shoten, 1939.

Waley, Arthur. *The Life and Times of Po Chü-i, 772–846 A.D.* London: George Allen and Unwin, 1955.

Warder, A. K. *Indian Buddhism*. 2d revised edition. Delhi: Motilal Banarsidass, 1980.

Watson, Burton. "Buddhism in the Poetry of Po Chü-i." *The Eastern Buddhist* 21, 1 (1988): 1–22.

———, trans. *The Complete Works of Chuang Tzu*. New York: Columbia University Press, 1968.

———, trans. *Records of the Grand Historian of China Translated from the Shih Chi of Ssu-ma Ch'ien*. 2 vols. New York: Columbia University Press, 1961.

———, trans. *Records of the Historian: Chapters from the Shih Chi of Ssu-ma Ch'ien*. New York: Columbia University Press, 1969.

Wayman, Alex and Hideko. *The Lion's Roar of Queen Śrīmālā: A Buddhist Scripture on the Tathāgatagarbha Theory*. New York: Columbia University Press, 1974.

Weber, Max. "Theodicy, Salvation, and Rebirth." In *The Sociology of Religion*. Boston: Beacon Press, 1964.

Wechsler, Howard J. *Mirror to the Son of Heaven: Wei Cheng at the Court of T'ang T'ai-tsung*. New Haven: Yale University Press, 1974.

Wei Tat, trans. *Ch'eng Wei-Shih Lun: Doctrine of Mere-Consciousness*. Hong Kong: The Ch'eng Wei-Shih Lun Publication Committee, 1973.

Weinstein, Stanley, *Buddhism under the T'ang*. Cambridge: Cambridge University Press, 1987.

———. "Buddhism, Schools of: Chinese Buddhism" In *The Encyclopedia of Religion*. Edited by Mircea Eliade et al. New York: Macmillan, 1987.

———. "The Concept of the Ālaya-Vijñāna in Pre-T'ang Chinese Buddhism." In *Bukkyō shisō ronshū*. Tokyo: Daizō shuppan, 1964.

———. "Imperial Patronage in the Formation of T'ang Buddhism." In *Perspectives on the T'ang*. Edited by Arthur Wright and Denis Twitchett. New Haven: Yale University Press, 1973.

Wen, Yü-ch'eng 温玉成. "Chi hsin ch'u-t'u-te Ho-tse ta-shih Shen-hui t'a-ming" 记新出土的荷泽大师神会塔铭. *Shih-chieh tsung-chiao yen-chiu* 2 (1984): 78–79.

Witzling, C. "Chia Tao." In *The Indiana Companion to Traditional Chinese Literature*. Edited by William H. Nienhauser, Jr. Bloomington: Indiana University Press, 1986.

Woodward, F. L., trans. *The Minor Anthologies of the Pali Canon*. London: Oxford University Press, 1948.

Woodward, F. L., and E. M. Hare, trans. *The Book of Gradual Sayings (Aṅguttara-Nikāya) of More-Numbered Suttas*. 5 vols. London: Luzac & Co., 1960–65.

Yamazaki, Hiroshi 山崎宏. "Keihō Shūmitsu kō" 圭峯宗密考. *Ryūkoku shidan* 56–57 (1967): 104–115.

———. "Keihō Shūmitsu ni tsuite" 圭峯宗密について. *Indogaku bukkyōgaku kenkyū* 15, 2 (1965): 16–21.

———. *Shina chūsei bukkyō no tenkai* 支那中世仏教の展開. Tokyo: Shimizu shoten, 1942.

———. "Tōdai kōki no koji Hai Kyū ni tsuite" 唐代後期の居士裴休について. *Bukkyō shigaku* 16, 4 (1969): 189–204.

———. *Zui tō bukkyō shi no kenkyū* 隋唐仏教史の研究. Kyoto: Hōzōkan, 1967.

Yampolsky, Philip B. *The Platform Sutra of the Sixth Patriarch*. New York: Columbia University Press, 1967.

Yanagida, Seizan 柳田聖山, trans. *Chūgoku senjutsu kyōten I: Engaku kyō* 中国撰述経典 I —円覚経. Bukkyō kyōten sen, vol. 13. Tokyo: Chikuma shobō, 1987.

———. "Chūgoku zenshū shi" 中国禅宗史. In *Zen no rekishi: Chūgoku* 禅の歴史—中国, Kōza zen, vol. 3. Edited by Nishitani Keiji 西谷啓治. Tokyo: Chikuma shobō, 1974.

———. "Jinne no shōzō" 神会の肖像. *Zenbunka kenkyūjo kiyō* 15 (1988): 215–243.

———. "The *Li-tai fa-pao chi* and the Ch'an Doctrine of Sudden Awakening." Translated by Carl W. Bielefeldt. In *Early Ch'an in China and Tibet*. Edited by Whalen Lai and Lewis Lancaster. Berkeley: Berkeley Buddhist Studies Series, 1983.

———. "Mujū to Shūmitsu: Tongo shisō no keisei o megutte" 無住と宗密—頓悟思想の形成をめぐって. *Hanazono daigaku kenkyū kiyō* 7 (1976): 1–36.

———. *Rinzai-roku* 臨済録. Butten kōza, no. 30. Tokyo: Daizō shuppansha, 1972.

———. *Shoki no zenshi I: Ryōga shiji ki, Den hōbōki* 初期の禅史 I: 楞伽師資記・伝法宝紀. Zen no goroku, vol. 2. Tokyo: Chikuma shobō, 1971.

———. *Shoki no zenshi II: Rekidai hōbō ki* 初期の禅史 II: 歴代法宝記. Zen no goroku, vol. 3. Tokyo: Chikuma shobō, 1976.

———. *Shoki zenshū shisho no kenkyū* 初期禅宗史書の研究. Kyoto: Hōzōkan, 1967.

———, ed. *Ko Teki zengaku an* 胡適禅学案. Kyoto: Chūbun shuppansha, 1962.

Yanagida, Seizan, and Umehara Takeshi 梅原猛. *Mu no tankyū: Chūgoku zen* 無の探求：中国禅. Bukkyō no shisō 7. Tokyo: Chikuma shobō, 1969.

Yoshioka, Yoshitoyo 吉岡義豊. *Dōkyō to bukkyō* 道教と仏教, vol. 1. Tokyo: Gakujutsu shinkōkai, 1959.

Yoshizu, Yoshihide 吉津宣英. "Chōkan no kegon kyōgaku to Tojun no *Hokkai kanmon*" 澄観の華厳教学と杜順の法界観門. *Komazawa daigaku bukkyō gakubu kenkyū kiyō* 38 (1980): 145–165.

———. "Chōkan no zenshū kan ni tsuite" 澄観の禅宗観について. *Shūgaku kenkyū* 22 (1980): 206–211.

———. "Engi no yōrei to Hōzō no hokkai engi setsu" 縁起の用例と法蔵の法界縁起説. *Komazawa daigaku bukkyō gakubu kenkyū kiyō* 40 (1982): 176–205.

———. "Engi to shōki: yakukyō kara kyōgaku keisei e no isshiten" 縁起と性起—訳経から教学形成への一視点. *Tōyō gakujutsu kenkyū* 22, 2 (1983): 48–65.

———. "Hōzō-den no kenkyū" 法蔵伝の研究. *Komazawa daigaku bukkyō gakubu kenkyū kiyō* 37 (1979): 168–193.

———. "Kegon gokyōshō no kenkyū" 華厳五教章の研究. *Komazawa daigaku bukkyō gakubu kenkyū kiyō* 39 (1978): 169–191.

———. "Kegon kyōhan-ron no tenkai" 華厳教判論の展開. *Komazawa daigaku bukkyō gakubu kenkyū kiyō* 39 (1981): 195–226.

———. *Kegonzen no shisōshi-teki kenkyū* 華厳禅の思想史的研究. Tokyo: Daitō shuppansha, 1985.

———. Review of *Shoki chūgoku kegon shisō no kenkyū*. *Komazawa daigaku bukkyō gakubu ronshū* 9 (1978): 279–286.

———. "Shōsō yūkai ni tsuite" 性相融会について. *Komazawa daigaku bukkyō gakubu kenkyū kiyō* 41 (1983): 300–321.

———. "Shūmitsu no *Daijō kishin ronshū* ni tsuite" 宗密の「大乗起信論疏」について. *Indogaku bukkyōgaku kenkyū* 30, 2 (1982): 796–800.

———. "Shūmitsu no honrai jōbutsu ron" 宗密の本来成仏論. *Shūgaku kenkyū* 25 (1983): 157–162.

———. "Tonkyō ni taisuru Chōkan no kaishaku ni tsuite" 頓教に対する澄観の解釈について. *Shūgaku kenkyū* 23 (1981): 209–214.

Yūki, Reimon 結城令聞. "Chūgoku bukkyō no keisei" 中国仏教の形成. In *Chūgoku bukkyō* 中国仏教. Kōza bukkyō, vol. 14. Tokyo: Ōjura, 1973.

———. "Kegon no shoso Tojun to *Hokkai kanmon* no chosha to no mondai" 華厳の初祖杜順と法界観門の著者との問題. *Indogaku bukkyōgaku kenkyū* 18, 1 (1969): 32–38.

———. Shotō bukkyō no shisōshi-teki mujun to kokka kenryoku to no kōsaku" 初唐仏教の思想史的矛盾と国家権力との交錯. *Tōyō bunka kenkyūjo kiyō* 25 (1961): 1–28.

———. "Zuitō no chūgoku shin-bukkyō soshiki no ichirei to shite no *Kegon hokkai kanmon* ni tsuite" 隋唐の中国新仏教組織の一例としての華厳法界観門について. *Indogaku bukkyōgaku kenkyū* 6, 2 (1985): 587–592.

Yusugi, Ryōei 湯次了栄. *Kanwa taishō genninron shinyaku* 漢和対照原人論新釈. Kyoto: Bukkyō daigaku shuppan, 1935.

Zengaku Daijiten Hensansho 禅学大辞典編纂所, ed. *Zengaku daijiten* 禅学大辞典. 3 vols. Tokyo: Taishūkan shoten, 1978.

Zürcher, Erik. *The Buddhist Conquest of China: The Spread and Adaptation of Buddhism in Early Medieval China*. 2 vols. Leiden: E. J. Brill, 1959.

INDEX

Abhidharma, 5n.2, 97

Abhidharmakośabhāṣya, 285

advanced teaching: according to Chih-yen, 121–22, 123–24; according to Fa-tsang, 132, 137, 139, 140, 146, 158, 162, 163; and *Awakening of Faith*, 157, 185; and *li-shih wu-ai*, 158; and *Scripture of Perfect Enlightenment*, 167–70

ālayavijñāna: according to Fa-hsiang, 189, 208; and *Awakening of Faith*, 189, 310; Chinese Buddhist understanding of, 108–10; and conditioned origination, 157–58; and gradual cultivation, 192; and latent conditioning, 275; and tathāgatagarbha, 157–58, 179, 180–82, 232; two modes of, 182–83, 310–11

Analects (Lun Yü). See *Confucian Analects*

Ānanda, 94

Aṅguttara-nikāya, 95–96

An Lu-shan rebellion, 18, 27, 39, 39–40n.49, 44, 86, 135

anuloma (shun), 177, 200, 203, 266

arhat, 100, 220

arhatship, 100, 101, 102

Asaṅga, 69

Aśvaghoṣa, 176

ātmagrāha, 186

ātman (self), 96

Avataṃsaka Sūtra. See *Hua-yen Sūtra*

Awakening of Faith (Ta-sheng ch'i-hsin lun): and advanced teaching, 157, 185; and ālayavijñāna, 189, 310; Ch'eng-kuan's study of, 64; and cosmogony, 19, 173–87, 196, 208; and delusion, 198; and experiential enlightenment, 182, 203; Fa-tsang's commentary on, 157, 164, 182–83, 187; five practices enumerated in, 201; importance of for Tsung-mi, 14, 19, 52, 71, 81, 151, 154, 173, 187, 295; and intrinsic enlightenment, 182, 243, 247; and legitimation of Ch'an teachings, 57; and *li*, 6–7n.8; and *li-shih wu-ai*, 157–62, 255; and nature origination, 189; and no-thought, 44; and phenomenal evolution, 292;

and tathāgatagarbha, 13, 58, 139, 167, 219, 221, 222, 232, 255, 296, 306, 310; Tsung-mi's commentary on, 164, 174, 177, 178, 179, app. II-2; and two aspects of mind, 139–40, 157, 160–61, 179–83, 232, 240, 242; and water and waves metaphor, 151, 160–61, 181, 193, 205

awareness (*chih*): empty tranquil (*k'ung chi chih*), 215–16, 241, 245, 247; as single word, 213, 214; and tathāgatagarbha, 216–18; Tsung-mi's emphasis on, 245–47; as underlying basis of all mental states, 243–44

Bhallika (Po-li), 282

blind men and the elephant, parable of, 229

Bodhidharma, 15, 17, 18, 39n.45, 43, 226

Bodhiruci, 109

bodhisattva, 54, 99, 101, 102, 112, 119, 138, 152, 191

body of the senses (*ken-shen; sendriyaka-kāya*), 292

Book of Rites (Li chi), 32, 264, 268

Buddha: and interpretation of doctrine, 93–98; and patriarchal succession, 16; recitation of name of, 43, 52; supreme perfect enlightenment attained by, 100, 101, 194, 195. See also Śākyamuni Buddha

Buddhabhadra, 9, 67, 118, 157, 166

Buddhacarita, 176

Buddha-nature: and tathāgatagarbha, 12–13; universality of, 20

Buddhatrāta (Fo-t'o-to-lo, Chüeh-chiu), 54, 55

Buddhism, Tsung-mi's study of, 30, 31, 34

Chinese: historical precedent for schisms in, 94–95; in Six Dynasties period, 3, 116, 126, 127; in Sui–T'ang period, 3–5, 10, 111, 127; Tsung-mi's articulation of, 21. See also China